The Rough Guide to
Sweden

There are more than two hundred Rough Guide titles
covering destinations from Alaska to Zimbabwe and subjects from
Acoustic Guitar to Travel Health

Forthcoming travel guides include

Dordogne & the Lot • Menorca • Tenerife • Vancouver • Malta & Gozo

Forthcoming reference guides include

100 Essential Latin CDs • Videogaming • Personal Computers
Pregnancy & Birth • Trumpet & Trombone

Rough Guides online
www.roughguides.com

ROUGH GUIDE CREDITS

Text editor: Richard Lim
Series editor: Mark Ellingham
Editorial: Martin Dunford, Jonathan Buckley, Jo Mead, Kate Berens, Amanda Tomlin, Ann-Marie Shaw, Paul Gray, Helena Smith, Judith Bamber, Orla Duane, Olivia Eccleshall, Ruth Blackmore, Sophie Martin, Geoff Howard, Claire Saunders, Gavin Thomas, Alexander Mark Rogers, Polly Thomas, Joe Staines, Lisa Nellis, Andrew Tomičić, Claire Fogg, Duncan Clark, Peter Buckley (UK); Andrew Rosenberg, Mary Beth Maioli, Don Bapst, Stephen Timblin (US)
Production: Susanne Hillen, Andy Hilliard, Link Hall, Helen Ostick, Julia Bovis, Michelle Draycott,

Katie Pringle, Robert Evers, Niamh Hatton, Mike Hancock
Cartography: Melissa Baker, Maxine Repath, Nichola Goodliffe, Ed Wright
Picture research: Louise Boulton, Sharon Martins
Online editors: Kelly Cross (US)
Finance: John Fisher, Gary Singh, Edward Downey, Mark Hall, Tim Bill
Marketing & Publicity: Richard Trillo, Niki Smith, David Wearn, Jemima Broadbridge (UK); Jean-Marie Kelly, Myra Campolo, Simon Carloss (US)
Administration: Tania Hummel, Charlotte Marriott, Demelza Dallow

ACKNOWLEDGEMENTS

The authors jointly thank Ann-Charlotte Carlsson and Jane Wilde from the Swedish Travel and Tourism Council in London, the former for arranging accommodation and flights, the latter for providing last-minute information on the ever-changing airline situation; and Åsa Ericson at SJ in Stockholm, for arranging rail tickets and providing information on fares.

In addition, **James** thanks Juliet Schaffer's flexible lamps for correctly locating Sweden on the map; Per Henriksson in Stockholm for his *Jansson's frestelse*, cloudberry yoghurt and generous helping of good humour; John Porter in Dalama for advice on hiking routes around Grövelsjön and opinions on Idre; Christer Andersson at Allt om Stockholm for eating his way round the capital and Mårten Skånman for clubbing info; Jason Christie for cool advice on young person's Stockholm; and above all Lance Price, who kept it all together at home and whose patience is never tried when Sweden enters conversation – yet again.

For providing inspiration, information, smiling faces and most importantly, friendship, **Neil** would like to thank Stigake Berkin, Inger Eide-Jensen of Wettergrens, Ingvar Grimberg and Erik Soderlund, all of Gothenburg; Christina Fjällrud of Mölltorp; Ove Persson, Martin Holmberg and Mikka Karlson of Halmstad; Christer Hagström of Helsingborg; Charlotte Lindell of Lund; Torbjörn Persson and Claus Feldthusen of Malmö; Kalle Sundin and Janis Sundin-Straupenieks of Borgholm, Öland; Johan Alsen of Linköping; Anders Karlson of Norrköping; and Peter Doolk of Romakloster, Gotland.

The editor thanks Robert Mackey and Silke Kerwick for Basics research, Gillian Armstrong for proofreading, Mandy Muggridge of Geographic Services Ltd and Maxine Repath for cartography, Judy Pang, Neil Cooper and Mike Hancock for typesetting, Gavin Thomas for additional map enhancements, and Luis for the surplus croissants.

PUBLISHING INFORMATION

This second edition published May 2000 by Rough Guides Ltd, 62–70 Shorts Gardens, London, WC2H 9AH. Reprinted June 2001.
Distributed by the Penguin Group:
Penguin Books Ltd, 27 Wrights Lane, London W8 5TZ
Penguin Putnam, Inc., 375 Hudson Street, New York 10014, USA
Penguin Books Australia Ltd, 487 Maroondah Highway, PO Box 257, Ringwood, Victoria 3134, Australia
Penguin Books Canada Ltd, 10 Alcorn Avenue, Toronto, Ontario, Canada M4V 1E4
Penguin Books (NZ) Ltd, 182–190 Wairau Road, Auckland 10, New Zealand
Typeset in Linotron Univers and Century Old Style to an original design by Andrew Oliver.
Printed in England by Clays Ltd, St Ives PLC
Illustrations in Part One and Part Three by Edward Briant.

Illustrations on p.1 & p.489 by Henry Iles
© James Proctor and Neil Roland 2000
No part of this book may be reproduced in any form without permission from the publisher except for the quotation of brief passages in reviews.
544pp – Includes index
A catalogue record for this book is available from the British Library
ISBN 1-85828-537-2

The Rough Guide to

Sweden

written and researched by

James Proctor and Neil Roland

with additional research by

Jules Brown

ROUGH GUIDES

TRAVEL GUIDES • PHRASEBOOKS • MUSIC AND REFERENCE GUIDES

 We set out to do something different when the first Rough Guide was published in 1982. Mark Ellingham, just out of university, was travelling in Greece. He brought along the popular guides of the day, but found they were all lacking in some way. They were either strong on ruins and museums but went on for pages without mentioning a beach or taverna. Or they were so conscious of the need to save money that they lost sight of Greece's cultural and historical significance. Also, none of the books told him anything about Greece's contemporary life – its politics, its culture, its people, and how they lived.

So with no job in prospect, Mark decided to write his own guidebook, one which aimed to provide practical information that was second to none, detailing the best beaches and the hottest clubs and restaurants, while also giving hard-hitting accounts of every sight, both famous and obscure, and providing up-to-the-minute information on contemporary culture. It was a guide that encouraged independent travellers to find the best of Greece, and was a great success, getting shortlisted for the Thomas Cook travel guide award, and encouraging Mark, along with three friends, to expand the series.

The Rough Guide list grew rapidly and the letters flooded in, indicating a much broader readership than had been anticipated, but one which uniformly appreciated the Rough Guide mix of practical detail and humour, irreverence and enthusiasm. Things haven't changed. The same four friends who began the series are still the caretakers of the Rough Guide mission today: to provide the most reliable, up-to-date and entertaining information to independent-minded travellers of all ages, on all budgets.

We now publish more than 150 titles and have offices in London and New York. The travel guides are written and researched by a dedicated team of more than 100 authors, based in Britain, Europe, the USA and Australia. We have also created a unique series of phrasebooks to accompany the travel series, along with an acclaimed series of music guides, and a best-selling pocket guide to the Internet and World Wide Web. We also publish comprehensive travel information on our Web site:

www.roughguides.com

HELP US UPDATE

We've gone to a lot of effort to ensure that the second edition of *The Rough Guide to Sweden* is accurate and up-to-date. However, things change – places get "discovered", opening hours are notoriously fickle, restaurants and rooms raise prices or lower standards. If you feel we've got it wrong or left something out, we'd like to know, and if you can remember the address, the price, the time, the phone number, so much the better.

We'll credit all contributions, and send a copy of the next edition (or any other Rough Guide if you prefer) for the best letters. Please mark letters: "Rough Guide Sweden Update" and send to:
Rough Guides, 62–70 Shorts Gardens, London WC2H 9AH, or Rough Guides, 4th Floor, 345 Hudson St, New York NY 10014. Or send email to: *mail@roughguides.co.uk*
Online updates about this book can be found on Rough Guides' Web site at *www.roughguides.com*

THE AUTHORS

James Proctor first travelled to Sweden as a student. Attracted by the open nature of Swedish society, he taught himself Swedish and finally fulfilled a long-standing desire to live in Stockholm while working for the BBC. Now back in Britain, he resides in London and Brighton with his long-suffering partner who's learning to develop an interest in all things Nordic. James is also the co-author of the forthcoming *Rough Guide to Iceland*; when not updating or writing travel guides, he works as the Europe Correspondent for BBC Radio 5 Live and News 24.

Neil Roland is a law graduate living in Didsbury, Manchester, who has worked as a freelance features writer since escaping the clutches of the legal profession. He has been editor of the *Greater Manchester Theatre* magazine and of the *Jewish Gazette* newspaper, and has written on travel, sex, the law and entertainment in a variety of publications. He has also broadcast several short stories for radio and is now concentrating on writing fiction.

READERS' LETTERS

Thanks to all the readers who wrote in with comments on the first edition of this guide, in no particular order: Esra Bayoglu, S.E. Howett, Ulrika Sandberg, Diana Chitty, Jessica Dodd, Brendan Kirwan, Christian Ohman, Colin Gibson, Kate Wilford, S. Hermiston, Duncan Kilby, Annette Ferrier, Malcolm Inglis, Richard Wilmot, Charles Patmore, Harvey Woolf, Mike Day and Jennifer Ahlstrom.

CONTENTS

Introduction x

• CHAPTER 3: THE SOUTHWEST 183

• CHAPTER 4: THE SOUTHEAST 278

• CHAPTER 5: THE BOTHNIAN COAST: GÄVLE TO HAPARANDA 355

• CHAPTER 6: CENTRAL AND NORTHERN SWEDEN 410

PART THREE CONTEXTS 489

LIST OF MAPS

MAP SYMBOLS

▪▬▪▬▪	International boundary	☼	Viewpoint
▬ ▪ ▪ ▪	County boundary	✈	Airport
▬ ▬ ▬	Chapter division boundary	✈	Airfield
═══	Motorway	Ⓣ	T-bana station
═══	Major road	★	Bus stop
───	Minor road	🅟	Parking
-----	Path	◉	Accommodation
─┼─	Railway	⚠	Campsite
▪▪▪▪	Wall	☺	Swimming pool
─ ─ ─	Ferry route	ⓘ	Tourist office
───	Waterway	⊠	Post office
⊥⊥⊥⊥	Canal	ℭ	Telephone
♦	General point of interest	▨	Building
♖	Castle	✚	Church
🏛	Stately home	✝✝✝	Cemetery
♦	Museum	▨	Park
✡	Synagogue	▨	National park/reserve
☉	Statue	◥	Forest
∴	Ruin	▨	Beach
▲	Mountain peak		

INTRODUCTION

The mere mention of **Sweden** conjures up resonant images: snow-capped peaks, reindeer wandering in deep green forests and the 24-hour daylight of the midnight sun – not to mention notions of a standard of living that's one of the highest in the world. But beyond the household names of ABBA, IKEA and Volvo, Sweden is relatively unknown. The largest of the Scandinavian countries, with an area twice that of Britain (and roughly that of California), but a population of barely nine million, Sweden is still one of Europe's best-kept secrets. Its **cities** are safe, carefree places where the cheap public transport runs on time and life is relaxed. Sweden's **countryside** boasts pine and birch forest as far as the eye can see, crystal-clear lakes perfect for a summer afternoon dip, not to mention possibly the purest air you'll ever breathe; the country's south and west **coasts** feature some of the most exquisite beaches in Europe.

Forget anything you've heard about Sweden's reputedly high prices — over recent years, the Swedish *krona* has depreciated significantly against most other Western currencies, putting Sweden within the scope of many visitors' budgets. For accommodation, there's a range of decent hotels, guesthouses and hostels to suit every pocket, and many hotels drop their prices in summer (and at weekends all year round). What's more, Sweden is now one of the least expensive countries to reach from within Europe: air fares of just £99 from London to Stockholm have opened up the country as never before.

The Swedes

The other Nordic nations love to make fun of the **Swedes**. Witness the joke about the ten Nordic men stranded on a desert island. On day one, the two Finns have felled half the trees on the island for firewood. On day two, the two Norwegians have constructed a fishing boat from some of the wood to catch fish for supper. On day three, the Danes have set up a co-operative to organize all the work. On day four, the Icelanders decide to lift everyone's spirits with tales of the brave men of the ancient sagas. And on day five, the two Swedes are still waiting to be introduced to each other.

It is certainly true that the Swedes aren't the easiest of people to get to know, and are often thought of by foreigners as being distant and reserved. On the whole, Swedes are straight-talking, saying what they mean with a minimum of words and fuss. Many visitors interpret this as lack of interest in conversation or even downright rudeness, but both are unlikely to be the case; it's worth noting the fact that the Finns think the Swedes are too talkative. In short, overt expressions of emotion and raucous conversations punctuated with wild gesticulations are not the name of the game in Sweden – at least until the weekend when, in many parts of the country, beer and aquavit help people throw off their inhibitions.

Many tourists come to Sweden looking forward to wild sex and easy pick-ups. Most return home disappointed. Somehow over the years the open Swedish attitude to nudity and sexuality has become confused with sex. Contrary to popular belief though, Sweden isn't populated solely with people waiting for any opportunity to tear their clothes off and make passionate love under the midnight sun. People may talk about sex openly, but when it comes down to it the Swedes can be rather puritanical. **Nudity**, though often seen, is not really looked at, and is

quite unrelated to sex: go to a beach in Sweden on a hot summer's day and you'll doubtless see people sunbathing naked, but this state of affairs is certainly not an invitation for a love-in. However, the Swedes' **liberal** and open attitude to virtually every aspect of life is certainly one of their most enviable qualities; people are generally left to do their own thing providing it doesn't impinge on the rights and freedoms of others. In Sweden, rights go hand-in-hand with duties, and there's a strong sense of civic obligation (count how few times you see people dropping litter, for example), which in turn makes for a well-rounded and stable society.

Where to go

Sweden is principally a land of **forests** and **lakes**. Its towns and cities are small by European standards and mostly to be found in the southern third of the country, where most Swedes live. Of the **cities**, serenely beautiful **Stockholm** is supreme. Sitting elegantly on fourteen different islands, where the waters of Lake Mälaren meet the Baltic Sea, the city boasts some fantastic architecture, fine museums and by far the best culture and nightlife in the country. Its wide tree-lined boulevards, the narrow medieval streets of the Old Town and some modern, state-of-the-art buildings make Stockholm one of the most beautiful cities in Europe. The 24,000 islands which comprise the Stockholm **archipelago** begin just outside the city limits and are a perfect antidote to the bustle of the capital, offering endless opportunities to explore unspoilt island villages — and, of course, to go swimming. On the west coast, **Gothenburg**, the country's second city, is also one of Sweden's most appealing destinations. Gothenburgers have a reputation for being among the friendliest people in Sweden, and the city's network of canals, and spacious avenues is reminiscent of Amsterdam, whose architects designed it.

The **south** is the most cosmopolitan part of the country, owing to the proximity of Denmark and the rest of the European continent. Its surprisingly varied western coast has bustling towns all the way along its length. **Helsingborg**, near where the Danish island of Zeeland and Hamlet's Elsinore is situated, is small yet breezily continental. To the north lies the Bjäre peninsula, offering some of the country's best cycling and hiking, with the home of Swedish tennis, **Båstad**, nestling at the peninsula's base. Just over 50km south of Helsingborg is the gloriously ancient university seat of **Lund**, so different from any other Swedish city; hardly any distance away is **Malmö**, Sweden's third city, which heaves with youthful nightlife around its medieval core. The south coast is brimming with chocolate-box villages and a few cultural surprises; inland, southern Sweden boasts some handsome lakes, the two largest of which, Vänern and Vättern, provide exceptional fishing and splendid backdrops to some beautiful towns, not least the evocative former royal seat and monastic centre of **Vadstena**. To the east of the mainland lie the islands of **Öland** – featuring some stunning scenery – and **Gotland**, justifiably raved about as a haven for summer revelry within the medieval walls of its unspoilt Hanseatic city, **Visby**.

Central and **northern Sweden** are what most outsiders imagine Sweden to look like. In the country's centre is **Dalarna** (literally, "The Dales"), an area of rolling hills and villages of red-and-white wooden houses that is, for Swedes, the most quintessentially Swedish part of the country; it's also home to **Lake Siljan**, one of Sweden's most beautiful lakes. From Dalarna, the private Inlandsbanan train line strikes north through some of the country's most beautiful scenery, with reindeer – and occasionally bears – having to be cleared off the track as the trains make their way from village to village. To the east, the other train line linking the north with the south runs close to the **Bothnian coast**. Most towns and cities in the north are located along here: **Sundsvall, Umeå** and **Luleå** are all enjoyable, lively places to break your journey on the long trek north. Equally, the **High Coast** north of Sundsvall is an excellent introduction to northern Sweden, with its array of pine-clad islands and craggy inlets, which extend deep inland around a patchwork of flower meadows and rolling hillsides.

Both train lines eventually meet in the far north of Sweden, within the **Arctic Circle**, in the home of the Lapps or **Sámi** – Sweden (and Scandinavia's) oldest indigenous people. The further north you travel into **Lapland**, the more isolated the towns become – you'll often be covering vast distances in these regions just to get to the next village, and you shouldn't be surprised if you drive for hours without seeing a soul. This is the land of reindeer and elk, of swiftly flowing rivers and coniferous forest, all traversed by endless hiking routes. The **Kungsleden**, a trail which stretches for 500km from Hemavan to Abisko, passes through some of Sweden's wildest and most beautiful terrain, offering the chance to experience nature in the raw. Two of Sweden's northernmost towns, **Kiruna** and **Gällivare**, make excellent bases for exploring Lapland's **national parks**, which can all be reached easily from there by train or bus. Lapland is also where you will experience the **midnight sun**: in high summer the sun never sets, allowing you to read the newspaper outdoors or play golf at midnight. In midwinter the opposite is true, and months of complete darkness (not to mention temperatures as low as -30°C) can make this one of the most magical parts of the country to travel through, as the sky is lit up by the multi-coloured patterns of the **northern lights**, or Aurora Borealis. An eerie, shifting shimmer in the sky, in the shape of long wisps, and generally green, blue or pale orange in colour, they are created when charged particles from space interact with the earth's magnetic field.

When to go

In general, **May to September** is a good time to visit Sweden – north or south. **Summer** in Sweden, though short, can be hot; recent summers in Stockholm have seen temperatures pushing 30°C. Most Swedes take their summer holiday between mid-June and mid-August, which is when the weather is at its best and festivals are thick on the ground. Generally, if southern Sweden is having a hot summer, it'll be miserably cold and rainy in the north – and vice versa.

By the end of August, in northern Sweden, the leaves are starting to turn colour and night frosts are not uncommon. The first snows fall in the north in September. In Stockholm, snow starts to fall in October but doesn't generally settle; by November, though, the ground is usually covered in a blanket of snow, which will last until the following March or even April, when there can still be snow showers. **Winters** in the south of Sweden are often mild, and the southern province of Skåne often escapes snow completely. Swedes go to great lengths, however, to point out that a cold, snowy winter is far better than a milder, greyer one: a cover of snow on the ground acts as a reflector for the little light there is in the winter months and goes a long way to brightening things up. In the south of the country, the winter snow has generally gone by the end of March or beginning of April, when temperatures are slowly starting to rise. Bear in mind, though, that if you're heading north in late spring you're likely to encounter snow until well into May.

Daylight is in short supply in winter. In December, it doesn't get light in Stockholm until around 9.30am, and it's normally dark again by 3pm. North of the Arctic Circle – in Kiruna, for example – there's twenty-four darkness from mid-

DAYTIME TEMPERATURES (°C) AND AVERAGE MONTHLY RAINFALL (MM)							
Average daily temperatures (°C, max and min) and precipitation (mm)							
Jan	Mar	May	June	July	Aug	Oct	Dec
Jokkmokk							
°C							
-17	-8	6	12	14	12	1	-14
mm							
30	24	35	48	78	74	41	32
Umeå							
°C							
-9	-4	7	13	15	14	4	-7
mm							
49	41	41	44	53	78	65	56
Östersund							
°C							
-7	-4	7	12	13	12	4	-6
mm							
27	23	35	57	76	60	37	31
Stockholm							
°C							
-3	0	11	16	17	16	8	-1
mm							
39	26	30	45	72	66	50	46
Gothenburg							
°C							
-2	1	11	15	16	16	9	0
mm							
62	50	51	61	68	77	84	75
Visby							
°C							
-1	0	10	14	16	16	8	1
mm							
48	32	29	31	50	50	50	51
Lund							
°C							
-1	2	11	15	17	17	9	1
mm							
54	44	43	54	66	63	60	65

December to mid-January, and the merest glow of light at noon during the months immediately either side. This is also the time of year when the **northern lights** are at their most spectacular in the far north of the country. Conversely, at the height of summer there's no part of Sweden which is dark for very long. Even the south of the country only experiences a few hours of darkness; in Stockholm it doesn't get properly dark at all in June. From 11pm or midnight there's a sort of half-light, with the sun only just below the horizon, which lasts just a few hours; at 3am it's bright daylight again. In the far north there's 24-hour daylight from the end of May to the end of June, and April and July are very light months.

BASICS

GETTING THERE FROM BRITAIN

Given the long distances involved in reaching Sweden, especially the northern stretches of the country, flying is by far the best and cheapest option. The decision in recent years by the cut-price Irish airline, Ryanair, to target the Swedish market and introduce several daily London–Stockholm flights has seen prices plummet. As a result, Sweden is now one of the cheapest European countries to reach from the UK, with off-season one-way fares to Stockholm sometimes as low as £30. The train from London to the Swedish capital takes at least 25 hours – the plane takes two. But if you're planning to travel around Sweden by train, it's worth considering getting there on an InterRail or ScanRail ticket to help cut the cost. To take your car to Sweden, there are direct, if expensive, ferries from Newcastle to Gothenburg; driving on Sweden's straight and quiet roads is a joy (but bear in mind the high cost of petrol once you're there, generally around 8.5kr per litre). Travel by long-distance bus is the stuff horror movies are made of, and isn't recommended – it will nearly always be cheaper to fly.

FLIGHTS

Contacting airlines apart, a good way to find **cheap flights** is to look in the classified sections in the Sunday newspapers or, if you live in London, *Time Out* magazine or the *Evening Standard*, which sometimes throw up good offers. Failing that, go straight to a discount flight agent like Strata Travel (who specialize in cheap scheduled fares to

Sweden) or Trailfinders, STA Travel or usit CAMPUS; the last two specialize in youth and student flights, as well as discounted fares for the over-26s.

From **London Stansted**, Ryanair flies to two airports in Sweden: **Skavsta** (euphemistically called "Stockholm South" in the airline trade) and **Kristianstad**. Near the town of Nyköping, southwest of Stockholm, Skavsta is about a hour's drive from the capital; Ryanair's return fare generally hovers around the £99 mark (Mon–Thurs), rising by around £10–20 for departures involving travel on a Friday, Saturday or Sunday. Kristianstad is on the southeast coast of Skåne, within easy reach of Malmö, and the return fare with Ryanair is £69. Special promotions are often run when business is slow; for information on these, contact Ryanair direct (see box on p.4 for details).

It's worth trying other **airlines** who operate to Sweden, not just for the option of flying from Heathrow or Gatwick, but also because these companies now try to match the fares offered by Ryanair – the most useful ones are Scandinavian Airlines (SAS) and British Airways (BA). The cheapest non-discounted deals require your stay to include a minimum of one Saturday night, and generally have to be booked at least one day in advance, sometimes more. Flights in June, July and August (particularly at weekends) are often sold out months before at these lower fares. If you're under 25, ask about the availability of youth fares, although generally they're nothing to write home about. All the prices quoted below are the cheapest scheduled fares.

Of all the airlines, SAS has the most direct flights to Sweden from the largest number of British cities, with five flights a day from **Heathrow to Stockholm** (from £99; 2hr 25min) and two a day from **Heathrow to Gothenburg** (from £163; 1hr 55min). BA also operate direct flights to **Stockholm** and **Gothenburg** for around the same prices (see "Airlines and agents" for a full run-through of all the possibilities). SAS also flies from **Stansted to Stockholm** in competition with Ryanair and can therefore often be a good source of cheap fares (£99; 2hr 10min) – SAS has the advantage of flying into Stockholm's more central Arlanda airport, not Skavsta. The Swedish domestic airline Braathens Malmö Aviation flies from **London City Airport to Malmö** (from £139; 1hr 45min). Finnair flies direct twice daily (Sat & Sun 1 daily) from

AIRLINES

Braathens Malmö Aviation ☎01293/530839, *www.malmoaviation.com* London City to Malmö (2 daily except Sat); Edinburgh to Gothenburg (Tues & Fri 1 flight in summer only).

British Airways ☎0345/222111, *www.british-airways.com* Heathrow to Stockholm (5 daily); Gatwick–Stockholm (3 daily); Heathrow to Gothenburg (2 daily); Gatwick to Gothenburg (1 daily). Also flights to Copenhagen.

British Midland ☎0870/607 0555, *www. britishmidland.com* Edinburgh and Glasgow to Copenhagen, with connections on SAS to Gothenburg and Stockholm.

Finnair ☎020/7408 1222, *www.finnair.com* Manchester to Stockholm (Mon–Fri 2 daily; Sat & Sun 1 daily).

KLM UK ☎0870/507 4074, *www.klmuk.com* Frequent departures from UK regional airports to Stockholm and Gothenburg, via Amsterdam.

Go ☎0845/605 4321, *www.go-fly.com* Stansted to Copenhagen (Mon–Fri 3 daily; Sat & Sun 2 daily).

Maersk Air ☎020/7333 0066, *www. maersk-air.com* Gatwick to Copenhagen (2 daily); Birmingham to Copenhagen (2 daily).

Ryanair ☎0870/333 1250, *www.ryanair.com* Stansted to Stockholm South (3 daily); Stansted to Kristianstad (1 daily).

Scandinavian Airlines ☎0845/6072 7727, *www.sas.se* Heathrow to Stockholm (6 daily); Stansted to Stockholm (2 daily); Edinburgh to Stockholm (May–Sept Sat 1 daily); Heathrow to Gothenburg (2 daily); Heathrow to Copenhagen (5 daily); Stansted to Copenhagen (3 daily); Manchester to Stockholm (Mon–Fri 2 daily, Sat & Sun 1 daily). SAS offers connections through Copenhagen to Stockholm, Borlänge, Gothenburg, Jönköping, Kalmar, Karlstad, Malmö (by hovercraft), Norrköping, Örebro, Västerås and Växjö. Connections to destinations in northern Sweden can be made in Stockholm.

Widerøe ☎0141/887 1381, *www.wideroe.no* Summer-only flight (July to mid-Aug Thurs & Sun 1 daily) from Sumburgh in Shetland to Bergen. Connections available in Bergen to Stockholm and Gothenburg.

DISCOUNT TRAVEL AGENTS

Benz Travel, Regent St, London W1 (☎ 020/7462 0000).

STA Travel, 117 Euston Rd, London NW1 2SX, and branches elsewhere in London and in other major cities (☎020/7361 6145, *www. statravel. co.uk*). Worldwide specialists in low-cost flights and tours for students and under-26s.

Strata Travel, 9 Central Parade, Green St, Enfield EN3 7HG (☎020/8805 1555). Discount fares on scheduled flights.

Trailfinders, 215 Kensington High St, London W8 6BD, and branches elsewhere in London and in other major cities (☎020/7937 5400, *www.trailfinder.com*). One of the best-informed and most efficient agents.

Travel Bug, 597 Cheetham Hill Rd, Manchester M8 5EJ (☎0161/721 4000). Large range of discounted tickets.

Travel Cuts, 295 Regent St, London W1 (☎ 020/7255 1944).

usit CAMPUS, 52 Grosvenor Gardens, London SW1W 0AG and branches elsewhere in London and in other major cities (☎0870/240 1010, *www.usitcampus.co.uk*). Student/youth travel specialists, with branches also in YHA shops and on university campuses all over Britain.

usit Council, 28a Poland St, London W1V 3DB (☎020/7437 7767). Flights and student discounts.

Manchester to Stockholm (£185; 2hr 20min); SAS' Manchester–Stockholm flights (Mon–Fri 2 daily, Sat & Sun 1 daily) cost about the same. On Saturdays from April to October, SAS also flies direct **from Edinburgh to Stockholm** (£213; 2hr 10min); while from mid-June to late September, Braathens Malmö Aviation fly from Edinburgh to **Gothenburg** (£150; 1hr 45min). Flying to Stockholm from any other British city will involve a change of plane, most conveniently in Copenhagen, London or Amsterdam, although given the disproportionately higher fares to Stockholm from regional airports, it's probably worth considering travelling to London and taking a cheaper direct flight.

VIA DENMARK AND NORWAY

Flights to **Copenhagen** can be useful for **southern Sweden**, particularly Malmö. An inexpensive jetfoil service runs from Copenhagen city centre to Malmö, and from the summer of 2000, Copenhagen Airport will be linked directly to Malmö by train, via the new Öresund bridge. For bus services from Copenhagen airport to Sweden, see p.6. Airlines flying from **London to Copenhagen** include SAS (from Heathrow and Stansted), BA (Heathrow and Gatwick), Maersk (Gatwick) and Go (Stansted). Fares from London to Copenhagen start at £105. Flights from regional cities to Copenhagen include SAS, flying from **Manchester**; BA from Belfast via **Newcastle**; British Midland from **Glasgow** and **Edinburgh**; while Maersk is the only airline to operate out of **Birmingham**. Fares from regional cities to Copenhagen are around £180–200 with all these airlines; connections on to Stockholm or Gothenburg bring the price up to £250 or £230 respectively.

From Aberdeen, SAS offers **flights to Sweden via Norway** – first to Stavanger (from £200; 1hr; then onward connections to both Stockholm and Gothenburg for roughly another £100). From Orkney and Shetland, the best option to avoid the long and expensive haul south to Glasgow or London is the summer-only flight from Sumburgh to Bergen with the Norwegian carrier, Widerøe, and then travelling onwards to Sweden overland or by air.

SAS Airpasses are sold in connection with the company's return flights and can be useful for travelling around Sweden by air (see "Getting around", p.26).

TRAINS

Taking the **train** is much more expensive than flying, and is only worth considering if you're travelling on a rail pass. A number of discounted tickets and passes make it possible to cut costs (see below).

From London, trains to Sweden go via Brussels, Cologne, Hamburg and Copenhagen: a typical journey will involve changing trains four or five times. The fastest and easiest connection in summer is to take the Eurostar, leaving Waterloo in the early morning for Brussels Midi. From there, you should be able to take a mid-morning train to Cologne, where you change again for a lunchtime train to Hamburg, changing again in Hamburg for a late-afternoon train to Copenhagen, from where you pick up the connecting sleeper up to Stockholm. The times of trains can change, particularly if you're travelling outside the summer

season, but the above pattern generally holds. With the optimal choice of connections, the total journey takes around 24 hours, otherwise it could take up to 36 hours. The standard London–Stockholm return fare is around £470. From the summer of 2000, there will be direct trains from Copenhagen to Stockholm via the new Öresund bridge rather than via Helsingör and Helsingborg; this should cut the Copenhagen–Stockholm train journey time by an hour or two.

Travelling **from the north of England or Scotland**, you may well prefer to take the overnight P&O North Sea Ferries service from Hull to Rotterdam (passenger fare £59 one-way with cabin; students, under-26s and over-60s £37), and then a mid-morning train from Rotterdam for Utrecht, changing there for Oberhausen in the late morning, changing again in Oberhausen for a lunchtime train to Münster West, from where you get a mid-afternoon service to Hamburg; thereafter follow the route to Stockholm via Copenhagen detailed previously. There is no through ticket for this journey; the cheapest way to do it is with an InterRail pass (see below). Despite all the connections on this route, it's the fastest way to get from Holland to Sweden by train.

DISCOUNT TICKETS AND PASSES

If you're under 26, a **BIJ** ticket gives up to fifty-percent discount on ordinary fares. Available through Eurotrain or Wasteels (see "Train information", p.6, for details) and from youth and student travel agents (see p.4), these allow as many stopovers as you like and are valid for two months. You buy a ticket to more or less anywhere in Sweden, and follow a choice of routes to get there.

Better value by far, especially if you are taking in a number of other countries on the way, is an **InterRail pass**, available to anyone resident for six months in the participating European countries. A zoning system applies to all of the countries covered by the scheme, and the price of the pass is determined by the number of zones you want to travel in and for how long. Supplements for certain types of train (such as Sweden's InterCity and X2000 services, see p.27), seat reservations, couchettes and/or sleeping cars are extra, but you do get discounts on British trains and on Eurostar, and some hefty discounts on ferries within Scandinavia, including Sweden. To reach Sweden you'll need a pass covering zone E (France, Belgium, Netherlands, Luxembourg), zone

TRAIN INFORMATION

Eurostar, Eurostar House, Waterloo Station, London SE1 8SE (☎0990/186 186, www.eurostar.com).

Eurotunnel, Customer Service Centre, jct 12 off M20, PO Box 300, Dept 302, Folkestone, Kent CT19 4QD Centre (☎0990/353 535, www.eurotunnel.com).

Rail Europe, 179 Piccadilly, London W1V 0BA (☎0990/848 848 www.raileurope.co.uk).

Wasteels, Victoria Station (by platform 2), London SW1V 1JY (☎020/7834 7066).

BUS INFORMATION

Eurolines, ticket office opposite Victoria Station at 52 Grosvenor Gardens, London SW1W 0AU (bookings and enquiries ☎020/7730 8235 or ☎0900/143 219).

C (Germany, Switzerland, Austria and Denmark), and zone B (Sweden itself; also covers Norway and Finland) if you intend to see the country by train. A one-month pass for three zones currently costs £229. The equivalent **InterRail "26-Plus" pass** for those over 26 costs £309. The passes are available from Rail Europe and youth/student travel agencies.

A serious rival to InterRail, and invaluable if you're planning to visit the rest of Scandinavia as well, is the **ScanRail pass**. Valid on the rail networks of all four countries, the pass comes in two forms, ScanRail and ScanRail Flexi. A full 21-day ScanRail pass in standard class costs £212; 12- to 25-year-olds pay £160; over-60s £189. ScanRail Flexi is available for travel on any five days in a fifteen-day period (adult £139; youth £105; over-60s £124) or any ten days in a month (adult £187; youth £141; over-60s £166). More expensive passes for first-class travel are also available. ScanRail passes are valid on the Inlandsbanan (see p.30) as well as on buses connecting Boden, Haparanda and Kemi in Finland. They also give discounts on a number of ferry routes, including Stockholm–Helsinki, Stockholm–Turku, Umeå–Vaasa and Gothenburg–Fredrikshavn. The pass must be bought from Rail Europe before you leave (see box above).

Another alternative for travelling in Sweden (and through Scandinavia) is the **Freedom pass**, which offers unlimited train travel (including supplements for high-speed trains) within any one of 25 European countries includ-ing Sweden, Denmark, Finland and Norway. For each country you have to buy a separate pass, which is good for a certain number of travel days within a one-month period, and comes in under-26 and standard-class versions. The prices for Sweden are: three days for £99 (under-26) and £119 (standard-class); five days for £119 and £149; and eight days for £159 and £199. Exactly the same deal can also be purchased from Eurotrain, which calls its pass a **EuroDomino**.

Finally, if you're 60 or over, the **Rail Europe Senior Card** gives thirty-percent discounts on train travel in 25 European countries, including Eurostar and on sea crossings that connect with trains; more details on this card can be obtained from train-ticket agents. Information on Swedish rail passes is given in "Getting around" on p.27.

BUSES

Bus services from the UK to Sweden are an endurance test, and don't really save you money over a discounted flight. **From London**, Eurolines operate a service up to three times a week from Victoria Bus Station to Stockholm (31hr; from £161 return) with stops at around sixteen destinations in Sweden. **From the north of England and Scotland**, National Express run direct daily bus services to the Hull ferry terminal for the sailing to Rotterdam. Principal pick-up points are Bradford, Edinburgh, Glasgow, Leeds, Manchester, Middlesborough, Newcastle, Oldham, Sunderland and York; details from Eurolines (see box above).

Travellers flying to Copenhagen's main Kastrup airport can take advantage of a useful bus service that connects the airport with the south of Sweden. Kustlinjen buses (buy tickets on the bus with either Danish or Swedish currency; www.swebus.se/sweb9/flygbus2.html) depart from right outside the Arrivals terminal building and run eight times a day, linking Kastrup with Helsingborg (115kr one-way), Ängelholm (115kr), Båstad (115kr) and Halmstad (160kr). At Helsingborg you can connect up with the Swedish rail network and take a direct train to Stockholm; Halmstad is on the main Malmö–Gothenburg line, with frequent services between these two cities. There are also frequent daily buses from Copenhagen to Malmö (100kr). However, once the Öresund bridge opens to commercial traffic in July 2000, it will be much easier to get to Sweden by train, with direct services from Copenhagen airport all the way to Stockholm.

FERRIES

Only one ferry company, **DFDS Seaways**, provides a direct link between Britain and Sweden. It's possible to head for Sweden using ferry routes to other parts of Scandinavia and Europe; for a list of useful routes and details of the operators, see below. Although direct crossings to Sweden are long, they do save a lot in petrol and frayed tempers – don't underestimate the length of the drive up from France or Belgium through the Netherlands, Germany and Denmark before southern Sweden finally comes into sight. The drive from Copenhagen to Stockholm itself will take around eight to ten hours depending on the weather, and much longer in winter. This long haul north makes taking your car across to France on Eurotunnel services not worth the bother, unless you are doing a really extensive tour (see "Train Information" opposite for Eurotunnel details). The only other ferry routes that make any sense are those to the Netherlands, giving you a head start on the drive to Sweden.

DFDS Seaways' **fares** are expensive; the cheapest ticket from Newcastle to Gothenburg for a car and five passengers, with couchette accommodation, costs £493. For foot passengers, the cheapest tickets start at £99. Students get a fifty-percent discount. Facilities on board are extremely good, with saunas, cinemas and discos helping to while away the long hours. Bear in mind, though, that a 24-hour crossing of the North Sea can be a stomach-wrenching experience, especially in winter.

PACKAGE TOURS

Don't be put off by the idea of an inclusive **package**, as it can sometimes work out the cheapest way of doing things, and may be a much easier way of reaching remote areas of northern Sweden in winter. **City breaks** invariably work out less costly than arranging the same trip independently: prices include return travel, usually by plane, and accommodation ranging from hostels to luxury-class hotels. As a broad guide, four-night stays in Stockholm and Gothenburg go for around £250–300 a head. Go for a week, and rates per night fall considerably.

There are also an increasing number of operators (see box, p.8) offering **special-interest holidays** to Sweden, from camping tours to Arctic expeditions. Many also offer good-value

USEFUL FERRY ROUTES

Route	Company	Frequency	Duration
Newcastle–Gothenburg	DFDS Seaways	2 weekly	25hr 30min
Harwich–Esbjerg	DFDS Seaways	3–4 weekly	20hr
Hull–Rotterdam	P&O North Sea Ferries	1 daily	14hr
Lerwick–Bergen	Smyril Line	mid-May to mid-Sept only 1 weekly (Mon)	13hr 30min
Harwich–Hook of Holland	Stena Line	2 daily	4hr

FERRY OPERATORS
DFDS Seaways ☎0990/333000, www.dfdsseaways.co.uk
P&O North Sea Ferries ☎01482/377177, www.ponsf.com
Smyril Line www.smyril-line.fo, or c/o P&O Scottish Ferries (☎01224/572615).
Stena Line ☎0990/707070, www.stenaline.com

SPECIALIST TOUR OPERATORS

Anglers World Holidays, 46 Knifesmith Gate, Chesterfield, S40 1QR (☎01246/221717). Angling holidays; cottage and hotel stays.

Arctic Experience, 29 Nork Way, Banstead, SM7 1PB (☎01737/218800, *www.arctic-discover.co.uk*). Specializes in trips to Lapland.

Crystal Holidays, Crystal House, The Courtyard, Arlington Rd, Surbiton, Surrey KT6 6BW (☎020/8399 5144). The biggest ski operator on the market, with packages to Åre and Storlien at reasonable prices.

DFDS Seaways, Scandinavia House, Parkeston Quay, Harwich, CO12 4QG (☎0990/333000, *www.dfdsseaways.co.uk*). Extensive range of motoring and cabin holidays as well as city breaks – good out-of-season deals.

Mountain & Wildlife Ventures, Compston Road, Ambleside, Cumbria LA22 9DJ

(☎015394/433285). Vastly experienced company dealing in Nordic ski touring, skiing courses, mountain skiing and expeditions.

Norvista, 227 Regents St, London W1R 8PD (☎020/7409 7334). Hiking holidays around Arvidsjaur, and a four-day Arctic safari – but neither is worth the exorbitant prices.

Scantours, 21–24 Cockspur St, London, SW1Y 5BN (☎020/7839 2927). City breaks, cruises on the Göta canal, and trips out to lakes and mountains.

Tracks Travel, Evegate Park Barn, Smeeth, Ashford, Kent TN25 6SX (☎01797/344667). Group camping tours for 18- to 38-year-olds.

Travellers, Waterside, Kendal, Cumbria LA9 4HE (☎015396/20196). Dog-sledging holidays in Arctic Sweden, with accommodation in mountain cabins in the national parks.

skiing and **winter sports holidays**: a week in one of the major resorts, Storlien, costs around £300 (including flight and half board) in January with Ski Scandinavia. General information on skiing holidays in Sweden can be obtained from the Swedish Travel and Tourism Council's **Ski Sweden Information Line**, on ☎020/7724 5868. For more on skiing and winter sports in Sweden, see "Sports and outdoor pursuits", p.47.

GETTING THERE FROM IRELAND

With no ferry services from Ireland to any Scandinavian port, the most straightforward way to travel to Sweden is to fly. If you are planning a wider European tour, travelling by train on an InterRail pass is an option worth considering. Alternatively, you might find it more economical to make your way to London and pick up a flight, bus or package deal from there – all of which are detailed in "Getting there from Britain" (see p.3).

The cheapest airline ticket from Ireland is an **Apex**; these require you to stay for a minimum of one Saturday night and to book at least seven days in advance (all the prices quoted below are Apex fares). In general, there isn't much in the way of seasonal special deals, but since the airlines' fare structures change regularly, it's always a good idea to check with them or with your local travel agent.

It's possible to cut costs further by approaching a **discount agent**. Several of the discount agents (for addresses, see below), in particular usit NOW, are good for discount deals; if you're under 26 or a student, you can generally secure fares from Dublin to Stockholm for around IR£238.

From the Republic of Ireland, Finnair are the only airline offering direct flights to Sweden, with daily services (not Wed) **from Dublin** to **Stockholm** (IR£210; 3hr 50mln); and flights to **Gothenburg** via Copenhagen (IR£230; 4hr). It's likely to be cheaper to fly with Ryanair from Dublin to **Stansted**, and then pick up a connecting flight on to either Stockholm or Kristianstad with the same airline. Another possibility is to catch a flight from Dublin to **Copenhagen** on Aer Lingus (1 daily; 2 hr) or SAS (2 daily; 2hr), and get a connection to Stockholm from there.

AIRLINES

Aer Lingus Reservations ☎01/886 8888 in the Republic, ☎0845/973 7747 in Northern Ireland, *www.aerlingus.ie* Daily flights to Copenhagen.
British Airways Reservations ☎1-800/626747 in the Republic, ☎0345/222111 in Northern Ireland, *www.british-airways.com* Belfast to Heathrow, with three daily connections to Stockholm.

British Midland ☎01/283 8833 in the Republic, ☎0870/607 0555 in Northern Ireland. Belfast to Heathrow, then onward flights on SAS to Stockholm and Gothenburg.
Finnair 01/844 6565 in the Republic. Direct daily flights from Dublin to Stockholm.
Scandinavian Airlines ☎01/844 5888 in the Republic. Daily direct flights from Dublin to Copenhagen.

FERRY OPERATORS

Irish Ferries In the Republic ☎01/638 3333 and 24hr information 661 0715, *www.irishferries.ie* Dublin–Holyhead and Rosslare–Pembroke; once in Britain, you hook up in Newcastle with Scandinavian Seaways to Sweden.

DISCOUNT TRAVEL AGENTS

Discount Travel, 4 South Great Georges St, Dublin 2 (☎01/679 5888).
Flight Finders International, 13 Baggot St Lower, Dublin 2 (☎01/676 8326).
Joe Walsh Tours, 8–11 Baggot St, Dublin (☎01/676 3053). General budget fares agent.
Liffey Travel, Abbey Mall, 13 Lower Liffey St, Dublin 1 (☎01/873 4900). Package tour specialists.
Neenan Travel, 12 South Leinster St, Dublin 2 (☎01/676 5181). European city breaks.
Student & Group Travel, 71 Dame St, Dublin 2 (☎01/677 7834). Student specialists.

Thomas Cook, 118 Grafton St, Dublin (☎01/677 1721); 11 Donegal Place, Belfast BT1 5AJ (☎028/9088 3900). Package holiday and flight agent, with occasional discount offers.
Travel Shop, 35 Belmont Rd, Belfast 4 (☎01232/471717).
usit NOW, O'Connell Bridge, 19–21 Aston Quay, Dublin 2 (☎01/602 1600) and branches elsewhere in the Republic; Fountain Centre, Belfast BT1 6ET (☎028/9032 4073). *www.usitnow.ie* Student and youth specialists for flights, trains and European city breaks.

From Belfast, British Airways flies to **Copenhagen** (with a brief stop in Newcastle) from £190, where connections can be made to Stockholm for around another £100. Alternatively BA offer flights to London Heathrow with onward connections to Stockholm (from £295; 6–8hr). British Midland also fly from Belfast to Heathrow and offer connections and through fares with their partner airline, SAS, to Stockholm for the same price. It's better to buy two separate tickets instead of one through fare, for example a Belfast–Heathrow return (from around £60) plus Heathrow–Stockholm return (from £99).

If you want to travel to Sweden **by train**, then buying an **InterRail pass** (available from usit NOW) makes a lot of sense, especially if you are taking in a number of other countries on the way. From both the North and the Republic, you need the same pass as someone travelling from Britain. Another useful train pass is the **ScanRail pass**, which allows free travel within Sweden, Denmark, Norway and Finland. For full details of both passes see "Getting there from Britain".

Attempting to take the **bus** all the way to Sweden would involve connecting up with services from Britain and would take up to three days; for the money it saves it really isn't worth the hassle. Similarly, anyone wanting to take their car to Sweden is facing a long and tiring journey. Irish Ferries' "Landbridge" tickets allow you to travel via Britain and link up with Scandinavian Seaways **ferries** to Sweden (see "Getting there from Britain" for a full run-through of their routes), while P&O services to France are only worth it if you are touring the other countries on the way. On the Larne–Cairnryan route from Northern Ireland, P&O offer an inclusive onward fare for their services from Newcastle to Gothenburg (see the box on p.7 for ferry company details).

As yet there are very few **packages** available from Ireland to Sweden, and the agents listed on p.9 only have a limited range of city breaks and skiing holidays on offer. Probably your best bet is to connect up with one of the packages offered by the Britain-based tour operators (see p.8).

GETTING THERE FROM NORTH AMERICA

With only two airlines operating direct flights from the USA to Sweden, and with no direct flights from Canada, you will more than likely have to transit via another European city. To reduce costs you might consider flying to London first and continuing from there by plane, train or ferry (see "Getting there from Britain"). If you're visit-ing Sweden as part of a wider European tour, buying a Eurail pass can be one of the most cost-effective ways to travel (see the box on European passes on p.14).

SHOPPING FOR TICKETS

Special offers aside, the cheapest of the airlines' published fares is usually an **Apex** ticket, although this will carry certain restrictions: you have to book – and pay – at least 21 days before departure and spend at least seven days and no more than three months abroad; there tend to be penalties if you change your schedule. On transatlantic routes, there are also winter **Super Apex** tickets, sometimes known as "Eurosavers" – slightly cheaper than an ordinary Apex, but limiting your stay to between 7 and 21 days. Some airlines also issue Special Apex tickets to people younger than 24, often extending the maximum stay to a year. Many airlines offer youth or student fares to **under-26s**, though these tickets are subject to availability and can have eccentric booking conditions. It's worth remembering that most cheap return fares involve

DISCOUNT AGENTS, CONSOLIDATORS AND TRAVEL CLUBS

Adventure Travel Network ☎1-800/467-4595, *www.atntravel.com* Discount travel agency.

Air Brokers International ☎1-800/883-3273 or 415/397-1383, *www.airbrokers.com* Consolidator.

Air Courier Association ☎303/278-8810, *www.aircourier.org* Courier flight broker.

Airhitch ☎1-800/326-2009 or 212/864-2000, *www.airhitch.org* Stand-by seat broker: for a set price, they guarantee to get you on a flight heading as close to your preferred destination as possible, and departing within a week of your preferred travel date.

Airtech ☎1-800/575-TECH or 212/219-7000, *www.airtech.com* Stand-by seat broker; also deals in consolidator fares and courier flights.

Cheap Tickets, Inc US offices nationwide (☎1-800/377-1000 or 212/570-1179, *www.cheaptickets.com*). Consolidator.

Council Travel, 205 E 42nd St, New York, NY 10017 (☎1-800/226-8624 or 212/822-2700, *www.counciltravel.com*), and branches in many other US cities. Student/budget travel agency.

Educational Travel Center ☎1-800/747-5551 or 608/256-5551, *www.edtrav.com* Student/youth and consolidator fares.

International Student Exchange Flights, 5010 E Shea Blvd, Suite 104A, Scottsdale, AZ 85254 (☎1-800/255-8000 or 480/951-1177, *www.isecards.com*). Student/youth fares, student IDs.

Last Minute Travel Services, offices nationwide (☎1-800/LAST-MIN). Specializes in stand-by flights.

Nouvelles Frontières/New Frontiers, 1001 Sherbrook East, Suite 720, Montréal, H2L 1L3 (☎514/526-8444); in the US 12 E 33rd St, New York, NY 10016 (☎1-800/366-6387); *www.nouvelles-frontieres.com* French discount travel firm.

Now Voyager, 74 Varick St, Suite 307, New York, NY 10013 (☎212/431-1616). Courier flight broker and consolidator.

Skylink, 265 Madison Ave, 5A, New York, NY 10016 (☎1-800/892-0027 or 212/682-3111, *www.pltravel.com*). Consolidator.

STA Travel, 10 Downing St, New York, NY 10014 (☎1-800/781-4040 or 212/627-3111, *www.statravel.com*), and other branches. Worldwide discount travel firm specializing in student/youth fares.

TFI Tours International ☎1-800/745-8000 or 212/736-1140. Consolidator.

Travac ☎1-800/872-8800 or 212/563-3303, *www.thetravelsite.com* Consolidator and charter broker. If you have a fax machine you can have a list of fares faxed to you by calling toll-free ☎1-888/872-8327.

Travel Avenue ☎1-800/333-3335 or 312/876-6866, *www.travelavenue.com* Full-service travel agent that offers discounts in the form of subsequent rebates.

Travel CUTS, 187 College St, Toronto, ON M5T 1P7 (☎416/979-2406, *www.travelcuts.com*), and other branches all over Canada. Canadian student travel organization specializing in student fares, IDs and other travel services.

Travelers Advantage ☎1-800/548-1116, *www.travelersadvantage.com* Travel club; annual membership required.

UniTravel ☎1-800/325-2222 or 314/569-2501, *www.flightsforless.com* Consolidator.

Worldtek Travel ☎1-800/243-1723 or 203/772-0470, *www.worldtek.com* Discount travel agency.

Worldwide Discount Travel Club ☎305/534-2082. Travel club; annual membership required. Call for membership kit.

---

spending at least one Saturday night away and that often only a partial refund can be made if you need to cancel or alter your journey, so check the restrictions carefully before buying.

You can normally cut costs further by going through a **specialist flight agent** – either a **consolidator**, who buys up blocks of tickets from the airlines and sells them at a discount, or a **discount agent**, who in addition to dealing with discounted flights may offer special student and youth fares, and a range of other travel-related services such as travel insurance, rail passes, car rentals, tours and the like. Bear in mind, though, that penalties for

changing your plans can be stiff. Remember, too, that these companies make their money by dealing in bulk – don't expect them to answer lots of questions. Some agents specialize in **charter flights**, which may be cheaper than any scheduled ones, but again departure dates cannot be changed and withdrawal penalties are high (check the refund policy). If you travel a lot, **discount travel clubs** are another option to consider – the annual membership fee may be worth it for benefits such as cut-price air tickets and car rental.

Don't assume that tickets purchased through a flight specialist will be the cheapest – once you get

AIRLINES AND ROUTES FROM NORTH AMERICA

Air Canada US ☎1-800/776-3000, Canada 1-800/555-1212 for local toll-free number, *www.aircanada.ca* Toronto to Copenhagen, Frankfurt, or London, with connections to Stockholm on SAS and Lufthansa.

Air France US ☎1-800/237-2747, Canada 1-800/667-2747, *www.airfrance.fr* Flies daily from many major US and Canadian cities to Paris with connections to Stockholm.

American Airlines ☎1-800/433-7300, *www.americanair.com* Direct flights to Stockholm from Chicago.

British Airways US ☎1-800/247-9297, Canada 1-800/668-1059, *www.british-airways.com* Flies daily from 26 different US and Canadian cities to London, with connecting flights to Stockholm.

Continental Airlines ☎1-800/231-0856, *www.continental.com* New York to Paris, Frankfurt or Madrid connecting to flights to Stockholm on Air France or SAS.

Delta Airlines ☎1-800/241-4141, *www.delta-air.com* Direct flights from New York to Stockholm; or from Atlanta or New York to Brussels or Zürich with connections on Sabena or Swissair.

Finnair ☎1-800/950-5000 or in Canada 1-800/461-8651, *www.finnair.com* Flights from New York to Stockholm via Helsinki (6–7 weekly); also from San Francisco (summer only; 3 weekly), Fort Lauderdale (Sun in winter only), and Toronto (summer only; 2 weekly).

Icelandair ☎1-800/223-5500, *www.icelandair.com* Flies to Stockholm via Reykjavik from New York (daily), Minneapolis (daily), Baltimore (6 weekly), Boston (4 weekly), Orlando (3 weekly) and Halifax (2 weekly) – frequencies given here are for high season; they vary throughout the year. You'll have the option to break your journey with 1–3 nights' stay in Reykjavik.

Scandinavian Airlines ☎1-800/221-2350, *www.flysas.com* Direct daily flights from New York and Chicago to Stockholm; also operates daily flights from Seattle to Stockholm, via Copenhagen. You can connect up on United with all their flights from other North American cities.

TWA ☎1-800/892-4141, *www.twa.com* Services from major cities in North America to European cities such as Paris, London and Madrid, with connections on Air France or SAS to Stockholm.

United Airlines ☎1-800/538-2929, *www.ual.com* Connects most major North American cities with SAS direct flights from New York or Chicago to Stockholm.

US Air ☎1-800/622-1015, *www.usairways.com* Flies from Philadelphia to many major European cities, with connecting flights to Stockholm on other carriers.

Virgin Atlantic ☎1-800/862-8621, *www.virgin-atlantic.com* Daily flights from the major US and Canadian cities to London, with connections to Stockholm.

---

a quote, check with the airlines and you may turn up an even better deal. Be advised also that a few operators are sharks – exercise caution and never deal with a company that demands cash upfront or refuses to accept payment by credit card.

Students might be able to find cheaper flights through the major student travel agencies, such as STA Travel, Nouvelles Frontières or, for Canadian students, Travel Cuts (see the box on p.11 for details).

Another option for finding air fares is the **World Wide Web**. In addition to the Web sites of the discount travel firms, there are a number of Web-based companies that allow you to look up fares and book tickets. You can search the travel sections of the main Web directories for these, or try Travelocity, *www.travelocity.com*; and FLIFO Cyber Travel Agent, *www.flifo. com.*

Regardless of where you buy your ticket, the fare will depend on the **time of year** you travel:

fares are highest between June and August, when the weather is best; they drop during the "shoulder" seasons of mid-March to May and September to October, and are cheapest during the low season, November to mid-March (excluding Christmas and New Year when prices are hiked up and seats are at a premium). Double-check with each airline for specific season dates. Flying on Fridays and at weekends adds about US$50–60 to the round-trip fare.

FLIGHTS AND FARES

Non-stop flights from the **US** to Sweden are operated by Scandinavian Airlines (SAS), which flies from New York to Stockholm daily, and by American Airlines, with daily flights from Chicago to Stockholm. Icelandair, Finnair and SAS also fly from numerous US cities to Stockholm, with one stop en route in their respective hubs of Reykjavik, Helsinki and Copenhagen – see the box above for

SPECIALIST TOUR OPERATORS

Abercrombie & Kent ☎1-800/323-7308, *www.abercrombiekent.com* Tours of Scandinavia by land and sea.

American Express Vacations ☎1-800/446-6234, *www.americanexpress.com/travel* Flight-plus-hotel packages to Stockholm.

Bennett Tours ☎1-800-221-2420, *www.bennett-tours.com* Scandinavia specialists offering cheap weekend breaks (in winter) or fully escorted bus tours (in summer) throughout Scandinavia.

Bergen Line ☎1-800/323-7436, in Canada call Finncharter on ☎1-800/461-8651, *www.coastalvoyages.com* For cruises along the Norwegian coast, with ferry connections to Sweden.

Borton Overseas ☎1-800/843-0602, *www.borton.com* Company specializing in adventure vacations (hiking, mountain biking, cross-country skiing, horse riding).

Contiki Tours ☎1-800/CONTIKI. Tours of Scandinavia and Russia for 18- to 35-year-olds.

Euro-Bike ☎1-800/321-6060. Offers a summer bicycling tour of Sweden and Denmark.

EuroCruises ☎1-800/688-3876, *www.eurocruises.com*. For cruises of the Baltic Sea and the canals of Sweden.

Euroseven ☎1-800/890-3876, *www.euroseven.com* Independent hotel-plus-flight packages from New York, Baltimore or Boston to Scandinavia.

Passage Tours ☎1-800-548-5960, *www.passagetours.com* Specializes in Scandinavia. Offers escorted and unescorted tours and cheap weekend breaks.

Pedersen World Tours in Canada 1-800/973-3377. A Canadian tour operator specializing in Swedish tours.

Scanam World Tours ☎1-800/545-2204 or 201/835-7070, *www.scanamtours.com* Specializes in Scandinavian tours and cruises for groups and individuals. Also cheap weekend breaks.

Scandinavian Airlines ☎1-800/221-2350, *www.flysas.com* Offers tours and fly-drive deals.

Scantours ☎1-800/223-7226, *www.scantours.com* Major Scandinavian holiday specialists offering vacation packages and customized itineraries, including cruises and city sightseeing tours.

Vantage Deluxe World Travel ☎1-800/322-6677. Deluxe group tours and cruises in Scandinavia.

---

full details of airlines and routings. Otherwise, you can choose from a number of other carriers offering flights from across the States to major European cities, from where you can pick up a second flight to Stockholm with another airline.

Although direct flights are usually cheaper than indirect or connecting flights, there is really very little difference in price, and it is always worth shopping around to get the cheapest fares for the dates you want to travel. The price ranges quoted below are all based on the airlines' Apex tickets and exclude taxes and airport fees.

From **New York**, a round-trip midweek **fare** to Stockholm (8hr on a non-stop flight; otherwise around 10hr) will cost US$600–1000 in high season, US$750–850 during the shoulder seasons, and anywhere between US$450 and 650 in the low season. Icelandair are currently offering some of the best deals, at the lower end of the price range in summer or winter. From **Chicago** (9hr on a non-stop flight; at least 11hr otherwise), prices are much the same, although some

airlines charge US$100 more than the top fares from New York. American Airlines' direct flight is the cheapest Midwest option, although SAS is now competing with them for the same route, so it is a good idea to compare fares. Travelling from the **West Coast** (journey time at least 12hr), you'll pay around US$1250 in high season, US$1050 in the shoulder seasons, and US$650–900 in low season. Some of the cheapest fares are with SAS from Seattle, and on Finnair from San Francisco (a summer-only flight which can cost as little as $715).

Travellers in **Canada** can fly to Stockholm from **Toronto** via Helsinki with Finnair (summer only), or from **Halifax** via Reykjavik with Icelandair. Several other airlines also operate flights from Toronto and Vancouver to European cities, with connections on to Stockholm – see the box on p.12 for full details of airlines and routings.

Fares from Toronto (journey time 9–13hr depending on connections) are CAN$1100–1400 in high season, CAN$900–1050 in shoul-

EUROPEAN RAIL PASSES

There are a number of **European rail passes** that can only be purchased before leaving home, though consider carefully how much travelling you are going to be doing: these all-encompassing passes only really begin to pay for themselves if you intend to see a fair bit of Sweden and the rest of Europe.

The best-known and most flexible is the **Eurail Youthpass** (for under-26s), which costs US$388/A$575 for fifteen days, and there are also one-month and two-month versions; if you're 26 or over you'll have to buy a first-class **Eurail** pass, which costs US$554/A$720 for the fifteen-day option. You stand a better chance of getting your money's worth out of a **Eurail Flexipass**, which is good for a certain number of travel days in a two-month period. This, too, comes in under-26/first-class versions: ten days for under-26s

costs US$458/A$635, for over-26s US$654/A$895; and fifteen days costs US$599/A$855 and US$862/A$1175.

North Americans and Australasians are also eligible to purchase a pass specifically for travel in Scandinavia only (Sweden, Denmark, Finland and Norway) called the **ScanRail pass**. These also come in under-26/over-26 versions and are valid for five days of travel within fifteen days (under-26s US$140/A$177; over-26s US$187/A$236) and ten days within one month (US$226/A$294; US$301/A$392). These fares are for the well-regarded second-class ticket; there are also first-class versions for both youth and adult passengers that are slightly more expensive. Scanrail also also offers one-month passes. For information on passes that you can buy at home for travel in Sweden only, see "Getting Around", p.26.

RAIL AGENTS IN NORTH AMERICA

CIT Tours ☎1-800/223-7987, www.fs-on-line.com Eurail passes only.
DER Tours/German Rail ☎1-800/421-2929 or in Canada ☎416/695-1209, www.dertravel.com Eurail and ScanRail passes.

Rail Europe US ☎1-800/438-7245, Canada ☎1-800/361-RAIL, www.raileurope.com Official Eurail pass agent in North America; also sells the ScanRail pass.
ScanTours ☎1-800/223-7226, www.scantours.com Eurail and ScanRail passes.

RAIL AGENTS IN AUSTRALIA

CIT, 123 Clarence St, Sydney (☎02/9267 1255); offices in Melbourne, Adelaide, Brisbane and Perth (☎09/322 1090). No NZ office – enquiries

and reservations via Australian offices. Comprehensive range of rail passes.

der season, and CAN$850–1150 in low season. In comparison, fares from Vancouver (13–18hr) are around CAN$400 higher in all seasons. The cheapest fares are with Finnair and Icelandair. It might well also be worth investigating cheap flights to New York, Chicago or Seattle and linking up with one of SAS' or American Airlines' non-stop flights from there (see box on p.12).

If Sweden is only one stop on a wide-ranging tour, you might want to consider buying a **Round-the-World (RTW) ticket**. As Stockholm and the other Scandinavian capitals are not among the most popular destinations, you will most likely need a customized RTW ticket. This will allow you to touch down in about half a dozen cities aside from your Scandinavia stopoff, but is apt to be more expensive than a standard RTW ticket – up to US$3000, depending on your route.

PACKAGES AND ORGANIZED TOURS

There are a large number of companies operating **package holidays** and **tours** of Sweden (see p.13), ranging from deluxe cruises to bicycling holidays. Group tours can be very expensive, and prices occasionally do not include the air fare, so it's important to check exactly what's included. To visit just Stockholm, you could simply book a hotel-plus-flight package, which can work out cheaper than booking the two separately. Bennett Tours, Scanam and Passage Tours offer very reasonable weekend deals in the low season. You can get a round-trip flight on SAS from New York (Newark) and two nights in a Stockholm hotel for as little as US$469 per person (based on double occupancy). For general information on package tours, the Swedish Travel and Tourism Council (see box, p.24) can provide tour brochures and useful advice.

GETTING THERE FROM AUSTRALIA & NEW ZEALAND

There are no direct flights from Australia or New Zealand to Sweden; instead you have to fly to a gateway city in either Europe or Asia, from where you can get a connecting flight or alternative transport. Fares are pretty steep, so it's worth heading to London (see "Getting there from Britain"), Amsterdam or Frankfurt first, as it's easier to get a cheap onward flight from there. If you intend to take in a number of other European countries on your trip, it might well be worth buying a Eurail pass before you go (see box, p.14).

FLIGHTS AND FARES

Air fares vary significantly with the **season**. For most major airlines, low season is mid-January to

AIRLINES AND ROUTES

Air New Zealand Australia ☎13/2476, NZ 09/366 2424, *www.airnz.com* Several flights weekly to London from Australia, via Auckland and LA; also daily flights to Bangkok (to connect with SAS) from major cities in Australia and New Zealand.

Airtours/Britannia Airways Australia ☎02/9247 4833. During their charter season (Nov–March), there are several charter flights each month to London and Manchester from major Australian cities and from Auckland, via Singapore and Bahrain.

British Airways Australia ☎02/8904 8800, NZ 09/356 8690. Daily flights to London from major Australian cities via Asia, and from New Zealand cities via Los Angeles, in conjunction with Qantas. Free side-trips to Europe, including to Stockholm, and fly-drive deals.

Canadian Airlines Australia ☎1300/655 767, NZ 09/309 0735. Twice weekly to Vancouver and Toronto from Sydney, Melbourne and Auckland; connects with SAS to Copenhagen, then on to Stockholm and Gothenburg.

Finnair Australia ☎02/9244 2299, NZ c/o World Aviation, 09/308 3365. Three flghts weekly from Sydney and Auckland to Helsinki via Singapore (code-share with Qantas) and then on to Stockholm and Gothenburg.

Garuda Australia ☎1300/365 330, NZ 09/366 1862. Flies several times weekly to London Gatwick and Amsterdam from major Australian cities, via Jakarta or Denpasar, and from Auckland twice weekly.

Japan Airlines Australia ☎02/9272 1111, NZ 09/379 9906. Daily flights to London from Brisbane and Sydney, via Tokyo or Osaka, plus several flights weekly from Cairns and Auckland.

Korean Airlines Australia ☎02/9262 6000, NZ 09/307 3687. Several flights a week to London from Sydney, Brisbane, Auckland and Christchurch, via Seoul.

Lauda Air, 143 Macquarie St, Sydney (Australia ☎02/9251 6155, NZ 09/308 3368). Several flights weekly to Stockholm from Sydney and Melbourne via Vienna and Kuala Lumpur, in conjunction with Austrian Air.

Lufthansa, 143 Macquarie St, Sydney (Australia ☎02/9367 3888, NZ 09/303 1529). Daily flights to Frankfurt from major Australian cities and Auckland, through arrangements with Singapore Airlines and Thai Airways, connecting with Lufthansa flights in either Singapore or Bangkok.

Malaysia Airlines Australia ☎13/2627, NZ 09/373 2741. Several flights weekly to London, Amsterdam, Paris and Zürich from major Australian and New Zealand cities, via Kuala Lumpur.

Qantas Australia ☎13/1313, NZ 09/357 8900. Daily to London, Singapore and Bangkok from major cities in Australia and New Zealand, connecting with SAS and Finnair to Stockholm and Gothenburg.

Scandinavian Airlines Australia ☎02/9299 9800, NZ c/o Air New Zealand, 09/366 2424. SAS, through a partnership with Qantas and Air New Zealand, have several flights weekly to Stockholm and other destinations in Scandinavia from major cities in Australia and New Zealand, via Bangkok, Singapore or Tokyo and Copenhagen.

Singapore Airlines Australia ☎13/1011, NZ 09/379 3209 and 0800/808 909. Several flights weekly to London from major Australian cities, via Singapore, and twice weekly from Auckland.

Thai Airlines Australia ☎1300/651 960, NZ 09/377 3886. Several flights weekly to Stockholm from major Australia cities and from Auckland (connects with Lufthansa).

DISCOUNT AGENTS

Anywhere Travel, 345 Anzac Parade, Kingsford, Sydney (☎02/9663 0411, *anywhere@ozemail.com.au*).

Budget Travel, 16 Fort St, Auckland (☎09/366 0061, toll-free 0800/808 040).

Destinations Unlimited, 3 Milford Rd, Milford, Auckland (☎09/373 4033).

Flight Centres 82 Elizabeth St, Sydney (☎02/9241 2422; nearest branch ☎13/1600, *www.flightcentre.com.au*), plus branches nationwide; 205–225 Queen St, Auckland (☎09/309 6171), with other branches countrywide.

STA Travel, 702 Harris St, Ultimo, Sydney (nearest branch ☎13/1776, telesales 1300/360 960, *www.statravel.com.au*), and other offices in major cities; Travellers Centre, 10 High St, Auckland (☎09/309 0458, telesales 366 6673), and other offices in major cities.

Status Travel, 22 Cavenagh St, Darwin (☎08/8941 1843).

Student Uni Travel, 92 Pitt St, Sydney (☎02/9232 8444) plus branches in Brisbane, Cairns, Darwin, Melbourne and Perth.

Thomas Cook, 175 Pitt St, Sydney (local branch ☎13/1771, *www.thomascook.com.au*), plus branches in other state capitals; 159 Queen St, Auckland (☎09/359 5200).

Trailfinders, 8 Spring St, Sydney (☎02/9247 7666).

Travel.com.au, 80 Clarence St, Sydney (☎02/9290 1500, *www.travel.com.au*).

usit Beyond, corner of Shortland St and Jean Batten Place, Auckland (☎09/379 4224 or toll-free ☎0800/788 336, *www.usitbeyond.co.nz*).

the end of February, and October and November; high season is from mid-May to the end of August and from December to mid-January; shoulder seasons cover the rest of the year. There's no variation in price during the week. The fares we list for Australia are for flights from any of the major eastern Australian cities; in comparison, flying from Perth and Darwin via Asia costs A$100–200 less, or A$300–400 more via North America. The New Zealand fares we give are for flights out of Auckland; fares from Christchurch and Wellington cost NZ$200–300 more.

Tickets purchased direct from the airlines tend to be expensive, with published fares listed at A$2499/NZ$2799 (low season); A$2799–2999/NZ$2999–3250 (shoulder season); and A$3199/NZ$3599 (high season). Travel agents offer better deals on fares and have the latest information on limited special deals, such as free stopovers en route and fly-drive/accommodation packages. Flight Centres and STA (which has fare reductions for ISIC-card-holders and under-26s) generally offer the best discounts – see the box above for details. All the prices quoted below are for discounted fares.

Scandinavian Airlines and Finnair, in conjunction with airlines operating out of Australia and New Zealand, offer the best connections for Sweden, with daily flights to **Stockholm** and **Gothenburg**, via Copenhagen and Helsinki, for around A$1600/2000/2500 and NZ$2200/2600/3000 (low/medium/high season). Lauda Air, in conjunction with Austrian Air, has several flights weekly from Sydney and Melbourne to Stockholm, via Kuala Lumpur and Vienna, for similar prices.

Of fares to other European cities, the lowest are on Airtours/Britannia to **London** – during their limited charter season, from November to March, prices are A$1100/1430/1760 and NZ$1620/1820/2110. Generally you can expect to pay A$1500–A$1800/NZ$2000–NZ$2500 on Garuda, Gulf, Korean or Japan Airlines; A$1800–A$2100/NZ$2300–NZ$2700 on Malaysia Airlines, Thai Airways and Lufthansa; and A$1850–A$2600/NZ$2250–NZ$3150 on British Airways, Qantas, Singapore Airlines, Air New Zealand and Canadian Airways. For details of all the airlines and a full run-down of routes, see the box on p.15.

Airpasses for discounted flights within Europe, including Sweden, are only available if you fly with the issuing airline, and must be purchased before you depart. Examples include SAS' Visit Scandinavia Pass and the BA-Qantas Airpass. Expect to pay A$115–175/NZ$140–210 per coupon.

For extended trips, **Round The World (RTW) tickets**, valid for up to a year, make good sense. Star Alliance (*www.star-alliance.com*), a grouping of airlines including SAS, Thai, United, Varig, Lufthansa, Air New Zealand and Ansett, issues tickets (A$2699/NZ$3299) that allow for six stopovers, open-jaw travel and limited backtracking. The Qantas-BA "Global Explorer" and "One World" tick-

SPECIALIST TOUR OPERATORS

Bentours, Level 11, 2 Bridge St, Sydney (☎02/9241 1353, *scandinavia@bentours.com.au*). Ferry, rail, bus and hotel passes, and a host of scenic tours throughout Scandinavia, including a four-day ferry journey down the Göta Canal between Stockholm and Gothenburg (from A$1410/NZ$1700, including meals).

European Travel Office, 122 Rosslyn St, West Melbourne (☎03/9329 8844); 407 Great South Rd, Penrose, Auckland (☎09/525 3074). Stockholm hotel twin-share accommodation from A$148 and sightseeing tours by bus or boat.

Explore Holidays, 2nd Floor, 155 Blaxland Rd, Ryde, NSW (☎02/9857 6200). Wholesaler of Stockholm mini-stays, from A$730/NZ$880 twin sharing for three nights' accommodation with city sightseeing tour and evening meals.

Wiltrans/Maupintour, Level 10, 189 Kent Street, Sydney (☎02/9255 0899). Luxury, all-inclusive thirteen-day tours of Scandinavia and the Baltic, departing by boat from the UK, from US$6250 (when you buy, prices are converted to A$ at the prevailing exchange rate).

ets (each A$2499–2999/ NZ$2999–3499) also offer flexible routings, including stops in Sweden.

PACKAGE TOURS

Travellers who want to take a **package holiday** to Sweden will find there are very few to choose from, with only a small number of tour operators offering holidays to Scandinavia. Your best bet is Bentours (see box above for details), who will put together a package for you and are about the only agents willing to deal with skiing holidays. Alternatively you could wait until you get to Europe, where there's a greater choice of holidays and prices (see "Getting there from Britain"). Note that all prices given in the list of Australian tour operators (see above) exclude air fares.

RED TAPE AND VISAS

American, Canadian, Australian and New Zealand citizens need only a valid passport to enter Sweden, and can stay for up to three months. If you want to stay longer, you can often get a short extension via the local police. There's no fixed period for these, and you may have to leave the country first to get one; once this extension has expired, you won't be allowed back into Sweden, or any of the other Nordic countries, for a further six months. European Union and European Economic Area nationals can stay in Sweden for an unrestricted period but require a residency permit (*uppehållstillstånd*) for visits longer than three months. For further information on where to obtain the permits contact the Swedish embassy in your home country (see p.18). Non-EU nationals should consult their local Swedish embassy about visa requirements.

In spite of the relative lack of restrictions on entering Sweden, checks are sometimes made on travellers at the ports in Malmö, Helsingborg, Gothenburg and Stockholm. Especially if you are young and have a rucksack, be prepared to prove that you have enough money to support yourself during your stay. You may also be asked how long you intend to stay and what you are there for; be polite in your responses, and you'll avoid unnecessary trouble. There are few border formalities between the Nordic countries so once you're in Sweden, in effect, you've made it into the rest of Scandinavia.

CUSTOMS ALLOWANCES

Visitors arriving from the EU can take into Sweden 300 cigarettes, or 150 cigarillos, or 75 cigars, or 400g of pipe tobacco; one litre of spirits (more than 22° of alcohol by volume), 3 litres of wine and 15 litres of strong beer (more than 3.5 percent alcohol by volume), provided the tax on all these has already been paid in another EU country. Allowances for people arriving from North America, Australia and New Zealand are lower – but are duty-free.

HEALTH

EU nationals can take advantage of Sweden's health services under the same terms as residents of the country. For this you'll need form E111, available in the UK through post offices and DSS offices. You'll have to show your E111 if you need medical treatment. Citizens of non-EU countries will be charged for all medical services; US visitors will find that medical treatment is far less expensive than they are accustomed to at home. Even so it is advisable to take out travel insurance (see p.19).

There's no local doctor system in Sweden: go to the nearest hospital with your passport (and E111 if applicable) and they'll treat you; the casualty department is called Akutmottagning. For a hospital clinic visit, the charge is 60–120kr; overnight stays in hospital cost 80kr per 24 hours (free for children under 16).

For **dental treatment**, EU citizens have to pay in full any bill up to 700kr, then 65 percent of the next 650kr of the cost, and 30 percent of any remaining charge. You can spot a **dental surgery** by looking out for the sign "Tandläkare" or "Folktandvården". An emergency dental service is available in most major towns and cities out of hours – look in the windows of the local pharmacy for contact telephone numbers.

Medicines may be taken into Sweden if intended for your own use; you must have a medical certificate proving that you need them. **Prescriptions** can be taken to the nearest pharmacy (Apotek); those from Scandinavian doctors will be filled routinely, but if your prescription is from another EU country you'll also need to show your E111 form to get your medicine. Minor painkillers, such as aspirin, are not available over the counter in Sweden, so bring some with you – otherwise you'll need a prescription to get them.

COPING WITH MOSQUITOES

The **mosquito** goes by the rather fetching name of *mygg* in Swedish – it's a word you'll become uncomfortably familiar with during your stay. If you're planning to spend any time at all outside the confines of towns and cities (and even in built-up areas the little critters can be merciless), it's imperative that you protect yourself against bites. Swedish mosquitoes don't carry diseases, but they can torment your every waking moment from the end of June, when the warmer weather causes them to hatch, until around mid-August.

They are found in their densest concentrations in the north of the country, where there's swampy ground; there the sky has been known to darken when swarms of the things appear from nowhere.

Mosquitoes are most active early in the morning and in the late afternoon/early evening; the best way to protect yourself is to wear thick clothing (though not dark colours, which attract them) and apply mosquito **repellent** to any exposed skin. When camping, make a smoky fire of (damp) peat if feasible, as mosquitoes don't like smoke. And, easier said than done, don't scratch mosquito bites (*myggbett*); treat them instead with Salubrin or Alsolsprit creams, or something similar, available from local chemists.

KEEPING WARM AND SAFE IN WINTER

There's no two ways about it: seven to eight months of snow can make **winter in Sweden** pretty grim. But visiting in the depths of winter can be quite fun if you protect yourself against the extreme cold – temperatures are often below -30°C in the north of the country. Swedes cope by wearing several **layers of clothes**, preferably cotton, which is good at keeping out the cold. A warm winter coat alone won't suffice. You'll need a good woolly hat, snug-fitting gloves or mittens, and thick socks as well – between thirty to fifty percent of body heat is lost from the feet and head. Be prepared, though, to shed layers when you go into shops and other buildings, which are often heated to seemingly oven-like temperatures.

Bring **boots** or stout shoes with good grips which will hold onto the finely polished compacted snow that covers streets and pavements in winter. Venturing onto the ice isn't advisable, but if you feel you must do so, first ask the advice of local people as to whether it'll hold your weight. **Drivers** often take shortcuts in their cars across frozen lakes in winter – if you're going to do this, too, make sure you stick to the route that has either been marked out or the existing well-worn tracks in the ice. In towns and cities, keep your eyes peeled for **icicles** hanging from roofs and gutters; sooner or later they'll come crashing to the ground and you don't want to be underneath when that happens.

INSURANCE

It's essential to take out comprehensive travel insurance, but before buying, check if you already have some degree of cover. Bank and credit cards (particularly American Express) often have certain levels of medical or other insurance included, especially if you use them to pay for your trip. This can be quite comprehensive, covering anything from lost or stolen luggage to missed connections. Similarly, a good "all risks" home insurance policy may well cover your possessions against loss or theft even when you're overseas, and many private medical schemes also cover you when abroad.

If you plan to **ski** or do some **hiking**, you'll probably have to pay an extra premium; check carefully that any insurance policy you're considering will cover you in case of an accident in the course of such activities. Note also that very few insurers will arrange on-the-spot payments in the event of a major expense or loss; you will usually be reimbursed only after going home. In all cases of loss or **theft** of goods, you'll have to contact the local **police** to have a **report** made out so that your insurer can process the claim; for medical claims, you'll need to provide supporting bills.

TRAVEL INSURANCE BROKERS

AUSTRALIA AND NEW ZEALAND

AFTA, 181 Miller St, North Sydney (☎02/9956 4800).
Cover More, Level 9, 32 Walker St, North Sydney (☎02/9968 1333, toll-free 1800/251 881).

Ready Plan, 141–147 Walker St, Dandenong, Victoria (toll-free ☎1800/337 462); 10th Floor, 63 Albert St, Auckland (☎09/379 3399).
UTAG, 347 Kent St, Sydney (☎02/9819 6855, toll-free 1800/809 462).

BRITAIN AND IRELAND

Columbus Travel Insurance ☎020/7375 0011, www.columbusdirect.co.uk.
Endsleigh Insurance ☎020/7436 4451 in Britain, www.endsleigh.co.uk.
Frizzell Insurance ☎01202/292333 in Britain.

STA Travel ☎020/7361 6262 in Britain.
usit Campus ☎ 020/7730 8111 in Britain.
usit NOW ☎028/9032 4073 in Northern Ireland, ☎01/679 8833 in the Republic.

US AND CANADA

Carefree Travel Insurance US & Canada ☎1-800/323-3149.
Desjardins Travel Insurance Canada ☎1-800/463 7830.
International Student Insurance Service (ISIS; US & Canada ☎1-800/777-0112. Sells STA travel insurance.

Travel Assistance International ☎1-800/821-2828.
Travel Guard US ☎1-800/826-1300, Canada ☎715/345-0505.
Travel Insurance Services US ☎1-800/937-1387.

Keep **photocopies** of everything you send to the insurer, and always make sure you know the **procedure** for claims, including which phone numbers to use and any time-frame within which claims must be lodged.

In **Britain** and **Ireland**, travel insurance schemes (from around £23 for a month) are sold by many **travel agents** and **banks**, and by **specialist insurance companies**. Policies issued by usit Travel, usit NOW, STA, Endsleigh Insurance, Frizzell Insurance or Columbus Travel Insurance are all good value. Columbus also does an annual multi-trip policy which offers twelve months' cover for £125.

In the **US** and **Canada**, the best **premiums** are usually to be had through student/youth travel agencies – ISIS policies, for example, cost US$48–69 (depending on level of coverage) for fifteen days, US$80–105 for a month, US$149–207 for two months, and US$510–700

for a year. Most North American travel policies apply only to items lost, stolen or damaged while in the custody of an identifiable, responsible third party – hotel porter, airline, luggage consignment, etc. Holders of official **student/teacher/youth cards** (see p.23) are entitled to accident coverage and hospital in-patient benefits – the annual membership is far less than the cost of comparable insurance. **Students** may also find that their student health coverage extends during the vacations and for one term beyond the date of last enrolment.

The various travel insurance policies available in **Australia** and **New Zealand** are broadly comparable in terms of premiums and coverage: typically A$190/NZ$220 for one month, A$270/NZ$320 for two months and A$330/NZ$400 for three months. Policies can be bought from travel agents or insurance companies (see box above).

TRAVELLERS WITH DISABILITIES

There are organized tours and holidays specifically for people with disabilities – the contacts in the box below will be able to put you in touch with any specialists in trips to Sweden. Once you're there, you'll find Sweden in many ways a model of awareness in terms of disabled travel, with assistance forthcoming from virtually all Swedes, if needed. A useful holiday guide for people with disabilities is available from Swedish tourist offices (see

"Information and maps" for their addresses outside Sweden).

PLANNING A HOLIDAY

If there's an association representing people with your specific disability, it's worth contacting them early in the planning process. The more independent you want to be when travelling, the more important it is to become an authority on where you must be self-reliant and where you may expect help, especially regarding transport and accommo-

CONTACTS FOR TRAVELLERS WITH DISABILITIES

AUSTRALIA AND NEW ZEALAND

ACROD (Australian Council for Rehabilitation of the Disabled), PO Box 60, Curtin, ACT 2605 (☎02/6282 4333).

Disabled Persons Assembly, PO Box 10, 138 The Terrace, Wellington (☎04/472 2626).

BRITAIN AND IRELAND

Disability Action Group, 2 Annadale Ave, Belfast BT7 3JH (☎028/9049 1011).

Holiday Care Service, 2nd floor, Imperial Building, Victoria Rd, Horley, Surrey RH6 9HW (☎01293/774535). Information on all aspects of travel.

Holiday Scandinavia Ltd, 28 Hillcrest Rd, Orpington BR6 9AW (☎01689/824958).

Irish Wheelchair Association, Blackheath Drive, Clontarf, Dublin 3 (☎01/833 8241). A

national voluntary organization working for people with disabilities, and supplying disability-related services for holidaymakers.

RADAR, 12 City Forum, 250 City Rd, London EC1V 8AS (☎020/7250 3222, minicom ☎7250 0212, *www.radar.org.uk*). A good source of advice on holidays and travel abroad.

Tripscope, The Courtyard, Evelyn Rd, London W4 5JL (☎0345/585641, minicom ☎020/8994 9294).

SWEDEN

De Handikappades Riksförbund, Katrinebergsvägen 6, S-117 43, Stockholm (DHR; Swedish Federation of Disabled Persons; ☎08/18 91 00, fax 645 65 41).

Svenska Handikappidrottsförbundet, Idrottenshus, S-123 87, Farsta, Sweden (☎08/605 60 00, fax 724 85 40). Information on sports facilities for people with disabilities.

US AND CANADA

Mobility International USA, PO Box 10767, Eugene, OR 97440 (☎541/343-1284, *www.miusa.org*). Information and referral services, access guides, tours and exchange programs. Annual membership $25 (includes quarterly newsletter).

Society for the Advancement of Travel for the Handicapped (SATH), 347 5th Ave, Suite 610, New York, NY 10016 (☎212/447-7284, *www.sath.org*). Non-profit travel-industry referral

service that passes queries on to its members as appropriate; allow plenty of time for a response.

Twin Peaks Press, Box 129, Vancouver, WA 98666-0129 (☎360/694-2462 and 1-800/637-2256, *home.pacifier.com/~twinpeak*). Publisher of *Directory of Travel Agencies for the Disabled*, listing more than 370 agencies worldwide; *Travel for the Disabled*; *Directory of Accessible Van Rentals* and *Wheelchair Vagabond*, loaded with personal tips.

dation. Assess your limitations and make sure other people – travel agencies, insurance companies and travelling companions – know about them, too.

People with a pre-existing medical condition are sometimes excluded from travel **insurance policies**, so read the small print carefully. To make your journey simpler, ask your travel agent to notify airlines or bus companies of your arrival, as they may be able to arrange assistance, for example, providing a wheelchair at airports and staff primed to help. A **medical certificate** of your fitness to travel, provided by your doctor, is also extremely useful; some airlines or insurance companies may insist on it. Make sure that you have extra supplies of drugs – carried with you if you fly – and, in case of emergency, a prescription that includes the generic name of any medicine you need. Carry spares of any clothing or equipment that might be hard to find. If you use a wheelchair, it's always wise to have it serviced before you go, and carry a repair kit. If you don't use the wheelchair all the time, but your walking capabilities are limited, remember that you are likely to need to cover greater distances while travelling than at home (sometimes over rougher terrain and in hotter/colder temperatures than you are used to), and plan your route with this in mind.

DISABLED TRAVEL IN SWEDEN

Getting to Sweden is becoming easier for disabled visitors: DFDS Seaways ferries now have specially adapted cabins, and Silja Line offers discounts for travellers with disabilities on its routes between Sweden and Finland. **Public transport** throughout the country is also geared up for people with disabilities. Wheelchair access is usually available on **trains** (InterCity trains have wide aisles and large toilets, and often have special carriages with hydraulic lifts), and there are lifts down to the platforms at almost every Stockholm metro station. In every part of the country there'll be some taxis in the form of minivans specially converted for disabled use.

Accommodation suitable for the disabled is often available: most **hotels** have specially adapted rooms, while some chalet villages have cabins with wheelchair access. Any building with three or more storeys must, by law, have a lift installed, while all public buildings are required by law to be accessible to people with disabilities and have automatic doors. Generally, hotels, hostels, museums and other public places are very willing to cater to those with disabilities.

COSTS, MONEY AND BANKS

It's a widely held belief that Sweden is the most expensive country in Europe. This is simply not true any more. There's no doubt that it can be expensive, but Sweden is cheaper than all the other Nordic countries and no more expensive than, say, France or Germany. If you like drinking coffee and eating cakes all day long, travelling by taxi and tripping off to the theatre of an evening, you'll leave Sweden a pauper. If, however, you don't mind having your main meal of the day at lunchtime, like the Swedes, or having picnics under the midnight sun with goodies bought from the supermarket, travelling by the efficient public transport system and going easy on the nightlife, you'll find Sweden isn't the financial drain you thought it was going to be.

CURRENCY

The Swedish **currency** is the *krona* (kr; plural *kronor*), made up of 100 *öre*. It comes in coins of 50 *öre*, 1kr, 5kr and 10kr; and notes of 20kr, 50kr, 100kr, 500kr, 1000kr and 10,000kr. There's no limit on the amount of Swedish and foreign currency you can take into Sweden. Currently there are 13kr to £1, or 7.5kr to US$1.

COSTS

Accommodation in Sweden is good value: youth hostels are of a very high standard and charge only 75–175kr a night for members (£6–13.50/US$9–20); hotels offer special low prices to tourists in summer; and campsites are plentiful and cheap. **Admission prices** to museums and galleries are also low or nonexistent; and if you flash an ISIC card (see below), it's likely to bring a reduction. At most places, there are also reductions of around thirty to fifty percent for children and senior citizens, and younger children often get in for free.

When shopping for **food**, look for produce marked "*extrapris*", which denotes a special offer, or "*fynd*", which is supposed to be literally that – a bit of a find. Avoid anything frozen or in tins, as fresh food is reasonably priced in comparison.

Restaurant eating can work out a good deal if you stick to the *Dagens Rätt* (dish of the day), served at lunchtime in most restaurants and cafés, and generally consisting of salad, a main meal (often a choice between two or three dishes), bread, a drink and a coffee – for 40–60kr all-in (£3–5/US$5–8). What will cost you serious money in Sweden is **alcohol**: a strong beer in a bar costs a dizzy 35–55kr (£2.70–4.20/US$5–8); a bottle of wine in a restaurant will set you back around 200kr (£16/US$24); and the cost of a whisky or cognac is likely to bring on heart trouble.

Put all this together and you'll find you can exist – camping, self-catering, hitching, no drinking – on a fairly low budget (around £15/$22 a day), though it will be a pretty miserable experience and only sustainable for a limited period of time. Stay in hostels, eat the *Dagens Rätt* at lunchtime, get out and see the sights and drink the odd beer or two and you'll be looking at doubling your expenditure. Once you start having restaurant meals with wine, taking a few taxis, enjoying coffees and cakes and staying in hotel accommodation, you'll be getting through considerably more (£60–75/US$90–115).

YOUTH AND STUDENT DISCOUNTS

Full-time students are eligible for the **International Students Identity Card (ISIC)**, which entitles the bearer to special fares on local transport and discounts at museums, theatres and other attractions. For Americans there's also a health benefit, providing up to US$3000 in emergency medical coverage and US$100 a day for up to sixty days in hospital, plus a 24-hour hotline to call in the event of medical, legal or financial emergency. The card, which costs £5 in the UK, £7 in Ireland, US$16 in the US and CAN$15 in Canada, is available from branches of usit in Ireland, and from Council Travel, STA and Travel CUTS around the world.

If you're 25 or younger you qualify for the **International Youth Travel Card**, which costs the same as the ISIC card and offers the same benefits. It can be purchased through Council Travel in the US and Hostelling International in Canada (see "Accommodation", p.34), and from STA in Australia, New Zealand and the UK.

STA also sells its own ID card that's good for some discounts, as do various other travel organizations. A university photo-ID might open some doors, too.

TRAVELLERS' CHEQUES, CASH AND CARDS

Although you're unlikely to be mugged in Sweden, it's safest to carry your money as **travellers' cheques**, available for a small commission from most banks and building societies, and from branches of Thomas Cook and American Express. You must always keep the purchase agreement and a record of cheque serial numbers separate from the cheques themselves.

The major **credit and charge cards** (Visa, Mastercard, American Express and Diners Card) are accepted almost everywhere in return for goods or cash. Visa and to a lesser extent Mastercard can also be used in Swedish ATMs. British and Irish chequebooks don't work in Sweden; bank cards only work if they have a Visa or Mastercard facility on them. **Cirrus** cards are by far the most preferable way of accessing money in your bank account at home: ATMs almost everywhere in Sweden accept Cirrus cards – simply look out for the double blue circle logo.

In the UK, banks can also issue current-account holders with a **Eurocheque card** and chequebook. The former works like a Cirrus card, while the latter can be used to pay bills in Sweden using money drawn direct from your own bank account.

BANKS AND EXCHANGE

Banks (Mon–Wed & Fri 9.30am–3pm, Thurs 9.30am–5.30pm; in some cities, banks may stay open to 5.30pm every weekday) have standard exchange rates but commissions can vary enormously, so it's always worth shopping around. Some places charge per cheque, others per transaction, so it's common sense to take large denominations with you, or to try to change in one go as much as you feel you can handle. Banks at airports, ports and main train stations generally have longer opening hours – but often inferior rates of exchange. All banks are closed at weekends and on public holidays.

The **best place to change money** is at the yellow **Forex** offices, which offer 3–18 percent more *kronor* for your currency than the banks. You'll find Forex branches in city centres – in Stockholm, Gothenburg, Malmö, Lund, Uppsala, Norrköping and Västerås. There are also branches at Stockholm's Arlanda airport (Terminal 2) and Central Station, at Landvetter airport in Gothenburg, Sturup airport in Malmö and at the ferry terminals in Helsingborg and Ystad.

It's also possible to change money in **post offices**: look out for the *"Växel"* (exchange) sign; rates here are little different from those at Forex branches. In the more remote areas, you'll often find that hostels, hotels and campsites will change money, but the rates at hotels are abysmal.

WIRING MONEY

The quickest way to get **money sent out** to Sweden is to contact your bank at home and have them wire the cash to the nearest bank. You can do the same thing through Thomas Cook, American Express or Western Union. Make sure you know when it's likely to arrive, since you won't be notified by the receiving office. Remember, too, that you'll need some form of identification when you pick up the money.

INFORMATION AND MAPS

Before you leave, it's worth contacting the **Swedish Travel and Tourism Council (the national tourist board)** in your own country (see box) for free maps and brochures – though you don't need to go overboard, as the same can easily be obtained once you're in Sweden. Any timetables for trains, planes and buses are worth taking along with you, as are the booklets listing accommodation.

SWEDISH TRAVEL AND TOURISM COUNCIL

Australia: No office but the Swedish Embassy handles tourist information (see p.18).

Britain: 11 Montagu Place, London, W1H 2AL (☎020/7870 5600, fax ☎020/7724 5872).

Canada: Contact the Swedish Embassy for tourist information (see p.18).

Ireland: No office but the Swedish Embassy handles tourist information (see p.18).

New Zealand: The Swedish Consulate supplies tourist information (see p.18).

US: PO Box 4649, Grand Central Station, New York, NY 10163–4649 (☎212/885-9700, fax 885-9764).

TOURIST OFFICES IN SWEDEN

All towns – and some villages – have a **tourist office** from where you can pick up free town plans and information, brochures and other literature. Many tourist offices can book private rooms (and sometimes youth hostel beds), rent bikes, sell local discount cards and change money. During the summer they're open until late evening; out of season it's more usual for them to

MAP OUTLETS

AUSTRALIA AND NEW ZEALAND

The Map Shop, 16a Peel St, Adelaide
(☎08/8231 2033).

Mapland, 372 Little Bourke St, Melbourne
(☎03/9670 4383).

Perth Map Centre, 891 Hay St, Perth, WA 6000
(☎08/9322 6733).

Specialty Maps, 58 Albert St, Auckland
(☎09/307 2217).

Travel Bookshop, Shop 3, 175 Liverpool St
(☎02/9261 8200).

BRITAIN

Blackwell's Map and Travel Shop, 53 Broad
St, Oxford OX1 3BQ (☎01865/792792, *book-
shop.blackwell.co.uk*).

Daunt Books, 83 Marylebone High St, London
W1 (☎020/7224 2295).

John Smith and Sons, 57–61 St Vincent St,
Glasgow G2 5TB (☎0141/221 7472).

National Map Centre, 22 Caxton St, London
SW1 (☎020/7222 2466, *www.mapsworld.com*).

Stanfords, 12–14 Long Acre, London WC2
(☎020/7836 1321, *sales@stanfords.co.uk*).

The Travel Bookshop, 13–15 Blenheim
Crescent, London W11 2EE (☎020/7229 5260,
www.thetravelbookshop.co.uk).

CANADA

Open Air Books and Maps, 25 Toronto St,
Toronto, ON M5R 2C1 (☎416/363-0719).

Ulysses Travel Bookshop, 4176 St-Denis,
Montréal (☎514/843-9447).

World Wide Books and Maps, 1247 Granville
St, Vancouver, BC V6Z 1E4 (☎604/687-3320).

IRELAND

Easons Bookshop, 40 O'Connell St, Dublin 1
(☎01/873 3811).

Fred Hanna's Bookshop, 27–29 Nassau St,
Dublin 2 (☎01/677 1255).

Hodges Figgis Bookshop, 56–58 Dawson St,
Dublin 2 (☎01/677 4754).

Waterstone's, Queens Bldg, 8 Royal Ave,
Belfast BT1 1DA (☎028/9024 7355).

US

The Complete Traveler Bookstore, 199
Madison Ave, New York, NY 10016 (☎212/685-
9007); 3207 Fillmore St, San Francisco, CA 92123
(☎415/923-1511).

Map Link, 30 S La Petera Lane, Unit #5, Santa
Barbara, CA 93117 (☎805/692-6777).

Phileas Fogg's Books & Maps, #87 Stanford
Shopping Center, Palo Alto, CA 94304
(☎1-800/233-FOGG in California;
☎1-800/533-FOGG elsewhere in US).

Rand McNally, 444 N Michigan Ave, Chicago,
IL 60611 (☎312/321-1751); 150 E 52nd St, New
York, NY 10022 (☎212/758-7488); 595 Market St,
San Francisco, CA 94105 (☎415/777-3131); call
☎1-800/333-0136 (ext 2111) for other locations,
or for maps by mail order.

Sierra Club Bookstore, 6014 College Ave,
Oakland, CA 94618 (☎510/658-7470).

Travel Books & Language Center, 4437
Wisconsin Ave NW, Washington, DC 20016
(☎1-800/220-2665).

keep shop hours, and in the winter they're normally closed at weekends. You'll find full details
of individual offices throughout the text.

MAPS

The **maps and plans** printed in this guide are
fine for general reference, but drivers, cyclists
and hikers will probably require something more
detailed. Tourist offices give out reasonable
road maps and town plans, but anything better
you'll have to buy – see the map shops listed
overleaf.

The most useful **map of Stockholm** can only
be bought in the city itself: the Stockholmskartan

(35kr) is available from the local transport authority, Storstockholms Lokaltrafik, at their offices underneath the central train station, and also at the entrance to Sergels Torg metro station and at Slussen metro. This map has the particular advantage of showing all bus and metro routes in the capital, and includes a street index. For maps of the whole country, go for the Terrac (1:1,000,000) or Hallwag maps. There are also regional maps produced by Kartförlaget (1:400,000), which are excellent.

If you're staying in one area for a long time, or are **hiking** or **walking**, you'll probably need something more detailed still, with a minimum scale of 1:400,000 – though preferably much larger for serious trekking. The 1:300,000 Esselte Kartor are excellent, but the ones to beat them are the Fjällkartan series, covering the northwestern mountains; these maps, produced by Lantmäteriet, at a scale of 1:100,000, are unfortunately rather expensive, both in Sweden and abroad. You'll find that the larger tourist offices usually have decent hiking maps or leaflets giving descriptions of local hiking routes. Svenska Turistföreningen (Swedish Touring Club; Box 25, S-101 20 Stockholm; ☎08/463 21 00) also has a good selection of maps and guides.

GETTING AROUND

The public transport system in Sweden is Europe's most efficient; it operates on time in all weathers. There's a comprehensive train network in the south of the country; in the north travelling by train isn't quite so easy – many branch lines have been closed as Swedish State Railways tries to save money on loss-making routes. However, it's still possible to reach the main towns in the north by train, and where train services no longer exist, buses generally cover the same routes (rail passes are valid for some of these journeys).

Look out for city and regional **discount cards**, which often give free use of local transport, free museum entry and other discounts. Often these cards are only on sale during the summer (notable exceptions are those in Stockholm, Gothenburg and Malmö); the most useful ones have been detailed in the text. Elsewhere, it's worth asking at local tourist offices as discount schemes frequently change.

TIMETABLES

All train, bus and ferry schedules are contained in the giant **Rikstidtabellen** (*National Timetable*), which currently costs 80kr and is available from train stations. It's not really worth buying and carrying with you, given its size; instead ask for photocopies of the relevant pages from tourist offices or travel agents. Alternatively, for train times pick up a copy of the handy and free **Tur & Retur** booklets available from stations, which give listings of services to major destinations in Sweden. But the most useful booklets if you're doing a lot of travelling by train are the **Tågtider** (*Train Times*) and **Tåg Till Utlandet** (*Trains Abroad*), again available free from train stations. The former lists most train departures on most routes within Sweden, the latter connections to destinations in the rest of Europe – both booklets are in Swedish but are easy to figure out. Each train route also has its own timetable leaflet, available free from the local station.

In winter, train and bus services are reduced, especially in the north (where they may even dry up altogether). At holiday times (see "Opening hours, holidays and festivals", p.46) and between mid-June and mid-August, services are often heavily booked; it's worth making reservations (often compulsory) as far in advance as you can (email *swedenbooking@gtsab.se*).

If you're planning on jetting round the country by **plane** using the airpass system operated by SAS, you'll find it handy to have a copy of the **Inrikestidtabellen** (*Domestic Timetable*), which lists every route within Sweden operated by SAS and its partner airline, Skyways; the booklet is available free from airports, tourist offices, travel agents and airline offices.

TRAINS

Other than flying, train travel is the quickest and easiest way of covering Sweden's vast expanses. Whether you travel on Swedish State Railways (usually abbreviated to "SJ"), or on one of the regional services (Länstrafiken) operated by Sweden's county councils, or on the increasing number of private services, such as those to Lapland operated by Tågkompaniet, the service is excellent and prices are not that expensive. The standard-class one-way fare from Stockholm to Gothenburg, for example, is 520kr, and from Stockholm to Kiruna 780kr including a couchette; return fares are double the one-way price. Rail passes are accepted on the Länstrafiken, and generally accepted on private services.

X2000 ROUTES AND JOURNEY TIMES

Stockholm–Malmö	4hr 15min (InterCity 6hr 15min)
Stockholm–Gothenburg	3hr 15min (InterRegio 5hr 15min)
Stockholm–Mora	3hr 30min (InterCity 4hr)
Stockholm–Karlstad	2hr 30min (InterRegio 2hr 50min)
Stockholm–Sundsvall	3hr 20min (InterCity 4hr)
Stockholm–Härnösand	3hr 50min (InterCity 5hr 15min)
Stockholm–Växjö	3hr 25min (InterCity 5hr 30min)
Malmö–Gothenburg	3hr (InterRegio 3hr 50min).

Swedish State Railways (Statens Järnvägar; ☎0046/8 696 75 40 from abroad, or toll-free within Sweden on ☎020/75 75 75, *www.sjpersontrafik.sj.se*) has an extensive network, stretching from the far south of the country up through northern Sweden, into the Arctic Circle, and across the border to Narvik in Norway – the last of these is the northernmost line in Europe. You can email *swedenbooking@gtsab.se* to book tickets, buy rail passes and obtain general information on trains before you arrive in Sweden.

HIGH-SPEED TRAINS (X2000)

Sweden is currently expanding its network of **high-speed trains**, the X2000, which operate on main routes (see box). Using these services can save you a couple of hours, particularly on the Stockholm–Gothenburg and Stockholm–Malmö runs. The trains have overhead sockets for listening to the radio (bring your own headphones), telephones, a bistro car and, in first-class only, fax machines and photocopying services. Fares are, not surprisingly, higher: for example, the X2000 Stockholm–Gothenburg one-way fare in standard class is 920kr – 400kr more than on a normal service. When you buy an X2000 ticket, the price includes a charge for an X2000 supplement and a seat reservation, which are mandatory; if you have a rail pass, you'll pay only for the seat reservation and supplement (50kr). During the summer school holidays, at weekends, and on public holidays all year round, X2000 fares fall to the same prices as on ordinary InterCity or slower Inter Regio trains. You always have a choice of trains on most major routes, as all three types operate on all the routes listed in the box; see p.29 for discounts on all these fares.

From January 2001, SJ expect to operate a full X2000 service between Stockholm and Copenhagen (via Copenhagen airport) across the Öresund bridge.

TICKETS AND DISCOUNTS

Individual **train tickets** are rarely cost-effective, despite the comprehensive (and downright confusing) system of discounts, which seem to change as soon as they've been brought in. Visitors doing a lot of touring by train are much better off buying a train pass (see p.29). If you do need to buy an individual ticket, it's worth checking if any special deals are available. In Sweden, one-way tickets cost half of the return price.

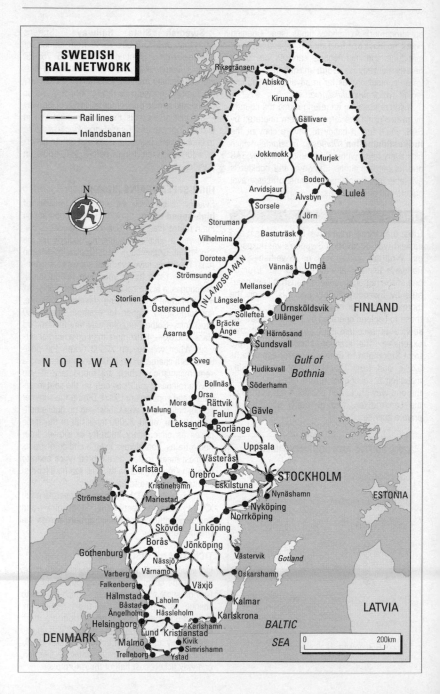

SWEDISH RAIL NETWORK

Rail lines
Inlandsbanan

N

NORWAY

FINLAND

Gulf of Bothnia

Riksgränsen
Abisko
Kiruna
Gällivare
Jokkmokk
Murjek
Boden
Arvidsjaur
Älvsbyn
Luleå
Sorsele
Jörn
Storuman
Bastuträsk
Vilhelmina
Dorotea
Vännäs
Umeå
Strömsund
Mellansel
Storlien
Långsele
Örnsköldsvik
Östersund
Sollefteå
Ullånger
Bräcke
Åsarna
Ånge
Härnösand
Sundsvall
Sveg
Hudiksvall
Bollnäs
Söderhamn
Orsa
Mora
Rättvik
Malung
Falun
Gävle
Leksand
Borlänge
Uppsala
Västerås
Karlstad
Örebro
STOCKHOLM
Kristinehamn
Eskilstuna
Nynäshamn
ESTONIA
Strömstad
Mariestad
Nyköping
Skövde
Norrköping
Linköping
Borås
Jönköping
Gothenburg
Nässjö
Västervik
Gotland
Varberg
Värnamo
Falkenberg
Oskarshamn
Halmstad
Växjö
Båstad
Laholm
Ängelholm
Hässleholm
Kalmar
Helsingborg
Karlshamn
Karlskrona
LATVIA
Lund
Kristianstad
BALTIC
DENMARK
Malmö
Kivik
SEA
Trelleborg
Simrishamn
Ystad

INLANDSBANAN

0   200km

Seat reservations are only compulsory for travel by X2000, and are included in the price of the ticket. A rail-pass holder, though, pays an X2000 supplement of 50kr, which includes the cost of reserving a seat. Reservations are not required on InterCity and InterRegio trains but are strongly recommended, particularly in summer and during school holidays, when trains are often fully booked. Rail-pass holders pay 30kr per seat reservation. Tickets without seat reservations, called "*obokad biljett*" – literally "an unbooked ticket" – cost the same as those with, but give you the added flexibility of being able to break your journey en route on the day of travel. Paradoxically, such tickets allow you to travel on trains which are fully booked; head for the restaurant car for a seat. Reserved seats on Swedish trains are not marked, so although it may appear that a seat is free it may not be so – always ask "*är det ledigt här?*" – is anyone sitting here – before you sit down. Incidentally, "*några nya påstigare*" is what you're likely to hear the conductor saying as he/she comes through the train after each station, which literally means "any new boarders": only show your ticket if you've just got on. "*Biljetterna, tack*", on the other hand, is "all tickets please".

The main **discount** option is **Reslust** (literally "wanderlust") **tickets**, which are available on every train. However, you'll need a **Reslustkort** (valid for one calendar year; 150kr) to be eligible for the discounted Reslust prices. The Reslustkort also includes a number of other discounts, and one card entitles two people travelling together to the same discount. Reslust tickets come in two varieties – either **rosa** (pink) or the cheaper **röd** (red – these are valid on the same trains as the pink tickets and so sell out fast); they're valid on both X2000 and InterCity trains, including all-night trains in couchette and sleeping-car accommodation. For example, a Rosa Reslust ticket from Stockholm to Gothenburg costs 390kr; a Röd Reslust ticket costs just 260kr (this compares with 520kr by InterCity train and 920kr by X2000). A restricted number of both pink and red tickets is available on every. Both pink and red tickets must be bought at least seven days before departure. Under-26s can buy a Reslustkort Max 25 card (150kr; proof of age required when purchasing), which entitles them to a thirty percent discount on all fares, including the Reslust tickets. It's worth pointing out that nearly all train staff in

Sweden speak good English, which means that you've got a sporting chance of buying the right ticket every time; conversely it's difficult to be convincing if you're caught by the conductor in possession of an invalid or wrong ticket.

In the end most people are best off avoiding the headache of choosing discount tickets by getting a **pass** instead, such as InterRail, Eurail or ScanRail (see the relevant "Getting there" section for details) or, if you are touring Sweden only, a **Sweden Rail Pass**. This gives unlimited travel throughout the country on all SJ trains. A seven-day pass costs £130 in standard class and £171 in first class; a fourteen-day version costs £174 and £226 respectively. Supplements are payable on InterCity and express services. You have to buy the pass before you leave home; it is not available in Sweden. In countries where there is no agent, for example, Australia or New Zealand, you can email *swedenbooking@gtsab.se* to buy the pass before you leave home.

Bicycles cannot simply be taken on board the train. As in most European countries, you'll need to register the bike as luggage and send it ahead; in Swedish this service is called *pollettera*, and generally costs around 150kr. SJ guarantee that your bike will arrive within three days, although the time needed can often be much less.

OVERNIGHT TRAIN JOURNEYS

If you're travelling overnight in Sweden, it's worth paying for a **couchette** or a **sleeping car** – Swedish train seats don't pull out to form a bed, unlike their equivalents in many other European trains. If you want to travel by couchette or sleeper without a rail pass, you have to buy an all-in-one ticket which includes your train fare, sleeping accommodation and supplement. Prices vary according to distance: for example, a couchette on the Stockholm–Luleå journey costs 550kr one-way (625kr in a three-berth sleeper) whereas a couchette on the Stockholm–Kiruna trip costs 630kr one-way (705kr in a three-berth sleeper).

With a rail pass, prices are low: a couchette costs 90kr on journeys within Sweden (roughly the same as a night in a youth hostel). A three-berth standard-class sleeping car is a little more at 165kr (200kr Oslo–Copenhagen; not available Stockholm–Copenhagen); a two-berth costs 280kr per person (251kr for Stockholm–Copenhagen; 250kr Oslo–Copenhagen). Couchettes in women-only compartments, unique to Sweden, are available.

Sleepers run on several routes out of Stockholm, including those terminating at Malmö, Östersund, Luleå and Kiruna, but there are no sleepers between Stockholm and Gothenburg in either direction. On the Stockholm–Copenhagen and Oslo–Copenhagen via Helsingborg runs, there are no longer any sleepers between Stockholm and Oslo. From Gothenburg there are through sleepers to Luleå; from Malmö to Stockholm, and abroad to Berlin (there are no longer direct services to Prague and Budapest); from Helsingborg to Stockholm and Oslo (these are all final destinations). There's a hot shower and a hair dryer in the end of every sleeping car (modern carriages have toilet and shower in the compartment itself) as well as a socket for the radio (bring your own headphones). Sleepers are single-sex only; straight couples are permitted to share a two-berth compartment.

Run by the private **Tågkompaniet** (*www.tagkompaniet.se*), the night trains from Stockholm to Kiruna and Luleå and from Gothenburg to Luleå are an experience in themselves. There's even a cinema on board where you can catch up on the latest releases before heading off to the bistro for a bite or a quick jive to your favourite tunes from the jukebox – all as you slip painlessly through the Swedish night.

REGIONAL TRAIN LINES

If you're in Sweden for any length of time, travelling at least a section of the **Inlandsbanan** (Inland Railway; ☎063/12 76 95, fax 10 15 90, *www.inlandsbanan.se*), which runs through northern Sweden, is a must. The route takes in some of the country's most unspoilt terrain – kilometre after kilometre of forests, and several lakes (the train stops at two, Tandsjöborg and Varjisträsk, for passengers to take a quick dip), and offers a chance to see real off-the-beaten-track Sweden. For more information on the line, see p.421.

In Sweden's southernmost province, Skåne, a local private company, **Pågatågen**, operates trains between Helsingborg, Lund and Malmö, and between Malmö and Ystad. Prices on the short hops are low; ticketing is fully automated – you buy your tickets from a machine on the platform, which accepts coins and notes. InterRail and ScanRail cards are valid for travel on these routes.

BUSES

Although **bus** travel is about half as expensive as going by train, buses are generally less frequent, and so much slower that they aren't a good choice for long journeys (for example, Stockholm to Malmö takes 4hr 15min on the X2000, but 9hr 20min by bus). Most **long-distance buses** are operated by two companies, Swebus (from abroad ☎00468/655 00 90, in Sweden local rate 0200/21 82 18, *www.express.swebus.se*) and Svenska Buss (from abroad ☎08/440 85 70; in Sweden 020/67 67 67, *www.svenskabuss.se*). **Swebus** have the most extensive network in Sweden, with departures to over four hundred destinations ranging from Malmö in the south to as far north as Dalarna. **Svenska Buss** also operate in the south of the country, going no further north than Falun and Borlänge. Both companies run two types of buses: daily Expressbussar, usually complementing rather than competing with the train network; and the cheaper Veckoslutsbussar, on Fridays and Sundays. On Swebus, **fares** range from 20kr to 350kr depending on the length of the journey, with under-17s going for half price and children under 6 for free. Students and those aged 17–21 get a thirty percent discount, while senior citizens can travel at a fifty percent discount from Monday to Thursday and on Saturday; fares on Svenska Buss are similar.

Regional buses are particularly important in the north, where they carry mail to isolated areas. Several companies operate daily services, and their fares are broadly similar to one another's (usually 100–150kr for a 1hr to 2hr journey). Major routes are listed in the "Travel Details" at the end of each chapter, and you can pick up a comprehensive timetable at any bus terminal.

PLANES

The **domestic plane** network is operated by a number of companies, the key players being SAS and Skyways. Various deals can make flying a real steal, especially considering the time saved. Individual so-called Pleasure Saver tickets (much the same as an Apex), which must be booked either two weeks or one week before departure, aren't particularly cheap (around 1000–2000kr return depending on destination). Flying to or from Stockholm, anyone travelling with you goes for just

500kr or 700kr depending on the length of the flight – ask for a *medföljandepris*. This fare is supposed to be only for accompanying partners (male or female, gay or straight) – it's worth pretending even if you're not quite so familiar with your travelling companion.

SAS operates between **Stockholm** and the following destinations: Gothenburg, Kalmar, Karlstad, Kiruna, Kristianstad, Luleå, Malmö, Ronneby/Karlskrona, Skellefteå, Sundsvall, Umeå, Växjö, Ängelholm/Helsingborg, Östersund, Örnsköldsvik. **Skyways** flies between **Stockholm** and Arvidsjaur, Borlänge/Falun, Gällivare, Hemavan, Hultsfred, Kramfors/Sollefteå, Linköping, Lycksele, Mora, Oskarshamn, Storuman, Vilhelmina, Visby, Sveg, Söderhamn, Trollhättan/Vänersborg, Visby and Örebro; between **Gothenburg** and Borlänge/Falun, Sundsvall/Härnösand, Umeå and Västerås; between **Luleå** and Gällivare, Kiruna and Sundsvall/Härnösand; between **Umeå** and Gällivare, Luleå and Kiruna; and between **Malmö** and Västerås and Örebro. For information on domestic flights and fares in Sweden with both SAS and Skyways, call ☎020/72 70 00.

There are also a number of other smaller airlines which operate mostly regional routes; perhaps the most useful if you're planning hiking in Dalarna is Air Stord, which flies between Stockholm and Idre.

AIR PASSES AND STAND-BY TICKETS

SAS and Skyways offer a joint **Visit Scandinavia Airpass**, which can make flying a serious alternative to InterRail or ScanRail. The airpass has to be bought in conjunction with an SAS or Skyways return ticket to Sweden. With each international ticket, you can buy up to eight coupons, each valid on one flight; so two coupons are needed on journeys involving one change of plane (for example Malmö to Östersund via Stockholm). The coupons cost $75 on all flights within Sweden except on SAS' Stockholm–Kiruna route, for which a coupon costs $125. The passes are also valid on flights between Sweden and Finland and within and between Denmark, Norway and Sweden.

People under 26 can save substantially by flying **stand-by**. Buy tickets at any domestic airport when you arrive, and on the day you want to catch an internal flight, go to the airport and get in the appropriate queue. A single stand-by ticket (for example Stockholm–Luleå) currently costs a ridiculously cheap 200kr; for 350kr you can get priority on a particular flight. If you buy eight one-way stand-by tickets, (at either 200kr or 350kr) you get one return trip (for which you can reserve a seat) free. You can avoid lengthy waits at airports by checking seat availability first (☎020/72 78 88, *www3.sas.se/ungdom/se/stand_by/*), though this service is only in Swedish. If you don't speak Swedish, call SAS on ☎020/72 70 00 and ask them whether you're likely to get a seat.

FERRIES AND BOATS

Domestic ferry services in Sweden are few. The main route is between Visby, on the Baltic island of Gotland, and Nynäshamn, on the mainland near Stockholm and Oskarshamn. High-speed **catamarans** as well as regular ferries operate on both routes. Departures are very popular in summer and you should try to book ahead. The ScanRail pass gives a fifty percent discount on the Gotland crossings (for more details see p.339).

Each of the various archipelagos off the coast – particularly the **Stockholm archipelago** with its 24,000 islands – has ferry services which link up the main islands in the group. If you're in Stockholm, make sure you venture out into the archipelago – the peace and quiet, and the vistas of water, rocks and islets, are something special. A boat pass which covers travel within the archipelago is available in Stockholm; see p.99 for more details. There's also an extensive archipelago off Luleå which is worth visiting; details of boat services there are given on p.403.

It's possible to cross between Stockholm and Gothenburg on the **Göta Canal**, either on your own boat or by taking one of the expensive cruises along the route on an atmospheric old **steamboat**; ticket and journey details are given on p.167. Cheaper day cruises are possible along stretches of the Göta Canal and the Trollhättan Canal; more details are given in the text.

DRIVING AND HITCHING

As far as road conditions go, **driving in Sweden** is a dream. Traffic jams are rare (in fact in the north of the country yours will often be the only car on the road), roads are well-maintained and motorways, where they exist, are toll-free. The only real dangers are **reindeer** (in the north) and **elk** (everywhere), which wander onto the road without warning. It's difficult enough to see them at dusk, and when it's properly dark all you'll see is two red eyes as the animal leaps out in front of your car. The Swedes have now taken to spraying pungent-smelling artificial wolf urine on the edges of roads where accidents involving elk are common – elk and wolves don't get on at all well. If you hit an elk or deer, not only will you know about it (they're as big as a horse), you're bound by law to report it to the police.

To drive in Sweden you'll need a **full licence**; an international driving licence isn't required, though a green card or other insurance documents are essential. **Speed limits** are 110kph on motorways, 90kph on dual carriageways and many other roads, 50kph in built-up areas, and 70kph elsewhere if unsigned; for cars towing caravans, the limit is 80kph. You must drive with your headlights on 24hr a day (don't forget to turn them off when you leave the car!), and it's useful to fit a headlamp adaptor if you're bringing over a right-hand drive car to avoid dazzling oncoming traffic with your lights. Warning triangles are compulsory, as is the wearing of seat belts both in the back and in the front; children can use any seat but must use a seat belt or a special child safety seat. Studded tyres for driving on snow and ice are allowed between November 1 and the first Monday after the Easter holiday; when in use they must be fitted to all wheels. In northern Sweden, it's worth fitting mud-flaps to your wheels and stone-guards to the fronts of caravans.

Swedish **drink-driving laws** are among the strictest in Europe, and random breath tests are commonplace. Basically, you can't have even one beer and still be under the limit; the blood alcohol level is 0.2 percent. If you're found to be over the limit you'll lose the right to drive in Sweden, face a fine (often) and a prison sentence (not infrequently). Fines for **speeding** are levied on the spot.

The cost of **petrol** (*bensin*) is very high. Types of petrol normally available are 98 octane (equivalent to four-star), unleaded (*blyfri*) and diesel; a litre of petrol is currently around 8.5kr. Most filling stations are self-service (*Tanka själv*), where you either pay a machine at the pump that accepts 20kr or 100kr notes (though not for diesel), or head for the pumps marked "*Kassa*", which allow you to pay inside at the till.

If you **break down**, call either the police or the Larmtjänst (☎020/91 00 40 for towing; ☎020/22 00 00 for other accidents), a 24-hour rescue organization run by Swedish insurance companies. You should only use the emergency telephone number (☎112) in the event of an accident and

injuries. It's not mandatory to call the police in the event of an accident, but drivers must give their name and address to the other parties involved and shouldn't leave the scene until that's done. Drivers who don't stop after an accident may be liable to a fine or even imprisonment.

CAR RENTAL

Roads in Sweden may be a dream, but forking out for car rental and petrol is more the stuff of nightmares. **Car rental** is uniformly expensive; the only way to bring down the ludicrous prices is to hunt for special **weekend rates** (tourist offices are a good source of information on these, or try the national chain of filling stations, Statoil, which often rents out vehicles at near-bargain-prices over weekends (generally Friday afternoon to Monday morning). If you fail to find a special deal, in the summer months reckon on paying 3000kr and upwards a week for a VW Golf or similar-sized car, with unlimited mileage. Be warned, though, that deals in the remoter parts can be even more expensive than this. The major international companies are represented in all the main towns and cities (in out-of-the-way places, airports are often the only source of car rental). To rent a car in Sweden you must be over 21 and have held a driving licence for at least one year.

You may well find it cheaper, especially if you are travelling from North America, to arrange things before you go; airlines sometimes have special deals with car rental companies if you book your flight and car through them. Alternatively, if you don't want to be tied down, try an agency such as Holiday Autos, who will arrange advance booking through a local agent and can usually undercut the big companies considerably (see the box opposite for details of car rental companies).

HITCHING

Despite the amount of holiday traffic and the number of young Swedes with cars, **hitching** is rarely worth the effort, as long-distance lifts are few and far between. Shorter hops are easier to find, especially when travelling along the coasts and in the north, but don't rely on hitching as your main means of transport. If you do try it, always use a sign; be prepared for long, long waits and to be scoffed at by passing drivers.

CITY TRANSPORT

Taxi fares are quite simply horrific. Before you get in the taxi the meter will be showing at least 28kr;

CAR RENTAL FIRMS

AUSTRALIA
Avis ☎1800/225 533.
Budget ☎1300/362 848.
Hertz ☎1800/550 067.

BRITAIN
Avis ☎0990/900500.
Budget ☎0800/181181.
Eurodollar 01895/233300.
Europcar ☎0345/222525.
Hertz ☎0990/996699.
Holiday Autos ☎0990/300400.

IRELAND
Avis ☎0990/900500 in Northern Ireland,
☎01/874 5844 in the Republic.
Budget ☎0800/181181 in Northern Ireland,
☎0800/973 159 in the Republic.
Europcar ☎0345/222 525 in Northern Ireland,
☎01/874 5844 in the Republic.
Hertz ☎0990/996 699 in Northern Ireland,
☎01/660 2255 in the Republic.

Holiday Autos ☎0990/300 400 in Northern
Ireland; ☎01/872 9366 in the Republic.

NEW ZEALAND
Avis ☎09/579 5231.
Budget ☎0800/ 652 227.
Hertz ☎09/309 0989.

NORTH AMERICA
Auto Europe ☎1-800/223-5555,
www.autoeurope.com.
Avis International ☎1-800/331-1084,
www.avis.com.
Budget ☎1-800/527-0700,
www.budgetrentacar.com.
Dollar ☎1-800/421-6868.
Europe by Car ☎1-800/223-1516,
www.europebycar.com
Hertz International ☎1-800/654-3001, in
Canada ☎1-800/263-0600, *www.hertz.com*
Kemwel Holiday Autos ☎1-800/422-7737,
www.kemwel.com.

it will continue to tick over as you wait at traffic lights. A three-kilometre ride can easily set you back around 100kr. Given the phenomenal fares they charge, taxi drivers don't expect a tip. In some areas there are also surcharges for booking a taxi by phone. Save your money and take the excellent public transport instead. **Buses** in towns and cities can be very useful, as many hotels and especially hostels and campsites can be a fair distance from town centres. Flat fares are around 12kr to 20kr, the ticket usually being valid for an hour. Most large towns operate some sort of discount system allowing you to buy a book of tickets, which is better value than buying them individually – details of such schemes are in the text or can be obtained from the local tourist offices.

CYCLING

Some parts of the country are made for **cycling**: Stockholm, the southern provinces and Gotland, in particular, are ideal for a

leisurely bike ride. Many towns are best explored by bike, and tourist offices, campsites and youth hostels often rent them out from around 80kr a day, 400kr a week. Taking a bike on the train involves a bit of forward planning, however: you'll have to hand it in three days in advance so it can be sent ahead, for which you'll pay 125kr.

Sweden has a large number of signposted cycle trails; one of the most popular is the **Sweden Trail** (Sverigeleden), which stretches all the way from Helsingborg in the southwest to Karesuando near the Finnish border, taking in many of the country's main sights. Svenska Cyckelsällskapet (Swedish Cycling Association; Box 6006, S-164 06 Kista; ☎08/751 62 04, fax 751 19 35) has more information; also try Cyckelfrämjandet, Box 6027, S-102 31 Stockholm (☎08/32 16 80). The STF (see p.34) has details of Swedish cycling holidays that include hostel accommodation, meals and cycle rental.

ACCOMMODATION

Finding somewhere cheap to stay in Sweden isn't difficult. There's an extensive network of youth hostels (of an exceptionally high standard) and campsites, while private rooms and bed-and-breakfast places are common in the towns and cities. Discounts make hotels affordable during the summer months and at weekends all year round, and special deals which form part of the discount-card schemes available in many of the larger towns also help to bring down the cost.

YOUTH HOSTELS

Youth hostels in Sweden (*vandrarhem*: literally "wanderers' home") turn up in the unlikeliest of places. There are over three hundred of them dotted across the country, in converted lighthouses, old castles and prisons, historic country manors, schoolrooms and even on boats. Quite simply, they offer some of the best accommodation in the country. Forget any preconceptions about youth hostelling: in Sweden, dormitories are few, and rooms are family-oriented (usually sleeping four people), modern, clean and hotel-like.

The majority of hostels are run by STF – short for Svenska Turistföreningen (Swedish Touring Club; Vandrarhemsavdelningen, Box 25, S-101 20 Stockholm; ☎08/463 22 70, *www.stfturist.se*). To get members' rates at Swedish hostels you can either join the youth hostel association in your home country (see box below for details) or get a **Hostelling International (HI)** card at any Swedish hostel (250kr per calendar year); the cards also provide discounts on admission to some museums, ferry crossings and sightseeing trips. The cost of hostel accommodation varies between 75kr and 175kr per person per night for members; the surcharge for non-members is generally about 25kr a night, which can amount to a sizeable expense if repeatedly incurred over a couple of weeks, especially when compared to the low cost of annual membership. **Under-16s**

YOUTH HOSTEL ASSOCIATIONS

AUSTRALIA
Australian Youth Hostel Association, 422 Kent St, Sydney (☎02/9261 1111, *www.yha.com.au*).

CANADA
Hostelling International/Canadian Hostelling Association, Room 400, 205 Catherine St, Ottawa, ON K2P 1C3 (☎613/237-7884 or 1-800/663-5777).

ENGLAND AND WALES
Youth Hostel Association (YHA), Trevelyan House, 8 St Stephen's Hill, St Alban's, Herts AL1 2DY (☎01727/845047, *www.yha.org.uk*). London information office: 14 Southampton St, London WC2 7HY (☎020/7836 8541).

IRELAND
Youth Hostel Association of Northern Ireland, 22 Donegall Rd, Belfast BT12 5JN (☎028/9032 4733,

www.hini.org.uk); An Oige, 61 Mountjoy St, Dublin 7 (☎01/830 4555, *www.irelandyha.org*).

NEW ZEALAND
Youth Hostel Association of New Zealand, 173 Gloucester St, Christchurch (☎03/379 9970, *www.yha.co.nz*).

SCOTLAND
Scottish Youth Hostel Association, 7 Glebe Crescent, Stirling, FK8 2JA (☎01786/451181, *www.syha.org.uk*).

US
Hostelling International-American Youth Hostels (HI-AYH), 733 15th St NW, Suite 840, PO Box 37613, Washington, DC 20005 (☎202/783-6161, *www.hiayh.org*).

pay between 30–80kr per night if their parents are association members, 60–110kr if parents are non-members; **under-3s** who don't take up an extra bed go free.

Nearly all hostels have well-equipped self-catering kitchens and serve a buffet breakfast. If you're planning to cook for yourself using youth hostel kitchens, bear in mind that a few don't provide kitchenware and utensils – take at least basic equipment with you. To stay at an STF hostel you'll ideally have a **sheet sleeping bag**; these are on sale at camping shops and can be rented at the hostels; alternatively you can stitch a couple of old sheets together and take a pillowcase. You can use a different type of sleeping bag provided you put a sheet between it and the mattress to keep the latter clean.

Hostels are used by Swedish families as cheap hotel-standard accommodation and can fill quickly, so always **ring ahead**, particularly in the summer, to improve your chance of getting a place. They usually close between 10am and 5pm, with curfews commencing at around 11pm or midnight; some are closed out of season, particularly those in the north.

It would be impossible to list all youth hostels in Sweden in this guide; for details, see *Hostelling International: Europe and the Mediterranean*, available from your local youth hostel assocation. Apart from the STF hostels there are a number of **independently run hostels**, usually charging similar prices; we've mentioned the most useful in the text, and tourist offices will have details of any other local independent hostels.

FELL STATIONS AND MOUNTAIN CABINS

Fell stations (*fjällstationer*) provide hostel-like accommodation along mountain hiking routes; charging 150–380kr per person, depending on their standard and the time of year, they're slightly more expensive than hostels in towns and cities. They're also better equipped than the average youth hostel: each fell station has a sauna, a shop, a kitchen and – Sylarna fell station, south of Storlien, apart – a restaurant. There are eight fell stations in all, found in or near the chain of mountains which form the border between Sweden and Norway, and always located on walking paths.

Mountain cabins (*fjällstugor*), of which there are around ninety, are often no more than simple huts out in the wilds and are wonderful for getting away from it all. Run by the STF, they generally cost between 100–155kr depending on season (100–195kr for huts along the northern stretch of the Kungsleden between Abisko and Hemavan; see p.478) and are often located at convenient intervals along popular walking routes. Some of them have a warden who can sell you food supplies and, more often than not, there'll also be a kitchen where you can prepare your own food. The odd one or two also have saunas, making for a perfect end to a day's hiking. Both fell stations and mountain cabins allow you to use a sleeping bag without a sheet underneath.

HOTELS AND PENSIONS

Hotels and **pensions** needn't be expensive, and although there's little chance of finding any kind of room under 250kr a night, you can often find good-value hotel rooms in summer, especially in July, when business people who would otherwise fill the hotels during the week are on holiday (many Swedes also head south, out of the country, at this time of year). If you turn up at some of the larger hotels after 6pm without a booking in summer, you may find they drop their prices even lower than their usual discount rate. This is obviously a risky strategy (and breakfast often isn't included in these late deals), but it can land you

---

ACCOMMODATION PRICES

The pensions and hotels listed in the guide have been price-graded according to the scale given below; the price category given against each establishment indicates the cost of the least expensive double rooms there. Many hotels offer considerable reductions at weekends all year round, and during the summer holiday period (mid-June to mid-Aug); in these cases the reduction is either noted in the text or, where a discount brings a hotel into another price band, given after the number for the full price. Single rooms, where available, usually cost between 60 and 80 percent of a double.

① under 500kr	③ 700–900kr	⑤ 1200–1500kr
② 500–700kr	④ 900–1200kr	⑥ over 1500kr

some very cheap rooms. The only parts of the country where summer discounts don't apply are in some of the popular holiday destinations in southern Sweden, where prices can actually go up in summer.

Out of summer, rooms are much cheaper at weekends (when the business people are at home) than midweek; for example, a room with TV and bathroom will on average cost from 350kr for a single, and from 500kr for a double at weekends outside summer. Nearly all hotels include a huge self-service buffet breakfast in the price, which will keep you going for much of the day.

The best **package deals** are those operated in Malmö, Stockholm and Gothenburg, where 300–365kr gets you a double room for one night, with breakfast and the relevant city discount card thrown in. These schemes are often valid from mid-June to mid-August and at weekends throughout the year, but see the accommodation details under the city accounts for specific information.

The other option is to buy into a **hotel pass** scheme, where you buy in advance a series of vouchers that pay for a room or give you a discounted rate in various chain hotels throughout the country. These vouchers can be bought before you leave for Sweden; for the latest details, it's best to consult the Swedish Tourism and Travel Council (see p.24 for their addresses outside Sweden), whose publication *Hotels in Sweden* contains a comprehensive listing of hotels with information on the various discount schemes. The drawback of having a hotel pass is that you'll feel bound to stay in hotels all the time and will be limited to particular chains.

PRIVATE ROOMS, B&B AND SELF-CATERING

Another accommodation option is renting **private rooms** in people's houses. Most tourist offices can book such rooms for you in any reasonably sized town, and at around 90–140kr a head (plus a 30–50kr booking fee), they're an affordable and pleasant option. In the countryside, these rooms are advertised with roadside signs saying "*Rum*" or "*Logi*". All rooms have access to showers and/or baths and sometimes a kitchen; hosts are rarely intrusive.

Farms throughout Sweden offer **bed and breakfast** accommodation and self-catering facilities. For more information, contact local tourist offices or an organization called Bo på Lantgård (Living on a farm), Box 8, S-668 21 Ed,

SELF-CATERING APARTMENTS

STOCKHOLM
Hotelltjänst/Caretaker ☎08/10 44 37, fax 21 37 16.
Olssons ☎08/10 22 29, fax 21 01 76.

GOTHENBURG
Foretagsbostäder ☎031/17 00 25, fax 711 24 60.
SGS ☎031/81 33 71; fax 81 24 97.
Svenska Turistlägenheter ☎031/330 06 00; fax 332 29 99.

MALMÖ
City Room ☎040/795 94, fax 97 67 70.

Sweden (☎0534/120 75, fax 610 11, *www.bopalantgard.se*). Accommodation on a farm costs roughly 250–300kr a night per person, with discounts for children. The Swedish Travel and Tourism Council (see p.24) have the latest details on farm B&Bs and farm holidays, and should be able to help you book your accommodation before you leave for Sweden.

If you fancy renting a **self-catering** private apartment or a couple of rooms for a week or so, contact local tourist offices (details given in the text), where staff will book them for you, or approach one of the companies listed in the box above. Apartments for four people cost between 2000kr and 3000kr a week.

CAMPSITES, CHALETS AND CABINS

Practically every town or village has at least one **campsite**, and these are generally of a high standard. To pitch a tent at any campsite you'll need the **Swedish Camping Card** (Svenskt Campingkort), which costs 49kr and includes accident insurance while staying at the site. Cards can be issued at the first site you visit or before you leave; contact the Swedish Camping Site Owners' Association (Box 255, S-451 17 Uddevalla; *www.camping.se/index_en.html*).

It costs around 80–160kr for two people to pitch a tent at an official campsite. Most sites are open from June to September, some – including around two hundred in winter sport areas – throughout the year. A camping brochure with details of all sites, plus a detailed motoring and camping map, is available from offices of the Swedish Travel and Tourism Council (see p.24 for details). Note also that only **propane gas** – for example, Primus – is normally available in Sweden. It's illegal and also highly dangerous to burn propane in equipment designed for butane. Propane and the associated cooking, heating or lighting equipment are inexpensive, and widely available at more than two thousand Primus dealers in Sweden.

Thanks to a tradition known as *Allemansrätten* (Everyman's Right; see p.48), it's perfectly possible to **camp rough** throughout the country. This gives you the right to camp anywhere for one night without asking permission, provided you stay a reasonable distance (100m) away from other dwellings. In practice (and especially if you're in the north), there'll be nobody around to mind if you camp in one spot for longer, although it's as well – and polite – to ask first should you come across

someone. The wide open spaces within most town and city borders make free camping a distinct possibility in built-up areas too.

Many campsites also boast **cabins**, each of which is usually equipped with bunk beds, a kitchen and utensils, but not sheets. For a group or a couple, the cabins are an excellent alternative to camping; cabins go for around 250–350kr for a four-bed number. As usual, it's wise to ring ahead to secure one.

Sweden also has a whole series of cabins for rent in spots other than campsites, often in picturesque locations, such as in the middle of the forest, by a lakeshore or on the coast. On the whole, these cabins offer high-standard accommodation at prices to match. For information and to make a booking, contact the local tourist office or the Swedish Travel and Tourism Council.

EATING AND DRINKING

There's no escaping the fact that eating and drinking is going to take up a large slice of your budget in Sweden – though no more so than in any other northern European country. Swedish food – based largely on fish, meat and potato, and very varied in preparation – is always tasty and well presented, and, at its best, delicious. Unusual specialities generally come from the north of the country and include reindeer, elk meat and

wild berries; while herring and salmon come in so many different guises that fish fiends will always be content. Vegetarians, too, should have no problems, with plenty of non-meat options available especially in the bigger towns; elsewhere their choice will be limited to pizzas and salads . The availability of alcoholic drinks is more uniform, with lager-type beers and imported wines providing no surprises; the local spirit *akvavit*, however, is worth trying at least once – it comes in dozens of weird and wonderful flavours, from lemon to cumin-and-dill.

Eating well and eating cheaply needn't be mutually exclusive aims in Sweden. The best strategy is to fuel up on breakfast and lunch, both of which offer good-value options. Breakfast is often included in the cost of a night's accommodation, and most restaurants have lunchtime specials that time and again are the best-value meals you'll find. There are a large number of foreign restaurants – Chinese and Italian mostly, Indian less often – but don't expect them to serve up cheap evening meals. In Sweden Chinese food, in particular, can be really quite expensive and tasteless.

GLOSSARY OF SWEDISH FOOD AND DRINK TERMS

BASICS AND SNACKS

Bröd	Bread	*Knäcke*	Crispbread	*Ris*	Rice	*Tårta*	Cake
Bulle	Bun	*-bröd*		*Salt*	Salt	*Vinäger*	Vinegar
Glass	Ice cream	*Olja*	Oil	*Senap*	Mustard	*Våffla*	Waffle
Grädde	Cream	*Omelett*	Omelette	*Småkakor*	Biscuits	*Ägg*	Egg
Gräddfil	Sour cream	*Ost*	Cheese	*Smör*	Butter	*Ättika*	Vinegar for
Gröt	Porridge	*Pastej*	Paté	*Smörgås*	Sandwich		pickling
Kaka	Cake	*Peppar*	Pepper	*Socker*	Sugar		
Keks	Biscuits	*Pommes*	Fries	*Sylt*	Jam		

MEAT (KÖTT)

Biff	Beef	*Köttbullar*	Meatballs	*Renstek*	Roast reindeer
Fläsk	Pork	*Kyckling*	Chicken	*Rådjursstek*	Roast venison
Kalvkött	Veal	*Lammkött*	Lamb	*Skinka*	Ham
Korv	Sausage	*Lever*	Liver	*Älg*	Elk
Kotlett	Cutlet/chop	*Oxstek*	Roast beef		

FISH (FISK)

Ansjovis	Anchovies	*Kräftor*	Freshwater	*Sardiner*	Sardines
Blåmusslor	Mussels		crayfish	*Sik*	Whitefish
Fiskbullar	Fishballs	*Lax*	Salmon	*Sill*	Herring
Forell	Trout	*Makrill*	Mackerel	*Sjötunga*	Sole
Hummer	Lobster	*Räkor*	Shrimps/	*Strömming*	Baltic herring
Kaviar	Caviar		prawns	*Torsk*	Cod
Krabba	Crab	*Rödspätta*	Plaice	*Ål*	Eel

VEGETABLES (GRÖNSAKER)

Blomkål	Cauliflower	*Morötter*	Carrots	*Svamp*	Mushrooms
Brysselkål	Brussel sprouts	*Potatis*	Potatoes	*Tomater*	Tomatoes
Bönor	Beans	*Rödkål*	Red cabbage	*Vitkål*	White cabbage
Gurka	Cucumber	*Sallad*	Lettuce; salad	*Vitlök*	Garlic
Lök	Onion	*Spenat*	Spinach	*Ärtor*	Peas

FRUIT (FRUKT)

Ananas	Pineapple	*Hallon*	Raspberry	*Persika*	Peach
Apelsin	Orange	*Hjortron*	Cloudberry	*Päron*	Pear
Aprikos	Apricot	*Jordgubbar*	Strawberries	*Vindruvor*	Grapes
Banan	Banana	*Lingon*	Lingonberry;	*Äpple*	Apple
Citron	Lemon		red whortleberry		

CULINARY TERMS

Blodig	Rare	*Kall*	Cold	*Ungstekt*	Roasted/
Filé	Fillet	*Kokt*	Boiled		baked
Friterad	Deep fried	*Lagom*	Medium	*Varm*	Hot
Genomstekt	Well done	*Pocherad*	Poached	*Ångkokt*	Steamed
Gravad	Cured	*Rökt*	Smoked		
Grillat/halstrat	Grilled	*Stekt*	Fried		

DRINKS

Apelsinjuice	Orange juice	*Mellanöl*	Medium-strong beer	*Storstark*	Large strong beer
Chocklad	Hot chocolate			*Te*	Tea
Citron	Lemon	*Mineral-vatten*	Mineral water	*Vatten*	Water
Fruktjuice	Fruit juice	*Mjölk*	Milk	*Vin*	Wine
Grädde	Cream	*Rödvin*	Red wine	*Vitt vin*	White wine
Kaffe	Coffee	*Saft*	Juice	*Öl*	Beer
Lättöl	Light beer	*Starköl*	Strong beer	*Skål*	Cheers!

SWEDISH SPECIALITIES

Bruna bönor	Baked, vinegared brown beans, usually served with fried pork
Filmjölk	Soured milk
Fisksoppa	Fish soup usually including several sorts of fish, prawns and dill
Getost	Goat's cheese
Glögg	Mulled wine usually fortified with spirits to keep out the cold, and drunk at Christmas
Gravad lax	Salmon marinated in dill, sugar and seasoning; served with mustard sauce and lemon
Hjortron	A wild, orange-coloured berry, served with fresh cream and/or ice cream. Also made into jam
Janssons frestelse	A potato and anchovy bake with cream
Kryddost	Hard cheese spiced with seeds, sometimes caraway seeds or cloves
Köttbullar	Meatballs served with a brown creamy sauce and lingonberries
Kräftor	Crayfish, often served with *kryddost*, and eaten in August
Lingon	Lingonberry (sometimes known as red whortleberries), a red berry made into a kind of jam and served with meat dishes as well as on pancakes and in puddings eaten at Christmas
Långfil	A special type of soured milk from northern Sweden
Lövbiff	Sliced, fried beef with onions
Matjessill	Sweet-pickled herring
Mesost	Brown, sweet whey cheese; a breakfast favourite

Ostkaka	Curd cake made from fresh curds and eggs baked in the oven served with jam or berries
Pepparkakor	Thin, spiced gingerbread biscuits popular at Christmas
Plättar	Thin pancakes often served with pea soup
Potatissallad	Potato salad often flavoured with dill or chives
Pytt i panna	Cubes of meat and fried potatoes with a fried egg and beetroot
Semla	Sweet bun with almond paste and whipped cream; associated with Lent
Sillbricka	Various cured and marinated herring dishes; often appears as a first course in restaurants at lunchtime
Sjömansbiff	Sailor's beef casserole, thin slices of beef baked in the oven with potatoes and onion topped with parsley
Smultron	Wild strawberries, known for their concentrated taste
Strömming	Baltic herring
Surströmming	Baltic herring fermented for months until it's rotten and the tin it's in buckles – very smelly and eaten in very, very small quantities. Not for the faint hearted!
Ärtsoppa	Yellow pea soup with pork spiced with thyme and marjoram; a winter dish traditionally eaten on Thursdays
Ål	Eel, smoked and served with creamed potatoes or scrambled eggs (*Äggröra*)

FOOD

Sauces feature prominently in Swedish cooking, often flavoured with dill or parsley – making a wonderful complement to fish dishes – and there are many delicious creamy concoctions. Sweden's various **salmon** dishes are among the very best the cuisine has to offer – they're divine and delectable either warm or cold, and a mainstay of any Swedish *smörgåsbord* worth its salt. **Herring** is mostly served raw, but don't let that put you off as it tastes surprisingly good.

Of the dishes from the north, **reindeer** is the most obvious one to try; it has a delicious flavour when smoked and is akin to beef in taste and texture, but with virtually no fat; **elk meat** is decidedly less appetizing, but is good for burning up calories – you'll expend as many chewing the stuff as you'll get from it. Wild berries appear in many dishes, especially the **lingonberry**, which is something like cranberry, making a good accompaniment to Swedish meatballs, a combination praised by many a Swede as a delicacy of the country. You'll also be able to taste orange-coloured sweet **cloudberries**, which grow in the marshes of Lapland and are delicious with ice cream to follow any main dish.

BREAKFAST

Breakfast (*frukost*) is almost invariably a help-yourself buffet in the best Swedish tradition; you go up to the serving table as many times as you like and eat until you're fit to explode. There's generally an endless supply of breakfast cereals, muesli, cheeses, ham, salad, caviar (generally not the genuine article, but roe from fish other than sturgeon), paté, boiled eggs, Danish pastries, coffee, tea and juice. Swankier venues will usually also offer porridge, herring, yoghurt and fruit, as well as hot food, usually bacon, scrambled egg and sausages. Youth hostels charge around 50kr for breakfast; if you stay in a hotel, it'll be included in the price of your accommodation.

Something to watch out for is the jug of *filmjölk* (sometimes just called *fil*) or **soured milk** that you'll find next to the ordinary milk on the breakfast table. Swedes rave about the stuff and pour lashings of it on their cereals. It's thicker than normal milk, and you might find it tastes better if you mix it with some of the regular stuff. It's also eaten by itself, sometimes with a dollop or two of jam and a pinch of cinnamon.

Coffee is something the Swedes excel at: always freshly brewed, strong and delicious. Coffee breaks are a national institution, encapsulated in the verb *fika*, which is rendered rather longwindedly in English as "to put your feet up and enjoy a good cup of coffee". A coffee costs 10–15kr, but the price usually buys you more than one cup; the word *påtår* indicates that all cups after the first are either free or cost just a few *kronor*. **Tea** isn't up to scratch – weak Liptons as a rule – and costs just one or two *kronor* less than coffee. There are, however, some excellent speciality teas available in Sweden – look around for some when you're in a café, and if they have *Södermalmsblandning* (a variety that tastes of flowers and spices, and is named after Stockholm's south island), give it a try.

SNACKS AND LIGHT MEALS

For **snacks** and **light meals** you're really looking at the delights dished up by the **Gatukök** (street kitchen) or **Korvstånd** (sausage stall). A Gatukök is often no more than a hole in the wall – generally conspicuous by the snaking queue and gaggle of teenagers it attracts – serving sausages, burgers, chips, soft drinks and ketchup, and sometimes pizza slices or chicken pieces. Chips with a sausage or burger is generally around 45kr. The Korvstånds usually limit themselves to sausages, though some have chips and burgers as well. These outlets are to be found on every street, and until quite recently were often the only source of nourishment open after 5pm in the smaller towns and villages. Thankfully things have changed now. If you feel like really pushing the boat out, you could hit one of the country's **burger bars**: Clockburger is Sweden's own chain and usually a couple of kronor cheaper than McDonalds or Burger King. At the very best, these places offer the cheapest source of coffee – if you can stomach the surroundings.

For coffee, it's far better to hit the **konditori**, a coffee and cake shop of the first order. You should try at least one *konditori* while you're in Sweden, but unfortunately once may be all you can afford: coffee and cake will typically set you back 50–60kr (remember, though, that coffee refills are generally free). The *konditori* is as good a place as any to try a Swedish **open sandwich** (40–50kr), generally using white or rye bread, piled high with an elaborate variety of toppings. Favourites include prawns in mayo (with or without caviar), smoked salmon, egg slices and anchovy, cheese (often with green peppers or cucumber), paté, meatballs and, in the north, sometimes reindeer.

SELF-CATERING

For the cheapest eating it's hard to beat the **supermarkets** and **market stalls**. Of the supermarket chains, the cheapest is Vivo, followed by ICA and Konsum. Most of the supermarkets in Sweden aren't huge out-of-town affairs but small local affairs selling just the basics and a few other bits and pieces. If it's choice you're after, and you're in one of the bigger towns and cities, you should try the food halls in the department stores, Åhléns and Domus, which have a much wider selection than the average supermarket. Alternatively head for the indoor or outdoor markets, which often have fresher produce than the supermarkets, and at lower prices.

Fish is always excellent value, especially salmon. Pork and beef aren't too bad either; chicken is slightly more expensive. Sweden uses few preservatives in fresh produce.

As for **bread**, it's best to avoid the fluffy white loaves that you'll hardly notice you've eaten; go instead for those made from rye, which are darker and more filling. Sweden is a country rich in **cheeses**, all of which are reasonably good value and make great sandwich fillers; the range runs from stronger ripened cheeses such as Västerbotten and Lagrad Svecia to milder types like Grevé and Herrgårdsost; Prästost (literally "priest's cheese"), a medium-strong cheese akin to a crumbly cheddar, is also a particular favourite here. Also handy for sandwiches, though not especially cheap, are the packs of sliced ham that are available in all supermarkets, and **Kalles Kaviar**, packaged in blue tubes with a smiling little boy on the label – he's Kalle (Charlie) and something of a folk hero. The contents, which are orange in colour, aren't real caviar but made from cod roe; the stuff is especially good on **crispbread** (*knäckebröd*) – which is another area where the Swedes excel: it's easy to be overwhelmed by the different crispbread varieties available, and you can try a good few as prices are low.

There's also loads of different **yoghurts** and varieties of *filmjölk* (see p.40) to choose from – all very healthy and inexpensive – as is **milk**, which comes in three varieties: *lättmjölk* (skimmed), *mellanmjölk* (semi-skimmed) and *mjölk* (full-fat). **Fruit** and **vegetables** are expensive but not exorbitantly so, with bananas and mushrooms generally the most expensive items. A pack or jar of **coffee** constitutes a serious financial investment; tea less so, but it is still not especially cheap.

Pasta, rice, potatoes, eggs, onions and bacon are relatively inexpensive. The only goods to steer well clear of are those in tins (except mussels, mackerel and tomatoes), which are invariably extremely pricey for what they are.

VEGETARIAN FOOD

It's not too tough being **vegetarian** in Sweden: buffet-type meals are commonplace, and most are heavy with salads, cheeses, eggs and soups. For those who eat fish, there'll be no problem at all. The cities, too, have salad bars and sandwich shops, where you'll have no trouble feeding yourself; and if all else fails the local pizzeria will always deliver the non-meaty goods. At lunchtime you'll find that the *Dagens Rätt* (dish of the day) in many restaurants has a vegetarian option; it's always worth asking about if one isn't mentioned.

RESTAURANTS

Don't treat **restaurants** (*restaurang*) as no-go areas: they can be perfectly affordable, and offer some delicious high-quality food. Swedes eat their main meal of the day at **lunchtime**; do likewise and you'll save lots of cash. But you don't have to restrict yourself to eating out at lunchtime; many restaurants also offer special deals in the evening, and even if they don't you're bound to find something on their menu that will fit your pocket. A not-too-upmarket **evening meal** in a restaurant will cost you 70–100kr without alcohol. A three-course meal will naturally cost more; expect to pay something in the region of 150–200kr. Add around 40kr for a strong beer, or 200kr for an average bottle of wine. Dishes usually have some sort of salad accompaniment and come with bread. Many of the traditional Swedish dishes on offer in most restaurants are listed in the box on pp.38–39. Bear in mind that Swedes eat early; lunch will be served from 11am, dinner from 6pm.

At lunchtime, go for the **Dagens Rätt** or dish of the day, which costs between 40kr and 60kr and is one way to sample Swedish *Husmanskost* (home cooking). Served from 11am to 2pm, *Dagens Rätt* offers the choice of a main meal, along with salad and bread/crispbread, a soft drink or light beer, and coffee. Some Swedish dishes like *pytt i panna* (a fry-up of potatoes and meat with beetroot and a fried egg) and *köttbullar* (meatballs) are standards. You'll also find various pizza and pasta dishes on offer in Italian restaurants, basic meals in Chinese restaurants (sometimes a buffet-type spread). Most cafés also offer some sort of *Dagens Rätt* but their standard of cooking is often not as good as in restaurants; cafés in train stations and department stores, however, are worth trying. If you're travelling with children, look out for the places that have a **childrens' menu** (Barnmatsedel).

While you're in Sweden you should try a **smörgåsbord**, available in the larger restaurants and in hotels for around 150kr – expensive, but good for a blowout. A good table will be groaning under the weight of dishes: salmon (both boiled and smoked), *gravad lax*, shrimps, herring, eel, *Janssons frestelse*, scrambled eggs, oven-baked omelettes, fried sausages, smoked reindeer, liver paté, beef, hot and cold meats, eggs, fried and boiled potatoes, vegetables, salad, pastries, desserts, fruit, cheese – the list is endless. It's important to pace yourself: don't feel compelled to fill up your plate the first time you go to the table, as you can return as many times as you like. If you're a traditionalist you should start with *akvavit*, drink beer throughout and finish with coffee. Coffee will be included in the price – alcohol won't be, except on Sundays when fancier and dearer spreads generally include it.

A variation on the theme is the **Sillbricka** or herring table, made up of a dozen or so dishes based on Sweden's favourite food, cured and marinated herring. Once again this is excellent – if you like raw fish – and runs to about the same price as the *Smörgåsbord*.

FOREIGN RESTAURANTS

For years the only **ethnic** choice in Sweden was between pizzerias and the odd Chinese restaurant; in provincial towns this is often still the case, but even here the number of ethnic restaurants has increased dramatically. **Pizzerias** offer the best value; you'll get a large, if not strictly authentic, pizza for 50–60kr, usually with free coleslaw and bread. As well as the local restaurants, *Pizza Hut* can be found in Sweden, though the chain is a lot more expensive than in the US or Britain. **Chinese** restaurants nearly always offer a cheapish set lunch, but in the evenings prices shoot up. They aren't particularly good value for money and the food is often bland and inauthentic. If there's a group of you, however, putting dishes together can work out reasonably in terms of price. **Middle Eastern** kebab takeaways and cafés have also sprung up

over recent years; here you can find something substantial in pitta bread for around 30–40kr. **Japanese** is popular and not too pricey, but other options are not such good deals: **Indian** food is hard to find and quite expensive; while anything **French** is expense-account stuff and not worth the money.

DRINKS

Drinking in Sweden is notoriously expensive, but there are ways of softening the blow. Either you forgo bars and buy your booze in the state-run liquor shops, the Systembolaget (see p.43), or you seek out the **happy hours** (same term in Swedish) offered at many pubs and bars. The timing of happy hours has no rhyme or reason to it, so keep your eyes peeled for signs either in bar windows or on the pavement outside. During happy hours, the price of a strong beer can come down to under 25kr. If you miss happy hour, content yourself with the fact that Swedes, too, think booze is overpriced, and you won't be expected to participate in buying expensive rounds of drinks. It's also perfectly acceptable to nurse one drink through the entire evening, if that's all you can afford.

WHAT TO DRINK

Beer is the most common alcoholic drink in Sweden, and even though it's expensive it is very good. Competition among bars within Stockholm, Gothenburg and Malmö has brought down the price considerably; be prepared to pay a third more in the provinces for the same thing. Whether you buy beer in a café, restaurant or a bar, it'll cost roughly the same: on average 30–40kr for half a litre of lager-type brew; in nightclubs, it'll be more like 50–60kr.

Unless you specify a type, the beer you get in a bar will be *starköl* (also referred to as *storstark*), the strongest Class III beer with an alcohol content of five percent or slightly over. Outside bars, Class III is only available in the Systembolaget, where it's around a third of the price you'll pay in a bar. *Mellanöl*, another Class III brew, costs slightly less than a *starköl* because it contains less alcohol; a good brand is Three Towns (green-labelled bottle). Class II or *folköl* is very similar in strength to *mellanöl*. Cheapest of all is *lättöl*, the beer served with *Dagens Rätt* at lunchtime. It's palatable with food, though it contains virtually no alcohol; Pripps and Spendrups are the two main brands. Both *folköl* and *lättöl* are available in supermarkets.

THE SYSTEMBOLAGET: A USER'S GUIDE

In any Swedish town or city, the **Systembolaget** is the only shop that sells wine, strong beer and spirits. It's run by the state, is only open office hours from Monday to Friday (some stores are open Sat), and keeps all its alcohol on display in locked glass cabinets. Walking into any Systembolaget is a trip into the twilight zone, if you can find one at all: stores are often tucked away in obscure places, and they're forbidden by law to advertise.

Buying alcohol is made as unattractive as possible: first you take a queue number from the machine by the door. This will give you your place in the queue and may even state the likely waiting time: a quarter of an hour is about average, though on Friday afternoons it can be up to an hour and over. You select your bottles of the hard stuff by number (each bottle in the

cabinets has its number displayed alongside); when your turn comes you then quote your number to the cashier who scuttles off to retrieve your booty. Hand over your cash and the dirty business is over. Should you wish to choose your tipple from the comfort of your own armchair, the Systembolaget produces a handy catalogue, which you can take home to peruse at your leisure. You need to be at least 20 to buy alcohol, and may have to show ID.

The system is designed to make Swedes think about how much they drink, and prices are accordingly very high – 70cl of whisky costs 250kr. But it's estimated that for every four bottles of booze consumed in Sweden only two are bought from the Systembolaget; one is smuggled into the country while the last is moonshine, distilled illegally at home.

Wine in restaurants is pricey; a bottle will set you back something like 200kr, and a glass around 40kr. You can buy a good bottle of red or white in the Systembolaget for just 40–50kr.

It's also worth trying the **akvavit** or schnapps, which is made from potatoes, served ice-cold in tiny shots and washed down with beer. There are numerous different flavours of *akvavit*: spices, herbs or citrus fruits, to name a few, are added to the finished concoction, giving rise to some memorable headaches. If you're in Sweden at Christmas, don't go home without having sampled **glögg**: mulled red wine with cloves, cinnamon, sugar and more than a shot of *akvavit*.

WHERE TO DRINK

With the fall in the price of alcohol over recent years, more and more people are now going out to bars of an evening. On Friday and Saturday nights in particular, they're the place to be seen. You'll find **bars** in all towns and villages. In Stockholm and the larger cities the trend is towards **brasserie-type**

places – smart and flash. The British **pub** – and, more recently, the Irish pub – is also popular in Sweden, although the atmosphere inside never quite lives up to the original. Elsewhere – particularly in the north of the country – you'll come across more down-to-earth drinking dens, occasionally sponsored by the local trades union. Drink is no cheaper here, and the clientele is heavily male and usually drunk: they can be intimidating places for outsiders, especially in small provincial villages, where drinking seems to be the main way of coping with eight months of winter.

In the summer, **café-bars** spill out onto the pavement, which is a more suitable environment for children and handy if all you want is a coffee. When you can't find a bar in an out-of-the-way place, head for the local hotel – but be prepared to pay for the privilege. Bar opening hours are elastic and drinking-up time is generally some time after midnight; in the big three cities – Stockholm, Gothenburg and Malmö – you can go on drinking all night, if your wallet can take the pace.

MAIL AND TELECOMMUNICATIONS

Communications within Sweden and abroad are good; in general it is easy to phone or fax anywhere in the world, even from smaller towns. Most Swedes speak some English, and the operators are usually fluent (although you may have to use German with older employees). International mail services also work very efficiently and post offices are easy to use if you don't know Swedish, though in remoter places collections and deliveries can take a bit longer.

POSTAL SERVICES

Post offices are open Monday to Friday (9am–6pm) and Saturday (10am–1pm) but closed Sunday. You can buy **stamps** (*frimärken*) at post offices, most newspaper kiosks, tobacconists, hotels, bookshops and stationers' shops. International letters (*internationella brev*) and postcards (*vykort*) within Europe cost 7kr for up to 20g. Within Sweden, letters cost 5kr for "A-post" (first class) or 4.50kr for "Ekonomipost" (second class); letters sent to the other Nordic countries and the Baltic States cost 6kr. Stamps for anywhere else in the world cost 7kr for a letter up to 20g, 14kr for 50g and 20kr for 100g.

You can have letters sent **poste restante** to any post office in Sweden by addressing them "Poste Restante" followed by the name of the town and country. When picking up mail you'll need to take your passport, and make sure they check under middle names and initials as letters can get misfiled.

PHONING WITHIN SWEDEN

Major towns and their surrounding area each have an **area code**, which must be used when phoning from outside that zone. Area codes are included in telephone and fax numbers throughout the guide – omit them if dialling from within the area.

It's worth knowing that general information lines (SJ, SAS and the like) are often ☎020 numbers, which are **toll-free**. These numbers cannot

---

MAKING INTERNATIONAL CALLS TO AND FROM SWEDEN

To **call Sweden from abroad**, dial your country's international access code followed by **46 for Sweden**, then dial the area code (without its first 0) and the number. To **call abroad from Sweden**, dial 00 followed by the required country code (see below), then wait for the tone and dial the area code (without its first 0) and the number. Within Sweden, international directory enquiries is on ☎07977.

USEFUL COUNTRY CODES

Sweden ☎46	**Australia** ☎61
Britain ☎44	**Canada** ☎1
Ireland ☎353	**New Zealand** ☎64
USA ☎1	

---

be dialled from outside Sweden. For collect calls, use the Swedish operator on ☎020 0018; for domestic directory enquiries call ☎118 118. In **emergencies**, call ☎112 for the police, fire brigade or ambulance.

A **fax** service is widely available at most hotels across the country; residents pay for the call charges when using the service. Post offices in Sweden do not have fax machines for public use.

All public payphones in Sweden are **cardphones** and you'll generally find one in even the smallest village. You call anywhere in the world from a public cardphone using **phonecards**, which are sold at newsagents (Pressbyrån) in various units: 30 units (around 30kr), 60 units (55–60kr) and 120 units (100–120kr). The cards have no fixed price. English instructions on how to use a cardphone are generally displayed inside each booth. Alternatively, whip out your **credit card** and dial from a credit-card phone marked "CCC"; these are widely found. Calls within Europe cost 4.62kr per minute every day between 8am and 10pm and 3.88kr per minute at other times. Paying for international calls made from hotel rooms will give you nightmares for months after, and is only worth it in emergencies.

THE MEDIA

Stockholm is the centre of the Swedish media world; all national radio and television stations are broadcast from the capital, and the country's four main daily newspapers are also based here. As in most other countries, the media are justifiably accused of being obsessed with events in the capital and rarely venturing beyond the city's boundaries in their coverage. However, as you travel around the country, you'll doubtless come across the wide array of regional newspapers, as well as local TV and radio stations, that help to fill this gap. Every region or city has its own newspaper, for example *Göteborgsposten* in Gothenburg or *Norrbottens tidning* in Lapland. In remote parts of the country, particularly in the north, these local media really come into their own; in winter, people depend on them for accurate and up-to-date information on everything from local political machinations to snow depths in the vicinity.

Throughout the country the quality of the Swedish media is generally high. It's worth pointing out one cultural difference though: some interviews in Swedish news broadcasts can come across as rather plodding to outsiders, but will sound normal to Swedes. In Sweden, having long pauses between words shows that the speaker is talking in a considered way (to outsiders, it'll sound as if the interviewee is about to fall asleep).

NEWSPAPERS

Assuming you don't read Swedish, you can keep in touch with world events by buying **English-language newspapers** in the major towns and cities, sometimes on the day of issue, more usually the day after. The main **Swedish papers** are *Dagens Nyheter* and *Svenska Dagbladet* – their Friday supplements, often available free in the entrance to bookshops, may be useful for Stockholm listings – and the tabloids, *Expressen* and *Aftonbladet*. If you're in Stockholm you can pick up a copy of *Metro*, a free newspaper available at tube stations, which has lots of information about what's on in the capital; its listings are in Swedish only, but will be comprehensible enough even if you don't speak the language.

TV AND RADIO

Swedish **TV** won't take up much space on your postcards home. There are two **state channels**, Kanal 1 and TV2, operated by Sveriges Television (SVT), worth watching if only for the wooden invision continuity announcers. TV3 is a pretty dire **cable station** shared with Norway and Denmark, although there's a good chance of catching an old episode of *Kojak* – if you like that sort of thing. Sweden's only **commercial station** is TV4, whose evening news programme, *Nyheterna*, is an attempt to portray news as entertainment; unfortunately, though, the end result is pretty tasteless. On all the channels, foreign programmes are in their original language, which makes for easy viewing; Kanal 1 and TV2 show a lot of excellent BBC documentaries and comedy programmes.

On the **radio**, you'll find pop and rock music on P3, classical music on P2, and Swedish speech on P1 (frequencies differ throughout the country) – all operated by **Swedish Radio** (*www.sr.se*), the state broadcaster. Commercial stations have now sprung up in towns and cities across Sweden, and in Stockholm the ones worthy of your interest if you like pop music are Radio City 105.9 FM and Megapol 104.3 FM.

You'll find **news in English** courtesy of **Radio Sweden** (Swedish Radio's international arm; ☎08/784 7287, *www.radiosweden.com*). Their English news programme, *60 Degrees North*, can be heard weekdays in Stockholm on 89.6MHz FM at 2.30pm, 3.30pm, 7.30pm, 9.30pm and at 12.30am. The evening broadcasts should be audible on 1179kHz medium wave throughout Sweden, although reception can vary considerably. They also produce *Lunchbreak*, two hours of English chat and music between 11am and 1pm, and carried on their Stockholm FM frequency. These Stockholm FM broadcasts comprise a service called "Stockholm International" (*www.sr.se/rs/stockint/*), which additionally carries material from foreign broadcasters, including **BBC World Service** (also on 6195, 9410, 12095 and 15070 kHz short wave; *www.bbc.co.uk/worldservice*) and America's **National Public Radio** (*www.npr.org*).

OPENING HOURS, HOLIDAYS AND FESTIVALS

Opening hours are generally from 9am to 6pm on weekdays and 10am to 4pm on Saturdays. In larger towns, department stores remain open until 8pm or 10pm on weekdays, and some are also open on Sundays between noon and 4pm. In country areas, shops and petrol stations generally close for the day between 5pm and 6pm. Museums and galleries operate various opening hours, but are generally closed on Mondays. Banks, offices and shops are closed on public holidays (see box below). They may also close or have reduced open-ing hours on the eve of the holiday. For bank-ing hours, see p.23; for post office hours, see p.44.

Swedish **festivals** are for the most part organized around the seasons. Most celebra-tions are lively events as Swedes are great party people – especially when the beer begins to flow. The highlight of the year is the **Midsummer** festival when the whole country gets involved, and wild parties last well into the early hours. The date of Midsummer's Day varies from year to year but is the Saturday closest to the actual summer solstice.

PUBLIC HOLIDAYS IN SWEDEN

New Year's Day (Jan 1)
Epiphany (Jan 6)
Good Friday
Easter Sunday
Easter Monday
Labour Day (May 1)
Ascension Day (May 1)
Whit Sunday (the seventh Sunday after Easter)
Whit Monday (the Monday after Whit Sunday)

Midsummer's Eve (always on a Friday)
Midsummer's Day (the Saturday closest to the summer solstice)
All Saints' Day (Nov 2)
Christmas Eve (Dec 24)
Christmas Day (Dec 25)
Boxing Day (Dec 26)
New Year's Eve (Dec 31)

MAJOR FESTIVALS AND EVENTS

Valborgsmässoafton (April 30): Walpurgis Night; bonfires and songs welcome the arrival of spring nationwide.

Labour Day (May 1): a marching day for the workers' parties.

Stockholm Marathon (June 1): one of the biggest events of its kind.

Swedish National Day (June 6): in existence since 1983, a bit of a damp squib and not a pub-lic holiday; worthy speeches are delivered in the evening.

Midsummer (June 21–23): the celebration to beat them all, during which the Swedish Maypole, an old fertility symbol, is erected at popular gatherings across Sweden. The Maypole is raised in June because it's often still snowing in northern Sweden in May.

Crayfish parties (throughout Aug): held in the August moonlight across the country to say a wistful farewell to the short Swedish summer.

Stockholm Water Festival (Aug): special events and entertainment celebrating the capi-tal's close links with water, which constitutes a third of the area within the city boundaries – see also p.92.

Surströmming (late Aug): in northern Sweden, parties are held at which people eat foul-smelling fermented Baltic herring (see p.379).

Eel parties (Sept): held in the southern province of Skåne, a region known for its smokehouses and the smoked eel they produce.

St Martin's Eve (Nov 10): people from Skåne get together to eat goose – the traditional sym-bol of the province.

Nobel Prize Day (Dec 10): ceremonies are held in Stockholm.

St Lucia's Day (Dec 13): a procession of Swedish children, led by a girl with candles in her hair, sings songs to mark one of the darkest periods of the year.

SPORTS AND OUTDOOR PURSUITS

Sweden is a wonderful place if you love the great outdoors, with great hiking, fishing and, of course, skiing opportunities. Best of all you won't find the countryside overcrowded – there's plenty of space to get away from it all, especially in the north. You'll also find Swedish beaches refreshingly relaxed and always clean.

SKIING AND WINTER PURSUITS

During the winter months, **skiing** – a sport which began in Scandinavia – is incredibly popular; in the north of Sweden people even ski to work. Some of the most popular ski **resorts** include Åre, Sälen, Storlien, Jukkasjärvi and Riksgränsen; these and many others are packed out during the snow season when prices hit the roof. If you do intend to come to ski, it is essential to book accommodation well in advance or take a package holiday – see the relevant "Getting there" sections.

In northern Sweden you can ski from the end of October well into April, and at Riksgränsen in Lapland you can ski under the midnight sun from late May to the end of June when the snow finally melts; the ski lifts are open from 10pm to 1am. Riksgränsen is also the place to head for if you're into **snowboarding**. Kiruna is a good place to base yourself for other winter pursuits, whether you fancy dog sledging, snowmobile riding, a night in the world's biggest igloo (the **Ice Hotel** at Jukkasjärvi, see p. 476), ice fishing or even a helicopter tour out into the snowy wilderness. Bear in mind, though, that the area around Kiruna is one of the coldest in the country, and temperatures in the surrounding mountains can sink to -50°C during a really cold snap (also see "Keeping warm and safe in winter" on p.19). If the mere thought of such temperatures chills you to the bone, it's worth noting that milder Stockholm also has a ski slope within the city boundary.

HIKING

Sweden's **Right of Public Access**, *Allemansrätten*, means you can walk freely right across the entire country (see box on p.48, for more details). A network of more than forty long-distance footpaths covers the whole of Sweden, with overnight accommodation available in mountain stations and huts. The most popular route is the northern **Kungsleden**, the King's Route, which can get rather busy at times, but is still enjoyable. The path stretches for 460km between Abisko (on the train line between Kiruna and Narvik in Norway) and Hemavan, passing through some spectacular landscape in the wild and isolated northwest of the country; the trail also takes in Sweden's highest mountain, Kebnekaise (2078m). To find out more about walking in Sweden, contact the very helpful Svenska Turistföreningen (Swedish Touring Club; Drottninggatan 31–33 in Stockholm; Drottningtorget 6 in Gothenburg; *www.stfturist.se*). For a guide to the do's and dont's of hiking in Sweden, see p.471.

CANOEING AND WHITEWATER RAFTING

There are almost one hundred thousand lakes and thousands of kilometres of rivers and canals in Sweden. Needless to say, on summer afternoons taking to a **canoe** is a popular pastime; an excellent area for this is Strömsund (see p.447). For more fast-flowing action, the northern rivers are ideal for **whitewater rafting**, with particularly good spots including the Pite river near Moskosel, north of Arvidsjaur (handy for the Inland Railway); the Kukkola rapids in the Torne Valley, north of Haparanda (and the Torne river in general between Haparanda and Pajala in the far northeast, where there are various lengths and grades of difficulty); and the Indalälven river, in Jämtland on the border with Norway, which offers moderately-difficult-to-difficult rafting. The Strängforsen rapids in Värmland are somewhat tamer, with easy whitewater trips in paddle boats.

GOLF AND FISHING

Golf has become incredibly popular in Sweden in recent years. There are now over three hundred courses in the country; most are concentrated in the south and are playable year-round, but it's also possible to play north of the Arctic Circle in the light of the Midnight Sun. For more information, contact the Swedish Golf Federation (PO Box 84, S-182 11, Danderyd, Stockholm; ☎08/622 15 00, fax 755 84 39, *www.golf.se*).

THE COUNTRYSIDE – SOME GROUND RULES

In Sweden you're entitled by law to walk, jog, cycle, ride or ski across other people's land, provided you don't cause damage to crops, forest plantations or fences; this is the centuries-old **Allemansrätten** or Everyman's Right. It also allows you to pick wild berries, mushrooms and wild flowers (except protected species), fish with a rod or other hand-tackle, swim in lakes, and moor your boat and then go ashore where there are no nearby houses. But this right brings with it certain obligations: you shouldn't get close to houses or walk across gardens or on land under seed or crops; pitch a tent on land used for farming; camp close to houses without asking permission; cut down trees or bushes; or break branches or strip the bark off trees. Nor are you allowed to drive off-road (look out for signs saying "*Ej motorfordon*", no motor vehicles; or "*Enskild väg*", private road); light a fire if there's a risk of it spreading; or disturb wildlife.

It's also common sense to be wary of frightening reindeer herds in the north of Sweden; if they scatter it can mean several extra days' hard work for the herders; also avoid tramping over the lichen – the staple diet of reindeer – covering stretches of moorland. If you'd like to pick flowers, berries or mushrooms it's worth checking the latest advice from the authorities as to any health-risks this may pose – post-Chernobyl. As you might expect, any kind of hunting is forbidden without a permit. National parks have special regulations which are posted on huts and at entrances, and these are worth reading and remembering.

Sweden is an ideal country for **anglers**; in fact salmon are regularly caught from opposite the Parliament building right in the centre of Stockholm, because the water there is so clean and fishing there is free. Fishing is also free along the coastline and in the larger lakes, including Vänern, Vättern (particularly good for salmon and char) and Mälaren. In the north of the country, Hemavan (see p.542) is known for top-class mountain fishing for trout and char, whereas nearby Sorsele (see p.452) is good for fly-fishing for trout, char and grayling. For salmon fishing, the river running up through the Torne Valley (see p.482) is among the very best places. Char are said to be most easily caught in summer on flies and small spinners; for grayling, fly-fishing on late summer evenings using flies resembling mayflies, stoneflies or nymphs is likely to give the best results. In most areas you need a permit for freshwater fishing; ask at local tourist offices. For more information, contact Top 10 Fishing, S-566 93 Brandstorp, Sweden (☎0502/502 00, fax 502 02).

CRIME AND PERSONAL SAFETY

Sweden is in general a pretty safe country to visit, and this extends to women travelling alone. However, it would be foolish to assume that the innocent, trouble-free country of just a few years ago still exists. It doesn't, but although people no longer leave their doors unlocked when they go out shopping, Sweden is still a far cry from crime-ridden London or New York. As long as you take care, especially at night in the bigger towns and cities, you should have no problems. If you do meet trouble you can dial ☎112 for emergency assistance from the police, fire brigade or ambulance; emergency calls from cardphones are free of charge.

That said, Stockholm and the bigger cities have their fair share of **petty crime**, fuelled as elsewhere by a growing number of drug addicts and alcoholics after easy money. But keep tabs on your cash and passport (and don't leave anything valuable in your car when you park it) and you should have little reason to visit the **police**. If you do, you'll find them courteous, concerned and, most importantly, usually able to speak English. If you have something stolen, make sure you get a **police report** – it's essential if you want to make a claim against your insurance.

PETTY CRIME AND MINOR OFFENCES

As for **offences** *you* might commit, the big no-nos are **drinking alcohol in public places** (which includes on trains), and being drunk in the streets can get you arrested – **drink-driving** is treated especially rigorously (see p.32). **Drugs** offences, too, meet with the same harsh attitude that prevails throughout the rest of Europe.

Otherwise, Sweden is a pretty liberal place. **Topless sunbathing** is universally accepted in all the major resorts (elsewhere there'll be no one around to care). **Nude bathing** is best kept for quieter spots but is very common and perfectly accepted – you'll have no problems finding a beach or a shady glade in a forest where you can work on your all-over tan; should anyone stumble on you they'll either ignore you or apologize for cramping your style. **Camping rough** creates no problem and is a right enshrined in law (see opposite).

RACISM

The biggest problem you may encounter in Sweden is the ugly and fast-spreading **racism** stemming from a small but vocal neo-Nazi movement, VAM (their full name translates as "White Aryan Resistance"). Slogans like *"Behålla Sverige Svenskt"* (Keep Sweden Swedish) can sometimes be seen daubed on walls in towns and cities and on the Stockholm metro. In recent years, the unemployment rate has shot up from the steady 1–2 percent during the heyday of Social Democratic governments; now Sweden's skinheads blame the country's one million immigrants for stealing jobs from Swedes. There have been several racist murders and countless attacks on dark-skinned foreigners over the past couple of years, and it pays to be vigilant: keep your eyes and ears open and avoid trouble, especially on Friday and Saturday nights when drink fuels these prejudices.

WOMEN IN SWEDEN

Sexual harassment in Sweden is rare. In general the social and economic position of women is one of the most advanced in Europe – something that becomes obvious after just a short time here. Sweden has one of the highest percentages in the world of women in the workplace, and international surveys continually put Sweden at the top of the list when it comes to equality: half of Sweden's government ministers are women. Many women are in traditionally male occupations, which means that Swedish men have been forced to become more aware of the rights of women.

Women can walk around almost everywhere in comparative comfort and safety, although in Stockholm and Gothenburg you can occasionally expect to receive unwelcome attention. If you do have any problems, the fact that almost everyone understands English makes it easy to get across an unambiguous response.

The **women's movement** is strongly developed, riding on the back of welfare reforms introduced by the Social Democratic governments since World War II. You'll find women's centres in most major towns.

GAY AND LESBIAN SWEDEN

Swedish attitudes to gay men and lesbians are remarkably liberal – on a legal level at least – when compared to most other western countries, with both the government and the law proudly geared towards equality (the official age of sexual consent is 15 whether you are gay or straight) and the promotion of gay rights. In 1995, Sweden introduced its registered-partnership law, despite unanimous opposition in parliament from the right-wing Moderates and Christian Democrats (needless to say, the Swedish Church wasn't best pleased either). Under the law, gay couples can, in effect, marry, by registering their relationships with the state. They are then guaranteed the same legal rights enjoyed by married straight couples; the law even permits the exchange of rings.

That said, the acceptance of gays and lesbians in society as a whole can at best be described as paradoxical, and in fact homosexuality was regarded as a psychological disease in Sweden until 1979. Outside the cities, and particularly in the north of the country where the lumberjack mentality rules supreme, there can still be widespread embarrassment and unease whenever the subject is mentioned in public. On the other hand, some of Sweden's best-loved entertainers are gay – and accepted as such.

Sweden's **gay scene** is less visible than in countries with more regressive official policies towards minority sexuality; this is probably because the small-town mentality is still quite prevalent throughout the country. Even in Stockholm and Gothenburg, you're unlikely to see gay or lesbian couples holding hands or kissing in public. Gay community life in general is supported by the state-sponsored Riksförbundet för Sexuellt Likaberättigande, or **RFSL** (National Association for Sexual Equality; Sveavägen 57–59, PO Box 350, 10126 Stockholm; ☎08/736 02 13, fax 30 47 30, *www.rfsl.se*). Founded in 1950 as one of the first gay rights organizations in the world, RFSL today operates a switchboard and helpline in most of the larger towns, though it's usually necessary that callers leave messages for someone to ring them back. It runs discos and pub nights in local venues either once a week or, more likely, once a month. RFSL also organizes a Midsummer party in Stockholm to which foreign visitors are very welcome. Tourist offices invariably have no details of gay venues or events, so it's worth contacting the main RFSL offices in Stockholm or Gothenburg for information, or

checking out their regular publication *Kom Ut!*, available in most bars. The international gay guide, *Spartacus*, has lots of useful information about gay and lesbian happenings in Sweden, and listings of bars, discos, cafés and restaurants; it's best to stick to places described as "mainly gay", as many of the "mixed gay" venues are not particularly gay-orientated compared to those at home.

DIRECTORY

ADDRESSES In Sweden addresses are always written with the number after the street name. In multi-floor buildings the ground floor is always counted as the first floor, the first the second, etc.

ALPHABET The letters å, ä and ö come at the end of the alphabet after z.

ARCTIC CIRCLE An imaginary line drawn at approximately 66° 33' latitude that stretches across northern Sweden and denotes the limit beyond which there is at least one day in the year when the sun never sets and one on which it never rises.

BEACHES The southern province of Skåne has the sandiest beaches in the country. The further north you travel the rockier the beaches become. The Bohuslän coast north of Gothenburg has some gently sloping rocks which are ideal for sunbathing, and so do the islands in the Stockholm archipelago. Many of Sweden's thousands of lakes also have sandy stretches of shoreline.

BOOKS You'll find English-language books in almost every bookshop and in the bigger department stores, though at roughly twice the price you're used to paying. Libraries, too, stock foreign-language books.

CHILDREN Sweden is a model country when it comes to travelling with children. Most hotels and youth hostels have family rooms and both men's and women's toilets – including those on trains – usually offer baby-changing areas. Always ask for children's discounts as many activities, particularly during the summer months, are geared towards families.

CROSSING BORDERS The land borders with Norway and Finland are relaxed affairs, and in fact on minor roads you'll hardly notice you've passed from one country to the other. It's wise to have your passport with you though it's unlikely you'll be asked to show it.

ELECTRICITY The supply is 220V, although appliances requiring 240V will work perfectly well. Plugs have two round pins. Remember that if you're staying in a cottage out in the wilds, electricity may not be available, so take candles in case.

EMERGENCIES Dial ☎112 (free) for the police, ambulance and fire brigade.

LUGGAGE In most train stations, ferry terminals and long-distance bus stations there are lockers where you can leave your bags for a small fee. At some train stations you hand in your baggage for storage. Tourist offices may also watch your stuff bags, but generally make a charge.

MEDICATION You need a doctor's prescription even to get minor painkillers in Sweden, so bring your own supplies.

MIDNIGHT SUN The midnight sun can be experienced in the far north of Sweden for about two months during the summer. At Abisko and Riksgränsen it is visible from about May 27 to July 15; in Kiruna from 31 May to July 11; in Gällivare from June 4 until July 12; and at Jokkmokk between June 8 and July 3; all dates are approximate.

MUSEUMS AND GALLERIES As often as not there's a charge to get in, though other than for the really major collections, it's rarely very much; flash an ISIC card and it's likely to bring a reduction. Opening hours vary widely though more often than not Monday is closing day.

NORTHERN LIGHTS (*Aurora Borealis*) A shifting coloured glow visible during winter in northern Sweden, thought to be of electrical origin – though you'll need to be in luck to see a really good display. The sky often turns peculiar colours on winter nights in the far north.

NUDE BATHING Although there are few official nudist beaches in Sweden, the country does boast around 100,000 lakes and one of the lowest population densities in Europe which means that sooner or later you'll find your very own lake where you can swim and sunbathe naked undisturbed. If other people are around, show them consideration, but you're unlikely to meet opposition.

PHOTOGRAPHY Film is available in most supermarkets, generally at 35–100kr per roll; developing is also very expensive and slow. It's best to bring more rolls than you think you'll need.

SAUNAS Most public swimming pools and hotels, even in the smallest towns, will have a sauna. They're generally electric and extra steam is created by gently tossing water onto the hot elements. The temperature inside will range from 70–120°C. Traditional wood burning saunas are often found in the countryside and give off a wonderful smell. Public saunas are always single-sex and nude; you'll often see signs forbidding the wearing of swimming costumes, as these would collect your sweat and allow it to soak into the wooden benches inside. Take a small paper towel to sit on; these are often available in the changing rooms. It is common practice to take a cold shower afterwards or, if you're in the countryside, to take a dip in a nearby lake. In the winter people will even roll in the snow to cool off.

SMOKING Smoking is frowned upon in Sweden and is outlawed on most public transport and in many public buildings such as libraries. Smoking in restaurants is permitted (although some are completely no-smoking) but be aware of your fellow diners. A pack of twenty cigarettes costs 35–40kr, and the minimum age is 18.

SWIMMING Swimming pools are generally open every day and until late into the evening. You'll sometimes need your own padlock to secure your clothes in the changing-room lockers. Entrance fees are low. Much better though is taking a dip in one of the many thousands of lakes you can call your own.

TIME Sweden conforms to Central European Time (CET) which is always one hour ahead of Britain and Ireland. For most of the year Sweden is six hours ahead of New York; nine hours behind Sydney and eleven hours behind Auckland. Clocks go forward by one hour in late March and back one hour in late October (on the same days as in Britain and Ireland).

TIPPING In restaurants, the service charge is normally included in the price of your food so there's no need to tip. However it is customary to round the bill up to the nearest 10kr. Do not tip taxi drivers.

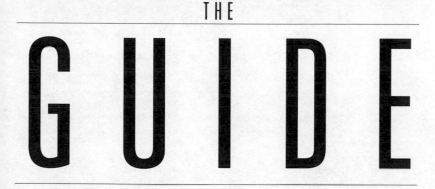

PART TWO

THE

GUIDE

CHAPTER ONE

STOCKHOLM AND AROUND

Stockholm is without a shadow of a doubt one of the loveliest cities in Europe. Built on no fewer than fourteen **islands**, where the fresh water of Lake Mälaren meets the brackish Baltic Sea, the city certainly lives up to the tourist-office hype of "Beauty on Water". Fresh air and open space are in plentiful supply here – one-third of the area within the city limits is made up of water, while another third comprises parks and woodlands, including the world's first urban national park, where you can swim and fish just minutes from the city centre. Broad boulevards lined with elegant buildings are reflected in the deep blue water, and alongside the cobbled waterfront, rows of painted wooden houseboats bob gently on the tide. Yet Stockholm is also a hi-tech metropolis, with futuristic skyscrapers and a bustling commercial hub. The modern centre is a consumer's heaven, full of stylish shops, and also home to the city's cinemas, and many of its bars and restaurants, of which Stockholm has more per capita than most other European capitals. Quality of life is important to Stockholmers – a seat on the metro and elbow room on even the most crowded shopping street are regarded as virtual birthrights. As a result, the capital is one of Europe's saner cities and a delightful place in which to spend time.

Move away from Stockholm, and it's not difficult to appreciate its unique geographical location. Water surrounds the city and, although you can travel by train

---

ACCOMMODATION PRICES

The pensions and hotels listed in the guide have been price-graded according to the scale given below; the price category given against each establishment indicates the cost of the least expensive double rooms there. Many hotels offer considerable reductions at weekends all year round, and during the summer holiday period (mid-June to mid-Aug); in these cases the reduction is either noted in the text or, where a discount brings a hotel into another price band, given after the number for the full price. Single rooms, where available, usually cost between 60 and 80 percent of a double. Where hostels have double rooms, we've given price codes for them also.

① under 500kr	③ 700–900kr	⑤ 1200–1500kr
② 500–700kr	④ 900–1200kr	⑥ over 1500kr

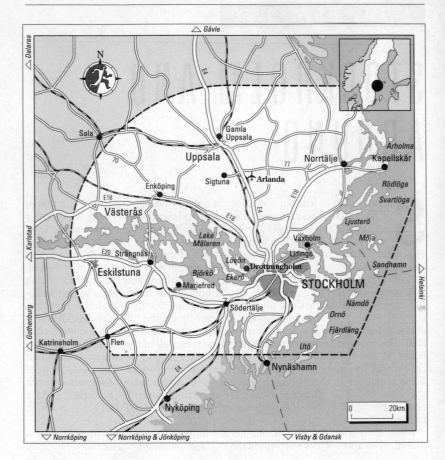

and bus, it's worth making the effort to ply the serene waters of Lake Mälaren or the Stockholm archipelago by boat. The **archipelago** is made up of a staggering 24,000 islands, islets and rocks, the Swedish mainland slowly splintering into the Baltic Sea. A summer paradise for holidaying city dwellers, the islands are easily accessible from the centre. Another must is a boat trip inland along Lake Mälaren, either to the Viking island of **Birka**, where you can see the remains of Sweden's most important medieval trading centre and a dizzying array of ancient finds, or to **Drottningholm**, the seventeenth-century royal residence right on the lakeside. Another easy trip on Lake Mälaren leads to the impressive castle of **Gripsholm** at Mariefred; and also within reach on a day-trip are the ancient Swedish capital and medieval university town of **Uppsala** and the country's oldest village, **Sigtuna**, complete with its rune stones and ruined churches; both these places are accessible by frequent train services from Stockholm's Central Station or by boat.

STOCKHOLM

"It is not a city at all," he said with intensity. "It is ridiculous to think of itself as a city. It is simply a rather large village, set in the middle of some forest and some lakes. You wonder what it thinks it is doing there, looking so important."

Ingmar Bergman, interviewed by James Baldwin

While **STOCKHOLM** is, perhaps, self-important, it is without doubt a disparate capital, its status as Sweden's most contemporary, forward-looking city at odds with the almost pastoral feel of its wide open spaces and ageing monumental buildings. First impressions of the city can be of a distant and unwelcoming place, and it comes as no surprise that provincial Swedes drawn to Stockholm for work sometimes dub the city "the Ice Queen". But don't be put off; on a Friday or Saturday night you'll see its other side – when Stockholmers let their hair down, and the night air is abuzz with conversation.

Gamla Stan (Swedish for "Old Town") was the site of the original settlement of Stockholm. Today the area is an atmospheric mixture of pomp and historical authenticity, ceremonial buildings surrounded on all sides by a latticework of medieval lanes and alleyways. Close by and easily reached by ferry is the tiny island of **Skeppsholmen** (pronounced "Shepps-holm-en"), from where there are fantastic views of the curving waterfront; conveniently, the island is also the site of the two most central youth hostels (see p.65). To the north of the Old Town, the district of **Norrmalm** swaps tradition for a thoroughly contemporary feel – shopping malls, huge department stores and a conspicuous, showy wealth; the lively **central park**, Kungsträdgården, and Central Station are here, too. Most of Stockholm's eighty or so **museums and galleries** are spread across this area and two others: to the east, the more residential **Östermalm**, with its mix of grand avenues and smart houses; and to the southeast, the green park island of **Djurgården**. Here the extraordinary seventeenth-century warship, **Vasa**, rescued and preserved after sinking in Stockholm harbour, and **Skansen**, oldest and best of Europe's open-air museums, both receive loud and deserved acclaim. The island of **Södermalm**, to the south of the Old Town, is sometimes known as "the Southside" (when Swedes talk about it in English) or as plain "Söder" (as its right-on inhabitants call it). This was traditionally the working-class area of Stockholm, but today is known for its cool bars and restaurants and lively street life. To the west of the centre, the island of Kungsholmen is fast becoming a rival to its southern neighbour for trendy restaurants and drinking establishments.

Arrival and information

Most international and domestic flights arrive at **Arlanda airport** (☎08/797 61 00), an inconvenient 45km north of Stockholm. Terminal 2 is used by Alitalia, Braathens Malmö Aviation (domestic), Crossair, Delta, Finnair, Sabena and Swissair; Terminal 5 by SAS and all other international airlines; Terminal 4 by SAS for its domestic flights; other domestic airlines, such as Skyways, use Terminal 3 (there isn't a Terminal 1). High-speed trains leave the dedicated Arlanda Express

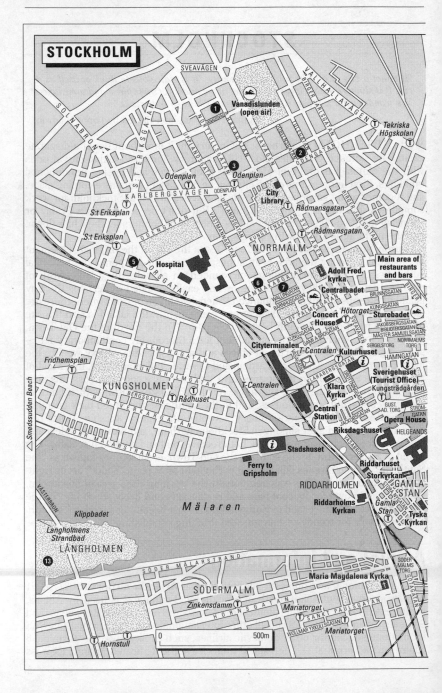

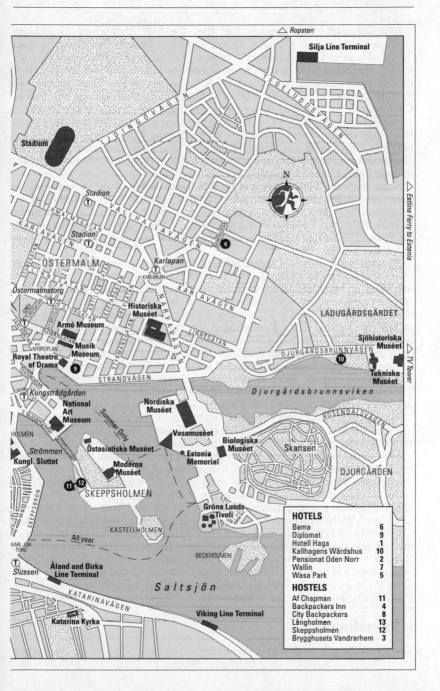

△ *Ropsten*

Silja Line Terminal

△ *Estline Ferry to Estonia*

△ *TV Tower*

Stadium

Stadion Ⓣ

Stadion Ⓣ

ÖSTERMALM

Östermalmstorg Ⓣ

Ⓣ

Karlapan
KARLAPLAN

Ⓣ

④

LADUGÅRDSGÄRDET

Historiska Muséet

Armé Museum

Musik Museum

Royal Theatre of Drama

⑨

DJURGÅRDSBRUNNVÄGEN

⑩

Sjöhistoriska Muséet

Tekniska Muséet

Kungsträdgården Ⓣ

STRANDVÄGEN

Djurgårdsbrunnsviken

National Art Museum

Nordiska Muséet

ROSENDALSVÄGEN

Vasamuséet

Biologiska Muséet

Skansen

HOLMEN

Östasiatiska Muséet

Estonia Memorial

Strömmen

Kungl. Slottet

Moderna Muséet

⑪ ⑫

SKEPPSHOLMEN

DJURGÅRDEN

KASTELLHOLMEN

Gröna Lunds Tivoli

All year

BECKHOLMEN

KARL JOH TORG

Ⓣ
Slussen

Åland and Birka Line Terminal

Saltsjön

Viking Line Terminal

KATARINAVÄGEN

Katarina Kyrka

HOTELS	
Bema	6
Diplomat	9
Hotell Haga	1
Kallhagens Wärdshus	10
Pensionat Oden Norr	2
Wallin	7
Wasa Park	5

HOSTELS	
Af Chapman	11
Backpackers Inn	4
City Backpackers	8
Långholmen	13
Skeppsholmen	12
Brygghusets Vandrarhem	3

station beneath the airport for the Central Station in Stockholm (5.05am–12.35pm; every 15min; 20min; 120kr); access to the station is from Terminal 5 as well as jointly from Terminals 2–4. SJ trains leave from a separate station, also beneath the airport, for most northbound destinations; for departure times see the yellow poster in the Arrivals hall. Airport buses, Flygbussarna, call at all terminals and run from Arlanda to Stockholm's long-distance bus station, Cityterminalen (6.40am–11.00pm; every 5min at peak times, otherwise every 10min; 40min; 60kr; ☎08/600 10 00); you buy your ticket on the bus. After 11pm bus departures are timed to coincide with incoming flights. **Taxis** from the airport into town should cost around 350kr – an affordable alternative for a group; choose those vehicles that have prices displayed in their back windows in order to avoid being cheated by cowboy operators.

Some domestic flights operated by Braathens Malmö Aviation arrive at the more central **Bromma airport**, which is also connected to Cityterminalen by Flygbussarna – buses run in connection with flight arrivals and departures. Ryanair flights arrive at Skavsta airport, 100km to the south of the capital close to the town of Nyköping; buses operate in connection with flight arrival and departure times (80min; 60kr).

By **train**, you'll arrive at **Central Station**, a cavernous structure on Vasagatan in the central Norrmalm district. Inside, there's a **Forex** money exchange office, cash machines, a post office and a very useful **room-booking service**, Hotellcentralen (see "Accommodation", p.65). All branches of the **Tunnelbana**, Stockholm's efficient metro system, meet at T-Centralen, the metro station directly below the main station. The regional trains, **Pendeltågen**, that run throughout Greater Stockholm leave from the main platforms at ground level – not from underground platforms.

By **bus**, your arrival point will be at the huge glass structure known as **Cityterminalen**, a hi-tech bus terminal adjacent to Central Station, handling all bus services: airport, ferry shuttle (see below), domestic and international. There's also a money exchange office here, and you can get to the northern end of Central Station's main hall using a series of escalators and walkways.

There are two main **ferry** companies that connect Stockholm with Helsinki and Turku in Finland and with Mariehamn in the Finnish Åland Islands. Viking Line services arrive at Vikingterminalen on the island of Södermalm, from where it's a thirty-minute walk along the water's edge and through Gamla Stan to the modern centre; or take a bus from outside the terminal to Slussen, from where the Tunnelbana leaves every couple of minutes to T-Centralen. Silja Line ferries arrive on the northeastern edge of the city at Siljaterminalen; it's a short walk to either Gärdet or Ropsten metro stations, on the red line, from where trains run into town. The third main operator is Estline, with sailings from Tallinn in Estonia. These arrive at Frihamnen, at the end of the #41 bus route which will take you all the way into town. If you're heading for Central Station, get off at the junction of Kungsgatan and Vasagatan and walk the short distance – the bus also goes directly past the Cityterminalen. The boats from Gothenburg that ply the Göta Canal dock at the quay on the island of Riddarholmen, just a couple of minutes' walk from Gamla Stan and the rest of the centre.

Information

You should be able to pick up a map of the city at most points of arrival, but you are best off visiting one of the city **tourist offices**. Each hands out fistfuls of free information, in the form of brochures and timetables, and carries *Stockholm This Week*, a free listings and entertainments guide. Most of the brochures and booklets will contain a functional (if tiny) **map** – it's probably worth paying 15kr for the better, larger plan of Stockholm and the surrounding area. You'll also be able to buy the valuable Stockholm Card (see p.63) from any of the tourist offices.

The main tourist office is on Hamngatan in Norrmalm, on the ground floor of **Sverigehuset** (June–Aug Mon–Fri 8am–7pm, Sat & Sun 9am–5pm; Sept–May Mon–Fri 9am–6pm, Sat & Sun 9am–3pm; ☎08/789 24 90, excursion information on ☎789 24 15, *www.stoinfo.se*). Upstairs, the **Sweden Bookshop** has a good stock of English-language books on Sweden as well as calendars, videos and the like; detailed factsheets on all aspects of Sweden (economy, geography, society, etc) cost 1kr each. There's also information to be had on working and studying in the country. Other tourist offices are in **Stadshuset**, at Hantverkargatan 1 on Kungsholmen (May–Oct daily 9am–5pm; Nov–April Fri–Sun 9am–3pm) and at the Kaknäs **TV tower** on Djurgården (May–Aug daily 9am–10pm; ☎08/789 24 35).

City transport

Stockholm winds and twists its way across islands, over water and through parkland, a thoroughly confusing place. To find your way around, the best bet is to equip yourself with one of the tourist maps and **walk**: it takes about half an hour to cross central Stockholm on foot, from west to east or north to south. Sooner or later, though, you'll have to use some form of **transport** and, while routes are easy enough to master, one thing to try to avoid is paying per trip on the city's transport system – a very expensive business. The city is zoned, a trip within one zone costing 16kr, with single tickets valid within that zone for one hour; cross a zone and it's another 8kr. Most journeys you will want to make will generally cost 24kr. It's better to make use of the bewildering array of **passes** and **discount cards** available, which we describe on p.63.

Storstockholms Lokaltrafik (**SL**) operates a comprehensive system of buses and trains (metro and regional) that extends well out of the city centre. Their main information office is the **SL-Center** at Sergels Torg (Mon–Fri 7am–6.30pm, Sat & Sun 10am–5pm), just by the entrance to T-Centralen. It stocks timetables for the city's buses and metro system, regional trains and archipelago boats, as well as a useful transport map (35kr; also available from Pressbyrå newsagents) that shows all bus routes and street names within the city centre. For details of other SL offices, see "Listings", p.95. Up-to-date information on the public transport system can also be obtained on ☎08/600 10 00.

The quickest and most useful form of transport is the **Tunnelbana** (T-bana), Stockholm's metro system, comprising three main lines (red, green and blue) and a smattering of branches. It's the swiftest way to travel between Norrmalm and Södermalm, via Gamla Stan, and it's also handy for trips out into the suburbs – to ferry docks and to distant youth hostels and museums. Station entrances are marked with a blue letter "T" on a white background, and displays above each platform give the final destination of each train, making the system easy to use. Trains runs from early morning until around midnight, but on Fridays and Saturdays there are services until 3.30am. The Tunnelbana is something of an artistic experience, too, many of the stations looking like Functionalist sculptures: T-Centralen is akin to one huge papier-mâché cave, and Kungsträdgården is littered with statues, spotlights and fountains. Other stations to look out for are

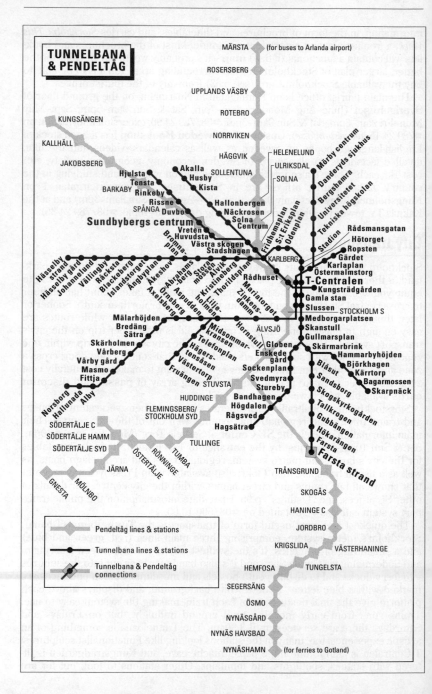

TUNNELBANA & PENDELTÅG

MÄRSTA (for buses to Arlanda airport)
ROSERSBERG
UPPLANDS VÄSBY
ROTEBRO
KUNGSÄNGEN
NORRVIKEN
KALLHÄLL
HÄGGVIK — HELENELUND
JAKOBSBERG ULRIKSDAL
Hjulsta Akalla SOLLENTUNA SOLNA
Tensta Husby
BARKABY Rinkeby Kista
Rissne Hallonbergen
SPÅNGA Duvbo Näckrosen
Sundbybergs centrum Solna Centrum
Vreten S:t Eriksplan
Huvudsta Fridhemsplan Odenplan
Västra skogen
Stadshagen KARLBERG

Mörby centrum
Danderyds sjukhus
Bergshamra
Universitetet
Tekniska högskolan
Rådmansgatan
Hötorget
Stadion
Ropsten
Gärdet
Karlaplan
Östermalmstorg
T-Centralen
Kungsträdgården

Hässelby strand
Hässelby gård
Johannelund
Vällingby
Råcksta
Blackeberg
Islandstorget
Ängbyplan
Åkeshov
Abrahamsberg
Brommaplan
Stora mossen
Alvik
Kristineberg
Thorildsplan
Rådhuset
Mariatorget
Zinkensdamm

Mälarhöjden
Bredäng
Sätra
Skärholmen
Vårberg
Vårby gård
Masmo
Fittja
Norsborg
Hallunada
Alby

Axelsberg
Ornsberg
Aspudden
Liljeholmen
Midsommarkransen
Telefonplan
Hägerstensåsen
Västertorp
Fruängen
STUVSTA

Hornstull
ÄLVSJÖ
Gamla stan
Slussen STOCKHOLM S
Medborgarplatsen
Skanstull
Gullmarsplan
Skärmarbrink
Hammarbyhöjden
Globen Björkhagen
Enskede gård Blåsut Kärrtorp
Sockenplan Sandsborg Bagarmossen
Svedmyra Skogskyrkogården Skarpnäck
Stureby
Bandhagen Tallkrogen
Högdalen Gubbängen
Rågsved Hökarängen
Hagsätra Farsta
Farsta strand

HUDDINGE
FLEMINGSBERG/ STOCKHOLM SYD
TULLINGE
SÖDERTÄLJE C
SÖDERTÄLJE HAMM
SÖDERTÄLJE SYD
ÖSTERTÄLJE
RÖNNINGE
TUMBA
JÄRNA
GNESTA MÖLNBO

TRÅNSGRUND
SKOGÅS
HANINGE C
JORDBRO
KRIGSLIDA VÄSTERHANINGE
HEMFOSA TUNGELSTA
SEGERSÄNG
ÖSMO
NYNÄSGÅRD
NYNÄS HAVSBAD
NYNÄSHAMN (for ferries to Gotland)

—◆— Pendeltåg lines & stations
—●— Tunnelbana lines & stations
Tunnelbana & Pendeltåg connections

Akalla (ceramic images of daily life), Rissne (maps of the world, each region labelled with key historical events and their dates) and Midsommarkransen (massive wooden sculptures of garlands of flowers).

Buses and ferries

Buses can be less direct than the metro, due to the city's layout – the route maps on the back of the *Stockholms Innerstad* bus timetable will give an idea as to how convoluted your journey might be. Tickets are bought from the driver; board buses at the front and get off at the back or in the middle. **Night buses** replace the metro after midnight, except on Friday and Saturday when trains run until around 2am. In an effort to cut pollution, many city buses now run on ethanol – supposedly better for the environment than diesel – partly produced from Spanish red wine; you'll notice a strange smell when one of these vehicles goes by. Stockholm's buses are also pushchair- and pram-friendly; a special area halfway down the bus has been set aside for these. If you're travelling with a dog, sit as far back as you can, as the seats at the front of the buses are intended for people with allergies.

Ferries provide access to the sprawling archipelago, sailing from outside the *Grand Hotel* on Strömkajen (see p.99 for more details); they also link some of the central islands: Djurgården is connected with Nybroplan in Norrmalm via the Vasa museum and Skeppsholmen (July & Aug only), and with Skeppsbron in Gamla Stan (year round). **Cruises** on Lake Mälaren leave from outside Stadshuset on Kungsholmen, and **city boat tours** leave from outside the *Grand Hotel*, as well as from round the corner on Nybroplan. **Tickets** for ferries linking the central islands cost 20kr one-way, and longer trips out into the archipelago up to 85kr, depending on how far you are going. They can be bought from the offices of the ferry company that operates the majority of sailings into the archipelago, Waxholms Ångfartygs AB (more commonly known as Waxholmsbolaget), on Strömkajen outside the *Grand Hotel*, or on the boats themselves. If you are intending to spend a week or so exploring different islands in the archipelago, there are a couple of cards available that will help cut costs; see "The archipelago", p.99.

Travel passes and tickets

The SL-issued Turistkort or **Tourist Card** is valid for 24 hours (70kr) or 72 hours (135kr) from the time you buy the card (it cannot be bought ahead of time because it is validated when sold). It gives unlimited travel on buses, metro and regional trains, and on the ferries and trams (the city's only line starts at

---

THE STOCKHOLM CARD

The best pass to have is the Stockholmskortet or the **Stockholm Card**, which gives unlimited travel on city buses, ferries, metro and regional trains; free entry to around seventy museums; discounts on boat trips and tours; plus free parking and many other discounts. Cards are sold undated and are stamped on first use, after which they're valid for 24 hours (199kr); one card will cover one adult and two children under eighteen. The card also covers the boat tours of the city which leave from in front of the *Grand Hotel* on Strömkajen (mid-May to end Aug; 1hr). It isn't valid, though, on ferries to Djurgården and the direct airport buses and trains to Arlanda. Buy the card from any tourist office in the city, or at Hotellcentralen in Central Station.

Norrmalmstorg) to Djurgården. The card really is excellent value, considering that a single journey in the city can cost up to 21kr. In addition, the 72-hour card gives you a fifty-percent reduction at Skansen and free admission to all other museums. As with all SL tickets, under-18s and senior citizens aged 65 and over travel at reduced rates (24hr card 40kr; 72hr card 80kr). Oddly, the cards are not available at metro station ticket offices to the metro stations – buy them instead from any Pressbyrå or SL-Center.

Otherwise you can buy a strip of twenty reduced-price SL **ticket coupons**, known as *rabattkuponger* (110kr) – you'll have to stamp at least two for each journey. Buy them at the ticket barriers to any metro station. If you're staying in Stockholm for a week or two, it's worth considering a Månadskort or **Monthly Card**, which brings fares tumbling down: for a mere 400kr, the card offers unlimited travel for 31 days on virtually everything that moves throughout the whole of Greater Stockholm. The card isn't specific to an individual, so any number of different people can use it – though not at the same time. If you're spending several months in the city, there are some great-value Säsongskort (**season cards**) available. Monthly and season cards can be bought from any SL-Center and once again, reduced fares are available on all cards for under-18s and senior citizens.

Bikes, taxis and cars

Bike rental is centrally available from Skepp O'Hoj at Galärvarvsvägen 10 (☎08/660 57 57), just over the bridge that leads to Djurgården, or from the nearby Cykel-och Mopeduthyrningen at Kajplats 24, along Strandvägen (☎08/660 79 59); reckon on 180kr per day or 800kr per week for the latest mountain bike, less for a bone-shaker. Other, less central, places include Cykelstallet at Sankt Eriksgatan 34 (☎08/650 08 04), to the northwest of Norrmalm; and Servicedepån at Kungsholmsgatan 34 on Kungsholmen (☎08/651 00 66), which also has tandems for rent.

You can either try to hail a **taxi** in the street, go to a taxi rank (there's one outside Central Station) or ring one of the three main operators: Taxi Stockholm (☎08/15 00 00), Taxi Kurir (☎08/30 00 00) and Top Cab (☎08/33 33 33). If you do phone for a taxi, the metre will show around 28kr when you get in and will then race upwards at an alarming speed: 93kr or thereabouts for every 10km during the day, 103kr per 10km between 7pm and 6am, and 110kr per 10km at weekends. A trip across the city centre will cost 100–150kr, more in the evenings and at weekends.

When **driving**, be extremely careful over **parking**: you aren't allowed to park within 10m of a road junction, whether it be a tiny residential cul-de-sac or a major intersection, and you'll often see people goose-stepping in an attempt to measure out the exact distance. Parking is also prohibited within 10m of a pedestrian crossing, and in bus lanes and loading zones. Disabled parking spaces are solely for the use of disabled drivers, a rule which is rigorously enforced – it can cost you over 800kr if you disobey. In the centre, parking isn't permitted one particular night a week to allow for cleaning (see the rectangular yellow street signs with days and times in Swedish, below the "no stopping" sign on every street) and, in winter, snow clearance. If a car is towed away (a regular occurrence), it goes to the compound at Gasverksvägen in Ropsten (Mon–Fri 8am–7pm, Sat 11am–2.30pm; ☎08/651 00 00) – a short walk from the metro station – where surly staff will demand at least 1500kr to hand it back, and more for every day it spends in the compound. In short, if in doubt, don't park there – look for the signs "Gatukontoret" or "Parkeringsbolaget" for valid spaces. For **car rental**, see "Listings", p.95.

Canoes and kayaks

The dozens of **canoes** and **kayaks** you see being paddled around Stockholm are a testimony to the fact that one of the best ways to see the city is from the water. Skepp O'Hoj, at Galärvarvsvägen 10 (☎08/660 57 57), and Tvillingarnas Båtuthyrning, just by Djurgårdsbron (☎08/663 37 39), are two of the best places in town to rent boats. Special weekend deals are often available from Friday evening to Monday morning, when a canoe can be rented for 400kr; otherwise one costs about 100kr per day. For canoes in the archipelago, try Skärgårdens kanotcenter on Vaxholm, one of the most popular islands (☎08/541 377 90), or ask locally on the other islands – corner shops often have canoes or boats for rent.

Accommodation

Stockholm has plenty of **accommodation** to suit every taste and pocket, from elegant upmarket hotels with waterfront views to youth hostels in unusual places – two on boats and another in a former prison. If you are looking for one of the cheaper hotel rooms or a hostel bed in the centre of town, don't turn up late in summer. In fact it is always a good idea to book your first night's accommodation in advance (especially during the Water Festival; see p.92), either through the **Sverigehuset** tourist office, on Hamngatan in Norrmalm, or directly with the hotel or hostel. An excellent room-booking service is provided by the **Hotellcentralen**, in the main hall of Central Station (daily: May–Sept 7am–9pm; Oct–April 9am–6pm; ☎08/789 24 25, *hotels@stoinfo.se*), which holds comprehensive listings of hotels and hostels. They score over ringing for yourself in that they have the latest special offers direct from the hotels; if you book accommodation through them you'll be charged a booking fee of 50kr for a hotel room, or 20kr for a hostel room. It's best to call at their office in person rather than phone, as they're often busy and not able to take that many phone calls. Hotellcentralen can also make bookings under the **Stockholm Package** scheme (see "Hotels and pensions", p.66).

Youth hostels and private rooms

Stockholm has a wide range of good, well-run **hostels**, nearly all in the city centre or within easy access of it, and costing 70–150kr a night per person. There are no fewer than six official STF youth hostels in the city, two of which – *Af Chapman* and *Långholmen* – are among the best in Sweden. There are also a number of independently-run places, which tend to be slightly more expensive.

Another good low-cost option is a **private room**; to book one, contact an agency called Hotelltjänst, Vasagatan 15–17 (☎08/10 44 67), just a few minutes' walk from Central Station. Tell them how much you want to pay, and where in the city you want to stay (some rooms are out of the centre), and they should land you somewhere with fridge and cooking facilities for around 250kr per person per night; you can usually arrange better-value deals for longer stays.

STF hostels

Af Chapman, Västra Brobänken, Skeppsholmen (☎08/679 50 15, fax 611 98 75, *info@chapman.stfturist.se*). Kungsträdgården T-bana or bus #65 direct from Central Station. This square-rigged 1888 ship – a landmark in its own right – has views over Gamla Stan that are unsurpassed at the price. Without an advance reservation (try to book a fortnight before you arrive), the chances of a space in summer are slim. The drawbacks to nautical accommodation are a lockout (11am–3pm) and the lack of a kitchen. Reception 7am–noon & 3–10pm, curfew at 2am. 130kr.

Backpackers Inn, Banérgatan 56, Östermalm (☎08/660 75 15, fax 665 40 39). Karlaplan T-bana, exit Valhallavägen, or bus #41. Quite central former school residence, with washing machines available. Three hundred beds in large dorms. Late June to mid-Aug. 95kr.

Hökarängen, Munstycksvägen 18 (☎08/94 17 65, fax ☎604 16 46). Out of the city on the green metro line in the direction of Farsta Strand; get off at Hökarängen and walk 10min from the station south along Pepparvägen. Nice old place with 46 beds. Swimming possible 2km from the hostel. Late June to early Aug. 100kr.

Långholmen, Kronohäktet, Långholmen (☎08/668 05 10, fax 720 85 75). Hornstull T-bana and follow the signs. On the island of Långholmen, Stockholm's grandest STF hostel is inside the former prison building (built in 1724), the cells converted into smart private and dormitory rooms, still with their original, extremely small windows. A great location, with beaches nearby, buses to Kungsholmen, and the whole of Södermalm on the doorstep. Fantastic views of Stockholm and of Lake Mälaren. 155kr.

Skeppsholmen, Västra Brobänken, Skeppsholmen (☎08/463 22 66, fax 611 71 55). Kungsträdgården T-bana or bus #65 direct. Right in the centre and immensely popular, this former craftsman's workshop is of a similar standard to *Af Chapman*, at the foot of whose gangplank it lies; there's no kitchen or laundry facilities here. Open all year; no lockout. 100kr, ①.

Zinkensdamm, Zinkens Väg 20, Södermalm (☎08/616 81 00, fax 616 81 20). Hornstull T-bana or Zinkensdamm. Huge hostel with 466 beds. Kitchen and laundry facilities (also see "Hotels and pensions"). 130kr.

Independent hostels

Brygghusets Vandrarhem, Norrtullsgatan 12N, Norrmalm (☎08/31 24 24, fax 31 02 06). Odenplan T-bana. Close to the top end of Sveavägen, around the lively area of Odenplan; has 57 beds. June to early Sept. 120kr.

City BackPackers Vandrarhem, Upplandsgatan 2A (☎08/20 69 20, fax 10 04 64). T-Centralen T-bana. Very central all-year hostel with forty beds. 120kr.

Columbus Hotell & Vandrarhem, Tjärhovsgatan 11, Södermalm (☎08/644 17 17, fax 702 07 64). T-bana Medborgarplatsen. A friendly hostel/hotel (also see "Hotels and pensions"). 120kr, ①.

Gustav af Klint, Stadsgårdskajen 153, Södermalm (☎08/640 40 77, fax 640 64 16). Slussen T-bana. Housed in a boat, this has rather cramped rooms; if they're full, don't be tempted to take one of its private rooms – they're not worth it. The place has a good central location, just a few minutes' walk from the Old Town. Beds in four-berth cabins for 130kr.

Hotels and pensions

Summer in Stockholm means a buyer's market for hotel rooms as business travel declines, with double rooms costing as little as 500kr. The cheapest choices on the whole are found to the north of Cityterminalen in the streets to the west of Adolf Fredriks kyrka. But don't rule out the more expensive places either: there are some attractive weekend and summer prices that make a spot of luxury nearer the waterfront a little more affordable. Most of the hotels and pensions also offer the **Stockholm Package** (mid-June to mid-Aug and at weekends year-round), an arrangement whereby accommodation booked at participating establishments is charged at a much reduced room rate, with a Stockholm Card (normally 199kr) thrown in free for each night's stay. At the bottom end of the scale it can work out cheaply: 485kr per person in a double room with breakfast, rising to around 700kr in quite a posh hotel. This package can only be booked through Hotellcentralen (see p.65); if you ring ahead you can specify which hotel you'd like, while if you book on the day you'll be given what's available. At the time of writing, all the hotels and pensions given below were part of the scheme, but the list of participants is prone to change. All the following establishments include breakfast in the price, unless otherwise stated.

Alexandra, Magnus Ladulåsgatan 42 (☎08/84 03 20, fax 720 53 53). Medborgarplatsen T-bana. Small, modern hotel in a peaceful Södermalm location. The summer and weekend reductions make this a pleasant and affordable option. ④/③.

Anno 1647, Mariagränd 3 (☎08/442 16 80, fax 442 16 47). Near Slussen in Södermalm; Slussen T-bana. A seventeenth-century building handy for the Old Town, with pine floors and period furniture; not recommended for people with disabilities. ③/②.

Bema, Upplandsgatan 13 (☎08/23 26 75, fax 20 53 58). Bus #47 or #69 from Central Station run here. Small pension-style hotel with twelve en-suite rooms, ten minutes' walk from the station. Modern Swedish decor, with beechwood furniture. Summer and weekend deals bring the cost down to the bottom of the price-code range. ③/②.

Castle, Riddargatan 14 (☎08/679 57 00, fax 611 20 22). Östermalmstorg T-bana. This fine, central hotel has jazz performances on summer evenings. All rooms have baths; there's a good breakfast buffet too. ⑤/③.

Central, Vasagatan 38 (☎08/566 208 00, fax 24 75 73). T-Centralen T-bana. A modern, comfortable place, handy for the station. ⑤/③.

Columbus Hotell & Vandrarhem, Tjärhovsgatan 11, Södermalm (☎08/644 17 17, fax 702 07 64). Medborgarplatsen T-bana. Simple rooms in a similarly unadorned, almost school-like building. Rooms not en suite. ③.

Diplomat, Strandvägen 7C (☎08/459 68 00, fax 459 68 20). Östermalmstorg T-bana or buses #47 or #69. Rooms with a view out over Stockholm's inner harbour and grandest boulevard. Although the suites at this turn-of-the-century town house are at the top end of the price range, they represent much better value than the cheaper rooms at the *Grand*. Out of season, double rooms start at 2095kr; there are summer and weekend discounts. ⑥.

First Hotel Reisen, Skeppsbron 12 (☎08/22 32 60, fax 20 15 59). Gamla Stan or Slussen T-bana. Traditional hotel with heavy wood-panelled interior. All rooms have actual bathtubs (not the norm in Sweden); excellent view over the Stockholm waterfront. ⑥.

Grand, Södra Blasieholmshamn 8, Norrmalm (☎08/679 35 00, fax 611 86 86). Kungsträdgården T-bana. A late nineteenth-century harbourside building overlooking Gamla Stan, Stockholm's most refined hotel provides the last word in luxury – with prices to match prices. Only worth it if you're staying in the best rooms – otherwise, the *Diplomat* has suites with a view for the same price as a double here. Out of season, double rooms start at 2700kr. Summer and weekend reductions. ⑥.

Haga, Hagagatan 29, Norrmalm (☎08/736 02 00, fax 32 70 75). Odenplan T-bana. In a quiet road a little out of the centre, within easy striking distance of the top of Sveavägen. Has 38 modern, good-value rooms. ④/③.

Källhagen, Djurgårdsbrunnsvägen 10 (☎08/665 03 00, fax 665 03 99). To get here, take bus #69 from Central Station or the town centre. Highly recommended. Twenty rooms painted in different colours in a fantastic spot overlooking the serene waters of Djurgårdsbrunnsviken. ⑥/④.

Lady Hamilton, Storkyrkobrinken 5 (☎08/23 46 80, fax 411 11 48). Gamla Stan T-bana. Traditional hotel with rooms done out in old-fashioned Swedish/British style – lots of antique furniture. ⑤.

Lord Nelson, Västerlånggatan 22 (☎08/23 23 90, fax 10 10 89). Gamla Stan T-bana. This cosy hotel is the narrowest in Sweden at just 5m wide. Small rooms with a maritime feel – teak floors and lots of mahogany and brass. Cheaper than the *Lady Hamilton* in summer. ⑥.

Mälardrottningen, Riddarholmen (☎08/24 36 00, fax 24 36 76). Gamla Stan T-bana. Moored by the side of the island of Riddarholmen, this elegant white ship was formerly the gin palace of American millionairess Barbara Hutton. Its cabin-style rooms are in need of a lick of paint and bit of a polish, but offer good value for such a central location. ④/③.

Pensionat Oden, Odengatan 38, Norrmalm (☎08/612 43 49, fax ☎612 45 01). Rådmansgatan T-bana. Second-floor hotel with elegant modern rooms which are excellent value for money. Good central location. Recommended. ②.

Pensionat Oden Söder, Hornsgatan 66B, Södermalm (☎08/612 43 49, fax ☎612 45 01). Mariatorget T-bana. A good-value choice in the heart of Söder, with tastefully decorated rooms at excellent prices. Recommended. ②.

Queen's, Drottninggatan 71A, Norrmalm (☎08/24 94 60, fax 21 76 20). Hötorget T-bana. Good mid-range pension-style hotel, with en-suite rooms and breakfast buffet. Summer and weekend deals. ②.

Rica City Gamla Stan, Lilla Nygatan 25 (☎08/723 72 50, fax ☎723 72 59). Gamla Stan T-bana. Really the only halfway affordable Old Town hotel. Wonderfully situated, elegant building with rooms to match; all 51 are individually decorated. ⑤/④.

Scandic Hotel Slussen, Guldgränd 8, Södermalm (☎08/517 353 00; fax 517 353 11). Slussen T-bana. Lots of wooden floors throughout this expensive chain hotel. Only worth it if you can get one of the rooms at the front with fantastic views out over Gamla Stan. ⑥/④.

Stockholm, Norrmalmstorg 1 (☎08/440 57 60, fax 611 21 03). Östermalmstorg or Kungsträdgården T-bana. A penthouse hotel on the top floor of a central office building, with good views out over Strandvägen and the harbour. Squeaky wooden floors and faded bathrooms – recommended. ⑥/④.

Tre Små Rum, Högbergsgatan 81, Södermalm (☎08/641 23 71, fax 642 88 08). Mariatorget T-bana. In the heart of Södermalm. Despite its name, this place has seven small rooms (not three). Clean and modern, with a Japanese flavour, it's very popular and often full. Summer and weekend deals. ②.

Wallin, Wallingatan 15, Norrmalm (☎08/506 161 00, fax 791 50 50). Buses #47 or #69 from Central Station. Decent central hotel with en-suite rooms; a 10min walk from the station. ⑤/③

Wasa Park, St Eriksplan 1, Norrmalm (☎08/34 02 85, fax 30 94 22). Sankt Eriksplan T-bana. A clean, simple hotel; a bit out of the centre but cheap. No en-suite rooms. Summer and weekend deals. ②/①.

Zinkensdamm, Zinkens Väg 20, Södermalm (☎08/616 81 10, fax 616 81 20). Hornstull or Zinkensdamm T-bana. Hotel rooms in a separate wing of the youth hostel (see p.66). ④/③.

Campsites

With the nearest year-round campsites well out of the city centre, **camping** in Stockholm can prove a bit of a burden. However, a summer-only city campsite does exist in Östermalm. The tourist offices have free camping booklets available, detailing facilities at all Stockholm's campsites. Pitching a tent costs around 100kr for two people in July and August, or 50kr at other times of year.

Bredäng (☎08/97 70 71, fax 708 72 62). Bredäng T-bana. Southwest of the city with views over Lake Mälaren. Bookings mandatory Nov–April.

Solna Vandrahems Camping, Enköpsvägen 16, Solna (☎08/655 00 55, fax 655 00 50). Solna Centrum T-bana, then bus #505 to Råstahem, 8km from Stockholm.

Ängby (☎08/37 04 20, fax 37 82 26). Ängbyplan T-bana. West of the city on the lakeshore. Bookings mandatory Sept–April.

The City

Visitors have been noting Stockholm's aesthetic qualities for the past 150 years, though the sights and museums have changed radically during that time. Once, in the centre, there were country lanes, great orchards, grazing cows, and even windmills. The downside then was the lack of pavements (until the 1840s) or piped water supply (until 1858), and the presence of open sewers, squalid streets and crowded slums. In the twentieth century, a huge **modernization** programme was undertaken as part of the Social Democratic out-with-the-old-and-in-with-the-new policy: Sweden was to become a place fit for working people to live. Old areas were torn down as "a thousand homes for a thousand Swedes" – as the project was known – were constructed. The result, unfortunately, can be seen only too clearly around Sergels Torg: five highrise monstrosities and an ugly rash of soulless concrete buildings that blot the city-centre landscape. There was even a plan to tear down the whole of the Old Town and build a modern city in its stead; thankfully the scheme was quickly rescinded.

Today, Stockholm is, for the most part, a bright and elegant place, and, with its great expanses of open water right in the centre, it offers a city panorama unparalleled anywhere in Europe. Seeing the sights is a straightforward business: everything is easy to get to, opening hours are long, and the pace is relaxed. The capital boasts an amazing range and number of **museums**; we've described the most interesting ones in detail.

Old Stockholm: Gamla Stan and Riddarholmen

Three islands – Riddarholmen, Staden and Helgeandsholmen – make up the **oldest part of Stockholm**, the whole history-riddled mass a cluster of seventeenth- and eighteenth-century Renaissance buildings backed by hairline medieval alleys. It was on these three adjoining polyps of land that Birger Jarl erected a fortification in 1255, an event that was to herald the beginnings of the present city. Rumours abound about the derivation of the name "Stockholm"; it's thought that wooden drying frames, known as "stocks", were erected on the island that is now home to Gamla Stan, thus making it the island, *holm*, of *stocks*. Incidentally, today the Swedish word *stock* means "log".

Although, strictly speaking, only the largest island, Staden, contains **Gamla Stan** (the Old Town), this name is usually attached to the buildings and streets of all three islands. Once Stockholm's working centre, nowadays Gamla Stan is primarily a tourist city, an eminently strollable concentration of royal palace, parliament and cathedral, and one that represents an extraordinary tableau of cultural history. The central spider's web of streets, especially if approached over Norrbron or Riksbron, invokes potent images of the past: sprawling monumental buildings and high airy churches form a protective girdle around the narrow lanes. The tall dark houses in the centre were mostly those of wealthy merchants, still picked out today by intricate doorways and portals bearing coats of arms. Some of the alleys in between are the most slender thoroughfares possible, steep steps ascending between battered walls; others are covered passageways linking leaning buildings. It's easy to spend hours wandering around here, although the atmosphere these days is not so much medieval as mercenary: there's a dense concentration of antique shops, art showrooms and chi-chi cellar restaurants. Not surprisingly, this is the most exclusive part of Stockholm in which to live.

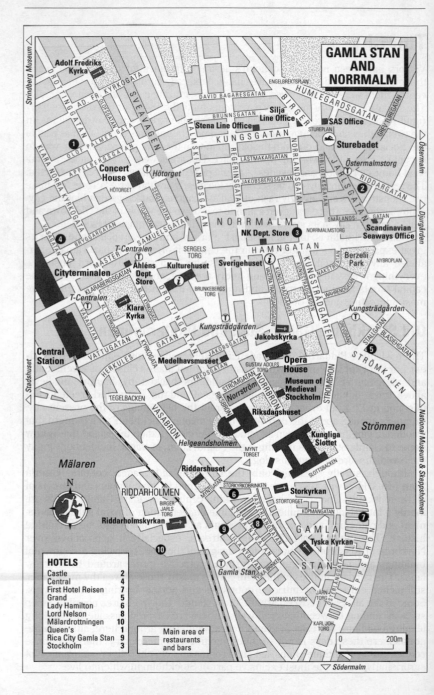

GAMLA STAN
AND
NORRMALM

HOTELS

Castle	2
Central	4
First Hotel Reisen	7
Grand	5
Lady Hamilton	6
Lord Nelson	8
Mälardrottningen	10
Queen's	1
Rica City Gamla Stan	9
Stockholm	3

Main area of
restaurants
and bars

0   200m

Riksdagshuset and the Medeltidsmuseum

Almost every time you enter or leave the Old Town, you'll walk past the **Riksdagshuset** (Parliament House; June–Aug Mon–Fri mandatory guided tours in English at 12.30pm & 2pm; free), the Swedish parliament building. Here, not only can Swedish politicians be observed nipping in and out, or lunching in nearby restaurants, but it's even been known for them to breastfeed their offspring in the chamber during particularly dull debates. This being Sweden, the seating for members is in healthy, non-adversarial rows, grouped by constituency and not by party. Just seventy years after it was built, the building was completely restored in the 1970s, and is a deceptive place today, as the columned, stately and original front (viewed to best effect from Norrbron) is hardly ever used as an entrance. The business end is the glassy bulge at the back (which you see when coming into Stockholm from the south by train), and it's around here that **guided tours** perambulate.

In front of the Riksdag (pronounced "Reeks-da"), accessed by a set of steps leading down from Norrbron, the **Medeltidsmuseum** (Museum of Medieval Stockholm; July & Aug Mon, Fri–Sun 11am–4pm; Tues–Thu 11am–6pm; Sept–June Tues–Sun 11am–4pm; 40kr) is a museum of medieval Stockholm. Ruins, tunnels and walls of the period were discovered during excavations under the parliament building, and have been incorporated into a walk-through underground exhibition. There are reconstructed houses to poke around, models and pictures, boats, skeletons and street scenes. With its detailed English labelling, it's a splendid display, and great fun for children, too.

Kungliga Slottet

Cross Norrbron or Riksbron from the Riksdagshuset and up rears the most distinctive monumental building in Stockholm, **Kungliga Slottet** (the Royal Palace) – a low, square, yellow-brown building, with two arms in front that stretch down towards the water. Stockholm's old Tre Kronor (Three Crowns) castle burnt down at the beginning of King Karl XII's reign, leaving his architect, Tessin the Younger (see p.98), a free hand to design a simple and beautiful Renaissance structure in its stead. Finished in 1754, the palace is a striking achievement: uniform and sombre outside, but with a magnificent Baroque and Rococo interior that's a swirl of staterooms and museums. Its sheer size and limited opening hours conspire against your seeing everything here on the same day.

The palace's **Apartments** (May–Aug daily 10am–4pm; Sept–April Tues–Sun noon–3pm; these times also apply to other buildings here unless stated; 50kr) form a relentlessly linear collection of furniture and tapestries, all too sumptuous to take in and inspirational only in terms of colossal size. The **Treasury** (50kr), on the other hand, is certainly worthy of the name. Its ranks of jewel-studded crowns grab the eye, the oldest being that of Karl X (made in 1650), the two most charming belonging to princesses Eugène (1860) and Sofia (1771). Also worth catching is the **Armoury** (60kr), not so much about weapons as ceremony – suits of armour, costumes and horse-drawn carriages from the sixteenth century onwards. It also displays the stuffed horse of King Gustav II Adolf, who died in the Battle of Lützen in 1632, and his blood- and mud-spattered garments, retrieved after the enemy had stripped him down to his shorts on the battlefield. Nearby, the **Museum Tre Kronor** (50kr) contains part of the older Tre Kronor castle, its ruins underneath the present building. There's also the **Museum of Antiquities**, complete with a mind-boggling collection of ancient sculptures (50kr), and – really only for real palace junkies – the **Hall of State**, a reception hall used by the royal family (20kr). The **Royal Coin Cabinet**, Slottsbacken 6 (Tues–Sun 10am–4pm; 45kr), is home to a stash of coins, banknotes and medals, as well as a number of silver hoards from Viking days.

Into Gamla Stan: Stortorget and around

South of the Royal Palace you're into Gamla Stan proper, the streets suddenly narrower and darker. The highest point of the old part of Stockholm is crowned by **Storkyrkan** (Great Church; daily: May–Aug 9am–6pm, 10kr; Sept–April 9am–4pm, free), consecrated in 1306, and almost the first building you stumble upon. Pedantically speaking, Stockholm has no cathedral, but this rectangular brick church is now accepted as such, and the monarchs of Sweden married and were crowned here. Storkyrkan gained its present shape at the end of the fifteenth century, with a Baroque remodelling having taken place in the 1730s. The interior is marvellous: twentieth-century restoration has removed the white plaster from the red-brick columns, and the effect has been to give a warm colouring to the rest of the building, although there's no evidence that this was intended in the original church. Much is made of the fifteenth-century Gothic sculpture of St George and the Dragon (see p.494), certainly an animated piece but easily overshadowed by the royal pews – more like golden billowing thrones – and the monumental black-and-silver altarpiece. Fans of organ music might find it worthwhile to visit on a Saturday around 1pm, as recitals generally take place then.

    Stortorget, Gamla Stan's main square, is handsome and elegantly proportioned. Crowded by eighteenth-century buildings, whose walls bear wrought-iron lamps, it's well placed for access to the surrounding narrow shopping streets. In 1520, Christian II used the square as an execution site during the "Stockholm Blood Bath" (see p.494), dispatching his opposition en masse with bloody finality. Now, as then, the streets **Västerlånggatan**, **Österlånggatan**, **Stora Nygatan** and **Lilla Nygatan** run the length of the Old Town, although today their time-worn buildings harbour a succession of art-and-craft shops and restaurants. Happily the consumerism here is largely unobtrusive, and in summer, buskers and evening strollers clog the narrow alleyways, making it an entertaining place to wander – and to eat and drink. There are few real targets, though at some stage you'll probably pass **Köpmantorget** (off Österlånggatan), where a replica of the George-and-Dragon statue can be seen. Take every opportunity, too, to scuttle up side streets, where you'll find fading coats of arms, covered alleys and worn cobbles at every turn.

    On Tyska Brinken, just off Västerlånggatan, is **Tyska kyrkan** (German Church; Sat & Sun noon–4pm; free). Once belonging to Stockholm's medieval German merchants, it served as the meeting place of the Guild of St Gertrude. A copper-roofed red-brick church atop a rise, it abandoned its secular role in the seventeenth century, which was when Baroque decorators got hold of it: the result, a richly fashioned interior with the pulpit dominating the nave, is outstanding. Sporting a curious royal gallery, designed by Tessin the Elder, in one corner, the church came complete with mini palace roof, angels and the three-crowns emblem that symbolizes Sweden.

Riddarhuset and Riddarholmen

From Storkyrkan, it's a five-minute stroll west along Storkyrkobrinken to the handsome, seventeenth-century Baroque **Riddarhuset** (House of Nobility; Mon–Fri 11.30am–12.30pm; 40kr), its Great Hall being where the Swedish aristocracy met during the Parliament of the Four Estates (1668–1865); their coats of arms – around two and a half thousand of them – are splattered across the walls. Take a look downstairs, too, at the Chancery, which stores heraldic bone china by the shelf-load and has racks full of fancy signet rings – essential accessories for the eighteenth-century noble-about-town.

Riddarhuset shouldn't really be seen in isolation. It's only a matter of seconds to cross the bridge onto **Riddarholmen** (Island of the Nobles) proper, to **Riddarholmskyrkan** (May–Aug daily 10am–4pm; Sept Sat & Sun noon–3pm; 20kr). Originally a Franciscan monastery, the church has been the burial place of Swedish royalty for over six centuries. Since Magnus Ladulås was sealed up here in 1290, his successors have rallied round to create a Swedish royal pantheon; among others, you'll find the tombs of Gustav II Adolf (in the green marble sarcophagus), Karl XII, Gustav III and Karl Johan XIV, plus other innumerable and unmemorable descendants. Walk around the back of the church for stunning views of Stadshuset, the City Hall, and Lake Mälaren. As you peer out west from Riddarholmen, you'll spot a bridge just over 1km away, Västerbron, with an island, Långholmen (p.85), to its left. In winter, people skate and take their dogs for walks on the ice as the water freezes most years from Riddarholmen right up to the bridge and beyond.

Skeppsholmen, Kastellholmen and the National Art Museum

Off Gamla Stan's eastern reaches lies the island of **Skeppsholmen** (a 10min walk from Stortorget: cross Strömbron, turn right and cross Skeppsholmbron; you can also take a ferry from Nybroplan, see p.63, or bus #65 from Central Station), home to many of Stockholm's less wealthy visitors, who end up at one of the island's two youth hostels. Other than these establishments, the reason to come here is an eclectic clutch of **museums**, the first of which, the National Art Museum, is actually just before the bridge, Skeppsholmbron. There's little else to detain you on Skeppsholmen or on the tiny, adjacent **Kastellholmen**, connected by a bridge to the south. The fact that both islands are in the Baltic proved attractive enough for the Swedish Navy to build camps here in the nineteenth century; some of the old barracks are still visible.

The National Art Museum

As you approach Skeppsholmsbron, on the way to Skeppsholmen, you'll pass the striking waterfront **National Art Museum** (Tues 11am–8pm, Wed–Sun 11am–5pm; 60kr), looking right out over the Royal Palace. This impressive collection of European fine and applied arts from the late medieval period to the nineteenth century is contained on three floors. Changing exhibitions of prints and drawings take up the **ground floor**, and this is where you'll have to leave your bags (in the lockers provided). There's a museum shop and café here, too. The **first floor** is devoted to applied art, and those with a penchant for royal curiosities will be pleased to find that this museum has the lot – beds slept in by kings, cabinets leaned on by queens, plates eaten off by nobles – mainly from the centuries when Sweden was a great power. There's modern work alongside the ageing tapestries and furniture, including Art Nouveau coffee pots and vases, and the intelligent simplicity of Swedish wooden chair design.

It's the **second floor**, though, that's most engaging. A plethora of European and Mediterranean sculpture can be found here, along with some mesmerizing sixteenth- and seventeenth-century Russian icons. The paintings on this floor are equally wide-ranging and of a similarly high quality, including works by El Greco, Canaletto, Gainsborough, Gauguin and Renoir. Something of a coup for the museum is Rembrandt's *Conspiracy of Claudius Civilis*, one of his largest monumental paintings, in room 33. Picturing a scene from Tacitus's *History*, the bold work shows a gathering of well-armed chieftains. There are also some fine works by **Swedish artists** from the sixteenth to early twentieth centuries – most notably paintings by the nineteenth-century masters Anders Zorn and Carl Larsson, and one, by Carl Gustav Pilo, a late eighteenth-century painter, depicting the coronation of Gustav III in Gamla Stan's Storkyrkan. The detail here is interesting, since it shows the church with white plaster columns and not the red brick of today.

So much is packed into this museum that it can quickly become confusing and overwhelming. To wade through it all, splash out on the **guidebooks**, available at the museum shop (40kr for a guide to the paintings only, 150kr for a book on the entire museum).

Skeppsholmen's museums

On Skeppsholmen itself, Stockholm's **Moderna Muséet** (Museum of Modern Art; Tues–Thu 11am–10pm, Fri–Sun 11am–6pm; 60kr) is one of the better modern art collections in Europe, with a comprehensive selection of work by some of the twentieth-century's leading artists. View Dali's monumental *Enigma of William Tell*, showing the artist at his most conventionally unconventional, and Matisse's striking *Apollo*. Look out for Picasso's *Guitar Player* and a whole host of Warhol, Lichtenstein, Kandinsky, Miró and Magritte. Next door is the **Arkitekturmuséet** (Architecture Museum; same times as Moderna Muséet; 45kr, ticket for both museums 75kr), serving up a taste of Swedish architecture in one of the most inspired buildings in the city – all glass and air. Perhaps one for a rainy day, the museum also stages temporary exhibitions on various aspects of architecture and urban planning within the country.

A steep climb up the northern tip of the island brings you to **Östasiatiska Muséet** (Museum of Far Eastern Antiquities; Tues noon–8pm, Wed–Sun noon–5pm; 40kr). A visit here is half a day well spent: you'll be rewarded by an array of objects displaying incredible craftsmanship, including many exhibits from China – the favourite hunting ground of Swedish archeologists. You can wander past fifth-century Chinese tomb figurines, intricate ceramics from the seventh century onwards and fine Chinese paintings on paper and silk. Alongside these, take a look at the astounding assembly of sixth-century Buddhas, Indian watercolours and gleaming bronze Krishna figures, and a magnificent set of Samurai armour, a gift from the Japanese Crown Prince in the 1920s.

Norrmalm and Kungsholmen

Immediately to the north and west of Gamla Stan, modern Stockholm is split into two distinct sections. **Norrmalm**, to the north, is the commercial heart of the city, a compact area full of shops and offices, restaurants, bars and cinemas, always bustling with people and streetlife – unfortunately, it also has a high count of ugly modern buildings. To the west, **Kungsholmen** has a very different feel, with wider, residential streets, larger parks, select shops and Stockholm's town hall. Norrmalm is easy to get round on foot, and from there it's only a short walk across Stadshusbron to Kungsholmen.

Around Gustav Adolfs Torg

Down on the waterfront, at the foot of Norrbron, is **Gustav Adolfs Torg**, more a traffic island than a square these days, with the nineteenth-century **Operan** (Opera House) its proudest, most notable – and ugliest – building. It was here, in an earlier opera house on the same site, that King Gustav III was shot at a masked ball in 1792 by one Captain Ankarström, an admirer of Rousseau and member of the aristocratic opposition. The story is recorded in Verdi's opera *Un ballo in maschera*, and you'll find Gustav's ball costume, as well as the assassin's pistols and mask, displayed in the Palace Armoury in Gamla Stan (see p.71). The opera's famous restaurant, *Operakällaren*, which faces the water, is hellishly expensive, the trendy café less so.

A statue of King Gustav II Adolf marks the centre of the square, between the Opera and the Foreign Ministry opposite. Look out, too, for fishermen pulling salmon out of **Strömmen**, the fast-flowing stretch of water that winds its way through the centre of the city. Since the seventeenth century, Stockholmers have had the right to fish this outlet from Lake Mälaren to the Baltic; landing a catch here isn't as difficult as it sounds, and there's usually a group of hopefuls on one of the bridges around the square.

Just off the square, at Fredsgatan 2, in the heart of government (several ministries are located in the surrounding streets), is **Medelhavsmuséet**, a sparkling museum devoted to Mediterranean and Near Eastern Antiquities (Tues 11am–8pm, Wed–Fri 11am–4pm, Sat & Sun noon–5pm; 50kr). Its enormous display on Egypt covers just about every aspect of life there up to the Christian era. As well as several whopping great mummies, the most attractive pieces are the bronze weapons, tools and domestic objects from the time before the Pharaohs. The Cyprus collections are also huge, the largest such assemblage outside the island itself, depicting life through a period spanning six thousand years; the museum also contains strong Greek displays and comprehensive collections of Etruscan and Roman art. A couple of rooms examine Islamic culture through pottery, glass and metalwork, as well as decorative elements from architecture, Arabic calligraphy and Persian miniature painting.

Walking back towards the Opera House and continuing across the main junction onto Arsenalsgatan, you'll soon come to **Jakobs kyrka** (daily 11am–5pm). The church is one of the many hidden away in Stockholm, and can easily be missed. It stands on the site of an earlier chapel of St James (Jakob in Swedish) and was completed some 52 years after the death of its founder, Johan III. Although the church's doors are impressive – check out the south door with its statues of Moses and St James on either side – it's the pulpit that draws the attention, a great, golden affair. The date of the church's completion (1642) is stamped high up on the ceiling in gold figures. There are weekly concerts here as well: organ and choir recitals, generally on Saturday at 3pm.

Kungsträdgården

Just beyond the Jacobs kyrka and the Opera House, Norrmalm's eastern boundary is marked by **Kungsträdgården**, the most fashionable and central of the city's numerous parks, reaching from the water northwards as far as Hamngatan. The mouthful of a name literally means "the king's gardens", though if you're expecting perfectly designed flower beds and rose gardens you'll be sadly disappointed – it's a great expanse of concrete with a couple of lines of trees, its days as a royal kitchen garden long gone. Today the area is Stockholm's main meeting place, especially in summer, when there's almost always something going on: free evening gigs, live theatre and other performances take place on the central open-air stage. Look out, too, for the park's **cafés** – the open-air one is popular in spring as a place for winter-weary Stockholmers to lap up the much-missed sunshine. In winter, the park is as busy as in summer: the **Isbanan**, an open-air ice rink at the Hamngatan end of the park, rents out skates (Oct–April daily 9am–6pm; 35kr). The main tourist office is here, too, at the corner of Hamngatan and Kungsträdgårdsgatan in Sverigehuset (see p.61 for details).

Hamngatan runs east to **Birger Jarlsgatan**, the main thoroughfare that divides Norrmalm from Östermalm and now a Mecca for eating and drinking, but until 1855 the site of two pillories and largely rural. Look out for the stone pillars near the water, with panels that light up, forming a sort of electronic display that gives an indication of the current levels of pollution (low compared to other capitals) in the city's air and water.

Sergels Torg to Hötorget

At the western end of Hamngatan, past the enormous NK department store, lies **Sergels Torg**, the ugliest part of modern Stockholm. It's an open-air meeting area and venue for impromptu music performances or demonstrations, centred around the five seething floors of **Kulturhuset** (Tues–Thu 11am–7pm, Fri 11am–6pm, Sat 11am–5pm & Sun noon–5pm; exhibitions 30kr), whose windows overlook the milling concrete square. Inside this building, devoted to contemporary Swedish culture, are temporary art-and-craft exhibitions, together with workshops open to anyone willing to get their hands dirty. The reading room (Läsesalongen) on the ground level is stuffed with foreign newspapers, books, records and magazines – especially handy when it's wet and windy outside. As you come in, check with the information desk for details of poetry readings, concerts and theatre performances. At the café on the top floor, you can indulge in delicious apple pie and custard – although the service here often leaves something to be desired – and take in the best **views** of central Stockholm. One thing you'll have a bird's-eye view of is the singularly ugly, tall, wire-like column, surrounded by a spewing fountain (sometimes clouded by soap suds – the local youth think it's a real wheeze to pour packets of washing powder into it), that dominates the massive square outside

Down the steps, below Sergels Torg, is **Sergels Arkaden**, a set of shabby underground walkways that are home to buskers, brass bands and the demented lottery ticket vendors. Look out for the odd demonstration, too, or oddball game: everything from young Stockholmers running around shivering in their underwear, having tied the rest of their clothes together in a line to see whose line is longest – a very Swedish pastime somehow – to political rallies. There's also an entrance to **T-Centralen**, the central T-bana station, as well as a gateway to Stockholm's other main department store, Åhléns, not quite as posh as NK, and an easier place to find your way around.

A short walk along Klarabergsgatan, west of Kulturhuset, brings you to **Central Station** and **Cityterminalen**, hub of virtually all Stockholm's transport. The area around here is given over to unabashed consumerism, but as you explore the streets around the main drag, **Drottninggatan** (Queen Street), there's little to get excited about – the run-of-the-mill shops selling clothing and twee gifts are punctuated by a *McDonald's* and the odd sausage stand. In summer, the occasional busker or jewellery stall livens up what is essentially a soulless grid of pedestrianized shopping streets. One highlight is **Klara kyrka** (Mon–Fri 10am–6pm, Sat 10am–7pm, Sun 8.30am–6pm), just to the south of Klarabergsgatan, another of Stockholm's overlooked churches, with only the spires visible from the streets around. Hemmed in on all sides, the church is particularly delicate, with a light and flowery eighteenth-century painted interior and an impressive golden pulpit. Out in the churchyard, a memorial stone commemorates the eighteenth-century Swedish poet Carl Michael Bellman, whose popular, lengthy ballads are said to have been composed extempore; his unmarked grave is somewhere in the churchyard.

Three blocks further up Drottninggatan in the cobbled square, **Hötorget**, you'll find an open-air fruit, vegetable and flower market, as well as the wonderful **Hötorgshallen**, an indoor market boasting a tantalizing array of Middle Eastern sights and smells. Just grab some ethnic snacks here and sit yourself on the steps of the **Konserthuset** in the square; you may even be here at the right time to catch one of the classical music recitals that are held within in summer (usually Sunday afternoons). From the steps, look out across the square to the tall building opposite, PUB; this former department store is where **Greta Garbo** began her working life as a sales assistant in the hat section. In its basement, the small commemorative Garbo Room contains a table, sofa, bureaux, lamps, carpets and paintings from her apartment at 450 East 52nd St in New York. Beside the room are several evocative pictures capturing the star at her best. Although she died in New York in 1990, it wasn't until 1999 that her ashes were returned to Stockholm and buried in the Skogkyrkogården cemetery. If you want to see a movie, you only have to walk across to the south side of the square where you'll find Stockholm's biggest cinema complex, Filmstaden Sergel; to the east, **Kungsgatan**, running down to Stureplan and Birger Jarlsgatan, has most of the rest of the city's cinemas (also see "Theatres and cinemas"), interspersed with agreeable little cafés and bars.

North to Adolf Fredriks kyrka

From Hötorget, the city's two main streets, **Drottninggatan** and **Sveavägen**, the latter with its excellent restaurants and bars, run parallel uphill and north as far as Odengatan and the Stadsbiblioteket or City Library, in its little park. In secluded gardens on Sveavägen, not far north of Hötorget, sits **Adolf Fredriks kyrka**, its yard popular with lunching office workers. Although the church has a noteworthy past – the French philosopher Descartes was buried in the church's cemetery for eleven years before his body was taken back to France in 1661 – it would have remained an unremarkable eighteenth-century church, were it not for one of the most tragic – and still unexplained – events in modern Swedish history: the murder of the former prime minister **Olof Palme** (see box, p.78).

Continuing north along Drottninggatan, you'll soon come to the excellent **Strindbergsmuséet** at no. 85 (Strindberg Museum; Tues–Sun 11am–4pm; 35kr), housed in the "Blue Tower", the last building in which the writer August Strindberg lived in Stockholm. The house, which was the writer's home between 1908 and 1912, has been preserved to the extent that you must put plastic bags over your shoes to protect the floors and furnishings. The study is as he left it on his death, a dark and gloomy place – he wrote with the venetian blinds and heavy

THE ASSASSINATION OF OLOF PALME

Adolf Fredriks kyrka is of immense significance to modern Swedes as the final resting place of **Olof Palme**; a simple headstone and flowers mark his grave. He was gunned down in front of his wife in February 1986, while they were on the way home from the Riviera cinema on Sveavägen. Like most Nordic leaders, Palme's fame was his security, and he was not under protection when he died.

Sweden's biggest-ever murder enquiry was launched, and as the years went by, so the allegations of police cover-ups and bungling grew. When Christer Pettersson was jailed for the murder (see p.499), most Swedes thought that was the end of the story, but his eventual release for lack of evidence only served to reopen the bitter debate, with consequent recriminations and resignations within a much-derided police force. Although it used to be that the finger of suspicion was most often pointed at immigrant Kurdish extremists, right-wing terror groups or even a hit-man from within the police itself, recent allegations suggest that Pettersson had a double who, although he was known to hate Palme and his policies, was never investigated. The murder weapon hasn't been found either; periodically the police carry out yet another abortive diving attempt (the weapon was apparently thrown into a lake) amid much public derision.

Palme's death sent shockwaves through a society unused to political extremism of any kind, and has sadly led to a radical rethink of the open-government policy Sweden had pursued for decades. Government ministers now rarely go unescorted; security guards and self-locking doors are now commonplace in all public buildings.

A simple **plaque** on the pavement, often respectfully bedecked with flowers, now marks the spot on Sveavägen, near the junction with Olof Palmes Gatan, where the prime minister was gunned down; the assassin escaped up the nearby flight of steps.

curtains closed against the sunlight. Upstairs is his library, a musty room with all the books firmly behind glass, which is a shame because Strindberg wasn't a passive reader: he underlined heavily and criticized in the margins as he read, though rather less eruditely than you'd expect – "Lies!", "Crap!", "Idiot!" and "Bloody hell!" tended to be his favourite comments. Good English notes are supplied free, and the nearest T-bana stop is Rådmansgatan, on the green line (direction Fridhemsplan and Hässelby Strand).

Heading further north, the city gradually peters out into a number of rather diverse parks and gardens (for more on which see p.81). The closest to town – officially in the area north of the centre called **Vasastaden**, and only a twenty-minute walk along Sveavägen from Adolf Fredriks kyrka – is **Vanadislunden**. Inside the park is a watersports and activities centre called **Vilda Vannadis** (mid-May to mid-Sept daily 10am–6pm; 50kr), containing an outdoor pool and waterslides, where you can while away some hours splashing about in the water. To get there from the centre, you can either walk from the T-bana at Odenplan, or take bus #52 from Central Station or Sergels Torg towards Karolinska Sjukhuset.

Kungsholmen: Stadshuset

Take the T-bana back to the centre, get off at T-Centralen and it's only a matter of minutes from there, across Stadshusbron, to the island of **Kungsholmen** and Stockholm's City Hall. Finished in 1923, **Stadshuset** (obligatory guided tours daily: June–Aug at 10am, 11am, noon & 2pm; Sept at 10am, noon & 2pm; Oct–May 10am & noon; 40kr) is one of the landmarks of modern Stockholm and one of the first buildings you'll see when approaching the city from the south by train. Its simple, if somewhat drab, exterior brickwork is no preparation for the intriguing detail inside. If you're a visiting head of state you'll be escorted from your boat up the elegant waterside steps; for lesser mortals, the only way to view the innards is on one of the guided tours, which reveal the kitschy Viking-style legislative chamber and impressively echoing Golden Hall where the Nobel Prize ceremony is held (see p.414). The City Hall is also the departure point for **boats** to Drottningholm, Mariefred, Sigtuna, Skokloster and Uppsala (see "Around Stockhom", p.97).

But don't stop just at Stadshuset; venture further into Kungsholmen and you'll discover a rash of great new bars and restaurants (see p.85), and an excellent **beach** at Smedsudden (buses #4 and #62 to Västerbroplan, then a 5min walk). There's also the popular park, **Rålambshovsparken**; head through it to get to Smeduddsbadet, where you can swim in Lake Mälaren and enjoy fantastic views of the City Hall and the Old Town.

Östermalm

East of Birger Jarlsgatan, the streets become noticeably broader and grander, forming a uniform grid as far as Karlaplan. **Östermalm** was one of the last areas of central Stockholm to be developed and, with the greenery of Djurgården (see p.81) beginning to make itself felt, the impressive residences here are as likely to be consulates and embassies as fashionable homes. The first place to head for is **Nybroplan**, a square at the water's edge, just east along Hamngatan from Sergels Torg (from Gamla Stan, it's a 15min stroll across Strömbron, or take the T-bana to Östermalmstorg or bus #55) and marked by the white-stone **Kungliga Dramatiska Teatern**, Stockholm's showpiece theatre. The curved harbour in front is the departure point for all kinds of archipelago **ferries** and tours (see p.99), including a summertime ferry that makes the short journey to Djurgården via Skeppsholmen (July & Aug daily every 15min; 25kr).

At the back of the theatre, at Sibyllegatan 2, is the innovative **Musikmuséet** (Tues–Sun 11am–4pm; 30kr), charting the history of music in Sweden using photographs, instruments and sound recordings, and containing a range of instruments that visitors can play ("carefully", pleads the notice). Best are the sections that deal with the late nineteenth century, a time when *folkmusik* had been given fresh impetus by the growing labour movement. The concluding parts on "progressive" and "disco" music are very brief and uninteresting, with the merest mention of punk and, pathetically, hardly anything on Sweden's most famous pop export, ABBA, bar a couple of their stage costumes. You can, however, listen to some of their tunes on the museum's jukebox.

The chief feature of this end of the city was once the barracks: it's a link continued today by the presence of **Armémuséet** (Army Museum), opposite the Musikmuséet at Riddargatan 13. Hardly anyone used to visit for its displays of precision killing machines, uniforms, swords and medals; indeed, visitors were often outnumbered by the attendants, who seemed to consider an interest in the exhibits proof of social deviancy. Ask at the tourist office if the museum has reopened as planned in the spring of 2000, after repairs and alteration.

Just west of the museums, up the hill of Sibyllegatan, **Östermalmstorg** is an absolute find, the square being home to the quite ritzy **Östermalmshallen**, an indoor market hall. Although it looks very similar to Norrmalm's Hötorgshallen, the items here are more akin to what you might find in a delicatessen, along with various oddities – reindeer hearts, the wicked-smelling *surströmming* (see p.378) and the like – and attracts a chic clientele to match. Wander round at lunchtime and you'll spot well-heeled ladies and gents sipping Chardonnay and munching on shrimp sandwiches.

Historiska Muséet

As you wend your way around Östermalm's well-to-do streets, sooner or later you're bound to end up at the circular **Karlaplan**, a handy T-bana and bus interchange, full of media types coming off shift from the Swedish Radio and Television buildings at the eastern end of Karlavägen. From here, it's a short walk down Narvavägen – or you can jump on a #44 bus – to the **Historiska Muséet** at nos. 13–17 (Tues–Sun 11am–5pm; 60kr); from Norrmalm, hop on bus #56, which runs there via Stureplan and Linnégatan. The most wide-ranging historical display in Stockholm, it's really two large collections, a Museum of National Antiquity and the new Gold Room, with its magnificent fifth-century gold collars and other fine pieces of jewellery, housed in an underground vault. On the ground floor, the prehistory section has labelling in English, and highlights include the idealized Stone Age household – flaxen-haired youth amid stripped-pine benches and rows of neatly labelled herbs – and a mass of Viking weapons, coins and boats, including jewellery and bones from Birka (see p.98). Upstairs, there's a worthy collection of medieval church art and architecture, with odds and ends gathered up from all over the country, evocatively housed in massive vaulted rooms. If you're moving on from Stockholm to Gotland, be sure to take in the reassembled bits of stave churches uncovered on the Baltic island – some of the few examples that survive in Sweden.

Lidingö

Just northeast of the city centre, **Lidingö** is a residential, commuter island which you'll already have glimpsed if you arrived from Finland or Estonia by ferry, as the terminal is immediately opposite on the mainland. Where Stockholm's well-to-do live, the island is also home to the startling **Millesgården** at Carl Milles Väg 2 (May–Sept daily 10am–5pm; Oct–April Tues–Sun noon–4pm; 60kr), the outdoor sculpture collection of **Carl Milles** (1875–1955), one of Sweden's greatest sculptors and art collectors. To get to Millesgården, take the T-bana to Ropsten, then the rickety Lidingöbanan over the bridge to Torsvikstorg, and walk down Herserudsvägen.

Milles's statues are seated on terraces carved into the island's steep cliffs, many of the animated, Classical figures also perching precariously on soaring pillars, overlooking the distant harbour: phalanxes of gods, angels and beasts. A huge *Poseidon* rears over the army of sculptures, the most remarkable of which, *God's Hand*, has a small boy delicately balancing on the outstretched finger of a monumental hand. Those who've been elsewhere in Sweden may find much of the collection familiar, as it includes copies and casts of originals adorning countless provincial towns. If this collection inspires, it's worth tracking down three other pieces by Milles in the capital – his statue of *Gustav Vasa* in the Nordic Museum on Djurgården, the *Orpheus Fountain* in Norrmalm's Hötorget, and out at Nacka Strand (bus #404 from Slussen or Waxholm boat from Strömkajen), the magnificent *Gud på Himmelsbågen*, a claw-shaped vertical piece of steel topped with the figure of a boy, forming a stunning entrance marker to Stockholm harbour.

Lidingö is also the venue for the world's biggest cross-country race, the **Lidingöloppet**, held on the first Sunday in October. It's been staged since 1965, the thirty-kilometre course attracting an international field of around thirty thousand runners – quite a sight as they skip or crawl up and down the island's hills. For more information, or if you want to take part, ask the tourist offices in Stockholm.

Djurgården and around

Royal hunting grounds throughout the sixteenth to eighteenth centuries, **Djurgården** (pronounced "Yoor-gorn") is two distinct park areas separated by a channel, **Djurgårdsbrunnsviken** – a popular area for **swimming** in summer and **skating** in winter, when the channel freezes over. Besides taking time out from the city, you can also sample some of Stockholm's finest **museums**. Top of the list are the massive open-air **Skansen**, an amazing conglomeration of architecture and folk culture from around the country, and **Vasamuseet**, which houses a wonderfully preserved seventeenth-century warship. A full day is just about enough to see everything on Djurgården. You can walk here through the centre out along Strandvägen, but it's quite a hike. Using public transport, take bus #44 from Karlaplan; or from Norrmalm, buses #47 and #69 (only as far as the bridge, Djurgårdsbron, leading onto the island); or from Gamla Stan, the ferries from Skeppsbron (all year; see p.63) or Nybroplan (July & Aug only; see p.63).

Nordiska Museet, Skansen and Gröna Lunds Tivoli

Starting with the palatial **Nordiska Museet** (Tues–Sun 11am–9pm; 60kr), just over Djurgårdsbron from Strandvägen, is the best idea, if only because the same cultural themes pop up repeatedly throughout the rest of the exhibits on the island. The displays are a recent attempt to represent Swedish cultural history of the past five hundred years in an accessible fashion, and the *Sámi* section is particularly good. On the ground floor of the cathedral-like interior, you can't fail to spot Carl Milles's phenomenal statue of Gustav Vasa, the sixteenth-century king who drove out the Danes, and an inspirational figure who wrought the best from the sculptor (for more on whom, see p.421).

It's for **Skansen**, though, that most people come: a vast open-air museum with 150 reconstructed buildings, from a whole town to windmills and farms, laid out on a region-by-region basis (daily: May 10am–8pm, June–Aug 10am–10pm; Sept–April 10am–4pm; 60kr June–Aug, 30kr Sept–May). Each section boasts its own daily activities – traditional handicrafts, games and displays – that anyone can join in. Best of the buildings are the small *Sámi* dwellings, warm and functional, and the craftsmen's workshops in the old town quarter. You can also potter around a small **zoo** and a bizarre **aquarium**, fish cheek-by-jowl with crocodiles, monkeys and snakes. Partly because of the attention paid to accuracy, partly due to the admirable lack of commercialization, Skansen manages to avoid the tackiness associated with similar ventures in other countries. Even the snack bars dole out traditional foods and in winter serve up great bowls of warming soup.

Immediately opposite Skansen's main gates and at the end of the #44 bus route (bus #47 also goes by), **Gröna Lunds Tivoli** (May–Sept daily noon to midnight; rest of the year reduced hours; 45kr not including rides) is not a patch on its more famous namesake in Copenhagen, though decidedly cleaner and less seedy. It's definitely more of a place to stroll through rather than indulge in the rides (unlimited *åkbandet* ride-pass 195kr), most of which are fairly tame, a notable exception being the Fritt Fall – a hair-raising vertical drop of 80m in just six seconds; do lunch later. At night the emphasis shifts as the park becomes the stomping ground for hundreds of Stockholm's teenagers.

Vasamuséet

Housed in an oddly shaped building, close to Nordiska Museet, **Vasamuséet** (mid-June to mid-Aug daily 9.30am–7pm; mid-Aug to mid-June daily 10am–5pm, Wed until 8pm; 60kr) is without question head and shoulders above anything else that Stockholm has to offer in the way of museums. The *Vasa* warship, which was built on the orders of King Gustav II Adolf, sank in Stockholm harbour on its maiden voyage in 1628. Preserved in mud for over three hundred years, the ship was raised along with twelve thousand objects in 1961, and now forms the centrepiece of a startling, purpose-built hall on the water's edge. The museum itself is built over part of the old naval dockyard. Impressive though the building is, nothing prepares you for the sheer size of the **ship**: 62m long, the main mast originally 50m above the keel, it sits virtually complete in a cradle of supporting mechanical tackle. Surrounding walkways bring you nose-to-nose with cannon hatches and restored decorative relief, the gilded wooden sculptures on the soaring prow designed to intimidate the enemy and proclaim Swedish might. Confronted by its frightening bulk, it's not difficult to understand the terror that such ships must have generated. Adjacent **exhibition halls** and presentations on several levels take care of all the retrieved bits and bobs. There are reconstructions of life on board, detailed models of the *Vasa*, displays relating to contemporary social and political life, films and videos of the rescue operation, excellent English notes and regular English-language **guided tours** – in short, a must.

The Estonia Memorial

Adjacent to the museum, an altogether more frightening reminder of the power of the sea deserves your attention. Located on the Stockholm waterfront, the three 2.5-metre high granite walls of the **Estonia Memorial**, arranged in the form of a triangle, bear the engraved names of the 852 people who died on board the *Estonia* ferry which sank in the Baltic Sea in September 1994, while crossing from the Estonian capital, Tallinn, to Stockholm. The inscription reads simply "their names and their fate, we shall never forget".

Thielska Galleriet

At the far eastern end of Djurgården (bus #69 from Norrmalm), **Thielska Galleriet** (Mon–Sat noon–4pm, Sun 1–4pm; 40kr) is one of Stockholm's major treasures, a fine example of both Swedish architecture and art. The house was built by Ferdinand Boberg at the turn of the twentieth century for banker Ernet Thiel, and turned into an art gallery after he sold it to the state in 1924. Thiel, who knew many contemporary Nordic artists, gathered an impressive collection of paintings over the years, many of which are on display today – there are works by Carl Larsson, Anders Zorn, Edvard Munch, Bruno Liljefors and even August Strindberg. The views, too, are attractive enough to warrant a trip out here.

The TV tower and around

It's possible to walk from Djurgården to Stockholm's famous **Kaknästornet** (TV tower; daily: May–Aug 9am–10pm, Sept–April 10am–9pm; 25kr), in the northern stretch of parkland known as **Ladugårdsgärdet** (or more commonly as plain Gärdet) – head eastwards across the island on Manillavägen, over Djurgårdsbrunnsviken. At 160m, the tower is the tallest building in Scandinavia, providing excellent views over the city and archipelago, and there's a restaurant about 120m up for an elevated cup of coffee. Bus #69 from Norrmalm will also take you directly here. Beyond Ladusgårdsgärdet, north of the tower, where windmills used to pierce the skyline, lies first Frihamnen, where the ferries from Estonia dock, and just beyond that are Värtahamnen and the Silja Line ferry terminal for Finland.

Ekoparken

The royal park of Djurgården, together with its northern neighbours, Haga and Ulriksdal, make up Stockholm's National City Park, **Ekoparken**. This vast stretch of urban parkland reaches all the way to the shimmering chrome-and-glass headquarters of Scandinavian Airlines, which you may have glimpsed on the way if you came into Stockholm by bus from Arlanda airport. Once you tire of the city streets, this is the place to come, not least for the excellent **swimming** opportunities at Brunnsviken lake which runs through the northern section of the park. If you don't fancy walking all the way to the lake – and it's a good one-hour walk from the city centre – take the T-bana to Universitetet, from where you can walk through the woods to the lake. Incidentally, there's also a gay sunbathing area here, Freskati – see p.94.

Södermalm and Långholmen

Whatever you do in Stockholm, don't miss the delights of the city's southern island, **Södermalm**, more often known simply as "Söder", whose craggy cliffs, turrets and towers rise high above the clogged traffic interchange at Slussen. The perched buildings are vaguely forbidding, but venture beyond the main roads skirting the island and a lively and surprisingly green area unfolds, one that is at heart emphatically working class. On foot, you reach the island over a bridge from Gamla Stan onto Södermalmstorg, the square around the entrance to the Slussen T-bana. To get here by public transport, you can either take bus #46 or #48 from Norrmalm and get off at Bondegatan, or jump on the #53 to Folkungagatan; alternatively ride the T-bana to either Slussen or, to save an uphill trek, Medborgarplatsen or Mariatorget.

Just south of Södermalmstorg is the rewarding **Stadsmuséet** (Stockholm City Museum; June–Aug Tues, Wed & Fri–Sun 11am–5pm, Thurs 11am–7pm; Sept–May Tues, Wed & Fri–Sun 11am–5pm, Thurs 11am–9pm; 40kr), hidden in a basement courtyard. The Baroque building, designed by Tessin the Elder and finished by his son in 1685, was once the town hall for this part of Stockholm; now it houses a set of collections relating to the city's history as a seaport and industrial centre. Fifteen minutes' walk to the southeast, the Renaissance-style **Katarina kyrka**, on Högbergsgatan, stands on the site where the victims of the so-called "Stockholm Blood Bath" (see p.494) – the betrayed nobility of Sweden who had opposed King Christian II's Danish invasion – were buried in 1520. Their bodies were burned as heretics outside the city walls, and it proved a vicious and effective coup, Christian disposing of the opposition in one fell swoop.

It's worth wandering westwards to **Mariatorget**, a spacious square where the influence of Art Nouveau on the buildings is still evident. This is one of the most

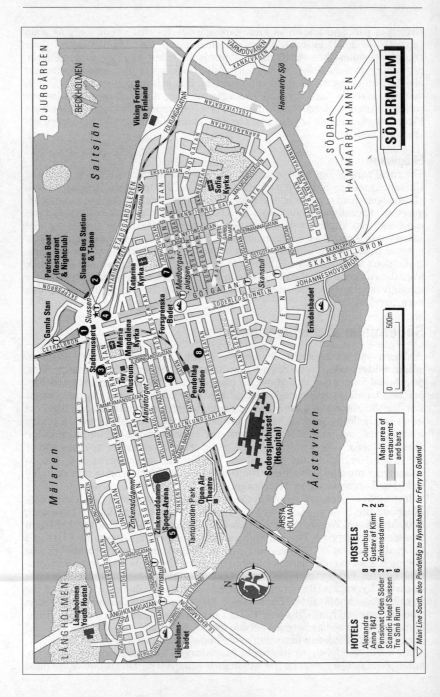

DJURGÅRDEN

BECKHOLMEN

Saltsjön

Mälaren

SÖDRA

HAMMARBYHAMNEN

Hammarby Sjö

Árstaviken

ÁRSTA HOLMAR

LÅNGHOLMEN

SÖDERMALM

VÄRMDÖVÄGEN

KANALVÄGEN

Viking Ferries to Finland

Patricia Boat (Restaurant & Nightclub)

Slussen Bus Station & T-bana

Gamla Stan

Slussen

Stadsmuseet

Katarina Kyrka

Maria Magdalena Kyrka

Forsgrenska Badet

Toy Museum

Mariatorget

Sofia Kyrka

Medborgar- platsen

Skanstull

Johanneshovsbron

Eriksdalsbadet

Skanstullbron

Pendeltåg Station

Södersjukhuset (Hospital)

Tantolunden Park Open Air Theatre

Zinkensdamm Sports Arena

Långholmen Youth Hostel

Liljeholms- badet

Hornstull

TANTOGATAN

GÖTGATAN

RINGVÄGEN

SÖDER MÄLARSTRAND

0   500m

Main area of restaurants and bars

HOTELS
Alexandra
Anno 1647   4
Pensionat Oden Söder   3
Scandic Hotel Slussen   1
Tre Små Rum

HOSTELS
Columbus   7
Gustav af Klimt   2
Zinkensdamm   5

8

6

N

▽ Main Line South, also Pendeltåg to Nynäshamn for Ferry to Gotland desirable places for Stockholmers to live and be close to the action, awash as it is with stylish bars and restaurants that are the favourite haunts of Stockholm's young and terminally hip. On bad-hair days, you can escape the latest fashions and regress to your childhood at the **Leksaksmuseum**, Mariatorget 1C (Toy Museum; Tues–Fri 10am–4pm, Sat & Sun noon–4pm; 40kr, children 20kr), which contains everything from tin soldiers to space guns, although there's more to interest big kids than little ones, as you can't actually play with most of the toys.

Södermalm is home to one of Stockholm's most popular parks, **Tantolunden**, located close to the Hornstull T-bana at the end of Lignagatan, and complete with an open-air theatre where performances are held in summer. The island is also the place to come for **swimming pools**, as there are three in fairly close proximity: Forsgrénskabadet (Medborgarplatsen T-bana); the newly built Erikdalsbadet (Skanstull T-bana). with an open-air pool; and the wonderful little Liljeholmsbadet (Hornstull T-bana), a pool in a boat-like pontoon contraption that floats in Lake Mälaren. The water at Liljeholmsbadet is never cooler than 30°C, and there's an excellent sauna and terrace from where you can look out over the waters of the lake. It also has single-sex nude swimming on certain days of the week (see p.96).

Although you'll probably end up in one of Söder's bars or restaurants (see p.91) when night falls, it's best to get your bearings during the day, as the streets become terribly confusing in the dark. The main streets to aim for are **Götgatan**, **Folkungagatan**, **Bondegatan** and **Skånegatan** (see p.91 for listings).

Långholmen

True to its name, which means "long island", **Långholmen** is a skinny finger of land that lies off the northwestern tip of Södermalm, crossed by the mighty Västerbron bridge linking Södermalm with Kungsholmen. There are a couple of popular beaches here: **Långholmens Strandbad** to the west of the bridge, rocky **Klippbad** to the east, and – over the bridge from here – at **Smeddsudden**, on Kungsholmen. Leafy and peaceful, Långholmen is a delightful place to take a walk; on the way you'll also get some stunning views of the city, towards Stadhuset and Gamla Stan. Get to Långholmen by taking the T-bana to Hornstull and following the signs to the youth hostel, or on bus #54, which crosses Västerbron on its way from Södermalm, Kungsholmen, Vasastaden (to the northeast of Norrmalm) and Östermalm – incidentally, this bus ride is an excellent way of seeing a lot of the city for very little cost.

One of the better places to stay in the city is the **youth hostel** (see p.66), sited in what used to be Långholmen's large prison building. There's a **café** here in the summer, where you can sit outside in the former exercise yard – full of narrow, bricked-up runs with iron gates at one end. Alternatively, you could nip back over onto Södermalm and sample the excellent *Lasse i Parken* café (see p.89).

Eating and drinking

Eating out in Stockholm needn't be expensive – observe a few rules and you'll manage quite well. If money is tight, switch your main meal of the day to lunchtime, when almost every café and restaurant offers an excellent-value set menu, known as *Dagens Rätt*, for 50–60kr, though this only applies Monday to Friday. For evening meals, don't assume that Italian and Chinese places will be the least expensive; more often than not they're overpriced, and serve food that's pretty tasteless. You're much better off seeking out one of Stockholm's many Swedish restaurants, where you're likely to find an extensive menu of traditional fare as well as some good international dishes. In fact the latest culinary craze in Stockholm is for "crossover" dishes, a blend of Swedish cooking with other world cuisines that can lead to some surprising and delicious combinations.

The scourge of Swedish nightlife – high alcohol prices – is gradually being neutralized due to increased competition. Over recent years, there's been a veritable explosion in the number of **bars and pubs** in Stockholm, in particular Irish theme pubs. **Beer prices** have dropped considerably and, on Södermalm especially, there are some very good deals. **Happy hours** at various places also throw up some bargains – watch out for signs outside bars and pubs advertising their particular times.

Breakfasts and snacks

Breakfasts are a Swedish speciality. If you're staying in a hotel, you're likely to be faced with a bewildering array of cereals, cheeses, cold meats and yoghurts for breakfast, to which you simply help yourself. You can return to the buffet table as many times as you want – needless to say coffee and other beverages, such as orange juice, are also included in the eat-and-drink-as-much-as-you-want spreads. Hotels are the only places that offer such extensive breakfasts, although you'll find plenty of good coffee, cakes and sandwiches at Stockholm's many cafés. For a cheap light meal or **snack**, you are best off avoiding burgers: at *McDonald's* you'll pay around 45kr for a large burger and fries (at least their coffee is cheaper than at most cafés) – only 10kr less than the *Dagens Rätt* at lunchtime elsewhere. When the hunger pangs strike, it's much cheaper to pick up a *korv*, a large grilled or fried sausage in bread for 10–15kr from one of the many street vendors.

Markets and supermarkets

Of the indoor **markets**, *Hötorgshallen* in Hötorget (see p.77) is cheaper and more varied than posher and downright expensive *Östermalmshallen* in Östermalmstorg (see p.79; both markets closed Sun). **Hötorgshallen** is awash with small cafés and ethnic snacks, but for **fruit and veg**, buy either from the cheaper open-air market outside, or from the summer stalls outside most T-bana stations, especially in the suburbs (conveniently, the ones outside Slussen and Brommaplan T-bana stations are open all year). Pleasant for a wander, **Östermalmshallen** has all kinds of unusual eats; however, most of what's on sale here can be bought at lower prices from the city's biggest **supermarket**, in the basement of Åhléns department store at Sergels Torg. There are also several other central supermarkets: try *Konsum* in Järntorget and *Metro* in the underground arcade at Sergels Torg – although neither will be particularly cheap. Out in the suburbs, look out for **Vivo** supermarkets – the cheapest chain in Sweden.

Cafés and restaurants

Day or night, the main areas for decent eating are, in the city centre, the triangle marked out by Norrmalmstorg, Birger Jarlsgatan and Stureplan; in Östermalm, Grev Turegatan; and in Södermalm, around Folkungagatan, Skånegatan and Bondegatan. In Kungsholmen, restaurants are more spread out, so it helps to know your destination before you set off. Several restaurants in Gamla Stan are also worth checking out, though they tend to be expensive. For the best choice in terms of price and variety, head south for Södermalm, where you'll find the more trendy and chic **cafés** and **restaurants**, and a broader range of cuisines.

In recent years, a rash of good daytime **cafés** has appeared, where you can sit over coffee and cake and just watch the world go by. It's worth noting the best ones: *Wayne's* in the city centre; *Saturnas* in Östermalm; and in Södermalm, *Indigo* and the studenty *String* and *Lasse i Parken* (see pp.89–90).

Some of the places listed below also appear in the "Nightlife and culture" section (p.91), as there's a fairly fine line between cafés, restaurants and bars in Sweden, with many places offering music and entertainment in the evening as well as food throughout the day.

Norrmalm

Biblos, Biblioteksgatan 9. A wonderfully trendy café and restaurant right in the centre of town – a good place to observe.

East, Stureplan 13. One of the city's finest restaurants. Trendy to a T, with excellent food – lots of fish and Asian-style dishes: lunch 74–106kr; dinner around 150kr.

Enzo & Matilde, Birger Jarlsgatan 9. A wonderful little Italian place tucked away in Birger Jarlspassagen, run by a lively Italian woman who serves up delicious home-made spinach-and-salmon lasagne and other pasta treats.

Fredsgatan 12, Fredsgatan 12. A delicious mix of Swedish and international cuisine, though on the expensive side. Check out the summer outside bar.

Halv trappa plus gård, Lästmakargatan 3, at Stureplan. This is one of Stockholm's most popular eateries, serving modern European dishes, particularly fish, with outside seating in summer. Bursting with fashion victims. Main courses for 150kr.

Hot Wok Café, Kungsgatan 44, in the eclectic *Kungshallen* foodhall. Generous portions of Chinese-style food (main courses cost under 100kr) and the largest glasses of wine anywhere in Stockholm.

IKKI, Kungsgatan 44, upstairs in the *Kungshallen*. A very popular Japanese sushi bar, especially at lunchtime. Lots of fish and things grilled on skewers. Main dishes from 150kr.

KB, Smålandsgatan 7. Excellent Swedish food in posh surroundings and a favourite haunt of authors and artists. Reckon on at least 250kr for a main course.

Konditori Kungstornet, Kungsgatan 28. Popular 1950s style Swedish coffee house with excellent cakes and sandiches.

Köket och en bar, Sturegallerian 30. Very popular (though rather pricey) place for snacks when the nightclubs have closed. From Thursday to Sunday it stays open until 3am.

Lao Wai, Luntmakargtan 74. This was Sweden's first East Asian restaurant and is decidedly good, though not especially cheap. Main courses around 200kr.

Leonardo, Sveavägen 55. Some of the tastiest pizzas (made in the only wood-burning oven in town) and pasta in Stockholm – always fresh and delicious.

Operakällaren, Operahuset, Gustav Adolfs Torg. A bill at the famous Opera House restaurant will seriously damage your wallet (starters from 150kr) but the daily smorgasbord (Mon–Sat 11.30am–3pm, Sun noon–6pm) is fabulous and just about affordable – around 250kr per person for a spread beyond compare. A better bet is the *Bakfickan* around the back where simpler (and much cheaper) dishes are served from the same kitchen.

Peppar, Torsgatan 34. Attractive, moderately-priced Cajun restaurant with decent-sized portions.

Prinsen, Mäster Samuelsgatan 4. Old and traditional place frequented by artists, musicians and the like.Very expensive.

Restaurangen, Oxtorgsgatan 14. No starters or main courses here – you simply put together a meal consisting of three or five small dishes. Run by one of Stockholm's top chefs.

Roberts Coffee, Kungsgatan 44. Just inside the door of the *Kungshallen* food hall, and a popular place to meet friends for a good cup of coffee.

Rolfs Kök, Tegnergatan 41. Popular central restaurant close to Hötorget with a special line in Asian and Cajun stir-fried food; fairly expensive prices.

Sawadee, Olofsgatan 6. Next to Hötorget T-bana. Attractive Thai restaurant with a wonderful 150kr special dinner and reasonably priced drinks.

Svea Bar & Matsal, Sveavägen 53, just by Rådmansgatan T-bana. Excellent place for a cheap and filling lunch for around 60kr. Set menus in the evenings with dishes for around 100kr; cheap beer.

TipTop, Sveavägen 57. If you want to eat among gay people, this is the place to come, but the food – standard Swedish home cooking – can be pricey for what it is (for more on gay Stockholm see p.94).

Wayne's, Kungsgatan 14. A popular café for smart city types and trendy young things, who sip cappuccinos while pretending to read foreign newspapers.

Östermalm

Aubergine, Linnégatan 38. An upmarket and expensive place on one of Östermalm's busiest streets. Lots of wood and glass. The separate bar menu brings prices within reach – chicken on a skewer is good at 85kr.

Elverket, Linnégatan 69. Tasty international food served up in a restaurant attached to a theatre. Spacious lounge for drinks before dinner or relaxation afterwards.

Grevens Bakficka, Fisk och Vilt, Grev Turegatan 7. Affordable and cosy place for lunch with meat, fish and game dishes for around 100kr each.

Grodan, Grev Turegatan 16. Swedish for "the frog", hence the name *La Grenouille* on the outside, and a favourite haunt for many Stockholmers. French cuisine at moderate prices.

Gröna Linjen, Mäster Samuelsgatan 10, second floor. A nineteenth-century building housing the oldest vegetarian restaurant in all Scandinavia, with a good buffet.

Il Conte, Grev Turegatan 16. Rumoured to be the best Italian place in town. The pasta is excellent and very good value.

Meaning Green, Norrlandsgatan 2. Decent veggie food served at one of the city's better vegetarian restaurants.

PA & Co, Riddargatan 8. Fashionable restaurant with international dishes, some good old Swedish favourites and a few inventive "crossovers".

Samuraj, Kommendörsgatan 40. A good Japanese place known for its fine food and friendly staff. Expensive.

Saturnus, Erikbergsgatan 6. Good, moderately priced pasta, huge cakes and massive sandwiches – a café by day, with a formal restaurant service in the evening.

Stockholms Glass och Pastahus, Valhallavägen 155. Excellent fresh pasta and home-made ice cream at this inexpensive place. Closed evenings.

Stolen, Sibyllegatan 47, close to T-bana exit at Östermalmstorg. The name means "chair", and fittingly there are dozens of different kinds here. Good Italian-style food at reasonable prices – the chicken dishes are especially delicious.

Vassilis Taverna, Valhallavägen 131. Stockholmers say this is the best Greek restaurant in town – try the moussaka, which slips down a treat.

Wedholms Fisk, Nybrokajen 17. Classy fish restaurant.

Örtagården, Nybrogatan 31. Top-notch vegetarian fare dished up under a huge chandelier in turn-of-the-century surroundings. Dozens of different salads, hot main courses and soups.

Gamla Stan

Bistro Ruby and **Grill Ruby**, Österlånggatan. At no. 14, *Bistro Ruby* is a pricey French bistro in the heart of the Old Town, tastefully done up in Parisian style. A wide selection of beers. Expensive. Next door is *Grill Ruby*, serving up American-style grills and weekend brunches.

Costas, Lilla Nygatan 21. Good central Greek restaurant with an ouzo bar, *C2*, next door.

De Fyras Krog, Järntorgsgatan 5. As good a place as any to eat traditional Swedish food – choose between the posh, more expensive restaurant or the simple farmhouse-style section.

Den Gyldene Freden, Österlånggatan 51. Stockholm's oldest restaurant, "The Golden Peace" was opened in 1772; around 350kr is a lot to pay for just two courses, without drinks, but the atmosphere, food and style are unparalleled in Stockholm.

Gondolen, Stadsgården 6. At the top of the Katarina lift. Breathtaking views over Stockholm from this high-level restaurant right on the seafront. The place is divided into two restaurants, one of which is dramatically cheaper (where main dishes go for about 150kr).

Hermitage, Stora Nygatan 11. Vegetarian restaurant well worth checking out for its hearty dishes; main courses cost 120kr or so. Mon–Sat till 8pm, Sun to 7pm.

Lilla Karachi, Lilla Nygatan 12. A Pakistani restaurant – an interesting change for Stockholm – with vegetarian options and moderate prices, housed in some of Gamla Stan's old cellar vaults.

Mårten Trotzig, Västerlånggatan 79. A classic known throughout Sweden for its excellent and stylish food (main courses at 300kr). Its lovely setting attracts city slickers from across Stockholm.

Pontus in the Green House, Österlånggatan 17. With main courses at around 300kr, this is the place to come if you want to splash out. Luxury food of all kinds served by one of the city's top chefs. Cheaper Asian dishes, including excellent sushi, available at the bar.

Södermalm

Blå Dörren, Södermalmstorg 6. Beer hall and restaurant with excellent, but expensive, Swedish food.

Bonden Mat & Bar, Bondegatan 1C. Small and cosy restaurant with rough brick walls. Main courses here go for around 160kr; try the delicious fillet of chicken with oyster mushrooms in red wine sauce and potato gratin – a winner every time.

Bröderna Olssons, Folkungagatan 84. If you like garlic this is definitely the place for you, with every conceivable dish laced with the stuff. Main courses from 200kr.

Creperie Fyra Knop, Svartensgatan 4. A rare treat in Stockholm – excellent, affordable crepes at around 50kr.

Dionysos, Bondegatan 56. Over-the-top Greek decor gives this place a friendly feel, and the food is excellent: moussaka for 85kr, chicken *souvlaki* for 70kr.

Folkhemmet, Renstiernas Gata 30. Very popular place serving Swedish home cooking and international dishes (150kr for a main course) to young trendies and media types. Packed at weekends.

Hannas Krog, Skånegatan 80. A firm favourite and popular haunt of Söder trendies. It's crowded and noisy with lunch deals for around 60kr, evening dishes for around 100–150kr. Also a popular drinking haunt; see p.91.

Hosteria Tre Santi, Blekingegatan 32. One of Södermalm's better Italian restaurants and excellent value for money – always busy.

Indigo, Götgatan. Near exit from Slussen T-bana. The ideal place to stop off for an afternoon cappuccino. Good pastries and cakes, too – the carrot cake is a house speciality. Small evening menu.

Indira, Bondegatan 3B. The area's biggest Indian restaurant, with a good tandoori-based menu. Takeaway food also. Main dishes cost 70–100kr.

Kvarnen, Tjärhovsgatan 4. Small beer hall with simple Swedish food – lunch for around 50kr. Evening dishes, fish and meat, for 80–90kr. Open till 3am at weekends.

Lasse i Parken, Högalidsgatan 56. Café housed in an eighteenth-century house, with a pleasant garden that's very popular in summer, and also handy for the beaches at Långholmen.

Mellis, Skånegatan 83–85. Another popular restaurant on this busy restaurant street. Greek, French and Swedish dishes – reasonable prices. A nice place for coffee and cakes, too.

Mosebacke, Mosebacke Torg 3. The place to come of a sunny lunchtime: sit outside and enjoy views over the harbour and the old town. The salmon is particularly good.

Pelikan, Blekingegatan 40. Atmospheric, working-class Swedish beer hall with excellent traditional food, such as *pytt i panna* for 58kr.

Sjögräs, Timmermansgatan 24. A modern approach to Swedish cooking, influenced by world cuisines; always packed.

Snaps/Rangus Tangus, Medborgarplatsen. Good old-fashioned Swedish food in a 300-year-old building. Very popular.

Soldaten Svejk, Östgötagatan 15. Lively Czech-run joint that draws in a lot of students. Simple menu with dishes around the 100kr mark. Large selection of Czech beers; Pilsner Urquell for 39kr.

String, Nytorgsgatan 38. If you fancy yourself as a brilliant writer, or if you just fancy yourself, you'll fit in well at this studenty café. Good for moderately priced cakes and snacks.

Tre Indier, Möregatan 2. Slightly tucked away in a tiny street off Åsögatan (take bus #55 in the direction of Södra Hammarbyhamnen), but well worth seeking out. A lively Indian restaurant. 150kr.

Österns Pärla, Götgatan 62. Reasonable Chinese food, at around 80kr a dish.

Kungsholmen

Bon Lloc, Bergsgatan 33. Catalan dishes with a hint of Swedish home cooking served up by award-winning chef Mathias Dahlgren. Bookings necessary.

Carls Bar, Scheelegatan 12. Good Thai food and a reasonable selection of more mainstream European dishes. Worth a look if you're in the area.

Hong Kong, Kungbrostrand 23. A popular good-value Chinese restaurant and deservedly one of the best in the city.

La Famiglia, Alströmergatan 45. One of Kungsholmen's better Italian places and a good one for that first date; even Frank Sinatra once ate here.

Mamas & Tapas, Scheelegatan 3. Delicious, reasonably priced Spanish food that deservedly attracts people from across Stockholm. Always packed.

Roppongi, Hantverkargatan 76. The best place on the island for sushi and other Japanese delights.

Salt, Hantverkaregatan 34. On the island's main road, it serves stodgy traditional Swedish fare, including elk burgers. Salt hasn't a bad name here either – ask for some water if you're eating the slabs of pork they serve up.

Bars, brasseries and pubs

The majority of Stockholmers do their drinking and eating together, and several of the places listed below also serve food. Those who want a place to do some serious drinking only will find the capital certainly has enough establishments to choose from, nearly all open seven days a week.

Norrmalm and Östermalm

Berns, Berzelii Park, Nybroplan. One of the chicest brasseries in town, with interior design by London's Sir Terence Conran. Originally made famous by writer August Strindberg, who picked up character ideas here for his novel, *The Red Room*.

Café Opera, Opera House, Gustav Adolfs Torg. If you don't mind your gear getting crumpled, and you can stand just one more Martini, join the queue outside. Daily till 3am.

Dubliner, Smålandsgatan 8. One of the busiest Irish pubs in town, with live music most evenings.

East Bar, Stureplan. Loud music, loud dress and loud mouths. Great fun.

Lydmar, Sturegatan 10. Definitely one of the most popular bars in Stockholm – and very elegant. Dress up a little to get in past the bouncers.

Silver Bar, Birger Jarlsgatan 5. Popular little bar with a nightclub downstairs. Attracts big crowds at weekends.

Storstad, Odengatan 41. A popular hang-out with Stockholm's media crowd and local celebrities. Crowded at weekends with card-flashing clientele.

Sturecompagniet, Sturegatan 4. Three floors of bars; something for everybody and worth a look. Expensive beer.

Svea Bar & Matsal, Sveavägen. By the exit to Rådmansgatan T-bana. Cheap beer and a upbeat atmosphere from early evening onwards.

Tranan, Karlbergsvägen 14. An atmospheric old workers' beer hall, in the basement.

Gamla Stan

Gråmunken, Västerlånggatan 18. Cosy café-bar, usually busy. Sometimes has live music to jolly things along.

Kaos, Stora Nygatan 21. An unpretentious crowd gathers here for a good time out. DJs at weekends.

Kleins, Kornhamnstorg 51. One of the better bars in Gamla Stan and definitely worth a look.

Magnus Ladulås, Österlånggatan 26. Rough brick walls and low ceilings make this bar-cum-restaurant an appealing place for a drink or two.

Mårten Trotzig, Västerlånggatan 79. Smart surroundings for an early evening drink before dinner – wear your finest garb.

Södermalm

Akkurat, Hornsgatan 18. Known for its 200 different types of whisky and extensive beer selection, including an impressive array of Belgian varieties.

Bonden Bar, Bondegatan 1B. Just along from the *Bonden* restaurant and down a sloping walkway. A good choice for an evening beer before strutting your stuff on the adjoining dance floor.

Fenix, Götgatan 40. A rough and ready American-style bar that's always busy and noisy.

Folkhemmet, Renstiernas Gata 30. Trendy hang-out for 20- to 30-somethings. Inordinately popular at weekends.

Gröne Jägaren, Medborgarplatsen. Some of the cheapest beer in Stockholm; *storstark* is 24kr until 9pm – perhaps inevitably, its clientele tend to get raucously drunk.

Hannas Krog, Skånegatan 80. A good place for a drink before eating in the excellent restaurant here of the same name.

Kvarnen, Tjärhovsgatan 4. Another busy beer hall – a favourite haunt of southside football fans.

O'Learys, Götgatan 11–13. Södermalm's most popular Irish pub – good for stumbling back to the nearby Slussen T-bana.

Pelikan, Blekingegatan 40. A fantastic old beer hall full of character – and characters.

Sjögräs, Timmermansgatan 24. A wonderful little local bar that's always busy and lively.

WC, Skånegatan 51. Very busy at weekends with people from across town – handy for the restaurants around Skånegatan and Blekingegatan.

Nightlife and culture

There's plenty to keep you occupied in Stockholm, from pubs, gigs and clubs to the cinema and theatre. In the bars and pubs, there's a good **live-music scene**, but you'll generally have to pay a cover charge of around 60–80kr. Also, if you don't want to feel scruffy, wear something other than jeans and training shoes –

many places won't let you in dressed in them anyway. Be prepared, too, to cough up around 10kr to leave your coat at the cloakroom, a requirement at many bars as well as at discos and pubs, particularly so in winter. Apart from the weekend, Wednesday night is an active time in Stockholm, with lots going on and queues outside the more popular places. Swedes, and especially Stockholmers, are fairly reserved, so don't expect to immediately get chatting to people – in fact it is positively fashionable to be cool and aloof. However, after a few drinks, it's usually easy enough to strike up conversation.

One of Stockholm's most popular events is the **Stockholm Water Festival**, a ten-day annual jamboree held in August, and featuring open-air gigs, street parties, fishing contests, exhibitions, sailing displays and children's activities; it closes with a stunning fireworks display. The tourist office has specific details about each year's events. If you're planning your stay to coincide with the festival, it's especially important to book accommodation in advance. You'll also have to brace your elbows and prepare to forge your way through the crowds that briefly transform Stockholm into a really bustling city.

For **information** on what's on – get someone to translate if your Swedish isn't up to it – there's a free monthly paper, *Nöjesguiden*, that details all manner of entertainments, from the latest films to club listings; you'll see it in bars and restaurants. *Stockholm This Week*, free from the tourist office, is particularly good for arts listings. It contains day-by-day information about a whole range of events – gigs, theatre, festivals, dance – sponsored by the city, many of which are free and based around Stockholm's many parks. Popular venues in summer are Kungsträdgården and Skansen, where there's always something going on. Another useful source of event listings is the Saturday supplement, *På Stan*, of the *Dagens Nyheter* newspaper. **Kulturhuset** in Sergels Torg has a full range of artistic and cultural events – mostly free – and the information desk on the ground floor has programmes to give away.

Clubs

The **club scene** in Stockholm is limited, and several clubs also function as restaurants – you are obliged to order food here – and bars. Cover charges aren't too high at around 40–50kr, but beer gets more expensive as the night goes on, reaching as much as 50kr, and in the places that function as restaurants you'll have to order food, too. In Stockholm, as in the rest of Sweden, there is very little real crossover with the gay scene. For more on gay Stockholm see p.94.

Aladdin, Barnhusgatan 12–14, Norrmalm. One of the city's most popular club-restaurants, close to Central Station – live bands often perform. Come here for an expensive night out.

Fasching, Kungsgatan 63, Norrmalm. Dancing to live jazz from midnight onwards.

G-Klubben, Kungsträdgården. Inside *Dailys*, a cheesy nightclub complex, complete with striplights on the stairs. This is where you'll find Stockholm's movers and shakers: be young, beautiful and trendy.

Patricia, Stadsgårdskajen, Slussen, Södermalm. A former royal yacht belonging to Britain's Queen Mother, today a restaurant-cum-disco-cum-bar, with fantastic views of the city out across the harbour, and Swedish stand-up-comedy nights. The menu, with a huge variety of imaginative main courses (from chicken *fajitas* to fresh lobster to Thai-style stir fries) is quite simply terrific. Wed–Sun; gay on Sun (see p.94).

Sturecompagniet, Sturegatan 4, Norrmalm. Strut to house and techno and a fantastic light show – also three floors of bars. Very popular.

Theatres and cinemas

There are dozens of **theatres** in Stockholm, but only one has regular **English-language performances**: the Regina, Drottninggatan 71 (☎08/20 70 00), which features touring productions – tickets and more information from the theatre. For productions at other theatres, which are occasionally in English, it's often worth waiting for reduced-price stand-by tickets, available from the tourist office at Sverigehuset.

Cinemas are incredibly popular, with screenings of new releases nearly always full. The largest city-centre venue is Filmstaden Sergel in Hötorget, but there's also a good number of cinemas along the stretch of Kungsgatan between Sveavägen and Birger Jarlsgatan. For **art-house films** head for Zita at Birger Jarlsgatan 37 (☎08/23 20 20); tickets cost around 70kr and films are always shown in their original language.

Live music

There's no shortage of venues that put on live music, the cafés and bars already listed among them. Classical music is always easy to find in Stockholm; there's generally something on at Konserthuset in Hötorget, Norrmalm (☎08/10 21 10); Berwaldhallen, Strandvägen 69, Östermalm (☎08/784 18 00); and Musikaliska Akademien, Blasieholmstorg 8, near the National Art Museum (☎08/20 68 18). Many museums – particularly Historiska Museet and Musikmuseet – stage regular performances. **Organ and choral music** can be heard at Adolf Fredriks kyrka and St Jakobs kyrka in Norrmalm, Gustav Wasa kyrka in Odenplan, and Storkyrkan in Gamla Stan; for more details consult *Stockholm This Week*. Operan, on Gustav Adolfs Torg, is Stockholm's main opera house (☎08/24 82 40); for less rarefied presentations of the classics, check out the programme at Folkoperan, Hornsgatan 72, Södermalm (☎08/658 53 00).

Rock and jazz

When there's live music at bars and cafés, it will mostly be provided by local bands, for which you'll pay around 60–70kr entrance. Nearly all the big names make it to Stockholm, playing at a variety of seated halls and stadiums – tickets for these are, of course, much more expensive. The main **large venues** are the Stockholm Globe Arena (supposedly the largest spherical building in the world); Johanneshov (T-bana Gullmarsplan; ☎08/600 34 00); Konserthuset in Hötorget (☎08/10 21 10); and the Isstadion, to the north of Östermalm (☎08/600 34 00) – ring for programme details or ask at the tourist offices.

Cirkus, Djurgården. Occasional rock and R&B performances.

Daily News, Kungsträdgården, Norrmalm. Part of the Dagens Nyheter complex, this central rock venue hosts the most consistent range of live contemporary music in town – everything from grunge to techno-influenced outfits.

Engelen, Kornhamnstorg 59, Gamla Stan. Live jazz, rock or blues nightly until 3am, but arrive early to get in; the music starts at 8.30pm (9pm on Sun).

Fasching, Kungsgatan 63, Norrmalm. Local and foreign contemporary jazz; also a place to go dancing; see p.92. Mon–Sat.

Hard Rock Café, Sveavägen 75. Occasional R&B bands, often American.

Kaos, Stora Nygatan 21, Gamla Stan. Live music from 9pm nightly; rock bands on Fri and Sat in the cellar; and reasonable late-night food.

Mosebacke Etablissement, Mosebacke Torg 3, Södermalm. Music and cabaret venue, putting on anything from jazz and swing to folk gigs (and even stand-up comedy).

Nallen, Regeringsgatan 74. *The* place to hear music in the 1940s–60s: even the Beatles were once booked to play here (they cancelled). Now offers jazz, swing and big band music.

Stampen, Stora Nygatan 5, Gamla Stan. Long-established and rowdy jazz club, both trad and mainstream; occasional foreign names, too.

Tre Backar, Tegnérgatan 12–14, Norrmalm. Good, cheap pub with a live cellar venue. Rock and blues every night Mon–Sat.

Gay Stockholm

Given that Stockholm is a capital city, the **gay scene** is disappointingly small and closeted. Attitudes in general are tolerant, but expectations of gay couples walking hand-in-hand or kissing in the street are just another false assumption about Sweden. Until just a few years ago, there was only one gay place in the whole of the city. Thankfully, the country has now freed itself from the tax rules that made it hard for the smaller bars to stay afloat, and gay bars are springing up all over the place. The five main **bars** and **clubs** to be seen at – and definitely to do the seeing – are listed below. However, they are all mostly male hang-outs; lesbians in Stockholm have an even lower profile, and even the beaches listed below are male only.

TipTop, at Sveavägen 57, is the city's main gay centre; the offices above house the headquarters of Sweden's **gay rights group**, Riksförbundet för sexuellt likaberättigande (the National Association for Sexual Equality; RFSL for short), which is a great source of information (☎08/736 02 12). Besides offering HIV advice (☎08/736 02 11), they run a free newspaper, *Kom Ut*; a bookshop, Rosa Rummet; a restaurant, café, bar and club (see below) and a radio station. A second newspaper, *QX*, is also available at gay bars and clubs and is handy for listings. **Gay Pride Week** is the second week of August and features special events ranging from live bands to discussion forums.

Bars and clubs

Häktet, Hornsgatan 82; Zinkensdamm T-bana. A wonderful place with two bars, front and back, as well as a quiet sitting room and a beautiful outdoor courtyard – a real haven in summer. Very popular on Wed nights, especially with women. Wed and Fri only.

Patricia, Stadsgårdskajen; Slussen T-bana. The Queen Mother's former royal yacht attracts queens and more from across Stockholm for fun on Sun evenings (no entrance fee). Eat here before you groove – a great place for romantic evenings staring out across the harbour. Often hosts drag acts or stand-up comedy.

Propaganda, Blekholmsterassen 15. Bar and nightclub, with a particularly hot dancefloor. Fri & Sat.

SLM, Wollmar Yxkullsgatan 18. Stockholm's only leather club, complete with handy shoe polishing service. Very dark and definitely not one for the faint-hearted. Men only.

TipTop, Sveavägen 57; Rådmansgatan T-bana (☎08/30 83 38 & 31 34 80). Stockholm's main gay men's venue – a club, restaurant and bar all rolled into one – and very popular, especially on Fri and Sat nights. Daily.

Gay beaches

Freskati, Universitetet T-bana. Turn left out of the underground station, past the Pressbyrån kiosk, walk under the bridge and towards the trees. A popular sunbathing spot.

Kärsön, Brommaplan T-bana, then buses #177, #301–323, #336 or #338 towards Drottningholm palace. Get off at the stop over the bridge and take the path to the right along the water's edge. If you want to sunbathe nude and swim in Lake Mälaren, this island is where to come: woodpeckers in the trees, deer in the forest and people dozing in the sunshine; a truly wonderful place.

Listings

Airlines Aer Lingus, Döbelnsgatan 40 (☎020/79 52 51); Aeroflot, Sveavägen 31 (☎08/21 70 07); Air France, Norrmalmstorg 16 (☎08/679 88 55); Air New Zealand, Kungsbron 1G (☎08/21 91 80); American Airlines, Nybrogatan 3 (☎08/24 61 45); Braathens Malmö Aviation (at Arlanda airport ☎08/797 61 00; at Bromma airport ☎08/797 68 74); British Airways, Hamngatan 11 (☎08/679 78 00); Cathay Pacific, at Arlanda airport (☎08/797 85 80); Delta Airlines, Kungsgatan 18 (☎08/796 96 00); Finnair, Norrmalmstorg 1 (☎08/679 93 30); Icelandair, Kungstensgatan 38 (☎08/690 98 00); KLM and Northwest at Arlanda airport (☎08/590 799 10); Lufthansa, Norrmalmstorg 1 (☎08/614 15 50); Qantas, Kungsgatan 64 (☎08/24 25 02); SAS, Stureplan 8 (international ☎020/72 75 55; domestic ☎020/72 70 00); Singapore Airlines, Grev Turegatan 10 (☎08/611 71 31); United Airlines, Kungsgatan 3 (☎08/678 15 70).

Airports Arlanda airport (airport enquiries ☎08/797 61 00; enquiries about SAS domestic flights from Arlanda on ☎08/797 50 50); Bromma airport (☎08/797 68 00); Skavsta airport (☎0155/28 04 00).

American Express Birger Jarlsgatan 1 (Mon–Fri 9am–5pm; ☎08/679 78 80).

Banks and exchange Banks are generally open later in central Stockholm than in the rest of the country: typical hours are Mon–Fri 9.30am–3pm, though some stay open until 5.30pm; the bank at Arlanda airport is open even longer hours, and there's a cash machine in the departures hall. Forex exchange offices offer better value than the banks and are located in the main hall at Central Station (☎08/411 67 34) and downstairs in T-Centralen (☎08/24 46 02); at Cityterminalen (☎08/21 42 80); at Vasagatan 14 (☎08/10 49 90); in Sverigehuset (☎08/20 03 89); and at Arlanda airport's Terminal 2 (☎08/593 622 71). Also try Valutaspecialisten at Kungsgatan 30 (☎08/10 30 00) and at Arlanda Terminal 5 (☎08/797 85 57).

Beaches City beaches are Långholmens Strandbad and Klippbad on Långholmen – T-bana Hornstull; Smedsudden on Kungsholmen – bus #62 from Central Station towards Fredhäll, get off at Västerbroplan; Hellasgården lake in Nacka (an eastern suburb of Stockholm) – bus #401 from Slussen; Saltsjöbaden – take the Saltsjöbanan train from Slussen. There are also good sandy beaches in the archipelago on the island of Grinda (see p.102) – boats from Strömkajen.

Bookshops English-language books are available at Akademibokhandeln, corner of Regeringsgatan & Mäster Samuelsgatan; Aspingtons second-hand bookshop, Västerlånggatan 54; Hedengrens Bokhandel, Sturegallerian, Stureplan 4; Sweden Bookshop, Sverigehuset, Hamngatan 27.

Buses For SL bus information see "SL travel information" below; for long-distance bus information call Swebus Express (☎0200/218 218, *www.express.swebus.se*) or Svenska Buss (☎020/67 67 67) or visit Busstop (a travel agent specializing in bus tickets) inside the Cityterminalen (Mon–Fri 9am–6pm, Sat 9am–4pm, Sun 11am–6pm) for tickets and information on domestic and international services.

Car breakdown recovery Larmtjänst (☎020/22 00 00).

Car rental Avis, Vasagatan 10B, and at Arlanda and Bromma airports (☎020/78 82 00); Budget, Klarabergsviadukten 92 (☎08/411 15 00) and at Arlanda airport (☎08/797 84 70); Europcar, Medborgarplatsen 25 and at Arlanda airport (☎020/78 11 80); Eurodollar/Holiday Autos, Klarabergsgatan 33 (☎08/24 26 55); Hertz, Vasagatan 26 and at Arlanda airport (☎020/211 211); (see above); also a desk at Arlanda airport; Statoil, service stations throughout Stockholm (information only on ☎08/669 24 45).

Dental problems Emergency dental care at St Eriks Hospital, Fleminggatan 22; daily 8am–8.30pm. Out of hours ring the duty dentist at the hospital (☎08/463 91 00).

Doctor Tourists can get emergency outpatient care at the hospital for the district they are staying in; check with the 24hr medical advice line (☎08/463 91 00).

Embassies and consulates Australia, Sergels Torg 12 (☎08/613 29 00); Canada, Tegelbacken 4 (☎08/453 30 00); Ireland, Östermalmsgatan 97 (☎08/661 80 05); New Zealand – use the Australian Embassy; UK, Skarpögatan 6–8 (☎08/671 90 00); US, Strandvägen 101 (☎08/783 53 00).

Emergencies Ring ☎112 for police, ambulance or fire services.

Ferries To Finland: Silja Line, Stureplan or Värtahamnen (☎08/22 21 40); and Viking Line, Resebutik inside the Cityterminalen (Mon–Sat 8am–7pm, Sun noon–7pm) and Stadsgårdsterminalen (all bookings on ☎08/452 40 00). To Estonia: Estline, Frihamnen (☎08/667 00 01). To the Stockholm archipelago: Waxholms Ångfartygs AB, Strömkajen (☎08/679 58 30).

Laundry Self-service launderette at Västmannagatan 61; or try the youth hostels.

Left luggage There are lockers at Central Station, the Cityterminalen bus station and the Silja and Viking ferry terminals. Central Station also has a left-luggage office (☎08/762 25 49). All these places charge around 20kr a day to store your baggage.

Lost property Offices at Central Station (☎08/762 20 00); Police, Bergsgatan 39 (☎08/401 07 88); SL, Rådmansgatan T-bana station, Mon–Fri 10am–5pm (☎08/736 07 80).

Newspapers Buy them at kiosks in Central Station, Cityterminalen or at the Press Center which has branches in the Gallerian shopping centre on Hamngatan and also at Sveavägen 52. Read them for free at Stadsbiblioteket (City Library), Sveavägen 73, or at Kulturhuset, Sergels Torg.

Pharmacy 24-hour service at C. W. Scheele, Klarabergsgatan 64 (☎08/454 81 30).

Police Headquarters at Agnegatan 33–37, Kungsholmen (☎08/401 00 00), but the main city-centre stations is at Bryggargatan 19, near the train station.

Post office Most useful office is in the Central Station (Mon–Fri 7am–10pm, Sat & Sun 10am–7pm). Poste restante mail can be addressed to any post office; you'll need to show your passport when collecting your letters.

SL travel information Bus, T-bana and regional train (Pendeltåg) information on ☎08/600 10 00. SL Centers at Sergels Torg, Mon–Fri 7am–6.30pm, Sat & Sun 10am–5pm; Slussen Mon–Fri 7am–6pm, Sat 10am–1pm; Gullmarsplan (Södermalm) Mon–Thurs 7am–6.30pm, Fri 7am–6pm, Sat 10am–5pm; Tekniska Högskolan, Mon–Fri 7am–6.30pm, Sat 10am–5pm; Fridhemsplan (Kungsholmen) Mon–Fri 7am–6.30pm, Sat 10am–5pm.

STF They supply information (by telephone only, on ☎08/463 21 00) on Sweden's youth hostels, mountain huts and hiking trails.

Swimming pools Outdoors at Vilda Vandis, in Vanadislunden park, Sveavägen, and at Eriksdalbadet, Eriksdalslunden, Södermalm. Indoors at Forsgrénskabadet, Medborgarplatsen 2–4; Centralbadet, Drottninggatan 88; Storkyrkobadet, at Svartmangatan 20–22 in Gamla Stan; Sturebadet, inside Sturegallerian shopping centre, Stureplan; and at Liljeholmsbadet, Bergsunds Strand, Liljeholmen, where there's nude male-only swimming sessions on Fri, women-only Mon; non-nude mixed sessions Tues–Thurs and Sat.

Systembolaget Norrmalm: Klarabergsgatan 62; Sveavägen 66. Gamla Stan: Lilla Nygatan 18. Södermalm: Folkungagatan 56 & 101.

Train information Tickets and information for domestic and international routes with SJ (Swedish State Railways) on ☎020/75 75 75; from abroad ring ☎08/696 75 40.

Travel agents KILROY travels, Kungsgatan 4 (☎08/23 45 15), for discounted rail and air tickets and ISIC cards; Ticket, at Kungsgatan 60 (☎08/24 00 90), Sturegatan 8 (☎08/611 50 20) and Sveavägen 42 (☎08/24 92 20); Transalpinó, at Wasteels resor, Stora Nygatan 37 (☎08/411 22 33). For cheap flights, it's also worth checking the travel section of the main *Dagens Nyheter* newspaper.

AROUND STOCKHOLM

Such are Stockholm's attractions that it's easy to overlook the city's surroundings, yet if you did so you'd be missing some of the country's most fascinating sights, like **Drottningholm**, Sweden's greatest royal palace. Further out is the little village of **Mariefred**, containing Sweden's other great castle, **Gripsholm** – like Drottningholm, accessible by a fine boat ride on the waters of Lake Mälaren. So too is the Viking island of **Birka**, with its magnificent archeological remains of Viking dwellings. The university town of **Uppsala** and Stockholm's stunning **archipelago** can, in principle, be visited on day-trips, though these places really merit a longer stay.

Stockholm Cards or Tourist Cards are not valid on the enjoyable boat services to Drottningholm or in the archipelago, but they can be used on the bus, T-bana and regional train services within Greater Stockholm, which helps cut travel costs for at least part of some journeys. With either card, the cheapest way to get to Uppsala is by regional train from Central Station – both cards are valid as far as Märsta, where the train terminates; there you'll have to change trains and buy a ticket for the remaining part of the journey. There's also a summer boat service to Uppsala, stopping at medieval **Sigtuna** and the Baroque castle at **Skokloster** on the way. Boats to Mariefred and Drottningholm leave from Stadshusbron.

West of the city: Drottningholm and Birka

Even if your time in Stockholm is limited, try not to miss the harmonious royal palace of **Drottningholm** (May–Aug daily 10am–4.30pm; Sept daily noon–3.30pm; 50kr). The finest way to reach the place is by **ferry**, which leaves daily every half-hour from Stadshusbron on Kungsholmen, taking just under an hour each way (60kr one-way; 85kr return); or take the T-bana to Brommaplan and then buses #177, #301–323, #336 or #338 from there – a less thrilling ride, but covered by the Stockholm Card or the Tourist Card.

Beautifully located on the shores of leafy **Lövön**, an island 11km west of the centre, Drottningholm is perhaps the greatest achievement of the two architects

Tessin, father and son. Work began in 1662 on the orders of King Karl X's widow, Eleonora, with Tessin the Elder modelling the new palace in a thoroughly French style – giving rise to the stock comparisons with Versailles. Apart from anything else, it's considerably smaller than its French contemporary, utilizing false perspective and trompe l'oeil to bolster the elegant, though rather narrow, interior. On Tessin the Elder's death in 1681, the palace was completed by his son, then already at work on Stockholm's Royal Palace.

Inside, good English notes are available to help you sort out each room's detail, a riot of Rococo decoration largely dating from the time when Drottningholm was bestowed as a wedding gift on Princess Louisa Ulrika (a sister of Frederick the Great of Prussia). No hints, however, are needed to spot the influences in the Baroque "French", and the later "English", **gardens** that back onto the palace. Since 1981, the Swedish royal family has slummed it out at Drottningholm, using it as a permanent home. This move has accelerated efforts to restore parts of the palace to their original appearance, so much so that the monumental **grand staircase** is now once again exactly as envisaged by Tessin the Elder. Another sight worth visiting is the **Court Theatre** (Slottsteater), nearby in the palace grounds (May–Sept mandatory guided tours 11.30am–4.30pm hourly; 50kr). It dates from 1766, but its heyday was a decade later, when Gustav III imported French plays and theatrical companies, making Drottningholm the centre of Swedish artistic life. Take the guided tour and you'll get a florid but accurate account of the theatre's decoration: money to complete the building ran out in the eighteenth century, meaning that things are not what they seem – painted papier-mâché frontages are *krona*-pinching substitutes for the real thing. The original backdrops and stage machinery are still in place, though, and the tour comes complete with a display of eighteenth-century special effects: wind and thunder machines, trapdoors and simulated lighting. Also within the extensive palace grounds is a **Chinese Pavilion** (50kr), a sort of eighteenth-century royal summer house.

You might be lucky enough to catch a **performance** of drama, ballet or opera here (usually June–Aug). The cheapest **tickets** cost around 100kr, though decent seats are more in the region of 300kr – check the schedule at Drottningholm or ask at the tourist offices in the city.

Further into Lake Mälaren: Birka

Björkö (the name means "island of birches"), in Lake Mälaren, is known for its rich flora, good beaches, ample swimming opportunities, and most of all, **BIRKA**, which is on the UNESCO World Heritage List. Sweden's oldest town (founded in around 750AD), Birka was once a Viking trading centre, at its height during the tenth century. A few obvious remains lie scattered about, including the remnants of houses and a vast cemetery. Major excavations began here in 1990 and a museum, named **Birka the Viking Town** (May to mid-Sept daily 10am–5pm; 200kr including boat trip here from Stockholm, otherwise 50kr) now displays historical artefacts as well as scale models of the harbour and craftsmen's quarters.

In Viking times, Björkö was actually two separate islands, with the main settlement located in the northwest corner of the one further north. As the land rose after the last Ice Age, the narrow channel between the two islands vanished, resulting in today's single kidney-shaped island; remains of jetties have been found where the channel would have been, as well as a rampart which acted as an outer wall for the settlement. It's reckoned that, from the eighth to the late tenth century, the population here was around a thousand, the inhabitants living a relatively properous life. The developed nature of their society is evident from modern finds: scissors, pottery and even keys have all been excavated. Among the remains of Viking-age life, the most striking is Birka's graveyard, which can be found outside the rampart; turn right from where the boat arrives and you'll come across around four hundred burial mounds, some with standing stones. A fort complete with earth ramparts was located at the island's highest point; today the rampart is still visible.

To get to Björkö, take the Strömma Kanalbolaget boat from Stadshusbron on Kungsholmen (May to late Sept daily 10am, return trip from Birka at 3.45pm); you buy your ticket on board. Unfortunately, you can't get to the island from Drottningholm without going back into Stockholm.

The archipelago

If you arrived in Stockholm by ferry from Finland or Estonia, you'll already have had a tantalizing glimpse of the **Stockholm archipelago**. In Swedish the word for archipelago is *skärgården* (pronounced "share-gord-en") – literally "garden of skerries" and a pretty accurate description: the array of hundreds upon hundreds of pine-clad islands and islets is the only one of its kind in the world. Most of the islands are flat and therefore wonderful places for **walking**; we've suggested a few routes which aren't meant to take you to any particular destination, but are the best way to take in the sweeping sea vistas and unspoilt nature here.

The archipelago can be split geographically into three distinct sections. In the inner archipelago, there's more land than sea; in the centre, it's pretty much fifty-fifty; and in the outer archipelago, distances between islands are much greater, such that sea and sky seem to merge into one, and the nearest island is often no more than a dot on the horizon. From November to April, life in the archipelago can be tough, with the winter ice stretching far out into the Baltic, throwing the boat timetables into confusion. But in summer the archipelago is at its best: the air is heavy with the scent of fresh pine, and seemingly endless forests are reflected in the deep blue of the sea. It's worth bearing in mind that when it's cloudy in Stockholm, chances are the sun is shining somewhere out in the islands. Of the vast number of islands in the archipelago, several are firm favourites with Stockholmers, notably **Vaxholm**; others offer more secluded beaches and plenty of opportunity for walking amid beautiful surroundings.

Travel practicalities

Getting to the islands is easy and cheap, with Waxholmsbolaget operating the majority of sailings into the archipelago. Most boats leave from Strömkajen in front of the *Grand Hotel* and the National Museum; others leave from just round the corner at Nybroplan, next to the Kungliga Dramatiska Teatern (see p.79). The boats usually have a cafeteria or restaurant on board. Tickets are very reasonable, ranging from 20kr to 80kr depending on the length of the journey, and can be bought on the boat or from the Waxholmsbolaget office on Strömkajen. If you're planning to visit several islands, it might be worth buying the **Båtluffarkort** (Interskerries Card; 275kr), which gives sixteen days' unlimited travel on all

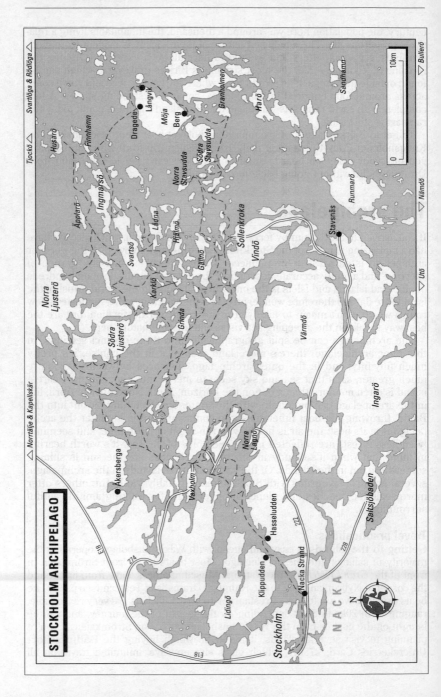

Waxholmbolaget lines. Alternatively, if you've already got an SL monthly travel card (see p.64), buy a supplementary **Waxholm card**, which gives you one month's free travel anywhere in the archipelago.

When boarding the boat, you'll be asked where you're heading for, as the boats don't stop at every island unless people want to get on or off there. If you're waiting for the boat out in the archipelago, you must raise the semaphore flag on the jetty to indicate that you want to be picked up; torches are kept in the huts on the jetties for the same purpose at night. **Departures** to the closest islands (around 4 daily) are more frequent than those to the outer archipelago; if there's no direct service, connections can often be made on the island of Vaxholm. In the **timetables** (free; available from the Waxholmsbolaget office, and sailing times are also posted on every jetty), the archipelago is divided into three sections: *norra* (northern), *mellersta* (central) and *södra* (southern); we have adopted these for our own coverage of the islands. The central section is easiest to reach from Stockholm.

In some parts of the archipelago, you'll be able to **row** across to nearby islands; for this purpose, there'll be a rowing boat either side of the water separating you from your destination. When you use the boats, you have to ensure there's always one left on either side – this entails rowing across, attaching the other boat to yours, rowing back to your starting point, where you leave one boat behind, and then rowing across one last time.

Accommodation

Though there are few hotels in the archipelago, it does have plenty of well-equipped and comfortable **youth hostels**, all of which are open in the summer; in our accounts of individual islands we mention any hostels they have. It's worth noting that there are several mainland hostels usefully located at points where boats sail for the archipelago: at **Kappelskär** (☎0176/441 69; 120kr), a good base from which to reach Tjockö in the northern archipelago; at **Nynäshamn** (☎08/520 208 34; 125kr), for the southern island of Utö; at **Skeppsmyra**, for Arholma (☎0176/940 27; 130kr); and **Kappelskär**, for Tjockö (☎0176/441 69; 120kr).

It's also possible to rent summer **cottages** on the islands for around 200kr per person per night or 1000–1500kr a week for four people – for more information on prices, contact the tourist office in Stockholm, where you can also pick up their *Bed & Breakfast in Stockholm's Archipelago* brochure. For longer stays, you'll need to book well in advance – at least six months before – or you may well find that you've been pipped to the post by holidaying Swedes.

Though **campsites** are surprisingly hard to find, you'll be fine camping rough – a few nights' stay here and there won't cause any problems. Remember though that open fires are prohibited all over the archipelago.

The central archipelago

The island of **Vaxholm** lies only an hour from the capital by boat, and is a popular weekend destination for Stockholmers. Its eponymous town has an atmospheric wooden harbour, whose imposing fortress once guarded the waterways into the city, superseding the fortifications at Riddarholmen. Successfully staving off attacks from Danes and Russians in the seventeenth and eighteenth centuries, the fortress nowadays is an unremarkable museum of military bits and pieces (June–Aug daily noon–4pm; 30kr).

Another firm favourite, though a much-overrated destination, is **Grinda** (2hr 30min from Stockholm by boat), a thickly wooded island typical of the central archipelago, with some sandy beaches. It's particularly popular with families and so can be busy, particularly at weekends. In its favour, Grinda has frequent **boat connections**, several ad-hoc **campsites**, a restaurant and a café in the centre of the island. To enjoy the sunshine on summer afternoons, head for beaches on the southern side of the island, as the tall trees on the northern side block out the sun. Boats dock at two jetties on the island, at its southern and northern ends; a walk between the two takes thirty to forty minutes.

Gällno and Karklö

A beautiful low-lying island covered with thick pine forest, **Gällnö** is the archipelago at its best. Home to just thirty people, a couple of whom farm the land near the jetty, the island has been designated a nature reserve: here you'll be able to spot deer in the forest or watch eider ducks diving for fish. It takes around two hours to get here from Stockholm. The idyllic **youth hostel** (☎08/571 661 17; 120kr; May–Sept), surrounded by low-hanging trees, is easy enough to find; the track leading to it is well signposted from the tiny main village, where there's also a small **shop** selling provisions. From here, there's the choice of two **walks**: either head east through the forest for Gällnönäs, from where you can pick up boats either back to Stockholm or further out into the islands, or alternatively, continue past the youth hostel, following signs for Brännholmen, till you arrive at a small bay popular with yachties. Now look for the hut where the toilet is, as one of its walls bears a map and sign on the outside showing the path leading from here to the rowing boats – these enable you to cross the narrow sound separating Gällnö from its neighbour, Karklö. When you head across, remember to leave one boat on either side of the sound (see p.101).

Karklö is one of the most unspoilt islands in the archipelago and, combined with Gällnö, makes for an excellent day-trip from Stockholm. There are no roads here, only tracks; these meander across the island and around farmers' fields, connecting the spot where the rowing boats are moored with the main jetty on the other side, where the boats from Stockholm dock. The paths can be difficult to find at times, so it's best to ask directions in the main village, which is close to the rowing boat moorings.

Svartsö

North of Gällno, **Svartsö** lies in what's considered to be the most stunning part of the whole archipelago. Known for its fields of grazing sheep, thick virgin forest and crystal-clear lakes, Svartsö has good roads, making the island ideal for cycling or walking. From the northern jetty, where most boats from Stockholm arrive, there's a pleasant walk, lasting about ninety minutes, which first takes you on the road towards the two lakes in the centre of the island. Just before you arrive at the lakes, turn right into the path that follows the lakeside, passing a few houses on the way. The road then becomes a track which heads into the forest. Continue past a couple of hayfields in a forest clearing, and eventually you'll glimpse the sea through the trees at the forest edge; this is an ideal place to sunbathe or stop for a picnic. Past a farmhouse and a couple of barns, the track eventually turns into a road again; from here it's another twenty- to thirty-minute walk to the village of **Alsvik**, with its shop, post office and ferry connections back to the capital (2hr).

Ingmarsö and Finnhamn

Ingmarsö is an excellent island for walkers. From the northern jetty, where most boats from Stockholm dock, you can do an enjoyable roundabout walk that takes you across the island and on to neighboring Finnhamn, where you can catch a boat back. You start by follow the main road away from the northern jetty; after about fifteen minutes, turn left at the signpost marked "Båtdraget and Femsund". The road to Femsund eventually turns into a track, marked by blue dots on tree trunks, which strikes out through the forest heading for Kålmårsön. After about an hour, the path skirts a wonderfully isolated lake, where you can swim and sunbathe, before passing through more unspoilt forest and emerging at a small bay filled with yachts. Look carefully here for the continuation of the path – still marked with blue dots – which will take you to rowing-boat moorings at the narrow sound between here and neighbouring Finnhamn. If you fail to locate the path, follow the coast round to the right for roughly ten to fifteen minutes while facing the yachts in the bay. It takes about two-and-a-half hours to get to the sound from the northern jetty, during which time you'll pass just one or two houses. Row over to **Finnhamn**, remembering to leave one rowing boat on either side of the sound (see p.101). A tiny island, Finnhamn is often busy because of its popular **youth hostel** (☎08/542 462 12; 140kr), a dramatically located yellow building perched on rocks looking out to sea, and complete with waterfront sauna. To walk from the rowing-boat moorings to the main jetty and the youth hostel takes around forty minutes; the journey time back to Stockholm is around three hours. If the crowds are too much here, head southeast from Finnhamn's tiny main village for the islet of Lilla Jolpan, where there are some good bathing opportunities.

Möja

One of the most popular islands to visit, **Möja** (roughly pronounced "Murr-ya") is home to around three hundred people, who make their living from fishing and farming. There's a small craft museum in the main town, **Berg**, and even a cinema, shop, post office and **restaurant**. A pleasant afternoon can be spent here doing an easy six-kilometre walk from the main ferry jetty, named Berg, where you should disembark when arriving from Stockholm. The walk takes you along the well-made road to the tiny settlement of **Långvik** in the north of the island, and gives you a chance to have a peep at some of the wooden cottages and well-tended gardens that help to keep people busy here. Just before Långvik, itself nothing more than a few houses grouped around a tiny harbour, a well-trodden path heads left into the forest, past a small store that sells bread, and on to **Dragede**, a cluster of a dozen or so wooden cottages romantically situated deep in the forest. It should take you about twenty minutes to arrive here from Långvik; once at Dragede you can catch a boat for Stockholm via Berg (journey time 3hr 30min).

Norrtälje, Grisslehamn and the northern archipelago

Heading for the northern islands, there's a fair chance you'll end up changing buses in the mainland town of **NORRTÄLJE**, where there's a tourist office at Lilla Torget (June to mid-Aug Mon–Fri 9.30am–7pm, Sat 9.30am–5pm, Sun 11am–5pm; mid-Aug to May Mon–Fri 9am–5pm; ☎0176/719 90). It's worth a quick look round between buses – this is an old spa town and capital of the Roslagen district, with a quirky cartoon museum and a separate regional museum (July & Aug daily noon–4pm; 15kr), housed in an old gun factory in the centre of town. Norrtälje is also a handy jumping-off point for trips to **GRISSLEHAMN** in the north, a small fishing village where you'll find the pretty home of the early-twentieth-century writer and artist Albert Engström, with paintings and knick-knacks displayed inside. Note that there are **ferry connections** from Grisslehamn to Eckerö on the Finnish Åland islands (3–5 daily; 2hr; 80kr one-way).

Close to the mainland is **Tjockö**, an island where life is much as it was decades ago. A wonderful little place with forests, meadows and open fields, Tjockö also has a good sandy beach, as well as smooth rocks that make for an ideal spot to soak up the sun. To get here, take bus #640 or #644 from Tekniska Högskolan T-bana to Norrtälje, then bus #631 to Rafsnäs, from where it's a ten-minute boat trip.

To the south, and much further out towards Finland, are Svartlöga and Rödlöga. **Svartlöga** is the only island in the archipelago whose forest is totally deciduous, and was one of the few to escape Russian incursions in 1719, during the Great Northern War. There are several good rocky beaches on which to relax after your long journey here. Neighbouring **Rödlöga** is a much tinier red-granite affair, with no roads, just leafy paths; overgrown hedgerows, thick with wild roses; and wonderful secluded beaches. The boat journey time is four hours from Stockholm, or ninety minutes from Furusund, a coastal town which is reached on bus #635 from Tekniska Högskolan T-bana.

Arholma

One of the most northerly islands in the Stockholm archipelago, **Arholma** was the scene of a dramatic confrontation with Russia in July 1719, when thirty Russian warships carrying five thousand men appeared on the horizon here. Their arrival was part of a strategic campaign mounted by the Czar, Peter the Great, to force Sweden to accept Russian dominance of the Baltic. As the terrified islanders fled to the mainland, their farms were set ablaze and animals slaughtered by the invading Russian forces. Today, Arholma is a working agricultural island, the countryside characterized not by forest, as with many other islands hereabouts, but by farmers' fields, the result of centuries of farming tradition. Other than the eighteenth century lighthouse to the east of the jetty served by boats to and from Stockholm, there's little else to see on the island; the main attraction is simply wandering around the country lanes and enjoying the tranquil setting.

A couple of minutes' stroll from the jetty is the **youth hostel** (☎0176/560 18; 110kr; advance booking required), located where the track from the jetty meets Arholma's main road. There's also a simple **campsite** in the tiny bay to the north of the jetty. The best **swimming** can be had south of the youth hostel in another tiny unnamed bay reached by following the main road south to the narrow inlet which marks the beginning of the Granö peninsula; from here, take the small road to the right which then becomes a track as it heads west to the sea. There are direct boats from Stockholm to Arholma (4hr).

The southern archipelago

In the southern stretch of the archipelago, **Bullerö** (three hours from Stockholm) is about as far out as you can go in the archipelago. This beautiful island is a nature reserve, with walking trails. To get here, take the Saltsjöbanan train from Slussen station to Saltsjöbaden, from where boats leave for the island of Nämdö; change at the Idöborg jetty on Nämdö for a shuttle service to Bullerö.

With its fine harbour, **Sandhamn** has been a destination for seafarers since the eighteenth century and remains so today, attracting large numbers of yachts of all shapes and sizes. The main village is a haven of narrow alleyways, winding streets and overgrown verandahs. The boat journey time is three-and-a-half hours from Stockholm; quicker by a couple of hours is to get bus #434 to Sollenkroka or Stavsnäs, from where you can get a boat to Sandhamn.

Fjärdlång was closely linked for a time with businessman Ernest Thiel, who established the Thiel Gallery on Djurgården in Stockholm. Inspired by his friend, Bruno Liljefors who once bought nearby Bullerö, Thiel purchased Fjärdlång (or Fjällång as the islanders call it) in 1909 and built a large and well-appointed villa on the island as his new residence. Today the building has been converted into a top-notch **youth hostel** (☎08/510 560 92; 110kr; early June to late Sept), which is next to the jetty where boats from Stockholm put in. Although the trees stretch down to the water's edge, rendering the island not suitable for bathing, Fjärdlång is an ideal place to commune undisturbed with nature, lying as it does on the very eastern edge of the archipelago and offering superb views of the surrounding skerries of the Baltic. To get here, either take the boat from Stockholm or pick up the train from Slussen to Saltsjöbaden and catch a boat there (journey times 3hr and 2hr respectively).

Lying far out in the southern reaches of the archipelago, **Utö** is flat and thus ideal for cycling around; it's not bad for bathing and picnics either. There are excellent views to be had from the island's windmill, on a hill, Kvarnbacken, a ten-minute walk southwest of the jetty. It takes three hours to get here by boat from Stockholm; alternatively you can get the Pendeltåg to Västerhaninge and get the boat from nearby Årsta Havsbad (1hr). The **youth hostel** is near where the ferry docks (☎08/501 576 60; 140kr).

Around Lake Mälaren

Freshwater **Lake Mälaren** dominates the countryside west of Stockholm and provides the backdrop to some of the capital region's most appealing destinations – all suitable for day trips. Frequent **train services** run to **Västerås**, a modern and thoroughly enjoyable city on the northern shore of the lake, about an hour from Stockholm, as well as to **Eskilstuna** on the southern shoreline, the town a showcase of Sweden's industrial prowess. Closer to Stockholm, however, it's the enchanting lakeside village of **Mariefred** that really steals the show with its magnificent castle, **Gripsholm**. Trains link these three places, making it possible to complete a circuit around the lake without having to return to Stockholm.

Mariefred and Gripsholm

If you've only got time for one boat trip outside Stockholm, make it to **MARIEFRED**, a tiny village about an hour west of the city, whose own peaceful attractions are bolstered by one of Sweden's most enjoyable castles. Its Swedish name derived from that of an old monastery, Pax Mariae ("Mary's Peace"), Mariefred is as quiet, and quintessentially Swedish, as such villages come. A couple of minutes up from the quayside and you're strolling through narrow streets, whose well-kept wooden houses and little squares haven't changed much in decades. The water and enveloping greenery make for a leisurely stroll around: if you call in at the central **Rådhus**, a fine eighteenth-century timber building, you can pick up a map from the **tourist office** inside.

Steam-train fans will love the **Railway Museum** in the village – you'll probably have noticed the narrow-gauge tracks running all the way to the quayside. There's an exhibition of old rolling stock and workshops, given added interest by the fact that narrow-gauge **steam trains** still run between Mariefred and **Läggesta**, a twenty-minute ride away. These trains leave Mariefred roughly hourly between 11am and 5pm (May & Sept Sat & Sun; mid-June to mid-Aug daily; ☎0159/210 06; 36kr return; half-price for children and rail-pass holders). From Läggesta, it's possible to pick up the regular SJ train back to Stockholm; check for connections on the timetable at the Mariefred tourist office. Of course, you could always come to Mariefred from Stockholm by this route too (see "Practicalities", below).

Gripsholms slott

Lovely though the village is, touring around it is really only a preface to seeing **Gripsholms slott**, the imposing red-brick castle built on a round island just to the south (April & Sept Tues–Sun 10am–3pm; May–Aug daily 10am–4pm; Oct–March Sat & Sun noon–3pm; 50kr). Walk up the quayside, and you'll be able to see the path to the castle running across the grass by the water's edge.

In the late fourteenth century, Bo Johnsson Grip, the Swedish High Chancellor, began to build a fortified castle at Mariefred, although the present building owes more to two Gustavs – Gustav Vasa, who started rebuilding in the sixteenth century, and Gustav III, who was responsible for major restructuring a couple of centuries later. Rather than the hybrid that might be expected, the result is rather pleasing – a textbook castle, whose turrets, great halls, corridors and battlements provide an engaging tour. There are guided tours (at noon and 2pm, not mandatory), on which the important bits and pieces here are pointed out: there's a vast portrait collection, which includes recently commissioned works depicting political and cultural figures as well as assorted royalty and nobility; some fine decorative and architectural work; and as at Drottningholm (see p.97), a private theatre, built for Gustav III. It's too delicate to be used for performances these days, but in summer, plays and other events are staged out in the castle grounds; more information can be obtained from Mariefred's tourist office.

Practicalities

To get here by public transport, take the Stockholm–Eskilstuna **train** to Läggesta (30min), from where connecting buses and, at certain times of year, steam trains (see above) shuttle passengers into Mariefred. In summer, you can even get here from Stockholm on a **steamboat**, the *S/S Mariefred*, which leaves from Klara Mälarstrand, near Stadshuset on Kungsholmen (mid-May to mid-June & mid-Aug to mid-Sept Sat & Sun 10am; mid-June to mid-Aug Tues–Sun 10am; 3hr 30min; 110kr one-way, 170kr return); buy your ticket on board. The **tourist office** is at the Rådhuset, the building with the large spire on top that's easily visible from the quay, a short walk away (daily: June–Aug Mon–Fri 10am–6pm; Sept 10am–4pm; ☎0159/297 90). You can ask here about **bike rental** (85kr per day; 400kr per week).

Mariefred warrants a night's stay, if not for the sights – which you can exhaust in half a day – then for the pretty, peaceful surroundings. There's only one **hotel**, *Gripsholms Värdhus*, Kyrkogatan 1 (☎0159/130 20, fax 109 74; ⑤), a beautifully restored inn (the oldest in Sweden) that's a wonderfully luxurious option, over-looking the castle and the water. The **youth hostel** is beyond the castle, in the Red Cross education centre (☎0159/361 00; 150kr, ③; mid-June to mid-Aug). Otherwise, ask in the tourist office about **rooms** in the village, which range from 150kr to 420kr per person per night. There are also six-person **cabins** (500kr), which you can rent at the tourist office.

As for **eating**, treat yourself to lunch in *Gripsholms Värdhus*. The food is excellent, and around 200kr will get you a turn at the herring table, a main course, a drink and coffee – all enhanced by the terrific views over to Gripsholm. Alternatively, try *Skänken* at the back of the *Värdhus*, where lunch goes for around 70kr. Another good spot is the classy *Strandrestaurangen* on the lakeside near the church, which serves up delicious fish dishes for 60kr; or there's the friendly but basic *Mariefreds Bistro* opposite the castle. For coffee and cakes, head for *Konditori Fredman* in the main square, opposite the town hall.

Eskilstuna and around

Around an hour west of Mariefred on the main train line from Stockholm, **ESKIL-STUNA** is a nasty industrial town known mostly for the precision tools and instruments manufactured here, but also for its higher-than-average incidence of violence and murders. Much is made of Eskilstuna's impressive industrial heritage in a series of fine **museums** based in and around the town's oldest houses, which date from the seventeenth century. In the **Radermachersmedjorna** museum, along Drottninggatan (Radermacher Forges; June–Aug daily 10am–4pm; Sept–May Tues–Fri 10am–4pm, Sat & Sun noon–3pm; free), smiths can be seen producing horseshoes and the like by traditional methods. Nearby, on an island reached by crossing the main Hamngatan and taking a narrow path over the river to Faktoriholmarna, is **Faktorimuséet** (Factory Museum; Tues–Sun 11am–4pm; free), which has three floors of displays about manufacturing processes, including several steam engines coaxed into life every Sunday between 1pm and 3pm. Next door is the dull **Vapentekniska Muséet** (Weapons Museum; June–Aug Tues–Sun 11am–4pm; Sept–May Tues, Sat & Sun 11am–4pm; free). To reach these museums from the train station, walk fifteen minutes down Drottninggatan and turn left. The tourist office is also out here (see "Practicalities", below).

A couple more museums can be found in the town centre. **Konstmuséet**, Kyrkogatan 9 (Art Museum; Tues–Sun noon–4pm; Thurs also 7–9pm; free) is worth a glance for its temporary exhibitions on the ground floor. On the first floor, there's a permanent collection of works of art from the seventeenth century onwards – look out for the thirty-odd paintings by local boy **Gustave Albert**. Born in Eskilstuna in 1866, he moved to France in 1891 and, heavily influenced by the Impressionist movement, become a respected and well-known artist by his death in 1905. In Sweden today he is still virtually unknown, but the museum is aiming to change all that by creating a special new exhibition on the artist's life.

Practicalities
Hourly **trains** leave from Stockholm's central station for Eskilstuna, whose **train station** is on Drottninggatan; east of here is the **bus station** at Kyrkogatan 20. The **tourist office** is in Munktellstorget, near the museums (June to late Aug Mon–Fri 9am–6pm, Sat & Sun 10am–4pm, Sept–May Mon–Thurs 9am–5pm, Fri

10am–5pm; ☎016/10 70 00, *www.eskilstuna.se*). For **accommodation**, the cheapest option is the **youth hostel** at *Vilsta Camping* (☎016/51 30 80; 130kr), a couple of kilometres south of the centre right by a nature reserve. To get there, turn right out of the station, head along Västermarksgatan to a roundabout, then right again onto Kyrkogatan, and follow the river until you come to the second bridge; the youth hostel is the other side of the river next to the open-air swimming pool. Of the central **hotels**, the cheapest is *City Hotell* at Drottninggatan 15 (☎016/13 74 25, fax 12 42 24; ⑤/②), but for greater luxury, try *Home Hotell*, Munktellstorget (☎016/13 76 90, fax 12 75 27; ⑤/③) or *Stadshotellet Best Western* at Hamngatan 9–11 (☎016/13 72 25, fax 12 75 88; ⑤/③).

The best **eating and drinking** places are concentrated in the central pedestrianized area. Popular with all ages, the best of the bunch is *Brasserie Oscar* at Kungsgatan 1, which has special student prices. Another brasserie-style restaurant-cum-bar with student discounts on food is *Perrongen*, nearby at Nybrogatan 1. For finer surroundings, check out *Restaurang Tingsgården* at Rådhustorget 2: the fish is particularly good, but the place is expensive. Greek food can be had at *Restaurang Akropolis* in Fristadstorget. For a good night's drinking there's *Oliver Twist*, a popular pub at Careliigatan 2; *Rolling Rock Café* in Fristadstorget and *Hamlet Pub Restaurang* at Teatergatan 1.

The Sigurd carving

Eleven kilometres north of town in a shady glade near **Sundbyholm**, the **Sigurd carving** is a thousand-year-old runic inscription running for 4m along a slab of stone. The runes are an epitaph for Sigrid, who built a bridge at the site; also on the stone are illustrations of scenes from the Icelandic epic poem, *Sigurd the Dragon Slayer*. To get here, take the #225 bus (5 daily; 19kr) from Eskilstuna's bus station – it passes very close to the stone. There's also excellent **swimming** to be had here in Lake Mälaren.

Västerås and around

Capital of the county of Västmanland and Sweden's sixth biggest city, **VÄSTERÅS** (pronounced Vest-er-ohs) is an immediately likeable mix of old and new, and frankly more worthy of your time and attention than nearby Eskilstuna. Today the lakeside city carefully balances its dependence on ABB, the industrial technology giant, with a rich history dating back to Viking times. If you're looking for a place that's lively and cosmopolitan, yet retains cobbled squares, picturesque wooden houses and even a sixth-century royal burial mound, you won't go far wrong here.

Arrival, information and accommodation

As the train pulls into Västerås, the first thing you'll notice is a sea of thousands of bicycles neatly standing in racks right outside the **train station** on Södra Ringvägen; arriving by **bus** you'll be dropped at the adjacent terminal. The **airport** is just 6km east of the city, from where **taxis** run to the centre (100kr). From the train station, the **tourist office** at Stora Gatan 40 is a ten-minute walk away (mid-June to mid-Aug Mon–Fri 9am–7pm, Sat 9am–3pm, Sun 10am–2pm; mid-Aug to mid-June Mon–Fri 9.30am–6pm, Sat 10am–2pm; ☎021/10 38 30, *www.vastmanland.se*), through Vasaparken towards the centre of town.

The **youth hostel** (☎021/18 52 30; 130kr; open all year), complete with sauna, is located at Lövudden, 5km west of the city on Lake Mälaren; take bus #25

(Mon–Sat roughly hourly, Sun restricted service) from the bus terminal. The following are some of the city's better **hotels**.

Aaros Metro, Vasagatan 22 (☎021/18 03 30, fax ☎18 03 37). The cheapest hotel in town and located right in the centre of the city. ③/②.

Arkad, Östermalmsgatan 25 (☎021/12 04 80, fax ☎83 00 50). New building done out in old-fashioned style. Good value for money in summer. ④/②.

Klipper, Kungsgatan 4 (☎021/41 00 00, fax ☎14 26 70). Centrally located, close to the charming Svartån river in the old town. Charming rooms and good service. ④/②.

Radisson SAS Plaza, Karlsgatan 9A (☎021/10 10 10, fax ☎10 10 91). Known locally as "the Skyscraper", this 25-storey glass-and-chrome structure is the last word in Scandinavian chic, and good value in summer. ⑤/③.

Stadshotellet, Stora Torget (☎021/10 28 00, fax ☎10 28 10). A Västerås fixture, the hotel has been here as long as anyone can remember. Good-quality modern rooms, right in the heart of the city. ⑤/③.

The City

From the tourist office, it's a short stroll up Köpmangatan to the twin cobbled squares of Bondtorget and Stora Torget. The slender lane from the southwestern corner of the square leads to the narrow **Svartån river**, which runs right through the centre of the city; the bridge over the river here (known as Apotekarbron) has great views of the old wooden cottages which nestle eave-to-eave along the riverside. Although it may not appear significant, the river was a decisive factor in making Västerås the headquarters of one of the world's largest engineering companies, Asea-Brown-Boveri (ABB); if you arrived by train from Stockholm you'll have passed their metallurgy and distribution centres on approaching the station. Back in the square, look out for the striking sculpture of a string of cyclists, the *Asea Stream*, which is supposed to portray the original workers of Asea as they made their way to work; today the sculpture is also a reminder of the impressive fact that Västerås has over 300km of cycle tracks and is a veritable haven for cyclists.

North of the two main squares, the brick **cathedral** (Mon–Fri 8am–5pm, Sat 9.30am–5pm, Sun 9.30am–7pm) dates from the thirteenth century, although its two outer aisles are formed from a number of chapels built around the existing church during the following two centuries. The original tower was destroyed by fire, leaving Nicodemus Tessin the Younger (who also built the Royal Palace in Stockholm, p.71) to design the current structure in 1693. The highly ornate gilded oak triptych, above the altar, was made in Antwerp and depicts the suffering and resurrection of Christ. Quite amazingly, the doors of the triptych can be opened further to display even more scenes. To the right of the altar lies the tomb of Erik XIV, who died an unceremonious death in Örbyhus castle in 1577 after eating his favourite pea soup – little did he realize it was laced with arsenic. Local rumour has it that the King's feet had to be cut off in order for his body to fit the coffin, which was built too small. Today though, his elegant, black-marble sarcophagus rests on a plinth of reddish sandstone from Öland. Beyond the cathedral is the most charming district of Västerås, **Kyrkbacken**, a hilly area which stretches just a few hundred metres. Here, steep cobblestone alleys wind between preserved old wooden houses where craftsmen and the petit bourgeoisie lived in the eighteenth century. Thankfully the area was saved from the great fire of 1714 — which destroyed much of the rest of the city – and the wholesale restructuring of the 1960s. The area's sleepy appearance today belies the fact that this was once the very centre of activity in the city, not least because it was here that the local students had their rooms. At the top end of Djäknegatan, the main street of the district, look for a narrow alley called Brunnsgränd, along which is a house bearing the sign "Mästermansgården": it was once the abode of the most hated and ostracized man in the entire district – the town executioner.

A quick walk past the restaurants and shops of Vasagatan will bring you back to Stora Gatan and eventually to the eye-catching modern **city hall** in Fiskatorget – the building is a far cry from the Dominican monastery which once stood on this spot. Although home to the city's administration, the building is best known for its 47 bells, the largest of which is known as The Monk and can be heard across the city at lunchtimes. Across the square, once home to a fish market, the old town hall has now been transformed into an **art museum** (Tues–Fri 5pm–8pm, Sat 11am–4pm, Sun noon–4pm; free) and might be worth a quick look for its contemporary collections of Swedish and other Nordic art – don't expect too much though. Continue across Slottsbron to the **castle**, today home to a dull collection of local paraphenalia inside the **county museum** (Tues–Sun noon–4pm; free). The best exhibit lies just inside the entrance: the most lavish female burial in Sweden, in the form of a Viking boat grave from nearby Tuna, Badelunda. The boat sat in clay for hundreds of years, which accounts for its remarkable state of preservation. The gold jewellery worn by the woman found in the boat dates from the Roman iron age, and is also on display.

Eating and drinking

Västerås easily has the best restaurants of any town around Lake Mälaren. Here, you'll find every sort of fare, from Thai to Greek, traditional Swedish to British-style pub food. The city also has a lively drinking scene – including one cocktail bar 23 floors up, from where there are unsurpassed views of the lake.

Atrium, corner of Smedjegatan and Sturegatan. Greek favourites from 125kr, starters from 32kr.

Bellman, Stora Torget 6. Very posh restaurant done out with eighteenth-century furniture and decor. Count on at least 150kr per dish.

Bill o Bob, Stora Torget 5. Handily located in the main square, with outdoor seating in summer. Usual meat and fish dishes, also salads; lunch from 65kr.

Bishops Arms, Östra Kyrkogatan. British-style pub with a large selection of beer and single malt whiskies. Age limit 23. Pub food also available.

Brogården, Stora Gatan 42 adjacent to the tourist office. Riverside café with good views of the water and old wooden houses.

Crille på hörnet, Stora Gatan 51. Definitely the best place hereabouts for traditional Swedish home cooking. Reckon on 100kr per dish.

Kalle på Spången, Kungsgatan 2. Great old-fashioned café with outdoor seating, close to the river. *The* place for coffee, cakes, grilled baguettes and fresh orange juice.

Karlsson på taket, Karlsgatan 9A. Chi-chi café-restaurant on the 23rd floor of the *Radisson SAS Plaza*. Expensive, but the views are fantastic.

Kina Thai, Gallerian 36. Next to the Filmstaden cinema. Usual Chinese and Thai dishes for around 100kr. Lunch for 59kr.

Möller Mat o Musik, Kungsgatan 4. Lunch for 59kr, tapas from 80kr. Restaurant which turns into a nightclub when evening comes.

Piazza di Spagna, Vasagatan 26 .The best pizzeria in town and a very popular place for lunch at 59kr. Pizzas from 67kr; pasta from 72kr; meat dishes start at 170kr.

Sky Bar, Karlsgatan 9A. On the 24th floor of the *Radisson SAS Plaza* hotel. Great cocktails and an unsurpassed view of the city. Light snacks also available.

Stadskällaren, Stora Torget. Smart restaurant with rough brick interior and windows looking out onto the square. Meat and fish dishes start at 150kr.

The Anundshög burial mound

Whilst in Västerås, try not to miss nearby **Anundshög**, the largest royal burial mound in Sweden, just 6km northeast of the city. Dating from the sixth century, the mound is thought to be the resting place of King Bröt-Anund and his stash of gold. Several other smaller burial mounds are located close by, suggesting that the site was an important Viking meeting place over several centuries. It's also known that Anundshög was additionally used for sessions of the local *ting*, or Viking parliament. Beside the main mound lie a large number of **standing stones** arranged end-to-end in the shape of two ships. The nearby **rune stone** dates from around 1000, its inscription reading "Folkvid erected all these stones for his son, Hedin, brother of Anund. Vred carved the runes". To get here, take **bus #12** from the centre of town to its final stop, Bjurhovda, from where it's a short walk of around 1km.

Trips on Lake Mälaren

It's easy to forget that Västerås is situated on Lake Mälaren, the centre of town being removed from from the waterfront. Yet it is very easy to get out onto the lake, with **boat trips** to Birka, Mariefred and even – via the nine locks of the Hjelmare canal – out to Örebro (see p.319). *M/S August Lindholm* sails from the Östra Hamnen, southeast of the train station, to **Birka** (mid-May to late August daily; 190kr) and **Mariefred** (late May to early June & late Aug Fri; 150kr). To **Örebro**, *M/S Nya Hjelmare Kanal* sails again from the Inner Harbour via its namesake canal (July to mid-Aug Tues; 6hr; 450kr one-way). More information from the boat operator (☎020/24 11 00, *www.strommakanalbolaget.com*), or the tourist office.

Listings

Airport 6km southwest of the city. Information on ☎021/80 01 60 or ☎80 11 00.

Banks FöreningsSparbanken, Hantverkargatan 5; Handelsbanken, Vasagatan 20A; Nordbanken, Stora Gatan 23; SEB, Vasagatan 12B.

Bike rental Available through the tourist office, Stora Gatan 40; ☎021/10 38 30.

Buses Operated by Västmanlands Lokaltrafik. Information on ☎0200/25 50 75 or *www.vl.se*.

Car rental Avis, at the airport, ☎021/80 01 88; Budget, Sjöhagsvägen 1, ☎021/14 39 27; Europcar, Kopparbergsvägen 47, ☎021/12 41 43; Hertz, Strömledningsgatan 11, ☎021/17 88 47.

Cinemas Filmstaden, Gallerian 34, opposite the *Radisson SAS Plaza*; Royal, Torggatan, close to Stora Torget.

Doctor Emergency service available by calling ☎021/17 30 00.

Ferries To Finland: Silja Line, at the corner of Torggatan and Smedjegatan, Mon–Fri 10am–6pm.

Left luggage Lockers available at the train station on Södra Ringvägen.

Newspapers Pressbyrån at the railway station.

Pharmacy Stora Gatan 34.

Police Västgötegatan 7 (☎021/15 20 00).

Post office Sturegatan 18.

Swimming In Lake Mälaren by the campsite at Lövudden. There's a sandy beach here, and you can rent pedal boats, windsurfing equipment and canoes.

Systembolaget Stora Gatan 48; Mon & Thurs 10am–6pm, Fri 9.30am–6pm.

Taxi Taxi Västerås (☎021/18 50 00); SAS Taxi (☎021/41 41 41); Taxi Direkt (☎021/12 22 22).

Trains Information on ☎020/75 75 75.

Travel agent Ticket, in Köpmangatan, next to the tourist office (Mon–Fri 9am–6pm, Sat 10am–2pm; ☎021/13 72 20).

Stockholm to Uppsala: Sigtuna and Skokloster

The medieval town of **SIGTUNA**, 40km north of Stockholm, makes an ideal destination for a day out. To reach Sigtuna from Stockholm, take the Pendeltåg to Märsta, from where **bus** #570 and #575 run the short distance to the town – total journey time is around an hour. In summer it's also possible to reach Sigtuna by **boat** from Stockholm (July to mid-Aug Tues–Sun; 2hr 30 min; single 90kr, return 140kr), services leaving Stadshusbron at 9.45am, returning from Sigtuna at 4.30pm.

Founded in 980, Sigtuna grew from a village to become Sweden's first town; fittingly, it contains Sweden's oldest street, Stora Gatan, and three **ruined churches**, dating from the twelfth century, which give a good idea of the important role the twon played in the Middle Ages. Two of these, the churches of **St Per** and **St Olof**, lie along Stora Gatan itself. Much of the west and central towers of St Per's still remain; experts believe it likely that the church functioned as a cathedral until the diocese was moved to nearby Uppsala. For its part, St Olof's has impressively thick walls and a short nave, the latter suggesting that the church was never completed. Close by is the very much functioning Mariakyrkan, containing several restored medieval paintings (daily: June–Aug 9am–5pm, Sept–May 9am–4pm; free). A number of rune stones can be seen close to the church of **St Lars** along Prästgatan, Sigtuna's third ruined church.

Having seen the churches, continue along the main road to the **museum** (June–Aug daily noon–4pm; Sept–May Tues–Sun noon–4pm; 20kr). Here you'll find archeological exhibitions on the town's history, including material on Sigtuna's past role as Sweden's foremost trading centre and its status as the first town in the land to mint coins.

Practicalities

Sigtuna's **tourist office** is at Stora Gatan 33 (June–Aug daily 9am–7pm; Sept–May Mon–Fri 9am–4pm; ☎08/592 500 20). Should you decide to stay, the best bet is the **youth hostel** at Manfred Björkquists allé 12 (☎08/592 584 78 or 592 582 00; 110kr; late June to mid-Aug), located at the bottom of the hill right by Lake Mälaren. There are a couple of places to **eat** located off the main street: *Tant Brun*, a café that specializes in home-made bread, at Laurenteegränd 3; and *Amandas Krug*, Långgränd 7, serving Swedish home cooking.

Skokloster

Leaving Sigtuna, you can continue by boat north to **Uppsala** (see p.113) via the seventeenth-century baroque castle at **Skokloster** (May–Aug mandatory guided tours, 11am–4pm; hourly; 60kr) with its collections of furniture, textiles, art and weapons. Boats leave Sigtuna for Skokloster at (July to mid-Aug), where you can change for the connecting boat to Uppsala; the total Stockholm–Uppsala fare is 230kr.

Uppsala and around

First impressions as the train pulls into **UPPSALA**, only an hour from Stockholm, are encouraging, as the red-washed castle looms up behind the railway sidings, the cathedral dominant in the foreground. A medieval seat of religion and learning, Uppsala clings to the past through its cathedral and university, and a striking succession of related buildings in their vicinity. The city is primarily regarded as the historical and religious centre of the country, and it's as a tranquil daytime alternative to Stockholm (and as a place with an active student-geared nightlife) that Uppsala draws the traveller.

Arrival, information and accommodation

Uppsala's **train** (several services an hour from Stockholm; 45min) and **bus stations** are adjacent to each other, separated only by an erotic statue of a man with an oversized penis by local sculptor and painter, Bror Hjorth (see p.116). It's a fifteen-minute walk down to the **tourist office** at Fyris Torg 8 (late June to mid-Aug Mon–Fri 10am–6pm, Sat 10am–3pm, Sun noon–4pm; mid-Aug to late June Mon–Fri 10am–6pm, Sat 10am–3pm; ☎018/27 48 00, *www.res.till.uppland.nu*), where you can pick up a handy English-language guide to the town. The **boats** from Skokloster, Sigtuna and Stockholm arrive and depart from the pier south of the centre, at the end of Bävernsgränd. Bus #801 runs between **Arlanda airport** and Uppsala bus station (daily; every 15–30min from 3.15am to midnight; 40min; 75kr).

Accommodation

Though it's so close to Stockholm, staying over in Uppsala can be an attractive idea. The youth hostel is at Sunnerstavägen (☎018/32 42 20; 160kr; May–Aug), 6km south of the centre at STF's beautifully sited *Sunnersta Herrgård* – take bus #20, #25 or #50 from Nybron, by Stora Torget. For a night's **camping**, head the few kilometres north to the open spaces of Gamla Uppsala (see p.116), or use the official campsite, *Sunnersta Camping*, at Graneberg, 7km out near the youth hostel (bus #20 from Nybron), offering two-person cabins by Lake Mälaren (☎018/27 60 84). Uppsala has a fair range of central **hotels** (see below), but the cheapest, *Hotell Årsta Gård*, is a bus-ride away in suburbia.

Basic, Kungsgatan 27 (☎ & fax 018/480 50 00). Simple, bright and clean rooms with en-suite bathroom and a tiny kitchen. Same price all year. ③.

Gillet, Dragarbrunnsgatan 23 (☎018/15 53 60, fax 15 33 80). A stone's throw from the cathedral but with run-of-the-mill, overpriced, rooms. Fans of kitsch should head for the restaurant. ⑤/③.

Grand Hotell Hörnan, Bangårdsgatan 1 (☎018/13 93 80, fax 12 03 11). A wonderfully elegant place with large old-fashioned rooms and restaurant. ④/②.

Linné, Skolgatan 45 (☎018/10 20 00, fax 13 75 97). Completely overpriced tiny rooms – a last resort when everything else is full. ⑤/③.

Provorbis Hotell Uplandia, Dragarbrunnsgatan 32 (☎018/10 21 60, fax 69 61 32). A modern hotel that's gone in for a lots of wood fittings – and small rooms. ⑤/③.

Svava, Bangårdsgatan 24 (☎018/13 00 30, fax 13 22 30). A newly built hotel with all mod cons, including specially designed rooms for people with disabilities and those with allergies. ⑤/③.

Årsta Gård, Jordgubbsgatan 14 (☎ & fax 018/25 35 00). This large cottage-style building in the outskirts is the cheapest hotel in town; take bus #7 daytimes or #56 evenings to Södra Årsta (15min). Same price all year. ②.

The City

A fifteen-minute walk west from the train station, the great **Domkyrkan** is Scandinavia's largest cathedral (daily 8am–6pm; free), and centre of the medieval town. Built as a Gothic boast to the people of Trondheim in Norway that even their mighty church could be overshadowed, it loses out to its rival by its building material – local brick rather than imported stone. Only the echoing interior remains impressive, particularly the French Gothic ambulatory, flanked by tiny chapels and bathed in a golden, decorative glow. One chapel contains a lively set of restored fourteenth-century wall paintings that recount the legend of Saint Erik, Sweden's patron saint: his coronation, subsequent crusade to Finland, eventual defeat and execution at the hands of the Danes. The Relics of Erik are zealously guarded in a chapel off the nave: poke around and you'll also find the tombs of the Reformation rebel Gustav Vasa and his son Johan III, and that of the botanist Linnaeus (see p.116), who lived in Uppsala. Time and fire have led to the

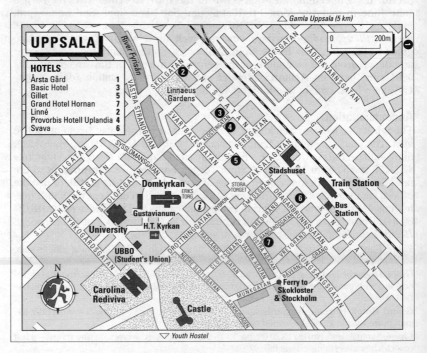

rest of the cathedral being rebuilt, scrubbed and painted to the extent that it resembles a historical museum more than a thirteenth-century spiritual centre; even the characteristic twin spires are late-nineteenth-century additions.

The other buildings grouped around the Domkyrkan can all claim a purer historical pedigree. Opposite the towers, the onion-domed **Gustavianum** was built in 1625 as part of the university (daily mid-May to mid-Sept 11am–4pm, Thurs till 7pm; mid-Sept to mid-May Wed–Sun 11am–4pm; 40kr), and is much touted by the tourist office for its **Augsburg Art Cabinet** – an ebony treasure chest presented to Gustav II Adolf – and its tidily preserved anatomical theatre. The same building houses a couple of small collections of Egyptian, Classical and Nordic antiquities with a small charge for each section.

The current **University** building (Mon–Fri 8am–4pm) is the imposing nineteenth-century Renaissance edifice opposite Gustavianum. Originally a seminary, today it's used for lectures and seminars and hosts the graduation ceremonies each May. Among the more famous alumni are Carl von Linné (Linnaeus) and Anders Celsius, inventor of the temperature scale. No one will mind you strolling in for a quick look, but to see the university properly, you'll need to join a **guided tour** (late June to late Aug daily noon & 2pm; 40kr).

A little way beyond the university is the **Carolina Rediviva** (Mon–Fri 9am–8pm, Sat 10am–4pm, Sun 11am–4pm; mid-May to mid-Sept 10kr, otherwise free), the university library and one of Scandinavia's largest, with around five million books. On April 30 each year the students meet here to celebrate the official first day of spring (usually in the snow), all wearing the traditional student cap that gives them the appearance of disaffected sailors. Adopt a studenty pose and you can slip in for a wander round and a coffee in the common room. More properly, take a look in the **manuscript room**, where there's a collection of rare letters and other paraphernalia. The beautiful sixth-century Silver Bible is on permanent display, as is, oddly, Mozart's original manuscript for *The Magic Flute*.

After this, the **castle** up on the hill, built by Gustav Vasa, is a disappointment (mid-June to mid-Aug daily 11am–4pm; rest of the year open sporadically; free). Much of it was destroyed in the 1702 fire that did away with three-quarters of the city, and only one side and two towers remain of what was once an opulent rectangular palace. But the facade, like a backless Hollywood set, still gives a weighty impression of what's missing.

The Linnaeus Gardens

Seeing Uppsala – at least its compact older parts – will take up a good half-day; afterwards, take a stroll along the river that runs right through the centre of town. In summer, there are several resting places here that are good for an hour or two's sunbathing, and enough greenery to make for a pleasant wander. One beautiful spot is **Linnaeus Gardens** (daily: May–Aug 9am–9pm; Sept 9am–7pm; free), over the river on Svartbäcksgatan, containing around 1300 varieties of plants. Relaid by Linnaeus (see box, p.116) in 1745, these were the university's first botanical gardens and are the oldest in Sweden; some of the species he introduced and classified still survive here. The adjoining **museum** (same times as above; 20kr) was once home to Linnaeus and his family, and attempts to evoke his life through a partially restored library, writing room and a collection of natural history specimens. While you're in Uppsala, you may also wish to visit Linné's former house at Hammarby, south of town (see box).

CARL VON LINNÉ

Born in Småland in 1707, **Carl Von Linné**, who styled himself Carolus Linnaeus, is undoubtedly Sweden's most revered scientist: any Swedish town of a decent size has a street named Linnégatan, one of Gothenburg's most appealing districts (see p.140) is named after him – and his face appears on all 100kr notes. His international reputation was secured by his introduction of **binomial classification**, a two-part nomenclature that's enabled plants to be consistently named and categorized into families. Only very recently has the basis of his classifications been undermined by genetic methods, resulting in the complete realignment of certain plant families.

Such was Linné's interest in plants that in 1732, when still a university student, he secured funds from the bishop of Växjö to undertake a botanical expedition to Lapland. His later expeditions to the Baltic islands of Öland and Gotland, and the mainland provinces of Västergotland and Skåne, were to provide the cornerstones for the creation of his ground-breaking system of plant classification. Becoming a professor at Uppsala in 1741, in 1754 he acquired an estate at **Hammarby**, 13km south of the town, and built a house there. Today, the place, a beautiful homestead with lush gardens, is managed by the university (May–Sept daily 8am–8pm; bus #808 runs here from town). The house contains some of Linné's own hand-coloured drawings of plants; also here is his private natural history museum, now the property of the Linnéan Society in London, in a stone pavilion on a hill nearby (Tues–Sun noon–4pm; 10kr).

The Bror Hjorth museum

Travelling around Sweden, you can't help but spot the work of Uppsala-born sculptor and painter, Bror Hjorth (1894–1968). Once Professor of Drawing at the Swedish Royal Academy of Fine Arts, today he's considered one of Sweden's greatest artists. A modernist with roots in folk art, his numerous public art commissions can be seen right across the country – perhaps most strikingly in the church in Jukkasjärvi in Lapland (see p.477). Arriving in Uppsala by train or bus, you'll have come face-to-face with one of his statues right outside the main stations, and will understand why his work caused so much controversy. The central theme in his sculptures and paintings, which concentrate mostly on love, life and music, was to seek out the intensity which art can evoke. His former home and studio in Uppsala have now been turned into a museum (June to mid-Aug Tues–Sun noon–4pm; mid-Aug to May Thurs, Sat & Sun noon–4pm; 30kr), containing the largest and most representative collection of his work in the country. Bus #6 or #7 run from Stora Torget to the museum, located a ten-minute ride west of the centre at Norbyvägen 26.

Out from the centre: Gamla Uppsala

Five kilometres to the north of the present city, three huge royal **burial mounds**, dating back to the sixth century, mark the original site of Uppsala, **Gamla Uppsala**. This was a pagan settlement – and a place of ancient sacrificial rites. Every ninth year, the deaths of nine people would be demanded at the festival of Fröblot, the victims left hanging from a nearby tree until their corpses rotted. The pagan temple where this bloody sacrifice took place is now marked by the Christian **Gamla Uppsala kyrka** (Mon–Fri 8.30am to dusk, Sat & Sun 10am to dusk), which was built over pagan remains when the Swedish kings first took baptism in the new faith. What survives of the church is only a remnant of what was, originally, a cathedral – look inside for the faded wall paintings and the tomb of Celsius, inventor of the temperature scale that bears his name. Set in the wall outside is an eleventh-century rune stone.

There's little else to Gamla Uppsala, and perhaps that's why the site remains mysterious and atmospheric. There's an **inn** nearby, *Odinsborg*, where – especially if you've got children – you might want to sample the "Viking lunch" smorgasbord: a spread of soup, hunks of meat served on a board, and mead, which comes complete with a horned helmet – an essential item if you're considering pillaging and plundering the afternoon away. To get to Gamla Uppsala, take **bus** #2 (3 hourly Mon–Fri) or #54 (Sat afternoon after 3pm & Sun 6pm–midnight; every 30min) from Dragarbrunnsgatan in Uppsala.

Eating, drinking and nightlife

Eating and **entertainment** are straightforward enough in this university town, and easier still if you have some form of student ID. For light daytime meals there are plenty of **cafés**, particularly in summer, when a glut of open-air places re-emerge, the most popular on the river. Many stay open until the early hours, an unusual bonus (also see "Bars and clubs" below). For **snacks** and cheap coffee you can also try the *Alma* café in the basement of the university building. The following all offer more substantial eating options.

Alexander, Östra Ågatan 59. Completely over-the-top Greek place with busts of famous Ancient Greeks at every turn. Lunch deal for 55kr.

Café Katalin, Svartbäcksgatan 19. Does reasonably priced veggie food in a similar set-up to *Sten Sture & Co* (see below), and just as popular.

Caroline's, Övre Slottsgatan 12. A cheap pizzeria up by the university. Lunch for 45kr.

Domtrappkälaren, St Eriks Gränd. One of the most chi-chi places in town – old vaulted roof and great atmosphere. Dishes around 200kr; excellent lunch upstairs for 60kr.

Elaka Måns, Smedsgränd. A modern bistro-style restaurant with the usual run of fish and meat dishes. Very popular, not too expensive and definitely worth a look.

Fågelsången, Munkgatan 3. Café and lunch place that's full of posey students.

Grisen, Östra Ågatan 11. Very small but oh-so-trendy restaurant with tiled walls and arty paintings. Moderately priced international fare.

Güntherska hovkonditori, Östra Ågatan 31. Old-fashioned café with simple lunch dishes.

Hambergs fisk o kräft, Fyris Torg 8. Located next to the tourist office and serving very good fish and seafood. Particularly popular at lunchtime.

Kung Krål, Gamla Torget. Across the river from the tourist office, in a fantastic old stone building with outdoor seating in summer. Swedish home cooking and international dishes.

Landings, Kungsängsgatan 5. Busy café in the main pedestrian area.

Ofvandahls, Sysslomangatan 3–5. Near the old part of town, this lively café originally opened in 1878. It has old wooden tables and sofas – don't leave town without trying the home-made cakes.

Sten Sture & Co, Nedre Slottsgatan 3. Trendy and inspired cooking at this large ramshackle wooden house immediately below the castle: plenty of young Uppsala folk come and there's often live jazz while you eat. Outdoor tables in summer. A must.

Svenssons krog/bakficka, Sysslomangatan 15. A wonderful restaurant decked out in wood and glass, with everything from Swedish home cooking to elaborate salmon dishes. The cheaper *bakficka* section serves good pasta.

Svenssons taverna, Sysslomangatan 14. Across from its neighbour, with an international menu. Large outdoor seating area in the shade of huge beech and oak trees. Dishes around 100kr. Recommended.

Svenssons åkanten, St Eriks Torg. Outdoor café right by the river and a wonderful place to chill out in summer.

Wayne's Coffee, Smedgränd 4. The best café in Uppsala – modern and airy with large windows which open right out onto the street.

Bars, clubs and live music

At night, most of the action is generated by the **students** in houses called "Nations", contained within the grid of streets behind the university, backing onto St Olofsgatan. Each a sort of college student club or association, they run dances, gigs and parties of all hues, and most importantly boast very **cheap bars**. The official line is that if you're not a Swedish student you won't get into most of the things advertised around the town; in practice being foreign and nice to the people on the door generally yields entrance, and with an ISIC card it's even easier. As many students stay around during the summer, functions are not strictly limited to term time. A good choice to begin with is *Uplands Nation*, off St Olofsgatan and Sysslomangatan near the river, with a summer outdoor café open until 3am. Among the non-student bars is *Svenssons Taverna*, Sysslomangatan 14, which is a great place for a beer and nibbles; but it's *O'Connors*, a first-floor Irish pub with food, tucked away in Stora Torget above the fast-food place *Saffet's*, which is *the* place to do your drinking – it's quite astounding just how many people can crowd into this pub. *Sten Sture & Co* puts on **live bands** in the evenings, while *Café Katalin* (see p.117) is open late and has **jazz** nights. *Club Dacke* is a student-frequented summer-only **disco** on St Olofsgatan, near the Domkyrkan.

Listings

Banks Handelsbanken, Vaksalagatan 8; Nordbanken, Stora Torget; SEB, Kungsängsgatan 7–9; Upplandsbanken at the corner of Östra Ågatan and Drottninggatan.

Buses City buses leave from Stora Torget; they're operated by Uppsalabuss (☎018/27 37 01); city buses leave from Stora Torget; long-distance buses from the bus station adjacent to the train station (see Stockholm "Listings" for phone numbers).

Car rental Avis, Spikgatan 1 (☎018/10 55 55); Budget, Kungsgatan 80 (☎018/12 43 80); Europcar, Kungsgatan 103 (☎018/17 17 30); Hertz, Kungsgatan 97 (☎018/16 02 00); Statoil, Gamla Uppsalagatan 48 (☎018/20 91 00).

Cinemas Filmstaden, Västra Ågatan 12; Fyrisbiografen, St Olofsgatan 10B; Royal, Smedsgränd 14-20.

Exchange Forex, Fyris Torg 8 (☎018/10 30 00), next to tourist office. Mon–Fri 8am–7pm, Sat 8am–3pm.

Pharmacy At Bredgränd; Mon–Fri 9am–6.30pm, Sat 10am–3pm.

Police ☎018/16 85 00. In emergencies call ☎112.

Post office Dragarbrunnsgatan (☎018/17 96 31).

Swimming pool Gamla Torget.

Systembolaget Svavagallerian, Mon–Wed 10am–6pm, Thurs 10am–7pm, Fri 10am–6.30pm.

Taxis Taxi Direkt (☎018/12 53 60); Taxi Uppsala (☎018/23 90 90).

Train station Information on ☎018/65 22 10.

Travel agent Kilroy, Bredgränd; Ticket, Östra Ågatan 33 & Bangårdsgatan 13.

travel details

Trains

Stockholm to: Boden (2 daily; 14hr); Gothenburg (21 daily; 3hr 10min by X2000, 5hr by InterCity); Eskiltuna (hourly; 1hr); Gällivare (2 daily; 16hr); Gävle (hourly; 1hr 20min); Helsingborg (14 daily; 5hr by X2000); Kiruna (2 daily; 17hr); Luleå (2 daily; 14hr); Läggesta (for Mariefred; 32 daily; 45min by X2000); Malmö (11 daily; 4hr 30min by X2000); Mora (11 daily; 3hr 30min by X2000, 5hr by InterCity); Sundsvall (9 daily; 3hr 30min by X2000); Umeå (1 daily; 11hr); Uppsala (50 daily; 40min); Västerås (hourly; 1hr 10min); Östersund (6 daily; 6hr).

Eskilstuna to: Läggesta (for Mariefred; hourly; 20min by X2000); Stockholm (hourly; 1hr by X2000); Västerås (hourly; 30min).

Läggesta to: Stockholm (hourly; 45min).

Uppsala to: Gällivare (2 daily; 15hr); Gävle (hourly; 40 min); Kiruna (2 daily; 16hr); Luleå (2 daily; 13hr); Mora (11 daily; 2hr 45min by X2000); Stockholm (50 daily; 40min); Sundsvall (9 daily; 2hr 45 min by X2000); Umeå (1 daily; 10hr); Östersund (6 daily; 4hr 30 min).

Buses

Stockholm: to Gothenburg (Mon–Wed 2 daily, Thurs 3 daily, Fri & Sun 5 daily, Sat 1 daily; 4hr 30min, or 7hr 20min via Kristinehamn or Jönköping); Gävle (daily; 2hr 20min); Halmstad (Fri & Sun 1 daily; 7hr 30min); Helsingborg (Mon–Thurs 1 daily, Fri & Sun 2 daily; 8hr); Jönköping (Mon–Thurs 1 daily, Fri & Sun 2 daily; 4hr 50min); Kalmar (5 daily; 6hr 30min); Kristianstad (Mon, Thurs, Fri & Sun 1 daily; 9hr 30min); Kristinehamn (Mon–Thurs & Sat 2 daily, Fri & Sun 3 daily; 3hr); Malmö (Fri 1 daily, Sun 2 daily; 10hr 20min); Norrköping (Mon–Wed 2 daily, Thurs 3 daily, Fri & Sun daily, Sat daily; 2hr); Sollefteå (1 daily; 8hr 15min); Umeå (1 daily; 9hr 20min); Östersund (1 daily; 8hr 30min).

Ferries

For details of Stockholm city ferries, see p.63; and for the services to the archipelago, see p.99.

International trains

Stockholm to Copenhagen (16 daily; 7hr); Narvik (2 daily; 20hr); Oslo (2 daily; 6hr 30min); Trondheim (1 daily; 10hr 30 min).

International ferries

Stockholm: to Helsinki (1 Viking Line & 1 Silja Line daily; 15hr); Turku (2 Viking Line & 2 Silja Line daily); Tallinn (summer 1 daily; 1 every other day); Eckerö on the Åland islands (3–5 daily; 3hr; a bus leaves Tekniska Högskolan T-bana 2hr before the ferry's departure from Grisslehamn).

CHAPTER TWO

GOTHENBURG AND AROUND

O f all the cities in southern Sweden, the grandest and most varied is the western port of **Gothenburg**. Designed by the Dutch in 1621, the city boasts splendid Neoclassical architecture, masses of parkland and a welcoming and relaxed spirit.

Gothenburg is Sweden's second largest city and Scandinavia's largest seaport; these facts, allied with its industrial heritage as a ship-building centre, have been enough to persuade many travellers arriving in the country by ferry to move quickly on into the surrounding countryside. Yet in common with other formerly industrial cities, the still-visible legacy of the gargantuan shipyards can now be relegated to a historical context, while the cityscape of broad avenues, elegant

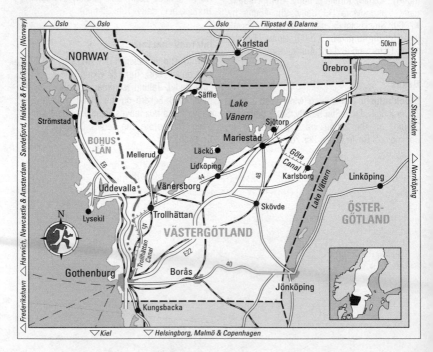

squares, trams and canals is not only one of the prettiest in Sweden, but also the backdrop to a burgeoning arts and youth scene, and a well-developed café society. While the city's image once suffered from the inevitable comparisons with the capital, and there is a certain resentment on the west coast that Stockholm wins out in the national glory stakes, Gothenburg's easier-going atmosphere – and its closer proximity to western Europe – makes it first choice as a place to live, ahead of the capital, for many Swedes. Talk to any Gothenburger and he or she will soon disparage the more frenetic lives of the "08-ers" – 08 being the telephone code for Stockholm. Yet Gothenburg has a buoyancy of its own – thanks to its highly visible student population – that inspires exploration; those who try soon discover that the place is worth a lot more time than most ferry arrivals give it.

The countless to the north and east of the city are prime targets for domestic tourists. To the north, the craggy **Bohuslän coastline**, with its uninhabited islands, tiny fishing villages and clean beaches, attracts thousands of holiday-makers all the way to the Norwegian border. The coast is popular with the sailing set, and there are many guest harbours along the way. One highlight is the glorious fortress island of **Marstrand**, which makes for an easy and enjoyable day-trip from Gothenburg, while further north, islands like the **Kosters** offer splendid isolation and unexpectedly exuberant wildlife.

To the northeast of the city, the vast and beautiful lakes of **Vänern** and **Vättern** provide the setting for a number of historic towns, fairy-tale castles and some splendid inland scenery, all of which are within an hour's train journey of Gothenburg. The lakes are connected to each other (and to the east and west coasts) by the cross-country **Göta Canal**, allowing you to travel all the way from Gothenburg to Stockholm by boat, a trip that's worth considering if you're inspired by the possibilities of water transport. The first leg of this journey is up the Trollhättan Canal to **Trollhättan**, a low-key, winning little town built around the canal, and a good place to aim for if you only have time for a short trip out from the city. Beyond here, though, other agreeable lakeside towns vie for your attention, with attractions including the so-called elk safaris on the ancient plateaux of Halleberg and Hunneberg, near **Vänersborg** on the tip of Lake Vänern; the historically fascinating natural haven of **Kinnekulle**, a hill rising to the east of Lake Vänern; the picturesque medieval kernel of **Mariestad**, further up the lake's eastern shore; and the huge military fortress at **Karlsborg**, on the western shore of Lake Vättern.

ACCOMMODATION PRICES

The pensions and hotels listed in the guide have been price-graded according to the scale given below; the price category given against each establishment indicates the cost of the least expensive double rooms there. Many hotels offer considerable reductions at weekends all year round, and during the summer holiday period (mid-June to mid-Aug); in these cases the reduction is either noted in the text or, where a discount brings a hotel into another price band, given after the number for the full price. Single rooms, where available, usually cost between 60 and 80 percent of a double. Where hostels have double rooms, we've given price codes for them also.

① under 500kr	③ 700–900kr	⑤ 1200–1500kr
② 500–700kr	④ 900–1200kr	⑥ over 1500kr

Trains and **buses** provide most of the region with a regular, efficient service; the only area you may find difficult to explore without a car is the Bohuslän coast. **Accommodation** is never a problem, with plenty of hotels, hostels and campsites in each town.

GOTHENBURG

With its long history as a trading centre, **GOTHENBURG** (Göteborg in Swedish; pronounced "Yur-te-boy") is a truly cosmopolitan city. Founded on its present site in the seventeenth century by Gustavus Adolphus, Gothenburg was the fifth attempt to create a centre not reliant on Denmark – the Danes had enjoyed control of Sweden's west coast since the Middle Ages, and had extracted extortionate tolls from all water traffic into Sweden. The medieval centre of trade had been 40km up the Göta River, but to avoid the tolls it was moved to a site north of the present city. It wasn't until Karl XI chose the island of Hisingen, today the site of the city's northern suburbs, as the location for Sweden's trading nucleus that the settlement was first called Gothenburg. This, however, fell to the Danes during the battle of Kalmar, and it was left to Adolphus to find the vast ransom demanded for its return. Six years later, when it had finally been paid off, he founded the city where the main square is today.

Although Gothenburg's reputation as an industrial and trading centre has been severely eroded in recent years – clearly evidenced by the stillness of its shipyard cranes – the British, Dutch and German traders who settled here during the eighteenth and nineteenth centuries left a rich architectural and cultural legacy. The city is graced with terraces of grand **merchant houses,** all carved stone, stucco and painted tiles. The influence of the Orient was also strong, reflecting the all-important trade links between Sweden and the Far East, and is still visible in the chinoiserie detail on many buildings. This trade was monopolized for over eighty years by the hugely successful **Swedish East India Company,** whose Gothenburg auction house, selling exotic spices, teas and fine cloths, attracted merchants from all over the world.

Today the city remains a sort of transit camp for business people, though their presence in the flashy hotels in the centre is much less striking for the visitor than restrained opulence of the older buildings, which echoes not only its bygone prosperity but also the understated tastes of its citizens. In the 1960s, parts of the city lost many of their grandest old buildings, and the new apartment blocks that replaced them, while lacking the beauty of their predecessors, are far less hideous than the equivalent monstrosities in other European cities. Gothenburgers may tell you that they think their surroundings are nothing special, but these assertions are simply an expression of Swedish reserve and Gothenburg modesty. They also have a reputation for friendliness, and though a one night stopover may not reveal it, there is a relaxed geniality among many of the city's folk, making this one of the few places in Sweden where the locals may strike up a conversation with you, rather than vice versa.

Arrival and information

All **trains** arrive at **Central Station,** which forms one side of Drottningtorget. **Buses** from towns north of Gothenburg use **Nils Ericsonsplatsen,** just behind train station; arriving from places south of Gothenburg, you'll disembark at

THE GOTHENBURG CARD

A boon if you want to pack in a good bit of sightseeing, the **Gothenburg Card** ("Göteborgskortet") provides unlimited bus and tram travel within the city; free entry to most of the city museums and the Liseberg Amusement Park (see p.138); free boat trips to Nya Elfsborg (see p.133); and two-for-one reductions at several other sights. The only transport not covered by the card are the special buses to and from the airport and port (see "Arrival and information", below). The Gothenburg Card comes with a second card entitling the holder to free parking in roadside spaces (but not at privately run or multistorey car parks). You can buy the Gothenburg card, which is valid on the day of purchase, from either of the tourist offices, and from hotels and Pressbyrån kiosks (75kr, children 40kr). An accompanying Gothenburg Card booklet explains in detail where and how it can save you money.

Heden terminal at the junction of Parkgatan and Södra Vägen, with easy tram connections to all areas of the city. From **Landvetter airport**, 25km east of the city, Flygbuss (airport buses) run every fifteen minutes into the centre (daily 5am–11.15pm; 30min; 45kr), stopping at Korsvägen, a junction just outside Liseberg Amusement Park to the south of the city centre, and in Drottningtorget outside Central Station.

DFDS Seaways **ferries** arrive at **Skandiahamn** on Hisingen, north of the river, from where buses run to Nils Ericsonsplatsen, behind the train station (40kr). Sea Cat's terminal, where its boats from Fredrikshavn in Denmark arrive, is at **Amerika House**, west of the city; tram #3 or #9 go from Stigbergstorget nearby. Stena Line also operates ferries from Fredrikshavn, which dock just twenty minutes' walk from the city centre, close to the Masthuggstorget tram stop on lines #3, #4 and #9; their services from Kiel in Germany put in 3km away from the city, from where bus #491 or trams #3 or #9 will bring you into the centre.

Gothenburg has two **tourist offices**; the one handiest for those arriving by train or bus is at the kiosk in Nordstan, the indoor shopping centre near Central Station (Mon–Fri 9.30am–6pm, Sat 10am–4pm, Sun noon–3pm). The main office is, however, on the canal front at Kungsportsplatsen 2 (May Mon–Fri 9am–6pm, Sat & Sun 10am–2pm; June & mid-Aug to late Aug daily 9am–6pm; July to mid-Aug daily 9am–8pm; ☎031/61 25 00, fax 61 25 01, *turistinfo@gbg-co.se*), just five minutes' walk from the train station, across Drottningtorget and down Stora Nygatan; the tourist office is opposite the "Copper Mare" statue (see p.136). Both offices provide information, free city and tram maps, a room-booking service, and restaurant and museum listings; the bilingual *Göteborg What's On*, a monthly publication in Swedish and English detailing events, music and nightspots in town, is available from either. The tourist offices also sell the Gothenburg Card (see above), obtainable on its own or with hotel accommodation as part of the Gothenburg Package (see p.126).

City transport

Apart from sights north of the river or out in the islands, it's easy to **walk** to almost anywhere of interest in Gothenburg. The streets are wide and pedestrian-friendly, and the canals and the grid system of avenues make orientation simple. The city is one of the best in Europe for **cycling**: most main roads have cycle

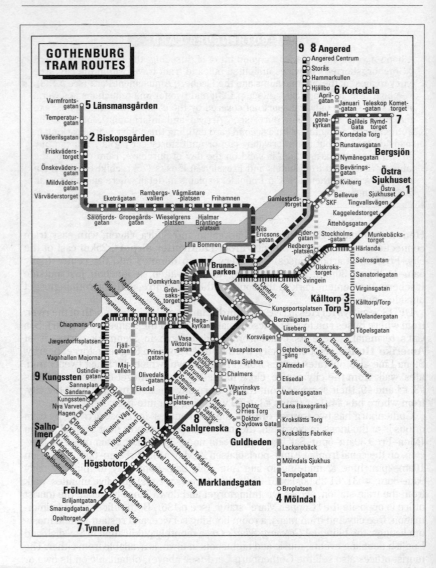

GOTHENBURG TRAM ROUTES

lanes, and motorists really do seem to give way to those on two wheels. The tourist office can provide you with the excellent *cykelcarte* which shows clearly all the cycle routes throughout the city, and out to the archipelago.

That said, access to some form of public transport is always handy, particularly if you've just arrived at one of the central transport terminals or end up staying further out from the centre. A free **transport map** (*Linje Kartan*) is available at both tourist offices.

Public transport

The most convenient form of public transport is the **tram** system (see map on p.124). A colour-coded system of nine tram lines serves the city and its outskirts, and a tram will pass through all central areas every few minutes – you can tell at a glance which line a tram is on, as the route colour will appear on the front. Trams run from 5am to midnight, after which there is a less frequent night service. The main pick-up points are outside Central Station and in Kungsportsplatsen. During summer, there are even vintage trams on the network, plying the Liseberg route (see below). Gothenburg also has a fairly extensive **bus** network, using much the same routes, but central pedestrianization can lead to some odd and lengthy detours. You shouldn't need to use buses in the city centre; routes are detailed in the text where necessary.

Tickets are available from tram and bus drivers. There are no zones, and fares cost a standard 16kr for adults, while 7- to 16-year-olds go for half price; tickets for the night service on the trams cost double the usual price. Ticket inspectors, in yellow jackets, are on the increase, and there's an instant fine of 600kr if you're caught travelling without a valid ticket – since all the ticket information is in English and posted on boards at bus and tram stops, ignorance is no defence.

If you are staying for a couple of days and travelling around the city quite a bit, it's better value to buy **carnets** from the Tidpunkten offices – travel information centres – at Brunnsparken, Drottningtorget and Nils Ericsonsplatsen, or from Pressbyrån kiosks. A ten-trip carnet costs 100kr. Stick these in the machines on a tram or bus, press twice for an adult, once for a child. With a **Gothenburg Card** (see p.123), most public transport within the city is free.

VINTAGE TRAMS AND PADDAN BOAT RIDES

An atmospheric way of seeing the city is to ride one of the **vintage trams** that spend the summer trundling noisily from the old town to both **Liseberg**, southeast of the centre, and **Slottskogen**, to the southwest. These trams run daily between July and August and on weekends in April and September; tickets cost the same as on ordinary trams. You can even take a **guided tour** of the city on one; the trips leave from Kungsportsplatsen and can be booked through the tourist office.

Since the beginning of the century, trams have played an important role in Gothenburg life, from those decked with ribbons as mothers jolted home with their newborn, to black-hearse trams pushing coffins with mourners in the front carriage. Today white-gloved enthusiasts steer exquisitely preserved models – dating from between 1902 and the 1940s – complete with all their original leather, polished wood, etched glass and candles. The pre-1933 models have swastikas on the hub caps, painted on before the ancient religious symbol was appropriated by the Nazis, and many still have doors on the left – a reminder that Sweden drove on the left from the late eighteenth century, when the British industrialists held sway, until 1967.

Another popular way to get acquainted with the city is to take a **paddan boat ride** (late April to mid-June 10am–5pm; mid-June to early Aug 10am–9pm; early Aug to mid-Sept 10am–5pm; mid-Sept to early Oct noon–3pm; 75kr). This thorough canal and harbour tour, on barges with bench seating, offers a worthwhile 55-minute trip past the city's historical sites. There are regular departures from their moorings on the canal by Kungsportsplatsen.

Cars, taxis and bikes

There is no shortage of **car parks** in the city, with a basic charge of 20kr per hour in the centre. The most useful of these are the new Ullevigarage at Heden, near the bus terminal; the Lorensbergs car park near Avenyn; Gamla Ullevi on Allen, south of Kungsportsplatsen; and two multistorey car parks: at Nordstan near Central Station, and at Garda-Focus, close to Liseberg. Guests at some of the larger hotels can claim a discount at the multistorey car parks. Roadside parking areas marked with blue signs, where you pay at machines, are cheaper than metered spaces. The Gothenburg Card comes with a second card entitling the holder to free parking in certain areas (see p.123). For information on **car rental**, see "Listings",p.151.

Taxis can be summoned by calling ☎031/65 00 00; you can also pick one up at the rank at Central Station. There is a twenty percent reduction for women travelling at night – check with the driver first.

Cycling in the city is easy and popular; there's a comprehensive series of cycle lanes and bike racks. You can rent a bike at Millennium Cykel at Chalmersgatan 19 (☎031/18 43 00), a street to the south of and parallel to Avenyn; the *Slottskogens* and *Stigbergssliden* hostels (see p.128) also rent bikes for 50kr a day.

Accommodation

Gothenburg has plenty of good accommodation to choose from, with no shortage of comfortable **youth hostels** (a couple of which are very central) and **private rooms**. Most of the central **hotels** are clustered around the train station; they offer a high standard of service, though they're designed with businessmen in mind, meaning they tend to be flashy but characterless. Summer reductions mean that even the better hotels can prove surprisingly affordable, and most places also take part in the **Gothenburg Package**, a scheme co-ordinated by the tourist office. This is a real bargain as it offers accommodation in a twin bedroom, breakfast and a Gothenburg Card, all for 390kr per person per night. With around thirty good, central hotels participating, the scheme operates every Friday to Monday from early June to the end of August, on all major holidays, and over Christmas. Some hotels also operate it on Thursdays, and others all year round. There is a fifty percent discount for **children** sharing with one parent at some hotels, while others allow extra beds in single rooms – the tourist office can advise. To take advantage of the Gothenburg Package, contact the tourist office.

You should have no trouble finding accommodation whenever you turn up, though in summer it's a good idea to book ahead if you are limited to the cheaper hotels, or if you want to stay in the most popular youth hostels (see the listings below). Summer and weekend prices are almost invariably dramatically cheaper than weekday options at other times of year.

Hotels and pensions

The prices given below are standard rates, with summer discounts where they exist. It's worth checking if rooms can be booked more cheaply using the Gothenburg Package; all the hotels we list were participants in the scheme at time of writing. Breakfast is included in our prices, unless otherwise stated.

Allen, Parkgatan 10 (☎031/10 14 50, fax 11 91 60). Very central, sensibly priced hotel close to Avenyn and the old town. Prices include room service and parking. ③/②.

City, Lorensbergsgatan 6 (☎031/708 40 00, fax 708 40 02). Not to be confused with *City Hotel Ritz*, this is a cheapish and popular place, excellently positioned close to Avenyn on a street named after the Lorensberg. En-suite rooms cost an extra 300kr. ①.

City Hotel Ritz, Burggrevegatan 25 (☎031/80 00 80, fax 15 77 76). Close to Central Station and the airport bus stop. All rooms in this comfortable hotel are en suite and have cable TV. Residents can take advantage of the free sauna and the solarium (30kr). ③.

Eggers, Drottningtorget (☎031/80 60 70, fax 15 42 43). The original station hotel, this very characterful establishment has individually furnished bedrooms and a wealth of grand original features; the place is believed to have been used during World War II for secret discussions between British and Nazi military negotiators. With a low Gothenburg Package price, this is one of the best-value central hotels. ⑤/④.

Europa, Köpmansgatan 38 (☎031/80 12 80, fax 15 47 55). With an amorphous facade adjoining the Nordstan shopping centre, this is reputedly the largest hotel in Sweden, with 460 rooms. The interior is very plush, with lots of marble, and unusually for Sweden, the bathrooms have actual bathtubs. For breakfast, a huge, international-style buffet is on offer. ⑤/③.

Excelsior, Karl Gustavsgatan 9 (☎031/17 54 35, fax 17 54 39), between Avenyn and Haga. A shabbily stylish 1880 building in a road of classic Gothenburg houses, this is the place to come for character. It's been a hotel since 1930; Greta Garbo and Ingrid Bergman both stayed here as, more recently, did Sheryl Crow. Classic suites – Garbo's was no. 535 – with splendid nineteenth-century features cost no more than ordinary rooms. ④/②.

Hotel 11, Maskingatan 11, at the harbour (☎031/779 11 11, fax 779 11 10). With views across to Hisingen and dramatic summer reductions, this is one of the city's most interesting and stylish places to stay, built on the site of an old shipyard. Take tram #5 to Lilla Bommen, then the boat, *Älv Snabben* (Mon–Fri 6am–11.30pm, shorter hours at weekend; every 30min; 16kr, free with Gothenburg Card), in the direction of Klippan – get off at Eriksberg. ⑤/③.

Lilton, Föreningsgatan 9 (☎031/82 88 08, fax 82 21 84). Close to the Haga district, this cosy, ivy-covered fourteen-bedroom place is one of Gothenburg's more unobtrusive bed-and-breakfast hotels. It's quiet and simple, with splendid National Romantic and Art Nouveau buildings directly opposite, and there's free tea and coffee and use of a kitchen. ③.

Maria Erikssons Pensionat, Chalmersgatan 27A (☎031/20 70 30, fax 16 64 63). With just ten rooms, this place is well positioned on a road running parallel with Avenyn. Breakfast not included. ①.

Novotel Hotel, Klippan 1 (☎031/14 90 00, fax 42 22 32). A glamorous pile converted from the old Carnegie Porter Brewery in delightful Klippan, just west of the city (see p.142). It's a mishmash of architectural styles on the inside, but has great views from the upper storeys. There's also a huge central atrium dripping with fake foliage, and an expensive, traditional restaurant, *Carnegie Kay*, attached. ⑤, at weekends ③.

Opera Hotel, Norra Hamngatan 38 (☎031/80 50 80, fax 80 58 17). A merger of two hotels has resulted in this big, central establishment close to the train station, with sauna, jacuzzi and cable TV. ④/③.

Robinson, Södra Hamngatan 2 (☎031/80 25 21, fax 15 92 91). Facing Brunnspark, this mediocre but economical hotel, housed in part of the old Fürstenburg Palace, still boasts the original facade. A few other original features, like the lift's etched windows depicting Skansen Leijonet (a fortress tower, one of two that survive in the city), have survived decades of architectural tampering. All rooms have cable TV. You'll need to pay 160kr more for one of the en-suite rooms; there are also some family rooms here. ②.

SAS Radisson Scandinavia, Södra Hamngatan 59–65 (☎031/80 60 00, fax 15 98 88). Opposite the train station. With glass lifts and fountains, the atrium foyer of what was until 1999 the *Sheraton* resembles a shopping mall; the bedrooms here are all pastel shades and birch wood. Also within the complex is a glamorous restaurant. ⑤/④.

Youth hostels and private rooms

The cheapest options for accommodation are **private rooms**, booked through the tourist office (175kr per person in a double room, 225kr for a single; booking fee 60kr), or staying in one of the **youth hostels**. All the hostels listed below are STF-run, and are open all year unless otherwise stated. For stays of a week or more, it is worth contacting SGS Bostader, Utlandgatan 24 (Mon–Fri 11am–3pm), who rent out **furnished rooms**, with access to kitchen facilities, for around 1200kr a week; sheets are provided, but not utensils. Most hostels have a range of rooms, from singles through to dormitories with up to ten beds.

Karralunds Vandrarhem, Olbergsgatan (☎031/84 02 00, fax 84 05 00), 4km from the centre, close to Liseberg Amusement Park (take tram #5, direction Torp, to Welandergatan). Has non-smoking rooms, and also offers cabins and a campsite (see below). Breakfasts can only be ordered by groups. Fills up quickly in summer, so book ahead. 145kr, ①.

Kviberg Vandrarhem, Kvibergsvägen 5 (☎031/43 50 55, fax 43 26 50), in Gamlestad (the Old Town before present-day Gothenburg was founded). Ten minutes by tram #6 or #7 from Central Station. 120kr, ①.

Masthuggsterrassen, Masthuggsterassen 8 (☎ & fax 031/42 48 20). Up the steps from Masthuggstorget (tram #3 or #4) and within a couple of minutes' walk of the Stena Line ferry terminal. 130kr, ①.

M/S Seaside, Packhuskajen (☎031/10 59 70, fax 12 23 69). Take tram #5 to Lilla Bommen. A moored ship at the harbour next to Maritima Centrum, with twenty cabins, each sleeping one to four people. A cabin to yourself costs 250kr; breakfast and sheets extra. April–Sept. 100kr.

Partille, Landvettervagen, Partille (☎031/44 65 01, fax 44 61 63). Fifteen kilometres east of the city; take bus #513 from Heden bus terminal to Astebo (30min). This hostel has a solarium and lounge with TV. 110kr.

Slottskogen, Vegagatan 21 (☎031/42 65 20, fax 14 21 02). Just two minutes' walk from Linnégatan and not far from Slottskogen Park (tram #1 or #2 to Olivedalsgatan). Superbly appointed, family-run hostel – the best in town – whose stylish apartment complex has a great living area/TV lounge, fine kitchen and well-designed rooms. The 40kr breakfast is excellent. 130kr, ①.

Stigbergssliden, Stigbergsliden 10 (☎031/24 16 20, fax 24 65 20). Along with the *Slottskogen*, a really good choice, and ideally placed for ferries to Denmark, being just west of the Linné area down Första Långgatan. Built in 1830 as a seamen's house, this friendly place has washbasins in all rooms, disabled access, laundry facilities (20kr) and a pleasant back courtyard. The buffet breakfast is an extra 40kr and bikes can be rented here for 50kr. 110kr, ①.

Torrekulla, Kallered (☎031/795 14 95, fax 795 51 40). Fifteen kilometres south of the city, this is a pleasantly situated hostel with a free sauna and a nearby lake where you can take a dip. Take bus #705 from Heden, or it's a 10min journey on a local train from Central Station (direction Kungsbacka) to Mölndal, followed by a 15min walk, or change to bus #705 there. 130kr, ①.

Cabins and campsites

Askims (☎031/28 62 61, fax 68 13 35). Twelve kilometres from the centre; take tram #1 or #2 to Linnéplatsen, then bus #83, or better still take the Blå Express bus, direction Saro, from Drottningtorget outside Central Station. Beside sandy beaches, *Askims* has four-bed cabins costing 615kr in the high season, otherwise 495kr. Early May to late Aug.

Karralunds, Olbergsgatan (same contact details as *Karralunds* hostel, see above). Set among forest and lakes, this campsite has four-bed cabins costing 615kr (695kr en suite).

Lilleby Havsbad (☎031/56 50 66, fax 56 16 05). Getting here from the centre takes about an hour: take bus #21 from Nils Ericsonsplatsen and change to the #23 at Kongshallavagen. The splendid seaside location is some compensation for the trek. May–Aug.

The City

Nearly everything of interest in Gothenburg is south of the **Göta River**, and with one exception – a trip to the **Volvo factory** on the northern island of **Hisingen** – there's no need to cross the water. At the heart of the city is the historic **old town**, about the best place to start, although Gothenburg's attractions are by no means restricted to this area. Tucked between the Göta River to the north and the zigzagging canal to the south, the old town's tightly gridded streets are lined with impressive facades, interesting food markets and a couple of worthwhile museums – the **Stadmuseum** and, up by the harbour, the **museum of maritime history**. Just across the canal that skirts the southern edges of the old town is **Trädgårdsforeningen** park, in summer full of floral colour and picnicking city dwellers.

Heading further south into the modern centre, **Avenyn** is Gothenburg's showcase boulevard, alive with showy restaurants and bars. However, it's the roads off Avenyn that hold the area's real interest, with more alternative 24-hour café-bars and some of Gothenburg's best museums: in a small district called **Vasastan** to the southwest, you'll find the **Röhsska Museum** of applied arts and, further south in **Götaplatsen**, the city's **Art Museum**. For family entertainment day or night, the classic **Liseberg Amusement Park**, just to the southeast of the Avenyn district, has been a focal point for Gothenburgers since the 1920s.

Vasastan stretches west to **Haga**, the old working-class district, now a haven for the trendy and monied. Haga Nygåtan, the main thoroughfare, leads on to Linnégatan, the arterial road through **Linné**. Fast establishing itself as the most vibrant part of the city, it's home to the most interesting evening haunts, with new cafés, bars and restaurants opening up alongside long-established antique emporiums and sex shops. Further out, the rolling **Slottskogen** park holds the **Natural History Museum**, but is more alluring as a pretty place to sunbathe.

Gothenburg is a fairly compact and easy city to get around, so you can cover most of the sights even if you only have a day or two here. But to get the most from your stay, give the city at least four days and slow your pace down to a stroll – which will put you in step with the locals.

The old town and the harbour

The **old town** is divided in two by the **Stora Hamn Canal**, to the north of which is the harbour, where the decaying, but still impressive, shipyards make for a dramatic backdrop. The streets south of the Stora Hamn stretching down to the southern canal are just right for an afternoon's leisurely stroll, with some quirky cafés, food markets and antique/junk shops to dip into, as well as mainland Sweden's oldest synagogue. Straddling the Stora Hamn is the stately main square, **Gustav Adolfs Torg**; an early start here will mean you can see the whole area the same day, without rushing.

Gustav Adolfs Torg

At the centre of **Gustav Adolfs Torg**, a copper statue of Gustavus Adolphus points ostentatiously at the spot where he reputedly declared: "Here I will build my city." This, however, isn't the original German-made statue of the city founder:

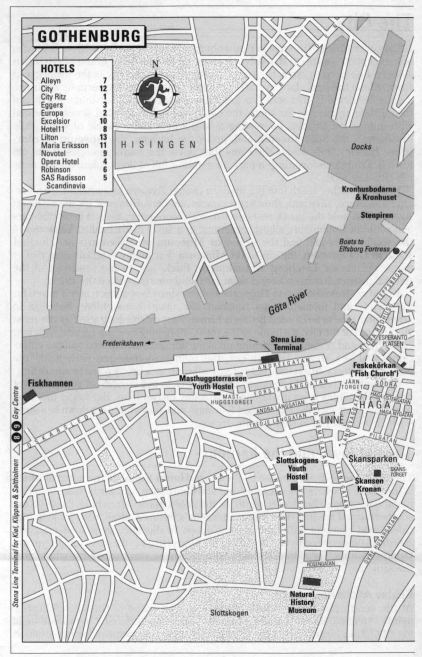

GOTHENBURG

HOTELS

Alleyn	7
City	12
City Ritz	1
Eggers	3
Europa	2
Excelsior	10
Hotel11	8
Lilton	13
Maria Eriksson	11
Novotel	9
Opera Hotel	4
Robinson	6
SAS Radisson Scandinavia	5

HISINGEN

Docks

Kronhusbodarna & Kronhuset

Stenpiren

Boats to Elfsborg Fortress

Göta River

Frederikshavn ←

Stena Line Terminal

ESPERANTO PLATSEN

Feskekörkan ('Fish Church')

Fiskhamnen

Masthuggsterrassen Youth Hostel

ANDREEGATAN

JÄRN TORGET

SÖDRA

HAGA ÖSTERGATAN

FORSTA LÄNGGATAN

ANDRA LÄNGGATAN

MAST-HUGGSTORGET

HAGA NYGATAN

HAGA

TREDJE LÄNGGATAN

LINNÉ

PILGATAN

OSKARSLEDEN

BANGATAN

FJALIGATAN

JUNGMANGATAN

Slottskogens Youth Hostel

Skansparken

SKANS-TORGET

Skansen Kronan

LINNÉGATAN

VEGAGATAN

ROSENGATAN

ÖVRE HUSARGATAN

Natural History Museum

Slottskogen

Stena Line Terminal for Kiel, Klippan & Saltholmen △ 8 9 Gay Centre

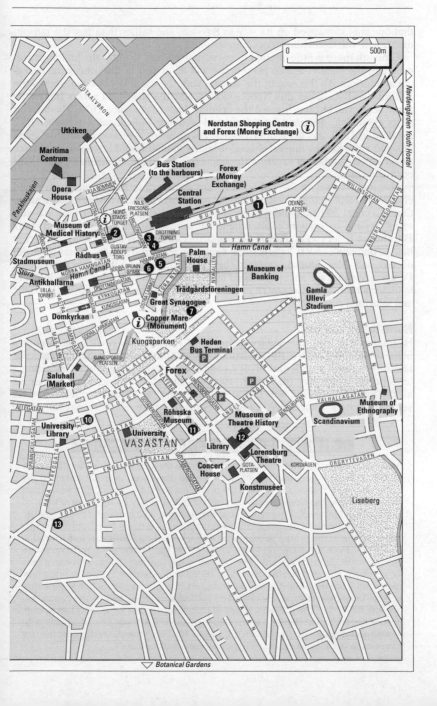

that one was kidnapped on its way to Sweden, and rather than pay the ransom demanded, the Gothenburgers commissioned a new one.

Although there is little attempt to encourage visitors to enter the buildings surrounding the square, a little persistence will allow you to discover some exceptional interiors. To the east of the square, with the canal behind you, stands the **Rådhus**, with its rather dull Neoclassical façade; the place isn't a town hall as the name suggests, but has housed the criminal law courts since 1672. The interior of its extension, designed by the ground-breaking Functionalist architect E.G. Asplund in 1936, has been internationally acclaimed; it retains its original glass lifts and also features mussel-shaped drinking fountains and huge panels of laminated aspen – the latter creating the impression of standing inside a giant 1930s cocktail cabinet.

Also tucked away in the old building are some rather fine rooms, with grand chandeliers and trompe l'oeil ceilings; to see them you'll have to attract the attention of a court assistant and wait for the rooms to be opened. Your time is better spent trying to convince attendants at the white, double-columned 1842 **Börshuset** to let you in. Facing the canal, this former Exchange has magnificent banqueting and concert halls of great opulence, while the smaller rooms are a riot of red and blue stucco, inspired by the eighteenth-century excavations at Pompeii. Visitors are not encouraged in any numbers as the fabric of the building is under strain, but once you're inside, the staff will usually give an enthusiastic and informed commentary.

North to the harbour

Heading north from the square along Östra Hamngatan, you'll pass Sweden's biggest shopping centre, the amorphous **Nordstan**. Despite valiant attempts at face-lifts, it's still a dark and dreary complex, its few saving graces including a late-opening pharmacy (daily 8am–10pm), a tourist office and ticket offices for all the ferry companies (see p.123). If you have time to spare and haven't yet seen the city's impressive **Central Station**, take a short detour along

NEW TRANSPORT LINKS TO THE HARBOUR

A far-reaching programme designed to eradicate the one non-user-friendly aspect of Gothenburg was launched in 1999 – and has been warmly received by Gothenburgers despite a certain chaos prevailing during the work. For years now, the harbourside has been effectively severed from the city by the huge amount of traffic along Marten Krakowsgatan and Skeppsbron, which makes crossing to the water a treacherous task from Lilla Bommen, and a tedious one from Nordstan. Now that the harbour area is becoming upmarket, a huge **traffic relief tunnel** is being built from the Järntorget area just south of the Feskekorka, right up to the Opera House. Apartments are to be built all along the waterfront, with car access for residents only. New tram lines will be added to the existing system to bring people to and from the area (the overall transport plan even extends to having a ring of tram lines right around the city), and getting around on foot in the centre will become far easier. The previous layout of tram lines around Järntorget has already been rejigged, and at the time of writing, the square itself was a building site, with new stops being built for trams #1, #3, #4 and #9. This project, the biggest the city has seen in decades, is expected to be completed around 2004.

NYA ELFSBORG

Boats leave from Lilla Bommen, near the Opera House, for the popular excursion to the island **fortress** of **Nya Elfsborg** (early May to Aug hourly 9.30am–3pm; 20min; 75kr, free with a Gothenburg Card), built in the seventeenth century to defend the harbour and the city. The surviving buildings here have been turned into a **museum** and café. On the guided tours (included in the price of the boat trip) of the square tower, chapel and prison cells, you'll hear about violent confrontations with the Danes and some of the methods used to keep prisoners from swimming away – check out the set of iron shackles weighing over 36kg.

Burggrevegatan to Drottningtorget. The oldest train station in the country (dating from 1856), its period facade fronts a grand and marvellously preserved interior – take a look at the wood beam-ends in the ticket hall, every one carved in the likeness of the city-council members of the day. Although it's usually behind closed doors, you might be able to persuade a guard to let you see the staff room, once the royal waiting room and still resplendent with its hand-painted ceilings and gilt-topped pillars.

Back on Östra Hamngatan is the **Museum of Medical History** (Tues, Wed & Fri 11am–4pm, Thurs 11am–8pm; 20kr), owned by the Sahlgren Hospital and charmingly set in the 200-year-old house which was home to the hospital during the mid-nineteenth century. The rooms exploring disease through the ages are not likely to inspire those without a ready interest in pathology. More diverting are an 1870s ambulance, like a vast wicker pram, and an old dental surgery, complete with hand-decorated dentist's chair.

At the northern end of Östra Hamngatan, on Lilla Bommen, Gothenburg's industrial decline is juxtaposed with its artistic regeneration to dramatic visual effect. To the west, beyond the harbour, redundant shipyard cranes loom across the sky, making a sombre background to the bronze and pink-granite sculptures dotted along the waterfront – most of which have an industrial theme. A couple of minutes' walk to the west is the **Opera House** (daily noon–6pm; ☎031/13 13 00, fax 10 80 51; guided tours July Tues & Wed noon–3pm; ☎031/10 82 03 for programme and tour details). It's no accident that it looks somewhat industrial – the idea was that its design should facilitate the manufacture of stage sets on the premises. Whether or not you're an opera buff, it's worth having a quick wander around inside. North along the river bank from the Opera House is the **Utkiken** (Lookout Point; Jan to mid-May & early Sept to mid-Dec Sat & Sun 11am–4pm; mid-May to early Sept daily 11am–7pm; 25kr); designed by the Scottish architect Ralph Erskine in the late 1980s, this 86-metre-high office building resembles a half-used red lipstick. Its top storey offers panoramic views of the city and harbour.

Walking west along the quay, it's just a couple of minutes to **Maritima Centrum** (Mon–Fri 9am–5pm, Sat & Sun 10am–5pm; 45kr, free with a Gothenburg Card; ☎031/61 29 01), which describes itself as "the largest ship museum in the world". Not a dull experience, even for non-enthusiasts of things maritime, the museum comprises a dozen boats, including a 1915 lightship, a submarine and a firefloat (a sort of nautical fire engine), each giving a glimpse of how seamen lived and worked on board. The most impressive ship is a monstrous naval destroyer, complete with a medical office, where the display showing the amputation of a leg and hand is more amusing than informative – far-fetched clothes-shop dummies do the honours. There is a rather good café-restaurant on the ship, too. Disabled access to the ship is good; anyone wanting to avoid its steep stairs can use a special route indicated by blue arrows.

The Kronhuset and the Stadsmuseum

From the maritime museum, it's a short walk southwest to Gothenburg's oldest secular building, **Kronhuset**, on Kronhusgatan (Tues–Fri 11am–4pm, Sat & Sun 11am–5pm). Built by the Dutch in 1642 as an artillery depot for the city's garrison, it was where 5-year-old Karl XI was proclaimed king in 1660. Set picturesquely in the eighteenth-century wings that flank the original building is **Kronhusbodarna** (Mon–Fri 10am–5pm, Sat 10am–2pm), a cluster of small, pricey shops specializing in making gold, silver and glass ornaments and jewellery. The silversmith here can sell you a replica of the city's oldest key, but your money would be better spent at the atmospheric vaulted café, which serves heaps of meringues as well as sandwich lunches.

A couple of blocks further south, the **Stadsmuseum**, Norra Hamngatan 12 (City Museum; May–Aug daily 11am–4pm; Sept–April Tues & Thurs–Sun 11am–4pm, Wed 11am–8pm; 40kr) has emerged, after an extensive reshuffle of the city's museums, as the mother of them all, incorporating several in the one building. It is located in the Ostindiska Huset, built in 1750, which housed the offices, goods store and auction house of the enormously influential Swedish **East India Company**. Envious of the major maritime nations, two Gothenburg-based industrialists, Colin Campbell and Niklas Sahlgren, set up the firm in the early eighteenth century. Granted the sole right to trade with China in 1731, the company monopolized all Swedish trade with the Far East for over eighty years, the only condition being that the bounty – tea, silk, porcelain, spices and arrack (an East Indian schnapps used to make Swedish punch) – had to be sold and auctioned in Gothenburg. The Chinese influence acquired on these great sea voyages pervaded Gothenburg society, and wealthy financiers adorned their homes and gardens with Chinese motifs. By 1813, the unrest of the French Revolution and competition from British and Dutch tea traders meant profits slid, and it was decreed in Sweden that "East India trade could be pursued by anyone so inclined". The headquarters, however, remains an imposing reminder of the power and prestige the company, and Gothenburg, once had. Very informative **guided walks** of the seventeenth-century streets, canals and buildings in the vicinity are organized by the museum (in English; cost included in the museum admission fee, otherwise 40kr or free with Gothenburg Card); it's no surprise that these tours emphasize the legacy of the East India Company.

The museum itself is well worth a browse, not least for its rich interior, a mix of squat, carved stone pillars, stained glass and frescoes. Your first port of call should be the third floor, where there are exhibitions on the East India Company. There is very little English labelling, but the numerous display cabinets, full of Chinese goods and treasures, give a wonderful insight into the company's history. The renovated hall where the city's grandest auctions took place is, however, surprisingly modest. From here you move on to the rather incongruously located exhibition of **1950s life**, based around fashions and film stars; among the displays are showcases of pointy bras and Vespa motorbikes.

The museum's most impressive section is the **industrial history** exhibition. Using sound effects, clever design and plenty of English commentary, the exhibition focuses on twentieth-century commerce, starting with the textile and timber trade, which were central to Gothenburg's wealth. At the beginning of the century, working conditions in the city's factories were extremely poor, and at some textile factories up to a third of the workforce was children. The main working-class neighbourhood was Haga (see p.140), and the exhibition highlights the importance of Järntorget (Iron Square), just northwest of Haga Nygatan, which was a hotbed of unrest during the great strike of 1909. The exhibition then moves on to the middle decades of the century, when massive industrial growth saw the building of the shipyards, and rise of the ball-bearings and motor-vehicle industries. By the 1950s and 1960s, the first foreign labour had to be recruited to deal with demand, and the present-day situation is summed up by a plaque at the end: "Once, the city had one engineer and one hundred workers to make a ship engine. Now, a large group of engineers design an engine part to be built by factories abroad."

South of Stora Hamn – Lilla Torget to Brunnsparken

Most of the city's smaller and none-too-thrilling museums have been incorporated within the Stadsmuseum, with the exception of one, the **Banking Museum**, Södra Hamngatan 11, on the south side of Stora Hamn canal (Sun noon–3pm, guided tours in English at 2pm; ☎031/40 11 05). You can visit the vaults inside, but the building's facade is really the best bit. Also on this side of the canal, and just to the west of the Stadsmuseum, is **Lilla Torget**. In itself, the square is nothing to get excited about, but having nodded at the statue of Jonas Alstromer here – the man introduced the potato to Sweden in the eighteenth century – it's worth taking the tiny opening on the western side of the square and making the steep but short climb to **Drottning Kristinas Jaktslott** (Queen Kristina's Hunting Lodge) at Otterhallegatan 16. Never a hunting lodge, and absolutely nothing to do with Queen Kristina, who died before it was built, it is now a quaint café that serves particularly good waffles (daily 11am–4pm).

A couple of minutes' walk west from the square brings you to the quayside where, at **Stenpiren** (Stone Pier), hundreds of emigrants said their last goodbyes before sailing off in 1638 to "New Sweden" in the United States. The granite **Delaware Monument** was carted off to America from Gothenburg in the early part of this century, and it wasn't until 1938 that celebrated sculptor Carl Milles cast a replacement in bronze, which stands here looking out to sea.

Back in Lilla Torget, it's only a short walk down Västra Hamngatan, which leads off from the southern side of the square, to the city's cathedral; on the way you'll pass **Antik Hallarna** (Mon–Fri 10am–6pm, Sat 10am–2pm), a clutch of pricey antique shops. The most affordable stuff here is towards the back, along with the tat. It's the building, however, that warrants your attention, with its fantastic gilded ceiling and regal marble stairs leading up to the second floor, where there's a decent enough café.

A few blocks south of Antik Hallarna and left off Västra Hamngatan is the Neoclassically styled cathedral, **Domkyrkan** (daily Mon–Fri 8am–8pm, Sat 9am–6pm, Sun 10am–3pm), built in 1827 – the two previous cathedrals were destroyed by fires at a rate of one a century. Four giant sandstone columns stand at the portico, and inside there's an altarpiece that's a picture of gilded opulence. The plain white walls concentrate the eye on the unusual post-resurrection cross – devoid of a Jesus, his gilded grave clothes strewn around, summoning images of an adolescent's bedroom floor. Another quirky feature is the twin glassed-in verandas that run down either side; looking like glamorous trams with net curtains, they were actually designed for the bishop's private conversations.

Continuing east past the cathedral and north towards Stora Hamn, the leafy square known as **Brunnspark** soon comes into view, with Gustav Adolfs Torg just across the canal. The sedate house facing the square is now a snazzy restaurant and nightclub called *The Palace* (see p.148), but in the late nineteenth century the house was home to Pontus and Gothilda Fürstenburg, the city's leading arts patrons of the time. They opened up the top floor as an art gallery, the first in Gothenburg to make use of electric as well as natural light, and later donated their entire collection – the biggest batch of Nordic paintings in the country – to the city's Art Museum. As a tribute to the Fürstenburgs, the museum made over the top floor into an exact replica of the original gallery (see p.138). Staff at *The Palace* know little of its history, but won't prevent you wandering upstairs to see the richly ornate plasterwork and gilding, much as it was.

West from Stora Nygatan along the canal

Following the zigzagging canal that marks the southern perimeter of old Gothenburg – a moat during the days when the city was fortified – makes for a fine twenty-minute stroll, past pretty waterside views and a number of interesting diversions. Just east of Brunnspark, **Stora Nygatan** wends its way south along the canal's most scenic stretch; to one side are Classical buildings all stuccoed in cinnamon and cream, and to the other is the green expanse of Trädgårdsföreningen park (see p.137). Amid all the architectural finery sits the **Great Synagogue**, inaugurated in 1855, making it mainland Sweden's oldest (call ☎031/17 72 45 to arrange a visit). Its simple domed exterior belies the presence inside of one of the most exquisite interiors of any European synagogue: the ceiling and walls are all covered in rich blues, reds and gold, and Moorish patterns are interwoven with Viking leaf designs – a combination that works to stunning effect. It also has some unusual features: the lofty interior contains two upper levels of women's galleries and at the back, a splendid organ – extremely rare in synagogues – first played at the inauguration ceremony. The original congregation were Orthodox German Jews, though it now serves as a Conservative synagogue for all the community.

South from the synagogue, you'll pass **Kungsportsplatsen**, in the centre of which stands a useful landmark, a sculpture known as the "Copper Mare" – though it's immediately obvious if you look from beneath that this is no mare. A few minutes further on, and one block in from the canal at Kungstorget, is **Saluhallen** (Mon–Fri 9am–6pm, Sat 9am–2pm), a pretty barrel-roofed indoor market built in the 1880s. Busy and full of atmosphere, it's a great place to wander through (for more on food markets in Gothenburg see "Eating", p.143); outside there's a flower market.

Five minutes' walk west from here is Gothenburg's oldest food market, the Neo-Gothic **Feskekörka**, or "Fish-church" (Tues–Thurs 9am–5pm, Fri 9am–6pm, Sat 9am–1.30pm), whose strong aromas may well hit you long before you reach its door. Despite its undeniably ecclesiastical appearance, the nearest this 1874 building comes to religion is the devotion shown by the fish lovers who come to buy here. Inside, every kind of fish, from smoked to shellfish, lies in gleaming pungent mounds of silver, pink and black flesh; while in a gallery upstairs, there's a very small, very good restaurant (see "Eating", p.145).

The Garden Society Park

From Kungsportsplatsen, cross the bridge over the southern canal, and the main entrance to the well-groomed **Trädgårdsföreningen** (Garden Society Park; May–Aug 7am–9pm; Sept–April 7am–6pm; May–Aug 10kr, rest of year free) is just to the east. There are a number of attractions to visit, the most impressive of which is the 1878 **Palm House** (daily: June–Aug 10am–6pm; Sept–May 10am–4pm; 20kr fee also gives entry to the Botanical Gardens; see p.141). Designed as a copy of London's Crystal Palace, and looking like a huge English conservatory, it contains a wealth of very un-Swedish plant life: tropical, Mediterranean and Asian flowers. Close by is the **Butterfly House** (April, May & Sept Tues–Sun 10am–4pm; June–Aug daily 10am–5pm; Oct–March Tues–Fri 10am–3pm, Sat & Sun 11am–3pm; 35kr), where you can walk among free-flying butterflies from Asia and the Americas who flit about here in eighty percent humidity. Further on is the **Rosarium**, a rose garden with nearly three thousand varieties, arranged in a veritable palette of colours. During summer the place goes into overdrive, with lunchtime concerts and a special children's theatre.

Avenyn and around

Running all the way from the canal southeast to Götaplatsen is the wide, cobbled length of Kungsportsavenyn. Known more simply as **Avenyn** or "the Avenue", this is Gothenburg's showiest thoroughfare, teeming with life. The ground floor of almost every grand old nineteenth-century home here has been converted into a café, bar or restaurant; the young and beautiful strut up and down sipping over-priced drinks while posing at tables that, from mid-spring to September, spill out onto the street. It's enjoyable enough to sit and watch people go by, but for all its glamour, the tourist-orientated shops and brasseries are mostly bright and samey, and the grandeur of the city's industrial past is easier to imagine in the less spoiled mansions along Parkgatan – running at right angles to Avenyn and parallel to the canal – and other roads to the southwest off the main drag. Here, in the area known as **Vasastan**, you'll find Gothenburg's **museum of applied arts**, and at the end of Avenyn on **Götaplatsen**, the extensive **fine art museum**.

Götaplatsen

At the top of Avenyn, **Götaplatsen** is modern Gothenburg's main square. in the centre of which stands Carl Milles's **Poseidon** – a giant, nude, bronze body-builder with a staggeringly ugly face. The size of the figure's penis caused moral outrage when the sculpture first appeared in 1930, and was subsequently dramatically reduced. Today, although from the front Poseidon appears to be squeezing the living daylights out of what looks like a large-fanged fish, if you climb the steps of the **Concert Hall** to the right, it becomes clear that the creature was actually Milles' revenge for his climbdown over Poseidon's manhood. To the left of the statue and standing back from the City Library is the columned **Lorensberg theatre**, one of Gothenburg's few private theatres, and originally designed as the first people's theatre in the country, having no expensive boxes, just standard-price stalls. Few tourists are likely to take in a show here, though, as the Lorensberg (like many other theatres in Sweden) is closed during the summer and only puts on shows in Swedish (for more on theatre in Gothenburg, see p.150).

Art Museum

Behind *Poseidon* stands the Götaplatsen's most impressive attraction, the much-respected **Konstmuseum** (Art Museum; May–Aug Mon–Fri 11am–4pm; Sept–April Tues, Thurs & Fri 11am–4pm, Wed 11am–9pm, Sat & Sun 11am–5pm; 35kr). Though its massive, symmetrical facade is reminiscent of the Fascist architecture of 1930s Germany, this is one of the city's finest museums, and it's easy to spend half a day absorbing the diverse and extensive collections. The following is only a brief guide to some of the highlights.

On the ground floor, the **Hasselblad Centre** shows excellent photographic exhibitions; while on the floor above, a display of post-1945 Nordic art gives space to changing displays of the work of contemporary Scandinavian painters and sculptors. Another room on this floor has some works by the celebrated masters of French Impressionism; the next couple of floors up hold a range of minor works by Van Gogh, Gauguin and Pissarro, a powerful and surprisingly colourful Munch and a couple of Rodin sculptures. Moving on to floor five, you'll find Italian and Spanish paintings from 1500 to 1750, including Rembrandt's *Knight with Falcon*, Rubens' *Adoration of the Magi* and works by Canaletto and Francesco Guardi.

Best of all, however, and the main reason to visit, are the **Fürstenburg Galleries** on the sixth floor. These celebrate the work of some of Scandinavia's most prolific and revered turn-of-the-century artists; well-known works here by Carl Larsson, Anders Zorn and Carl Wilhelmson reflect the seasons and landscapes of the Nordic countries and evoke a vivid picture of Scandinavian life at that time. Paintings to look out for include Larsson's *Lilla Suzanne*, which touchingly depicts the elated face of a baby and is one of his most realistic works; Anders Zorn's *Bathers*, flushed with a pale pink summer glow and exemplifying the painter's feeling for light and the human form; and the sensitive portraits by Ernst Josephson, most notably his full-length portrait of Carl Skånberg – easily mistaken for the young Winston Churchill. The Danish artist Peter Kroyer's marvellous *Hip Hip Hooray* again plays with light, and a couple of works by Hugo Birger deserve your attention, too. One depicts the interior of the original Fürstenburg Gallery (see p.136), complete with electric lights, while his massive *Scandinavian Artists' Breakfast in Paris,* dominating an entire wall, will help put some faces to the artists' names. Also worth a look is an entire room of Larsson's fantastical and bright wall-sized paintings.

A delightful little park, **Nackros Dammen** ("Waterlily Park"), lies just behind the museum; with its late-spring rhododendrons and big pond full of ducks, it's just the place to relax after a morning of intensive art appreciation.

Liseberg Amusement Park and Museum of Ethnography

Just a few minutes' walk southeast from Götaplatsen (or take tram #5 from the old centre), **Liseberg Amusement Park** (late April to June & late Aug daily 3–11pm; July to mid-Aug daily noon–11pm; Sept Sat 1–11pm, Sun noon–8pm; 45kr, under-7s free; all-day ride pass 215kr, tickets for a fixed number of rides 90kr or 150kr) is a riot of party lights and gum-pink paintwork. Opened in 1923, Scandinavia's largest amusement park, with its flowers, trees, fountains and clusters of lights, is great fun for adults as well as children, a league away from the hyped neon and plastic mini-cities that constitute so many theme parks around the world. Old and young dance to live bands most evenings, and although louder and more youth-dominated at night (especially on Saturdays), it is safe to stroll around. An attraction that's much in demand here is an ambitious roller coaster called "Hangover".

If you visit Liseberg during the day, it's worth teaming it up with the surprisingly interesting **Museum of Ethnography** at Avagen 24, a ten-minute walk north of the park (May–Aug Mon–Fri 11am–4pm, Sat & Sun 11am–5pm), just over the highway. The best exhibits are those on Native-American culture, with brilliantly lit textiles that are up to 2000 years old and some other more grisly finds, including skulls deliberately trephined (small circular sections of bone were removed) to ward off bad spirits.

Vasastan and the Röhsska Museum

Back at Avenyn, take one of the roads off to the west and wander into the **Vasastan** district, where the streets are lined with fine nineteenth-century and National Romantic architecture, and the cafés are cheaper, more laid-back. and much more charismatic. On **Vasagatan**, the main street through the district, is the excellent **Röhsska Museum**, Sweden's only museum of applied arts (May–Aug Mon–Fri noon–4pm, Sat & Sun noon–5pm; Sept–April Tues noon–9pm, Wed–Fri noon–4pm, Sat & Sun noon–5pm; 35kr). This 1916 museum is an aesthetic Aladdin's cave, with each floor concentrating on different areas of decorative and functional art, from early-dynasty Chinese ceramics to European arts and crafts of the sixteenth and seventeenth centuries. Most arresting is the first floor, devoted to twentieth-century decor and featuring all manner of recognizable designs for domestic furniture and appliances from the 1910s to the 1990s – enough to send anyone over the age of ten on a giddy nostalgia trip. Attached to the contemporary design shop is a pleasant café, serving light lunches (55–60kr). A little further down on the left, the glorious **University main building** stands in a small park; it's worth trying the doors of this 1907 classic to peek at the stunningly renovated interior – all pale marble coolness, an enormous Art Nouveau light fitting and a main hall with impressive wall paintings.

Back on Vasagatan, head to the west end of the street, where the Haga district begins, and on the right, overlooking Haga Park, is the original **University Library** now housing newspaper archives (☎031/773 27 20). Here you can read the British, American and French national daily and Sunday papers (though some are rather out of date) – but the real draw is that the whole place has been restored, with reading areas that are a feast for the eye, beneath vaulted, handpainted arches. In the main reading area, one wall is filled with a vast impressionistic **painting**, *The Giving of Wisdom*, which Pontus Fürstenburg (see p.136) commissioned for the library from Carl Wilhelmson, one of Sweden's most celebrated late-nineteenth-century artists (see p.158).

Along Vasagatan, and the parallel **Engelbrektsgatan**, you'll come across solid, stately and rangy buildings that epitomize Gothenburg's nineteenth-century commercial wealth and civic pride. White-stuccoed or red-and-cream brick facades are decorated with elaborate ceramic tiles, intricate stone-and-brick animal carvings, shiny metal cupolas and Classical window porticoes. With the detail spread gracefully across these six-storey terraces, the overall effect is of restrained grandeur. Many of the houses also have Continental-style wrought-iron balconies; it's easy to imagine high-society gatherings spilling out into the night on warm summer evenings. In contrast, interspersed among all this nineteenth-century swagger are some perfect examples of early twentieth-century National Romantic architecture, with rough-hewn stone and Art Nouveau swirls in plaster and brickwork; look particularly at the low-numbered buildings along Engelbrektsgatan, furthest from Avenyn.

Haga

A ten-minute stroll west up Vasagatan (alternatively take tram #1 or #2 to Olivedalsgatan) is the city's oldest working-class suburb, **Haga**, once so run-down that its demolition was on the cards, but today one of Gothenburg's most picturesque quarters. The transformation took place in the early 1980s, after some-one saw potential in the web of artisans' homes known as "governor's houses". These distinctive early-nineteenth-century buildings, made up of a stone ground floor and two wooden upper storeys, were built thus so as to minimize the devastation caused by city fires. After one particularly bad blaze, the city governor decreed that no building should have more than two floors of wood. At the time, stone was expensive, and heavy for the clay ground – hence the combination of materials ultimately used.

Haga is now Gothenburg's miniature version of Greenwich Village, the domain of well-off and socially aware 20- and 30-somethings. The thick smattering of cafés and shops along its cobbled streets are style-conscious and not at all cheap. Although there are a couple of good restaurants (see p.146) along the main thoroughfare, **Haga Nygatan**, this is really somewhere to come during the day, when tables are put out on the street and the atmosphere is friendly and villagey – if a little self-consciously fashionable. Apart from the boutiques, which tend to sell the likes of Art Deco light fittings, calmative crystals and nineteenth-century Swedish kitchenware, it's worth noting the intervening apartment buildings. These red-brick edifices were originally almshouses donated by the Dickson family, the city's British industrialist forefathers who played a big part in the success of the East India Company – the name of Robert Dickson is still emblazoned on the facades. Next door to the beautiful F.D. Dickson People's Library on Allegården, a real measure of Haga's social status is offered in the **Haga Badet**, a superbly renovated old working-class bathhouse whose construction was funded by Sven Renström, one of Gothenburg's non-British philanthropists at the end of the nineteenth century (Mon–Fri 7am–9.30pm, Sat 9am–6pm, Sun 10am–5pm). Today, the sort of customers that made up the original clientele wouldn't get a look in – it's a rather fine (and not cheap) health spa, with the prettiest of pools in an Art Nouveau-style setting, a Roman bath and a massage area. There's also a very pleasant café and buffet (Mon–Fri 11.30am–2pm, Sat 11.30am–3pm). The complex is certainly worth a peek; a one-day card letting you use the sauna, gym and pool costs 150kr.

Adjoining Haga to the south, **Skansparken** is hardly a park at all, being little more than the raised mound of land on which stands the **Military Museum** (Tues & Wed noon–2pm, Sat & Sun noon–3pm; 30kr; guided tour, included with admission, first Sunday of each month at 1pm; ☎031/14 50 00), housed in the newly gilded Skansen Kronan, one of Gothenburg's two surviving seventeenth-century fortress towers. The steep climb is worth it for the views north across the city to the harbour, rather than for the incredibly feeble museum, whose entire collection consists of wax models dressed in military uniforms through the ages.

Linné

To the west of Haga is the cosmopolitan district of **Linné**, named after the botanist Carl Von Linné, who originated the system for classifying plants used the world over (see p.116). In recent years, so many stylish cafés and restaurants have sprung up along the main thoroughfare, Linnégatan (turn south off Haga

Nygatan into Landsvagsgatan, which joins up with Linnégatan), that Linné is now considered Gothenburg's "second Avenyn" – but without the attitude. The street is lined with Dutch-inspired nineteenth-century architecture, tall and elegant buildings interspersed with steep little side roads.

However, it's the main roads leading off Linnégatan, prosaically named Long Street (Långgatan) First, Long Street Second, and so on up to Fourth, that give the area its real character. The not-very-long Second and Third streets contain a mix of dark antique stores, basement cafés and upfront sex shops. The antiques go for high prices here, so if you're interested, it's well worth checking out the popular **Auction House**, Trådje Långgatan 9 (closed July; ☎031/12 44 30), where a large amount of silver, porcelain and jewellery is mixed in with total tat; viewings (Mon 4pm–7.30pm, Tues 9am–noon) precede the weekly auctions (Wed & Thurs 9am–3pm).

On the right as you head up Linnégatan towards Järntorget is one modern apartment block that's worth a second glance, if only because King Oskar II had his private apartment – and his women – in the forbidding, dark building directly opposite, on your left. The block on the right replaced a property whose republican owner so hated both the monarchy and the morals of the king that he had a run of colourful ceramic panels, depicting the devil, set facing the royal apartment. Sadly, the Gothenburg propensity for doing away with its own past meant the "devil building", as it was known, was recently demolished, but two of the grotesque panels have been incorporated into the new apartment block.

Slottskogen, a five-minute walk south from Linnégatan (tram #1 or #2 to Linnéplatsen), is a huge, tranquil expanse of parkland, with farm animals and birdlife, including pink flamingos in summer. The rather dreary **Natural History Museum** (daily 11am–5pm), within the grounds of the park, prides itself on being the city's oldest museum, dating from 1833. Its endless displays of stuffed birds appear particularly depressing after seeing the living ones outside, and although the museum supposedly contains ten million animals, most of these are minute insects, which sit unnoticed in drawers that fill several rooms. The only items that really capture the attention are a bottle containing the macabre nineteenth-century pickled foetuses of conjoined twins, and the world's only stuffed blue whale. Harpooned in 1865, the whale now contains a Victorian café complete with red-velvet period sofas – the top half of the animal neatly secured to its underside by hinges. Unfortunately, these days the whale is only opened in election years – the Swedish for "election" is the same as for "whale". On the south side of Slottskogen are the large **Botanical Gardens** (daily 9am–dusk; glasshouses May–Aug daily 9am–6pm; Sept–April Mon–Fri 10am–3pm, Sat & Sun noon–4pm). Entrance is free with a ticket to the Palm House (see p.137), and costs 20kr otherwise.

West to Klippan and the Gothenburg Archipelago

On a fine day, Gothenburgers make for the nearest **coastal islands**, where bathing in the sea and sun are a real pleasure and it's hard to imagine you're so close to a city at all. One of the best ways of exploring the area just to the west of the city is to take a bike along the riverside from the Opera House (see p.133), a route which takes you past the ferry terminals used by Stena Line's Denmark services and on to the Seacat terminal in the old **Amerika House**, the building that once housed the shipping line operating services to the USA. This was where countless Swedes set foot on their native shores for the last time – and also the spot from where Sweden's small clutch of film stars (ie Garbo and Bergman) sailed. Around 1km on, the gold-topped spire of the Karl Johan Church appears in foliage to the left, and a small lane, also on your left, leads to the city's gay centre (see p.149); just on the right are Gothenburg's famed **fish auctions** at Fiskhamnen (see p.144) which make a dramatic sight at six in the morning.

A few hundred metres straight on is **Klippan**, a charming old enclave of old red houses once used in both the sugar and brewing industries; the area was at one time also the home port of the East India Company. Today, the buildings are largely converted for tourist purposes, the sugar mill having closed in the late 1950s and the brewery shut down in 1975. The first one you'll see is the old, wooden, red-painted East India Company warehouse, now a chic restaurant, *Sjömagasinet* serving lots of turbot and lobster at prices to test any expense account (Mon–Fri 11.30am–2.30pm & 5–11pm, Sat 5–11pm, Sun 2–9pm). A number of preserved houses are dotted about, including the low cottages of the workers at the Carnegie brewery and the East India Company, and the old sugar mill; taken over by Sir David Carnegie in 1836, the mill now houses artists' studios which are not really open to the public, but from the outside you'll be able to see work in progress. The most imposing building, the **Carnegie Porter Brewery** itself, is now a *Novotel* hotel (see "Accommodation", p.126). To rest a while, the best spot is the café/art gallery, in an old factory office (Mon–Fri 11am–8pm, Sat & Sun noon–8pm) which has views over the water to the Öresund, beyond the turquoise-painted Älfsborgs bridge. You'll also find the ruins of Älvsborg Castle hereabouts, but it's only a few paltry mounds of stones, and not to be confused with Nya Elfsborg fortress (see p.133), at the mouth of the river, to which boats make regular trips.

Just a few steps further west, the newest and most exciting development at Klippan for anyone interested in contemporary art is **Röda Sten** (daily noon–4pm; free), an old grafitti-covered warehouse which lacks charm in itself, but is being developed into huge gallery space for temporary exhibitions. The only permanent exhibits are outside, a smattering of large and powerful granite sculptures by Claes Hake, reflecting the once industrial character of the area.

From here, the riverside scenery relieves you of any sense of being in an urban area. A few metres beyond Röda Sten is a small inlet in which children like to splash about. It's said locally that in a seventeenth-century river battle between Swedes and Danes, one surviving Swede climbed up on the largest stone in the water and, while his own blood dripped onto it, declared a minor victory; today the biggest stone in the water is painted blood red. A cycle track leads from the inlet through to **Nya Varvet** (New Wharf), a pleasant harbour area filled with small pleasure boats. There's not much to do here except fill up at *Reveljen* (Mon–Fri 11am–2pm), a vast self-service eatery with scores of large bowls containing salads, fish or meat – excellent budget lunches at 60kr for as much as you can gorge.

Saltholmen and the offshore islands

Around 3km west of Klippan is **Saltholmen**, at the tip of Gothenburg's most westerly peninsula. There are lots of smooth rocky outcrops here, providing a multitude of hidden sunbathing areas, and nude bathing is quite the norm. You can climb Saltholmen's highest point for lovely views, while the zone around to your left, on the south side of the peninsula, has become a recognized gay bathing area. The views are quite idyllic, with boats flecking the water and the islands stretching out into the distance.

From Saltholmen, regular ferries make the short trips to the most popular islands, stopping first at **Brännö**, an island mainly given over to summer houses converted from fishermen's shacks, and crowded with Gothenburgers through the summer. **Styrsö** is the next island, with three hamlets where most of its residents live all year. The furthest of the main islands is **Vrångö**, which has one small village and a perfect lagoon with a great beach: leaving the boat here, turn left, follow the short path and you'll find a spit of flat stone forming one side of the lagoon.

Tram #4 runs all the way to Saltholmen, and the ferries cost 10kr (free with tram ticket). There's a delightful little outdoor **café** at Saltholmen run by a Thai family, selling coffee, cake and ice cream.

North of the river

There is little need to venture north across the Göta river onto Hisingen, Sweden's fourth largest island, though car enthusiasts might be tempted by a visit to the **Volvo Museum** (June–Aug Tues–Fri 10am–5pm, Sat & Sun 11am–4pm; Sept–May Tues–Fri noon–5pm, Sat 11am–4pm; 30kr; ☎031/66 48 14); take tram #2 or #5 to Eketrägatan, then bus #28 to Götaverken Arendal. There is little effort made at the museum to create a special ambience for the many pristine exhibits, but fans of classic cars will enjoy seeing rare examples of many models, including "Phillip", an unusual American-style Volvo with fins, of which only one was ever produced, and plenty of other gleaming specimens, such as Volvo Amazons and the sporty P1800s, along with some not very interesting commercial vehicles – lorries and the like.

The quite separate, and free, **Volvo factory** has more general appeal; the tourist office will have the current opening times. To reach the museum from the factory, take bus #28 to Eketrägatan and then change onto bus #29; or from the centre of town, bus #29 runs in summer from Drottningtorget platform M, outside the main post office, right up to the Volvo Factory (40min). From its humble beginnings in 1927, when the company was founded by two engineers from a Gothenburg ball-bearings factory, the Volvo of today has a factory that's a vast, city-like complex, with city buses wending their way across leafy hills and stopping at places called Volvo Hall and Volvo Park. Geared towards people who are contemplating buying a car, the (compulsory) tour here includes film shows and commentaries in English that are one long advertisement. To see just how advanced technology is used at each stage in a car's creation, take the more interesting **Blue Train tour** (free), on a tram-like series of carriages that transports visitors through the vast site and the two-kilometre-long factory building, where you can watch robots (and even a few humans) build the cars from start to finish. There's a full commentary in English, which thankfully steers clear of technical jargon.

Eating and drinking

Gothenburg has a multitude of **eating** places, catering for every budget and for most tastes. The city's status as a trading port has led to a huge number of foreign restaurants, everything from Lebanese to Thai (though these places tend to come and go very quickly); the only thing you won't see much of, at least at the lower end of the market, is Swedish food. The city is also a great centre for fish restaurants, and these are among the most exclusive around. For less costly eating, there is a growing trend towards low-priced pasta places to complement the staple pizza parlours and burger bars.

During the past few years, **café life** has really come into its own in Gothenburg, the profusion of new places throughout the city adding to the traditional **konditori** (bakery with tea-room attached). Nowadays, it's easy to stroll from one café to another at any time of day or night, and tuck into humungous sandwiches and gorgeous cakes. Cafés also offer a wide range of light meals and are fast becoming about the best places to go for good food at reasonable prices. The most interesting cafés are concentrated in the fashionable Haga and Linné districts.

There's an excellent choice of places to **drink** in Gothenburg, but even the hippest bars serve food and so have a bit of a restaurant atmosphere, the exceptions being a small number of British- and Irish-style pubs. Although it's not uncommon for Gothenburgers to drink themselves to oblivion, the atmosphere around the bars is generally non-aggressive. Avenyn, late on a Saturday night, is really the only place where you might feel even the slightest bit unsafe.

Markets and snacks

The bustling, historic **Saluhallen** at Kungstorget is a delightful sensory experience, with a great choice of meats, fish, fruits, vegetables and a huge range of delectable breads; there are also a couple of cheap coffee- and snack bars here. A more recent arrival on the market scene is **Saluhall Briggen**, on the corner of Tredje Långgatan and Nordhamsgatan, in the Linné area. Housed in the old fire station, and more Continental and much smaller than Saluhallen, it specializes in good-quality meats, fish and cheese and mouthwatering deli delights. For excellent fresh fish, **Feskekorka** (see p.136) is an absolute must; while for the serious fish aficionado, there's the auction at **Fiskhamnen** (Fish Harbour; Tues–Fri 7am), a couple of kilometres west of the centre – take tram #3 or #4 to Stigbergstorget. The conveniently located **Konsum** supermarket on Avenyn (daily till 11pm) sells a wide range of fruits, fish, and meats, and has a good deli counter. For excellent takeaway baguette and coffee deals, head for the Liseberg end of Södravagen, where a clutch of café-shops sell full-to-bursting sandwiches and coffee for just 20kr – and all just a couple of minutes' walk from the much pricier Avenyn.

Cafés and restaurants

If you want to avoid paying over the odds, then it's a good idea to steer clear of Avenyn, where prices (with just a few exceptions) are almost double what you'll pay in Haga or Linné. It also makes sense to have your main meal at **lunchtime**, when *Dagens Rätt* deals fill you up for not very much outlay (40–60kr). For a useful guide to night-time eating for under 100kr, consult the Friday edition of Gothenburg's daily paper, *Göteborgs Posten*. It's worth noting that places can rapidly go in and out of fashion, or even out of business.

The old town

Ahlstroms Konditori, Korsgatan 2. A classic café-bakery of the old school. The original features have been watered down by modernization, but it's still worth a visit for its good selection of cakes, and its *Dagens Rätt* at 52kr.

C & Co Artroom, Kyrkogatan 31 (☎031/74 03 27). Perfect example of Gothenburg's recent foray into cool little cafés and bagel bars, attracting people who just have to be graphic designers. Excellent filled bagels at 35–40kr, and really good coffee. Mon–Fri 10am–5pm, Sat 9am–2pm.

Cafe Bommen, at the harbour. Standard café food, but a lovely spot to have a coffee by the water's edge, facing the Opera House. Daily 11am–6pm.

Froken Olssons Kafe, Östra Larmgatan 14. Dunes of sandwiches, salads and sumptuous desserts in a country-style (but not twee) atmosphere. Look out for their mountains of giant meringues on tiered, silver cake-trays. Sandwiches 30–50kr.

Gabriel at Feskekorka, in the eponymous fish market (☎031/13 90 51). Excellent fish restaurant, but prices seem particularly high, especially when the market displays the ingredients and their real costs. Specializes in oyster, lobster, crab, sole and crayfish. Much cheaper is to fill up at the tiny eight-seat *Cafe Feskekorke* at the opposite end of the market, where a substantial snack comes to about 40kr. Tues–Thurs 9am–5pm, Fri 9am–6pm, Sat 9am–1.30pm.

Grande E.t.c. Kungsgatan 12 (☎031/701 77 84). A big brother to *E.t.c.* at Vasaplatsen (see below), this place opened in summer 1999, with similar, very fresh pasta dishes from 85kr.

Greta's, Drottninggattan 35. Stylish, casual bar-restaurant very popular as a gay venue, with pictures of the enigmatic screen goddess all over the walls. Good menu of fish, meat and vegetarian options, and wonderful cakes for dessert, all consumed to easy background music and friendly chat.

Mat & Dryck, adjoining Saluhallen market. A pleasant, if basic, place for salads and fresh, country breads. Daily lunch at 58kr and a choice of twenty beers.

Matilda's, by the side of Saluhallen market. This central, friendly café is good for a soup-bowl-sized *café au lait,* chunky sandwiches and cakes.

Ostindiska Huset Krog & Cafe, at Norra Hamngatan 12, next door to the Stadsmuseum. Delightful eatery in the vaulted white Ostindiska House. Lunch menu for around 60kr and more costly evening menu in a romantic setting.

Petersens, Korsgatan 15. A *konditori* with good cakes and the best breads in town. Mon–Fri 9am–7pm, Sat 8.30am–5pm.

Avenyn, Vasastan and around

Cafe Dali, Vasagatan 42. In an orange-painted basement. A friendly, stylish place for sandwiches and cakes.

Café Engelen, Engelbrektsgatan. Home-baked, excellent-value food (there's always a vegetarian selection) at this friendly, studenty café. Baked potatoes, lasagne or chunky sandwiches each cost 38kr. Also on offer are a good all-day breakfast (27kr), glorious home-made ice cream and a wide range of fruit teas. Open 24hr, seven days a week.

E.t.c., Vasaplatsen 4, Vasastan. With an elegant, cool-white basement interior, this Swedish- and Montenegran-owned restaurant makes wonderful home-made pasta. Lunch menu at 55kr; at dinner there are additional meat and fish dishes. Popular, and so fills up in the evenings.

Restaurant Frågetecken, Södra Vägen 20. With a name that translates as "restaurant question mark", this is a very popular spot, just a minute's walk from Götaplatsen. Eat in the conservatory, or inside where you can watch the chefs at work, carefully preparing Balkan-influenced food. Duck is the most expensive thing on the menu, at 219kr; a pasta dish is under 100kr. Mon–Fri 11am–11pm, Sat 2pm–midnight, Sun 2–10pm.

Garbo, Vasagatan 40. Not a place where you'd want to be alone, despite the name, this sociable, relaxed café serves good, light food. Same owners as *Greta's* (see "The old town" listings, above).

Gothia Hotel Restaurant, Massansgatan 24 (☎031/40 93 00). Panoramic views are afforded at this piano-bar restaurant, on the hotel's glass-walled top floor. They serve, among other fabulously expensive meals, superb king-prawn sandwiches at a whopping 110kr.

Java Café, Vasagatan 23, Vasaplan. There's a Parisian feel to this studenty coffee house that's stood the test of time, serving breakfasts at 28kr and a wide range of coffees. Decor includes a collection of thermos flasks dotted among shelves of books. A good Sunday-morning hangout. Mon–Fri 8am–10pm, Fri & Sat 8am–11.30pm, Sun 9am–10pm.

Junggrens Café, Avenyn 37. The only reasonably priced Avenyn café, with excellent snacks and sandwiches. Run for decades by a charismatic Polish woman and her sulky staff. Drop by just for its quirky, convivial atmosphere, its wall paintings and its chandeliers. Coffee at only 10kr, sandwiches 12–20kr.

Lai Wa, Storgatan 11, Vasaplan. One of the better Chinese restaurants with a wide variety of dishes at reasonable prices. Good lunches. Try what they've called "Peking soup", a meaty, sweet-and-sour concoction.

Skåne Café, Södra Vägen 59. Big, freshly made sandwiches – one with a smoked-salmon filling costs just 20kr, for example – in a very small, basic café, well worth the five-minute walk here from Avenyn or Liseberg.

Smaka, Vasaplatsen 3, Vasastan (☎031/13 22 47). A fine choice for traditional Swedish food at reasonable prices, in a modish setting of blue walls and steel floor tiles. Mon–Thurs 5pm–1am, Fri & Sat 4pm–2am.

Tai Pak, Arkivsgatan, just off Avenyn near Götaplatsen. A goodish, traditional-style Chinese restaurant serving a two-course special for 69kr; individual courses around 65–75kr. Open seven days a week; till 11.30pm on Sat & Sun.

Teatergatan Cafe, Teatergatan. A hip, even posey, café with black-and-white swivel chairs, sandwiches at 50kr and salads at 60kr. Cool on a hot afternoon.

Tintin Café, Engelbrektsgatan 22 (☎031/16 68 12). Very busy, 24hr café with a laid-back, studenty atmosphere, offering mounds of delicious cakes and pies. Prices are low – a big plate of chicken salad costs 40kr.

28+, Götabergsgatan 28. A very fine, expensive French-style gourmet restaurant in a street parallel to Avenyn. Its name refers to the fat percentage of its renowned cheese: there's a cheese shop (daily 9am–11pm) just inside the entrance. Specialities include goose-liver terrine. The service is excellent. Mon–Fri 11.30am–2pm & 6–11pm, Sat 6–11pm.

Haga

Allegården, Södra Allegatan 4, looking onto Feskekorka. Simple, friendly place for a coffee, set in a fairy-tale concoction of engraved stone and pink brick, originally built by F.D. Dickson as a people's library in 1897. Mon–Fri 8.30am–4pm.

Cafe Kringlan, Haga Nygatan 13. A recent arrival on the very good chocolate pie scene. Also serves bagels, strudel and generous open sandwiches, it's a popular place to sit outside in the summer.

Hemma Hos, Haga Nygatan 12 (☎031/13 40 90). Popular and expensive restaurant, full of quaint old furniture, serving upmarket Swedish food – reindeer and fish dishes.

Jacob's Café, Haga Nygatan 10. *The* place to sit outside and people-watch; amid the pretty decor are some fine Jugend (Swedish Art Nouveau) lamps.

Sjöbaren, Haga Nygatan 27. A small new fish and shellfish restaurant, with moderate prices, on the ground floor of a traditional governor's residence.

Solrosen, Kaponjargatan 4a (☎031/711 66 97). The oldest vegetarian restaurant in Gothenburg, with a wide range of dishes at moderate prices. Mon–Fri 11.30am–1am, Sat 2pm–1am.

Linné

Alten, at the junction of Linnégatan and Landsvägsgatan, below *Plus* (see p.147). A pure-1950s café and ice-cream parlour of the circular red leatherette bar stools and pistachio green walls variety. Sells ice creams and the cheapest espresso coffees in town.

Biblos Bar & Restaurant, Andra Långgatan 21 (☎031/42 35 53). Serves traditional Lebanese food with a fifteen-dish *mezze* for 195kr (minimum four people); the range of dishes is large and so are the portions. Try the wonderful couscous and lamb dishes; there's also a good salad buffet at 55kr and plenty of veggie options. Belly dancing on Fri and Sat nights. Mon–Thurs 11.30am–11pm, Fri 11.30am–midnight, Sat 2pm–midnight, Sun 1–9pm.

Café 3, Linnégatan 3, at the corner of Tredje Långgatan. A cosy, relaxed café serving baguettes with chicken, tuna or other fillings for 25kr, and lovely fruit crumbles. Mon–Thurs 7.30am–10pm, Fri 7.30am–9pm, Sat & Sun 11am–7pm.

Cyrano, Prinsgatan 7 (☎031/14 31 10). An absolute must: this superb, authentically Provencal bistro has a laid-back atmosphere and great service. They also do the best wood-fired pizzas. Gothenburgers have discovered this gem of a place, so book ahead. Mon–Fri 11am–11pm, Sat 2–11pm, Sun 2–9pm.

Den Lilla Taverna, Oliver Dahlsgatan 17 (☎031/12 88 05). A very good and very popular Greek restaurant, with paper tablecloths and Greek mythological scenes painted on false windows. Most dishes cost 65–90kr. Live bazouki music Wed & Sat. Mon–Thurs 4–11pm, Fri 4pm–1am, Sat 1pm–1am, Sun 1pm–11pm.

Hos Pelle, Djupedalsgatan 2 (☎031/12 10 31). Lovely and sophisticated wine bar off Linnégatan. Try their snack options or full meals, while surrounded by wonderful abstract artwork. Mon–Thurs & Sun 6pm–midnight, Fri & Sat 6pm–1am. Moderate.

Jazzå, Långgatan 4. Pleasantly dark bar and restaurant with jazz and blues nights and interesting modern art on the yellowing walls.

Johansson's Café & Curiosity Shop, Andre Långgatan 6. A pleasant café, where you can actually buy the antique ornaments and furniture around you. Sandwiches from 22kr.

Krakow, Karl Gustavsgatan 28 (☎031/20 33 74). Burly staff serve moderately priced and very filling Polish food in this large, dark restaurant.

Le Village, Tredje Långgatan 13 (☎031/24 20 03). Lovely, candle-lit restaurant whose management also runs a big antique shop. Everything you sit on and at is for sale, though at inflated prices. The smallish dishes are very well-presented. Eating in the main dining area is expensive; the trick is to pick a table at the cheaper bar area where meals start from 65kr. Mon–Thurs & Sun till midnight, Fri & Sat till 1am.

Linnés Trädgård, Linnégatan 38. This bar and restaurant is a popular, stylish meeting place, its huge windows taking full advantage of its corner position. It serves beautifully presented fish, meat and pasta dishes, though the menu's not extensive. For something sweet, try the blueberry mousse or the deliciously indulgent honey-and-pecan parfait.

Louice Restaurant, Värmlandsgatan 18, off Andra Långgatan (☎031/12 55 49). Justifiably popular and unpretentious neighbourhood restaurant, with occasional live music. Standard main courses are expensive, but look out for the excellent-value daily specials at 53kr. There's a full children's menu, with an English translation available, at 35kr.

Pasta Gambero, Övre Husargatan 5 (☎031/13 78 38). The best of a number of good, reasonably priced Italian eateries on this long street at the end of Linnégatan. The servings here are generous and the service very obliging. Next door is an excellent pizzeria, run by the same family. Mon–Thurs 11am–10pm, Fri 11am–11pm, Sat 3–11pm, Sun 2–9pm.

Petroshka, Oliver Dahlsgatan 10 (☎031/24 30 88). Bizarre Russian restaurant – the tables are decked out with cut-glass crystal and candelabras, but the atmosphere is that of a St Petersburg living room. Plentiful, traditional Russian food from borsch to caviar and blinis. This place manages to glitter grandly yet cheaply.

Plus (+) at junction of Linnégatan and Landsvägsgatan (☎031/24 08 90). In a beautifully restored old wooden house that was until recently a ramshackle home, nestling in the rough-hewn rock which cradles Linnégatan. Eat well-prepared meat and fish dishes with an international flavour (160–180kr) at polished tables beneath chandeliers. There's an extensive drinks list. Daily 5–11pm.

Saluhallen Briggan (see markets above). Amid the delicatessen, fish and cheese counters, a blackboard-menu café serves baked potatoes, pies, and pizzas for 55kr each; also pasta dishes and sizeable grills at 60kr.

Solsidan Café, Linnégatan 42. Lovely, long-standing café, very popular with Linné locals, with outside seating. Delicious cakes. Pasta salad and coffee 49kr. Daily 10am–11pm.

Thai Garden, Andra Långgatan 18 (☎031/12 76 60). Nothing special to look at, this place offers excellent service, moderate prices and large portions.

Bars

We've listed some of the city's most popular pubs and bar-restaurants below; however, it's worth noting that many of the cafés and restaurants given above are also good places to have a beer, especially in the busier night-time areas of Avenyn and Linné. In Vasaplan, just west of Avenyn, and in Haga, further west, the 24-hour studenty cafés listed earlier are great places to drink into the early hours, and on Avenyn itself, it's less a matter of choosing the best place than spotting a table. Although there are a number of long-established bars in the old town, the atmosphere is generally a bit low-key at night.

The old town

Beefeater Inn, Plantagegatan 1. One of a bevy of British-orientated neighbourhood pubs, very much in vogue with Gothenburgers. This one really goes overboard, with a stylistic mishmash of red-telephone-box doors and staff in kilts to match the tartan walls.

Dubliners, Östra Hamngatan 50b. Swedes have for a while been swept away with nostalgia for all things old and Irish – or at least what they imagine to be old and Irish. This is the most popular of Gothenburg's Irish-style pubs, offering a Swedish interpretation of Dublin *bonhomie*.

Esther, Kungstorget, behind Salluhall. Though it doesn't look like much from the outside, this is a pleasant bar with some striking art work on the walls; it does good cakes too.

Gamle Port, Östra Larmgatan 18. The city's oldest watering hole, with British beer in the downstairs pub and an awful disco upstairs (see "Clubs", p.149).

The Palace, Brunnsparken. In the rather splendid former home of the Fürstenburgs and their art galleries (see p.138), this upmarket bar and restaurant is very popular – and pricey.

Avenyn and around

Brasserie Lipp, Avenyn 8. No longer the hippest place on Avenyn, *Lipp* is expensive and so attracts a slightly older crowd – but a crowd it is, especially during summer. Also here is *Bubbles Nightclub* (see "Clubs", p.149).

Harley's, Avenyn 10. Very loud, young crowd. Not a place for a quiet chat, unless you hover just outside.

Napoleon, Vasagatan 11. It's the fabulous decor of this old house that makes a drink here fun: even the exterior walls are covered in delicate old paintings. Though really a bar, this lovely, dark, mellow place also serves light meals. Mon–Thurs & Sun 10am–midnight, Fri & Sat 10am–3am.

Niva, Avenyn 9. Bar and restaurant on separate levels. This stylish bar, with its modern, mosaic interior, is becoming ever more popular.

Scandic Rubinen Bar, Avenyn 24. Glitzy hotel-foyer-style bar, always packed with tourists and right at the heart of Avenyn.

Haga

Dog & Duck, Viktoriagatan 5. An all-British pub/restaurant that makes a valiant attempt at evoking a cosy, nineteenth-century atmosphere. Serves light meals, nachos, burgers and chicken shish-kebabs, each dish at around 65kr.

Indian Palace Pub, Järntorget 4. Just northwest of Haga Nygatan, this place is rather unappealing on the outside, with its neon arrows attempting to coax you in. There is a restaurant on the ground floor, and the basement pub has a pool table.

Studs, Götabergsgatan, off Engelbrektsgatan, behind Vasa Church. This is the hub of Gothenburg student life, with a pub, bar and restaurant. The main advantage of the student bar is its prices – there's a two-for-one offer every summer evening before 9pm. If you haven't got student ID, friendly bluffing should get you in.

Linné

Irish Rover, Andra Långgatan 12. Run-of-the-mill Irish/English pub selling Boddingtons beer with other lagers, ales and cider on tap, and a wide range of bottled everything. Lamb, steaks and trout dishes for 59–105kr, and fish and chips at 65kr for those who just can't leave home behind. Mon–Thurs 5pm–1am, Fri & Sat 5pm–2am, Sun 5pm–midnight.

1252, Linnégatan 52. The first of the bars to become trendy, this long-term survivor put the Linné area on the nightlife map. Reasonably priced food considering the location. Outdoor tables in summer.

Nightlife and entertainment

There's plenty of other things to do in Gothenburg at night besides drink. The city has a brisk **live music scene** – jazz, rock and classical – as well as the usual cinema and theatre opportunities. The details below should give you some ideas, but it's worth picking up the Friday edition of the *Göteborgs Posten*, which has a weekly supplement, *Aveny*, full of listings for bars, concerts, clubs and almost anything else you might want to know about – it's in Swedish but not very difficult to decipher. The notice boards in the main hall at the entrance to *Studs*, the student bar in Haga, are also good for information on gigs and what's going on generally in the city.

Clubs

There are no outstanding **clubs** in Gothenburg. The oldest nightclub in town, always crowded, is *Valand*, at Vasagatan 3, just off Avenyn. One of the city's liveliest haunts, the hip *Trägårn*, on Nya Alleyn, near Heden (☎031/10 20 90 for details of events), is located in the ugliest building Gothenburg has to offer, the outside looking like a half-finished sauna interior; inside there are five bars, a casino, a disco and show bands. The *Trägårn* is open daily 9pm–3am, with a minimum age of 25; if you get here before 10pm you get in for free. Otherwise, admission is 80kr (60kr on Friday nights, when the age limit drops to 22). *Park Lane*, Avenyn 36, is a hot, crowded club with three bars, a casino and live entertainment (☎031/20 60 58). Despite having three bars, a stage and a casino, *Yaki Da*, at Östra Larmgatan 18 (upstairs from *Gamle Port*, see p.148), makes for a pretty depressing atmosphere; similarly, *Bubbles Nightclub* at *Lipp* (see p.148) is a bit of a disappointment. Sweden's biggest dance floor (if that's a boast) is said to be at *Rondo*, the restaurant at Liseberg Amusement Park. There's always live bands here, with people of all ages dancing in a friendly atmosphere.

Gay Gothenburg

Gothenburg's **gay scene** appears surprisingly half-hearted to visitors. This state of affairs has been largely put down to the high levels of tolerance towards lesbian and gay sexuality in the wider community, though the situation may owe more to the strangely ambivalent attitude of the gay community towards itself, despite the most liberal official attitudes. In the past couple of years, however, things have been looking up, and there is now something approaching choice, though it's still very limited compared to most other cities of this size. In Gothenburg, the RFSL is based at Karl Johansgatan 31, in a charming old wooden vicarage inconveniently far from the town centre (☎031/775 40 10, *goteborg@rfsl.se*), with a rather feeble library and a café. By bike or on foot, head out west towards Klippan, and when you see the gold-topped spire of Karl Johan Church, follow the sign, under the freeway, pointing to Majorna. Their bar and disco, in the same building, is called *Next* (Thurs 3pm–1am, Fri & Sat 6pm–2am). Far more appealing – and open every evening (a first for Gothenburg's gay scene), is *Greta's*, a very friendly café-restaurant at Drottninggatan 35, (see p.145); open to everyone, this gay-run place attracts a principally gay crowd of both men and women.

Otherwise, the Greek restaurant *Satyros*, Karl Johansgatan 8, on the same street as the RFSL, goes gay on Saturday evenings for a down-to-earth, mixed-age club night called *Eros*. Much younger, hipper and more posey is *XLNT*, at Club Fobi, Vasagatan 43B, off Avenyn (gay on Fri & Sat 10pm–5am).

Live music

Gothenburg's large student community means there are plenty of **local live bands**. The best venue, with an emphasis on alternative and dance music, is *Kompaniet* on Kungsgatan. The top floor is a bar, while downstairs there's dancing to Eurotechno stuff. Very few tourists head for *Kompaniet*, so it's ideal for meeting locals. Another of its selling points is the fact that the drinks are half-price between 8pm and 10pm, and the place stays open until 3am daily in summer (winter Wed–Sat only). Other bars worth checking out are *Klara*, Vallgatan 8, which has wannabe poets by day and, on Monday nights, a diverse range of indie and rock bands; and *Dojan*, Vallgatan 3, a small, smoky and crowded rock pub, with a mixed-age clientele, and live bands every night. For **international bands**, there are some sizable stadia in the city, notably Scandinavium (☎031/81 10 20), which hosts some big-time acts, as does the colossal arena, Ullevi Stadium, not to be confused with Gamle Ullevi close by, where football matches are held. Both are off Skånegatan to the east of Avenyn; take tram #1, #3 or #6.

Jazz enthusiasts should head for the trendy *Neffertiti* jazz club at Hvitfeldtsplatsen 6 (Mon–Sat from 9pm) – you may have to queue. *Jazzhuset*, Eric Dahlbergsgatan 3 (Wed–Sat 8pm–2am), puts on trad and Dixieland jazz, and swing, and is something of a pick-up joint for executives. **Classical music** concerts are held regularly in the Konserthuset, Götaplatsen, and at the Stora Theatre, Avenyn; programme details can be obtained from the tourist office.

Cinema and theatre

There are plenty of **cinemas** around the city, and English-language films (which make up the majority of what's shown) are always subtitled in Swedish, never dubbed. The most unusual of the cinemas is Bio Palatset, on Kungstorget. In a building that was originally a meat market and then a failed shopping mall, this ten-screen picture house has an interior painted in clashing fruity colours; the foyer has been scooped out to reveal rocks, now flood-lit, studded with Viking spears. Another multi-screen complex is Filmstaden, at Kungsgatan 35, behind the cathedral. For a great **art-house cinema**, check out Hagabion on Linnégatan (Mon–Fri 6–9.15pm, Sat & Sun 2.30–9.15pm; ☎031/42 88 10). Converted from an old creeper-strewn school, it has a pleasant café for cake, soup and sandwiches. A remarkable range of films is offered at the **Gothenburg Film Festival** (Jan & Feb), at the Draken cinema on Järntorget, but the place is closed during summer.

Theatre in Gothenburg is unlikely to appeal to many visitors. Not only are all productions in Swedish, the city's council-run theatres put on plays that would make Strindberg look like farce – the lack of an audience is not a big concern. The Lorensberg, a privately run theatre on Lorensbergsgatan off Götaplatsen, goes for light comedy shows in Swedish only and is closed during the summer months.

Listings

Airlines British Airways, at the airport (☎020/78 11 44); Finnair, Fredsgatan 6 (☎020/78 11 00); KLM, at airport (☎031/94 16 40); Lufthansa, Fredsgatan 1 (☎031/80 56 40); SAS, at the airport (☎020/91 01 10).

Airport General information on ☎031/94 10 00.

Banks and exchange Most banks are found on Östra Hamngatan, Södra Hamngatan and Västra Hamngatan. There are four Forex exchange offices, which accept American Express, Diners Club, and travellers' cheques: Central Station (daily 8am–9pm; ☎031/15 65 16); Avenyn 22 (daily 8am–9pm; ☎031/18 57 60); Nordstan shopping centre (daily 9am–7pm; ☎031/15 75 30); and Kungsportsplatsen (daily 9am–7pm; ☎13 60 74).

Buses Reservations are obligatory for buses to Stockholm, Helsingborg and Malmö; book at Bussresebyra, Drottninggatan 50 (☎031/80 55 30).

Car rental Avis, Central Station (☎031/80 57 80) and at the airport (☎031/94 60 30); Budget, Kristinelundsgatan 13 (☎031/20 09 30), at the airport (☎031/94 60 55); Europcar, Stampgatan 22D (☎031/80 53 90), at the airport (☎031/94 71 00); Hertz, Stampgatan 16A (☎031/80 37 30), at the airport (☎94 60 20).

Doctor Medical Counselling Service and Information (☎031/41 55 00); Sahlgrenska Hospital at Per Dubbsgatan (☎60 10 00). A private clinic, City Akuten, has doctors on duty 8am–6pm at Drottninggatan 45 (☎031/10 10 10).

Emergency services Ambulance, police, fire-brigade on ☎112.

Laundry At Nordstan Service Centre, the shopping centre near Central Station.

Left luggage Lockers at Nordstan Service Centre and Central Station.

Pharmacy Apoteket Vasen, Götagatan 10, in Nordstan shopping centre, is open till 10pm every day (☎031/80 44 10).

Police Headquarters at Ernst Fontells Plats (Mon–Fri 9am–2pm; ☎031/61 80 00).

Post offices Main post office for poste restante is in Nordstan shopping centre (daily 10am–6pm); another is on Avenyn (Mon–Fri 10am–6pm, Sat 10am–12.30pm).

Public telephones Phone cards can be bought at Pressbyrån and the tourist offices.

Swimming The biggest and best pool is the 1950s Valhallabadet, on Skånegatan, next to the Scandinavium sports complex.

Train information Domestic trains on ☎020/75 75 75; international train information on ☎031/80 77 10).

Travel agents KILROY travels, Berzeliigatan 5, not far from Götaplatsen (Mon–Fri: 9.30am–5pm; ☎031/20 08 60).

AROUND GOTHENBURG

North of Gothenburg, the rugged and picturesque **Bohuslän coast**, which runs all the way to the Norwegian border, attracts countless Scandinavian and German tourists each summer. The crowds don't detract, though, from the wealth of natural beauty – pink-and-black-striped granite rocks, coves, islands and hairline fjords – nor from the many fishing villages that make this stretch of country well worth a few days' exploration. The most popular destination is the island town of **Marstrand**, with its impressive fortress and richly ornamental ancient buildings, but there are several other attractions further up the coast that are also worth visiting, not least the Bronze Age **rock carvings** at **Tanumshede**, near Strömstad.

Northeast of the city, the county of **Västergötland** encompasses the southern sections of Sweden's two largest lakes, **Vänern** and **Vättern**. Here the scenery is gentler, and a number of attractive lakeside towns and villages make good bases from which to venture out into the forested countryside and onto the **Göta Canal** proper. This connects the lakes with each other, and is part of a larger waterway, also referred to as the Göta Canal, running from the North Sea to the Baltic. There are a number of ways to experience the canal, from cross-country cruises to short, evening hops on rented boats or organized ferry rides. The use of **bikes** is a great alternative for exploration of Västergötland, by means of the canal's towpaths, countless cycling trails and empty roads. Nearly all tourist offices, youth hostels and campsites in the region rent out bikes, for around 80kr a day or 400kr a week.

The Bohuslän coast

A chain of **islands** linked by a thread of bridges and short ferry crossings make up the county of **Bohuslän** where, despite the summer crowds, it is still easy enough to find a private spot to swim. Sailing is also a popular pastime among Swedes, many of whom have summer cottages here, and all the way along the coast you'll see yachts gliding through the water. Another feature of the Bohuslän landscape you can't fail to miss is the large number of **churches** throughout the county. Although church crawls may not be everyone's idea of a holiday, for long stretches these are the only buildings of note. The county has a long tradition of religious observance, fuelled in the early nineteenth century by the dogmatic Calvinist clergyman Henric Schartau, who believed that closed curtains were a sign of sin within – even today, many island homes still have curtainless windows. The churches, dating from the 1840s up until the 1910s, are mostly white, simple affairs, looking like windmills without sails. They are almost all built 1300m from their villages, and all are surrounded by graveyards. Once you've seen the inside of one of these churches, you've seen most, but those few that are exquisite or unusual have been highlighted in the text. Each church is usually open between 10am and 3pm, but the clergyman invariably lives next door and will be happy to unlock the building.

Travelling up the coast by public transport is possible by **train**, with services from Gothenburg through industrial Uddevalla and on to **Strömstad** (the northernmost town of any size before you enter Norway), but you will be limited to visiting the main towns. Although **bus services** do run, these are patchy and infrequent (on some routes, there is only one bus a week). If you really want to explore Bohuslän's most dramatic scenery and reach its prettier villages, you'll need a car. From Gothenburg, the E6 motorway is the quickest road north, with designated scenic routes leading off it every few kilometres.

Kungälv and the Bohus Fortress

Just under 20km north of Gothenburg on the E6, the quaint old town of **KUNGÄLV**, overshadowed by the fourteenth-century ruins of Bohus Fortress, is a gem of a place to stop for a few hours. Rebuilt after the Swedes razed it in 1676 to prevent the Danes finding useful shelter during one of many skirmishes between the two, the town now consists of pastel-painted wooden houses, all leaning as if on the verge of collapse, and sprawling cobbled streets. The **tourist office** (☎0303/992 00, fax 171 06), in the square below the fortress, will provide

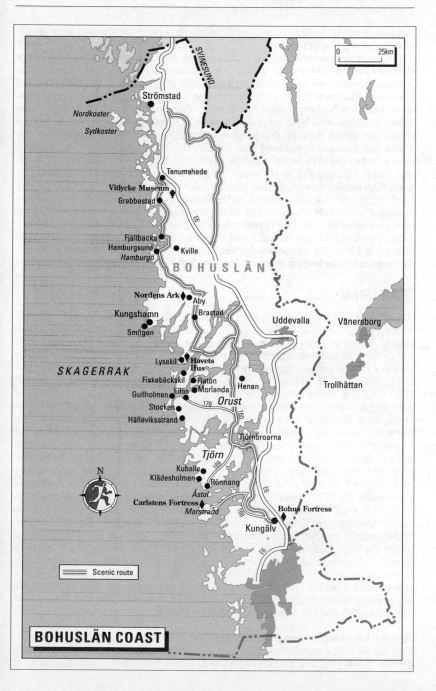

SVINESUND

Strömstad

Nordkoster

Sydkoster

Tanumshede

Vitlycke Museum

Grebbestad

Fjällbacka

Hamburgsund

Hamburgö

Kville

B O H U S L Ä N

Nordens Ark ◆ Åby

Kungshamn

Brastad

Uddevalla

Vänersborg

Smögen

Lysekil ◆ **Havets Hus**

SKAGERRAK

Fiskebäckskil ● Flatön

Gullholmen

Ellös ● Morlanda

Henan

Trollhättan

Stocken

Orust

Hälleviksstrand

Tjörnbroarna

Tjörn

N

Kuballe

Klädesholmen ● Rönnäng

Åstol

Carlstens Fortress ◆ *Marstrand*

Bohus Fortress ◆

Kungälv

━━━ Scenic route

BOHUSLÄN COAST

0 ─── 25km

you with a useful walking-tour map detailing the history of almost every seventeenth-century property here.

The main reason most people visit the town, though, is to see the remains of **Bohus Fortress** (May–Sept; guided tours, concerts and opera performances in July and August – for details call the tourist office). The first defensive fort here, a wooden affair, was built by the Norwegian king in the fourteenth century, on what was then Norway's southern border. This was replaced by a solid stone building, surrounded by deep natural moats, a complex which came to be known in Sweden for its impregnability. After withstanding six Swedish attacks in the 1560s, the colossal stronghold was rebuilt, this time enclosing a Renaissance palace. When the area finally became Swedish in 1658, Bohus didn't enjoy much of a respite: during the next twenty years, a further fourteen sieges here saw some spectacular bombardment by the Danes: records show that 15,000 men fired 30,000 red-hot cannonballs at the unfortunate fortress, which somehow managed not to fall. Where attack failed, Swedish weather has succeeded, however, and today the building is very much a ruin.

Once you've seen the fortress and wandered round the village, there is little else to do here. For **accommodation**, there's an STF **youth hostel** a stone's throw from the fortress at Farjevagen 2 (☎0303/189 00, fax 192 95; 110kr).

Marstrand

About 25km to the west of Kungälv, the island of **Marstrand** buzzes with summer activity, as holiday-makers come to sail, bathe and take one of the highly entertaining historical tours around its impressive castle, Carlstens Fästning. With ornate wooden buildings lining the bustling harbour, Marstrand is a really delightful place to visit and an easy day-trip from Gothenburg – it shouldn't be missed.

The town's colourful history – as so often in Sweden – mainly revolves around fish. Founded under Norwegian rule in the thirteenth century, it achieved remarkable prosperity through herring fishing in the following century, when the ruling king, Håkon of Norway, obtained permission from the pope to allow fishing in the town even on holy days. Rich herring pickings, however, eventually led to greed and corruption, and Marstrand became known as the most immoral town in Scandinavia. The murder of a cleric in 1586 was seen as an omen, and soon after, the whole town burned to the ground and the herring mysteriously disappeared from its waters. The fish – and Marstrand's prosperity – eventually returned in the 1770s. Around this time, the king announced an open-door policy, or *Porto Franco*, for Marstrand, which for the first time allowed foreigners to settle in Sweden, resulting in an influx of Jewish people onto the island. Unfortunately, in 1808 the fish disappeared again, and never came back. In his anger, the king abolished *Porto Franco*, forcing the Jewish community to move to Gothenburg (where pressure from the East India Company had brought a change in the law, allowing Jews to settle). Meanwhile, the town, without its main source of income, fell behind Gothenburg and Kungälv in importance. By the 1820s, the old herring salting-houses had been converted into bathhouses, Marstrand having reinvented itself as a fashionable bathing resort.

Arrival, information and accommodation

Coming by boat from Gothenburg, you can get two day-trip tickets for the price of one (160kr) with a Gothenburg Card. Boats leave from Lilla Bommen at

9.30am, arriving in Marstrand at 12.30pm (May & June selected dates; July & Aug daily). To save time, take **bus** #312 from Nils Ericsonsplatsen in Gothenburg to its terminus, where you can catch the ferry. If you buy a 100kr carnet at Tidpunkten, next to the bus terminal (once on the bus, insert the carnet into the machine and press "5"), it's half the cost of buying a ticket on the bus and covers the two-minute ferry journey from the mainland. By **car**, take the E6 north out of Gothenburg, and then Route 168 west, leading right to the ferry stop (15min; 13kr return). Cars are not permitted on the island; you must park on the mainland (25kr a day at car park close to terminal; 15kr a day if you use one of the car parks slightly further away). Leaving the island between midnight and 5am, you press a button at the ferry stop and they'll send a boat to pick you up.

At Marstrand harbour, the **tourist office** (June Mon–Fri 9.30am–4.30pm, Sat & Sun noon–4pm; late June to early Aug Mon–Fri 9.30am–6pm, Sat & Sun 11am–5pm; mid-Aug to May Mon–Fri 10am–4pm; ☎0303/600 87, fax 600 18) will book **private rooms** in an old barracks with a small kitchen; bookings must be for a minimum of two people (prices start from 370kr; no booking fee). There are also more pleasant en-suite rooms with their own kitchens in private homes or cottages (450kr for two people). The island's *Båtellet* **youth hostel** is wonderfully set in an old bathhouse (☎0303/600 10, fax 606 07; April & May 140kr, June to mid-Aug 200kr, Sept–March 100kr), and looks out onto idyllic islands. It boasts a sauna, laundry, a swimming pool and a restaurant (see p.156).

Of the several very pleasant **hotels** on the island, the 1892 *Grand Hotel*, at Paradis Parken (☎0303/603 22, fax 600 53; ⑤), just 50m from the tourist office and left through the park, is a real classic. Expertly refurbished, this very fine hotel lives up to its name, but ask for a room away from the street – loud late-night revellers can otherwise keep you awake. The more standard *Hotel Nautic*, at Långgatan 6 (☎303/610 30, fax 612 00; ③), has a lovely setting, surrounded by water and sailing boats.

The Town

Turning left when you leave the boat, head up cobbled Kungsgatan and past the Renaissance-style *Grand Hotel*. After about a minute, you'll arrive at a small square, surrounded by exquisite wooden houses painted in pastel hues; the locals play *boules* here beneath the shade of a huge, ancient beech tree. Across the square is the squat, white **St Maria kyrka**, named after a girl who was shipwrecked here in the twelfth century. The church, whose interior is simple and unremarkable, was originally called Maria Strand (Maria's Beach), hence the name of the island. From here, all the streets, lined with wooden villas, climb steeply to the castle.

Carlstens Fästning is an imposing sweep of stone walls solidly wedged into the rough rock above (June–Sept daily 11am–6pm; 25kr). You could easily spend half a day clambering around the castle walls and down the weather-smoothed rocks to the sea, where there are always plenty of places to bathe in private. The informal **tours** take an hour and, though none are officially in English, guides are happy to oblige. The most interesting tales they'll tell are down in the prison cells: Carlstens' most noted prisoner-resident was **Lasse Maja**, a thief who got rich by dressing as a woman to seduce and rob wealthy farmers. A sort of Swedish Robin Hood, Maja was known for giving his spoils to the poor. Incarcerated here for 26 years, Maja ingratiated himself with the officers by deploying his cooking skills in a kitchen not renowned for its cuisine. His culinary expertise eventually won him a pardon: when the new king, who was reputed to hate Swedish cooking, visited, Maja had the foresight to serve him French food.

In Maja's cell you can view the neck, waist and ankle shackles that prisoners wore for years on end. More unnerving, though, are the cell designs that were tried out here, with a floor area of just two metres by three metres and pitch dark; a prisoner would stand inside until he invariably lost his sanity and eventually died. In 1845, one prisoner was chosen for one of these cells on the grounds that he was the least observant Christian in the town; records show that the only person he was allowed to speak to was a pastor, just once a year, on Christmas Eve. His drawings in his own blood are still visible, as is the dip in the barred windowsill where his hand tapped constantly until his death.

For 40kr extra, you can take one of the special tours of the 100-metre-high towers (3 weekly; 40kr), built in 1658. The views from the top are stunning, but you have to be fit to get up there; the steep, spiral climb is quite exhausting. Once a year, around July 20, the fortress hosts a huge and colourful **festival**, with an eighteenth-century-style procession and live theatre, well worth catching.

On your way back down from the castle, you can take a detour and visit the remains of **Fredriksborg**, one of the original twelve fortresses on the island, reduced now to a neat wall around the shore. Walking down Villagatan, before you get to the shore there's a small gateway on the right that leads to a house covered with black, wooden tiles. Its friendly owner will allow you (if you ask first) to walk along his garden path to a vault, originally used to fire cannons at enemy boats, in the old fortress wall; inside are the dusty remains of Scandinavia's first synagogue, soon to be restored. To get back to the town centre, carry on down Villagatan to the shore and walk along the path till you reach Långgatan, which leads back to the main square.

Eating, drinking and nightlife

At night, the relaxed *American Bar* and neighbouring *Oscars*, close to the harbour, are good **drinking** haunts. *Oscars* became Sweden's first discotheque in 1964, and today part of it is a **nightclub** playing disco and popular rock music to 25- to 50-year-olds. The *Societetshuset* (see below) has a disco throughout the summer (Thurs–Sat; entrance 80kr after 10pm).

Marstrand is nowadays known as something of an **eating** Mecca, though the fare mostly comes at considerable cost. About the most interesting place to eat on the island is the *American Bar*, close to the harbour, which has an authentically worn feel of 1940s America with posters of cruise ships sailing between Sweden and the US. It serves huge portions of excellent food: chicken-and-cheese salad for 88kr, or, in the evenings, home-made burgers (108kr) – though coffee is a steep 20kr. Next door, *Oscar's* has recently been restored to its old glory as a glamorous restaurant (☎0303/615 54). Very popular is *Lasse Majas Krog*, in a cheerful old harbourfront house with yellow walls (☎0303/611 22). A wide-ranging meat and fish menu has main courses from 110kr to 220kr, as well as pizzas at around 80kr. Very pleasant lunches and dinners are also served in *Restaurant Drott*(☎0303/618 70), in a warm 1858 bathhouse attached to the youth hostel, with daily pasta dishes for 49kr, and meat or seafood meals for 90–130kr. Eating outside here affords delightful views, while the inside retains all the old style of the bathing days, with stripped floors and painted tongue-and-groove walls. To reach it, just turn right from the ferry pier and follow the water's edge from the harbour, as far as you can go. Bygone-era style is afforded just a few steps away at the old *Societetshuset*

(☎ 0303/606 00), where three restaurants, all serving a good range of meat and fish dishes, can be found within one classic old house. Very popular for eating at basic wooden tables outside is *Marstrands Värdshus* – chicken salad here costs 125kr, or try the smoked salmon with dill and potatoes, at 139kr. Also dear is the *Grand Hotel's* very popular *Restaurant Tenan*, which looks onto a classic bandstand, where you might catch a brass-band performance. Those in the market for cheap eats will be restricted to the very good smoked fish at *Arvidsons*, on the harbourfront, and the adjacent seafront stall, which does mediocre burgers; bread and other provisions are inexpensive at *Skepps Handel*, also on the harbourfront, at the corner of Drottninggatan (daily 7.30am–9pm). For a daytime coffee, the most atmospheric place is the café in the old officers' mess at the fortress.

Tjörn and Orust

Back on the mainland, Route 160, the first coastal scenic route north of Kungälv, begins 23km on from the town; if driving from Gothenburg, you can get to Route 160 off the E6. From Marstrand, though, it's far more appealing to cut east on Route 168, then north on the tiny road signed "Stenungsund", turning onto Tjörn island on Route 169. Once off the main road, you'll soon reach **Tjörnbroarna**, a five-kilometre sequence of three graceful bridges connecting the islands of Tjörn and Orust, and affording spectacular views over the fjords.

Tjörn, Klädesholmen and Åstol

Buses go from Nils Ericsonsplatsen in Gothenburg directly to the village of **Kuballe** (bus times from the Tidpunkten on ☎031/80 12 35), 2km from Tjörn's southernmost tip. The island is less visited than the more northerly Orust – indeed there's not much to do on Tjörn itself – but can be used as a base to visit two neighbouring islands.

From Kuballe, a bridge makes for an easy journey to **Klädesholmen**, an island of lovely wooden cottages on steep inclines. The landscape around here is all pink granite islets, smoothed down but still somehow raw. There are no trees, just little lakes with ducks and swans. Past the duller outskirts of this herring-canning island, a sign shows the way to a small museum, **Sillebua** (early June Sat & Sun 3–7pm, June to mid-Aug daily 3–7pm, late Aug Sat & Sun 3–7pm), depicting how life has always been in this tucked-away place.

Just south of Kuballe is the blandly built-up village of **Rönnäng**, from where ferries head out to **Åstol** (44kr return), a tiny island so filled with pretty houses, it's known locally as having no industry, no fishing and no soil. Plans are afoot to build a bridge here from Tjörn, but don't mention this to locals, who are fiercely protective of their isolation. Rönnang has a charming **youth hostel**, clearly signposted, in an appealing yellow-painted wooden house at Nyponvägen 5 (☎0304/67 71 98, fax 67 76 74; 115kr, ①). There's a decent little **pizza place** at Dalenvägen 12, also in Rönnang (June–Aug Mon–Fri 11am–11pm, Sat & Sun 1–10pm; Sept–May Mon–Fri 11am–9pm, Sat & Sun 1–9pm).

Orust and Gullholmen

A centre for boat building since Viking times, **Orust** is bare on its windward coasts, yet has forest right up to its eastern shores. Henan, its largest village, is unremarkable; you are much better off avoiding it altogether and heading west off Route 160 onto Route 178, for the town of **Ellös**, where there are places to stay and eat (see below). Due west is the island of **Gullholmen**, where there's a fine example of an unspoilt fishing village, reached by a frequent ferry crossing. Founded in the thirteenth century, the village has a substantial church around which red-and-white wooden homes huddle. The rest of the island is a nature reserve where birds nest undisturbed beneath smooth, granite rocks.

Back on Örust, the little village of **Morlanda**, a couple of kilometres northeast of Ellös contains a nineteenth-century **cholera cemetery**, where the locals who died of the disease are buried. To get there, take the narrow road just before the church (which, incidentally, contains Sweden's oldest organ, dating from the seventeenth century); follow it for about 700m and you'll see a path, which takes you into some gardens, where it peters out. From here, wander through a meadow and some lovely woodland until you see a sign, marked "Kolerakyrkogård". A crude stone wall surrounds the site and a bronze cross at the centre commemorates the 1834 epidemic.

For **accommodation** and **food**, head for Ellös, where there's an economical place to **stay**, *Ellös Brygga* apartments, signposted from the centre (☎0304/509 93; closed in winter). Here a two-room place with cooking facilities and a balcony overlooking the water costs 550kr in summer, 390kr spring and autumn. In summer the building is also home to a good **restaurant**, offering dishes of very fresh fish, such as cod with chilli sauce. In the centre is an unusual fish-shop and delicatessen, *Nabbens*, serving shellfish and great fish soup. Just outside the nearby village of **Stocken**, to the south of Ellös, is the splendidly situated STF **youth hostel** at Tofta (☎0304/503 80; 125kr; May to mid-Sept), a wooden manor built in 1770, and set in huge grounds, making a wonderful base from which to explore the locality.

Fiskebäckskil

Just north of Morlanda, a free car ferry carries you over to the next island where, having stopped at Malö, you reach Flatön. From here, the road leads on for a couple of kilometres, past undulating meadows and cottages, to another ferry ride (free), lasting just thirty seconds, to **FISKEBÄCKSKIL**. Although it's a wealthy place today, the locals once eked out a living making herring-oil lamps, until the advent of electric light put paid to that trade. The village is peppered with exquisite, imposing old wooden houses, many with fancily carved porchways and intricate glazed verandahs, perched high up on rocky rises. But the place is more than simply pretty, and has several attractions that are well worth exploring.

Arriving by road from the south, you'll find the remarkably stylish **art café**, *Salt Arvet* (☎0523/229 00, summer daily noon–6pm, winter Wed–Sun noon–6pm), just on the right where the road enters the village. The galleries (40kr) display constantly changing exhibitions of international standard, such as works by Lichtenstein and Picasso. The café is also a lovely spot for a bite – moussaka (60kr), filled baguettes (45kr) or home-made apple cake (60kr) can be enjoyed while looking out through the glass walls onto the picturesque natural harbour.

Fiskebäckskil's most famous son is the artist **Carl Wilhelmson**, who was born in a cottage near the marina. Having made his money and his name nationally with his powerful, evocative portraits and landscapes, which beautifully reflect west-coast Swedish life at the end of the nineteenth century, in 1912 he had a strikingly elegant cottage built close to his birthplace, with splendid views over the waters towards Lysekil. Today, Wilhelmson's grandson, a retired sea captain, still spends his summers in the airy, elevated wooden house, and is happy to show interested visitors around (☎0523/221 28). The cottage's sitting room is Wilhelmson's former studio, its double-height windows letting the light flood in. Reproductions of his work line the walls (the originals are mostly in the Göteborg Art Museum, see p.138; or the National Art Museum in Stockholm, see p.73), the settings depicted being mostly scenery just outside these windows. The most poignant of the prints, *On The Hill* (original in Göteborg), shows a scene from Wilhelmson's childhood. Aged 9, he had stood unnoticed behind a group of old men sitting on a rock in Fiskebäckskil, while they discussed a hurricane which had wrecked twenty ships the day before, killing his father, a sea captain. When they became aware of the boy's presence, they asked him not to say anything, and he kept the secret from his mother, who only learnt of her husband's death from the post-boat captain a month later.

Not far away, close to the marina, the 1772 **church** (daily 10am–9pm) has an opulent yet comfortable feel about its interior, as if it were a home furnished in grand style. There are chandeliers, gold-plated sconces, etched glass mirrors with hand-carved wood frames, and fresh flowers at the ends of each pew. The luxuriance of the decor is thanks to donations from Bohuslan's richest eighteenth-century land owner, Margareta Huidtfeldt, who also paid for the wrought-iron-and-sheet-metal spire, crowned with a gold-plated weathercock. Wooden and barrel-vaulted, the ceiling is worth a glance, too: it's covered in eighteenth-century murals, the oddest aspect of which are the scattering of angels' heads. The altarpiece is also strange, the centre panel showing the crucifixion of Christ, his legs chopped off below the knee. Outside in the graveyard is Wilhelmson's rather plain grave, his likeness carved into the granite tombstone.

Practicalities

The **ferry** from Lysekil (see p.160) to Fiskebäcksill, the *Carl Wilhelmson*, leaves from opposite the tourist office (Mon–Sat 6am–11pm, Sun from 8.30am; hourly; 15 min). It first stops briefly at modern and uninteresting Östersidan, separated from Fiskebäcksill by a river – stay on till the second stop. There is a small **tourist office** by the marina by the boat slipway (late June to Aug Mon–Sat 9am–7pm, Sun noon–4pm; Sept to late June Mon–Fri 10am–5pm; ☎0523/229 80, fax 228 03). Here you can book rooms and cottages for 150kr per person, plus a booking fee of 50kr, or have a hotel or hostel room booked (fee 20kr). Though Fiskebäckskil is a quiet, hidden-away sort of place, it does have a fine **hotel** and a couple of excellent eating opportunities. The glamorous *Gullmarsstrand Hotel* (☎0523/222 60, fax 228 05; ③) is right on the water, next to the Lysekil ferry pier (see above). The place also boasts a decent **restaurant**, which is open in July only for lunch and dinner (other times by arrangement). For a really exceptional meal, though, try *Kapten Sture's Restaurant*, its interior is done out like an old ship, up Kaptensgatan from the church (☎0523/221 25). The fish dishes are the best choices, with the main ingredient caught locally a few hours before. A new addition to the eating scene is the pleasant *Brygghuset,* close to the tourist office on the marina waterfront (Mon–Fri 6pm–1am, Sat & Sun noon–1am).

Lysekil and around

The largest coastal town in this area is **LYSEKIL**, at the tip of a peninsula with the Gullmar fjord twisting to the east and the Skagerrak to the west. While the journey by Route 162 into town does not suggest its appeal, the place has plenty to recommend it. From the tourist office, it's just five minutes' walk to **Havets Hus** (daily 10am–4pm; closed Jan; ☎0523/165 30; 50kr), an amazing museum of marine life. The chief attraction here is an eight-metre-long underwater tunnel with massive fish swimming over and around you. This view is a little distorted, however, as looking through the curved glass is a bit like gazing through someone else's glasses. Fish delighting in such names as Father Lasher, Picked Dogfish and Five Bearded Rockling feature, along with varieties usually associated with lemon-wedges in restaurants; children can enjoy feeling the texture of slimy algae or starfish by sticking their arms into the touch pool.

The villas en route to Havets Hus, with their intricately carved eaves, porticoes and windows, are worth a look, too. Lysekil was a popular and genteel bathing resort in the last century, and these ornate houses are a reminder of the time when the rich and neurotic came to take the waters. The bizarre, castellated rough granite house on the inland side of the main road was built as home for a Mr. Laurin, then Lysekil's wealthiest man; it now plays host to the offices of the local newspaper. A better-known local figure of the past is Carl Curman, a self-styled health guru. Of the town's ornate Hansel-and-Gretel houses, painted mustard and chocolate brown, his was the most fancy (a bronze bust of him stands behind it, at the water's edge). You'll find his and most of the other houses on the water side of the main road. In his day, Curman managed to convince his patients that sunbathing on the exposed rock was dangerous "as the amount of air must be regulated" – but it was rather more dangerous for his bank account if they bathed for free instead of paying to use the bathhouses, which he owned. Today, the classic old bathhouses, stretching into the water, are a popular place for (segregated) nude bathing (free).

Walk up any set of steps from the waterfront and you'll reach the town's **church** (daily 11am–3pm), the town's most imposing landmark visible for miles around, hewn from the surrounding pink granite, with beaten copper doors and windows painted by turn-of-the-century artist Albert Eldh.

Much of the shoreline has been turned into a **nature reserve** with over 250 varieties of plant life – all due to Carl Curman's wife Carla, who bought the whole coast here to prevent the local stone-cutting industry, which became big business locally in the nineteenth century, from destroying it. For guided botanical and marine walks (late June to Aug Wed; 30kr), ask at the tourist office.

In July, Lysekil has a sizeable **jazz festival** attracting some big (in Swedish terms) names. The tourist office has information on performances.

Practicalities

From Fiskebäckskil, an hourly passenger **ferry** goes to Lysekil from the end of Kaptensgatan. To get here by car, head back out of the village in an eastward direction (towards Uddevalla) for 10 km, then take the ferry over. Express **bus** #840 comes here from Gothenburg (2 hourly); or by **car**, take Road 162, which leads off the E6 at Uddevalla.

Lysekil's **tourist office** is located at Södra Hamngatan 6 (mid-June to mid-Aug daily 9am–7pm; mid-Aug to mid-June Mon–Fri 9am–5pm; ☎0523/130 50, fax 125 85, *info@lysekil.se*), the main road along the waterfront. For a place to **stay**, there's a hostel (contrary to its name), *Kust Hotel Strand*, Strandvägen 1 (☎0523/101 20, fax 122 02; 175kr, ①), nicely placed on the waterfront next to Havets Hus. The central, though very ugly, *Hotel Lysekil* at Rosiksstorg 1

(☎0523/66 55 30, fax 155 20; ③) allows more comfort. For somewhere with rather more character, *Lysekil Havshotell*, Turistgatan 13 (☎0523/797 50, fax 142 04; ②), is in an archetypal red and white house, built in 1904. Its sea views are all but obliterated by a huge granite boulder behind – though you can climb up for a windy panoramic view for miles around. For a meal of fish and a beer, *Pråmen*, a **restaurant-bar** actually jutting out over the water, makes for a pleasant spot, with views back over Fiskebäcksil. Nestling beneath the church, *Konditori Jönssons Katt* is best for light meals, salads and sandwiches (Mon–Fri 7am–8pm, Sat 8am–8pm, Sun 10am–8pm).

North to Nordens Ark and Smögen

A worthwhile diversion after Lysekil is to head back along Route 162 and turn left for Nordens Ark, a wildlife sanctuary near Åby. It's a twenty-minute drive from Lysekil, and on the way you'll pass a couple of notable churches, in particular the one at **Brastad**, an 1870s Gothic building with an oddly haphazard appearance: every farm in the neighbourhood donated a lump of its own granite towards its construction, but none of the bits matched.

Don't be put off by the yeti-sized inflatable puffin at the entrance to **Nordens Ark**, on the Åby fjord (daily: June–Aug 10am–6pm; Sept–May 10am–4pm; ☎0523/522 15; Jan–May 90kr, June–Aug 130kr, Sept–Dec 100kr). The place is a unique wildlife sanctuary for endangered animals, where animal welfare takes priority over human voyeurism. Red pandas, lynxes, snow leopards and arctic foxes are among the rare creatures being bred and reared at the sanctuary, where the mountainous landscape of dense forest and glades is managed so it's as similar as possible to the animals' natural surroundings. The enclosures are so large, and the paths and bridges across the site so discreet, that you may be disappointed to not see any animals at all. Your best bet for a glimpse is to follow behind the little truck that trundles around at feeding times. Tickets and a full English-language guide are available in the fine eighteenth-century Åby manor house on the grounds.

Smögen

The old fishing village of **SMÖGEN**, 15km west of Nordens Ark along the coast (there's no transport between the two), is all ice-cream parlours, boutiques in old seafront wooden houses, and a quay that runs for several hundred metres. In July and August, Bohuslan's entire teenage population besieges the village for an orgy of drinking – fascinating to watch, and impossible to sleep through.

For **accommodation**, *Smögens Havsbad*, Hotellgatan 26 (☎0523/310 35, fax 701 74; ④/③) is a stylish place five minutes' walk from the quay, away from all the summertime hubbub. In an attractive old house bordered by granite boulders, it also has a good **restaurant** and bar. There are plenty of other places for a cheap bite, though the real culinary draw is the terrace of open-fronted **fishmongers' shops** selling mounds of shrimp, langoustine, crab and all manner of smoked seafood. The most popular restaurant and bar in the village is *Brasserie Brygget* by the water, though drinking hordes raise the decibel levels alarmingly. *Lagergrens* close by is far more pleasant for a laid-back, quiet drink and a wide range of à la carte meals, or pizzas at 79kr. Once very popular as a nightclub-restaurant, *Magasinet*, on the other side of the water and reached by a small boat has lost its hip status – largely because it's on the wrong side of the quay. The nicest **café** here is *Cafe Oasen* at Sillgatan 10 (mid-June to mid-Aug daily 9am–8pm), just 50m from the foot of Storgatan. They serve a breakfast buffet, excellent home-baked bread and cakes, pasta and warm baguettes. Next door is the best of the old-fashioned sweet shops selling boxes of candy, *Sommar Godd.*

Fjällbacka

Thirty-five kilometres north along the coast from Smögen, **FJÄLLBACKA** was long regarded as a picture-perfect village: nestling at the base of a huge granite rock formation, its houses are painted in fondant shades, with a wealth of intricate gingerbreading known in Swedish as *snickargladje* ("carpenter's joy"). Today, though, that image is spoiled by all the rooftop television antennae and satellite dishes, while the rocks are mostly under safety netting. Coming here from Smögen, drive along Route 174 north, then either take the tiny, unnamed coastal route here, or head on up to Dingle from where you get Route 163.

When you arrive in Fjällbacka, it will immediately be apparent that a certain celebrated actress holds sway in the little town. Her statue, in the eponymous Ingrid Bergmans Torg, looks out to the islands where she had her summer house, and to the sea, over which her ashes were scattered. Steps behind Bergman's statue lead to a dramatic ravine between some cliffs, known as Kungskliftan (King's Cliff); in 1887, Oscar II etched his name into the rock here, and so started a trend for graffiti.

The **tourist office** (June–Aug erratic hours; ☎0525/321 20, fax 311 43) is in a tiny red hut on Ingrid Bergmans Torg. For a really glamorous **hotel**, there's the costly *Stora Hotellet,* Galärbacken (☎0525/310 03, fax 310 93; ④), with a host of stunning design features. There are plenty of **camping** opportunities in Fjällbacka, and a **youth hostel** a couple of minutes away on an unnamed island (May–Aug ☎0525/312 34; 100kr) – though its setting is more frustrating than romantic when the ferryman is too busy to carry visitors to the mainland. A more convenient hostel is *Badholmen*, just on the pier, two minutes' walk from the tourist office in a yellow house with a black roof (☎0525/32150; 150kr). It has just four rooms, and breakfast can be provided; a good non-STF hostel alternative is *Åsleröd Vandrarhem* (☎0525/312 77, fax 325 33), 2km north. There are a couple of pleasant places to **eat**. *Restaurant Mässen*, on the waterfront just off Ingrid Bergmans Torg, has a 55kr lunch, pizzas and à la carte items such as catfish with shrimp sauce for 120kr. Better for a relaxed beer and baguette is *Cafe Bryggan*, right on the square and with outside seating, nestling beneath the rock formation.

Tanumshede

The town of **TANUMSHEDE**, on the E6, has the greatest concentration of **Bronze Age rock carvings** in Scandinavia, with four major sites not far away in the surrounding countryside. The E6 express **bus** runs from Gothenburg to Tanumshede (5 daily; 2 hr); bus #875 runs here from Fjällbacka (Mon–Fri 6 daily; Sat & Sun 2 daily). Tanumshede was coastal during the Bronze Age, when the sea level was 15m higher than today. Between 1500 and 500 BC, Bronze Age artists scratched images into the ice-smoothed rock, and at Tanumshede you'll see some fine examples of the most frequent motifs: the simple cup mark the most common, and also boats, humans and animals. Since 1994, the Tanumshede carvings have been included in the UNESCO World Heritage List.

The carvings are mostly to be found on sloping, smooth rock surfaces (these are very slippery when wet) and it's well worth heading straight for the **tourist office** (June to mid-Aug Mon–Sat 10am–6pm; mid-Aug to June Mon–Thurs 9am–4.30pm, Fri 9am–3pm; ☎0525/204 00, fax 298 60, *tanum.turist@swipnet.se*), oddly sited in a Texaco filling station, which will provide you with English booklets (10kr) detailing the types of images at the four sites. You could get to the carvings on a **bike**, which you can rent from Westmans Tanumshede at Riksvägen 67, 500m south of the church in the town centre (☎0525/20100; 80kr a day).

The **Vitlycke Museum**, opened in Tanumshede in 1998, explores the meaning of the images in the carvings, in keeping with its theme, "pictorial communication". The interpretations it presents are wildly liberal and often contradictory: take, for example, the celebrated Fossum Woman, who is variously described as "giving birth to the egg of life", "a male trophy" or "displaying nether-region jewellery". One of the best-known is the so-called "Bridal Couple", who appear to be fornicating standing up. There's a good **restaurant** at the Vitlycke Museum, delighting in using what it calls "Bronze Age raw materials" – which actually means eschewing food processors. They serve venison, fish and shellfish, with sauces flavoured with parsley root, sorrel and chickweed.

Practicalities

There is a smattering of restaurants and nightlife opportunities at the caravan/camping Mecca of **GREBBESTAD**, just a couple of kilometres south-west of Tanumshede. Among the best **cafés** here are the very relaxed *Greby's*, where you can eat well in a 1901 former factory at Grebbestadsbryggan (☎0525/107 16); or try the waterfront *Skafferiet* at Nedre Långgatan 23 (☎0525/612 84 or 141 09), which serves good-value savoury pies and filling salads, as well as cakes and a wide selection of unusual ice creams. They also do **bed and breakfast** for 250kr per person (late May to Aug). Another good accommodation option here is *Grebbestads Vandrarhem & Mini Hotel* at Nedre Långgatan 15 (☎ & fax 0525/614 14), right on the waterfront in a pleasant, wooden house.

Strömstad

Once a fashionable eighteenth-century spa resort, **STRÖMSTAD** still has an air of faded grandeur, though these days it's pretty lifeless outside the height of midsummer. From its train station, everywhere of interest is easily accessible, and with ferry connections to the Norway towns of Sandefjord, Fredrikstad and Halden, the town makes for a brief breathing space before heading north. Aside from its close proximity to the Koster Islands (see p.165), Strömstad itself has a couple of quite remarkable public buildings that are well worth a look. Although you wouldn't guess it from its run-of-the-mill exterior, inside Strömstad's **church**, a few minutes' walk from the train and bus stations, there's an eclectic mix of unusual decorative features, including busy frescoes, model ships hanging from the roof, gilt chandeliers and 1970s brass lamps.

The town's most bizarre building is the massive, copper-roofed **Stadshus**, the product of a millionaire recluse. Born to a Strömstad jeweller in 1851, Adolf Fritiof Cavalli-Holmgren became a financial whizz kid, moved to Stockholm and was soon one of Sweden's richest men. When he heard that his poor home town needed a town hall, he offered to finance the project, but only on certain conditions: the building had to be situated on the spot where his late parents had lived, and he insisted on complete control over the design. By the time the mammoth structure was completed in 1917, he was no longer on speaking terms with the city's politicians, and he never returned to see the building he had battled to create, which was topped with a panoramic apartment for his private use. Much later, in 1951, it was discovered that his obsessive devotion to his parents led him to design the entire building around the dates of their birthdays – January 27 and May 14 – and their wedding day – March 7. The dimensions of each of the over one hundred rooms were combinations of the numbers in these dates, represented in metres, as were the sizes of every window, every flight of stairs and every cluster of lamps. Furthermore, in all the years of dealing with with city officials, he only ever responded or held meetings on these dates. Built entirely from rare local apple-granite (the stone is so named because it contains circular markings), the town hall is open to the public, but to view the most interesting areas you have to arrange a free private tour (ask at the town hall itself). Adolf's portrait, which bears a false date (unsurprisingly, one of his three favourites), can be seen in the main council chamber. Despite his animosity towards the city administration, Adolf still chose to be buried in the graveyard at Strömstad's church – his rough-hewn granite tombstone is by far the grandest here, its inscription translating as "From Stromstad town, with grateful thanks to this most memorable son".

Practicalities

Strömstad is reached by **train** from Gothenburg or by the E6 express **bus** between Gothenburg and Oslo; by car, take Route 176 off the E6. There's also a local bus here from Tanumshede. Both the **train and bus stations** are on Södra Hammen, opposite the **ferry** terminal for services to Sandefjord in Norway (Color Scandi Line; ☎0526/620 00). Ferries to Fredrikstad and Halden use Norra Hamnen, 100m to the north on the other side of the rocky promontory, Laholmen, as do the ferries to the Koster Islands.

The **tourist office**, on the quay (May to mid-June & mid-Aug to end Aug Mon–Fri 9am–6pm, Sat & Sun 10am–4pm; mid-June to mid-Aug Mon–Sat 9am–8pm, Sun 10am–8pm; Sept–April Mon–Fri 9am–5pm; ☎0526/623 30, fax 623 35, *info@stromstadtourist.se*), has full details of ferry times; they will help book **private rooms**, which cost from 150kr per person (plus a 50kr booking fee); and advise about renting **cabins.** The STF **youth hostel**, *Crusellska House*, is at Norra Kyrkogatan 12 (☎0526/101 93, fax 0708/41 01 95; 130kr), a kilometre or so from the train station along Uddevallavägen; there's also an independent hostel, *Gastis Roddaren Hostel*, at Fredrikshaldsvagen 24 (☎0526/602 01; 130kr), ten minutes' walk along the road fronting the Stadshus. For a central **hotel**, try *Krabban* on Södra Bergsgatan 15 (☎0526/142 00, fax 142 04; ②), or the modern, low-built *Hotel Laholmen* (☎0526/124 00, fax 100 36; ⑤/④), with a prime waterfront position enjoying wonderful views, and serving exceptional **breakfasts** (Mon–Fri 7–9am, Sat & Sun 8–10am; 65kr for non-residents). There is **camping** a kilometre from the train station, along Uddevallavägen, near the youth hostel, or at Dafto, 4km south in tiny triangular-shaped cottages (a bus runs here from the centre).

Strömstad has a number of places to **eat and drink**, most of which are easily found by just wandering around near the harbour area. Among the newer **restaurants** worth trying are *The Cod,* a few metres towards the centre from the Color Scandi Line terminal (☎0526/615 00), and opposite, the *Pråmen,* jutting into the water. Both specialize, unsurprisingly, in fresh fish dishes. The best of the bunch of **cafés** are *Backlund's* (Mon–Fri 8am–7pm, Sat 8am–3pm) a locals' haunt in the old bathhouse building just behind the tourist office, with sandwiches at about 18kr; *Café Casper*, on Södra Hamngatan, which does lunch specials for 35kr; and *Kaff Doppet*, a more characterful *konditori* by the station. There are also a number of fish shops doubling as **fish-snack cafés**. Excellent value is *Skaldjurs Cafe*, hidden away behind the Sandefjord ferry terminal in a row of red wooden sheds. For 20kr, you get smoked mackerel and bread, and for a little more they'll serve you a plateful of fish, bread and potato salad.

Nightlife in Strömstad is, unsurprisingly, not too hot. The only place that really comes alive on a summer evening is *Skagerack*, in a wedding cake of a building where the Stockholm elite once partied, but now looking tired; it's in the centre, opposite the church. At night in summer it is very loud, very young and the place for big-name bands to play, if they hit the Bohuslän coast at all. An older crowd fills the more sedate (and expensive) terraces of *Hotel Laholmen* (see p.164). Some awful singers can be heard at *Pub Rorbua* next door to the tourist office, where there's also reasonable, if simple, food.

The Koster Islands

Sweden's two most westerly inhabited islands (population 400), the **Kosters** enjoy more sunshine hours than almost anywhere else in the country. To **get here**, pick up the comfortable **ferry** at Norra Hamn, outside Strömstad's tourist office (80kr return). Outside high season, you'll have to take an early-morning ferry to North Koster (80kr) to see both islands; if you leave later, the only way of making it across onto the south island is to hitch a lift in a local's boat. The boat stops first at **North Koster** (35min), the more rugged of the pair; the island is a grand **nature reserve**, which takes a couple of hours to walk around. It's just another five minutes to Långegärde, the first stop on **South Koster**, an island three times the size of its neighbour. You could stay on another fifteen minutes to reach **Ekenäs**, the only settlement of any size, but it doesn't make much difference where you disembark as one spot is much like any other here. These boats apart, you can also get **taxi boats** to the islands from outside Strömstad's tourist office, which head to the islands (500kr); they are the only choice if you miss the last ferry back at 9.30pm.

No vehicles are allowed on either island except for curious, motorized buggy bikes with wooden trays in front for carrying provisions. There are no dramatic sights – the pleasure of being here is in losing yourself in an atmosphere of complete calm, the silence broken only by the screeching of birds. Mostly, the place is made for cycling in the sun, along the easy paths through wild-flowers meadows; once in a way you can have refreshments at the smattering of small cafés and ice-cream parlours. There's no crime and the pace is even slower than in mainland Bohuslän. During the summer, there are also **bird- and seal-watching expeditions** (late June to mid-Aug Tues–Thurs; 140kr; more information from Strömstad's tourist office).

Practicalities

Wherever on the Kosters you disembark from the ferry, you'll be met by a sea of **bikes** to rent, always for 50kr a day; they're the best way to explore the gently undulating landscape of the south island. You can also buy a **map** of the island (10kr), but you don't need one: all the tiny tracks lead to coves and also interconnect, so finding your way around should be simple. There's no tourist office here; it's best to get information at the one in Strömstad (see p.164).

Camping on North Koster is restricted to *Vettnet* (☎0526/204 66), though there are several sites on South Koster and a **youth hostel** (☎0526/201 25; 130kr; May–Sept), 1500m from the ferry stop at Ekenäs. Before you get there, though, expect to be inundated by people prepared to rent out their **apartments** for 250–300kr a night, excellent value if there are three or more of you. There's just one **hotel** on South Koster, and surprisingly stylish it is too: the *Skärgårdshotell* at Ekenäs, just 100m from the harbour (☎0526/202 50, fax 201 94; ④), with a warm apricot interior. There's a good **restaurant** here too, but outside high season you must ring to find out if they're open. A good **café** to try is located where the boat comes in at Långegärde. Called *Skaldjurscafe*, it's inside a big red wooden house, and serves meat and fish dishes, as well as light bites like *pytt i panna* (59kr), home-baked bread and shrimp (known locally as "Toast Koster"), and mussel soup.

The Göta Canal: Trollhättan, Vänersborg and around

The giant waterway that is the **Göta Canal** leads from the mouth of the River Göta to Sweden's largest lake, **Vänern**, via the **Trollhättan Canal**, then links up with another formidable lake, **Vättern**, and runs right through southeastern Sweden to the Baltic Sea. Centuries ago, it was realized that Vänern and Vättern could be linked as part of a grand scheme to create a continuous waterway across the country, from Gothenburg to the Baltic. This would not only make inland transport easier, but also provide a vital trade route, a means of both shipping iron and timber out of central Sweden, and of avoiding Danish customs charges levied on traffic through Öresund. It was not until 1810 that Baron Baltzar Von Platen's hugely ambitious plans to carve out a route from Gothenburg to Stockholm were put into practice by the Göta Canal Company. Sixty thousand soldiers spent seven million working days over a period of 22 years to complete the mammoth task, and the canal opened in 1832, shortly after Von Platen's death.

Without your own transport, some of the easier places to see from Gothenburg are the few small towns that lie along the first stretch of the river/canal to Lake Vänern, in particular **Trollhättan**, where the canal's lock system tames the force of the river to dramatic effect. A few kilometres north of Trollhättan, **Vänersborg**, at the southernmost tip of Lake Vänern, provides a useful base for exploring the natural beauty of the nearby hills, home to Sweden's largest population of elks.

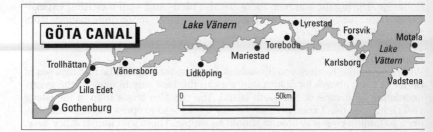

THE GÖTA CANAL BY BOAT

Although the Trollhättan Canal is still used to transport fuel and timber – the lakeside views from towns on the shores of Vänern are blotted by unsightly industrial greyness – the Trollhättan segment and the Göta Canal proper, between Vänern and Vättern, are extremely popular tourist destinations, with a wide range of canal trip deals on offer.

At the top end of the price range, Rederiaktiebolaget Göta Kanal, at Hotellplatsen 2 in Gothenburg (Göta Canal Steamship Company; ☎031/80 63 15, fax 15 83 11), offer what are dubbed "golden dollar" **cruises** aboard the historic steamers *M/S June* and *M/S Wilhelm Tham* for four- or six-day trips. The trips are slow-paced, wonderfully scenic and aim at making you feel you've stepped back in time, but glamour and sophistication are still piled on to justify the prices, with baskets of fruit and bathrobes thrown in for "A" category cabins (15,100kr for four days in a single cabin, or 10,000kr per person in a double); prices are cheaper downstairs on the main deck (9100kr for a single cabin, 8300kr per person in a double). The four-day trips from Gothenburg to Stockholm leave from Packhuskajen 10 at 8.45am, arriving in Stockholm at 2pm on day four. Leaving Stockholm, the journey begins at N. Riddarholmen.

To cut down on expenses and time, you can take in a selection of locks on a **day-trip** from towns along the canal route; any tourist office in the region will help organize the practicalities. You can also **rent a boat** or use your own; tourist offices (see "Mariestad", p.177) will advise on fees and mooring places, and on **renting a bike**, which is about the cheapest way to enjoy the canals (the towpaths being particularly picturesque).

From Gothenburg, there are regular **trains** stopping at Trollhättan, or by car, take Route 45; the area is even closer at hand from Uddevalla in Bohuslän, via Route 44.

Trollhättan

Seventy kilometres northeast of Gothenburg, **TROLLHÄTTAN** is the kind of place you might end up staying for a couple of days without really meaning to. Built around the fast river that powered its flour mills and sawmills for a couple of hundred years, Trollhättan remained fairly isolated until 1800, when the Göta Canal Company successfully installed the first set of locks to bypass the town's furious local waterfalls. River traffic took off, and better and bigger locks were

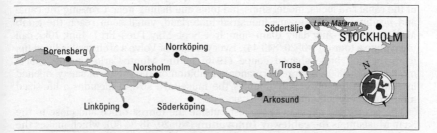

installed over the years. The main sights in town today are these locks and the falls themselves, with **paths** along the whole system, and orientation maps to guide you. Summer is the only time when the sluices are opened fully, allowing you to see the falls in all their crashing splendour (May & June Sat & Sun 3pm; July & Aug Wed, Sat & Sun 3pm).

Downtown Trollhättan is fairly mundane, but one worthwhile foray if you like contemporary art is a visit to the **Folketshus** on Kungsgatan, the pedestrianized main shopping street (Tues–Fri noon–4pm, Sat 10am–2pm; ☎0520/42 86 07). This impressive building contains a hall given over to dramatic, constantly changing exhibitions of modern art and installations. Three streets to the west and parallel to Kungsgatan is Strandgatan, where you can follow the river south, towards the locks. You'll soon be able to pick up the path for the Canal Museum (see below), which runs between the ordered network of canal locks and the beautiful winding river – it's a splendid half-hour walk there, passing a grand, English-style church perched on rocks between the waterways.

Considerably more enjoyable than you might imagine, the first point of interest you come to is the **Insikten Energy Centre** (mid-June to late Aug daily noon–4pm; telephone for times outside those dates; 10kr; ☎0520/888 82), which features none-too-scientific explanations of the workings of the nearby **Olidan hydroelectric power station** (June–Aug daily guided tours noon–4pm), a fine 1910 castle-like building with thirteen massive generators, and of the environmental advantages of hydroelectric power over coal and oil burning. The centre also explains the extraordinary salmon and eel ladders outside the power station: on their way from the sea to Lake Vänern, the migrating fish would die in the falls or at the power station, were they not caught in nets and hoisted out of the water in spring, deposited in Vänern by lorry, and returned with extra reserves from breeding stations in autumn, just in time to make the seaward trip.

Climbing beyond the power station, a road twists up to the striking **Elvius Lock**, the lowest in the system built in 1717 and known as Polhem's lock (you can see Polhem's irate-looking face peering out from all 500kr bank notes); it was never used as its design was regarded as flawed. From here, an evocative **forest walk** along the top of a steep, raised bank above the river provides a lovely twenty-minute saunter to the **Lower Locks**, built during the first forty years of the nineteenth century. These locks were rather more successful, being built away from the falls instead of directly in the course of the falls. If you carry on up Nedre Slussvägen, the road up by the side of the locks where the forest gives way to meadows, you'll reach the 1893 **Canal Museum** (mid-June to mid-Aug daily 11am–7pm; mid-Aug to mid-June Sat & Sun noon–5pm; 5kr; ☎0520/47 22 06) at Slussledsvägen 2–8 which puts the whole thing in perspective, covering a history of the canal and locks, model ships, old tools and fishing gear. Crossing the canal and heading into the town's industrial hinterland, you'll soon reach the **Saab Museum** (June–Aug daily 10am–6pm; free Sept–May Tues–Fri 1–4pm; 10kr, call to arrange a tour on ☎0520/843 44). Every model of Volvo's arch rival is lined up, from the first bullet-shaped coupé (1946) to the Monte-Carlo-winning sports model of the 1960s. A large permanent exhibition on the theme of safety, opened in summer 1999, effectively doubles the museum's size; it includes a life-sized model of an elk colliding a saloon car.

The newest attraction in town, just outside the tourist office and close to the Saab Museum, is the **cableway Innovatum** (☎0520/48 84 80), which makes the odd boast of being Sweden's most southerly cable-car ride. The futuristic cable cars make a four-minute journey 30m above the water, offering superb views over the river (early June noon–6pm, mid-June to mid-Aug 10am–6pm, mid-Aug to end Aug noon–4pm; 40kr). The trip starts at **Innovatum**, a centre dedicated to exhibitions on Swedish inventions, in the same building as the tourist office (mid-June to mid-Aug daily 10am–6pm; other times ☎0520/48 84 80). At the tourist office you can buy the **Innovatum Card** (valid mid-June to mid-Aug; 90kr), which allows free entrance to Innovatum, Insikten, and the Saab and Canal museums, plus free cable-car trips.

There are **boat trips** on *M/S Strömkarlen* (late June to mid-Aug; ☎0520/321 00; 100kr), heading to the locks and Canal Museum at 11.30am, 1.30pm and 3.30pm; the boats leave from outside *Strandgatan Cafe* (see below). To take full advantage of all Trollhättan's watery activity, the best time to visit is during the **Fallensdagar**, a three-day festival of dancing and music based around the waterfalls, starting on the third Friday in July.

Practicalities

The **train station** is on Järnvägsgatan, just north of the town centre. Next door to the Saab museum is the **tourist office**, at Åkerssjövägen 10 (mid-June to mid-Aug daily 9am–7pm; mid-Aug to mid-June Mon–Fri 10am–noon & 1.30–4pm; ☎0520/876 54, fax 310 13, *tourist@trollhattan.se*); they can book **private rooms** costing from 100kr (booking fee 26kr). There is an STF **youth hostel** a couple of blocks from the train station at Tingvallavägen 12 (☎ and fax 0520/129 60; 120kr); it has double and family rooms, serves breakfast and also rents bikes. You can find out about a range of central **hotels** from the tourist office. For a central, comfortable hotel, try *Hotel Swania*, Storgatan 49 (☎0520/890 00, fax 890 01; ⑤/④). As well as having an attached brasserie and nightclub (see p.170), it serves an exceptionally varied breakfast buffet, available to non-residents at 65kr. *Hotel Turisten*, Garvaregatan 18 (☎0520/41 11 39) also has cheap rooms with shared bathrooms. Overlooking the river is another hotel, *Stromsberg* (☎0520/129 90, fax 133 11; ③/②) which has an interesting history (see below). There's a **campsite** close to the centre by the river (June–Aug; ☎0520/306 13), with a heated swimming pool close by, and also offering bike rental, tennis and golf.

The best **cafés** are mostly along Strandgatan by the canal. Among the most popular is *Strandgatan*, not surprisingly on Strandgatan (daily 10am–11pm), in a workers' house built in 1867. Attracting a relaxed crowd who while away the evenings outside in summer, the café serves filled bagels (39kr) and good-value cooked meals, along with beers, wines and spirits also on offer. *Sluss Caféet,* overlooking the locks (daily: May & Aug 10.30am–9pm; June & July 10.30am–10pm), is a summer outdoor café; and *Pingst Café* on Strandgatan (Mon–Sat 9.30am–7pm, Sun noon–7pm) does lunch from 39kr and belongs to Sweden's free church, the Pingst Church – a fact unlikely to escape your notice once inside. The most delightful of them all is *Café Smulan* on Foreningsgatan (Mon–Thurs 9am–10pm, Fri & Sat 9am–5pm, Sun 11am–5pm), with excellent cakes and a cosy atmosphere. Its superb soups and filling pies also make it the best choice for vegetarian home cooking.

For fine dining, the best bet is *Warf 36* (☎0520/102 22; Mon–Sat 6–11pm) for luscious fish and meat dishes. The restaurant at *Hotel Stromsberg* is also well worth a visit (Mon–Fri 3–10pm, Sat & Sun 1–10pm): this charming old house was home to Edward Albert, a German who came to Trollhättan in 1880 and designed the first organized street system of working-class housing in Sweden (many of which remain intact in the town today). After his wife Maria died in childbirth, he founded a hospital; the house has lots of pictures of how his family lived. There's a good lunch special for 55kr and stylish evening meals are served. The most popular **pubs**, which are also good for evening meals, are *Oscar's* at Storgatan 44 (Mon & Tues 5–11pm, Wed–Sat 5pm–1am), and *Butler's*, at no. 35, a traditional late-opening Irish-style pub.

Despite being a small town set amid peaceful river surroundings, Trollhättan nevertheless manages to pack in plenty of offbeat entertainment. Nightlife revolves around the **nightclubs** at *Hotel Swania*, entrance in Strandgatan (till 2am), and *KK's Bar & Nightclub* at Torggatan 3, which has a young crowd, except on Thursdays, when 25- to 30-year-olds hit the dance floor. Trollhättan's **gay** community is served by RFSL Trestad (covering Trollhättan, Vänersborg and Uddevalla; ☎0520/41 17 66), who run the friendly *Rainbow Cafe* (Wed & Thurs 6–10pm), serving cheap coffee and cakes at Stridsbergsgatan 8 (just continue down Garvaregatan heading away from the town centre).

Vänersborg and around

On the tip of Lake Vänern, 14km north of Trollhättan, **VÄNERSBORG** was dubbed "Little Paris" by the celebrated local poet Birger Sjoberg. The similarities would be lost on anyone who has visited the French capital, though Vänersborg is a pleasant enough little resort town. Its main attractions are the nearby twin plateaux of **Hunneberg** and **Halleberg** (see p.171), both of which are not only of archeological interest but also support a wide variety of wildlife.

Vänersborg's old town is compact, if a bit lacklustre, pivoting around a central market square; it's pleasant to stroll past the numerous grand buildings – though all are overlooked by the bleak old prison at the end of Residensgatan. **Skräcklan Park**, just a few minutes from the centre, is a pretty place to relax, with its 1930s coffee house and promenade. The bronze statue of Sjoberg's muse, Frida, always has fresh flowers in her hand – even in winter, when the lake is solid ice, locals brave the sub-zero winds to thrust rhododendrons through her fingers.

Vänersborg's **museum**, behind the main square (June–Aug Tues noon–7pm, Wed, Thurs, Sat & Sun noon–4pm; Sept–May Tues noon–4pm, Sat & Sun noon–4pm; 20kr), is worth viewing not so much for its contents per se (a sequence of stuffed birds obscured by century-old dust) but rather for the sheer antiquity of the presentation: nothing is meant to be touched, and the pervading darkness means not much more can be seen. It's the oldest such museum in the country, and the gloomy interior and the collections have hardly altered since the doors first opened to the public in 1891. The biggest collections are of African birds, perched in massive glass cases in a room with a hand-painted ceiling. Also worth a glance is the caretaker's apartment, preserved in all its 1950s gloom, and a reconstruction of Sjoberg's home, which is darker still.

Practicalities

The **tourist office** is forever threatening to move, but at time of writing it remains at Kungsgatan 15 (June–Aug Mon–Fri 9am–8pm, Sat & Sun 11.30am–4pm; Sept–May Mon–Fri 10am–4pm; ☎0521/27 14 00, fax 27 14 01). The cheapest **B&B** is the friendly and central *Hoglunds* at Kyrkogatan 46 (☎0521/71 15 61; 550kr for a double including breakfast). For a **hotel**, there's the *Strand*, a decent enough place at Hamngatan 7 (☎0521/138 50, fax 159 00; ③, summer ②). You can **camp** at the lakeside *Ursands Camping* (☎0521/186 66, fax 686 76); get there on

bus #661 (6 daily); you need to book a place at least an hour ahead on ☎020/71 97 19. A good place to **eat** is *Konditori Princess* at Sundsgatan, a pleasant bakery with a café popular with locals, or make the two-kilometre journey to Värgon's top hotel restaurant (see below). **Nightlife** is pretty limited, the only options being *Club Roccad* on Kungsgatan 23 and *Oslagbar* at Edsgatan 8.

The tiny town of **Värgon**, just a kilometre from Vänersborg and reached along Östravägen (or take bus #62) is home to a renowned, ultra-chic restaurant and hotel, *Ronnums Herrgård* (☎0521/26 00 00, fax 26 00 09). A double room here in summer is 950kr, and though some of the rooms are rather less sophisticated than the hotel's reputation suggests, breakfast does live up to expectations. If you stay, insist on a room in the main building (the ones further away are less glamorous). The restaurant offers Swedish and international cuisine (☎0521/26 00 30; Sept–June lunches only, 200kr for two courses; evening meals in summer only, 350kr for three courses). Alternatively, you can save your *kronor* and get a good pizza and salad for 40kr at *Pizzeria Roma*, Nordkroksvagen 1 (☎0521/22 10 70; Mon–Fri 11am–10.30pm, Sat & Sun noon–10.30pm), on the opposite side of the main road from *Ronnums*.

East of Vänersborg: Halleberg and Hunneberg

East of Värgon, the road runs between the twin plateaux of **Halleberg** and **Hunneberg**, difficult to get to without your own transport, but well worth the trouble. There are regular **buses** to Hunneberg from Vänersborg, which are replaced in summer by a **taxi** service for the same price; there are just three a day and you need to ring an hour ahead (☎020/71 97 19). From Trollhättan, bus #619 runs straight to Hunneberg.

Thought to be five hundred million years old, the hills are remarkable structures, the result of water and sun cracking and grinding down the rock until the original peaks were reduced to their present flat-topped form. They're covered in a forest of blueberry and spruce where ospreys feed, which in turn is surrounded by dense clumps of oaks and pine. At the foot of the mountains are deciduous trees like linden, ash and maple; it's not uncommon to see hawfinches, herons and greenfinches here.

Early human remains have been found in the vicinity, as well as the traces of an old Viking fort, but these ancient places are best known as the home of Sweden's biggest herd of elks. **Elk safaris** run from late June to mid-August from Vänersborg's central square (150kr), but the old practice of offering money back if no sightings are made has been dropped, since a disease has reduced the stock to just 120. Oscar II began shooting elk here in 1872, and the Royal Hunt continues to claim elk lives: the present king shoots a maximum of fifty during two days at the beginning of October (new animals are then brought in to keep the number steady). Without going on a safari, the easiest way of spotting the elks is to be on the five-kilometre track around Halleberg at dawn or dusk; you can drive, cycle or walk up. The elks are well worth the trouble: leggy and long-faced, these massive creatures are so inquisitive they have no qualms about eating apples from your hand.

The excellent **youth hostel**, at Bergagårdsvägen 9, is housed in a building dating from 1550 at the foot of Hunneberg (reception daily 9–11am & 5–8pm; ☎0521/22 03 40, fax 684 97; 140kr; closed mid-Dec to mid-Jan); in the seventeenth century the place was used by Danish soldiers as a base from which to drive the Swedes into the hills. You can walk or cycle (bike rental at youth hostel; 60kr) along the Swede's line of retreat up Hunneberg, a route that brings you to the **Naturskola Nature Centre** (daily: mid-May to mid-Aug 11am–8pm; mid-Aug to mid-May 11am–4pm; ☎0521/22 37 70; free). A web of nature trails begins outside the centre, including special trails for wheelchair users; there's also a great **café**, which serves home-made cakes and endless refills of coffee for 12kr, and has lots of information about the wildlife in the hills.

Between the lakes: Västergötland

The county of **Västergötland** makes up much of the region between lakes Vänern and Vättern – a wooded, lakeland landscape that takes up a large part of the Gothenburg-to-Stockholm train ride. The most interesting places lie on the southeastern shore of Lake Vänern, notably the fascinating countryside around **Kinnekulle**, and the pretty town of **Mariestad**, easily reached from Gothenburg. With more time, you can cut south to the western shore of Lake Vättern, and in particular to the colossal fortress at **Karlsborg**. In between the lakes runs the **Göta Canal** which, along with the **Tiveden National Park**, is the main regional target for Swedes taking their holidays in July and August.

Lidköping

Flanking a grassy banked reach where the River Lidan meets Lake Vänern, **LIDKÖPING**, around 140km northeast of Gothenburg, won't detain you long, though its layout is pleasant enough due to an age-old decree that the height of a house may not exceed the width of the street on which it stands. On the east bank, the old town square, dating from 1446, faces the new town square, Nya Stadens Torg, created on the west bank by Chancellor Magnus de la Gardie in 1671, and graced by a wooden hunting lodge brought from his estate. Both squares enjoyed a perfect panorama of Vänern until an unsightly concrete screen of coal-storage cylinders and grain silos was plonked just at the water's edge; the squares still make for a pleasant-enough wander though. The most appealing section of town to stroll around is along Esplanaden where it runs across Mellbygatan overlooking the park, ablaze with flowers in summer. All the houses here seemed modelled on Norman Bates' home in *Psycho*.

The town's chief claim to fame, however, is the **Rörstrand Porcelain Factory** (Mon–Fri 10am–6pm, Sun noon–4pm; free, with guided tours in June & Aug only for 15kr; ☎0510/823 48). Run by Europe's second oldest porcelain firm (Rörstrand was founded in Stockholm in 1726), it is situated at the heart of the bleak industrial zone near the lake, and easily spotted as a giant version of their signature-style logo looms up in front of you as you head down Norra Torngatan. Though the company is revered by many Swedes, the museum here is pretty uninspiring. There are some pleasing classical designs on sale, supposedly at bargain prices, at the factory.

Lidköping itself has little else to offer, but it does make a good base for visiting the picturesque **Läckö castle**, on the Kalland peninsula west of the town (see p.175). Jutting into Vänern, this finger of land is brimming with scenic routes and a number of other architectural gems. Lidköping is also convenient for visiting **Kinnekulle** (see p.175), just a few kilometres to the northeast, which has even more surprises.

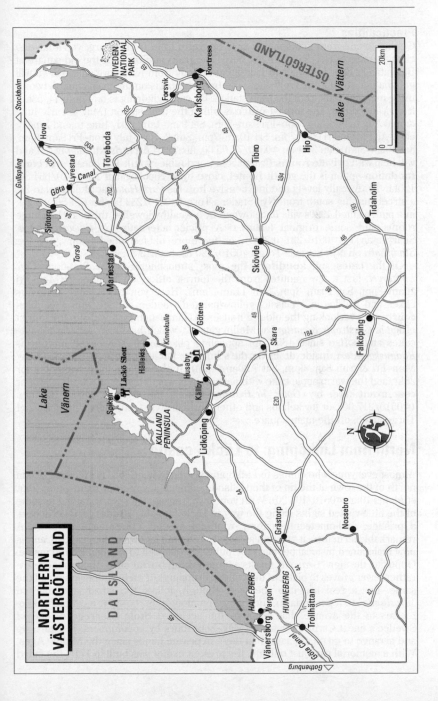

NORTHERN
VÄSTERGÖTLAND

Practicalities

Getting to and from Lidköping is easy by **train**; from Gothenburg, you'll have to change trains at Herrljunga to get here. The **train station** is by the old square at Bangatan 3. **Bus** #1 comes to Lidköping directly from Karlsborg, and bus #5 will get you into town from Trollhättan; the **bus station** is on the main square, two or three minutes' walk from the train station. By **car**, Lidköping is on Route 44, 53km from Vänersborg. The **tourist office** is within the train station (May to early June & mid-Aug to end Aug Mon–Fri 9am–5pm, Sat 9am–1am; early June to end June & early Aug Mon–Fri 9am–7pm, Sat 10am–7pm, Sun 2–7pm; July Mon–Fri 9am–8pm, Sat 10am–8pm, Sun 2–8pm; ☎0510/77 05 00, fax 77 04 64, *turist@lidkoping.se*), and will help with **private rooms** (from 350kr per double room). The cheapest **accommodation** option is the **youth hostel**, close by at Nicolaigatan 2 (☎0510/664 30; 120kr, ①). A really lovely and inexpensive **hotel** is *Park Hotell* at Mellbygatan 24, a street running south from Nya Stadens Torg (☎0510/243 90; fax 611 50; ②/①); in a pink-painted 1920s villa once owned by a wealthy jeweller, the place has huge rooms and some original features. A pricier alternative is *Edward Hotell*, Skaragatan 7 (☎0510/221 00; ③), or for more old-fashioned luxury, try the *Stadtshotel* on Nya Stadens Torg (☎0510/220 85, fax 215 32; ⑤/③).

Of the **cafés** and **konditori**, the most atmospheric is the first-floor *Café Limtorget*, just a few minutes from the tourist office, on Limtorget (Mon–Fri 10am–8pm, Sat 10am–3pm, Sun 11am–7pm). Here you can devour gorgeous cakes and waffles in a classic, yellow-painted wooden cottage with a cobbled courtyard, overlooking the old red houses in Gamlastad. Just opposite the tourist office is *Garstroms Konditori* at Mellbygatan 2, which has been serving reliable cakes and coffee since 1857. An appealing place for freshly-baked muffins is *Rådhuskonditori*, inside de la Gardie's hunting lodge in the new square (daily: Mon–Fri & Sun 8am–6pm, Sat 7.30am–4pm). It also serves filled baguettes for 28kr, and the warm apple cake with ice cream is worth trying at 20kr. For proper **restaurant** fare, try *Gotes Festvaning*, across the river at Östra Hamnen (☎0510/217 00), or for kebabs and other Turkish-style food, there's *Madonna*, at Torggatan 6, off the main square.

North from Lidköping: to Läckö castle

Almost everyone who comes to Lidköping seems to head for Läckö castle, 25km north of the town at the tip of the Kalland peninsula (May–Sept 10am–6pm; 40kr, students 10kr; ☎0510/103 20). With your own transport, it's worth taking in some of the little-visited sights along the way to Läckö, notably **Riddargardskvarnen**, a pristine, mid-nineteenth-century windmill around 11km north of town. A remarkable structure, it was run as a flour mill until its owner died in 1978, and is now maintained by local people – the public are allowed to wander around inside. Opposite, the sign "*Gravfalt*" marks a huge **Viking burial site** – though there are rather fewer graves to pick out than sheep droppings, it's a beautiful setting all the same. For a real trip into the past, though, follow the small lane marked "*Froslunda*" to a potato farm, then carry on along this route for a couple of kilometres to the avenue that leads to the secluded **Stola Herregård**, one of Sweden's finest Carolean estates (May–Sept tours by appointment; just turn up and arrange to go on one later that day), in private hands since the Middle Ages. With a memorial park just outside, the present manor was built in 1713, the faded grandeur of its interior a wonderfully authentic example of Rococo ornamentation. The whole area has changed very little in several hundred years.

Officially billed as being on its own island, but surrounded by water on just three sides, **Läckö** is everyone's idea of a fairy-tale castle, looking as though it's been dipped in yoghurt, its turrets and towers all creamy white. The castle dates from 1290, but was last modified and restructured by Lidköping's chancellor, de la Gardie, when he took it over in 1652. Inside, there is a wealth of exquisite decoration, particularly in the apartment that belonged to de la Gardie's wife, Princess Marie Euphrosyne. There are celebrated annual art exhibitions here in summer (ask at tourist office for details) and frequent guided tours (May–Aug daily 10am–4pm, Sept daily 11am–1pm; 30kr). Läckö's charms are no secret, so if you visit during summer, be prepared for the crowds. **Bus** #132 from Lidköping travels out here every hour during summer (20kr), via the tiny village of **Spiken**, 3km south of Läckö, which is a haven for lovers of smoked fish, sold at little stalls here.

East from Lidköping: Kinnekulle

Unlike many other areas of southern Sweden known primarily for their natural beauty, the delightful **Kinnekulle** region, stretching east from Lidköping along the southeastern edge of Vänern, is peppered with points of historical and social interest and makes for a splendid day amid a picturesque wilderness. Although the area is very much of the mainland, it has an insular feel, with the locals seeing themselves as living autonomously. The region has always been considerably wealthy, a fact not widely known in Sweden, with some magnificent manor houses, some of which continue to be run privately (one or two have become hotels, see p.177); each has its own immaculate railway station, where tiny trains still stop regularly.

Källby and Husaby

Twelve kilometres east of Lidköping and the first stop on the Kinnekullebanan regional train from Lidköping, **KÄLLBY** has an Iron Age burial site (turn left at the road junction), where two impressive stones face each other, one carved with a comical, goblin-like figure, supposedly the god Thor. Not far beyond, **HUSABY** village makes for a tranquil diversion, but one of great religious and cultural significance. It was at the church here that, in 1008, the English missionary St Sigfrid baptized Olof Skotkonung, the first Swedish king to turn his back on Viking gods and embrace Christianity. The present, three-towered church was built in the twelfth century, and just to the east is the well where the baptism is said to have taken place. A remarkable sight is afforded close by if you take a path just a few metres west of the church and follow a sign to **Lasse i Bergets Grotta** (Lasse's Grotto), 200m off the main road. Sunk into the rock and entirely camouflaged by trees, the grotto is where a local man, Lars Eriksson, and his wife made their home in 1881; they remained in this two-chambered cave until his death in 1910. Born in 1828 and known as Lasse, this illiterate man made his own guns, hunted and picked all his own food, and was said to practise witchcraft; more mundanely, his wife made clothes which she sold in the area. Today, you can walk into the dark rock "rooms" which are made additionally fascinating by the photographs, on the display board outside, taken in 1907 of Lasse and his cosy, cluttered interior. From outside, there's no sign that anyone ever lived here.

From Husaby to Hällekis

A couple of kilometres onward from Husaby lies the "flowering mountain", **Kinnekulle** (all the trains from Källby will take you there), an area of woods and lakes all interwoven with paths and boasting hundreds of varieties of flowers, trees, birds and other animals. The strange, flat-topped shape of the hill is due to its top layer of hard volcanic rock, which even four hundred million years of Swedish weather has not managed to wear down, making for something of a botanical and geological treasure trove. For views of the surrounding landscape and the water beyond, pop in to **Högkullen**, a wooden look-out tower on the hill, built in the Romantic style in 1892; it's close to the tourist office (p.177).

At the northernmost point of the region, the only town as such is **HÄLLEKIS**, an unglamorous little place where concrete-making was the local industry until the 1970s, but which now concentrates on the insulation trade. The unlovely buildings connected with this business are thankfully restricted to the periphery of the town. An unexpected diversion here is **Falkängen,** a street of former workers' cottages renovated and prettified into a sort of Swedish *Stepford Wives* village where all the pretty pastel former homes sell appallingly twee hand-crafted knick-knacks. The village is a must-see, though, for the unlikely combination of permanently smiling women (no men seem to be involved) making clothes and ornaments, and the charming coffee houses serving home-made cakes. The youth hostel is right in the middle of all this (see p.177), and sheep and ducks have been encouraged to live among the houses, creating the appearance of a toy farm.

Around Hällekis

Heading back south from Hällekis, the grand Naples yellow facade of **Hönsäter Slott**, just half a kilometre away, comes as quite a surprise. Now a fine restaurant and an exquisite place to stay (see p.177), this castle dates from the fourteenth century, though most of the present building was constructed in the 1660s. Even if you're not staying, staff are relaxed about visitors peeking into the beautiful rooms with antiquated square pianos. Note the run of glorious first-floor rooms, each one opening onto the next, as though an image infinitely reflected in two facing mirrors.

Three kilometres south of Hönsäter, **Hällekis castle** is a very grand mansion at the end of an avenue lined with horse-chestnut trees and cut through the forest. A dreary clothes shop specializing in tartans and V-neck sweaters is to be found within the building nearest the entrance, but otherwise the grounds of this private estate contain a range of design workshops, all worth a look (June–Aug Tues–Sun noon–4pm, July daily; Sept–May Sat & Sun noon–4pm); their products range from ceramics to ironware and glassware. It is the **gardens** (10kr), however, that are the real draw. The headily scented perennial borders were devised by the British garden designer Simon Irvine, who also created the gardens at Läckö Castle (see p.175). There's an appealing, vine-covered **café** here, open in summer. At the start of the avenue by which you enter the grounds, a long flight of half-hidden, mossy stone steps leads to a path through some of the prettiest forest here. The stairs were built for King Oscar II to enable him to climb Kinnekulle without having to hike, and an inscription commemorating his first visit is engraved on gravestone-like tablets at the foot of the stairs. Once at the top, follow the path to the right, opening onto a clearing blushing with wild roses. From here, there's a striking vista down into the huge quarry below, as big as a canyon.

Just a little further on from Hällekis Castle is an extraordinarily fine mansion named **Råbäcks**, fronted by yellow-striped awnings and framed by climbing roses and honeysuckle. A few strides away, Råbäck station is doll's-house perfect. Wild poppies grow on the track undisturbed by the trains, six of which run through each day, stopping at each mansion. Just a few metres on, Munkängarna is a meadowland **nature reserve** owned by the monastery at Vadstena (p.316) until the fifteenth century. In spring, the whole area is fragrant with wild flowers but sadly, the only English text amid the masses of information posted is an injunction to visitors "not to collect any kind of animals or drive a horse with cart". Of the three churches found just south of here – Medelplana, Österplana and Västerplana – the most rewarding interior by far is that at **Västerplana** (May–Sept daily 8am–8pm), its medieval core being the tower and nave. An appealing hall church with wide arches, it has beautiful eighteenth-century roof paintings. Its reredos and pulpit, all dark reds and gold, are also worth a look. Directly opposite is a particularly good **antique curio shop**, Kinnekulle Kuriosa (Sun 1–5pm; ☎0510/54 15 06), evocatively housed in an unrenovated old wooden house. Inside are some real finds, both among the items for sale and in the form of the hand-painted original decor.

Practicalities

There's an excellent **tourist office** on Kinnekulle, just south of Hällekis at Högkullen (☎ and fax 0510/54 42 10; early June to mid-Aug daily 11am–4pm; at other times of year, call to check if they're open before visiting). It's attached to a prettily sited restaurant and café called *Kinnekulle Gården*, which does sumptuous cakes and coffee at 15kr, including refills. The beautifully renovated STF **youth hostel** *Falkängen* (☎0510/54 06 53, fax 54 00 85; 110kr, ①), amid the former workers' cottages close to Hällekis, has a real community atmosphere. The hostel **rents bikes** for 50kr a day or 200kr a week. A gorgeous, though expensive, **hotel** is *Hönsäter Slott* (☎0510/54 05 90; ⑤/④), just south of Hällekis (see p.176); the price does, however, include a two-course dinner which is a gastronomic delight – delicately flavoured fish and meat dishes. For less money, the General Harald Stakes **bar** here (daily noon–9pm; 65kr), named after the castle's former owner, stays open till 1am and the terrace is a great place for lunch, while the dinner special is good value for fine Swedish cooking (175kr for two courses).

Mariestad and around

Lakeside **MARIESTAD** is smaller, prettier and more welcoming than Lidköping, from where it's just an hour's train ride north. With its splendid medieval quarter and harbour area, Mariestad is a good place for a day or two's stay, and an excellent base for exploring its surroundings. The compact centre is brought to life by either the self-guided walking tour (pick up a map from the tourist office, see p.178) or the guided tours organized by the tourist office in summer (mid-June to mid-Aug Mon & Thurs; 20kr). What lifts the town beyond mere picture-postcard status is the extraordinary range of building styles crammed into the centre – Gustavian, Carolean, Classical, Swiss-chalet style and Art Nouveau – a living museum of architectural design. It's also worth taking a look at the late-Gothic **cathedral**, on the edge of the centre, whose construction at the end of the sixteenth century was fuelled by spite. Duke Karl, who named the town after his wife, Maria of Pfalz, was jealous of his brother, King Johan III, and so built the cathedral to resemble and rival the king's Klara kyrka in Stockholm. Karl ensured the the new building was endowed with over-the-top Baroque features and some odd niceties – note the stained-glass windows, depicting mint green and yellow wheat sheaves, and set with numerous real insects. The Baroque pulpit is dramatic too, covered in cherubs with silver or black bodies, all dressed in gold wreaths.

Once you've inspected Mariestad's fine architecture, there is little else to do in town – the clutch of seven folk museums in the vicinity aren't up to much. Better prospects are offered at the nearby island of **Torsö**, which now has a bridge connecting it with the mainland and offers good fishing and bathing opportunities (fishing equipment available at the tourist office). To reach Torsö, head up Strandgatan past Snapen, from where the route is signposted; it's a fifteen-minute cycle ride. Perhaps best of all, Mariestad is also an ideal base from which to **cruise** up Lake Vänern to the start of the Göta Canal's main stretch at Sjötorp. There are 21 locks between Sjötorp and Karlsborg (see p.179), with the most scenic section up to Lyrestad, just a few kilometres east of Sjötorp and 20km north of Mariestad on the E20. Lake and canal cruises cost 190kr, no matter where you choose to disembark; the boats return to Mariestad on the same day (contact Mariestad's tourist office for details).

Practicalities

The **train station** is in a beautiful Art Nouveau building about five minutes' walk from the harbour. Besides providing the usual information, the **tourist office**, by the harbour on Hamngatan (June–Aug Mon–Fri 8am–7pm, Sat & Sun 9am–6pm; Sept–May Mon–Fri 8am–4pm; ☎0501/100 01, fax 121 40, *turistbyran@mariestad.se*), **rents bikes** at 60kr per day. Opposite is the hugely popular STF **youth hostel** (☎0501/104 48; mid-Aug to mid-June advance booking necessary; 120kr), with galleried timber outbuildings and an excellent garden café (daily 11am–7pm); it's a great place to stay, close to all the sights. The oldest **hotel** is the 1698 *Bergs Hotell*, in the old town at Kyrkogatan 18 (☎ and fax 0501/103 24; ①). It's quite basic inside, with no en-suite rooms, though comfortable enough and quiet. Other good-value central hotel options include *Hotel Aqua*, Viktoriagatan 15 (☎0501/195 15, fax 187 80; ①), which is mundane but cheap, and has breakfasts at 40kr extra; and the far cosier and more appealing *Hotel Vänerport*, Hamngatan 32 (☎0501/771 11, fax 771 21; ③). Rather more luxurious is the *Stadshotellet* on Nya Torget (☎0501/138 00, fax 77640, ④/③), just five minutes' walk away in the modern centre. The nearest **campsite** is *Ekuddens*, 2km down the river (☎0501/106 37, fax 186 01; 100kr; May–Sept); alternatively you can stay on Torsö at *Torsö Camping* (☎0501/213 02; May–Sept).

In the new town area, Mariestad's trendiest coffee-house hang-out is *Café Stroget* at Österlånggatan 10 (Mon–Fri 9am–6pm, Sat 9am–2pm), a laid-back place that's popular with young locals. More welcoming, though, is the *Garden Cafe* at the youth hostel (see above) which serves baguettes for around 30kr, ice cream and cakes. The liveliest **bar-restaurants** are *Buffalo* at Österlånggatan 3 and *Hjorten* at Nygatan 21; the latter also has occasional live music. A very pleasant place for a drink and cheapish meal in summer is the *Old Ox*, a bar-restaurant on a boat moored just 300m from the tourist office (☎0501/130 50; Mon–Sat 7pm–midnight), and serving steaks, chicken and home-made burgers for

Royal Palace, Stockholm

T-bana mural, Stockholm

Östermalm food hall, Stockholm

Front door, Ystad

Vasa galleon, Djurgården, Stockholm

Stockholm archipelago

Millesgården, Stockholm

Opera House, Gothenburg

Rural scene, Skåne

Kallbadhuset, Varberg

HUBERT STADLER/CORBIS

Helsingborg harbour

CHRIS COE/AXIOM

Marina, Bohuslän coast

MACDUFF EVERTON/CORBIS

68–98kr, with an ambitious drinks menu. The best pizza place (and almost the only place open on a Sunday for a bite) is *Candy's Bistro*, Österlånggatan 17A (☎0501/106 20), a simple café popular with the locals; besides tasty pizzas (48kr), it also serves pies, pasta and salad dishes. The hippest of very few **nightclubs** is *Aquavit Blå Bar* at Kungsgatan 5 (☎0501/711 00), which is popular with a 20-something crowd and also has good food.

North of Mariestad: Gullspång
Buses head 40km north from Mariestad to **GULLSPÅNG**. Between here and Torved to the south runs 20km of railway track, rebuilt in 1965 in an abortive attempt to run standard trains. In the mid-1980s a craze for railway cycling took hold, and the rusting tracks were cleared for self-propelled trips on pump-action buggies like those in Hollywood westerns. These carry one or two people and can be rented at the tourist office (May–Sept; 30kr for an hour, 300kr per day); the buggies must be returned to the spot where they were rented. The route, which can also be cycled (around 5hr there and back), lies alongside the eminently swimmable Gullspång River. Gullspång is the more convenient end at which to rent a buggy, since there's an STF **youth hostel** there (110kr). You can book both the buggy rides and the youth hostel through the Gullspång's **tourist office** (☎0551/361 40; fax 202 77). They also offer a **package** at the hostel: accommodation, breakfast and a packed lunch for 350kr per person.

Karlsborg and around

Despite the great plans devised for the fortress at **KARLSBORG**, around 70km southeast of Mariestad on the western shores of Lake Vättern, it has survived the years as one of Sweden's greatest follies. By the early nineteenth century, Sweden had lost Finland – after six hundred years of control – and had became jumpy about its own security. In 1818, with the Russian fleet stationed on the Åland Islands and within easy striking distance of Stockholm, Baltzar Von Platen (see p.166) persuaded parliament to construct an inland fortress at Karlsborg, capable of sustaining an entire town and protecting the royal family and the treasury – the idea being that enemy forces should be lured into the country, then destroyed on Swedish territory. With the town pinched between lakes Vättern and Bottensjön, the Göta Canal – also the brainchild of Von Platen and already under construction – was to provide access, but while Von Platen had the canal finished by 1832, the fortress was so ambitious a project that it was never completed. It was strategically obsolete long before work was finally abandoned in 1909, as the walls were not strong enough to withstand attack from new weaponry innovations. However, parts are still in use today by the army and air force, and uniformed cadets mill around here, lending an authenticity to your visit.

The complex, which is as large as a small town, appears austere and forbidding, but you are free to wander through and to enter the **museum**, where you'll find endless military uniforms on display (mid-May to mid-June Mon–Fri 10am-4pm, Sat & Sun noon–5pm; mid June to early Aug daily 10am–6pm; early Aug to end Aug daily 10am–5pm; Sept to mid-May Mon–Fri 10am–3pm; 30kr). The **guided tour** (60kr), with special sound and smoke effects, is a must for children. Apart from the fortress, Karlsborg has one of the most delightful family-run hotels you'll find in Sweden, and a couple of good places to eat.

Practicalities

There is no train service to Karlsborg, and you'll have to come on one of the regular **bus** services from either Lidköping or Mariestad; by road, take the 202 from Mariestad, which brings you to Storgatan when you reach town. Turn left into Strandgatan for the **tourist office** (June–Aug daily 9am–5pm; Sept–May Mon–Fri 9am–3pm; ☎0505/188 30, fax 188 39). During summer they are in a lovely old building at the entrance to the fortress, and at other times of year in the big yellow house close by; they will book **private rooms** for around 150kr per person. The STF **youth hostel** (☎ & fax 0505/446 00; 120kr) is at the fortress entrance too (signposted *"Fästningen"*). Karlsborg's **campsite** is on the banks of Lake Bollensjön (☎0505/449 16, fax 449 12; May–Sept), 2km north along Storgatan. **Bikes** can be rented here for a steep 80kr a day, but they're cheaper to rent from Cykel och Sport on Strandvägen (☎0505/101 80), which has excellent bikes for 70kr per day. One of the real treats of Karlsborg is staying at its most stylish **hotel**, *Kanalhotellet* at Storgatan 94 (☎0505/121 30, fax 127 61; ②), built in 1894 when the present owner's grandparents returned from America after working for President Cleveland at The White House. The dining room here, with stately dark panels, oil-paint portraits and glinting chandeliers, overlooks the Göta Canal.

The **restaurant** here is very fine too, with classic Swedish dishes – try the speciality, red-belly salmon fresh from Lake Vättern – and a sumptuous breakfast. Another good eating option is *Ida's Brygga* (☎0505/131 11; Mon & Tues 11.30am–11pm, Wed & Thurs 11.30am–midnight, Fri & Sat noon–1am, Sun noon–10pm) just opposite the *Kanalhotellet*. With its canal backdrop, it's a romantic spot for dinner, and there's live music in the evenings. Next door, *Klangahamns Fiskrokeri* is good for smoked fish (☎0505/130 93). To fill yourself up on a tight budget, a fair choice is *Järnhandel* (Mon–Thurs 4–11pm, Fri & Sat 4pm–3am) on Storgatan, at the junction with Strandgatan. This pub-cum-café, much frequented by locals, plays every ageing rock hit you've ever heard; it serves inexpensive *pytt i panna*, chicken sandwiches and fish and chips. Also cheap is *Restaurant San Remo* on Storgatan 15 (Mon–Sat 11am–11pm, Sun noon–10pm), a somewhat uninspired pizza restaurant in the disused train station, with pizzas for 45kr and a range of salads.

Forsvik

As far back as the early fourteenth century, the Karlsborg area maintained an important monastic flour mill, 8km northwest at the village of **FORSVIK** (the monastery was founded by Sweden's first female saint, Birgitta). The height differential between lakes Viken and Bottensjön meant that energy could be extracted, first by means of waterwheels and later with turbines, which allowed a sizable industry to emerge, producing all manner of metal and wood products. During the Reformation, the Crown confiscated Forsvik from the monastery. The creation of the Göta Canal gave the place new life: it once again became a busy industrial centre, its paper mill operating until the 1940s, its foundry until the Swedish shipyard crises of the 1970s. Today, the area makes for a charming excursion: the mill has been restored to its 1940s condition and converted into an impressive **museum** (June–Aug 9am–5pm; 30kr), providing a stimulating picture of Forsvik's industrial past. There's a thorough English booklet about all that's on show and an English-language video for the super-interested. Close by, in the old shipbuilding area, you can observe the work that's currently afoot to build a **steamboat** which, it is hoped, will be ready for use by 2003. The boat will be named *Eric Nordvall II* after the first paddle steamer of that name, which sank in 1856 to the bottom of Lake Vättern, where it has remained ever since.

Bus #420 runs to Forsvik from Karlsborg two or three times a day in summer. Within the clutch of dark red wooden buildings here is a matching, well-appointed STF **youth hostel** at Bruksvägen 11 (☎0505/411 37 in summer, 411 27 in winter), formerly a workmen's dwelling from the 1860s, while 250m on down the main road is *Forsvik Cafe*, a relaxing spot for a **light meal**, with home-baked cakes and savouries.

Tiveden National Park

Located 15km northeast of Karlsborg, **Tiveden National Park** is part of a much larger expanse of forest, lakes and ice-age boulders. One of southern Sweden's few remaining areas of virgin land, the park has never been inhabited – though charcoal has been produced at the periphery of the area since the seventeenth century. The park, unlike more managed forests, aims to maintain an environment close to that of a primeval forest, with no human intervention, and the old or dead trees throughout Tiveden provide the habitat for a number of rare birds and animals. There are 25km of trails here passing though some spectacular scenery, with organized hikes tailored for differing abilities (ask at Karlsborg tourist office for details). The Tiveden wilderness is also the site used by the Karlsborg **Survival Training Centre** for its courses (☎505/188 34, fax 188 39), each of which usually lasts one to three days. Activities such as baking in a Siberian sauna (complete with birch-twig beatings) on the shores of Lake Vättern, mountain biking and abseiling are also on offer.

Among the easier **trails** to try is the **Stenkälla**, running close by Ödlesjön, a lake. Almost all the forest here originates from after 1835, the date of the last massive fire to devastate the region. A recently added route, and one of the best parts, is the Stenkälleklack, a short but steep two-hundred-metre trail off the main track. The landscape you see here was shaped hundreds of millions of years ago when the plains cracked and formed valleys, one of which became Lake Vättern.

Just north of the trail, fire marks are still visible on the 250-year-old pines from the 1835 disaster. In order that the bogs here could be crossed in summertime, primitive footbridges were subsequently built; having been trampled down into the peat, their preserved remains can still be seen. **Fishing** is very popular at Tiveden, but comes with a flurry of rules. You can get a licence at various places, among them Karlsborg's tourist office and Olssons Fiske, back in Mariestad (110kr for 24hr; covers eight lakes in the area); however, you're only allowed to catch three fish. For more information on fishing here, contact Hökensås Sportfiske (☎0502/230 00, fax 230 10).

Horse-riding excursions have taken off at Tiveden recently. Tivedens Hästskjuts, based at Uggletorp, just north of Karlsborg does guided horseback excursions through the forest (summer 10am–7pm, winter 10am–3pm; book a week in advance on ☎0505/250 44 or 070/512 73 58). The horses are all of the a Scandinavian breed known as Nordsvensk. A beginner's excursion costs 175kr, but among the longer trips for more experienced riders are a half-day trip (4hr; 475kr) and a two-day outing offering ten hours' riding and an overnight stay in primitive conditions (1200kr).

travel details

Trains

Gothenburg to: Kalmar (Mon–Fri 3 daily, Sat & Sun 2 daily; 4hr 20min); Karlskrona (Mon–Fri 2 daily, Sat & Sun 1 daily; 4hr 40min); Lidköping (6 daily; 45min); Malmö (Mon–Fri 12 daily, Sat 8 daily, Sun 9 daily; 3hr by X2000, 3hr 50min by InterCity); Stockholm (Mon–Fri 13 daily, Sat 9 daily, Sun 12 daily; 3hr 15min by X2000, 4hr 30min by InterCity); Strömstad (Mon–Fri 9 daily, Sat 8 daily, Sun 7 daily; 2hr 40 min); Trollhättan (Mon–Fri 15 daily, Sat 12 daily, Sun 8 daily; 40min); Vänersborg Mon–Fri 10 daily, Sat & Sun 4 daily; 1hr 5min).

Buses

Gothenburg to: Falun/Gävle (Mon–Thurs & Sat 1 daily, Fri & Sun 3 daily; 10hr 30min); Halmstad (Fri & Sun 3 daily; 2hr); Karlstad (Mon–Thurs & Sat 3 daily; Fri 5 daily, Sun 4 daily; 4hr); Linköping/Norrköping (Mon–Thurs & Sun 3 daily, Fri 4 daily, Sat 1 daily; 4hr 35min); Mariestad (Mon–Fri & Sun 5 daily, Sat 4 daily; 3hr); Oskarshamn (Fri & Sun 2 daily; 5hr 20min); Tanumshede/Strömstad (Mon–Fri 5 daily, Sat & Sun 4 daily; 2hr 30min); Trollhättan (Mon–Thurs & Sun 5 daily, Fri & Sat 2 daily; 1hr 5min); Varberg/Falkenberg (Fri & Sun 2 daily; 50min/1hr 20min).

Gullspång to: Mariestad (Mon–Thurs & Sun 2 daily, Fri 3 daily; 40min).

Lidköping to: Vånersborg/Trollhättan (Fri & Sun 2 daily; 45min/1hr).

Mariestad to: Gävle (Mon–Fri 1 daily; 7hr 30min); Örebro (Mon–Fri 2 daily, Sat & Sun 1 daily; 1hr 30min); Skövde/Jönköping (Mon–Thurs & Sun 3 daily, Fri 4 daily, Sat 1 daily; 1hr 30min/2hr 10min).

International buses

Gothenburg to: Oslo (Mon–Fri 5 daily, Sat & Sun 4 daily; 4hr 45min).

International trains

Oslo–Copenhagen trains involve changing at Gothenburg. There are two trains daily.

International ferries

Gothenburg to: Frederikshavn (4–8 daily; 3hr 15min; by catamaran 3–5 daily; 1hr 45min); Harwich (2 weekly; 24hr); Kiel (1 daily; 14hr); Newcastle (1 weekly June to mid-Aug).

Strömstad to: Fredrikstad (mid-June to mid-Aug Mon–Sat 5 daily; 1hr 15min); Halden (mid-June to mid-Aug Mon–Sat 3 daily; 1hr 15min); Sandefjord (mid-June to mid-Aug 2 daily; 2hr 30min).

CHAPTER THREE

THE SOUTHWEST

There is a real historical interest to the southwestern provinces of **Halland**, **Skåne** and **Blekinge**, not least in the towns and cities that line the coast. In the fourteenth to seventeenth centuries, the flatlands and fishing ports south of Gothenburg were almost constantly traded between Denmark and Sweden; several fortresses scattered about the region bear witness to its status as a buffer in medieval times.

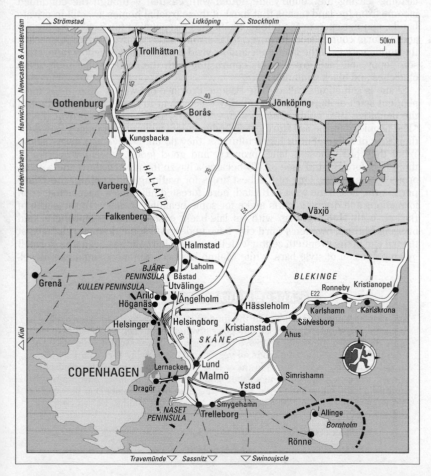

Halland, a finger of land facing Denmark, has a coastline of smooth, sandy beaches and bare, granite outcrops, punctuated by a number of small, distinctive towns. The most charismatic of these is the old society bathing resort of **Varberg**, dominated by its tremendous thirteenth-century fortress; also notable is the small, beautifully intact medieval core of **Falkenberg**; while the regional capital, **Halmstad**, is popular for its extensive beaches and nightlife.

Further south, in the ancient province of **Skåne**, the coastline softens into curving beaches backed by gently undulating fields. This was one of the first parts of the country to be settled, and the scene of some of the bloodiest battles during the medieval conflict with Denmark. Although Skåne was finally ceded to Sweden in the late seventeenth century, the Danish influence died hard; indeed it is still evident today in the thick Skåne accent, often incomprehensible to other Swedes, and in the province's architecture. The latter has also been strongly influenced by Skåne's agricultural economy, the wealth generated by centuries of profitable farming leaving the countryside dotted with **castles** – though the continued income from the land means that most of these palatial homes are still in private hands, and not open to the public. Skåne has a reputation for fertile, mainly flat and uniform countryside; however, it takes only a day or two here to appreciate the subtle variety of the landscape and its vivid beauty: slabs of yellow rape, crimson poppy and lush green fields contrasting with the castles, charming white churches and black windmills.

Skåne is sometimes called "The Basque Province of Sweden" due to the independent spirit of its people. This quality was evident to James Steveni, author of the definitive 1925 guide, *Unknown Sweden*; he wrote, somewhat provocatively: "The people of Skåne are sturdy, very independent and not particularly noted for their love of refinement or high culture. . . they do not believe in outward show. What they prize most is land, property and good food." Steveni was writing, though, before **Båstad** (see p.203) became a haven to outward show and a glamorous tennis capital. One of the best areas for **walking** and **cycling**, the **Bjäre peninsula**, lies to the west of Båstad; here, forested hill ranges, spectacular rock formations and dramatic cliffs make for some beautiful scenery. To the south of Båstad, both **Helsingborg**, with its laid-back, cosmopolitan atmosphere, and bustling **Malmö**, Sweden's third city, have undergone some dramatic changes at the tail end of the twentieth century. Helsingborg's harbour has been transformed by an explosion of style bars, while Malmö has seen the most significant devel-

---

ACCOMMODATION PRICES

The pensions and hotels listed in the guide have been price-graded according to the scale given below; the price category given against each establishment indicates the cost of the least expensive double rooms there. Many hotels offer considerable reductions at weekends all year round, and during the summer holiday period (mid-June to mid-Aug); in these cases the reduction is either noted in the text or, where a discount brings a hotel into another price band, given after the number for the full price. Single rooms, where available, usually cost between 60 and 80 percent of a double. Where hostels have double rooms, we've given price codes for them also.

① under 500kr	③ 700–900kr	⑤ 1200–1500kr
② 500–700kr	④ 900–1200kr	⑥ over 1500kr

opment of all – the completion of the sixteen-kilometre-long **bridge** linking the city to Copenhagen, and thus Sweden to the rest of Europe. Just north of Malmö, the university town of **Lund** has a distinctive bohemian atmosphere that's in contrast with Malmö's Social Democratic, more down-to-earth heritage; with its wealth of classic architecture, Lund is a must for anyone travelling in the south.

The southwest corner of Skåne boasts excellent beaches around some minor resorts. Moving east, you encounter the pretty medieval town of **Ystad** along the south coast, and then enter the splendid countryside of **Österlen**, whose pastoral scenery is studded with Viking monuments, such as the Swedish Stonehenge at **Ales Stennar**. Lined with brilliant white beaches backed by several nature reserves, the area also offers some of Sweden's most enjoyable cycling. As you edge north, the land becomes green and more hilly, the coast dotted with a number of interesting little places at which to stop, such as **Kivik**, with its apple orchards and Bronze Age cairn, and the ancient and picturesque resort of **Åhus**. At the northeast of the county, **Kristianstad**, built as a flagship town by the Danes, retains its fine, Renaissance layout.

Beyond here to the east, the ledge of land running to the Baltic is **Blekinge** province. Among its several small, not particularly distinguished resorts, **Karlskrona** stands out, a naval base built on a number of islands.

Travel practicalities

South of Gothenburg, the SJ **train** line follows the coast, with frequent trains stopping at all towns as far as Ystad, from where it cuts northeast to Kristianstad. The comfortable, Danish-built Kustpilen Express trains run west–east across the country, linking Malmö, Helsingborg and Lund with Kristianstad and Karlskrona. However, some of the most beautiful and less-frequented areas are not covered by the train network, and the **bus** service is skeletal at best, especially along the south coast. There are also certain transport anomalies to look out for: there are trains but no buses between Malmö and Ystad, whereas there are no trains from Ystad to Kristianstad (to do this route by rail you'll have to take the inland Osterlenaren train from Ystad to Malmö and change). More generally, some train and bus services stop running early in the day. The best places to pick up timetables for the region are Gothenburg and Malmö's train and bus stations and tourist offices.

With no really steep hills, the southwest is wonderful country for **cycling**, and bike rental outlets are numerous; most tourist offices, youth hostels and campsites also rent out bikes. There are several recognized **walking trails**, many of which are referred to in the text.

Kungsbacka, Tjolöholm and Äskhult

Just beyond the southernmost suburbs of Gothenberg, the small town of **KUNGSBACKA** is a residential backwater that's of no particular interest to travellers, unless you time your trip to arrive on the lively market days (the first Thursday of every month). Although Kungsbacka dates from the thirteenth century, when it shared growth and prosperity with many other Hanseatic towns along the south coast, there's not much of a sense of history about the place: the town was razed by fire in 1846, and now just two old houses stand as testimony to its past. It's altogether better to use the town simply as a means of reaching the splendid and unique manor house on the coast at **Tjolöholm,** 15km south, and the immaculately preserved historic farmstead village at **Äskhult**, just on the other side of the E20 from Tjolöholm.

Trains run here from Gothenburg (20min); Kungsbacka's **tourist office**, opposite the station (mid-May to mid-June Mon–Fri 9am–5pm, Sat 10am–2pm; mid-June to end June Mon–Fri 9am–6pm, Sat 10am–2pm; July Mon–Sat 9am–6pm, Sun 10am–2pm; Aug Mon–Fri 9am–6pm, Sat & Sun 10am–2pm; Sept to mid-May Mon–Fri 9am–5pm; ☎0300/345 95, fax 131 34), will book **private rooms** at 170kr per person. The STF **youth hostel** is 2km from the train station, on the road to Särö (☎0300/194 85; 110kr; mid-June to mid-Aug) – turn left from the station, then right onto the main road. The only central hotel is Hotel Halland at Storgatan 35 (☎0300/775 30, fax 162 25; ④/②), a couple of doors down from the tourist office. It's a bland but reasonable place, where all the rooms are en suite and have TVs. The nearest **campsite** is 3km away at the Kungsbacka Sportscenter (June–Aug ☎0300/148 29; Sept–May ☎0300/346 48). Unfortunately there are no buses here; you can get to it on foot from the centre by heading out along Storgatan.

Tjolöholm

The manor house at **TJOLÖHOLM** (pronounced "chewla-home"; June–Aug daily 11am–4pm; Sept & Oct Sun 11am–4pm; 45kr; ☎0300/54 42 00) was once the dream home of the Scottish merchant and horse-breeder James Dickson. Enormously wealthy, he wanted a unique house that reflected a combination of his British ancestry, the then current Swedish fascination for Romanticism, and the latest comfort innovations of the day. The design of the house was the object of a grand competition in the 1890s, won by the architect Lars Israel Wahlman, and the result of his work is a stunning Elizabethan-style stately home. Dickson, however, never saw Tjolöholm completed: he died after he cut his finger on a bottle of vintage champagne he was opening (he fatally poisoned himself by wrapping the lead cap around the wound). To get to Tjolöholm, take the **train** from platform 15 at Gothenburg's Central Station to Kungsbacka (20min), from where you catch bus #732 (covered by the train ticket) which goes to within 3km of the estate, from where you'll have to walk or hitch. By **car**, turn off the E6 highway just south of Kungsbacka at Fjärås and follow the signs to Åsa for 2km, from where there are signs for Tjolöholm.

In 1901, the Dicksons had a village built around the house to provide accommodation for the staff; its little red and white wooden cottages, each with just one room and a kitchen, have been immaculately preserved. Walking up the main driveway, you pass the huge stables and indoor riding track, which have been converted into an airy **café** (April to mid-June & mid-Aug to Oct Sat & Sun 11am–5pm; mid-June to mid-Aug Tues–Fri 11am–5pm). It's worth peeking inside the carriage museum next to the stables (same opening times as the house), where among the many stylish carriages and London-built hansom cabs, the most bizarre exhibit is an amazing four-wheeled, horse-drawn electric vacuum cleaner, as large as one of the cabs. Horses gave the carpets a not-so-quick once-over from outside by means of a forty-metre hose, hoisted up through the windows.

The **interior** of the house deserves a good hour or so. Excellent pamphlets describing the rooms are available free at reception, making it easy to guide yourself. Among the many highlights of the finely detailed interior is the **billiard room**, where the walls are lined with Belgian marble and punctuated by hot-air vents (part of the avant-garde central heating system). Sweeping through

Blanche Dickson's boudoir and her four fabulous bathrooms (with sunken baths and showers that once sprayed Mrs Dickson from above, below and the sides), you're led on to the Charles Rennie Mackintosh-inspired children's nursery, with its simple, white motifs.

The **grounds**, with their ash and oak woods, and the nearby beach, beyond the gardens, are wonderful places to while away a warm summer's afternoon. The transition here from the dramatic rocky cliffs of Bohuslän, to the north, to the open beaches of Halland in the south, made the area a subject for the Varberg group of painters (see p.189).

Äskhult

Just a few kilometres inland, **Äskhult** is a rare example of a hamlet of four immaculately preserved farmsteads, making for a fascinating insight into the lives of Swedish country folk of the eighteenth and early nineteenth centuries. You can get here from Gothenburg by **car** by taking the E6/E20 to Kungsbacka, then Route 135 heading southeast, off which Äskhult is signposted.

At the end of the eighteenth century, **land reforms** meant small patches of cultivated land had to be amalgamated into larger units. The result, all over Sweden, was that villages were split up as people were resettled on larger farms elsewhere. These reforms were brought into force at Äskhult in 1825, but the four local farmers banded together to defy the authorities and kept their land together. By the turn of the century, 15 of the 35 people living here had emigrated to America, thanks to the hardships resulting from the reforms; by the 1930s, there were only six inhabitants. Today, you can wander inside and upstairs through the homes (20kr), seeing the primitive wooden bed-chambers and inside the cowshed, where a dead snake was placed, in accordance with local superstition, to protect the animals from snake bites. The **café**, built into one of the farms, has a plainness about it that's very pleasantly in keeping with its surroundings.

Varberg

More atmospheric than any other town in Halland, the fashionable little nineteenth-century bathing resort of **VARBERG** boasts surprisingly varied sights (its imposing fortress the most obvious), a laid-back atmosphere and plenty of good places to eat. Bathing and windsurfing opportunities are also plentiful here.

Arrival, information and accommodation

Varberg is a handy entry point to southern Sweden: a year-round **ferry** service comes here from Grenä in Denmark. Regular **trains** run down the coast here from **Gothenburg**, and local **buses** cover the 45-kilometre trip south from Kungsbacka. From the **train** and **bus stations**, turn right down Vallgatan, and you'll find the town centre is off to the left, and the fortress to the right. The central square is dominated by the grand Warbergs bank, opposite which is the **tourist office** (April & May Mon–Fri 8am–5pm, Sat 10am–7pm; June–Aug Mon–Sat 9am–7pm, Sun 3–7pm; Sept–March Mon–Fri 8am–5pm; ☎0340/887 70, fax 61 11 95), where you can pick up a free map of the town. Varberg itself is easy to get around on foot, but to explore the coast around the town, you can **rent a**

bike from Erlan Cykel och Sport, Västra Vallgatan 41 (☎0340/144 55; 70kr a day); or from B.F. Cykelsport at Östralånggatan 47 (☎0340/61 12 55; 70kr a day), both of which are in the centre. Cheaper, and, for those who are camping here, more convenient, is hiring a bike at *Getteröns Camping* or *Apelvikens Camping* (see below), which both charge 50kr per day.

Accommodation

There's a wide variety of really good places to stay in Varberg – some of them representing excellent value. It's worth booking well in advance for the **youth hostel** (☎0340/887 88; 130kr), housed in the former prison at the fortress; outside the summer season you have to book through the tourist office. Apart from its now being spotlessly clean, the place is much as it was: each cell has its own key and original door, complete with spy-hole. Cell 24 on the upper floor has been preserved, without redecoration: push the door open for a chilling glimpse of past conditions. If you do want to stay, ask for Cell 13, the only one with a full-sized (although barred and curtainless) window and a great sea view. Another decent, very central hostel is *Platsamas Vandrahem* at Villagatan 13 (☎0340/61 16 40; 140kr). As a last resort, 8km south of town is an STF **hostel** (☎0340/410 43; 110kr) at the village of **Himle** – from Varberg's bus station, bus #652 runs down E6 to within a kilometre of the hostel.

There are a number of **campsites**, the nearest to the centre being the family-oriented *Apelvikens Camping*, 3km south of the fortress along Strandpromenaden (☎0340/141 78, fax 875 38; April to early Oct); it adjoins sandy beaches and a couple of good eating places (see p.190). Close by, *Apelviken Stugby* has neat, clean **cabins** sleeping four to six (a cabin for six costs 4300kr a week in summer); book at the tourist office. *Getteröns Camping* is near the nature reserve area (see p.191), 5km to the north of the town (☎0340/168 85, fax 104 22). Three-person cabins here cost 335kr a night; from July to early August you can only book for the week at 2300kr. To camp for free, there are plenty of places beyond the nudist beaches (see p.191).

For a B&B, there's **Nils Mårtensgård** (☎ & fax 0340/408 37; ①), fifteen minutes' drive east, just off the E6. In a comfortable old farmhouse surrounded by woodland, they serve home-made bread as part of their excellent breakfasts. **Hotels** in Varberg itself include the following.

Hotel Bergklinten, Västra Vallgatan 25 (☎0340/61 15 45). Close to the station. A slightly dilapidated old hotel with a spartan wartime feel, but clean and comfortable enough; the cheapest in town. ①.

Hotel Fregatten, Hamngatan (☎0340/67 70 00, fax 61 11 21). In a former cold storage warehouse, overlooking the harbour and within a few steps of the fortress. Quite luxurious, boasting a jacuzzi and sauna. ④/②.

Hotel Gästis, Borgmästaregatan 1 (☎0340/180 50, fax 138 50). Far more appealing inside than out: witty paintings of dishevelled men getting dressed fill false windows outside. All rooms are en suite. You'd never guess the hotel dates from 1786 – it has a sauna, jacuzzi, and a gym. It also offers excellent value, as the cost of a room includes an evening meal, afternoon coffee and even cycle hire. There's a good breakfast buffet. ③.

Kust Hotellet, Nils Kreugers Vägen 5 (☎0340/62 98 00, fax 62 98 50). In what was once the sanatorium, at Lilla Apelviken (see p.191). For unexpected glamour in an interesting setting, this sumptuous – and costly – hotel is the place. Full of new Art Nouveau and Tiffany features, it even has its own pool. ⑥.

Hotel Varberg, Norrgatan 16 (☎0340/161 25, fax 159 02). Built in 1899, this place retains some of its former grandeur and character. A very friendly, family-run hotel, it offers excellent value: the tariff includes a voucher worth 100kr in the restaurant next door, *Knopen*. There's a great breakfast too. ③/②.

Stadshotell, Kungsgatan 24–26 (☎0340/161 00, fax 67 86 52). Very central, close to the main square. Similar in price to the *Fregatten*, though a more traditional place, with some Art Nouveau features. It has a good restaurant, and a jacuzzi. ④/③.

The Town

All of Varberg's sights are concentrated along or near the seafront. The thirteenth-century moated **fortress**, set on a rocky promontory, is Varberg's most prominent attraction. It was home to the Swedish king Magnus Eriksson, who signed important peace treaties with Denmark here in 1343. The great bastions were added for protection by Danish king Christian IV in the seventeenth century; ironically, they were completed just in time for him to see the fortress fall, permanently as it turned out, to Sweden in 1645. Standing outside, it's easy to imagine how impenetrable the fortress must have appeared to attackers in the past – and to conclude that it still seems unwelcoming today, given the lack of signposting. The entrance is on its seaward side, either through the great archways towards the central courtyard or by a side route, the uneven stone steps which lead up to a delightful terrace **café** (June–Sept noon–10pm).

Tours in English will take you into the dungeons and among the impressive dark-cocoa-coloured buildings that make up the inner courtyard (daily 11am–4pm, with hourly tours July to mid-Aug; 30kr; children's tours July Mon–Fri 11am, 1pm & 3pm; 30kr). It's the **museum**, though, that deserves most of your attention (mid-June to mid-Aug daily 10am–6pm, 40kr; mid-Aug to mid-June Mon–Fri 10am–4pm, Sat & Sun noon–4pm, 20kr). The most unnerving exhibit is **Bocksten Man**, a murder victim who was garrotted, drowned, impaled (three stakes were thrust through his body, in the belief this would stop his spirit seeking out his murderers) and buried in a local bog six hundred years ago – until 1936, when a farmer dug him up while planting crops. His entire garb preserved by the acidity of the bog, Bocksten Man sports the Western world's most complete medieval costume: a cloak, a hood, shoes and stockings. His most shocking feature is his thick, ringletted red hair, which cascades around his puny-looking skull.

In the neighbouring room, a great deal is made of a small, spot-lit brass button that sits on a rotating velvet cushion. The button not only matched those on the uniform of King Karl XII, but exactly fitted the hole in his regal cranium, punctured when he was shot dead while attacking a Norwegian castle in 1718. Convinced that the king had special powers, his assailants believed his life could only be ended by something that belonged to him and so, having stolen the button, had it filled with lead. In the same room, an oil painting of the rather unattractive king lets you see whose life they were so keen to end.

The rest of the museum is, for the most part, dispensable, with sections on farming and fishing in Halland from the 1750s onward and some southern-Swedish peasant wall hangings. A signposted room devoted to the sensitive work of Richard Bergh, Nils Kreuger and Karl Nordström – the so-called **Varberg School** – is, however, worth viewing. These three artists linked up in the last years of the nineteenth century and developed a plein-air national painting style, reflecting the moods and atmosphere of Halland, and Varberg in particular. Night scenes of the fortress beneath the stars show a strong Van Gogh influence; in other paintings, the misty colours create a melancholy effect, evoking the atmosphere of the time.

Overlooking the sea, and painted custard and cream, the 1850 **fortress prison** seems like a soft option next to the looming fortress in whose shadow it lies. The first Swedish prison built following the American practice of having cells for individual inmates, it housed lifers until 1931, when the last one ended his days here. Today you can stay in a private youth hostel in the fortress, which has been carefully preserved to retain most of its original features (see p.188).

Back at the main entrance to the fortress, a **bicycle museum** (same ticket as for guided tours of fortress; otherwise 40kr, children 10kr) is largely given over to celebrating the Monark bicycle company, Sweden's biggest. Its founder, Birger Svensson, was born in Varberg; you'll not fail to notice that the company has funded the permanent exhibition and provided the bikes. Among the most interesting exhibits is a bizarre, ungainly wooden Draisne bike from 1820.

A couple of fine remnants from Varberg's time as a spa resort are within a minute of the fortress. On the side of the fortress facing the town is the grand Societeshuset, a wedding-dress-like confection of cream-and-green carved wood, set in its own small park. This was where upper-class ladies took their meals after bathing in the splendid **Kallbadhuset** nearby (Cold Bathhouse; mid-June to mid Aug daily 9am–6pm, Wed till 8pm; ☎0340/173 96; 37kr for cold bath and sauna), just to the north of the fortress and overlooking the harbour; there's a pleasant **café** here too. Beautifully renovated to its original splendour, this dainty bathhouse has single-sex nude bathing areas and is topped at each corner by Moorish cupolas, lending it an imperial air. While in the harbour area, take a look inside the busy **Konsthall** (Tues–Fri noon–6pm, Sat & Sun noon–5pm), in a fine old warehouse building, where glass-blowers, silversmiths and several ceramics artists sell their wares.

Eating and drinking

There are plenty of good places to eat in Varberg, mostly along Kungsgatan, which runs north of the main square; we list a selection below. Away from the town centre, at Apelviken, there are a couple of very popular **beach eateries** – the laidback, stylish *Maja's Strand Cafe*, which has live bands on summer evenings and a full à la carte menu; and *John's Steak House and Bar*, in a rustic wood building which is seafront, serving great meat dishes. One popular place to **drink** is *O'Brien's*, opposite *Harry's Pub & Restaurant*. Part of the Irish-style pub chain, this one has live music in summer (Wed–Sat), and a happy hour 5pm till 7pm.

Harry's Pub & Restaurant, Kungsgatan 18. Next door to *Cafe Mignon*. A large eating place with a rather jumbled identity, its dark interior adorned with chandeliers and statuettes of Liberty and Hiawatha. It has a range of pastas, meat and fish dishes from 75kr; service can be less than attentive. There's a wide selection of malt whiskies and beers, and a popular happy hour (4–7pm). Daily noon–midnight.

Kärleksparkens Servering, Strandpromenaden. A few minutes' walk from the centre, this small café has filled baguettes at 30kr, ice cream and filling lunch specials at 55kr.

Knopen, Norrgatan 16. Next door to the *Hotel Varberg* (see p.188). A down-to-earth, cosy place serving good but overpriced steaks. Really only worth it if you're staying at the hotel and so are entitled to the guests' discount.

Kunst Kafe, on the corner of Norrgatan and Västra Vallgatan. The best café in town, with home-made cakes to die for and delicious breakfasts too, all in a friendly setting.

Maja's, Kungsgatan 28. This is where to chill out with a relaxed, studenty crowd. A few old wireless sets and a chequered floor give it a slight 1950s feel. Mon–Fri 7am–7pm, Sat 7am–4pm, Sun 10am–4pm.

Matt & Go, Brunnsparken 6 (☎0340/14390). On the pricey side, this place serves Swedish cuisine, such as marinated salmon with a dill/caramel sauce. Mon–Sat 11am–11pm.

Cafe Mignon, Drottninggatan. Opposite Varberg Church. A good, if plain, café serving half baguettes at 23kr. Mon–Fri 7.30am–9pm, Sat 7.30am–6pm, Sun 9.30am–7pm.

Ny Fiket, Kungsgatan 18. A pleasant café that also serves full meals. Mon–Thurs 8am–9pm, Fri & Sat 8am–1pm.

Societen, in Societets Park (☎0340/676500). Directly behind the fortress. *Dagens Rätt* is 69kr here; for a fine gourmet lunch, it's worth spending a little extra (179kr). The place comes alive in the evenings, with foxtrots on Fridays, and live bands or discos on Saturdays.

Around Varberg

Halland's coastline becomes less rocky the further south you go, turning into open beaches at Falkenberg (see p.192). Although it's still a little rocky around Varberg, there are several excellent spots here for bathing; for the best ones, head south, to the left of the fortress as you face the sea, down Strandpromenaden. In summer, this stretch of the track, built in 1912 as a route from the fortress to the sanatorium 4km beyond, is filled with an assortment of strolling couples, roller skaters and cyclists. After about five minutes, two well-known **nudist beaches** are signposted, with not very private fencing delineating the separate-sex areas, called Goda Hopp ("Good Hope"; the men's zone) and Kärringhålan (provocatively, "Pit of Bitches"). A little further along, at **Lilla Apelviken**, is a small sandy beach popular with families. The large grey-and-cream buildings ahead once comprised the Apelviken Hospital, set up at the beginning of the twentieth century as a **sanatorium** for impoverished tuberculosis sufferers; now, it's a glamorous hotel (see p.188). Just by the hotel is a specially designed **handicapped bathing beach**, with wheelchair access into the water.

Behind the hotel, **Apelviken cemetery** is a remarkable looking place, featuring a chapel like a miniature Parthenon and carpeted with wild flowers. Created in 1927, the boulder-walled enclosure is the resting place of dozens of children who died of TB in the 1920s and 1930s. The only adult's grave is that of Johan Almer, who created the sanatorium, his huge granite tomb overlooking the rest from one corner of the plot. The north side of Lilla Apelviken is sheltered by a hill, Subbeberget, where you'll find several Bronze Age burial mounds – nothing much to look at. More dramatic is the windy panorama from the secluded **lighthouse**, which looks back towards the fortress across the water. Built in 1934, the lighthouse only takes a few minutes to reach, and is set on a rocky promontory covered with a threadbare carpet of tiny wild orchids and honeysuckle, the waves crashing beneath.

North of Varberg: Getterön

There are regular **buses** in summer from Varberg north to **Getterön**, a fist of land jutting into the sea, where you can bathe amid the secluded coves and among the wild flowers that fill the rock crevices in early summer. Just before you reach Getterön, there's a nature centre and extensive bird reserve, **Getterön Naturum**, off on the right of the main road (Getterön Nature Centre; July & Aug daily 10am–6pm, Sept–June Fri–Sun 10am–4pm). Contained in striking thatched houses, the centre is a must for anyone interested in the wildlife – particularly bird-life – of the area. The staff are enthusiastic and well informed about the site, though you only get the full benefit of their knowledge on the guided tours of the surrounding area (750kr for groups of up to ten).

Bexell's Talking Stones

An intriguing oddity in the landscape near Varberg is **Bexell's Talking Stones**. The name was given to the numerous rocks hidden away in a beech forest at Torstorp, 20km east of Varberg, which were engraved in the 1880s with the names of famous people of the time and a range of quotations. An MP who owned the land then, Alfred Bexell, had the stones carved with the words of people he believed important (from Aristotle to Voltaire), grouped into categories such as the ancient Greeks, luminaries of the French Revolution, statesmen, authors and philosophers. Along with well-known quotations were a wide range of clichéd sayings of the day, unsurprisingly all in Swedish. After his death in 1900, the stones were forgotten and were soon lost under the moss, until 1925, when picnickers rediscovered the first names; more have come to light every year or so since (mostly through random discovery). To get there, head east from Varberg following signs for Grimeton and Rolfstorp until you reach Torstorp, where a signposted track for the stones leads off past a golf course into the forest. The rocks cover an area of around two-and-a-half kilometres square, mostly in identifiable clumps; signs to them have been posted along the forest roads. The tourist office at Varberg has information on guided tours (in English by arrangement).

Falkenberg

It's a twenty-minute train ride south from Varberg to the well-preserved and decidedly likeable medieval town of **FALKENBERG** (falcons were once hunted here, hence the name), with some lively museums and a long beach. It's a little town that really comes alive in July and August, when most of the tourists arrive.

Falkenberg has a long-standing reputation as a centre for **fly-fishing**, which is to be had on the River Ätran that runs through it. In the 1820s, Sir Humphrey Davy, the inventor of the miner's safety lamp, visited the town, having heard about its excellent fly-fishing. A succession of wealthy **English countrymen** came here throughout the nineteenth century, their numbers swelling as Falkenberg's reputation for good fishing spread; one such devotee, London lawyer William Wilkinson, went so far as to write a book about the experience, *Days In Falkenberg* (1894). In it, he described the place where the well-to-do visitors stayed as "an ancient inn with a beautiful garden leading down to the river". This building, one of the few here to have escaped every town fire, now houses *Falkmanska Caféet*, the best café in town (see "Eating and drinking").

These upper-class Englishmen brought considerable wealth with them, and had a tremendous influence on the town. Predictably enough, they made no attempt to adapt to local culture; as a result Falkenbergers had to learn English for the first time, and throughout the latter half of the nineteenth century, baby boys here were named Charles instead of the Swedish Karl, while the most popular girls' name was Frances, after Wilkinson's daughter. English influence can be seen even today: near the post office there is a classic British telephone box, donated by Oswaldtwistle, the English town with which Falkenberg is twinned. Another legacy of the English connection is the current low level of fish stocks;

the waters have been so overfished that it now costs relatively little to try your hand at fishing in the two-kilometre stretch of river around the splendid 1756 stone Tullbron ("toll bridge"). The tourist office (see below) will sell you a one-day **licence** that allows you to catch up to three fish (available March–Sept; 80kr).

Arrival, information and accommodation

Regular **buses** and **trains** drop you close to the centre on Holgersgatan, from where it's a couple of hundred metres along to the **tourist office** in Stortorget (mid-June to mid-Aug Mon–Sat 9am–7pm, Sun 3–7pm; Sept to mid-June Mon–Fri 9am–5pm; ☎0346/174 10, fax 145 26; *falkenberg.tourist@mailbox.calypso.net*); they'll book **private rooms** from 120kr per person, plus 30kr booking fee. The comfortable and well-equipped STF **youth hostel** (June to mid-Aug; ☎0346/171 11; 110kr) is in the hamlet of **Näset**, 4km south of town, which you can get to on local buses #1 or #2 (no services after 7pm). From the hostel, the southern end of the beach is just a few minutes' walk away, through the neighbouring **campsite** (☎0346/171 07). The tourist office will also **rent bikes**, which makes trips to the beaches easier (June–Aug; 100kr per day, 145kr for two days or 300kr a week).

The cheapest **hotel** is the plain *Hotel Steria*, a ten-minute walk away from the river up Arvidstorpsvägen (☎0346/155 21, fax 101 30; ①); it's plain but the price includes breakfast. In the town centre, the smart *Grand Hotel* overlooks the historic Tullbron bridge (☎0346/144 50, fax 829 25; ⑤/④). Its upmarket restaurant offers good but pricey meals, while the bar and disco are popular night-time haunts for the young. Rather more interesting, and almost next door, the riverside *Hvitan* overlooks a picturesque open courtyard surrounded by low-built houses dating from 1703 (☎0346/820 90, fax 597 96; ③/②). The best placed hotel for the beach is *Hotel Strandbaden* (☎0346/71 49 00, fax 161 11; ④/③), 2km from the old town centre (follow Strandvägen all the way to the beach). A plush modern hotel, it lacks any design niceties but does have an excellent lounge with an uninterrupted view of the sea. The cost of a room here includes a fine, varied breakfast and free entry to Klitterbadhuset (see p.194).

The town and around

Fishing apart, Falkenberg offers several disparate pleasures. The **old town**, to the west of the curving river, comprises a dense network of low, wooden cottages and cobbled lanes. Nestling among them is the fine twelfth-century **St Laurentii kyrka**, its ceiling and interior walls awash with seventeenth- and eighteenth-century paintings. An electronic box by the door lets you choose a taped commentary in a range of languages; if you press the wrong language, there's no way to reverse your selection, and for twenty minutes you'll be regaled with information in the wrong tongue at a frightening volume. It's hard to believe that this gem of a church was – in the early twentieth century – variously a shooting range, a cinema and a gymnasium; indeed its secular usage saved it from demolition after the Neo-Gothic "new" church was built at the end of the nineteenth century. When St Laurentii kyrka was reconsecrated in the 1920s, it was decided to try to locate its sixteenth-century font and silverware, which were traced to, and recovered from, places all over northern Europe.

The local museum on St Lars Kyrkogatan, with its collections tracing the town's history until 1900, is a pedestrian place that's best bypassed; head straight for the

Falkenberg Museum, in an old four-storey grain store near the main bridge at Skepparesträtet (June to early Sept Tues–Fri 10am–4pm, Sat & Sun noon–4pm; mid-Sept to May Tues–Fri & Sun noon–4pm; 20kr). Although there are the usual archeological collections here, the enthusiastic curator has chosen to devote most of the museum to the 1950s, considering the decade to be the most interesting and educational for visitors. The fact that Falkenberg had over one hundred dance bands up until the 1970s provides the basis for another of the permanent exhibitions, along with original interiors of a shoe repair shop and stylized café (complete with jukebox) – though labelling in English is minimal.

Falkenberg is full of quirky **sculptures** which make for amusing viewing. You'll find one right outside Falkenberg Museum, a diverting piece called *Wall* – which you may not realize is a sculpture. Per Kirkeby, a celebrated Danish sculptor, built the two brick walls here for a major exhibition in 1997, to close off the wide space below the museum building down to the river. A series of entrances and window openings are designed to let shadows fall at striking angles, and somehow complement the old grain store – though predictably, the more conservative among the locals loathe the sculpture. The most fun sculpture, though, is one taking up the whole wall at the corner of Nygatan and Torgatan in the centre: *Drömbanken*, by Walter Bengtsson, is a witty, surrealist explosion of naked women, cats, mutant elks, bare feet and beds.

The town also boasts a rather unusual **Fotomuseum** (late June to Aug Tues–Thurs 1–7pm; Sept to late June Tues–Thurs 5–7pm, Sun 2–6pm; 30kr) at Sandgatan 13, the home of Falkenberg's first purpose-built 1907 cinema. It has over one thousand cameras and a remarkable collection of cinematic paraphernalia, including some superb local peasant portraits, taken in 1898. The oldest pictures on show are English and date back to the 1840s. There's also an impressive section on Sweden's well-loved author Selma Lagerlöf at her celebrated home in Mårbacka (see p.420). For a completely different sort of experience, head to the local **Falken Brewery** (July & Aug Mon–Thurs 10am & 1.15pm; 20kr; book tours through the tourist office), where Sweden's most popular beer, Falken, has been brewed since 1896, and is available for sampling at the end of the tour.

One of the most relaxing ways to spend a warm summer's evening is to walk along the **promenade** set up in 1861 by a local physician, who encouraged everyone to stroll down it. Today you can walk the romantic stretch along either the river's north bank (follow Ågatan, which becomes Laxpromenade), or, even lovelier, the south – known as Doktorspromenaden. This former heathland was planted with forest in the 1890s, and now massive alders shadow the river here.

Skrea Strand and Klitterbadhuset

Over the river and fifteen minutes' walk south from town, **Skrea Strand** is a fine, four-kilometre stretch of sandy beach. At the northern end, a relaxing diversion is the large bathing and tennis complex of **Klitterbadhuset** (mid-June to mid-Aug Mon–Fri 9am–7pm, Tues & Thurs from 6am, Sat 9am–5pm, Sun 9am–4pm; mid-Aug to mid-June Tues & Thurs 6–9am & noon–8pm, Wed noon–8pm, Fri 9am–noon), which has a fifty-metre pool (with a shallow children's pool nearby), a vast sauna, jacuzzi and steam rooms, all for 30kr (gym costs 15kr extra). At the southern end of the long beach lie some secluded coves, all the way down past the busy wooden holiday shacks; in early summer the marshy grassland here is full of wild violets and clover. It's a great place for

birdwatching: ungainly cormorants nest here, while oyster-catchers, shell ducks and plover are also thick on the ground.

Eating, drinking and nightlife

In this, the birthplace of Sia Glass – a popular ice cream made by Sweden's oldest family firm, established in 1569 – and Falcon beer, both readily available in the town, eating and drinking can certainly be a pleasure. Although the variety of food on offer isn't huge, Falkenberg's restaurants and bars are of a standard to make eating and drinking here a pleasure.

Restaurants

The poshest **restaurant** is *Gustav Bratt*, Brogatan 1, near the main square (☎0346/103 31; Mon–Fri 11.30am–2pm & 6pm–midnight, Sat & Sun 3pm–midnight), built as a grain warehouse in 1860; however, its à la carte menu is a disappointingly ordinary selection of fish and pizza dishes; lunch costs around 150kr. There are fine restaurants at two of the town's hotels, the *Grand Hotel* and the *Hvitan*. For good-value meals, there's the friendly *D.D.* on Hotelgatan 3 (June–Aug daily noon–2am; Sept–May Wed–Sat noon–2pm). A smallish restaurant, its lamps consisting of old converted cartwheels, it serves à la carte pasta dishes and baguettes at very reasonable prices; lunch is 55kr. Fans of salmon will find it a must to travel 9km north on the old E6 (parallel to the present one) to *Laxbutiken*, in a white building off the highway (☎0345/511 10; summer daily 10am–8pm); their superb dishes have salmon exclusively as the main ingredient. Down at the beaches, the *Kattegat Restaurant*, attached to Strandbaden Hotel (Mon–Sat 7–11pm), offers outside dining overlooking the sea, serving lots of grilled meats, pasta dishes and baked potatoes.

Cafés, bars and nightlife

About the best **café** in town is the *Falkmanska Caféet*, Storgatan 42 (Mon–Fri 10am–6pm, Sat 10am–2pm), housed in the oldest (1700) secular building in town, and featuring a stripped wood floor, mellow furnishings and a lovely garden. This place has a welcoming atmosphere and the food's pretty fine, too: huge baguettes (30–35kr) and decadent home-made cakes. Another excellent café is *Cafe Antik*, sandwiched between *Hotel Hvitan* and the *Grand Hotel* on Ågatan (Mon–Sat 10am–1pm, Sun 10am–10pm): here you can gorge on sweet, gooey confections, at tables consisting of cupboard doors plastered with old magazine pictures and set on Husqvarna sewing machines. For its setting, *Cafe Rosengården,* with its flowery, shaded outside area at the beginning of Doktorspromenaden (see opposite), just over the old bridge, would be hard to beat, though the cakes on offer aren't nearly as tempting as at *Antik*. On the main square, *Folkes Café* (Tues–Fri 1–10pm, Sat & Sun 1–5pm) is a basic place, usually full of older teenagers; it doubles as a solarium at 50kr a go.

Mixing American and British influences, *Harry's Bar* on Rådhustorget (noon till late) is always packed with eaters and drinkers. At night, a dance floor opens up at *D.D.* for a 20-something crowd. The owner of *Hotel Hvitan* (see above), Bo Persson, runs a popular jazz, blues and folk music **festival** in the second week of July, setting up stage in the courtyard. One-day tickets to this enjoyable event cost 200kr, from the tourist office.

Halmstad

The principal town in Halland, **HALMSTAD**, was once a grand walled city and an important Danish stronghold. Today, although most of the original buildings have disappeared, Halmstad has a couple of cultural and artistic points of interest, most notably the works, displayed nearby at Mjellby, of the Halmstad Group, Sweden's first Surrealists. The town also boasts extensive, if rather crowded, beaches not far away, and a range of really good places to eat – all in all, a sound choice for a day or two's relaxation.

In 1619, the town's **castle** was used by the Danish king Christian IV to entertain the Swedish king Gustav II Adolf; records show that there were seven solid days of festivities. The bonhomie, however, didn't last much longer, and Christian was soon building great stone-and-earth fortifications around the city, all surrounded by a moat, with access afforded by four stone gateways. However, it was a fire soon after, rather than the Swedes, that all but destroyed the city; the only buildings to survive were the castle and the church. Undeterred, Christian took the opportunity to create a contemporary Renaissance town with a gridwork of straight streets; today the main street, Storgatan, still contains a number of impressive merchants' houses from that time. After the final defeat of the Danes in 1645, Halmstad lost its military significance, and the walls were torn down. Today, just one of the great gateways, Norre Port, remains; the moat has been filled in and a road, Karl XIs Vägen, runs directly above where the water would have been.

Arrival, information and accommodation

It takes 25 minutes to get here from Falkenberg by train. From the **train station**, follow Bredgatan to the Nissan river, and just by Österbro, the easternmost of the bridges, is the tourist office; across the bridge is the main square. The helpful **tourist office** (May & late Aug Mon–Fri 9am–6pm, Sat 10am–1pm; June & early to mid-Aug Mon–Fri 9am–6pm, Sat 10am–3pm, Sun 1–3pm; July Mon–Sat 9am–7pm, Sun 3–7pm; mid-Aug to April Mon–Fri 9am–5pm; ☎035/10 93 45, fax 15 81 15, *info@tourist.halmstad.se*) will book **private rooms** from 125kr per person, plus a booking fee (25kr if you visit the office – essential in summer, 50kr by phone).

A good way to get to the beaches or the Mjellby Arts Centre (see p.199) is on a **bike**. There is currently only one place in town to rent them, Arvid Olsson Cykel, Norra Vägen 11 (Mon–Fri 9.30am–6pm, Sat 9.30am–1pm; ☎035/21 22 51), which charges a steep 100kr per day for a five-speed bike, though two days is just 140kr; trailers are 80kr extra. Much cheaper is renting at *Kronocamping* in Tylösand (see p.198; ☎035/305 10; 75kr a day or 285kr a week). No deposit is needed if you're camping there; otherwise there is a 400kr refundable deposit to pay.

Accommodation

The most beautiful **hotel** in town is *Hotel Continental*, Kungsgatan 5 (☎035/17 63 00, fax 12 86 04; ④/③), just two minutes' walk from the train station. With a bright, well-preserved interior, this graceful, elegant building was built in 1904 in National Romantic and early Jugend style. There's a free sauna and solarium, with massages are available; the breakfasts are very good. Another fine choice is the very comfortable old *Norre Park Hotel*, at Norra Vägen 7 (☎035/21 85 55, fax 10 45 28; ④/③), overlooking the beautiful Norre Katt Park; the hotel is reached through the Norre Port arch, north of Storgatan. The price here includes the use of saunas and the fitness room, and an excellent buffet breakfast. The long, low *Hotel Tylösand*, on the Tylösand beach (☎035/305 00, fax 324 39; ④), is owned by Per Gessle, better known as the singer/songwriter from the Swedish rock duo Roxette, who hail from the town. It has a big, international restaurant with shows and a casino, plus a pool, sauna and solarium; plans are afoot to revamp the place for a younger market.

The central **youth hostel** is at Skepparegatan 23, 500m to the west of St Nicolai church (☎035/12 05 00; 135kr; ③; mid-June to mid-Aug); all rooms are en suite. **Camping** is a popular option here, the best site being *Hägons Camping* at Östra Stranden, about 3km from the centre (☎035/12 53 63, fax 12 43 65); there are also **cabins**, each sleeping up to five people (3200kr a week, or 4500kr en suite). The site is next to a nature reserve, to the east of the town centre (see p.199).

The Town

At the centre of the big and lively market square, **Storatorg**, is Carl Milles's *Europa and the Bull*, a fountain with mermen twisted around it, all with Milles's characteristically muscular bodies, ugly faces and oversized nipples. Flanking one side of the square is the grand **St Nikolai kyrka** (8.30am–3.30pm). Dating from the fourteenth century, its monumental size attests to the town's former importance. Today, the only signs of its medieval origins are the splodges of bare rock beneath the plain, brick columns. Adjacent to the church, the **Tre Hjärtan** (Three Hearts) *konditori* is a vast, proud building with a crossbeamed ceiling; its name derives from the three hearts that make up the town's emblem, Christian IV having granted the town the right to use it in gratitude for their loyalty to Denmark. It's worth taking your coffee and cake upstairs, where the beams and ceiling are beautifully hand-painted, and historical photographs of nineteenth-century Halmstad adorn the walls.

Not far from Österbro, **Halmstad Castle** is a mellow, cinnamon-red affair half hidden by trees; the private residence of the governor, it is closed to the public. Moored in front is *Najaden*, a small, fully rigged sailing ship built in 1897, once used for training by the Swedish navy (July & Aug Tues & Thurs 5–7pm, Sat 11am–3pm). With children in tow, a reasonable, though not outstanding, diversion is a trip to the **Tropic Centre**, a few minutes along the river from the tourist office (daily: July 10am–6pm; Aug–June 10am–4pm; adults 60kr, under-15s 30kr), where snakes, monkeys, crocodiles and spiders are on display in a sort of miniature menagerie. A more active time is to be had at the **Sannarpsbadet**, Växjövägen (June–Aug Tues & Thurs 11am–8pm, Wed & Fri 11am–5pm, Sat 10am–4pm; Sept–May Tues–Fri 10am–8pm, Sat & Sun 10am–4pm; ☎035/13 96 50; 45kr, families of two adults and up to three children 120kr), a swimming complex with a solarium (40kr), slides and jacuzzis.

Leading north from the square, pedestrianized **Storgatan** – the main thoroughfare for restaurants and nightlife (see p.199) – is a charming street, with some creaking old houses built in the years following the 1619 fire; the great stone arch of **Norre Port** marks the street's end. To the right is the splendid **Norre Katt Park**, a delightful, shady place that slopes down towards the river; the park is dotted with mature beech, copper beech and horse-chestnut trees, with great weeping willows by the water. The town's most serene spot is at the park's centre, where there's a lily pond crossed by a bridge. A popular **café**, housed in an ornate former bandstand, overlooks the spot (June–Aug daily noon–8pm); it serves waffles smothered in jam and cream at 20kr, as well as cakes and ice cream.

The Halmstad Museum and Hallandsgården

At the northernmost edge of the park, by the river, is the fine **Halmstad Museum** (early June to late Aug daily 10am–7pm, Wed till 9pm; late Aug to early June 10am–4pm, Wed till 9pm; 20kr). While the archeological finds and basement collections are unlikely to set many pulses racing, the first-floor displays (rooms 6, 7 & 8) of home interiors from the seventeenth, eighteenth and nineteenth centuries are not at all stuffy; indeed they're a lot of fun. You can wander through, among others, a room of glorious Gustavian harps and square pianos from the 1780s; some exquisitely furnished doll's houses are also worth seeing. The shipping room here avoids the usual nautical maps and bits of old boats, instead showing a charismatic collection of ghoulish figureheads from ships wrecked off the Halland coast.

The museum is noted for its tapestries from southern Sweden; the full English commentary amusingly explains the pictorial stories. The top floor is devoted to a fair sampling of the work of the **Halmstad Group** (see opposite). There are also some contemporary sculptures – arresting glass pieces using prismic forms to intriguing effect.

Close by, on so-called Gallows Hill, is a small collection of Halmstad's older houses moved to the site to form a miniature outdoor museum, **Hallandsgården** (early June to mid-Aug 11am–5pm; guided tours 2pm each day and at other times by arrangement on ☎035/15 63 29; free).

Martin Luther Church

For a completely different church to any other you may have visited in Sweden, head to the gleaming 1970s **Martin Luther Church** 1km east of the centre on Långgatan (9am–3pm), one of the main roads out of town. The first church in Scandinavia to be assembled entirely of steel – it is known by locals as the Tin Factory – this unique Art Deco/Futuristic creation looks from the outside like a clumsily opened sardine can, with jagged and curled edges, and stained glass. Inside it's just as unusual: all the walls are a rust-orange version of the outer skin, and there are some striking ornaments. The building is famed for its acoustics, and plays host to concerts (Sun evenings in summer) and a seven-day music festival held during the first week of July (☎035/15 19 61 for details).

Out from the centre: Halmstad's beaches and the Mjellby Arts Centre

Eight kilometres west of the town centre, Halmstad's most popular **beach** is at **Tylösand** (regular buses run here from town), which in July and August becomes packed with bronzing bodies; by night the same bodies fill the surrounding bars and restaurants. There's a smuggler's cove to wander around at **Tjuvahålan**, signposted directly off the beach, and plenty of excellent spots for bathing, including **Svärjarehålan**, a little further north, where a bathing beach has been adapted for the disabled.

The best beach to the east of town is at **Östra Stranden**, where there is also a large, well-equipped campsite. It's reached by crossing the river from Stora Torg and heading along Stationgatan past the train station, then turning southeast for a couple of kilometres down Stälverksgatan. The long beach – deep, sandy and less crowded than at Tylösand – is excellent for children as the waters are particularly shallow here. Further south is **Hagön**, a secluded **nudist beach**, where privacy is afforded by the deep hollows between the dunes; behind it is a nature reserve.

Mjellby Arts Centre

Five kilometres north of the town centre is the **Mjellby Arts Centre** (road signs still use the original "Mjällby"; ☎035/316 19; mid-March to June & mid-Aug to Oct Tues–Sun 1–5pm; July to mid-Aug Tues–Sun 1–6pm; Nov to mid-Dec Sat & Sun 1–5pm; 40kr) containing the largest collection of works by the **Halmstad Group**, a body of six local artists from the 1920s who championed Cubism and Surrealism in Sweden. To get here by car, head out along Karlsrovägen past the tiny airport into the countryside, then take the first road on the left for about 1km; bus #350 from the centre will drop you just after the turning.

The Halmstad Group, comprising brothers Eric and Axel Olson, their cousin Waldemar Lorentzon and three others, is reputedly the only artists' alliance to have kept together for fifty years. The group's members, strongly influenced by Magritte and Dalí (having studied in Berlin and Paris), produced work that caused considerable controversy back in the 1920s and for the next two decades. They sometimes worked collectively on a project – an almost unheard-of practice in Swedish art (a good example of one of these group efforts is at the Halmstad City Library, where a fourteen-metre-long work in six sections hangs above the shelves). If Viveka Bosson, the daughter of Eric Olson, is around (she works here), you may get a free guided tour around Mjellby. There's also an excellent café here, *Cafe Blå*, a cool blue-and-white place serving superbly prepared food.

Eating, drinking and nightlife

People congregate in the restaurants, bars and clubs along cobbled, pedestrianized **Storgatan**, lined with trendy eating places, most of which have shaded outdoor areas along the street. Prices can be steep, but there are also plenty of cheaper cafés and light meal options. **Tylösand** is a night-time spot for the beach crowd, with most of the action concentrated on *Hotel Tylösand* (see p.197). For mouthwatering picnic fare, try the deli section of **Strömbergs Ost & Delikatessen** (Mon–Fri 10am–6pm, Sat 10am–2pm).

Cafés and restaurants

Fribergs Konditoria, Norregatan, next to *Norre Park Hotel*. Traditional bakery and coffee house with a relaxed atmosphere, overlooking the park and serving mouthwatering cakes and plates of white-chocolate truffles. A coffee and sandwich is 40kr. Mon–Fri 8am–7pm, Sat & Sun 9am–7pm.

Nygatan, Nygatan 8, off Storatorg. Quite ordinary check-tablecloth café-diner that does a good-value three-course dinner at 129kr. Mon–Sat 9am–midnight, Sun 6pm–midnight.

Pio & Co, Storgatan 27. Half the restaurant is a bistro, the other half is for more formal eating. A lovely place, where the speciality is steaks served on wooden planks with clouds of mashed potato at 172kr. There's also a massive drinks list.

Skånska Hembageriet, Bankgatan 1. Rustic seventeenth-century cake shop and *konditori* just off Storgatan. Mon–Fri 8.15am–6pm, Sat 9am–2pm.

Strömbergs Ost & Delikatessen, Storgatan 23. The eating area has a relaxed atmosphere and does great light lunches like pasta with chicken, onions and cream (62kr). July & Aug Mon–Sat 11am–11pm, Sun 4–9pm.

Tre Hjärtan, Storatorg. Cakes, sandwiches and light meals are served within this impressive *konditori* (also see p.197).

Ulle's Café, Brogatan 7. Café serving snacks and sandwiches. Boasts surreal ceiling paintings and great little garden at the back. Mon–Fri 9am–6pm, Sat 9.30am–2.30pm.

Yoss, Storgatan. This cosy restaurant serves meat, fowl, fish and shellfish main courses, each for 100–200kr, plus several slightly cheaper veggie options. They also do lots of different liqueur coffees for 64kr each.

Bars and discos

Bull's Pub, Lilla Torg, a step away from Storgatan. Very popular, English-style bar with live music. 1960s sounds on Mon nights. Mon–Fri 11.30am–1am, Sat & Sun noon–midnight.

Daltons, Storgatan. An alternative-music bar offering Swedish music upstairs and dancing on the ground floor, with a bar open to the sky in summer. Entry is by a small doorway two doors down from *Pio & Co* (see above).

Harry's, Storgatan. On the corner of Klammerdammsgatan. Massively popular, attesting to the delight taken by some Swedes in all things purporting Britishness. This one has an English phone box and a life-sized Charlie Chaplin dummy. It also does reasonably priced meat, fish and pub meals. Mon–Thurs & Sun 5pm–1am, Fri 5pm–2am, Sat noon–2am.

Kavaljeren, Storgatan. Known locally as "Kavven", this popular nightclub is in the basement of the building still called Gamla Rådhuskällaren – it housed Halmstad's law courts in the seventeenth century. The vaulted cellars lend something to the atmosphere.

Svea Bryygen On the river bank opposite the castle. The only watering hole not around Storgatan, and very popular throughout summer when there's live bands. From midsummer until around October, this is the place for prawns – 69kr for as many as you can gorge. Mon–Thurs noon–midnight, Fri & Sat noon–1am, Sun 3pm–midnight.

Gay Halmstad

Halmstad now boasts an exceptionally well-designed and lively **gay club**, run by RFSL, called *Nightlife*, at Stålverksgatan 2; to get there, head north down Stationgatan from the train station and take the first left, following signs to Östrastranden. Built out of an old wall-tie factory, the place has a striking dance floor and friendly bar area, though the real eye-opener is in the basement – the main room of which has walls lit up to reveal wall-hanging plaster buttocks, all modelled from the bodies of club members. There's a disco party every Saturday night during summer; you'll have to join RFSL to get in (80kr for three months, which gives you entry to all RFSL venues around Sweden). On Monday and Wednesday there's a welcoming pub night, and Thursday night is women only.

East of Halmstad: Simlångsdal

Leaving Halmstad on Route 25, the first turning off the road is to the village of **Åled**. The high ridge here, a product of the last ice age, was until the eighteenth century a place where Swedish grandparents came to throw themselves off, in order to be not to be a burden on their descendants; the way to the spot where they did so is signposted.

To fully discover the natural beauty of the region, head 15km east from Halmstad along Route 25 towards **SIMLÅNGSDAL** (bus #340 runs here twice daily, but it's difficult to make your way around by public transport once you arrive). A deeply picturesque eight-kilometre chain of lakes marks the start of the forested landscape, making for perfect vistas on summer nights, when the sunsets are reflected in the tranquil waters. It's possible to cycle here from Halmstad following the old railway track, and you might want to try the seven-kilometre **hiking trail** east of the lakes – ask at Halmstad's tourist office for more details.

Simlångsgården Youth Hostel (☎ & fax 035/780 60; 155kr) has basic **accommodation** in a lovely setting: a small river called Fylleån ("drunk stream") meanders all the way from here to the sea, with several waterfalls within walking distance along the way. One, Dansken Fallet, is named after horrific battles which took place close by in the 1640s, turning the waters red, while Tolarps Fallen is a popular bathing area today. To get to the youth hostel, take the signposted road off Route 25 for Marhult, and head over a bridge towards Gyltige. In Simlångsdal, *Simlångdalen Gästgivaregård* has five good-value double rooms (☎ & fax 035/701 20; ①).

There are several eating places, some surprisingly renowned, in Simlångsdal and along Route 25. Just beyond Selsbo, a few kilometres east of Toftasjö along Route 25, is the rather grand *Tallhöjden Värdshus Restaurant and Hotel* (☎035/702 45, fax 705 71), a sedate eatery in an oddly hacienda-like house, all whitewashed walls and wrought iron. In Simlångsdal itself, there's *Pizza butik* (☎035/707 04, daily noon–10pm), serving decent pizzas; for more of a culinary treat, try just opposite – *Simlångdalen Gästgivaregård* (☎ & fax 035/701 20; Tues & Wed noon–3pm, Thurs–Sat noon–6pm, Sun noon–5pm) where the à la carte and lunch specials (59kr) are beautifully cooked. The place is famed for its herring and salmon buffet.

Laholm and around

Just 10km south of Halmstad, **LAHOLM** is the oldest, smallest and most southerly town in Halland. It is also the most underrated and undermarketed place on Sweden's west coast and consequently is often ignored. Yet Laholm is a pleasant little resort, its chief attraction being its proximity (6km) to the outstanding beach at **Mellbystrand**.

Established in the twelfth century, Laholm ping-ponged between the Danes and the Swedes until 1645, when all the fortifications were torn down on the orders of Karl XI. It has a village feel to its centre, marked by **Stortorget**, with its small, colourful daily fish and flower market, and there are some delightful strolls to be taken around the lanes of half-timbered houses that lead off from the square. However, the most remarkable thing about Laholm is the number of witty contemporary **sculptures** that are dotted around the town and its park. The 28 official works that adorn the tiny centre were all funded by Axel Malmqvist, who wrote and staged 36 outdoor theatrical productions in the 1930s to fund the restoration of Laholm Castle; so successful were the plays that the leftover money was enough to pay for all the art work. A self-guided tour is available at the tourist office (see p.202), but you'll stumble across the majority without it. One of the most amusing is *Women Picking Potatoes*, in the little square near the tourist office. Great fun, yet entirely omitted from all tourist information, is an unofficial collection of quirky wood sculptures in the park up behind the youth hostel (see below). Created as part of an environmental project by local unemployed people, the sculptures form part of a children's playground: wooden slides and round-abouts with finely carved animal images stand among the trees, while other pieces bob up and down on springs.

Laholm has plenty to offer in terms of fishing. Almost entirely concentrated on the southern bank of the River Lagan, **salmon fishing** has been a big activity here since the sixteenth century. Unlike at Falkenberg (see p.192), salmon breeding programmes were developed in Laholm back in the nineteenth century, so fishing here is still a rewarding pastime. The salmon hatchery, centrally situated by the power station in Lagavägen, operates surprisingly interesting summer tours (details from the tourist office) showing each stage of the life cycle. You can get a **licence** for the salmon fishing season (March 8–Dec 31) from the tourist office; fishing is allowed from the power station to the river estuary, a distance of 8km. If you catch the season's biggest salmon, you win the much-sought-after title "King [or Queen] of Salmon", and a seasonal fishing licence.

Other river activities include a **steamboat trip** (July & Aug; 2hr; 75kr, tickets from the tourist office) on the tiny wooden steamer *Sofiero*, built in 1888 and owned and run by the local brewery of the same name. You're never far from the steam pipes, however, so on a hot day the boat is like a sauna and the trip rather too long. You can go on one of the tours of the old brewery itself (July Tues & Thurs 9.30am; ask at the tourist office for details); the factory is a fifteen-minute walk east from the town centre.

Practicalities

Trains run hourly here from Halmstad, the trip taking twelve minutes. The **train station** is an inconvenient 3km from Laholm. There are buses to take you to the disused old station in the heart of town (11kr); they are timed to coincide with train arrivals, but you have to be quick as they don't hang around once the train has come in. **Bikes** can be rented from Blåkulla Cykel, Angelholmsvägen 11 (☎0430/132 50; 75kr per day or 160kr per week). The **tourist office** is on the central square, close to the old station (mid-June to Aug Mon–Fri 10am–6pm, Sat 10am–3pm, Sept to mid-June Mon–Sat 10am–2pm; ☎0430/154 50).

The STF **youth hostel** at Parkgårdens, Tivolivägen 4 (☎0430/133 18, fax 153 25; 100kr plus 40kr for breakfast; closed mid-Dec to mid-Jan), is a central, well-appointed **place to stay** ideally situated beneath the park and a few metres from Stortorget. **Private rooms** can be booked by the tourist office for a fee of around 130kr. A quite stylish central **hotel** is the stately, white-stuccoed *Stadshotellet* at Hästtorget 3 (☎0430/128 30, fax 127 30; ①).

For daytime **eating**, a worthwhile **café** on the main square, *Conditori Cecilia* serves a wide range of scrumptious cakes in its down-to-earth café area. As for evening meals and **nightlife** in town itself, your choice is restricted to three venues (most people head off to Mellbystrand or Halmstad). *Annabelle's*, on Hästtorget off Stortorget (Mon–Fri 11am–2pm & 5–10pm, Sat & Sun 4–10pm), is a restaurant serving meat and pizzas – try the moose with noodles, their speciality. There's also a popular restaurant on the square: *Brasseriet* (Mon–Fri 11.30am till late, Sat & Sun from 1pm), serving meat and fish dishes, with main courses at 100–150kr. From either of these, the locals move on to *Bakfickan*, a regular pub just a few feet from *Annabelle's*.

Mellbystrand

A beach holiday Mecca, **Mellbystrand**, 6km west of Laholm, is a twelve-kilometre-long stretch of wide beaches, fringed by dunes and scrubland, behind which lie endless campsites for caravans, tents and cabins. Popular with Swedes, Mellbystrand gets very crowded in summer. Nude bathing sections are indicated by signs showing a rear view of a family.

Mellbystrand is something of a public transport oversight, with no train service and infrequent buses; **taxis** here from Laholm (☎0430/713 10) cost 100kr. **Bikes** are a good option for getting around, with cycle paths all the way here from Laholm; you can rent a bike in Laholm (see opposite) or, in Mellbystrand, at the very cheap Sturesson, Tärnvägen 13 (25kr per day or 100kr per week). In summer, there's an information point at a café, *Maxi* (☎0430/278 44). **Camping** is the most popular form of accommodation here, and *Marias Camping* the best campsite (☎0430/285 85), with excellent roomy cabins; you can pitch tents here, too. There are a couple of **restaurants** here, mainly pizza places attached to the campsites. Set in the prettiest wooden lodge trimmed with fancy carving, the *Strand Hotel*, 200m from the beach, is no longer a hotel – it's now a busy restaurant, pizzeria and grill.

Hishult

Established in the twelfth century, Hishult was an old farming village, and its homes all boasted furnaces in which ore taken from the local swamps was turned into iron. Today the place is very much a backwater, though one set in exquisite forest and lake surroundings. It makes a glorious cycle ride east from Halmstad (40km) or Laholm (20km). One historic sight worth a peek along the way (signposted off the main road) is the ruins of **Sjöboholm**, once the manor of old Hishult County, now reduced to little more than its foundations, its chief attraction being its verdant setting, jutting out into the lake 3km west of Hishult.

The real reason to seek the village out, though, is **Hishult Gästgivaregård** and **Konsthallen** at Markarydsvägen 10 (gallery May–Aug Tues–Fri 1–8pm, Sat & Sun 1–5pm, Sept–April Wed–Fri 2.30–6pm, Sat & Sun 1–5pm; ☎0430/403 21 or 400 55, fax 403 63); it's well signposted once you reach the village. An old inn had existed here in the middle of Hishult for centuries; it was inherited by its present owner, the amicable Kjell Åke Gustafsson, who set about converting part of it into a sensational art gallery. The design is full of inspired ideas, juxtaposing old and new, such as the steel spiral staircase and old stoves which came from old industrial buildings; outside, the gardens are peppered with wacky sculptures. Despite its apparent backwater location, the place is packed in summer. The ground-breaking exhibitions, of which there are six a year, provide much aesthetic stimulation. There's also a substantial collection of art books, mostly in Swedish, to browse or buy.

In the grounds, a fine **café**, a good spot for a light lunch, serves almond cream slices and chocolate cake. The inn is a delightful place to **stay**, with nine rooms (①); dinners can be ordered by arrangement.

Båstad

It's only a seven-minute train ride south from Laholm into the small town of **BÅSTAD**, the northernmost town in the ancient province of **Skåne**, yet its character is markedly different from other towns along the coast. Cradled by the **Bjäre peninsula** (see p.205), which bulges westwards into the Kattegat (the waters between Sweden and Jutland), Båstad is Sweden's elite **tennis centre**, where the Swedish Open is played at the beginning of July. The rest of Båstad boasts sixty other tennis courts, five eighteen-hole golf courses and the Drivan Sports Centre, one of Sweden's foremost sports complexes. It's all set in very beautiful surroundings, with forested hills on the horizon to the south.

There is a downside, though, which can blunt enthusiasm for the place. Ever since King Gustav V chose to take part in the 1930 tennis championships and Ludvig Nobel (nephew to Alfred of the Nobel Prize) gave financial backing to the tournaments, wealthy retired Stockholmers and social climbers from all over Sweden have flocked here. The result is an ostentatious smugness about the town, reflected in the clothes boutiques and shops selling overpriced oriental antiques that line Köpmansgatan, the main thoroughfare. The locals themselves, however, are quite down-to-earth, and most view the alleged arrogance of the "08-er"s (referring to folk from Stockholm – after its telephone prefix), which they endure during the tennis season, as a financial lifeline. Despite all this, Båstad isn't a prohibitively expensive place to stay, and makes a good base from which to explore the peninsula.

Arrival, information and accommodation

There are around twenty **trains** a day here from Laholm (7min). Båstad's **train station** is a lamentably long walk from the main part of town, a good 25-minute hike east down Köpmansgatan. The new station, to open early in the twenty-first century, will be even more inconveniently far away. Båstad's **tourist office**, on the main square (mid-June to mid-Aug Sun–Fri 10am–6pm, Sat 10am–3pm; mid-Aug to mid-June Mon–Sat 10am–4pm; ☎0431/750 45, fax 700 55, *turistbyran@bastad-tourism.se*) will book **private rooms** from 140kr per person. The main place to **rent bikes** is Svenn's Cykel, Tennisvägen 31 (Mon–Fri 8am–1pm & 2–5pm, Sat 8am–noon; ☎0431/701 26), which charges 80kr per day or 300kr per week. Another good option is at *B&B Malengården* (see below), also charging 80kr per day.

Accommodation in Båstad is plentiful, but to find somewhere to stay during the tennis tournament, you'll need to book months in advance. The STF **youth hostel** (☎0431/685 00, fax 706 19, Sept–May call ☎0431/710 30; 110kr) is next to the Drivan Sports Centre at Korrödsvagen, signposted off Köpmansgatan. It's open all year, but tends to be reserved for groups in winter; popular with sports-playing youngsters, it's one of the noisiest places to stay here. The cheaper **hotels** are mostly close to the station end of town, and unlike the rest of Sweden, prices are likely to increase dramatically during the summer due to the tennis tournament, which takes place just off the main square towards the harbour. *Hotel Pension Enehall* at Stationsterrasen 10 (☎0431/750 15, fax 724 09; ②) is a modern hotel just a few metres from the train station. In a pleasant, traditional wooden house, *Bed & Breakfast Malengården* is at Åhusvägen 41 (☎ & fax 0431/36 95 67; ①), reached by the same turning off Köpmansgatan as the youth hostel. *Hotel Pension Furuhem*, Roxmansvägen 13 (☎0431/701 09, fax 701 80; ①), close to the train station, is the town's oldest pension; it's an appealing old place that was once used as a posh boarding school. For a harbourside setting, there's *Hotel Skansen* (☎0431/720 50, fax 700 85; ③), in a century-old cream bathhouse. It has a restaurant, *Slamficken* (see p.205) and is right at the heart of the tennis action. Real glamour can be enjoyed at *Hotel Buena Vista* on Tarravägen 5 (☎0431/760 00, fax 791 00; ③), which has a splendid interior, though it doesn't look so good from the outside. This vast villa, built out of Cuban stone by a wealthy Cuban émigré, has two grand dining rooms, one overlooking Laholm Bay. To reach it, turn off Köpmansgatan around 500m east of the church. The reasonable *Hotel Borgen* on Köpmansgatan (☎ & fax 0431/750 80; ②; June–Aug). **Camping** is not allowed on the dunes – locals can be stuffy if you try; you are better off heading to the Bjäre peninsula.

The Town

From the train station, it's a half-hour walk eastwards down Köpmansgatan to the central, old square and tourist office (see p.204). Once you get close to the centre, you'll see that the street's architecture is unusual for Sweden; indeed it's somewhat reminiscent of provincial France, with shuttered, low-rise shops and houses. In the square is the fifteeth-century **St. Maria Church**, a cool haven on a hot summer's day. The altar painting is unusual, depicting Jesus on his cross with a couple of skulls and haphazardly strewn human bones on the ground beneath. To reach the **beach**, head down Tennisvägen, off Köpmansgatan, through a glamourous residential area, until you reach Strandpromenaden, where you can take a lovely evening stroll as the sun sets on the calm waters. West of here, the old 1880s bathhouses have all been converted into restaurants and bars, and beyond lies the harbour, thick with boat masts. To get involved in any **sports activities**, ask at the tourist office for information on booking tennis courts or renting out sports equipment.

Eating, drinking and nightlife

In Båstad, **eating and drinking** is as much a pastime as tennis, and most of the waterside restaurants and hotels here have two-course dinner offers, with menus changing weekly. *Pepe's Bodega* is a swish pizza place at the harbour (Mon–Thurs 7pm–1am, Fri 7pm–2am, Sat & Sun noon–1am), with a pizza-for-two offer at 98kr; next door is *Fiskbiten*, a busy fish restaurant, set in a turn-of-the-century bathhouse. *Slamficken* (also known as *Grandslam*) in a neighbouring old bathhouse, has a popular grill from 6pm, and is also open for breakfast and lunch. The fine restaurant at *Hotel Buena Vista* (see p.204) has a summertime grill buffet, with meat, fish and salad for 185kr. To eat cheaply right at the harbour, wander past all the restaurants to the little wooden hut (nameless) at the water's edge, serving smoked mackerel with salad, dill, potato salad and salad for 50kr and fresh filled baguettes for just 30kr.

Although it has a few **nightclubs**, Båstad is much more geared up for those who prefer to sip wine in restaurants; only teenagers fill the naff clubs along Köpmansgatan. *Madison's*, next to *Hotel Borgen* on Köpmansgatan, is grim-looking on the outside but is better inside; it's a blackjack joint (June–Aug).

The Bjäre peninsula

Deserving of a couple of days' exploration, the **Bjäre peninsula**'s natural beauty has a magical quality to it. Its varied scenery includes wide fertile fields, where potatoes and strawberries are grown (on New Potato Day, in June, part of the potato crop is sold in Båstad at up to 200kr a kilo); splintered red-rock cliff formations; and remote and seal-ringed islands, thick with birds and historical ruins.

Travel practicalities

To help you find your way around, it's best to buy a large-scale map of the area from Båstad tourist office (40kr). The well-known **Skåneleden walking trail** runs around the entire perimeter; it can be cycled and indeed makes for a great ride (having a bike with a choice of gears helps, as it can get hilly). **Public transport** around Bjäre is adequate, with **buses** connecting the main towns and villages. Bus #525 leaves Båstad every other hour for **Torekov** (Mon–Fri; 20min; 16kr), running through the centre of the peninsula en route; it stops at the small hamlets of Hov and Karup, on the peninsula's southern coast. For transport to Torekov at weekends, call Båstad taxi (☎0431/696 66) an hour before you want to leave (same charge as the bus; book your return journey on the outward trip). To move on to Ängelholm (see p.208) from Torekov, take bus #523 (6 daily; 50min). **Staying** on the Bjäre peninsula is no problem; there are plenty of spots to pitch a tent for free, several official places to camp and plenty of good hotels in the main towns.

The northern coastline

Heading north out of Båstad along the coast road, it's just a couple of kilometres to **Norrvikens Gardens** (May to mid-Sept daily 10am–6pm; 35kr), a paradise for horticulturists and lovers of symmetry. With the sea as a backdrop, these fine gardens were designed by Rudolf Abelin at the end of the nineteenth century; he is buried in a magnificent hollow of rhododendrons near the entrance. The best walk is the "King's Ravine", ablaze in late spring and early summer with fiery azaleas and blushing rhododendrons, and leading to a fine Japanese-style garden. At the centre of the grounds there's a villa with a **café-restaurant**. Around July 10, the biggest **classic car show** in Sweden is held in the grounds here (100kr, under-14s free).

Two to three kilometres further, past the *Norrvikens Camping Site* for caravans (☎0431/691 70; April–Oct), is **KATTVIK**. Once a village busy with stone-grinding mills, it is now largely the domain of wealthy, elderly Stockholmers, who snap up the few houses on the market as soon as they are up for sale. Kattvik achieved its moment of fame when Richard Gere chose a cottage here as a venue for a summer romance; otherwise, it contains little more than the friendly and peaceful *Delfin Bed & Breakfast* (☎0431/731 20; ①), offering vegetarian gourmet cooking and breakfast (featuring home-baked bruschetta) in the garden or on the terrace. With sparkling clean rooms, it's an idyllic base for exploring the region.

A kilometre from Kattvik off the Torekov road (follow the sign "*rökt fisk*") is Kai's fish smokery, an old farm where a seasoned fisherman smokes fish in little furnaces fired by sawdust from the nearby clog factory. Here you can have a taste of – and buy – the very best smoked fish in the area; as well as the usual mackerel and salmon, you can sample *horngadda*, a scaly fish with bright green bones, and *sjurygg*, an extraordinarily ugly, seven-crested fish with oily, flavoursome flesh. Just a couple of minutes walk from Kattvik, in the hills just behind *Delfin B & B*, is *Westfield Häst Safari* (☎ & fax 0431/45 13 53); signposted off the Torekov Route, it's a base for **horse trekking** – a wonderful way to explore the region. The treks are run by an Irishman, John Slattery; courses range from a two-hour guided trip (250kr, including lunch), to a two-day trek (1300kr including accommodation) from the forests close by across the valleys to Hovs Hallar (see opposite).

Heading north along the coast road or the signposted walking trail, the undulating meadows and beamed cottages you'll encounter have a rural, peculiarly English, feel. To continue along the coast after taking the trail from Kattvik, follow the path for **Hovs Hallar nature reserve**, leading off at the T-junction (around a 20min walk). Wandering across to the reserve from the car park, you can clamber down any of several paths towards the sea. The views are breathtaking – screaming gulls circling overhead (particularly unnerving if you've just bought fish) and waves crashing onto the unique red-stone cliffs.

Overlooking the cliffs, *Hovs Hallar Värdhus* is famed as a **restaurant** serving fine à la carte meals and lunch specials (☎0431/651 09; daily noon–9pm). Unfortunately, it's rested on its laurels as custom has been easy to come by recently – the area is now a bit of a tourist trap – and the standard is not what it has been. There are pretty, four-bed **cabins** just behind the restaurant (June–Aug from 695kr per night for the cabins, Sept–May 455kr). Double rooms are also available between June and August (①), and there's a **café** here too (10am–10pm; closed outside summer).

Torekov and Hallands Väderö

Leaving Båstad along Route 115 for the sleepy village of Torekov, consider stopping for a bite at *Solbackens* waffle bakery and café (daily noon–6pm), on Italienskavägen, 2km from town. Nestling amid wild flowers near the start of the peninsula, this place, in a wooden house above a babbling brook, has been dishing up excellent waffles (24kr each) since 1907. Rough-hewn steps lead upwards from the café to countless hidden hillside coves, with tables and chairs and spectacular views.

On the peninsula's western coast, **TOREKOV** is just 4–5km from Hovs Hallar. The village is named after a little girl, later known as St Thora, who, so the story goes, was drowned by her wicked stepmother; the body was washed ashore and given a Christian burial by a blind man, who then miraculously regained his sight. There's precious little to do here, other than have a look at the cut-in-half sailing ship (free), a **museum** with a collection of shipping memorabilia. One odd sight is the daily ritual of elderly men in dressing gowns wandering along the pier – so sought after is the property here, these old gents promenade in bathrobes to set themselves apart from the visitors.

Torekov's **tourist office** is at the back of Hamnmagasinet, close to the harbour (June–Aug Mon–Sat 10am–6pm; ☎0431/631 80, fax 645 53). To **stay** in Torekov itself, try the century-old *Hotel Kattegat*, to be found on its cobbled main street (☎0431/630 02; ③); this fine old building has en-suite rooms with TVs (room no. 9 has the finest view), and a lovely, frescoed dining room. A more rustic, very charming option is found 3km out of Torekov; follow the signposted turning from the main road towards Påarp. This will bring you to *Sjöbyggargården Bed & Breakfast* (☎0431/36 53 85; ①; April–September), in a converted stables dating from the eighteenth century; it oozes country character with hollyhocks outside the front door. Advance reservations here are a good idea, particularly in spring and autumn. For a place to **camp**, there's *Kronocamping* (☎0431/36 45 25, fax 36 46 25), 1500m out of Torekov on the Båstad road; it has four-bed, modern cabins with showers and cable TV.

There are three very popular, though rather expensive, **restaurants**. *Hotel Kattegat* has its own restaurant, boasting the revered chef Richard Nilson and international/European food, while just opposite, the glass-roofed *Svenson's* has maintained its high standards, serving fine fish dishes (Tues, Thurs & Sun 6–11pm, Fri & Sat 6pm–1am). By the harbour, *Hamn Krogan* restaurant looks the cosiest of the three, but its food is the least special. To avoid blowing a packet on rarefied dining, step inside the bright and breezy *Hamn Magasinet*, in between *Hamn Krogan* and *Svenson's*. Without pretentious trappings, you can enjoy home-baked baguettes for 55kr or à la carte dishes like entrecôte for around 130kr. Alternatively, you can buy smoked fish and baguettes (18kr) from the harbour fish shop.

Hallands Väderö

Old fishing **boats** regularly leave from Torekov's little harbour for the island nature reserve of **Hallands Väderö** (June–Aug hourly; Sept–May every 2 hr; 15min; 60kr return); the last one back leaves at 4.30pm, so it's well worth setting off early (first boats at 9am or 10am at weekends) to give yourself a full day to take in its awesome beauty. You can buy a map (30kr) of Hallands Väderö from Torekov harbour ticket office before you leave. The island is a scenic mix of trees and bare rocks, isolated fishermen's cottages dotted around its edges, while the skies above are filled with countless birds – gulls, eiders, guillemots, cormorants. One particularly beautiful spot is at its southernmost tip, where weather-smoothed islets stand out amid the tranquil turquoise waters. If you're lucky, you may be able to make out the colony of seals which lives on the furthest rocks; there are organized "**seal safaris**" there (11.30am & 5.30pm; 100kr; ask at Torekov tourist office). Also on the south of the island is the English graveyard, surrounded by mossy, dry-stone walls. It holds the remains of English sailors who were killed here in 1809, when the British fleet were stationed on the island in order to bombard Copenhagen during the Napoleonic Wars. Torekov church would not allow them to be buried on its soil as the sailors' faith was, strangely, considered unknown.

There is no camping on the island (heads are counted on the boats' return journeys to check if anyone tries), so if you do want to **stay** overnight, you'll have to rent one of the two idyllic cottages by the northern lighthouse (ask at Torekov tourist office for details).

Ängelholm

The best aspects of peacefully uneventful **ÄNGELHOLM** are its 7km of popular golden beach and its proximity to two places of interest – Helsingborg (see p.212) is just thirty minutes south by train, while the Kullen peninsula (see p.210) beckons enticingly to the west. With a range of accommodation, some agreeable restaurants and a surprisingly lively nightlife, Ängelhom isn't at all a bad place to base yourself.

Arrival, information and accommodation

There are regular **trains** here from Båstad (17 daily; 25min), and **buses** from Båstad and Torekov. Turn right out of the station and then left onto Järnvägsgatan, carrying on for 300m past the church to get to the old rådhus (town hall), in the main square, containing the **tourist office** (early June & late Aug Mon–Fri 9am–6pm, Sat 9am–2pm; mid-June to mid-Aug Mon–Fri 9am–7pm,

Sat 9am–4pm Sun 11am–3pm; Sept to early June Mon–Fri 9am–5pm; ☎043/821 30, fax 192 07, *turistbyran@engelholm.se*). Central Ängelholm is easy to get around on foot; one useful **bus** route is the #50, which runs from the train station to the square and on to the harbour. To **rent a bike** – the best way to head out to the Kullen peninsula (see p.210) – the only option is Harry's Cykel, Södra Kyrkogatan 9 (Mon–Fri 9am–6pm, Sat 9am–1pm; ☎0431/143 25; 100kr per day or 450kr per week) with seven-speed bikes and excellent service. The shop is a bit tricky to find; head down Storgatan, then around the back of the building on which the "Harry's Cykel" sign appears.

For **accommodation**, the tourist office can book hotel rooms (20kr fee) or **private rooms** (from 110kr, with a 30kr fee). There is an STF **youth hostel** at Magnarp Strand (☎ & fax 0431/45 23 64; 100kr; bookings necessary Nov–March), 10km north of the train station, and beyond the beaches detailed below (local buses ply the route). For a friendly **hotel** that's good value, try *Hotel Lilton* at Järnvägsgatan 29, just a few steps from the square (☎0431/44 25 50, fax 44 25 69). There are several **campsites**; the most convenient for the beach is *Råbocka Camping*, at the end of Råbockavägen (☎0431/105 43, fax 832 45). Just opposite is *Klitterbyn*, a large, leafy holiday village of wooden chalets and apartments (☎0431/586 00, fax 195 72; ①).

The Town

Ängelholm's efforts to sell itself concentrate not on its beaches but on its mascot, a musical clay cuckoo – unglazed and easily broken toy versions of the bird are sold everywhere – and **UFOs**. The latter have been big business here since 1946, when a railway worker, Gösta Carlsson, convinced the authorities that he had encountered tiny people from another world, who travelled in a discus-shaped craft. He produced as evidence a piece of stone allegedly harder than diamond, a strange other-worldly ring, and the supposed imprints made by the spaceship while landing; being a UFO guru has made him a rich man. Today, Ängelholm hosts international UFO conferences, and the tourist board, recognizing the potential of the theme, runs tours throughout the summer to the mysterious site 4km away where the spaceship is meant to have landed.

The town itself has a small historic core, created when the Danish king Christian II ("the Good" to the Danes, "the Tyrant" to the Swedes) forced the people of nearby Luntertun to relocate here in 1518; it's pleasant enough to wander around but has little to detain you. From the train station, it's just a few minutes' walk over the Rönneå river to the main square (where you'll find the tourist office; see opposite). Not far from here, up Kyrkogatan, is a **handicrafts museum** (May–Aug Tues–Fri 1–5pm, Sat 10am–2pm; 10kr). Housed in what used to be the town prison, the museum has a rather unexciting collection of tannery and silversmith artefacts, eighteenth-century peasant furniture and a ceramics collection dominated by pottery cuckoos. Should you want to see more of the town, the least strenuous way is a **boat trip** up the river from the harbour (early June to mid-Aug; 4 daily 40min trips, 45kr; or one daily 2hr return trip, 60kr; book on ☎0431/203 00). For more freedom of movement, *Skåne Marin*, which runs the tours, also rents out boats and canoes.

Having seen the town, head for the **beaches**, 2–3km west of the centre. You can take the free bus that runs from the main square in summer (late June to mid-Aug every hour 10am–4pm), or walk (15–20min): from the main square, head down

Järnvägsgatan, and turn left onto Havsbadsvägen; this soon turns into Råbockavägen, from where several overground paths lead to the beaches. There are no official demarcations, but in practice, 30-something singles seem to gravitate to the stretch of sand nearest the town; a little further south is the best of the family beaches; to its south is a section for the style gurus and body beautifuls; while the most southerly beach is nudist (both sexes).

Aside from the clay cuckoos, UFOs and beaches, Ängelholm has one further boast – a **Rose Festival**, held during the second weekend of July, when fifty thousand roses imported from Holland festoon the town, and a Rose Queen (indistinguishable blonde beauties each year) is chosen to parade round town. Though not much else happens, the visual impact is considerable.

Eating, drinking and nightlife

The best place for **food** is at the harbour, where *Hamn Krogen*, its walls decorated with maritime artefacts, serves the best fish dishes in Ängelholm (April to mid-Aug daily 11am–1am). Their speciality is Toast Skagen – shrimps and red caviar on toast; starters cost from 23kr, main courses from 85kr. The restaurant at *Klitterhus Pensionat* is costly and on the pretentious side (one dish here is "lemon and saffron polenta with black truffle and zucchini yoghurt"). A few metres up the beach, in a whitewashed wartime bunker, *Bunken* restaurant and bar (daily 11am–2am) is much more straightforward, a buzzing, friendly place serving a diverse choice of eats, from barbecue fare to lavish fish and seafood dishes. With local and imported beers, and regular live music, it makes a perfect place to chill out till late in the evening. Back in town, *Nick's*, a bar-restaurant on Stortorget (☎0431/12900, fax 800 07), has made a valiant attempt at Mexican-ranch styling; it serves burger-type meals at 70–80kr, and grills, fish and fowl dishes at reasonable cost. Nearby, the *Hotel Lilton*, Järnvägsgatan 29, has a great garden **café** (June & Aug noon–6pm; July noon–8pm), tucked away beneath a cluster of beech trees near the river.

The most popular **nightclub** is *Bahnhoff Bar*, a cavernous, industrial-looking place (Thurs 7pm–2am, Fri 9pm–3am, Sat 7pm–3am). Occupying old railway buildings just beyond the present train station, it packs out with a crowd of 18- to 30-year-olds. Not quite as hip and rather small is *Club 57*, in the basement of *Hotel Paletten* at Östergatan 57. *Factory*, on Nybrovägen (off Industrigatan, a continuation of Järnvägsgatan), is a loud, relaxed sort of place, catering for a younger crowd. A hundred metres up the road is *Rönneå River*, an equally popular summertime outdoor club and bar.

One of the country's biggest venues for a taste of the peculiarly Swedish obsession with **foxtrots** is *Ekebo*, in the Ängelholm suburb of Hjärnarp, around 15km east of town (bus #507 heads there). The place has a live band playing nothing but foxtrots on Saturdays, and live music every night in summer. Attracting a mainly 35-plus clientele, it's quite an eye-opener.

The Kullen peninsula

Jutting out like a stiletto heel, the **Kullen peninsula**, west of Ängelholm (though more easily reached by public transport from Helsingborg), is a highlight along the west coast. It is far flatter than the Bjäre peninsula to the north, and so makes for much easier cycling, but still undulates enough to ensure there are some great vistas. The most sensational sight is the sculptural creation of Nimis (see below), but this wealthy yet unpretentious triangle of land also boasts **Arild**, one of the most glorious villages you could hope to find, and the salubrious town of **Mölle**.

Arild

Nothing prepares you for the almost unreal prettiness of the village of **ARILD**. To get here from Ängelholm (see p.208), take Järnvägsgatan in the opposite direction from the beaches and harbour, initially following directions to Höganäs. At Utvälinge, take the much more scenic northern coastal road leading northwest, which will take you to Arild after a short drive. This waterfront cluster of homes and streets is like a picture postcard come to life – all cottages with fancy gingerbreading; grander houses standing behind. Strolling down Sankt Arilds Väg, parallel to the waterfront, you'll find a simple white chapel, **Arildskapell**, at the end of the street. Inside, the pews all take the form of compartments with hand-painted doors. The most appealing place to **stay** is the charming *Strand Hotel* on Storavägen 42, just up the hill from the chapel (☎042/34 61 00, fax 34 61 85; ③). With romantic, elegant bedrooms and exquisitely presented **food**, this friendly hotel has touches that lend much character – old books and antiquated Swedish tiled stoves.

Nimis

Continuing northwest along the coast road from Arild, you'll soon reach a right turn signposted for **Himmelstorp**, a well-preserved eighteenth-century farmstead which you can wander through at will. Mostly, though, people come here to down ice cream and fruit juice on their way to or from the stupendous **Nimis**. Arguably Sweden's most sensational – and controversial – **living sculpture** (one that's subject to constant alteration), *Nimis* is the creation of the eccentric sculptor Lars Vilks, Professor of Art at Oslo University. A brilliantly conceived, fantastical structure comprising a tower and corridors, built entirely out of driftwood and occasional items of furniture, the huge design looks as if it ought to collapse at the first breeze, but is so cleverly made that it supports the hundreds of eager visitors who clamber daily over its fascinating bulk. The reason for the controversy is that *Nimis*, as a building of sorts, contravenes the protected status of the surrounding area. Vilks argues, however, that it is art and, being built from driftwood, it enhances rather than detracts from the surroundings – a view accepted by anyone you'll meet hereabouts.

A little further to the right as you face out to sea here, what looks like a medieval ruined castle is in fact a stone structure also made by Vilks, entitled *Book* and looking nothing like its name. If you get close, you'll see almost all the stones are numbered – there are over three hundred stone "pages".

You have to be reasonably fit to get to *Nimis*, as doing so involves a steep clamber down from Himmelstorp into the Kullen ridge, negotiating rough stone steps en route. Yellow "N"s are painted on trees as you head down to the shore, as if the area is part of a treasure hunt.

Mölle

The steep, forested hill that shields the pretty harbour at **MÖLLE** is jollied up with lots of substantial old homes, the wealth of the locals apparent in the gleaming cars and the prices charged by the sedate, glamorous restaurants. The largest town on the peninsula, Mölle is just 300m from the majestic landscape of

Kullaberg, the forested rocks at Kullen's western tip, topped with a stately light-house, from where the views are superb. From *Nimis*, you simply carry on north along coastal road for a few minutes to reach Molle, which will be signposted to left. From Helsingborg (see below), **bus #222** runs to Mölle bus station almost hourly until after midnight.

At the harbour, the French-Renaissance-style splendour of *Hotell Kullaberg* sums the town up (☎042/34 70 00, fax 34 71 00; ⑥). Built in 1907, the hotel has a very popular restaurant where main courses alone are 185–235kr; better value is the bistro special at 85kr. For a place to **camp**, the best option is *Möllehässle Camping* (☎042/34 73 84, fax 34 77 29; May to mid-Aug). It's on the main coastal road just northwest of *Nimis*, and has small cabins (①), a very well-stocked shop, a laundry and a sauna.

Mölle's dearest places to **eat** are just metres from the cheapest – there are plenty places to fill up inexpensively. Right at the end of the harbour, *Rödspättan* is a plastic-tables-and-chairs outfit, with fish and meat dishes, served with chips and salads, for 50kr; pancakes are 30kr. Equally down-to-earth and also at the harbour edge, *Knafves Cafe* has freshly baked baguettes and savoury crepes. A good mid-price option is *Klubbhotellet Restaurant & Bar*, serving delicious fish soup with walnut bread at 75kr; to find it (signposting is very poor), head up Gyllenstiernas Alle from the harbour and head left up a steep winding hill for about 500m – *Klubbhotellet* is the last building you come to.

Helsingborg and around

The locals of **HELSINGBORG** used to joke that the most rewarding sight here was Helsingør, the Danish town whose castle – Hamlet's celebrated Elsinore – is clearly visible, just 4km across the sound, Öresund. This comment had less to do with any failings the bright and pleasing town of Helsingborg might have had, and much more to do with the appeal of Denmark's cheaper alcohol outlets. Trolley-lugging Swedes converge on Helsingborg from all over the country, both to stock up on beer across the water, and to spend entire nights on the **ferries**, becoming increasingly drunk for fewer *kronor* than they could on land. The building of the Malmö–Copenhagen bridge (see p.238) is expected to undermine this pastime.

In the past, the links between Helsingborg and Copenhagen were less than convivial. After the Danes fortified the town in the eleventh century, the Swedes conquered and lost it again on six violent occasions, finally winning out in 1710 under Magnus Stenbock's leadership. By this time, the Danes had torn down much of the town and on its final recapture, the Swedes contributed to the destruction by razing most of its twelfth-century castle – except for the five-metre-thick walled **keep** (*kärnen*), which still dominates the centre. By the early eighteenth century, war and epidemics had reduced the population to just seven hundred, and only with the onset of industrialization in the 1850s did Helsingborg experience a new prosperity. Shipping and the railways turned the town's fortunes round, as is evident from the formidable late nineteenth-century commercial buildings in the centre and some splendid villas to the north, overlooking the Öresund.

Today, a constant through traffic of Danes, Germans and Swedes are beginning to realize that being here only long enough to change trains is a mistake. They stay a couple of days – as should you – in order to savour the youthful, Continental feel of this instantly likeable town, with its warren of cobbled streets, burgeoning nightlife, historical sights and enjoyable day excursions. Very recently, Helsingborg has been lent a new vibrancy by an explosion of brilliantly styled bars on the ground floors of the ultramodern, super-trendy apartment blocks that have risen up across its regenerated North Harbour area.

Arrival, information and transport

Unless approaching by car on the E6, chances are you will arrive at the harbourside **Knutpunkten**, the vast, glassy expanses of which incorporate all **car-** and **passenger ferry** and **train** terminals. On the ground floor, behind the main hall, is the **bus station**, while ticket offices and transport enquiries are in the main hall itself. Below ground level is the **train station**, handling the national SJ trains and the lilac-coloured local Pågatåg services, the latter running south down the coast to Lund and Malmö; and north up to Ängelholm. There is a Forex **currency exchange** office at ground level (daily 8am–9pm). The **Sundsbussarna** passenger-only ferry from Helsingør (see p.217) is just outside at Hamntorget, 100m away.

Currently on the first floor of Knutpunkten, the **tourist office** (June–Aug Mon–Fri 9am–8pm, Sat & Sun 9am–5pm; Sept–May Mon–Fri 9am–6pm, Sat 10am–2pm; ☎042/12 03 10, fax 12 78 76, *turistbyran@helsingborg.se*) is expected to move elsewhere within the building. Here you can get free maps and *Helsingborg This Month*, an events guide with sections in English; or pick up the very comprehensive English-language *Helsingborg Guide* (free). A huge wall map outside the tourist office has every Helsingborg sight, museum, hostel and campsite you may want to check out; there's a push-button for each, which lights the corresponding location on the map when pressed.

Central Helsingborg is all within easy walking distance of Knutpunkten, but for the youth hostel, the gardens of Sofiero and surrounding sights to the north (see p.217), or Råå to the south (p.220), you'll need to get a **bus**. Tickets bought on board cost 13kr and are valid for two changes within an hour. **Bike rental** is an enjoyable option, as all the best sights are within 5km of town. The tourist office is the obvious outlet, with three-gear bikes (75kr a day, plus a 50kr returnable deposit); or try Pålsjöbaden, the old bathhouse on Drottninggatan, 3km north of town (same prices, see p.217).

Accommodation

The tourist office will book **private rooms** for upwards of 125kr per person, plus a steep 70kr booking fee; if staying four days or more, the booking fee is 200kr. The **youth hostel**, *Villa Thalassa*, is 2.5km north of the town centre at Dag Hammarskjöldsväg (☎042/21 03 84, fax 12 87 92; June–Aug 180kr, Sept–May 165kr), next to peaceful forest. The villa, now the hostel's main building, was built in 1903 by Von Dardel, a courtier to King Gustav Adolf (the present king's grandfather) at nearby Sofiero castle. Accommodation is not in the villa itself but in cabins behind, with showers an unwelcome short trek away, but the rooms at least have adjoining toilets. There are also more comfortable holiday cottages (①) here. Breakfasts (40kr) are served in *Thalassa*'s dining room, with wonderful views over the Öresund. Bus #7 runs north from Knutpunkten to Pålsjöbaden, the old bathhouse (every 20min), from where the hostel is a signposted one-kilometre walk through really beautiful forest; after 7pm, bus #44 follows the route to the bathhouse.

Hotels

There are plenty of central **hotels**. The most glamorous are around Stortorget, while cheaper establishments are to be found opposite Knutpunkten and along the roads leading away from it. All the following include breakfast in the price.

The Grand, Stortorget 8–12 (☎042/12 01 70, fax 11 88 33). New ownership has meant the loss of *The Grand*'s former exclusivity, though it's still pretty posh. ⑤/②.

Hotel Helsingborg, Stortorget 20 (☎042/12 09 45, fax 21 54 61). At the foot of the steps up to the castle keep. A lovely hotel, with marble stairs, comfortable rooms and a perfect location. ④/③.

Kärnen, Järnvägsgatan 17 (☎042/12 08 20, fax 14 88 88). Opposite Knutpunkten. This comfortable, newly-renovated hotel prides itself on "personal touches". These include ominous English-language homilies on each room door; the one for room no. 235 reads: "He who seeks revenge keeps his wounds open". There's a small library, cocktail bar and sauna. ④/②.

Linnea, Prästgatan 4 (☎042/21 46 60, fax 14 16 55). Centrally located, this hotel has recently been remodelled in a simple, pleasing style. Good value. ②.

Marina Plaza, Kungstorget 6 (☎042/19 21 00, fax 14 96 16). Right at the harbourside, next to Knutpunkten. A big, modern and well-equipped hotel, featuring a popular restaurant, *Hamnkrogen*; a nightclub, the *Marina*; and the much-frequented *Sailor Pub*. Lively and less austere than other top-class hotels. ⑤/③.

Mollberg, Stortorget 18 (☎042/37 37 00, fax 37 37 37). Every bit a premier hotel, with a grand nineteenth-century facade, elegant rooms and a salubrious brasserie. ⑤/③.

Hotel Nouveau, Gasverksgatan 11 (☎042/18 53 90, fax 14 08 85). Despite lacking the grandeur of other Stortorget hotels, it's pretty central and has all the comforts of the top hotels, including a swimming pool and a sauna. Serves exceptionally good breakfasts (also available to non-residents). Terrible views from the windows, though. ④/③.

Hotel Viking, Fågelsångsgatan 1 (☎042/14 44 20, fax 18 43 20). A very appealing, quiet old hotel with a good location, close to some of the town's loveliest old buildings. ④/③.

The Town

The most obvious starting point is on the waterfront, by the copper **statue** of Magnus Stenbock on his charger. With your back to the Öresund and Denmark, to your left is the **Rådhus** (town hall), a heavy-handed, Neo-Gothic pile, complete with turrets and conical towers. The extravagance of provincial nineteenth-century prosperity, and the architect's admiration for medieval Italy, make it worth seeing inside (tours mid-June to Aug Mon–Fri at 10am; 40min) – in particular for the many fabulous ecclesiastical-style stained-glass windows, which tell the entire history of the town. The ones to look out for are those in the entrance hall, depicting Queen Margaretta releasing her rival, Albert of Mecklenburg, in Helsingborg in 1395; and the last window in the city-council chamber, showing John Baptiste Bernadotte arriving at Helsingborg in 1810, having accepted the Swedish crown. When he greeted General Von Essen at the harbour, farce ensued as their elaborate gold jewellery and medals became entangled in the embrace. The windows were all donated by the town's wealthiest industrial magnates; such is their value that they were all taken out and hidden for the duration of World War II. The original wall and ceiling frescoes – deemed too costly to restore and painted over in 1968 – are currently being uncovered.

Crossing over the road towards the Kattegat from the Magnus Stenbock statue, you'll see the **harbour**, divided in two by the new bridge to the pier. To the south of the bridge, the new **Henry Dunker city museum** is due for completion in 2001, while to the north, a chain of stylish contemporary apartment

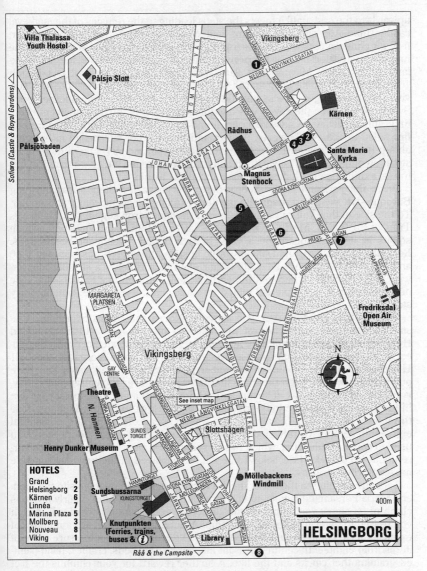

HELSINGBORG

HOTELS

Grand	4
Helsingborg	2
Kärnen	6
Linnéa	7
Marina Plaza	5
Mollberg	3
Nouveau	8
Viking	1

blocks has transformed the area from wasteland into a residential haven with sea views. The ground floor of each block is a bar-cum-café-restaurant, with hip colour schemes and plenty of beams and steel columns. The whole area is made for summer-evening strolling, sipping wine and serious eating (see p.218), usually by candlelight.

Returning to the statue, you'll find yourself at the bottom of **Stortorget** – the central "square" so elongated that it's more like a boulevard – which slopes upwards to the east, until it meets the steps leading to the remains of the medieval castle (June–Aug daily 10am–8pm; Sept–May Mon–Fri & Sun 10am–6pm; 5kr, free for children & wheelchair users); there is a lift to the side. At the top is the massive castellated bulk of **kärnen** (the keep), surrounded by some fine parkland (daily: April, May & Sept 9am–4pm; June–Aug 10am–7pm; Oct–March 10am–2pm; 15kr). The keep and St Maria kyrka (see below) were the sole survivors of the ravages of war, but the former lost its military significance once Sweden finally won the day. It was due for demolition in the mid-nineteenth century, only surviving because seafarers found it a valuable landmark. What cannon fire failed to achieve, however, neglect and the weather succeeded in bringing about: the keep was a ruin when restoration began in 1894. Like a huge brick stood on end, the keep is worth climbing today more for the views than the historical exhibitions (with descriptions in English) within.

From the parkland at the keep's base, it's just a few steps to a charming Baroque-style **rose and magnolia garden**, exuding scent and colour all summer. To the side of this, you can wander down a rhododendron-edged path, Hallbergs Trappor, to the **St Maria kyrka** (Mon–Sat 8am–4pm, Sun 9am–6pm), which squats in its own square by a very French-looking avenue of beech trees. Resembling a basilica, and Danish Gothic in style, the church was begun in 1300 and completed a century later. Its rather plain facade belies a striking interior, with a clever contrast between the early seventeenth-century Renaissance-style ornamentation of its pulpit and gilded reredos, and the jewel-like contemporary stained-glass windows.

Walking back to Stortorget, you arrive at **Norra** and **Södra Storgatan** (the streets that meet at the foot of the stairs to the *kärnen*), which comprised Helsingborg's main thoroughfare in medieval times and so are lined with the oldest of the town's merchants' houses. As you head up Norra Storgatan, the 1681 **Henckelska house** is hidden behind a plain stuccoed wall; once you have pushed your way through the trees that have grown over the entrance archway, you'll see a rambling mix of beams and windows, with a fine little topiary garden hidden beyond a passage to the right. This garden was laid out in 1766 to please the future wife of King Gustav III, who was to spend one night at the beautiful eighteenth-century **Gamlegård house** opposite. To the south, Södra Storgatan used to contain a museum, which has closed down – many of its exhibits are currently at Fredriksdal (see below) but will be displayed in the new harbour-side museum when it opens.

Take the opening to the left of the old cream brick building, opposite the modern Maria Församling House, to find a real historical gem. After a fairly arduous climb of 92 steps, you'll find a handsome nineteenth-century **windmill**, which you're free to enter using a narrow ramp. Around the windmill are a number of exquisite farm cottages, and inside the low (120cm) doors is a treasure trove of items from eighteenth-century peasant interiors: straw beds, cradles, hand-painted grandmother clocks and the like. A further reward for your climb is the fact that at one house, built in 1763 and brought to this site in 1909, there's a waffle servery, *Möllebackens Våffelbruk* (May–Aug daily noon–8pm). Established in 1912, they still use the original recipes, and you can enjoy your snack sitting on an eighteenth-century settee, or outside beneath the windmill.

To see some of the city museum's exhibits, take bus #1 or #6 from outside the Rådhus for the two-kilometre trip to **Fredriksdal** (May–Sept 10am–6pm; Oct–April more limited hours; ☎042/10 59 81; 20kr). Here a large, open-air museum is set around a fine eighteenth-century manor house; there's plenty to look at, with parks, peasant homes and extensive botanical gardens.

North of the centre: the Royal Gardens of Sofiero

An excursion it would be a shame to miss is to the **Royal Gardens of Sofiero** (May to mid-Sept 10am–6pm; 30kr); take bus #219 Mon–Fri, or #221 Sat & Sun, from Knutpunkten; or cycle the 4km north along the coast. Built as a summer residence by Oscar II in the 1860s, the house is not particularly attractive, looking more like an elaborate train station – its architect was in fact the designer of many of Sweden's stations. The thrill here is in seeing the gardens, given by Oscar to his grandson, Gustav Adolf, on the occasion of the latter's marriage to Crown Princess Marghareta in 1905. Marghareta created a horticultural paradise, and, as she was a granddaughter of Queen Victoria, the gardens are strongly influenced by English country-garden design. After Marghareta died, aged 38, in 1920, the king's second wife Louise continued her work and the English theme. The rhododendron collection here really is something special, one of Europe's finest, with a stunning array of ten thousand plants and over five hundred varieties, spreading a blanket of rainbow colours all the way down to the Öresund.

A couple of kilometres south of Sofiero, near the youth hostel (see p.213), is **Pålsjö Slott**, an immaculate eighteenth-century toy-town palace. While the building has nothing to see inside – it's been converted into offices – the public are free to wander behind to its gardens. Walking through a long, narrow avenue of gnarled beech trees, which have become knotted together overhead, and on towards the Öresund, you'll come to a beautiful pathway, Landborgspromenade. Head south along it, back towards town, and you'll pass some large, Art Nouveau villas in fine gardens. At the end of the path (where bus #7 runs into town) stands **Pålsjöbaden**, a classic 1880 bathhouse on stilts (Mon, Wed & Thurs 9am–7.30pm, Tues 6.45am–9pm, Fri 6.45am–6.30pm, Sat & Sun 8am–5pm; 30kr).

Eating, drinking and nightlife

Some excellent food shops, useful for picnic fare, are clustered on the square containing St Maria kyrka (see p.216), notably *Maratorgets* on the south side of the square, selling fresh fruit, and the adjacent *Bengtsons Ost,* a specialist cheese shop. The city has a good range of excellent **restaurants**, including a host of styl-

---

FERRIES TO HELSINGØR

For a taste of what the locals have traditionally done for fun – and in order to get away from the expensive restaurants and bars – buy a **ferry** ticket to **HELSINGØR** at Knutpunkten (ticket office on second floor). Scandlines' ferries run every twenty minutes (35kr return; children 6–11 half price; ☎042/18 60 00), as do Sundbussarna's (20kr one-way, 30kr return, children 6–14 half price; ☎042/21 60 60); while Tura offer back-and-forth ferry trips (50kr, with a 40kr discount per person on meals). Ask to go on the Swedish boat, *Aurora*, as it has better restaurants and bars than the Danish ones (*Hamlet* and *Tycho Brahe*). The idea is to go back and forth all night; the only reason to get off at Helsingør, apart from having a closer look at **Helsingør Castle** (Hamlet's Elsinore – less thrilling than you may imagine), is to buy duty-free drink (which can't be bought on the boat). **Car ferries** to Denmark cost 495kr for up to five people.

ish new eating and drinking opportunities in the **bar-restaurants** along the restored harbourfront. These places can seem samey, though, and it's the older restaurants that continue to provide the variety.

During the day, there are some great **cafés** and *konditori*. At night, locals recommend "taking the boat to Helsingør", the entertainment being the boat itself, not landing in Denmark (see p.217). Helsingborg also has some happening **clubs** for a young crowd.

Cafés and restaurants

Bunker Bar, near the far end of North Harbour, just 50m from *Sill & Mackerella* (see below). Very crowded, for both lunch and dinner.

Café Annorledes, Södra Storgatan 15. A friendly café with a subdued 1950s atmosphere. Still popular, but no longer quite the best place for cakes. Mon–Fri 9am–6pm, Sat 10am–4pm.

Le Cardinal, Södra Kyrkogatan 9. A meat-oriented restaurant, part of a nightclub establishment (see p.219). The speciality here is char-grilled steaks at 150kr; three-course specials are also available at the same price. 6pm–1am.

Cyber Space Cafe, Karlsgatan 9 (☎042/21 13 01). Plenty of screens – and espresso to keep you hyper – await here. There's no minimum charge; computer use is charged by the minute, with 30min costing around 25kr. Daily 10am–10pm.

Ebba's Fik, Bruksgatan 20 (☎042/28 14 40). The most fun café in town: its owners have collected an amazing jumble of 1950s and 1960s furnishings, with the jukebox belting out mambo, bebop and jive. It's not kitsch, though every detail of the era – from crockery to menu board – is here. The cakes are very good. At the back is a bookshop and bric-a-brac store, both stocking items that 30- and 40-somethings will have grown up with.

Fahlmans, Stortorget. This bakery/café has been serving elaborate cakes and pastries since 1914 and is *the* place for decadent apple meringue pie – a meal in itself. Also try the coconut and marzipan confections or filling sandwiches at this Helsingborg classic.

Grafitti, Knutpunkten. On the first floor. The ideal place if you're hungry, skint and it's past 9pm. Generously filled baked potatoes and baguettes, with a young, sometimes rowdy crowd.

Hotel Nouveau Dining Room, Gasverksgatan 11 (☎042/18 53 90, fax 14 08 85). Exceptional breakfasts (70kr) make it worth coming here: a massive range of fresh breads, fish, patés and jams (including ones suitable for diabetics), all served in relaxing surroundings.

Louise Cafe, Norra Strandgatan 11. Not particularly atmospheric and not at all trendy, this place offers very good value *bruschetta*, ciabattas and a vast range of fresh salads from 25–40kr. Mon-Fri 10am–6pm, Sat 10am–2pm

K & Co, Nedre Långwinkelsgatan. Try here first – the best of the laid-back style cafés in town. Very friendly, serving great muffins, cakes and filling ciabattas and baguettes.

Oasen, Bruksgatan 25 (☎042/12 80 74). A packed-out, excellent fondue restaurant with meat, fish, cheese-and-red-wine or oriental fondues (150kr). Booking always necessary as it tends to get packed out.; Tues–Sat 6pm–midnight, Sun 5–10pm.

Olsoní's Skafferi, Mariagatan 6 (☎042/14 07 80). Right outside the front of the St Maria Church. Despite its Swedish name, this is the very best Italian restaurant in town right outside the front. Not a pizza in sight: they simply offer wonderfully prepared fish, meat and pasta dishes. There's zabaglione to drool over. June–Aug daily 10am–10.30pm, Sept–May Mon–Wed 10am–7pm & Sat 10am–10.30pm.

Oscar's, Sundstorget (☎042/11 25 21). At the harbour. The simple decor belies how posh and expensive this fish restaurant is. Best suited to those with expense accounts. Mon–Sat 6–11pm.

Pålsjökrog (☎042/14 97 30). Attached to the old bathhouse, Pålsjöbaden, 2km north of the centre. This fine place is run by an architect, who designed it to feel like a Swedish country eating-house. With traditional, well-presented Swedish food, it's a place for special occasions. Main courses 150kr.

Signe Bergqvist, Drottininggatan. Dating from 1889, this *konditori* is the oldest in town, but far less busy than *Fahlmans* (see opposite) and not quite as good.

Sill & Mackerella, at the end of the North Harbour, as far as you can walk, past the style bars. This simple-looking place – the one with the white roof – is excellent for fresh fish dishes.

Utposten, Stortorget 17 (☎042/28 15 50). Beneath the post office at the steps to *kärnen*. Very stylish decor – a pleasing mix of rustic and industrial – at this great, varied Swedish restaurant. Try the delicate and filling seafood-and-fresh-salmon stew at 89kr. Two courses 140kr. Mon–Fri 5pm–1am Sat noon–2am.

Vegeriet, Järnvägsgatan 25 (☎042/24 03 03). Opposite Knutpunkten. A good vegetarian café, with simple food that's very good value. There's an elaborate menu, including a range of starters, and a small wine list. Hot dishes cost 59–110kr. Mon–Wed 11.30am–7pm, Thurs–Sat 11.30am–10pm.

Wayne's, Stortorget. One of the hippest cafés *not* at the harbour, this place is housed within a grand old building on the main square. The coffee's great, though the cakes can look better than they taste. A relaxed spot, well worth a visit.

Bars and clubs

Mostly opened in 1999, the glamorous North Harbour **bars** are seen more as places for wine and beer drinking than as restaurants, though they do serve food – along new-European lines, with varying specializations. All located at ground level in the area's upmarket apartment buildings, the bars share a smart, casual clientele of 20- to 40-somethings, in designer-industrial surroundings. At the northern end of the harbour, you'll find *Bunker Bar* and *Sill & Mackerella*, two good-value eating places (see "Cafés and restaurants", p.218).

Le Cardinal, Södra Kyrkogatan 9. The first floor is a popular disco, the second a quieter piano lounge with roulette (9.30pm–3am). Cover charge is 70kr on Sat, 60kr other nights. Age limit for nightclub is 25 (the clientele are mostly in their 30s and 40s). There's also a restaurant here (see p.218).

Jazz Clubben, Nedre Långvinkelsgatan 22. Sweden's biggest jazz club. Live sessions, not just jazz in its various forms, but also blues and Irish folk. Well worth a visit. Open Wed, Fri & Sat evenings.

Marina, Kungstorget 6. At *Marina Plaza*, a hotel by the harbour. A nightclub with a Continental atmosphere; minimum age 24. Gets very crowded. Thurs–Sat 10pm–3am.

OZ emellan, North Harbour. (☎042/146161). The first bar you encounter as you walk north from Hamn Torget along the harbour. Serves light meals and à la carte meat, fish and vegetarian dishes. Noon–1am.

Piren, Hamn Torget. At the harbour, opposite Sundsbussarna, in the old black wooden building that was once the train station. A café by day, it comes alive at night, when it's a club with a 1970s student-dive atmosphere. Very popular.

Sailor's Inn, Kungstorget 6. Part of the *Marina Plaza* hotel at the harbour. A post-dinner, pre-disco drinking spot – extremely popular, too. Mon–Wed 3pm–midnight, Thurs & Fri 3pm–1am, Sat 2pm–1am.

Stones Coffee & Bar, North Harbour. Next door to *OZ emellan*, and cheaper, with Greek salad, Thai chicken, and ciabattas, *panini* or baguettes (49kr). Daily 11am till late.

Telegrafen, Norra Storgatan 14. A long-term favourite, this cosy bar and restaurant is full of oddities such as stuffed animals wearing sunglasses. Lively atmosphere; good lunches at 52kr. Daily 11.30am–midnight.

Tivoli, Hamn Torget. Next door to *Piren* (see above), in the main part of the old train station. A club with lots of concerts, dances and events, and theme nights such as "Boogie Fever 1970s". There's an attached restaurant, *Vinyl Baren*, filled with red vinyl bench seats.

Gay Helsingborg

Gay life in Helsingborg revolves around the RFSL-run **Gay centre** at Pålsgatan 1 (☎042/12 35 32), close to the concert hall, ten minutes' walk from Knutpunkten. Inside, there's a welcoming **café** (Mon–Fri 10am–5pm) and a **pub** (Fri 10am–2am). There's also a **disco** night called *Empire* on alternate Saturdays (11pm–3am; 40kr for RFSL members, or 80kr for membership and entry).

Listings

Airport The nearest airport is at Ängelholm, 30km north of town (☎0431/45 80 00); for domestic departures take the bus from Knutpunkten (1hr before flight departure). For international services, you'll need to use Copenhagen's Kastrup airport (☎00945/32 31 32 31) – take the Kustlinjen bus from Knutpunkten (a 2hr journey).

Buses The daily bus for Stockholm leaves from Knutpunkten; buy tickets on the bus. For the daily Gothenburg buses, tickets must be bought from the bus information section at the train booking office.

Car rental Avis, Garnisonsgatan 2 (☎042/15 70 80); Budget, Gustav Adolfsgatan 47 (☎042/12 50 40); Europcar, Muskötgatan 1 (☎042/17 01 15); Hertz, Bergavägen 4 (☎042/17 25 40).

Exchange Forex, on the first floor of Knutpunkten or at Järnvägsgatan 13 (June–Aug 7am–9pm; Sept–May 8am–9pm); maximum 20kr fee.

Ferries See the "Ferries to Helsingør" box, p.217, for details.

Left luggage Lockers at Knutpunkten (20kr) and at the Sundsbussarna terminal (5kr).

Pharmacy Björnen, Drottninggatan 14 (☎042/12 07 25); Apotek Kärnen, at the main entrance of the hospital (☎042/14 82 02; Mon–Fri 8.30am–9pm, Sat 4–9pm, Sun 11am–9pm).

Post office Stortorget 17 (Mon–Fri 9am–6pm, Sat 10am–1pm). You can exchange money here (35kr per transaction).

Taxis. Taxi Helsingborg (☎042/18 02 00); Alltaxi (☎042/21 97 00).

Trains Tickets for the Pågatåg trains from Knutpunkten are bought from an automatic machine on the platform; international rail passes are valid.

Around Helsingborg: Råå, Ven and Ramlösa Spa

It's just 7km south of Helsingborg to the pretty, if sleepy, fishing village of **RÅÅ**. To get there, take city bus #1 (direction Landskrona/Rydebäck) from the Rådhus, or ride along the cycle lanes heading south out of town on Malmöleden. Råå's main street, **Rååvagen**, is a subdued place. Signs indicate the twelfth-century **Raus kyrka** (left up Lybecksgatan, over the highway and along Rausvägen), but it's nothing special. The village's main attraction is its **harbour**, dense with boat masts (ferries leave from here to Ven; see p.221); it's uncommercialized and more attractive than many of its counterparts. The **Maritime Museum** here is run by a group of Råå's residents and displays a comprehensive collection of seafaring artefacts. A fascinating, although somewhat stomach-churning, sight at the harbour is that of eel sorting: the squirming creatures are slopped into a box, appropriately shaped like a coffin, with a trap door at one end through which they slide, to be separated into sizes by fishermen using claw-shaped pincers.

Places to **stay** are limited to *Råå Camping Site* (☎042/10 76 80, fax 26 10 10), advertised as being "waterfront" – it is, but its most obvious views are not of the sea but Helsingborg's industrial smog, to the north. Around the museum are a couple of places to **eat**. Next door to the museum is the long-established *Råå Wärdshus*, serving pricey fish dishes at around 150kr, with lighter snacks and lots of salad choices for around 50kr. To the left as you face the front of the museum, *Råå Hamnservering* (daily 8.30am–midnight) is the best bet for a less expensive

---

TYCHO BRAHE

The son of a Danish nobleman, **Tycho Brahe** (1546–1601) began studying **astronomy** at the University of Wittenberg (though he never completed a degree). Among other discoveries, he found a star which he proved lay beyond the moon, contradicting Aristotle's hitherto-accepted theory that nothing beyond the moon could move. Brahe was known for his irascible nature; the tip of his nose was cut off in a duel following one of his fits of rage, and he spent the rest of his life with an artificial nose made of gold. He worked in Ven for over twenty years, but in 1597, after a row with the king, he left Sweden and settled in Prague, where he remained till his death.

---

lunch. The lunch buffet at 58kr is excellent and, unlike at the *Wärdhus*, which faces inland, here you get plenty of sea views; the restaurant is built on the pier and has water on three sides.

Ven
Little ferries regularly make the 35-minute trip from Råå to the tiny island of **VEN** (9.30am–5.30pm; every 2hr). With a population of about 350, Ven, apart from being scenic, is where the celebrated and impossibly temperamental astronomer **Tycho Brahe** built his **observatory** in the sixteenth century. Funded by Frederick II, the building was by all accounts an exquisite Dutch Renaissance-style creation; unfortunately, hardly any of it's left. The sights here are all to do with Brahe – a museum, the remains of his observatory, and his attractive, now partly restored, garden.

Ramlösa Spa
The Pågatåg **train** stops at **RAMLÖSA**, just three minutes from Helsingborg and a kilometre or so northeast of Råå, on its way to Malmö. Ramlösa's **Brunnspark** offers the chance for a delightful wander of an hour or so, beneath huge horse-chestnut trees and among the shocking-pink rhododendrons of early summer. This nineteenth-century park is also full of elegant, wooden pavilions with carved verandahs and balconies; the buildings were originally constructed as accommodation for the wealthy characters who came to take the waters here. It all began in 1707, when a health spa was set up in the park by Dr Johan Döbelius after he discovered two springs here, one high in iron, the other in calcium. People flocked to the spot, apparently undeterred by the unappealing orange colour of the iron-filled water in which they had to douse themselves. Rather more appetizing are the waffles served down by the Water Pavilion (May–Aug), from where you can retrace the shady "Philosophical walk", a beautiful half-hour stroll through the park – as encouraged by the doctor. The guests at the spa clearly took time out from philosophizing, for they carved their names on the trees along here in a seemingly acceptable bout of nineteenth-century vandalism.

Lund

"There is a very tangible Lund spirit – those with it have... an ironic distance to everything, including themselves and Lund, a barb to deflate pompous self-importance," wrote the Swedish essayist Jan Mårtensson. His compatriot, poet Peter Ortman, for his part once described what he termed "Lund syndrome": "a mix of paranoia, exhibitionism and megalomania". Whatever it is about the place, there is indeed a special spirit to LUND – a sense of tolerance (it's more relaxed than other Swedish cities), and a belief that people should be judged by what they do, not by their money.

A few kilometres inland and 54km south of Helsingborg, Lund's reputation as a glorious old **university city** is well founded. An ocean of bikes, some of them ancient, is the first image to greet you at the train station, and like Oxford in England – with which Lund is usually (aptly) compared – there is a bohemian, laid-back eccentricity in the air. With its justly revered twelfth-century Romanesque **cathedral**, its medieval streets lined with a variety of architectural styles, and its wealth of cafés and restaurants, Lund is an enchanting little city that could well captivate you for a couple of days. It also has a wide range of **museums** that may seem daunting in their scope, but with the exception of two excellent ones, they are largely of minority interest and can be bypassed. Cultural attractions aside, it is the mix of architectural grandeur and the buzz of student life that lends Lund its unique charm, distinctive among Swedish cities. Lund does lose much of its atmosphere during the summer months, though, when the students have left for vacation, and a number of its cafés and bars close until they return.

Arrival, information and accommodation

Trains arrive at the western edge of the centre. **Buses** use the station south of Mårtenstorget, with many also stopping outside the train station. Flying into Sturup **airport**, located to the east of Malmö, you can catch the hourly Flygbuss into the centre (Mon–Fri 5.30am–7.30pm, Sat 6.30am–5.30pm; 40min; 65kr).

From the train station, the centre is two minutes' walk away, and everything of interest is within easy reach, with all the sights no more than ten minutes' walk away. The **tourist office** is at Kyrkogatan 11, opposite the Domkyrkan (May & Sept Mon–Fri 10am–5pm, Sat 10am–2pm; June–Aug Mon–Fri 10am–6pm, Sat & Sun 10am–2pm; Oct–April Mon–Fri 10am–5pm; ☎046/35 50 40, fax 12 59 63, *bitte.saur@lund.se*); they can provide maps and copies of *I Lund*, a monthly diary of events with museum and exhibition listings (from June to August it's bilingual, with English listings).

You can **rent a bike** at Harry's *Cykelaffar*, Banvaktsgatan 2 (☎046/211 69 46; Mon–Fri 9am–6pm; 90kr a day); for weekend use you'll have to pay to keep the bike until the following Monday, when the shop reopens. The frequent sales of military bikes, most of which take place in Clemenstorget (a couple of minutes' walk northwest of the tourist office), offer excellent value (a typical price is 300kr), particularly if you plan to do a lot of cycling around the region. Large, sturdy and khaki green, these bikes are almost indestructible; you can always sell them back once you're finished with them.

There is a decent range of **accommodation** on offer in Lund – nearly all of it in the centre. The tourist office will book **private rooms** for 175kr per person, plus a 50kr booking fee. You may be surprised at the sight of the town's STF **youth hostel**, *Tåget,* housed in the carriages of a 1940s train at Vävaregatan 22, through the tunnel behind the train station (☎046/14 28 20, fax 32 05 68; 110kr). The novelty soon wears off, however, when you're crammed in three-tier bunks with rope hoists to help pull yourself up; furthermore, the kitchens and showers are pretty basic. An alternative is the *La Strada* hostel, at Brunnshögsvägen (☎046/32 32 51, fax 30 39 31; 130kr, ①). It's a bit far from the centre, though: take bus #4 from west of Martens Torget to Klosterängsvägen, a four-kilometre trip, then follow the bicycle track under the motorway for 1km. Back in town, there's a range of **hotels**, most of which have good summer reductions.

Hotels

Ahlström, Skomakaregatan 3, just south of the Domkyrkan (☎046/211 01 74). Old-fashioned, very central cheapie with the option of en-suite rooms. Closed June to mid-Aug. ②.

Concordia, Stålbrogatan 1 (☎046/13 50 50, fax 13 74 22). A couple of streets southwest of Stortorget. A very homely hotel with attentive service, though rather plain inside. It boasts a sauna, a pleasant courtyard area and parking. Just across the street, August Strindberg spent his time trying in vain to produce gold before his rather more successful writing career took off. ④/③.

The Grand, Bantorget 1 (☎046/280 61 00, fax 046/280 61 50). A grand nineteenth-century hotel, this pink-sandstone edifice straddles an entire side of a small, stately and central square. Without any of the pomp associated with premier hotels, the bedrooms are comfortable and well decorated. The breakfast buffet in the lovely dining room is enormous. ⑥/③.

Petri Pumpa, St Petri Kyrkogatan 7 (☎046/13 55 19, fax 13 56 71). An exclusive hotel, now without its nationally-renowed restaurant, which has moved to the *Savoy* in Malmö, leaving the *Petri Pumpa* bar only. ⑤/③.

The Town

Lund is a wonderful town to just wander around, its cobbled streets festooned with climbing roses. To help get your bearings, it's worth noting that the main thoroughfare changes its name several times. In the centre, it's called Kyrkogatan; to the north, Bredgatan (there's no need to venture further north than the pretty old brick house at no. 16); to the south, Stora Södergatan. **Lundagård** (the city's academic heart), the **Domkyrkan** (its ecclesiastical centre), and **Stortorget** (the people's square) are all along this route. Lund's crowning glory is its cathedral; just 100m north of Stortorget, and only a short walk east from the station, the Domkyrkan is the obvious place to begin.

The Domkyrkan

The magnificent **Domkyrkan** (Mon, Tues & Fri 8am–6pm, Wed & Thurs 8am–7.15pm, Sat 9.30am–5pm, Sun 9.30am–7.30pm; guided tours 3pm, free) is built of storm-cloud charcoal and white stone, giving it an imposing monochrome appearance. Before going inside, have a look round the back of the building; on the way there, you'll notice the grotesque animal and bird gargoyles over the side entrances, their features blunted by eight centuries of weathering. At the very back, the most beautiful part of the exterior, the three-storey **apse** above the crypt, is revealed, crowned with an exquisite gallery.

The majestic **interior** is surprisingly unadorned, an elegant mass of watery-grey, ribbed stone arches and stone-flagged flooring. One of the world's finest masterpieces of Romanesque architecture, the cathedral was built in the twelfth century when Lund became the first independent archbishopric in Scandinavia, laying the foundation for a period of wealth and eminence that lasted until the advent of Protestantism. There are several striking features to admire, such as the elaborately carved fourteenth-century choir stalls depicting Old Testament scenes, and the grotesque carvings hidden beneath the seats. The most vividly coloured feature is just to the left of the entrance, an amazing **astronomical clock** dating from the 1440s, which shows hours, days, weeks and the courses

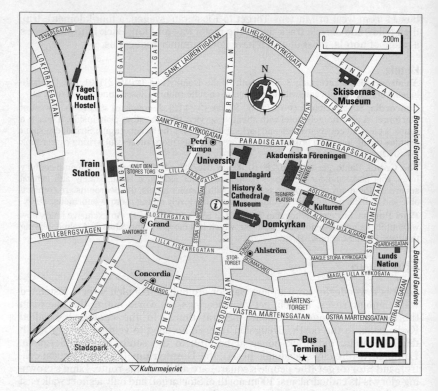

of the sun and moon in the zodiac. Each day at noon and 3pm, the clock also reveals its ecclesiastical Punch-and-Judy show, as two knights pop out and clash swords as many times as the clock strikes, followed by little mechanical doors opening to trumpet-blowing heralds and the Three Wise Men trundling slowly to the Virgin Mary.

The dimly lit and dramatic **crypt**, beneath the apse, has been left almost untouched since the twelfth century, and should not be missed. Here, the thick smattering of what look like tombstones is really comprised of memorial slabs, brought down to the crypt from just above; but there is one actual tomb – that of Birger Gunnarsson, Lund's last archbishop. A short man from a poor family, Gunnarsson chose the principal altar-facing position for his tomb, dictating that his stone effigy above it should be tall and regal. Two **pillars** here are gripped by stone figures – one of a man, another of a woman and child. Local legend has it that Finn the Giant built the cathedral for St Lawrence; in return, unless the saint could guess his name, Finn wanted the sun, the moon, or the saint's eyes. Lawrence was just preparing to end his days in blindness when he heard Finn's wife boasting to her baby, "Soon Father Finn will bring some eyes for you to play with." The relieved saint rushed to Finn declaring the name. The livid giant, his wife and child rushed to the crypt to pull down the columns, and were instantly turned to stone. Even without the fable, the column-hugging figures are fascinating to view.

Around the Domkyrkan: museums

Just behind the cathedral, the **History and Cathedral Museum**, on Sandgatan (Tues–Fri 11am–1pm; free), is for the most part rather dull unless you have specialist interests in ecclesiastical history. The statues from Scånian churches, in the medieval exhibition, deserve a look though, mainly because of the way they are arranged – a mass of Jesuses and Marys bunched together in groups. The crowd of Jesuses hanging on crosses have an ominousness worthy of Hitchcock, while in the next room all the Madonnas are paired off with the baby Jesuses.

A few minutes' walk north, on Tegnerplatsen, is the town's best museum, **Kulturen** (May–Sept daily 11am–5pm, Thurs till 9pm; Oct–April daily noon–4pm, Thurs till 9pm; 40kr). It's easy to spend the best part of a day just wandering around this privately owned open-air museum, a virtual town of perfectly preserved cottages, farms, merchants' houses, gardens and even churches, brought from seven Swedish regions and encompassing as many centuries. The displays don't have English translations, though you can buy a guidebook in English covering all the exhibits (100kr).

Walking further north from the square along Sankt Annegatan, it's worth stopping on the corner of Tomegapsgatan to have a look at Larsson's Sweet Shop (May–Sept noon–5pm); opened in 1814, it still has all its original fittings and sells nineteenth-century-style confections. Continuing north along Sandgatan, and then taking a right onto Finngatan, you'll soon find another stimulating museum, **Skissernas Museum**, Finngatan 2 (Museum of Sketches; Tues–Sat noon–4pm, Sun 1–5pm; free; 30kr for special exhibitions). Inside is a fascinating collection of preliminary sketches and original full-scale models of works of art from around the world. One room is full of work by all the major Swedish artists, while in the international room are sketches by Chagall, Matisse, Leger, Miro and Dufy; the best-known sculptural sketches here are by Picasso and Henry Moore. Outside, the sculptures on display include preliminary versions of pieces found in town squares all over Sweden.

Botanical Gardens

An antidote to museum fatigue, the **Botanical Gardens** are as much a venue for picnicking and chilling out as a botanical experience (mid-May to mid-Sept 6am–9.30pm; mid-Sept to mid-May 6am–8pm, greenhouses noon–3pm). From Finngatan, the gardens are a few minutes' stroll away; head southeast down to the end of the street, then turn left into Pålsjövägen and right into Olshögsvägen. The greenhouses and rock gardens are the best areas to view; the rarest sights here are the Far Eastern paper-mulberry trees and the huge tulip trees – part of the same family as magnolias – with masses of flowers in June.

Eating, drinking and nightlife

There are plenty of great places to eat and drink in Lund, many of them associated with the university: certain **coffee houses** are institutions with the students, and a number of the better **restaurants** are attached to student bodies or museums. This student connection keeps prices low, especially for beer; however, Lund also boasts some celebrated restaurants that are so expensive only those with business accounts can afford them. During the past couple of years, the range of establishments has been complemented by a rash of new, very appealing cafés which have opened up along Kyrkogatan, close to the Domkyrkan.

For provisions, the **market** at Mårtenstorget, *Saluhallen*, sells a range of fish, cheeses and meats, including Lund's own tasty speciality sausage, Knake. Next door to the *Espresso House* (see below) on Sankt Petri Kyrkogata, *Widerbergs Charkuteri* is a long-established food shop, brimming with cooked meats and baguettes for the ultimate picnic, while *Bentsons Ost*, Klostergatan 9, is a must for cheese lovers (Mon–Fri 9.30am–6pm, Sat 9.30am–2pm).

When it comes to **nightlife**, it's worth knowing that the university is divided into "Nations", or colleges, each named after different geographical areas of Sweden and with its own strong identity. Each nation has its own bar that's active two nights a week, and there are also regular discos. Perhaps unsurprisingly, *Lund Nation*, based in the big red-brick house on Agardhsgatan, is the biggest, with an inexpensive bar. *Småland's Nation* on Kastanjatan, off Mortenstorget, is the hippest, most left-wing nation. Both are known for supporting music, hosting regular gigs by all the best indie bands. Another lively place on the alternative music scene is the bright lilac-painted **Mejeriet** at the end of Stora Södergatan (daily 9am–5pm), the street running south from the main square. Converted into a music and cultural centre in the 1970s, this one-hundred-year-old former dairy has a **concert hall**, attracting artists as diverse as Iggy Pop and the Bulgarian Women's Choir; and an **art-house cinema** (concert information on ☎046/12 38 11, cinema details on ☎046/14 38 13). Its stylish café, whose walls are decorated with 1950s vacuum cleaners, serves fragrant suppers and wonderful chocolate cake.

Cafés and restaurants

Bantorget 9, Bantorget 9. A very chic restaurant within rumbling distance of the railway track, with old, painted ceilings; an established haven for gourmets, the place has a Swedish-international menu. It's expensive, but you can get away with one course, had as a bar meal, for under 100kr. Mon–Fri 11.30am–2pm & 6–11pm, Sat 6pm–midnight.

Café Ariman, Kungsgatan. Attached to the Nordic Law Department, a striking red-brick building. This deliberately shabby place is a classic left-wing coffee house and a place for wannabe writers – posey beards, ponytails and blond dreadlocks predominate. Cheap snacks and coffee. Mon–Fri 11am–6pm, Sat 11am–4pm, Sun 1–5pm. Closed Sun outside summer.

Café Baguette, Grönegatan. A simple, Mediterranean-style central café serving mostly Greek food, with baguettes from 20kr, and fish- and meat-based meals for 70–110kr. Mon–Thurs 11am–midnight, Fri & Sat 11am–1am, Sun noon–10pm.

Café Borgen, at the Botanical Gardens. A pleasant café, with a basic selection of food, in a castellated building overlooking the lily pond. June–Aug daily 10am–6pm.

Café Credo, behind the cathedral. This 500-year-old refectory serves coffee and snacks; though the food's nothing special, the very peaceful setting is. Tues–Fri 9am–5.30pm, Sat 10am–3pm.

Café Stortorget, Stortorget. Housed in a National Romantic-style building that was formerly a bank, this place has walls covered with theatrical black-and-white shots of musicians and actors. A large focaccia with a crab-meat, cheese or meat filling costs 48kr.

Conditori Lundagård, Kyrkogatan. *The* classic student *konditori*. A delightful institution with excellent caricatures of professors adorning the walls. Justly famous for its apple meringue pie.

Espresso House, Sankt Petri Kyrkogata 5. Opposite the library. The first of a breed of stylish, mellow coffee houses, this one serves a big range of delicious flavoured coffees for 13–26kr, and bagels, cakes and baguettes. There's a branch at Stora Grabrodersgatan, open similar hours. Mon–Sat 9am–7pm, Sun 10am–7pm.

Fellini, opposite train station (☎046/13 80 20). Stylish and popular Italian restaurant. All chrome and stripped wood. Two-course meals for 135kr. Mon–Thurs 11.30am–midnight, Fri & Sat till 2am, Sun till 10pm.

Gloria's, Sankt Petri Kyrkogata, near the *Espresso House*. Serving American food, *Gloria's* is very popular with students and tourists of all ages. Local bands play Friday and Saturday nights. There's a big, lively garden area at the back. Mon 11.30am–midnight, Tues–Thurs 11.30am–1am, Fri & Sat 11.30am–2am, Sun 1pm–midnight.

Grand Hotel restaurant, Bantorget 1. Part of the *Grand Hotel* (see p.223). Since the flight of *Petri Pumpa* to Malmö, Lund's got its own back on the glamorous restaurant front by gaining revered chef Mats Petersson from Malmö's *Kocksa Krogen* to the hotel restaurant.

Hemma Hos Greken, Sandgatan (☎046/32 44 33). A cheap Greek restaurant with basic decor in the basement of an old, ornate brick house. Serves tzatziki and bread for 25kr, along with non-Greek dishes, each for 35–40kr. Mon–Fri 10am–4pm, Sat 11am–3pm.

I-Internet Cafe, Paradisgatan 1. Housed in an eighteenth-century former stable set in a charming cobbled courtyard, this place lets you catch up on your emails (Internet use 55kr per hour, charged by the minute), in surroundings so pleasant they don't quite seem apt. If you're in town for a week or more, or need to use the Internet a lot, it's worth taking out membership. Coffee and snacks are pretty simple. Mon–Fri 11am–1am, Sat & Sun noon–1am.

Kulturen just in front of the Kulturen museum. Beneath a giant copper beech and facing ancient rune stones, this busy café, bar and restaurant attracts a 20- to 30-something crowd who enjoy the cheap beer (28kr). A great place to just watch people – sometimes for extended periods, as the service can be less than speedy. There's a good lunch with a vegetarian option (59kr). Mon–Wed 11.30am–1am, Thurs–Sat till 2am, Sun noon–6pm.

Lundia, Knutdenstorestorg. Serves good lunches in ugly, 1980s surroundings. Also a nightclub (see below). Mon–Thurs 11.30am–midnight, Fri & Sat 11.30am–1am, Sun 1–10pm.

Mondo, corner of Sankt Petri Kyrkogatan and Kyrkogatan. In a quaint, beamed house, this newcomer to the café scene serves bagels, cheesecake and brownies. The large baguettes are good value. Mon–Fri 8am–8pm, Sat 9am–7pm, Sun 10am–7pm.

Restaurant Staket, Stora Södergatan. Just down from Stortorget. A step-gabled vaulted house built in 1570 plays host to this place specializing in meat dishes – seemingly every type of steak can be had, each for 140–175kr. Mon–Thurs & Sun 11am–11pm, Fri & Sat to midnight.

Sandkakan Cafe, Sandgatan 14. For cheap baguettes, toast and baked potatoes – not really for atmosphere. Mon–Thurs 9.30am–6pm, Fri 9.30am–5pm

Stadspark Café, in the popular Stadspark at the end of Nygatan. This old wooden pavilion, fronted by a sea of white plastic garden furniture, is busy with families munching on snacks. Big baguettes will fill you up for 35–40kr.

Tegners Terass, in the building of the same name next to Akademiska Föreningen, the student union. Forget any preconceptions about student cafés being tatty, stale sandwich bars. Lunch for 55kr (49kr with student card) is self-service: you eat as much as you like from a delicious spread. Daily 11.30am–2.30pm.

Bars and clubs

Easy, in the Tegners Terass building next to the student union. A student nightclub (free entry till midnight, then 20kr) with its own restaurant. To get in, you'll simply need to be aged over 23, or be over 18 and have a student card. Restaurant Thurs 7pm–3am, nightclub Thurs 7pm–3am.

John Bull Pub, Bantorget, adjacent to *Grand Hotel*. Shabby, traditional English-style pub, with Art Nouveau details on the exterior.

Lundia, Knutdenstorestorg. This club fills with tourists, though the atmosphere is rather soulless. Wed–Sat 11pm–3am.

Palladium, Stora Södergatan 13 (☎046/211 66 60, fax 12 20 90). The newest, hip place just a few steps south of Stortorget, playing host to events and concerts. The club here hosts a soul night every Thursday (minimum age 20). Huge drinks list (shots are 39kr, cocktails 53kr). Its *News Cafe* has buffets with American and Asian fare, and shellfish, all very reasonably priced for late night eats. Mon, Wed & Thurs 11am–11pm, Tues 11am–1am, Fri & Sat 11am-3am.

Petri Pumpa Bar, next to *Gloria's*. A glamorous place – the sort of bar that has roasted hazelnuts rather than peanuts. Serves beer – at an imported French bar – and excellent Continental lunches (74kr).

Listings

Buses Information on local and regional buses on ☎020/567 567.

Car rental Avis, Byggmästaregatan 11 (☎046/14 50 30); Budget, Banggatan 13 (☎046/211 34 67); Europcar, Malmövägen Höjebro (☎046/19 79 39); Hertz, Winstrupsgatan 8 (☎046/30 60 12).

Currency exchange Forex, Bangatan 8 (☎046/32 34 10). Daily 8am–9pm.

Medical treatment University Hospital, Getingevägen 4. ☎046/17 10 00.

Police Byggmästaregatan 1. ☎046/16 50 00.

Post Office Knut den Stores Torg 2 (☎046/10 99 00). June and late Aug Mon–Fri 8am–6pm, Sat 10am–2pm; July to mid-Aug Mon–Fri 9am–6pm, Sat 10am–1pm.

Taxis Minitaxi (☎046/12 12 12); Taxi Skåne (☎046/33 03 30); Taxi Kunren (☎046/15 01 60).

Malmö

Founded in the late thirteenth century, **MALMÖ** was once Denmark's second most important city, after Copenhagen. The high density of herring in the sea off the Malmö coast – it was said that the fish could be scooped straight out with a trowel – brought ambitious German merchants flocking to the city; the striking fourteenth-century St Petri kyrka in the city centre is heavily influenced by German styles. Eric of Pomerania gave Malmö its most significant medieval boost, when, in the fifteenth century, he built the castle, endowed with its own mint, and gave Malmö its own flag – the gold-and-red griffin of his own family crest. It wasn't until the Swedish king Karl X marched his armies across the frozen Öresund to within striking distance of Copenhagen in 1658 that the Danes were forced into handing back the counties of Skåne, Blekinge and Bohuslän to the Swedes. For Malmö, too far from its own (uninterested) capital, this meant a period of stagnation, cut off from nearby Copenhagen. Not until the full thrust of industrialization, triggered by the tobacco merchant Frans Suell's enlargement of the harbour in 1775 (his jaunty bronze likeness, on Norra Vallgatan opposite the train station, overlooks his handiwork), did Malmö begin its dramatic commercial recovery. In 1840, boats began regular trips to Copenhagen, and Malmö's great Kockums shipyard was opened; limestone quarrying, too, became big business here in the nineteenth century.

Today, Malmö's attractive medieval centre, a myriad of cobbled and mainly pedestrianized streets, full of busy restaurants and bars, gives a misleading impression of economic wellbeing. In reality, the city has been facing commercial **crisis** after a series of economic miscalculations, which included investing heavily in the shipping industry just at the time of its great decline in the 1970s. These mistakes have stripped Malmö, Sweden's third city, of its wealth, a fact apparent from the carcasses of industry left scattered around its environs. Desperate mea-

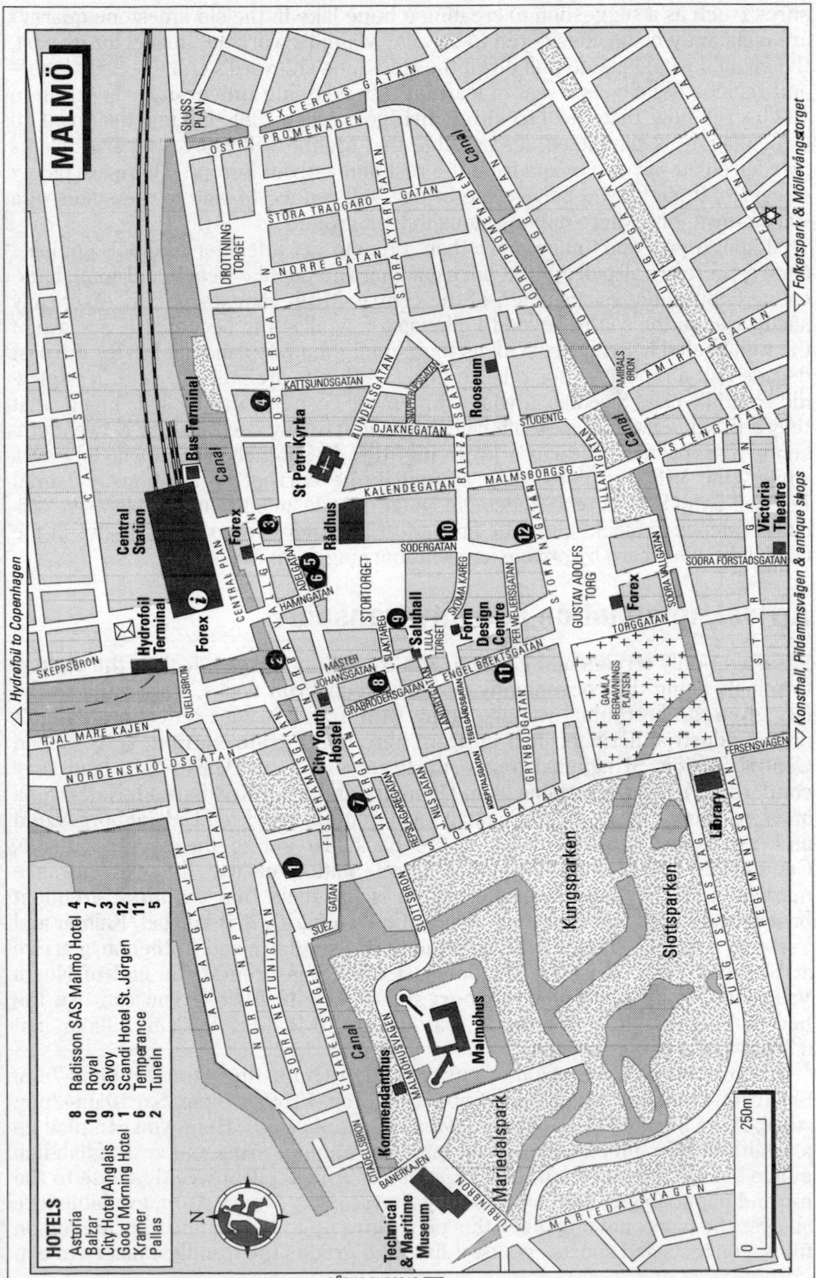

MALMÖ

◁ Hydrofoil to Copenhagen

△ Folketspark & Möllevångstorget

▷ Konsthall, Pildammsvägen & antique shops

△ Öresund bridge

HOTELS

Astoria	8
Balzar	10
City Hotel Anglais	9
Good Morning Hotel	1
Kramer	6
Pallas	2
Radisson SAS Malmö Hotel	4
Royal	7
Savoy	3
Scandi Hotel St. Jörgen	12
Temperance	11
Tuneln	5

N

250m

Central Station
Bus Terminal
Hydrofoil Terminal
Forex
St Petri Kyrka
Rådhus
Rooseum
Stortorget
Saluhall
Form Design Centre
City Youth Hostel
Gustav Adolfs Torg
Victoria Theatre
Gamla Begravnings Platsen
Kungsparken
Slottsparken
Malmöhus
Kommendanthus
Mariedalspark
Technical & Maritime Museum
Library

SLUSS PLAN
EXCERCIS GATAN
ÖSTRA PROMENADEN
STORA TRÄDGÅRDS GATAN
DROTTNING TORGET
NORRE GATAN
STORA KVARN GATAN
KATTSUNDSGATAN
DJAKNEGATAN
RUNDELSGATAN
KALENDEGATAN
BALTZARSGATAN
MALMSBORGSG
STUDENTG
SÖDERGATAN
ÖSTERGATAN
HAMNGATAN
MÄSTER JOHANSGATAN
SLAKTARG
BRÄDERNAS GATAN
ULLA KÄRE
ULLA TORGET
PER WEIJERSGATAN
ENGELBREKTSGATAN
TEGELGÅRDSGATAN
STORA NYGATAN
SKOMAKAREG
SÖDRA FÖRSTADSGATAN
TORGGATAN
FERSENSVÄGEN
GRYNBODGATAN
NILS GATAN
VÄSTERGATAN
REPSLAGAREGATAN
SLOTTSGATAN
FISKTÅNGSGATAN
ÖRBY GATAN
NORRA VALLGATAN
SÖDRA VALLGATAN
SKEPPSBRON
HJALMARE KAJEN
NORDENSKIOLDSGATAN
SUELLSBRON
BASSÄNG KAJEN
NORRA NEPTUNIGATAN
SÖDRA NEPTUNIGATAN
SÜEZ GATAN
CITADELLSVÄGEN
MALMÖHUSVÄGEN
BANERKAJEN
TURBINGRÄND
MARIEDALSVÄGEN
KUNG OSCARS VÄG
REGEMENTSGATAN
CARLSGATAN
CENTRAL PLAN
Canal
AMIRALS BRON
AMIRALSGATAN
KAPTENSG
ST PÅLS GATAN
GEORG GATAN

sures (such as a suggestion to creating a huge lake in the old limestone quarry) are constantly being considered to salvage Malmö's worn-out image; for its part, the council would like to pull down the Kockums shipyard's crane – a city icon – and refocus the city as a seat of learning (its fledgling **university** was set up in 1998). Yet now that the **Öresund bridge** (see p.238), linking the town to Copenhagen, is completed, it's possible that Malmö will enjoy a renaissance as Sweden's gateway city to and from the rest of mainland Europe. There are plenty of cynics, though, who believe the bridge will reduce Malmö to the status of a transit town, one where nobody stops to look around.

Although you won't need more than a day to get a feel for Malmö's compact centre, there are also delightful **parks**, a long and popular **beach** and some interesting cultural diversions south of the centre. **Möllevångstorget**, the exotically seedy area in the south, beyond Folketspark, is all set to become the enclave of the well-heeled bohemians. With its high immigrant population, it has for the past decade had a reputation for relative poverty. But its architecture is rather splendid – middle-class Swedish cravings for a more cosmopolitan lifestyle being what they are, white Swedes are tentatively beginning to buy into these early twentieth-century properties. The city's lively **nightlife** is another inducement to stay a while. One VIP who does hang around is the current prime minister Göran Persson (who lives here at Regementsgatan 10), despite having an extensive official residence in Stockholm. The first prime minister ever to refuse to live in the capital, he flies there by private jet each morning from Malmö.

Arrival, information and city transport

Passenger-only **ferries** and **catamarans** from Copenhagen dock at the various terminals along the conveniently central Skeppsbron docks. This route to the city gives the best initial vantage point, with grand facades reflecting Malmö's proud industrial heritage. Just up from here is the **train station**, aptly named Central Station. SJ national trains run here, as do the Danish-built (and very comfortable) Kustpilen trains from Denmark and from Kristianstad, Karlskrona and Linköping. The frequent Pågatåg local trains to and from Helsingborg/Lund and Ystad use platforms 9–13 at the back. To get to the square outside, Centralplan, either walk through Central Station or use the exit/entrance marked "Lokal stationen". In the square is the main **bus terminal**; frequent buses to and from Lund, Kastrup airport (in Denmark), Kristianstad/Kalmar and Ystad all stop here. Buses from Stockholm, Helsingborg and Gothenburg arrive at Slussplan, east of Central Station just over Slussbron at the end of Norra Vallgatan. Flying into Sturup **airport** to the east of Malmö, you can use the hourly Flygbuss to get into the city centre (Mon–Fri 5.30am–7.30pm, Sat 6.30am–5.30pm; 40min; 60kr).

The **tourist office** is inside Central Station (June–Aug Mon–Fri 9am–7pm, Sat 10am–2pm, Sun 10am–2pm; Sept–May Mon–Fri 9am–5pm, Sat 10am–2pm; ☎040/30 01 50, fax 611 18 34, *info@tourism.malmo.com*). Here, you can pick up a wealth of free information, including several good maps and an English-language listings brochure, *Malmö This Month*. An excellent weekly guide to the hip and happening is the Swedish-only *Sydsvenskan Dygnet Runt,* available free all over the place; not only does this paper give up-to-the-minute information on films, concerts and sports events, it lists and grades the trendiest places to eat, with categories ranging from "*absolut*" (the best) to "*aldrig*" (meaning "don't touch"). Opposite the tourist office is a Forex **currency exchange** office (daily 8am–9pm).

City transport

Although the city centre is easy to walk around, its central squares and streets all interlinked, you'll need to use the city **bus** service to reach some of the sights and places to stay. Each ride costs 14kr (tickets valid for 1hr); a 100kr magnetic card is also available, which reduces bus fares and can be used by several people at the same time. All tickets are sold on the bus. A useful two-day ticket is the **Öresund Runt** (Round the Öresund; 149kr, children 70kr), which covers whichever ferry, train and hydrofoil route you choose (or any part of it) to Lund, Helsingborg, Helsingør and across to Copenhagen. You can buy tickets at the tourist office, or by calling ☎020/567 567.

When using **taxis**, it's worth stopping several until you find one at a reasonable rate. If you use a minicab (cheaper than using taxis), be on your guard against being cheated on fares, an increasingly common practice used on tourists. To give a rough idea of costs, a trip from Malmö centre to the airport is around 225kr.

There are several **tours** around the city that are worth considering. A one-hour guided **sightseeing tour** (late June to early Aug 1 daily at noon 80kr; half price with Malmö Card, see box) leaves from the tourist office, but it's pricey and conducted in Swedish, English and German, so progress through the streets is necessarily slow. Alternatively you can do your own guided tour on city bus #20; the tourist office will sell you a specially designed brochure that details areas of interest (12kr) en route. The buses also leave from outside the tourist office (several buses an hour; both the bus ride and brochure are free with the Malmö Card). **Canal boat tours** leave daily from the canal opposite the *Savoy* hotel (June to August 11am–4pm; book on ☎040/611 74 88; 1hr; 70kr). Alternatively, **pedal boats** let you tramp around the canal network at your own pace. They're moored at Södertullstrappan (mid April to Aug daily 11am–7pm; 90kr per hour, half price with Malmö Card).

To strike out further afield, or just to head south of the city, **bike rental** is a good idea. The most central place is Cykel Kliniken (☎040/611 66 66), at the back of the car park directly behind the train station (summer Mon, Wed & Fri 10am–6pm, Tues & Thurs 10am–7pm, Sat 11am–2pm; rest of year shorter times), where standard bikes can be rented for 60kr a day; but check you're not getting a really ropey one. Newer and better mountain bikes are a very steep 120kr a day. Another place to try is Fridhems Cykelaffär at Tessinsvägen 13 (☎040/26 03 35), just beyond Malmöhus.

THE MALMÖ CARD

The very useful **Malmökortet** (Malmö Card; available for 1, 2 or 3 days; 150kr, 275kr or 400kr respectively) entitles you to free museum entry, free parking at public car parks, a guided bus tour of the city and unlimited bus journeys within town. It also gives various other discounts on transport and certain sights around the city, and at cinemas and concerts. With the card, you'll get fifty percent off at Sibbarps and Ribersborgs, each of which is an open-air bathhouse and sauna (see p.232 and p.239).

Accommodation

Of Malmö's two **youth hostels**, the central *City Youth Hostel,* Västergatan 9 (☎ & fax 040/23 56 40; 100kr; single rooms 125kr; June–Aug), is the friendlier and more convenient. The place is really student accommodation that's let out as a hostel over summer; as its dormitories are all in the basement and crammed with beds, it's worth getting your own room (ask for no. 24, the best furnished and the only one with a sea view). The STF-run *Vandrarhem,* Backavägen 18 (☎040/822 20; 100kr; closed mid-Dec to mid-Jan) is 5km from the city centre, pushed up against the E6 motorway; it's not particularly friendly and only to be considered if *City Youth Hostel* is full or closed. To get there, take bus #21A from Centreplan to Vandrarhemmet, cross over the junction past the traffic lights and take the first right; the hostel is signposted to left. The nearest **campsite**, *Camping Sibbarps,* is at Strandgatan 101 in Limhamm (☎040/34 26 50), not far from the new Öresund bridge. Conveniently near the campsite is Sibbarps Saltsjöbad, a fine, open-air bathhouse with a wood-fired sauna (a 10min ride on bus #82).

There are some really good and surprisingly affordable **hotels** in Malmö: the city is eager to attract tourists, and competition between the hotels can be fierce. Being a commercial city, prices are likely to plummet at the weekend, which for the hotel trade means Friday and Saturday nights; it's worth trying to persuade your hotel to charge you the weekend rate on Sunday night as well. Some hotels also reduce their rates in the summer. The **Malmö Package**, sold by the tourist office, provides visitors with a double room in a central hotel with breakfast and a Malmö Card (see p.231) thrown in, too. The scheme – along the lines of those in Stockholm and Gothenburg – runs from June to late August throughout, and at weekends only during the rest of the year; it costs from 365kr to 650kr per person, depending on the hotel. Though it's a good deal, the usual summer reductions at many non-participating hotels may prove even better value. All the hotels we list participate in the scheme, except for the cheapest, *Hotel Pallas.*

Hotels

Astoria, Gråbrödersgatan 7 (☎040/786 60, fax 788 70). A few minutes from the train station across the canal, this is a good, though plain, hotel. ③.

Balzar, Södergatan 20 (☎040/720 05, fax 23 63 75). Very central hotel between the two main squares. A swanky, traditional place, the decor all swags and ruches; some rooms have superb painted ceilings. None of it is remotely Swedish in style. ④/②.

City Hotel Anglais, Stortorget 15 (☎040/660 95 50, fax 660 95 59). A grand, turn-of-the-century hotel. With tasteful rooms, this is a fine choice on the city's premiere square. ⑤/②.

Good Morning Hotel, Citadellvagen 4 (☎040/23 96 05, fax 30 39 68). Five minutes' walk to the west of the train station, in the direction of Malmöhus. Its comfortable, pleasant interior is belied by the facade, which looks like a 1950s apartment tower. Price includes a good breakfast and free parking. ②.

Kramer, Stortorget 7 (☎040/20 88 00, fax 12 69 41). Beautiful, white-stuccoed, turretted establishment from the 1870s, once the top hotel in town. A very luxurious, beautifully preserved classic. Big weekend discounts. ⑥.

Pallas, Norra Vallgatan 74 (☎040/611 50 77, fax 97 99 00). A deceptively pretty, ornate old building that's not quite so attractive inside, looking more like a hostel. ①.

Radisson SAS Malmö, Östergatan 10 (☎040/698 40 00, fax 698 40 01). Just beyond the octagonal Caroline Church. Behind the unimposing facade hides a really delightful hotel. The rooms are massive – 43 square metres each, with stylish and innovative decor. Breakfast is served in a New-Orleans-inspired area, while the restaurant is set in one of Malmö's oldest timbered houses at the front of the main building. ⑤/③.

Royal, Norra Vallgatan 94 (☎040/97 63 03, fax 12 77 12). Just up from the train station. A small, family-run hotel. The price includes breakfast, which is taken in a pleasant garden area at the back. Weekend discounts. ③.

Savoy, Norra Vallgatan 62 (☎040/702 30, fax 97 85 51). Still the most expensive in town – but only just – this is the essence of style, with splendid furnishings and excellent food at its *Petri Pumpa Restaurant* (see p.241). Former guests are commemorated by brass plaques in the lobby – from Eartha Kitt to Lenin, Bardot to Dietrich, and the Bergmans, Ingmar and Ingrid. Large weekend discounts. ⑥.

Scandic Hotel St. Jörgen, Stora Nygatan 35 (☎040/693 46 00, fax 693 46 11). Rather dull and shabby on the outside, but all Chesterfield furniture and chandeliers within. Rooms are spacious, quite plush and sizeable; the en-suite bathrooms have actual baths. ⑤/③.

Temperance, Engelbrektsgatan 16 (☎040/710 20, fax 30 44 06). A pretty, central hotel. The price includes use of their sauna and solarium, and a big buffet breakfast. Weekend discounts. ③.

Tuneln, Adelgatan 4 (☎040/10 16 20, fax 10 16 25). Dating from the Middle Ages (it was built as a mansion in the 1340s), this is the finest of Malmö's small hotels. The room are all in Gustavian-style pastel or dark cherry colours, and the place is beautifully appointed. Good breakfasts and weekend discounts. ④.

The city centre

Heading south from the heavy-handed nineteenth-century opulence of the train station, with its curly-topped pillars and red-brick ornate arches, the **canal** is immediately in front of you. Dug by Russian prisoners in 1815, it forms a rough rectangle encompassing the **old town** to the south and the moated **castle** to the west. The castle is also surrounded by the first in a series of lovely, connecting **parks**. First off, though, head down Hamngatan to the main square. On the way you'll pass the striking sculpture of a twisted revolver, a monument to non-violence, standing outside the grand 1890s building that is the former Malmö Exchange.

Stortorget and St Petri kyrka

The laying out of **Stortorget**, the proud main square, necessitated the tearing down of much of Malmö's medieval centre in the mid-sixteenth century. Among the elaborate sixteenth- to nineteenth-century buildings, the 1546 **Rådhus** draws the most attention. It's an impressive pageant of architectural fiddling and crowded with statuary: restoration programmes in the last century robbed the building of its original design, and the finicky exterior is now in Dutch Renaissance style. To add to the pomp, the red-and-gold Scånian flag, of which Malmö is so proud, flaps above the roofs. The interior remains closer to its original form, and there are occasional tours within; check with the tourist office for the ever-changing times. The cellars, home to *Rådhus Källaven Restaurant* (see p.241), have been used as a tavern for more than four hundred years. To the south of the town hall, have a look inside **Apoteket Lejonet** (Lion Pharmacy – Swedish pharmacies are always named after creatures of strength): the outside is gargoyled and balconied, the inside a busy mix of inlaid woods, carvings and etched glass. From here, **Södergatan**, Malmö's main pedestrianized shopping street, leads down towards the canal. At the Stortorget end, there's a jaunty troupe of sculptured bronze musicians; further down, a run of lively cafés and restaurants. On the opposite side of the square, the crumbling, step-gabled red-brick building was once the home of the sixteenth-century mayor and master of the Danish mint, Jörgen Kocks. Danish coins were struck in Malmö on the site of the present Malmöhus castle (see p.235), until irate local Swedes stormed the building and destroyed it in 1534. The cellars of Jörgen's pretty home contain the *Kockska Krogan* restaurant (see p.241), the only entry point for visitors today. In the centre of the square, a statue of Karl X, high on his charger, presides over the city he liberated from centuries of Danish rule.

A block east, on Göran Olsgatan behind the Rådhus, the dark, forbidding exterior of the Gothic **St Petri kyrka** belies a light and airy interior (Mon–Fri 8am–6pm, Sat 9am–6pm, Sun 10am–6pm). The church has its roots in the fourteenth century, and, although Baltic in inspiration, has ended up owing much to German influences, for it was beneath its unusually lofty and elegantly vaulted roof that the German community came to pray – probably for the continuation of the "sea silver", the herrings that brought them to Malmö in the first place. The ecclesiastical vandalism, brought by the Reformation, of whitewashing over medieval roof murals started early at St Petri; almost the whole interior turned white in 1553. Consequently, your eyes are drawn not to the roof but to the pulpit and a four-tiered altarpiece, both of striking workmanship and elaborate embellishment. The only part of the church left with its original artwork was a side chapel, the **Krämare** (merchant's) **Chapel** (from the entrance, turn left and left again). Added to the church in the late fifteenth century as the Lady Chapel, it was considered redundant during the Reformation and was sealed off, so protecting the paintings from the zealous brush of the reformers. The paintings on the vaulted ceiling are in better condition than those on the walls, and depict mainly New Testament figures surrounded by decorative foliage, including the boy Jesus with a parrot and a fig. Beneath you, the chapel floor is a chessboard of tombs in black and white stone, with a few in red. Unfortunately, the paintings in the rest of the church were scraped away in the course of nineteenth-century restorations.

Lilla Torg

Despite the size of Stortorget, it still proved too small to suffice as the town's sole main square, so in the sixteenth century **Lilla Torg** was tacked on to its southwest corner, over a patch of marshland. Looking like a film set, this little square, with its creaky old half-timbered houses, flowerpots and cobbles, is everyone's favourite part of the city. During the day, people congregate here to take a leisurely drink in one of the many bars and wander around the summer jewellery stalls. At night, Lilla Torg explodes in a frenzy of activity, the venues all merging into a mass of bodies – mostly belonging to a casual, well-dressed crowd in their 20s and 30s – who converge from all over the city and beyond (see also "Eating and drinking", p.239).Head under the arch on Lilla Torg to get to the **Form Design Centre** (Tues, Wed & Fri 11am–5pm, Thurs 11am–6pm, Sat 10am–4pm, Sun noon–4pm; free). Built into a seventeenth-century former grain store, it concentrates on Swedish contemporary design in textiles, ceramics and furniture. It's all well presented, if a little pretentious. The courtyard entrance contains several small trendy boutiques; a simple café here serves not very much for not very much.

From the end of the nineteenth century until the 1960s, the whole of Lilla Torg was a covered market, and the sole remnant of those days, **Saluhallen**, is diagonally opposite the Design Centre. Mostly made up of specialist fine food shops, *Saluhallen* is a pleasant, cool retreat on a hot afternoon.

Rooseum

A few streets removed from the other sights of the old town, **Rooseum**, on Stora Nygatan (Tues–Sun 11am–5pm, Thurs till 8pm; guided tours Tues–Fri 6.30pm, Sat & Sun 2pm; 30kr, free with a Malmö Card), is well worth a visit if you're interested in contemporary art. This elaborately designed building – a cross between a miniature castle and a shuttered cottage – dates from 1900, and originally housed the Malmö Electricity Company's steam turbines. The main turbine hall is now the central gallery, revealing an imaginative use of space, playing host to experimental installations and interesting photographic works. There are regular new exhibitions and an excellent little café for the sweet-toothed (see p.240).

Malmöhus and around

Take any of the streets running west from Stortorget or Lilla Torg and you soon come up against the edge of **Kungsparken**, within striking distance of the fifteenth-century castle of **Malmöhus** (June–Aug daily 10am–4pm, Sept–May noon–4pm; 40kr, free with the Malmö Card). For a more head-on approach, walk west (away from the station) up Citadellsvägen; from here the low castle, with its grassy ramparts and two circular keeps, is straight ahead over the wide moat. There are free guided tours, in English, of Malmöhus (3pm) and the art museum (2pm).

Following the destruction of Denmark's mint, on this site, by the Swedes in 1534, the Danish king Christian III built a new fortress two years later. This was only to be of unforeseen benefit to his enemies who, once back in control of Skåne, used it to repel an attacking Danish army in 1677. For a time a prison (its most notable inmate the Earl of Bothwell, Mary Queen of Scots's third husband), the castle declined in importance once back in Swedish hands, and it was used for grain storage until becoming a museum in 1937. Today the exterior looks like an old, partly demolished factory, while most of the inner walls are concealed by the large, modern museum complex here.

Once in the museum, pass swiftly through the natural history section, a taxidermal Noah's ark holding no surprises; the most rewarding part of the museum is upstairs in the so-called **art museum**, part of the historical exhibition, where an ambitious series of furnished rooms covers most modern styles, from the mid-sixteenth-century Renaissance period through Baroque, Rococo, pastel-pale Gustavian and Neoclassical. A stylish interior from the Jugendstil (Art Nouveau) period is also impressive, while other rooms have Functionalist and post-Functionalist interiors, with some wacky colour and texture combinations. It's a fascinating visual feast; unfortunately though, there is no English labelling. Other sections of the historical exhibition include a display of medieval skeletons from Malmö's churchyards, showing the signs of infection with contemporary diseases like leprosy and tuberculosis – less gruesome than you might imagine. It's more interesting to head into the castle itself, with its spartan but authentic interiors.

Just beyond the castle, to the west along Malmöhusvagen, is **Kommendanthuset** (Governor's House; same times as Malmöhus), containing the strange marriage of a military and toy museum. The military section is a fairly lifeless collection of neatly presented rifles and swords, and the usual dummies sporting eighteenth- and nineteenth-century uniforms; its most interesting exhibit is an 1890 ambulance carriage. Upstairs, along with cases of glittering medals and the like, are some fine portraits of war heroes. The toy section is more fun, and contains the link between the two museums: a brigade of toy soldiers – of the British army, oddly enough.

A little further west, running off Malmöhusvagen, is a tiny walkway, **Banerkajen**, lined with higgledy-piggledy fishing shacks selling fresh and smoked fish – a rare little area of traditional Malmö that contrasts with the lively pace of the rest of the city. Just beyond the lane is the **Technical and Maritime Museum** (same times as the Malmöhus; 15kr). The technical section has displays on transport, power and local industries (sugar, cement); while upstairs in the science section the main display is a model of Tycho Brahe's observatory on the island of Ven (see p.221).The castle **grounds**, peppered with small lakes and sporting an old windmill, are good for a stroll, with paths leading all the way down to Regementsgatan and the City Library in the southeastern corner of the park. You can continue walking through the greenery, as far as Gustav Adolfs Torg, by crossing Gamla Begravnings Platsen, a rather pretty cemetery.

Malmö is justifiably proud of its collection of beautiful **parks**, a chain of which run southwards from the grounds of Malmöhus. Heading south from the castle, the first of these you encounter is Kungspark, with its graceful trees and classic sculptures, bordering the canal.

South of the centre

Tourists rarely head further south of the city than the canal banks that enclose the old town, but this is set to change now that Swedes are beginning to discover the multi-ethnic district around **Möllevågen** (see p.237), with an influx of "alternative" people helping this area – known more for crime than anything else during the past decade – gain in the hipness stakes. The buildings and areas off **Amiralsgatan**, to the southeast, give an interesting insight into Malmö's mix of cultures and its Social Democratic roots (for all of the twentieth century, the city has been at the forefront of left-wing politics, and was central to the creation and development of Sweden's Social Democratic Party). Around **Fersensvägen**, a couple of blocks west of Amiralsgatan, there are some charming enclaves of antique shops, cafés and quirky buildings, and the impressive art exhibition centre, Konsthall.

There's plenty of pleasure to be had from simply strolling around the chain of **parks** that continues south of Kungspark, with free guided tours of the flora and royal history of these appealing green swathes also available (ask at the tourist office). Just on the south side of the curving river is Slottspark, with graceful, mature trees and places to picnic; further south is the largest of the parks, Pildammspark, boasting tranquil lakes and a choice restaurant (see p.241).

South towards the Konsthall

Heading south from Malmöhus along Slottsgatan, peer upwards at Regementsgatan 10 as you cross over that street; the building is home to Sweden's current Prime Minister. Now cut across one block east to cobbled Södra Förstadsgatan; at no. 4 is a splendid house designed in 1904 as a National

Romantic gem, its facade covered with flower and animal motifs. A little further along the same road, the **Victoria Theatre** is Sweden's oldest cinema (Mon–Fri 11am–6pm), all fine Art Nouveau swirls of dark oak and bevelled glass. Now a place to watch art-house films, it occasionally plays host to theatrical productions.

Back on Fersensvägen, the southward continuation of Slottsgatan, you'll pass the city **theatre** on your right, with its complex and amusing sculpture of tiers of people – the naked supporting the clothed on their shoulders. Arriving at St. Johannesgatan, head for the single-storey glass and concrete building at no. 7: the **Konsthall**, (Art Hall; daily 11am–5pm, Wed till 10pm; free), an enormous white-painted space showing vast contemporary works in regular temporary exhibitions; there's lots of room to stand back and take in the visual feast.

The area between Regementsgatan and the Konsthall is also the best in town for interesting and esoteric **antique** and **curiosity shops** – Kärleksgatan (which runs between Davidshallsgatan and Davidshallstorg) is lined with them. You'll find lovely old silver samovars at Mats Kuriosa, Kärleksgatan 6 (☎040/11 82 23); the more costly Säljer & Köper Kuriosa, on the corner of Davidshallgatan (☎040/97 34 34; Mon & Wed–Fri noon–6, Sat 11–2pm), is one of the biggest antique stores here, selling silverware, glass, furniture – the lot.

South to Möllevången

From the canal, head east along Regementsgatan and turn right into Amiralsgatan, where, a few hundred metres down and off to your left along Föreningsgatan, you encounter the restored **Malmö Synagogue**, a splendid copper-domed Moorish building (ask the tourist office to make arrangements if you wish to see inside). It serves an Orthodox community, who came mostly from Germany in the latter part of the nineteenth century and during the 1930s. Designed and built in 1894 by the same architect responsible for the neighbouring Betania kyrka, the synagogue is decorated with concentric designs in blue and green glazed brick. The unrenovated interior is rather fine, with its original, German-inspired octagonal wooden ceiling, ark and enormous chandelier of dull brass; there's a separate women's gallery (visitors are permitted access to all parts).

Back on Amiralsgatan, it's a ten-minute walk south to **Folketspark**, Sweden's oldest existing working people's park and was once the prize of the community. Now rather shabby, Folkespark contains a basic amusement park, and at its centre, a ballroom named the **Moriskan**, an odd, low building with Russian-style golden domes topped with sickles. Both the park and the ballroom are now privately owned, a far cry from the original aims of the park's Social Democratic founders. Severe carved busts of these City Fathers are dotted all over the park. The Socialist agitator August Palm made the first of his several historic speeches here in 1881, which marked the beginning of a 66-year period of unbroken Social Democratic rule in Sweden.

More interesting than the giant twirling tea-cup fun rides in the park is the multicultural character of the city south from here. Strolling from the park's southern exit down Möllevången to **Möllevångstorget**, you enter an area populated almost entirely by non-Swedes, where Arab, Asian and Balkan émigré families predominate. The vast square is a haven of exotic food stores, side by side with shops selling pure junk and more recently established Chinese restaurants and karaoke pubs. On a hot summer afternoon it's easy to forget you're in Sweden at all, the more makeshift and ramshackle atmosphere around the bright fruit and veg stands contrasting with the clean, clinical order of the average Swedish neighbourhood. It's worth taking a close look at the provocative **sculpture** at the square's centre: four naked, bronze men strain under the colossal weight of a huge chunk of rock bearing carved representations of Malmö's smoking chimneys, while two naked women press their hands into the men's backs in support. It's a poignant image, marrying toil in a city founded on limestone quarrying with the Social Democratic vision of the working man's struggle.

This area has most recently fallen prey to the attentions of middle-class Swedes, who are already buying up the stylish, Art Nouveau apartment houses here, and renting them out until the area becomes smartened up enough for them to move in themselves. For a taste of the sort of architecture which is making the area so popular, turn right at Folketspark from Amiralsgatan up to Södra Parksgatan, where a stately roundabout is surrounded by Art Nouveau houses. Already the first trendy design shops are opening around here, though it's the sort of area where visitors are still reluctant to park their bikes for fear they'll be stolen.

South of the city: Malmö's beaches and the Öresund bridge

Separated from the city centre by the delightful **Öresund park** (bus #20 heads here), Malmö's long stretch of sandy beach reaches all the way to the old limestone-quarrying area of Limhamn in the southwest. Grand old villas set in glorious gardens overlook the Öresund, and the whole stretch is known as the Golden Coast because of the wealth of its residents. Fringed by dunes and grassland, the beaches here are popular with young families as the water remains shallow for several metres out to sea; throughout the summer months, the area also plays host to groups of youths letting their hair down. One bathing area further west (signposted a couple of kilometres from town; bus #20 comes here) is specially adapted for people with disabilities.

THE ÖRESUND BRIDGE

Linking Malmö with Copenhagen in Denmark (and thus Sweden with the rest of continental Europe), the **Öresund bridge** was finally completed in the summer of 1999, an event marked by the symbolic embrace, halfway along the then newly-finished structure, of Sweden's Crown Princess Victoria and Denmark's Crown Prince Frederick. From Lernacken, a few kilometres south of Malmö, the bridge runs to a four-kilometre-long artificial island off the Danish coast, from where an immersed tunnel carries traffic and trains across to the mainland – a total distance of 16km. The bridge itself has two levels, the upper for a four-lane highway and the lower for two sets of train tracks, and comprises three sections: a central high bridge, spanning 1km, and approach bridges to either side, each over 3km long.

Whether the bridge should be built at all was debated for some forty years (the late 1990s saw numerous demonstrations in Malmö proclaiming "make love not bridges"), with much concern expressed over the environmental damage that might result from its construction and subsequent operation. Yet now that the bridge is a reality, even its detractors are proclaiming it Sweden's most significant construction achievement of the twentieth century. Understandably though, Stockholmers have played down the bridge's importance, as it will undoubtedly draw attention to Sweden's west coast, away from the capital.

A classic Malmö experience at the town end of the beach is the **Ribersborgs kallbadhuset**, a cold-water bathhouse (mid-April to mid-Sept Mon–Fri 8.30am–7pm, Sat & Sun 8.30am–4pm; mid-Sept to mid-April Mon–Fri noon–7pm, Sat & Sun 9am–4pm) and sauna (mid-April to mid-Sept Mon–Fri 11am–7pm, Sat & Sun 9am–4pm; rest of year same as bathhouse); admission is 28kr, reduced to 14kr with a Malmö Card. Alongside the beaches runs the **Ribersborgs Recreation Promenade**, fringed by dunes and grassland, where groups of young people hold barbecues and play music (take bus #20 from the train station).

Further south is Limhamn (reached by bus #81 from the centre), close to the start of the new Öresund bridge (see box, p.238), where there's an **exhibition centre**, Öresunds Utställningen (June–Aug Mon–Fri 10am–6pm, Sat & Sun 11am–5pm; Sept–May Tues–Fri 10am–5pm, Sat & Sun 11am–5pm; 30kr; ☎040/16 44 60). An exhibition celebrating and explaining the massive structure is being held here until mid-2001, after which the striking contemporary building will be used for conferences and other events. The bridge exhibition offers more information on the structure than most people can take in, with a myriad of slides, models, videos and interactive displays. No reference is made to the Malmö tradition of spending an evening on board the Limhamn–Denmark car-ferries eating and drinking to oblivion, a pastime relegated to nostalgic memory with the advent of the bridge. Rather more fun than the exhibition is having something to eat or drink at the very pleasant **restaurant** here, with good views of the bridge from its terrace.

Eating and drinking

Among Malmö's **eating places** you'll find some with interesting interiors – check out the Industrial *Espresso Rooseum* – and much fine food. By day, several **cafés** serve good lunches and sumptuous cakes, while at night, there are a couple of top-notch places at which to eat, notably the Italian *Spot Restaurant*. Most of Malmö's restaurants, brasseries and cafés are concentrated in and around its three central squares, with Lilla Torg attracting the biggest crowds.

For cheaper eats and a very un-Swedish atmosphere, head south of the centre to Möllenvångstorget, the heart of Malmö's immigrant community. More inexpensively still, try *Saluhallen* at the corner of Lilla Torg, an excellent indoor **market** that sells wholefoods; there are also specialist food stores here, like *Krydboden*, which stocks herbal and fruit teas, coffees and crystallized fruits. Cheese fanatics will appreciate the tremendous *Ost huset* at Skomaregatan 10 (Mon–Fri 9am–6pm, Sat 9am–3pm), where the variety is exceptional. There's a good charcuterie, *Spot's Deli*, selling fresh pasta, meats and cakes next to the Italian restaurant at Stora Nygatan 33.

Cafés

Bageri Café Saluhallen, corner of Lilla Torg. Excellent bagels, baguettes, sweet pies and health foods – with outside eating, too. Mon–Fri 8am–6pm, Sat 10am–4pm.

Bro's Jazz Café, Södra Vallgatan 3. By the canal south of Gustav Adolfs Torg. Features good-value, filling sandwiches named after jazz greats. Mon–Fri 10am–1am, Sat & Sun noon–1am.

Cafe Bagels, Västergatan 18B. Pleasant basement bagel bar. Mon–Fri 9.30am–6pm, Sat 10am–5pm.

Cafe Horisont, Davidshallgatan 9. This no-smoking eco-café is a very likeable, quiet place, with home-made cakes, cheesecakes, muffins and lots of salads and milkshakes. Try their blueberry, honey and yoghurt shake at 24kr.

Cafe Rooseum, Gasverksgatan 22. Inside Rooseum, the contemporary art museum (see p.235); it's worth trying for the superb cheesecakes in twelve varieties along with the great cookies and filled bagels. Seating is around the edge of the room, with a giant generator taking up most of the remaining space. Tues–Sun 11am–5pm.

Café Siesta, Ostindiefararegatan. Turn right at the western end of Landbygatan, and it's on the next corner on the left. A fun little café specializing in home-made apple cake. Mon 10am–6pm, Tues–Fri 10am–midnight, Sat 10am–6pm, Sun noon–6pm.

Cafe Systrar & Bröder, Östra Ronneholmsvägen 26 (☎040/97 34 70). With a great-value breakfast buffet at just 38kr, and a hip young crowd reading the papers. Mon–Fri 7.30am–4pm, Sat 8am–1pm.

Conditori Hollandia, Södra Förstadsgatan. South of Gustav Adolfs Torg, across the canal. Classic, pricey *konditori* with a window full of chocolate fondants. The inside is sedate – Klimt prints cover the walls. Speciality is strawberry cheesecake. Mon–Fri 8.15am–7pm, Sat 9am–5pm, Sun 11am–6pm.

Cyber Space Café, Engelbrektsgatan 13, just east of Stortorget. A new Internet café. Surf the net while sipping coffee or soda and eating baguettes and pastries. All drinks 10kr. Half an hour's Internet use costs 20kr. Daily 2–10pm.

Espresso House, Skomakaregatan 2. Close to both Stora and Lilla Torg. Part of the excellent chain, this one serves great chocolate cake, muffins and ciabattas, and a delicious Oriental *latte* (24kr) flavoured with cardamom. There's another popular branch at Södra Förstadsgatan 11, just south of the city. Mon–Fri 8am–midnight, Sat 9am–midnight, Sun 10am–11pm.

Gustav Adolfs, Gustav Adolfs Torg. A popular spot, in grand, white-stuccoed building with seating outside, serving coffee (18kr). Also has a morning coffee and snacks menu. Open late at weekends.

Hos Den Blinda Åsnan Cafe, Norregatan 13. A cool hangout in a classic Jugend house, with marble walls that make it look like the interior of an expensive tomb. Relaxed, cheap and groovy. Varied menu including soups, sandwiches, and tortillas. Mon–Fri 10am–5pm. Closed July.

Nyhavn 8, Möllevångtorget 8. A Danish café-restaurant run by a Danish-Turkish émigré – it could only make sense on this square. Chief among the offerings are *smorrebrod* with all manner of possible toppings for 30–50kr, plus rich Danish meals, all for under 100kr.

Pelles Café, Tegelgårdsgatan 5. In a quaint period house, this simple café does generous, cheap baguettes and bottles of cold chocolate milk. Also has a popular leafy area for outside eating. Mon–Fri 7am–7pm, Sat & Sun 9am–7pm.

Slottspark Cafe, in the park south of the Malmöhus. An appealing spot, overlooking an old black windmill, for home-made carrot or chocolate cake. Tues–Sun 11am–4pm.

Restaurants

Adelgatan Restaurant, Adelgatan. Next to *Hotel Tuneln*. Part of the *Trocadero* nightclub, this place specializes in flambé dishes, tournedos and seafood. Mon–Sat 4pm–midnight.

Azteken, Landbygata (☎040/12 50 45). Just off Lilla Torg. A mellow, modern restaurant with a lovely outdoor courtyard which looks like something out of a film set. Inside is a cosy bar with animal-skin wall hangings, wooden log walls and a rough-hewn floor. Great atmosphere, though Aztec it isn't. Mon–Sat 5pm–1am.

Brasserie Slottsparken, Kung Oscarsvägen (☎040/97 11 11). On the road running through both Slottspark and Kungspark. One of Malmö's two parkland eateries, this place is much cheaper than the other, *Olga's* (see p.241), though not as beautifully set. Baguettes, open sandwiches and fish or meat dishes, with outside eating and a friendly, relaxed atmosphere. You can easily fill up here for 80–90kr.

Golden Restaurant, corner of Södra Parkgatan and Simrishamnsgatan. In Möllevången, this spartan place serves cheap crepes, pizza and kebabs.

Green, Södergatan l. In a splendid red-stone building and looking out onto the fancy carved facade of the Handelsbank. Popular, inexpensive vegetarian fast food – Thai wok dishes, pizzas or soup and bread for 25–45kr. Mon–Sat 11am–9pm, Sun noon–8pm.

Gokboet, Lillatorg 3. With a name that means "cuckoo's nest", this place has a friendly, youthful atmosphere. Mexican food from 45kr, baguettes 35kr, and unusual and delicious cakes.

Indian Side, Lilla Torg. Very popular Indian dishes, with house specialities all costing 100–140kr. Within staggering distance of the main bars.

Johan P. Fish Restaurant, Saluhallen. Black-and-white chequered, this place serves only fairly pricey fish dishes.

Kockska Krogan, corner of Stortorget & Suellgatan (☎040/703 20). Also known as *Arstiderna*, this fine old basement restaurant is within the former home of Malmö's sixteenth-century mayor Jörgen Kock. Overpriced but worth the splash. Daily lunch specials from 75kr. Mon–Fri 11.30am–11pm, Sat 1pm–midnight.

Krua Thai, Mollevangtorget 12 (☎040/12 22 87). In the big square south of the city centre, this place serves the best Thai food in town, with an informal atmosphere that's more domestic than *haute cuisine*.

Le Beau Monde, Vastergatan 16. On a quiet street, only a few minute's walk from the Stortorget action, this place has a reputation is for excellence. The gourmet menu is a wallet strainer at 445kr for a three-course meal, but there are cheaper, à la carte options.

Olga's, Pildamms Parken (☎040/12 55 26). Superbly set in a wooden lakeside pavilion, this is an expensive place, but a good one, serving Swedish and international cuisine. A vast portrait of the very substantial Olga adorns the wall.

Petri Pumpa, Norra Vallgatan 62. At the *Savoy* hotel (see p.233). This splendid restaurant – with prices to match – was Lund's culinary pinnacle before moving here. Elegant fine dining surrounded by dark panels and a white arched ceiling. Two courses at 295kr.

Rådhus Källaven, Stortorget. In the cellars of the gloriously decorated town hall. Main dishes cost 200kr, but there's an excellent daily economy lunch at 65kr. Outside seating in summer. Mon–Fri 11.30am–11pm, Sat 3–11pm, Sun 3–9pm.

Rinaldo's, Saluhallen. Serving generous, fresh salads that are a rainbow of colours, and some wicked desserts.

Spot Restaurant, Stora Nygatan 33 (☎040/12 02 03). A chic Italian restaurant. During the day, light meals based on ciabatta and *panini* breads, with great fillings, are served; in the evening there's a menu of fish, cheese and meats. Reasonably priced, this is a really great place to eat. Mon 9am–6pm, Tues–Sat 9am–midnight.

Tempo, Norra Skolgatan 30. Near Möllevångstorget, to the south of the city. (☎040/12 60 21). A quirky, hip place, whose patrons come to savour the very well-prepared and intriguing food. The menu is short, but inspired, with an emphasis on herbs. Service is friendly, but can be absurdly slow.

Bars

For **drinking**, Lilla Torg is *the* place to go in the evenings. The square buzzes with activity, as the smell of beer wafts between the old, beamed houses, and music and chatter fill the air. With a largely 20- and 30-something crowd, the atmosphere is like that of a summer carnival – orange-jacketed bouncers keep the throng from suffocating. It doesn't make a huge difference which of the six or so bars you go for – expect a wait to get a seat – but roughly speaking, *Mello Yello* is for the 25-plus age group, *Moosehead* for a younger crowd, and *Victors* is even younger and more boisterous. At the *Savoy Hotel*, the *Bishop's Arms* is a cosy but rather staid pub with a heavy-handed insistence on looking British. On Möllenvångstorget, south of the centre in the immigrant quarter, the Danish-style *Nyhavn* at no. 8 is a laid-back place to drink. A striking addition to the bar scene is *Club Trocadero*, next door to *Hotel Tuneln* on Adelgatan (Fri & Sat 10pm–3am; cover charge 60kr). Done out like a futuristic metallic tunnel by Argentinian designer Aberlardo Gonzalez, it's one of the few places in town welcoming a wide age range.

Entertainment and nightlife

It used to be that the only entertainment in Malmö was watching rich drunks become poor drunks at the blackjack table in the Central Station bar. Nowadays there are some decent **live music** venues and **discos**, most of which are cheaper to get into than their European counterparts. The best place to see live music is *Matssons Musikpub*, Göran Olsgatan 1, behind the Rådhus (daily 9.30pm–2am), with a variety of Scandinavian R&B and rock bands. Check out *Malmö This Month* for information on what's on here. The cellar bar at *Club Trocadero*, on Adelgatan, boasts a wild dancefloor, all steel and mirrors. Classical **music** performances take place at the Concert Hall, Föreningsgatan 35 (☎040/34 35 00; two for one with Malmö Card), home of the Malmö Symphony Orchestra, and at Musikhögskolan, Ystadvägen 25 (☎040/19 22 00); check with the tourist office for programme details.

Malmö plays host to two annual **festivals**. The **Folkfesten** takes place in early June and is devoted to progressive and classic rock. Begun in the early 1970s and now enjoying a renaissance in popularity, this mini-Woodstock is held in Kungsparken and draws a young, tie-dyed and beaded crowd. Much broader in scope is the **Malmö Festival** in August, which mainly takes place in Stortorget. Huge tables are set out here, with crayfish tails being served up for free. In Gustav Adolfs Torg, other stalls are set up by the immigrant communities, with Pakistani, Somali and Bosnian goodies and dance shows, while at the canal, rowing competitions take place.

Gay Malmö

Though most gay Malmöites head off to Copenhagen for a really good night out, Malmö's **gay nightlife** is surprisingly lively. The very friendly *Club Fyran* is Sweden's oldest exclusively gay club (Fri & Sat 11pm–3am; 70kr); to get there, head right down Kalendegatan from the St. Petri Church, left into Snapperupsgatan, and you'll find it at no.4, above the *Mandarin House* Chinese restaurant. From the outside, the place looks like it hasn't been open for a while; once inside – you get in by pressing the buzzer – you'll find that there can be a real party atmosphere. Another place you might want to try is *Club Trocadero* (see above), which is mostly gay on Friday nights.

The RFSL-run **gay centre** is at Monbijougatan 15, to the south of the city centre (head down Amiralsgatan and turn off to the right just before the Folketspark). This is home to *Club Indigo*, at its busiest after midnight (Fri & Sat nights from 10pm). It's a sizeable and friendly place, where all the gay anthems of the past couple of decades are played on disco nights. The first Saturday of the month is women-only and there's a pub night on Wednesdays. Entry is 80kr, but attitudes are relaxed and if you can get in as a guest of someone who's already a member, it's 40kr.

Listings

Airlines British Airways, Sturup airport (☎020/78 11 44); Finnair, Baltzarsgatan 31 (☎020/78 11 00); KLM, Sturup airport (☎020/50 05 30); Lufthansa, Gustav Adolfs Torg 12 (☎040/717 10); SAS, Baltzarsgatan 18 (☎040/35 72 00).

Buses Services run from Värnhemstorget to Lund (#130 or, from Aug–June, the much faster #131 express), Kristianstad/Kalmar (#805) and Ystad (#330).

Car rental Avis, Skeppsbron 13 (☎040/778 30); Budget, Baltzarsgatan 21 (☎040/775 75); Europcar, Mäster Nilsgatan 22 (☎040/38 02 40); Hertz, Jörgenkocksgatan 1B (☎040/749 55). Agencies also inside the SAS hovercraft terminal on Skeppsbron and at Sturup airport.

Catamarans and hovercrafts Catamarans to Copenhagen: Flygbåtarna, Skeppsbron ☎040/10 39 30); and Pilen (☎040/23 44 11). Hovercrafts direct to Kastrup airport are operated by SAS from Skeppsbron (☎040/35 71 00).

Consulate British Consulate at Gustav Adolfs Torg 8c (☎040/611 55 25).

Doctor On call daily 7am–10pm; ☎040/33 35 00; at other times ☎33 10 00.

Exchange Best rates are at Forex, Norra Vallgatan 60 and at the train station (June–Aug daily 7am–9pm). The Central Station post office also changes foreign currency (Mon–Fri 8am–6pm, Sat 9.30am–1pm).

Left luggage Lockers in Central Station are at the entrance to platforms 3–6 and are graded in three sizes (10, 15 or 20kr); the largest takes just about any size of case or backpack.

Pharmacy 24hr service at Apoteket Gripen, Bergsgatan 48 (☎040/19 21 13) or Lejonet in Stortorget.

Post office Skeppsbron 1 (Mon–Fri 8am–6pm), or in Arkaden, Stora Nygatan 31A (Mon–Fri 8am–6pm, Sat 9.30am–1pm).

Taxis Call ☎040/97 97 97 or 23 23 23 to book one.

Trains Pågatåg information office inside the Lokalstationen, within the train station (Mon–Fri 7am–6pm, Sat 8am–3pm, Sun 9am–3pm).

Southeastern Skåne: from Malmö to Ystad

The people of this province speak a guttural dialect which betrays their Danish origin; a peculiarity so marked that the Swedes playfully say that the Skåne folk "are born with gruel in their throats." They have a great difficulty in managing the letter 'r'. . . They consider themselves as quite as a separate nationality – as indeed they really are; for the typical Skåne man is neither a Swede nor a Dane, but distinct from both.

From *Unknown Sweden* (1925) by James Steveni.

Leaving Malmö, the local Pågatåg train and the E6 and E14 highways cut directly east towards Ystad (see p.251). Though direct, the route bypasses some picturesque, minor resorts and a couple of the region's best beaches along Sweden's most southwesterly tip; also missed out this way are a remarkable Viking-style settlement at Foteviken (see p.245) and an extensive Baltic amber workshop at Kämpinge (see p.247), the latter set in picture-perfect countryside. With time to explore, and particularly with your own transport, this quieter part of the south makes for a few days of delightful exploration.

As you head south along the old coast-hugging E6 road, you'll pass the **Hyllie water tower**, an impressive structure like a white flying saucer on four legs (mid-June to mid-Aug Mon & Thurs–Sun 11am–4pm; 20kr, 10kr with the Malmö Card). Special-effects shows with light, sounds and smoke are well worth catching here in the afternoon (call ☎040/34 16 48 for times). You can also get to the tower on **bus** #14 (direction Lindesborg) or bus #13 (to Holma), or on the **cycle trails** that head south out of the city: they actually start right from Malmö's train station, cutting through the city's parks and down Pildammsvägen, from where the tower is signposted off to the right.

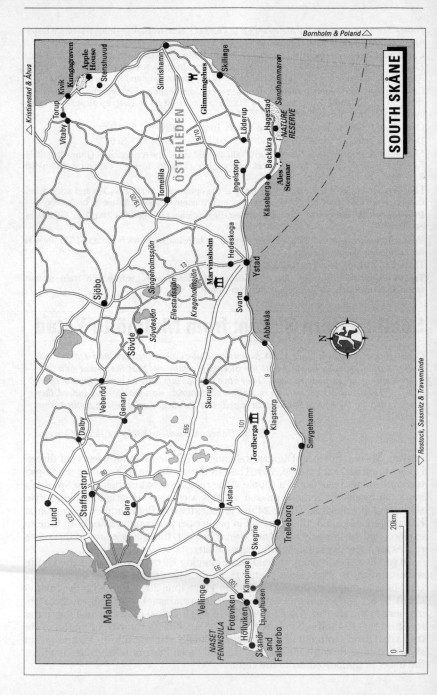

SOUTH SKÅNE

Bornholm & Poland △

△ Kristianstad & Åhus

▷ Rostock, Sassnitz & Travemünde

ÖSTERLEDEN

NATURE
RESERVE

NÄSET
PENINSULA

Skanör
and
Falsterbo

Malmö

Lund

Staffanstorp

Bara

Dalby

Veberöd

Genarp

Sövde

Sjöbo

Söydesjön

Ellestadssjön

Snogeholmssjön

Krageholmssjön

Marvinsholm

Hedeskoga

Ystad

Svarte

Abbekås

Skurup

Jordberga

Klagstorp

Smygehamn

Alstad

Skegrie

Trelleborg

Kämpinge

Ljunghusen

Höllviken

Foteviken

Vellinge

Tomelilla

Simrishamn

Stenshuvud

Apple
House

Kungagraven

Kivik

Torup

Vitaby

Löderup

Glimmingehus

Skillinge

Ingelstorp

Käseberga

Backåkra

Hagestad

Ales
Stennar

Sandhammaren

E22

80

E65

E6

E6

101

9

9

9/10

19

19/20

13

N

20km

0

Twenty-five kilometres south of the city on the old E6 is the village of **VEL-LINGE**, also reachable on bus #150 from Malmö's Centreplan, or on the same buses or cycle trails for the water tower (by bike, once out of Malmö, follow signs first for Tygelsjö and then to Vellinge; around 90min one-way). Look out for the old town hall here, with its deep thatched roof and perfectly preserved courtyard: opposite is one of Sweden's oldest **inns**, a gastronomic landmark called *Hvellingegästgifvaregård* (Mon 11.30am–3pm, Tues–Thurs 11.30am–10pm, Fri 11.30am–11pm, Sat 1–11pm, Sun 1–6pm). Genuine Skånian inns, revered by locals, are deceptively basic in appearance and well worth seeking out; this one dates from the early seventeenth century and offers such delights as beer-cooked eel with scrambled eggs (80kr), deer chops with prunes (180kr) and *äggakaka*, a Skånian egg pancake with lingonberries (150kr); there is also a good-value 70kr daily lunch option. Moving on just west of Vellinge (by car or bus #150), you cross an expanse of heathland to which birdwatchers flock every autumn. Their goal is to spot nesting plovers and terns, as well as millions of migratory birds fleeing the Arctic for the Stevns peninsula, south of Copenhagen.

Foteviken Viking Museum

From Vellinge, it's just a couple of kilometres southwest to Höllviken, on the way to Skanör and Falsterbo (see p.246). Höllviken itself has nothing to detain you, but signs here point the way to the **Foteviken Viking Museum**, just 500m away (mid-May to Aug daily 11am–4pm; ☎040/45 68 40, *www.foteviken.se*; 30kr, 75kr family ticket). An ancient coastal village and reputedly also a pagan sacrificial site, **Foteviken** was a market town and centre for herring fishing during Viking times. Today, the whole area has been transformed into a working **Viking-style village** comprising houses, workshops, a sacrificial temple and shipyard – a virtually self-sufficient settlement with an astonishing ring of authenticity, and more thought-provoking than any traditional museum could hope to be. The idea was to show the way of life here in the twelfth century, but more than this, the place has become a Mecca for people from all over Europe who want to live as Vikings, together with a not inconsiderable number of characters, sporting wild beards and lots of beads, who firmly believe they *are* Vikings.

The resulting atmosphere is that of a hippy commune in a time warp. Everyone dresses entirely in home-spun garments of loose, coarse linen, coloured with dyes made from local grasses and herbs (the clothes all end up muddy beige or green, as natural red and blue dyes are hard to come by). The villagers' simply-crafted footwear is made from leather which they cure themselves, and if you wander into the **cure-houses**, you'll see the pelts of locally caught mink – along with elk and wild-boar hides donated by local abattoirs more interested in the meat. Dotted around the ever-growing village are **kilns** and **clay ovens** looking like ant hills; these are used to bake bread, and fire the bowls from which the villagers eat.

There are currently twelve complete houses, though it is intended that the village will eventually comprise forty homes. Among the highlights is a **weavers' cottage** containing the village's answer to the Bayeux Tapestry: a wall-hanging here depicts the Battle of Foteviken of June 4, 1134, in which King Nils of Denmark is seen trying to reconquer Skåne from the rebellious pretender Erik Emune. It's also worth heading down to the shore, where **Viking-style ships**, based on the designs of excavated wrecks, are built.

From mid-May to August there are Viking **plays** (call for details) and **guided tours** in English at 11.30am, 1pm and 2.30pm. Two of the most dramatic times of year to arrive are June 12–13, when the battle is commemorated with a historical **re-enactment**; and July 2–4, when hundreds of people who have chosen to live as Vikings converge on the place from all over Northern Europe for a get-together and giant Viking **market**. For those who want to have a taste of the Viking life, there are many two-day **summer courses** from which to choose, ranging from bead-making (250kr) to how to sail a Viking ship (500kr); call or email for full details. There is also the possibility of **staying** here in Viking tents or houses (or you can camp for free), with access to showers and toilets. All participants are expected to wear Viking or medieval clothing, which the organizers can provide. For **food**, there's a café and restaurant here, serving the likes of smoked salmon and roasted pig.

The Naset peninsula

With a distinctly well-heeled population, the appropriately golf-club-shaped **Naset peninsula**, marking the southwest tip of the country, is well-known for its many golf courses. Heading west from Foteviken, you cross the Falsterbo canal (dug by Swedes during World War II to bypass to occupied Danish coastal waters), before arriving in the early-medieval town of **SKANÖR**. Once an important commercial centre, the town was founded as part of the Hanseatic commercial system, its existence thanks to the abundance of herring off this stretch of the coast. In the early twentieth century, Skanör and neighbouring **Falsterbo**, a couple of kilometres to the south, became fashionable bathing resorts for rich Malmö families. Both have since gone in and out of fashion; currently, they are once again desirable destinations for much the same set. Aside from the admirably pretty houses, there's not much to see in Skanör, but its **beaches** are superb: long ribbons of white sand bordering an extensive **bird** and **nature reserve**. From the beach, you can see across the reserve to Skanör's **church**, one section medieval, the other High Gothic. When the herring stocks disappeared in the sixteenth century, the town lost its importance, and so the church was never updated, making it all the more appealing today. From the harbour, it's a pleasant walk to the town square and the lovely old cottages lining Mellangatan.

A few kilometres to the south, beyond Falsterbo is Sweden's oldest **nature reserve**, **Nabben**, one of twelve on the peninsula. It's home to a huge population of birds – on a good day in September or October you can spot more than fifty species. Between November and January it's all off-limits to protect the birds and, to a lesser extent, seals. To the north of the peninsula lies the splendid **Flommen Nature Reserve**, dominated by wetland meadows carpeted with blue butterfly iris, with sea-holly sprouting between the sand dunes. You can walk southwards, towards the tip of the peninsula, to Sweden's oldest **lighthouse**, Kolabacken, whose beam was created by burning charcoal. At the very tip is **Maklappen Island**, a nature reserve known as a refuge for both grey and harbour seal (closed Feb–Oct).

The Amber Museum

After heavy storms, dull yellow nuggets of rough-textured **Baltic amber**, from submerged prehistoric forest, are regularly washed up on the shores around this part of southwest Sweden, particularly at Skånor beach. Appropriately enough, the hamlet of **Kämpinge**, 5km east of Falsterbo on Route 100 (bus #152 runs here from Höllviksnas), is home to a remarkable **amber workshop and museum** (June to mid-Aug 10am–6pm; to visit at other times call ☎040/45 08 61 or 45 45 04). Isolated among fields of yellow rape, the museum is signposted off the main road – look for "Bärnstenssnideri 500m". This remarkable centre was set up by one man, Leif Brost, who has dedicated himself to studying all aspects of this fossilized pine-tree resin. The most valuable pieces on show are those with insects trapped inside (known as "inclusions"), most strikingly mating pairs or hapless creatures caught in a web, complete with spider. In the 1990s, Brost's collections even drew the attention of the makers of *Jurassic Park* and *The Lost World,* who used some of his specimens in the films. English-language **tours** of the museum, giving you a full run-down on amber and all its uses, are available by prior arrangement.

Practicalities

At Rådhustorget 6, a few metres from Skanör's town hall, *Hotell Gässlingen* is a charming place to **stay**, with weekend discounts outside summer (☎040/47 30 35, fax 47 51 81; ④). They will **rent bikes** at 50kr a day. Another pleasant, small hotel is *Spelabacken* at 58 Mellangarten (☎040/47 53 00, fax 47 32 42; ④), which boasts a sauna and solarium. There are plenty of places nearby to **camp** for free, but be careful not to pick a protected area for birds, which are signposted. The town's little harbour boasts a terrific **restaurant**, *Skanör's Fiskroken* (☎040/474050), where you can savour superb fish dishes in a simple, elegant setting. Perhaps the best way to sample the remarkable range of smoked and pickled fish is to have them make up a picnic plate (around 90kr) – in particular, try herring roe marinated in rum and hot smoked salmon with black bread. At the corner of Dykengatan, near the square, is another quintessential Scånian inn, *Gästgivaregården* (March–Sept Mon & Wed–Fri 5–10pm, Sat 1–11pm, Sun 1–6pm).

Trelleborg

Heading east along the coast from the country's southwest corner, you'll see rolling fields punctuated by World War II concrete bunkers, some of which have been converted into unlikely looking summer houses. Around 15km from Kämpinge, you encounter **TRELLEBORG**, which greets traffic with a curtain of low-level industry blocking all views of the sea. Yet behind the graceless factories there's a busy little town; its main attractions are the inspired reconstruction of a recently discovered Viking fortress and a gallery of works by the sculptor Axel Ebbe.

From the train station or ferry terminals, walk up Kontinengatan to get to the tourist office (see p.248). They supply a good leaflet, *A Couple of Hours in Trelleborg* (free), its title an accurate reflection of how long most people will stay. A few minutes' further on is the **Axel Ebbe Gallery** (Tues–Sun: early June to early Sept 11am–5pm; early Sept to early June 1–4pm; 20kr) in a compact, 1930s Functionalist building that once was the local bank. Ebbe's superb sculptures make for a powerful collection of sensual nudes in black or white stone, all larger than life. At the turn of the century, Ebbe's gently erotic work was celebrated in Paris, though in Copenhagen, his graceful, sprawling female, *Atlas's Daughter,* was regarded as too erotic for public display. Embracing many of the new styles of the era – Art Nouveau, Neoclassical and National Romanticism – his sculptures are elegant, rhythmic and romantic. The exhibition also includes his distinctive, though less interesting, goblin-like figures that provide a lighter touch. A few steps into the **Stadsparken**, opposite, is Trelleborg's main square, dominated by Ebbe's *Sea Monster,* a fountain comprising a serpentine fiend twined around a characteristically sensual mermaid.

The main shopping promenade here is **Algatan**, running parallel with the sea front. Walking up the street from the ferry terminal end, you'll soon come to **St Nicolai's kyrka**, which has some bright ceiling paintings, elaborate sepulchral tablets, and chairs from a Franciscan monastery destroyed during the Reformation. A couple of minutes' stroll from here is Trelleborg's most dramatic attraction, the **Trelle Fortress** (open all year; free). Dating from around 980 AD, the original circular fortress was built entirely of earth and wood at the behest of King Harald Blue Tooth; it would have encircled a seventh-century settlement of pit houses and itself been surrounded by a moat. The fortress's heyday was over by the eleventh century, when Vandals had raged along the Skånian coast and the inhabitants had fled inland. By making comparisons with four almost identical forts in Denmark and employing a certain amount of guesswork, archeologists have come up with today's impressive reconstruction, built using split oak logs. Though the fortress obviates any need to visit the less impressive run-through of local Viking life at the town **museum**, Östergatan 58 (☎0410/530 50), any visitors here seriously interested in Viking matters would be even better off heading west to **Foteviken** (see p.245).

Practicalities

The **train station** is very close to the ferry terminal; three trains a day run from Malmö to Trelleborg, their arrival timed to connect with the ferry to Sassnitz. **Buses** stop at the bus terminal behind the main square. There's a Forex **exchange** at Friisgatan 1, just outside the Rostock ferry terminal (Mon–Fri 7am–7pm, Sat 7am–1pm, Sun 10am–7pm).

The **tourist office**, just off Kontinengatan at Hamngatan 4 (mid-June to mid-Aug Mon–Fri 9am–8pm, Sat 9am–6pm, Sun 1–6pm; mid-Aug to mid-June Mon to Fri 9am–5pm; ☎0410/533 22, fax 134 86), boasts its own pleasant café, *Garvaregården,* and will book **private rooms** for 130kr plus a 35kr booking fee. For a place to **stay**, there's the *Night Stop* hostel at Östergatan 59, dismal-looking on the outside, though clean inside (100kr, ①); open all night, it's ideal for late ferry arrivals. To get in, walk back to the box on the corner of Johan Kocksgatan and dial 15* on the keypad. The cheap and central *Hotel Standard,* Österbrogatan 4 (☎0410/104 38, fax 71 18 66; ①), has large rooms that are better than the somewhat shabby entrance suggests. At the other end of the quality spectrum, *Hotel Dannegården,* Standgatan 32 (☎0410/481 80, fax 481 81; ⑤/②), is a beautiful 1910 villa surrounded by scented bushes, with five double rooms in their original Art Nouveau style (other rooms are within a much more mundane extension).

The *Hotel Dannegården* is the finest place for a romantic **meal** (Mon–Fri noon–2pm & 6–10pm; closed July), with a good international menu; three courses here will set you back 275kr. On Algatan, a couple of reasonable *konditori* **cafés** include *Billings,* with its verandah, and the similar *Palmblads.* The 1912 National Romantic water tower, behind the bus station, is a pleasant place for a coffee, and convenient when you're waiting for a bus.

Smygehamn and Smygehuk

Around a third of the way from Trelleborg to Ystad along coast Route 9 (bus #183 from Malmö stops here hourly Mon–Fri), the hamlet of Smygehamn prides itself on being Sweden's most southerly point. Half a kilometre before you reach this tiny harbour village, neighbouring **SMYGEHUK** has little to it except a particularly cosy **youth hostel** (for details see below), part of a cluster of pretty, old wooden houses around a quaint **lighthouse**. Built in 1883 and now disused (it's been superseded by an automatic offshore beacon), the lighthouse affords a panoramic sea view, though you'll have to climb its spiral staircase (not especially hard) to partake of the privilege. At its base is Captain Brincks' Cabin: this old lighthouse laundry is crammed with seafaring artefacts from the travels of the old sea captain, who lives in another little cottage nearby and who is more than happy to regale you with nautical tales.

Walk east through the profusely flowering, and even more profusely nettley, low-growing vegetation along the coast, and you'll soon reach **SMYGEHAMN**. Arranged around the tiny harbour are a few summer-only restaurants, a café and a particularly fragrant smoked-fish shop (daily 10am–6pm), which sells excellent salmon marinated in cognac, and also has bread and cutlery – enough ingredients for a cheap picnic. The only other shop here sells souvenirs and is full of wooden geese, recalling the magic bird in the Swedish children's favourite *The Wonderful Adventures of Nils*, by Selma Lagerlöf (see p.420); in the book, the young hero flew the length and breadth of the country on a magic goose, his travels beginning on the Skånian coast.

The harbour has its origins in a coastal limestone quarry; indeed, lime burning was big business here from Smygehamn's heyday in the mid-nineteenth century until the 1950s. The area is still dotted with lime kilns – odd, igloo-like structures with cupola roofs. You can crawl on all fours to get inside the oldest one, just a few metres from the harbour, where limestone was once burned at a thousand degrees.

Just a hundred metres east of the road sign leaving Smygehamn is a sign for **Spettkaka Bageri**. As its name suggests, this is a bakery specializing in *spettkaka*, concoctions of eggs, sugar and potato starch which taste like done-to-death meringues. It's a two-kilometre walk from this sign, through rape fields, to the quaint vine-covered farm where Gudrun Olander famously turns out these Skånian specialities. The *spettkaka* batter is wrapped round and round skewers, then cooked over low heat for up to six hours; the cheapest way of sampling it here is to buy a twenty-centimetre-long arch of the stuff for 15kr.

Practicalities

The **tourist office** in Smygehuk is by the harbour (June–Aug daily 10am–6pm; ☎0410/240 53), inside a fine, early nineteenth-century corn warehouse; it's worth a visit if only for the very cheap coffee (8kr including refills). The nearest hotels proper are in Trelleborg, 13km away, but the area around Smygehuk offers a wide variety of other **accommodation** options. The tourist office can book **private rooms** for just 90kr per person, plus a 35kr booking fee. Smygehuk's **youth hostel** is in what was the lighthouse-keeper's house (☎0410/245 83, fax 245 09; 100kr; mid-May to mid-Sept), with a spacious kitchen and homely living area packed with books. Just 500m away is *Smygehus Havsbad*, in a former bathhouse (☎0410/243 90, fax 293 43), with four-bed cabins for 850kr, including breakfast;

there's a reasonable restaurant, sauna and swimming pool here, too. About 12km east of Smygehuk, and 16km west of Ystad on Route 101, the *Adalen* farm in Skivarp has immaculate self-catering **apartments** (☎0411/307 02) in a converted old barn, an economical choice at 500kr per night.

The hamlet of Boste, 3km inland (signposted off Route 9), has a rather fine **B&B** called *Hedman's* (☎0410/234 73, fax 234 71; ③), celebrated locally for its Thai restaurant and extensive wine list (daily noon–3pm & 8–10pm; main courses 150–200kr). However, the best **restaurant** in the area is *Albinslunds Krog*, Ostra Vemmenhog 7 at Skateholm (☎0411 53 23 10, fax 53 23 11; Tues–Sat 6–11pm, Sun 1–8pm), about 4km east of Smygehuk, serving international gourmet dishes.

East to Ystad: Jordberga and Marvinsholm castles

Between Smygehamn and Ystad, the wedge of countryside south of the E65 highway contains a range of attractive **castles**. In southern Skåne, these are rarely castellated fairy-tale confections, more often taking the form of splendid country houses. Not merely pretty, they warrant a visit for the insight they offer into the wealth of this historic region; we've selected a couple that are particularly rewarding.

From Smygehamn, it's only a few minutes' drive to the spectacular manor house of **Jordberga**: turn off Route 9 at the signpost and head 3km north, first to the village of Klagstorp, then on to another village, Kallstorp. Turn left here at the red brick church; a single sign on the right points the way into the pretty estate of thatched cottages. To get here by **bus**, get the #184 from Trelleborg, which stops at Klagstorp, just 2km away. A house was first built here in the 1350s, though the present house dates back only to 1906 (the preceding incarnation having been ruined by a fire). Rebuilt in classic Baroque style, the house's very setting makes the foray here worthwhile, with a lake surrounding the house like a moat and formal gardens. In the first week of June, it's well worth checking out the annual **Jordberga Festival** (☎0410/261 09 or 264 25 for information) – a diverse musical celebration attracting well-known Swedish musicians and singers running the gamut from classical to rock.

Driving on past the manor for another 3km brings you to the exceptionally pretty **Marsvinsholm Castle**. Here, amid intricate old outbuildings that practically amount to a village, stands an architectural confection regarded as the finest example of Renaissance splendour in southern Sweden. The present building was constructed for Otto Marsvin, a local aristocrat, and stands on piles in the middle of a lake; though renovated in the 1850s, it retains all the dolphin-shaped door handles (*marsvin* being Danish for "dolphin"). The castle has been in the hands of the Iacobaeus family since 1903, who are happy for visitors to stroll in its grounds beyond the immediate garden. Three hundred metres further is an outsized church, second only in size to Lund Cathedral in the whole of Skåne. It once had the highest spire for miles around, but in the 1850s, the castle's owner decreed that his home must rise higher, and so had lofty towers built to overshadow it.

Every July and August, a wide variety of shows in Danish and Swedish are staged in an open-air **theatre** by the castle (for details ☎0411/600 15). A pleasant restaurant and café open during performance evenings, also the only time that the Pågatåg trains stop at Marvinsholm.

Ystad and around

An hour by Pågatåg train from Malmö, the medieval market town of **YSTAD** is exquisitely well preserved. The prettiness of the centre may, however, come as a surprise if you've arrived at the train station down by the murky docks or seen the town's sprawling outskirts. Once in the centre though, you can marvel at the quaint, cobbled lanes, lined with cross-timbered cottages, and the town's chocolate-box central square, oozing rural charm. With the stunningly beautiful coastal region of Österlen stretching northeast from town all the way to Kristianstad (see p.262), and some excellent walking in the forests 20km to the north of town (see p.255), Ystad is a splendid place to base yourself for a day or so.

Arrival, information and accommodation

From the **train station**, cross over the tracks to a square, St Knuts Torg, where you'll find the **tourist office** (May to mid-June Mon–Fri 9am–7pm, Sat 11am–2pm, Sun 11am–6pm; mid-June to mid-Aug Mon–Fri 9am–7pm, Sat 10am–7pm, Sun 11am–6pm; mid-Aug to April Mon–Fri 9am–5pm; ☎0411/776 81, fax 55 55 85, *turistinfo@ystad.se*). Among other things, they can supply copies of a 1753 map of Ystad, still a serviceable guide to the old streets. The square is also where buses from Lund, Kristianstad and Simrishamn will drop you off. The **ferry terminal** is 300m southeast of the train station. **Bikes**, a great way to see the surrounding cycle-friendly landscape, can be rented from Roslins Cykelaffär, Apgränd, close to the tourist office (☎0411/123 15; 65kr a day). Slightly cheaper is Gösta Svenssons Cykel, St. Petri Kyrkoplan 4 (☎0411/55 51 23; 60kr a day), hidden away behind the monastery museum (see p.253).

Accommodation

There are two **youth hostels** in Ystad. One is on the beach at Sandskogen, close to the Saltsjöbaden (☎0411/665 66; 120kr) – take bus #572 or #304; it only takes group bookings from September to May. Much more convenient, and under the same management, is the recently renovated hostel in the old part of the train station (☎0708/57 79 95; 120kr). Next to the *Saltsjöbaden* hostel is the **campsite** (☎0411/192 70; 110kr). There are several good and reasonably priced **hotels** in town, and one at the beach, listed below.

Bäckagården, Bäckagården 36 (☎0411/198 48, fax 657 15). Just behind the tourist office. More a guesthouse than hotel. Price includes breakfast. ②.

Continental, Hamngatan 13 (☎0411/137 00, fax 125 70). A fine hotel touted as Sweden's oldest; its substantial stuccoed facade has been freshened up and opens onto a grand lobby of Corinthian pillars, marble floors and crystal chandeliers. The breakfasts are a treat. ④.

Prins Carl, Hamngatan 8 (☎0411/737 50, fax 665 30). A middle-of-the-range place; some rooms are reserved for non-smokers, while others are adapted for people with disabilities or allergies. ②.

Saltsjöbaden, Saltsjöbadsvägen 6 (☎0411/136 30, fax 55 58 35). This large seaside hotel is over one hundred years old – though you'd never know it, with all the modern corridors that have been tacked on. There's a sauna and summer-only pool, and a restaurant (see p.254). ④.

Sekelgården, Stora Västergatan 9 (☎0411/739 00, fax 189 97). In a former merchant's house dating from 1793, this family-run place boasts a courtyard garden and a great breakfast (included in the price). For a real treat, the attic suite (room no. 49) is a beamed expanse of polished wood, with sea views and its own sauna. The most charming hotel in the heart of Ystad. ②.

Tornväktaven, Stora Östergatan 33 (☎0411/129 54, fax 729 27). Plain and cheap, with breakfast buffet included. A reasonable choice. 595kr.

The Town

Leaving the train or bus stations or the ferry terminals, head west until you reach Hamngatan, where you take a right up the street. This brings you to the well-proportioned **Stortorget**, a grand old square around which twist picturesque streets. West of the church here is Mattorget, a small square, away from which leads Lilla Västergatan, the main street in the seventeenth and eighteenth centuries; strolling down it today, you'll see the best of the town's Lilliputian cottages.

In Stortorget itself, the thirteenth-century **St Maria kyrka** is a handsome centrepiece (daily 10am–4pm), with additions dating from nearly every century since it was built. In the 1880s, these rich decorative features were removed, as they were thought "unsightly", and only the most interesting ones were put back during a restoration programme forty years later. Inside, the Baroque early seventeenth-century pulpit is worth a look for the fearsome face carved beneath it, while opposite is the somewhat chilling medieval crucifix, placed here on the orders of Karl XII to remind the preacher of Christ's suffering. The figure of Christ wears a mop of actual human hair – sacrificed by a local parishioner in the nineteenth century, in an attempt to make it look realistic. Notice also the green box pews to either side of the entrance, which were reserved for women who had not yet been received back into the church after childbirth.

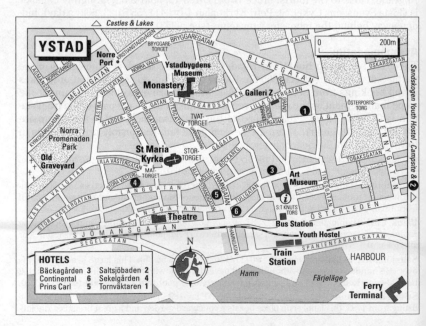

THE NIGHT BUGLER OF YSTAD

Staying in Ystad, you'll soon get acquainted with a tradition that harks back to the seventeenth century: from a room in the church's watchtower, a night watchman sounds a **bugle** every fifteen minutes from 9.15pm to 3am. The haunting sound isn't disturbing, though it's audible wherever you stay in the centre. The sounding through the night was to assure the town that the watchman was still awake (until the mid-nineteenth century, he was liable to be executed if he slept on duty); however, the real purpose of this activity was as a safeguard against the outbreak of **fire**. The idea was that if one of the thatched cottages went up in flames, the bugle would sound repeatedly for all to go and help extinguish the blaze. The melancholic bellowing only ceased during World War II – and then the residents complained they couldn't sleep in the unbroken silence. If you look carefully from Stortorget, you can see just the instrument appear at little openings in the tower walls each time it's played.

Not far from Stortorget, up Lilla or Stora Norregatan, is **Norra Port**, the original northern arched entrance to the town. From here, you can stroll through **Norra Promenaden**, an avenue lined with mature horse-chestnut trees and surrounded by parkland. Here you'll find a white pavilion, built in the 1870s to house a genteel café and a dance hall, with a brass band. Today, the café here, *Café Promenaden* (see p.254) is something of a favourite spot for funeral teas (the small park borders on a graveyard), with many of Ystad's older residents wanting to be remembered at the place where most of them met their loved ones and danced to the band.

Another short stroll from Stortorget, past Garvaregränd's art-and craft workshops (one of which, Krukmakaren, is in a remarkably higgledy-piggledy house on the right), then up Klostergatan, brings you to **Ystadbygdens Museum** (Mon–Fri noon–5pm, Sat & Sun noon–4pm; 20kr, under-16s free). Set in the thirteenth-century Gråbröder (Greyfriars) Monastery, the contents comprise the usual collections on local history, but are given piquancy by their medieval surroundings. After the monks were driven out during the Reformation, the monastery declined and was used as a hospital and a distillery, among others, before becoming a museum in the early twentieth century. The museum has a small café serving coffee and cake for just 20kr. Brightly painted low cottages line the streets around here; a brief stroll down the most picturesque of these, **Vädergrand**, off Lilla Östergatan and just one block up from the *English Book Café* (see p.254), makes for a worthwhile foray. The charismatic owner of the café also runs the impressive **Galleri Z** at Lilla Östergatan 28, which stages temporary exhibitions of contemporary art.

Eating, drinking and nightlife

There is a fair selection of places to eat in Ystad, with some atmospheric **cafés** and fine **restaurants**; most of the latter are on or around Stortorget. To start the day, you can stuff yourself at the *Continental* hotel's huge **breakfast buffet** (75kr). **Nightlife** is pretty minimal, though things are slowly improving; the only trendy club is *Starshine* at Osterportstorg, east from Stortorget (follow

Stora Östergatan, sometimes referred to just as Gågatan). There's a disco and bar here (minimum age 18 on Thursday, 20 on Saturday) and, just once a month, there's "Stardust", an evening for those aged 35 and up. The most recent addition to the scene is *Laura's* on Stora Östergatan (enter through same door as the *Ronsum* supermarket), with a minimum age of 20, though most who turn up are over 25; free entrance makes this disco and casino particularly popular. Otherwise, locals tend to take a bus thirty minutes north to **Tingballa**, where there are a couple of dance halls.

Ystad stages its annual **opera festival** through most of July at Ystad Teater at Skansgatan 36, a charming 1890s building just a few hundred metres from heart of the old town. You can get information on performances and book tickets there (☎0411/105 19).

Cafés, restaurants and bars

Bröderna Pehrsson, corner of Stora Östergatan and Vädergrand (Mon–Fri 8am–6pm, Sat 8am–2pm). Known locally as "The Cup", it's where the town's students and intellectuals come to sip coffee and devour little cakes.

Bruggeriet, Langgatan 20 (☎0411/699 99). Rough-beamed interior dominated by two copper beer casks makes for a welcoming ambience at this fine restaurant. Try the veal with asparagus and nettle sauce. Main courses 130kr. Mon–Sat 11.30am–midnight, Sun 12.30pm–midnight.

Café Promenaden, Norra Promenaden. A pleasant café-restaurant serving fruit pies with coffee, and a range of beers. The new ownership has removed the old velvet settees and silver samovar, robbing this old classic of some its character. Still, there's a good menu, with salmon the speciality. Lunches at 45kr; good-value evening dishes for 85–100kr. June–Aug Mon–Fri 11am–9pm, Sat & Sun 11am– 10pm.

The English Book Café, Gäsegränd (☎0411/16050). Down a tiny, cobbled street off Stora Östergatan. It's all old English china inside this leaning eighteenth-century wooden house, and there are books to read while you eat your home-made scones and tea. The gardens are a real treat, kept close to their 1778 shape. Opening times, like the delightful owner, are a little eccentric.

Kaffestugan Backahasten, Tvattorget. At the western end of Lilla Ostergatan. A charming red and yellow cottage close to the old monastery, with ducklings wandering among the tables. Serves full meals, with an appealing à la carte menu (main courses from 80 kr). Also has cream cakes, cheap baguettes and open sandwiches. Daily 10am–6pm.

Lotta's, Stortorget. The most popular restaurant in town (justifiably so), it packs with locals every summer evening. Try crayfish or butterfish (132kr) or pasta dishes at around 75kr. Even the bread here is like cake: sweet, dense and fragrant. Mon–Fri 5–11pm.

Lotta's Kellare, in the cellars of *Lotta's*. On Stortorget. For a 25–50 age range, Ystad's newest nightlife spot is a cosy bar with several English beers – a popular choice being Manchester United's own brew. June–Aug Mon–Sat 6pm–1am.

Prince Charles Pub, Hamngatan. Next door to the *Prins Carl Hotel*. An English-style pub and restaurant, with lots of maroon velour. There's an extensive meat and fish menu, and live music on Fri and Sat nights. July daily noon–1am, Aug–June Mon–Sat 4pm–1am, Sun noon–10pm.

Rådhuskälleren, Stortorget. In the cellars of the Rådhus. Rather more sedate than *Lotta's* opposite, with candle-lit lunches (55kr) and dinners (200kr), this pricey restaurant is housed in what was once a prison within in the 700-year-old town hall. The atmospheric is romantic, and the place now boasts a celebrated chef. Mon–Fri 11.30am–3pm & 6–11pm, Sat 11.30am–11pm.

Saltsjöbad, Saltsjöbadsvägen 6. The hotel's restaurant does daily lunches (50kr) and has a wide-ranging à la carte menu (main dishes 80–200kr); in July there's live music.

North of Ystad: lakeside hikes and castles

The forested lakes region 20km north of Ystad provides plenty of **hiking** possibilities, both along organized trails and in undeveloped tracts where you can camp rough. The trails, some of which have special tracks for wheelchairs, begin just north of the E65. Take any local bus north in the direction of **Sjöbo** (by car take Route 13), and you'll link up with the **Skåneleden**, a trail, which takes a hundred-kilometre circular route from just outside Ystad. The tourist office (see p.251) can provide route plans as well as details of where to find places to eat and stay en route. You can also head north on foot from Ystad to Hedeskoga and then follow trails that run past a chain of forest-fringed **lakes**: Krageholmsjön, Ellestadssjön, Snogeholmssjön and Sövdesjön (a 20km hike).

Taking Route 13 north out of Ystad, the first village you'll see is **Sövestad**, which has nothing to detain you except a good café-bakery, two doors up from the church, serving home-made cake and coffee. The first lake, with its accompanying castle, **Krageholms Slott**, is at Krageholm, a hamlet 13km further north, from where a four-kilometre signposted track through cornfields all fringed with cornflowers and poppies makes for the prettiest stroll to the castle. Built in the fifteenth century, the castle, now in private hands, is a disappointingly plain cream-stuccoed affair, set in similarly unexceptional grounds.

While there is another lake, Ellestadssjön, a few kilometres north, it's far more interesting to carry on past until you reach the next sizeable lake, **Snogeholmsjön**. Though the original castle here, built in the fifteenth century, was sited on Hagerholmen, the now-overgrown island in the middle of the lake, the present house, in French Baroque style, dates from 1870s; it's one of the few castles in this part of Sweden which are run as a commercial proposition, in this case as a hotel. From the outside, it looks like a French chateau in need of a lick of paint, but the inside is a revelation, all antique wardrobes, glittering chandeliers and elegant drawing rooms., The pictures of the current owners, leaning on guns, and the sight of their hunting trophies – boars, ferrets, deer and owls – peering from plinths above every doorway, waver between splendid and grotesque.

Just 3km northwest lies another beautifully sited lake, Sovdesjön, close to the idyllic hamlet of **Sövde**, which boasts some immaculate cottages. The real draw hereabouts, though, is the smallest of Sweden's six remaining traditional-style apple-presses, **Sövde Musteri**, on Sövdevagen (Fri 9am–5pm, Sat 9am–noon). The affable owner Goran Banke took over this 1890s dairy in 1984, and built their remarkable contraption for pressing apples for the finest juice, cider and scrumpy you'll find anywhere. A bottle of their headily delicious Sovde Glogg, perfumed with cloves, cinnamon, cardamom and ginger, costs just 16kr here.

Just a few minutes' walk away is the enchanting castle, **Sövdeborg Slott**. Only a couple of walls of the original Renaissance manor remain; its fairy-tale medieval facade was in fact the product of renovation in the 1840s. In the 1640s the pile was owned by one Otte Thott, whose two wives were a Miss Gyllenstierne and Miss Rosenkrantz, each from very wealthy, prominent Danish families (which were the inspiration for the characters in *Hamlet*). The grounds are delightful, the castle's moat featuring miniature thatched houses built on stilts; to see the interior, whose highlight is a magnificent ceiling of German baroque gilded oak in the red drawing room, you'll need to make arrangements in advance with Ystad's tourist office (see p.251).

Another 3km northwest of Sövde, **Kulturens Ostarp** is signposted off the road to Veberod (also reachable off Route 11 between Malmo and Sjöbo). In the gently hilly setting stands a **gammelgarden**, an eighteenth-century farm, recreated today as a working farm, with animals drawn from popular breeds of that time. Amid the meadows here are a windmill, and thatched cottages with water wheels. The greatest pleasure here, though, is lunch at the *gästgivaregård* (see below).

Practicalities

Getting around this region is tricky without a car. **Bus #341** between Ystad and Lund stops at Sövde (Mon–Fri every 2hr, Sat & Sun 2 daily). The driver will also drop you off at Ostarp, though you might be stranded once there if you're reliant on the infrequent buses. For a place to **stay**, there's the **hotel** at Snogeholms Slott, perched at the lake's edge (☎0416/162 00, fax 160 18; ⑤/④); it has a fine **restaurant** that takes advantage of the local produce. In Sjöbo, *Sjöbo Gastgiveri* serves excellent meals with daily lunch specials at 55kr. The *gästgivaregård* in Ostarp has a good à la carte menu and, on Sundays, a smorgasbord special (Tues–Thurs 11.30am–6pm, Fri 11.30am–3pm, Sat & Sun 12.30–6pm).

Österlen and the coast to Åhus

It's easy to see how the landscape of the southeastern corner of Skåne, known as **Österlen**, has lured writers and artists to its coastline and plains: here, standing out against the cobalt-blue skies of summer, are sunburst-yellow fields of rape, punctuated only by white cottages, fields of blood-red poppies and the odd black windmill. Along with the vivid beauty of its countryside, Österlen has a number of engaging sights, notably pretty villages, plenty of smooth, sandy beaches, and the Viking ruin of **Ales Stennar**. Moving further northeast are the orchards of Sweden's apple-growing region, **Kivik**, with its fragrant and surreal Apple House museum and a nearby Bronze Age cairn. At the far northeastern end of this stretch of the coast lies **Åhus**, a fairly low-key resort famous for smoked eels.

Unfortunately, **getting around** this part of the country isn't straightforward; the only major road, Route 9 to Kristianstad via Simrishamn, bypasses the most interesting southeastern corner of Österlen. The whole area is poorly served by buses, and the only train service is the Pågatåg from Ystad to Simrishamn. If you haven't got a car, the best way to get around is to use a combination of public transport, walking and cycling.

From Ystad to Ales Stennar

There are two ways to get to Ales Stennar from Ystad: either take **bus #322** (20min) or rent a bike and follow the coastal cycle track for the twenty-kilometre journey. The track runs through an area of pine forest opening onto white sandy beaches, with excellent bathing opportunities. From here (following signs to the hamlet of Kåseberga), you'll pass through a wedge of attractive, but uneventful, rolling fields that stretch for several kilometres. Near Kåseberga is **Ales Stennar**, an awe-inspiring Swedish Stonehenge. Believed to have been a Viking meeting place, it consists of 56 **stones** forming a 67-metre-long boat-shaped edifice, prow and stern denoted by two appreciably larger **monoliths**.

The site was hidden for centuries beneath shifting sands, which were cleared in 1958; even now, the bases of the stones are concealed in several metres of sand. It's difficult to imagine how these great stones, not native to the region, might have been transported here. Ales Stennar stands on a windy, flat-topped hill, which most of the tourists snapping away don't bother to climb; once at the top, though (it's a steep, 10min hike), there's a majestic timelessness about the spot that more than rewards the effort.

On the way to the site from the nearby car park, you'll pass a string of single-storey, white cottages, one of which houses the *Café Solståndet* (the owners live here, so opening hours are flexible), where you can have filling baguettes (40kr) or an excellent breakfast. They also do **B&B** (☎ & fax 04115/272 73 or 52 72 80; 150kr).

The Hagestad Nature Reserve

For a day in really splendid natural surroundings, it's hard to beat the **Hagestad Nature Reserve**, the best of the three reserves around the village of **Backåkra**, a signposted drive 5km east of Kåseberga. Thousands of pines were planted here in the eighteenth and nineteenth centuries to bind the sandy earth, and, together with oaks and birches, they make up a densely forested area; the clumps of gnarled, stunted oaks are particularly distinctive. It's especially beautiful in mid-summer when orchids and heathers colour the forest floor; if you're lucky, you may also see elk, badgers and roe deer, while buzzards and golden orioles are often sighted above. The reserve is also the home of the most glorious **beach** in Skåne: walk along any path towards the sea and you'll soon reach a bright white ribbon of sand – marked "Sandhammaren" on signs – backed by steep dunes and lapped by turquoise waters.

In the midst of the nature reserve, uphill on heathland towards Backåkra is an old farmstead (signposted from Backåkra) once owned by **Dag Hammarskjöld**, United Nations secretary-general in the 1950s. His love of the Skånian coast led him to buy the farm and the surrounding sixty acres in order to save it from developers. Killed in a plane crash in 1961, Hammarskjöld willed the farm and its contents to STF, which now runs the house as a **museum** (opening times vary; call ☎0411/260 10 or 261 51; 25kr). It contains intriguing pieces of art from all over the world, including an ancient Egyptian painting of the jackal-headed god Anubis, Greek bronzes from 200BC and contemporary pieces by Barbara Hepworth, Picasso and Matisse.

Practicalities

Backåkra village has a well-equipped STF **youth hostel**, in an old school house with a bus stop right outside (☎0411/260 80; 70kr, ①; mid-Aug to April advance booking necessary through Ystad's tourist office). You can **rent bikes** here at 30kr per day; though some of these have seen better days, they're functional and perfect for exploring the nature reserves. At **Löderups Strandbad**, just west of Backåkra, is a beautifully situated **campsite**, with a **café** and **restaurant**. About 8km east of Backåkra, on the road to Skillinge (see overleaf), there's another cheap place to stay: the *Villa Myrbacka* at Ornahusen (☎0411/200 76). Rooms in this simple house, located just 75m from the beach, cost from 150kr per person.

Skillinge

Just beyond the midway point on the road from Backåkra to Simrisham (see below), the sleepy fishing hamlet of **Skillinge** hasn't much in the way of things to do, but does have a couple of the best restaurants and places to stay in the region. Bus #573 stops here en route from Ystad to Simrisham (Mon–Fri 3 daily).

At the harbourfront, the tiny **sjofart** (sea-faring) **museum** doesn't take long to explore; down at the far end, past the fish-exporting warehouse, is **Skeppshandel** (April–Oct Mon–Fri 10am–6pm, Sat & Sun 11am–4pm) a museum-cum-store of sea-related antiquities, art and books. The place smells of smoked fish, which is unsurprising given the *fisk rokeri* round the back. During the summer, **musical evenings**, talks and suchlike take place at the rustic *Sjöbacka farm*, just 700m back from the sea, with views across to the Danish island of Bornholm from its raised setting amid the rape fields. The charming owners, who moved here from Gothenburg, run the place as a **bed and breakfast** (☎ and fax 0414/301 66; ①). Right on the waterfront is another B&B, *Ankarklyset,* in a cottage on the corner of Strandgatan and Kapellstraddet (☎0414/303 16; ①); its staircase was crafted out of wood from shipwrecks. Another pleasant option is the central *Skillinge Gastgard,* Byggmastaregatan 6, by the harbour (☎0414/303 90, fax 311 28; ①).

Two excellent **restaurants** make Skillinge worth a stop. A couple of centuries ago, *Bursen*, on Strandgatan, was where local sea captains gathered to swap news and do business; now, fish and meat dishes of exceptional quality are served here in a convivial family-run atmosphere (☎0414 /300 03; Mon noon–2pm & 6–10pm, Thurs & Fri 6–10pm, Sat & Sun 1–10pm). A hundred metres away, overlooking the sea, *Hamnkrogen* specializes in seafood (☎0414/308 25 Tues–Fri noon–10pm, Sat 1–10pm, Sun 1–6pm); for an inexpensive treat, try their hot, crunchy fried herring with cold sour cream. For a day-time **café**, *Gallerian Skillinge* on Killebacksgatan serves scones, waffles and coffee in an old black and white barn just metres from the harbourfront. Especially useful for self-catering is the surprisingly well-stocked **provisions shop** called *Köpmangarden* at 36 Strandgatan. To **rent a bike**, head to Skillinge Kiosk & Mack (☎0414 /302 84; 45kr a day).

Simrishamn and Glimmingehus Castle

There's not much to the little fishing town of **SIMRISHAMN** (about 25km north of Backåkra), though its old quarter of tiny cottages and its church, orginally built as a fishermen's chapel in the twelfth century, are pretty enough. On Storgatan, the unexceptional **museum** is full of the usual archeological finds and bits and pieces of farming and fishing equipment.

One impressive sight, just off Route 9, a few kilometres inland from Simrishamn, is the thirteenth-century **Glimmingehus Castle** (daily: April & Sept to mid-Oct 11am–4pm; May to mid Aug 10am–6pm; 45kr). Standing like an upright brick amid the flat landscape and visible for miles around, Glimmingehus lacks any of the aesthetic niceties of most of Sweden's castles, but is remarkably well preserved. One of the few projections on its flat facade is an oriel from which missiles could be dropped, clear evidence of its role as a fortification. In fact, the architect, Adam Van Duran was drafted in to dream up as many impenetrable features as possible, and his two-metre-thick walls and slits for windows certainly lived up to the brief. The only concession to comfort was an ingenious heating system spreading warmth from the kitchen upwards. Ironically, this was one castle that was never attacked; the only threat to its existence was Karl XI's desire to demolish Glimmingehus, after Skåne had became a Swedish province, in order to prevent Danish guerrillas getting hold of it.

Practicalities

Little Österlenaren **trains** run to Simrishamn from Malmö, stopping at Ystad; from Skillinge, you can get **bus** #575 here. **Bikes** can be rented at the *Ublivs* supermarket on the harbourfront, where they charge 30kr for the first day and 50kr for subsequent days; for longer periods, it's cheaper to use Österlens Cykel (☎0414/177 44; 60kr for the first day, therafter 30kr per day). The **tourist office** is by the harbour at Tullhusgatan 2 (☎0414/160 60); they can organize **cycling packages**, which include accommodation and cheap bike rental.

Housed in a renovated tavern, *Hotell Kockska Garden*, Storgatan 25 is a comfortable place to **stay** (☎0414/41 17 55, fax 41 19 78; ③). A couple of doors down, *Hotel Turistgarden* at no. 21 is pleasant enough (☎0414/166 22, fax 137 01; ③/②). The town's so-called premier hotel, *Hotel Svea*, by the harbour (☎0414/41 17 20, fax 143 41; ④/③) is more functional than stylish; its appealing **restaurant** serves a range of Swedish fish and meat dishes, with a couple of vegetarian options. Among other places to eat, one of the best is *Börje Olssons Skafferi*, Storgatan 13 (Mon–Fri 10am–6pm, Sat 10am–2pm), a charcuterie-cum-deli where you can serve yourself from a buffet of pastas, meats and breads for 40kr, or have a filled baguette, also for 40kr. *Hokarn's Cafe Krog*, on Storgatan (1–6pm), has daily specials for 60kr; next door, the *konditori* and café does good sandwiches and cake (Mon–Fri 6.30am–5.45pm, Sat 6.30am–5pm, Sun 8am–5pm). Equally pleasant is *Mans Byckare*, directly opposite (daily 11.30am–2pm), with lunch specials at 60 kr. More elegant evening dining can be had at the candle-lit *Maritim Krog* on Hamngatan 31, at the harbour, where you can also hear traditional jazz sounds at their **jazz club** (50kr).

Kivik and around

Not quite halfway along the coast from Simrishamn to Åhus (take Route 9 for about 9km), **KIVIK** is Sweden's **apple-growing region**, the dark forests and hilly green meadows giving way to endless orchards. As you wander through the countryside here, the pungent smell of wild garlic mixes with the fragrance of apple blossom. Kivik village has no obvious centre; the bus stops outside *Kivik Vardhus* hotel (see p.260). The uncommercialized harbour is just a few minutes away down Södergatan, and within a couple of kilometres are a number of sights: Sweden's most notable Bronze Age remains, **Kungagraven**; a cider factory with an **Apple House** that has to be seen to be believed; and **Stenshuvud National Park**, which offers fine walks. It all makes for a day's worth of enjoyable sightseeing and meandering. For two days around the middle of July each year, Kivik hosts one of the country's biggest **markets**, an enormous event with stalls and family entertainment centred around the main square.

Kungagraven

Just 500m from the Kivik bus stop lies **Kungagraven** (King's Grave; May–Aug daily 10am–6pm; 10kr), a striking 75-metre-wide Bronze Age cairn, an upturned saucer of rocks that was rediscovered by a farmer in 1748. A burial cist at its centre, entered by a banked entrance passage, contains eight flood-lit, three-thousand-year-old runic slabs bearing pictures of horses, a sleigh and what look like dancing seals. For coffee and cake in a gorgeous setting, try *Café Sågmöllan*, in the old thatched mill-cottage by the stream, next to the ticket kiosk.

Kiviksmusteri and the Apple House

Two kilometres from the grave (follow the signs), **Kiviksmusteri** is a cider factory, with a shop selling apple juices, sauces, ciders, dried apple-rings, and apple or pear wines by the crate. You can't tour the factory; in any case the attraction here is the **Apple House** (April & May 10am–5pm; June–Sept 10am–6pm; tours 20kr, under-16s free). A non-profit-making venture, the Apple House is aimed at making visitors as obsessed with apples as its dedicated workers, whose flowing smocks bear an apple print. In a new building painted in apple greens and reds is an entire apple museum, each room infused with a different smell. The room devoted to "great apples in history" (Adam and Eve's, Newton's etc) smells of cider, while the room detailing attempts to create an insect-resistant commercial apple smells of apple pie. Other less sane exhibitions concentrate on such topics as "the symphonic soul of apples", while an Internet facility allows addicts to send apple-related messages to one another around the world. You can ask one of the guides here to describe things in English (the displays themselves don't have English labelling).

Stenshuvuds National Park

After the Apple House, **Stenshuvuds National Park**, just 200m away, is the perfect place to come back to reality. The hill which comprises the park is almost 100m high, and the view from the top is superb, particularly over Hanöberg, a village to the east. A self-guided walk (descriptive leaflets are available from boxes at the starting point) will take you to the remnants of an ancient fortress, while wheelchair-accessible paths lead through the beautiful forested hillsides. Close to the car park is a charming café, with good pastries.

Practicalities

The frequent Skåne Express **bus** runs from Simrishamn to Kivik (30min) and from Kristianstad (55min). **Bikes**, a great choice for the local sights and in particular the orchards, can be rented at the harbour kiosk (mid-June to mid-Aug 10am–10pm; 75kr a day). Opposite the bus stop is a **hotel**, *Kivik Vardhus*, in a nineteenth-century vine-covered farmhouse, with pleasant rooms (☎0414/700 74, fax 710 20; ②; May–Aug). For cheaper accommodation, there's the STF **youth hostel** north of the harbour at Tittutvägen (☎0414/711 95; 130kr); just five minutes' walk from the bus stop. Three kilometres north of Kivik along Route 118 is another hostel, the basic, spotless *Angdala Vandrarhem* (☎0414/741 79 or 731/47), delightfully set amid the orchards and particularly lovely in May and June when the trees are a mass of pink and white blossom. A good choice for **camping** is 23km north of Kivik along Route 118, and 5km south of Åhus; follow the sign off Route 118 to *Martins Rokeri* and you'll come to the tranquil riverside site, where tents can be pitched for 100kr.

At the *Kivik Vardhus* **restaurant** (daily 11.30am–9pm), lunches cost 55kr; the dinnertime speciality is local venison. Another good **place to eat** is *Kärnhuset*, at the Apple House (see above). It serves only local produce, with an inevitable emphasis on apple desserts, and exceptionally good fresh-pressed cider. Back near the harbour, *Café Gallile*, on Eliselundsvägen (daily 7.30am–5pm) offers coffee, cakes and Skånian *spettkaka* (see p.249). There's also an excellent harbourside fish smokery called Buhres (daily 10am–5pm), where you can sample a dozen varieties of pickled herring and smoked eel before buying. They've also set up a burger bar – all they have are fish-burgers, of course.

Åhus

Once a major trading port, and in medieval times a city of considerable ecclesiastical importance, Åhus, 55km north of Simrishamn, relies on holidaying Swedes for its income today. The town is famed for its eels, which appear on menus all over the country, smoked and usually served with scrambled eggs, and for its popular (though unexceptional) ice cream.

From the tourist office (see below), it's a short walk up Köpmannagatan to the cobbled main square. On the left, the stylish modern building blending with an old red-brick factory behind (the latter best seen from the harbour) is the **Absolut Vodka Factory**. Not officially open to the public, it can be visited on a tour (call ☎044/28 81 13). Before leaving, note the remarkable sculpture outside, dotted with tiny, inebriated characters. A few steps away, also on the main square, is the **museum** (mid-June to mid-Aug daily 1–6pm; Sept Mon–Fri 1–6pm; free), in the strawberry-painted old Rådhus. There are no surprises here though; a more appealing sight is the wonderfully preserved twelfth-century **St Maria kyrka** behind, with its glistening altarpiece and high-ended pews; the church's sheer size attests to the town's former eminence. In the graveyard, take a look at the headstone of Captain Måns Mauritsson: according to the inscription, the captain's wife, Helena Sjöström, was 133 years old when she died, and her daughters were born when she was 82 and 95 years old respectively! The captain himself only lived to 101.

At nearby Västerport (walk to the end of Västergatan from the centre) is **Tobaksmonopolets Lada** (free), a building that contains tobacco labels and all the paraphernalia of tobacco processing. For 250 years, the crop was very important in Åhus; every household had a tobacco patch in their gardens, until 1964, when the government cancelled its contract with the growers and the industry here finally came to an end.

Beyond this, there's little more to do than cut through from the main square down Västra Hamngatan, a street opposite the museum, to the waterside. Pleasure boats line the harbour, which is quite a pretty spot – if you avert your eyes from the industrial area to the left. For the **beach**, head out on Järnvägsgatan, behind the tourist office, past a run of old train carriages – there are no trains running now – and left up Ellegatan, following signs for Åhus **Strand**. The twenty-minute walk takes you past some weather-worn but fine old houses, redolent of a bygone era. Every July, there's a **jazz festival** in town, organized in collaboration with Kristianstad; ask at the tourist office for details.

Practicalities

Arriving by bus, it's easiest to approach from Kristianstad (from where there are also sightseeing boat trips; see p.265), 20km to the northwest (#551; 25min). The bus stops at the **tourist office**, Köpmannagatan 2 (March–May, Sept & Oct Mon–Fri 10am–5pm; June–Aug Mon–Fri 9am–7pm, Sat 9am–6pm, Sun 2–6pm; Nov–Feb Mon–Fri 1–5pm, ☎044/24 01 06, fax 24 38 98, *touristinfo.ahus@kristianstad.se*), who **rent bikes** for 50kr a day; another bike shop to try, on Ellegatan (on the way to the beach), rents out double-pedalled buggy bikes (40kr an hour; the two riders sit side-by-side on these). The **youth hostel** is at Stavgatan 3, just a few metres away (☎044/24 85 35; 130kr; book through tourist office Sept–May). A central **hotel** is *Gästgivaregård*, at the harbour, whose pricey rooms all have sea views (④). Alternatively, you can stay on the bus for an extra few minutes to get to the beach, where there are plenty of hotels, such as *Hotel Åhus Strand* (☎044/28 93 00, fax 24 94 80; ②), a reasonable place, if plain. The inexpensive *Sports Hotel* nearby is owned by the *Åhus Strand* (you can book rooms through them; ①); it's dismal to look at though and feels more like a hostel. Åhus' **campsite** is in the forest near the beach (its location is signposted) and has a heated open-air pool and a restaurant (☎044/24 89 69).

There are some lovely places to **eat** in Åhus. Down by the harbour, the genteel *Gästgivaregård* specializes in Baltic fish dishes (Mon–Fri 11.30am–2pm & 6–10pm, Sat 3–10pm, Sun noon–4pm). Just 200m along the waterside from here, though, is the most enjoyable and relaxed place in town: *Ostermans* at Gamla Skeppsbron (May–Sept daily 3.30–10.30pm). At this small, wooden restaurant, Greenland prawns are the only item on the menu, and you buy your meal by weight – a kilogram costs 180kr. Most people manage half a kilo of the stuff, along with bread, sauces and beer. Also at the harbour, *Belle Époque Restaurant* and *Skylight Glassbar* both serve ice cream in the same old wooden boat, with a top-deck pub. For a cheap but delightful café-restaurant, head back up Västra Hamngatan to *Gallericaféet* at no. 4 (June–Aug daily noon–6pm), where the garden restaurant specializes in local seafood. Try their sandwiches filled with smoked eel, warm smoked salmon or herrings in dill (30–54kr).

Kristianstad

Twenty kilometres inland, eminently likable **KRISTIANSTAD** (for its correct pronunciation, try a gutteral "Krwi-chwan-sta") is eastern Skåne's most substantial historic centre and a perfect gateway to Sweden's southern coast. Dating from 1614, when it was created by Christian IV, Denmark's seventeenth-century "builder-king", during Denmark's 44-year rule here, it's the earliest and most evocative of his Renaissance towns. With its beautifully proportioned central squares and broad gridded streets flanking the wide river, it's a shining example of the king's architectural preoccupations. Christian nurtured plans to make the fortified town one of Denmark's most important, and it wasn't until the mid-nineteenth century that the fortifications were finally levelled, allowing the town to spill beyond the original perimeter. The late nineteenth century saw the creation of Parisian-style boulevards, so pleasant to wander through today, which earned the town the nickname "Little Paris".

Arrival, information and accommodation

The city's sparkling **airport** is 17km from the town centre; you can rent a car there from any of the major agencies. Buses from the airport to the centre are timed to leave shortly after flights arrive (20min; 40kr). Local buses from Ystad (1hr 30min), Simrishamn (1hr 30min) and Åhus (30min) all stop outside the central **bus station** on Östra Boulevarden. The fast, ultra-comfortable Kustpilen Express trains stop off here on their Malmö–Karlskrona runs; the **train station**, with left-luggage lockers, is centrally located just opposite the Holy Trinity Church. The **tourist office** is down Nya Boulevarden (mid-June to mid-Aug Mon–Fri 9am–7pm, Sat 9am–3pm, Sun 2–6pm; mid-Aug to mid-June Mon–Fri 10am–5pm, last Sat of each month 11am–3pm; ☎044/12 19 88, fax 12 08 98, *touristinfo@kristianstad.se*); to get here, turn right out of the train station and then take the second left. **Bikes** can be rented from them for 50kr a day or 250kr a week.

Accommodation

The tourist office can book **private rooms** from 150kr plus a 40kr fee (or you can check the list on the door and book yourself for free). There is a **campsite** at *Charlottsborg Camping*, 2km away (☎044/21 07 67; bus #22 or #23; Fri & Sat nights bus #17 to Vä from Busstorget, close to Lilla Torget). There's also a **youth hostel** here (same phone no. as campsite; 110kr); campers can use all the hostel facilities such as the TV and lounge room. As Kristianstad isn't a holiday resort, prices at its **hotels**, a selection of which appears below, come down in summer and at weekends.

Hotel Christian IV, Västra Boulevarden 15 (☎044/12 63 00, fax 12 41 40). Just south of Stora Torg, in a rather splendid building once home to Sparbank, retaining its original fireplaces and parquet floors; the old bank vaults are now a washroom and a wine cellar. ⑤/②.

Grand Hotel, Västra Storgatan 15 (☎044/10 36 00, fax 12 57 82). This modern, modest-looking place offers excellent friendly service and well-equipped en-suite rooms, with supremely comfortable beds. ⑤/③.

Lillemors B&B, (☎044/21 95 25, mobile 070/521 68 00). Built in the 1790s, this cosy hotel has exposed beams, a bright country-style attic dining room and spacious bedrooms. ②.

Stadshotel, Stora Torg (☎044/ 10 02 55, fax 10 25 80). Once the freemasons' hall. The lobby is all panelled opulence; the rooms, though, have modern decor. ④/②.

Hotel Turisten, Västra Storgatan 17 (☎044/12 61 50, fax 10 30 99). Off Stora Torg. With a friendly atmosphere, good breakfast and sauna, this is also the only hotel in town with actual baths in some of its bathrooms (the rest have showers only). Good value and very comfortable. ③/②.

The Town

The most obvious starting point is the 1618 **Trefaldighetskyrkan** (Holy Trinity Church; daily 9am–5pm) right opposite the train station. It symbolizes all that was glorious about Christian's Renaissance ideas: the grandiose exterior has seven magnificent spiralled gables, and the building's high windows allow light to flood the white interior. Inside, the most striking features are the elaborately carved pew ends: each is over 2m tall, and no two are the same; the gilded Baroque magnificence of the 1630 organ facade is also worth a look.

Diagonally across from the church, the main square, **Stora Torg**, contains the late nineteenth-century **Rådhus**, built in imitation of Christian's Renaissance design. Inside the entrance, a bronze copy of the king's 1643 bust is something of a revelation: Christian sports a goatee beard, one earring and a single dreadlock, and exposes a nipple decorated with a flower motif, itself a source of interest for a baby elephant round the royal neck. Opposite the town hall, and in marked contrast to it, the 1920s post office and the old Riksbank (the latter now home to a popular steakhouse and pub; see p.266), have an identical 1920s brick design; while the adjacent 1640s Mayor's House is different again, with a Neoclassical yel-

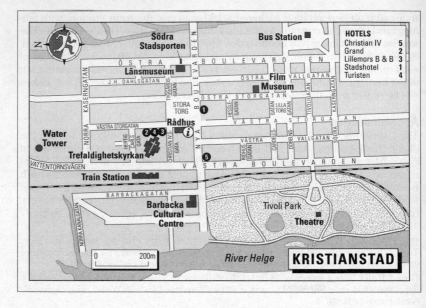

low-stuccoed facade. The square also boasts Palle Pernevi's splintered *Icarus* fountain, which depicts the unfortunate Greek soul falling from heaven into what looks like a scaffolded building site. The town's streets are peppered with modern **sculptures**; one of the best is Axel Olsson's bronze *Romeo & Juliet* at Östra Storgatan 3, close to Storatorg, depicting an accordion player serenading a woman emerging from a doorway.

Behind the post office and old bank is the **Länsmuseum** (June–Aug Tues, Thurs & Fri 10am–5pm, Wed 10am–6pm; Sept–May Tues & Thurs–Sat noon–5pm, Wed noon–6pm; free). Construction of its building was started by Christian in 1616; he intended to make it a grand palace, but, thanks to the bloody Skånian wars, work got no further than the low buildings. As soon as they were built, the stables here were turned into an arsenal containing ammunition for the pro-Danish partisans. Today, the museum is home to permanent exhibitions about the Snapphare (from the German *schnappen*, to snatch or steal), as these partisans were called.

It's a pleasant stroll up Nya Boulevarden to Östra Boulevarden, where you can see **Södra Stadsporten**, the southern town gate which dates from the 1790s; it was one of the few bits of fortification saved before the great demolition. There's a park close by, but it's considerably duller than the lovely Tivoli Park to the south (see p.265); more fun while you're here is to peep in at J.H. Dahlsgatan 8, one block south of the town gate, a gorgeous muddle of narrow outhouses framing a beautiful hidden courtyard around a Renaissance merchant's home. For a panoramic overview of both the town and the local lakes of Hammarsjön and Aradövssjön, connected by the River Helge, it's just a couple of minutes' walk west to the **water tower** (Mon–Sat 10am–6pm, Sun noon–6pm; free). A small lift takes you up the 42 floors to the top (the stairs are kept locked), where there are wall maps for orientation; there's also a café here.

Walking back through the town centre, a few minutes east of the Storatorg is the **Film Museum**, Ostra Storgatan 53 (Tues–Fri & Sun 1–4pm; free), a bronze model of an early twentieth-century movie camera stood outside its door. This was Sweden's oldest film studio; inside, you can watch some flickering old movie clips. Wander down any of the roads to the right and you'll reach **Tivoli Park**, known locally as the "English Park", where you can stroll down avenues of horse-chestnut and copper beech trees. In its centre is a fine Art Nouveau **theatre**, a stylish white building whose designer, Axel Anderberg, also designed the Stockholm Opera (p.75). Just to the south, **sightseeing boats** (*vattenriket*) splash their way up the river, the trips including commentary on history and river life (May to mid-June & mid-Aug to mid-Sept 3 daily at 11am, 2pm and 6pm; 2hr; 70kr, children 40kr).

Just to the west of the park is the **Barbacka Cultural Centre**, Barbackagatan (Sept to mid-July Mon–Fri 9am–5pm, Sat & Sun noon–4pm; ☎044/13 56 50), an ideal place to come with children, with hands-on science experiment rooms, live snakes coiled in glass columns and mountains of educational toys. There's a full programme of theatrical events (mostly for children), for which language barriers are not a problem. While you're here, you can grab a bite at their organic eco-café.

If you happen to arrive during the last week of May, expect hotels to be booked full for the five-day **South Swedish Rally**. Billing itself "the third largest car rally in Northern Europe", it is much advertised all over town; the tourist office can tell you the best vantage points.

Eating, drinking and nightlife

Kristianstad has a number of really good, stylish places to eat. The prettiest **café** is in *Fornstuga House*, which serves just waffles and coffee in an elaborately carved Hansel-and-Gretel lodge in the middle of Tivoli Park (daily 10am–5pm, stays open later if there are park concerts). A classic and central *konditori* is *Du Vanders*, Hesslegatan 6 (Mon–Fri 8am–7pm, Sat 8am–5pm, Sun 10am–5pm), which has been serving cakes and meringues since 1934. Nearby, at *Grafitti Café*, Västra Storgatan 45, you can fill up cheaply on baked potatoes (Mon–Fri 10am–6.30pm; Sat & Sun 10am–2pm). For excellent Swedish home cooking at very reasonable prices, it's worth jumping on the Kustpilen Express train for the fifteen-minute journey west to Vinslöv (by car, take Route E21 towards Hässleholm). Outside Vinslöv's train station, to the left, you'll find *Vinslöv Vardhus* (Mon–Thurs & Sat 11.30am–3pm, Fri 4–11pm) that prepares superb meat and fish dishes for the locals.

Bar-B-Ko, Tivoligatan (☎044/21 33 55). An inviting place, specializing in grilled meats. Main courses from 100kr. Mon–Thurs 6–11pm, Fri & Sat 6pm–midnight.

Christian Kock, Västra Storgatan. Next to the *Grand Hotel*. Serves Swedish delights like nettle soup and interesting combinations of meats, fish and fruits at 130kr. Fine cooking in candle-lit, modern elegance. Mon–Fri 11.30am–2pm & 5pm–midnight; Sat 5pm–midnight.

Classic,Nya Boulevarden 6. Just off Storatorg. The city's only Greek restaurant, with a wide range of main courses. Try the authentic moussaka. Main courses from just 60kr. Daily 4–11pm.

Restaurant Kippers, Östra Storgatan. In a building that dates from 1600. The eating area is in the original vaulted cellar, with crispbread hanging from the ceiling to dry. They specialize in steaks and poultry dishes. Dinner costs about 250kr, lunches 140kr. Mon 6–10 pm, Tues–Thurs 11.45am–1.15pm & 6–10pm; Fri 11.45am–1.15pm & 6pm–2am; Sat 6pm–2am.

Restaurant Roma, Östra Storgatan 15. An inexpensive Italian restaurant, worth trying for its generous pizzas at 65kr. Mon–Thurs 11.30am–2pm & 5–10pm, Fri till 11pm, Sat & Sun 6–9pm.

Restaurant Sparet, at the train station. Provides excellent value meals in modern surroundings, with the emphasis on fish dishes at around 100kr. Also filling staples like *pytt i panni* at 49kr. June–Aug Mon–Sat noon–2.30pm, 4–10.30pm; Sept–May Mon–Sat 4–10.30pm.

Skänken Pub and Restaurant, Stora Torg. In the dark old Riksbank building. One of the most frequented of the town's bars, with around three hundred beers, this place also has an eclectic dinner menu, ranging from the inevitable herring to kangaroo and alligator. Main courses from 150kr. Mon, Tues & Thurs 11.30am–11pm, Wed till 1am, Fri till 2am, Sat noon–2am.

Bars, clubs and entertainment

For loud rock **music**, try *Harry's Bar*, Östra Storgatan (not one of the southern Sweden *Harry's Bar* chain), with a 30-something crowd and has a very popular beer garden. German folk music, beers and food are to be had at a little German-owned pub, *Hesslebaren*, opposite the *Du Vanders konditori* on Hesslegatan (Mon–Fri 11am–2pm & every night till late except Mon). The most attractive **drinking venue**, though, has to be *Garvare Garden* on Tivoligatan (Mon–Fri 11am–10pm, Sat noon–11pm, Sun noon–9pm), in a lovely old house; there's good food here too. On weekdays, your only chance of a late night drink is at *Kong Christian,* Tivoligatan; this Irish theme bar is open till 1am, or 2am on Fridays and Saturdays.

There's not much choice in the way of **nightclubs**. *Uppblasbar*, above the *Sparet* restaurant at the train station, caters mainly for teenagers (Wed, Fri & Sat 9.30pm–2am). In the basement of the *Grand Hotel* is the glitzy *Grands Nightclub* (Thurs 8pm–2am, Fri & Sat 9pm–1am), for somewhat dated disco sounds and a mid-20s crowd. If you're 30 or older, it's probably best to head to the basement of the *Classic* restaurant (see p.265), which is liveliest Fri & Sat till 2pm.

The town hosts two annual festivals: **Kristianstadsdagarna**, a huge seven-day cultural festival in the second week of July; and the annual **Kristianstad and Åhus Jazz Festival**, around the same time; details of both can be obtained at the tourist office.

Into Blekinge: east to Ronneby

The county of **Blekinge** is something of a poor relation to Skåne in terms of tourism. Tourist offices here put out an endless stream of glossy brochures calling the region "the garden of Sweden", with each of its towns, predictably, the "heart" or "pearl" of that garden. The reality is that there are some good beaches, plentiful fishing, fine walking trails and enough cultural diversions to make Blekinge enjoyable for two or three days. The landscape is much the same as in northeastern Skåne: forests and hills, with grassland fringing the sea. A number of islands and a small archipelago south of Karlskrona make for picturesque destinations on short boat trips. If you only have a day or two in the region, it's best to head to the handsome and lively town of **Karlskrona**, the county capital (see p.271), from where the tiny, fortified hamlet of **Kristianopel** is just 30km away (see p.275).

The Kustpilen Express **train** runs from Malmö and Lund to Karlskrona, and stops at all the towns detailed below. **Public transport** in Blekinge requires some careful scrutiny of timetables to avoid being stranded in the evenings; at weekends in particular, there are likely to be no regional trains or buses between the towns. The taxi drivers are keenly aware of this fact, charging, for example, 250kr to take you between Ronneby and Karlshamn; hitching is nigh on impossible on this route.

Karlshamn

After **KARLSHAMN** was destroyed by fire in 1763, its wealthy merchants built themselves ever grander houses, some of which are still standing. The town saw its heyday in the nineteenth century, when it was a centre for the manufacture of such goodies as punch, brandy and tobacco – today, margarine and ice-cream factories flank the harbour. Karlshamn has some beautiful little streets of pastel-painted houses, a clutch of museums, including a splendid eighteenth-century merchant's house, a couple of summertime festivals that transform the town into a mini-Woodstock, and offshore islands (see box below) that offer wooded retreats and the chance of some swimming.

From the train station, turn left onto Eric Dahlbergsvägen, and right down Kyrkogatan, which is lined with old, wooden houses painted pale yoghurty shades. At its junction with Drottninggatan squats Karl Gustav kyrka, an unusually-shaped late seventeeth-century church. Walking down Kyrkogatan, you are retracing the steps of nineteenth-century emigrants on their way to "New Sweden" in America; for many this was the last bit of their homeland they would ever see. A grey house, on the left, with flights of external stairs either side of its

---

ISLAND TRIPS FROM KARLSHAMN AND RONNEBY

With a smattering of attractive **islands** punctuating the waters to the south of Karlshamn and Ronneby, there are a number of pleasant boat trips to choose from along this stretch of the coast – although at present military restrictions mean that certain islands are off-limits to non-Swedes. Before setting off for these islands you need to get a **permit**; if taking a boat from Karlshamn, you apply directly to the boat's captain (permits are free and don't take long to obtain); in Ronneby, ask the tourist office if a permit is needed and how to get one.

One of the most popular island destinations from Karlshamn is **Tjärö**, an hour off the coast (50kr). The island has some great bathing areas among the rocks and is a good place to camp – however, the island comes alive from June onwards with partying Swedes, so finding a secluded spot to camp may be difficult. Alternatively, you can stay at its very popular STF **youth hostel**, with its own restaurant, in an old farm building (☎0454/600 63, fax 390 63; 160kr, ①; early May to mid-Sept); it's advisable to book well in advance to stay here in summer. A **nature tour** of the island runs all summer and must be pre-booked through the youth hostel.

The only island trip possible from Ronneby is to **Karön**, just 500m off the mainland; take the bus from Ronneby train station to Ekenas, from where an old boat regularly makes the short trip. The island is a beautiful place to wander around during the day, with old wooden houses hiding among the trees. By night, the place is popular with an 18- to 25-year-old crowd. A restaurant-cum-nightclub here, *Restaurant Karön*, serves lunches (Tues–Sun noon–2.30pm) and has dancing four nights a week (Wed–Sat). There are boats back to the mainland after the place closes at night.

front door, is the former **Hotel Hoppet** (now offices), which was immortalized by Vilhelm Moberg's *The Emigrants*: the novel's idealistic peasant farmers, Karl and Kristina Oskar, spend their last night in Sweden here. If you carry on to the harbour, you'll see a poignant sculpture of the characters by the Halmstad Group's Axel Olson (a copy of which is at the House of Emigrants in Växjö, see p.300), depicting the husband staring out to sea and an unknown future, his wife glancing wistfully back for a final time at all she has known.

Traditionally a working people's town, Karlshamn is one of the few areas of the country where communist sympathizers still light a beacon for far-left politics. For a quick taste of this, pop into the **Röde** (red) **bookshop** at Ronnebygatan 42 (Wed–Fri 4–6pm, Sat 10am–1pm), its walls adorned with simple portraits of the likes of the Socialist agitator August Palm, who addressed the masses in Malmö (see p.237), and Anton Nilsson, who was imprisoned for life for blowing up a boat full of workers during strikes.

The third week of July sees Karlhamn stage its annual **Baltic Festival** – an impressive, all-consuming town celebration for all ages, with lots of eating, drinking and merriment to the sounds of live music. Karlshamn's annual **rock festival**, a laid-back and pleasingly dated affair, is staged 15km west of town at the small village of **Norje**; extra buses run there for the duration. The crowds, here to see such international acts as Status Quo and Deep Purple, seem to get bigger each year. Tickets cost 700kr for both days.

The museums

The best of the town's **museums** is the amazingly well-preserved eighteenth-century merchant's house, **Skottsbergska Gården**, on Drottninggatan (Tues–Sun noon–5pm; 10kr). Built after the fire that effectively obliterated the town, the place deserves a visit. On the ground floor, the kitchen is of most interest, furnished in eighteenth-century style; there's an enormous open fireplace, and all the pots and pans used over the centuries are here too. These were last used to fry up breakfast for Hanna Ljunggren, the final descendant of the original owner; she died in 1941, and her apartments on the ground floor remain as they were at her death. Upstairs there is some splendid Gustavian decoration, although, inexplicably, there don't appear to be any bedrooms; the wardrobes, which still have ancient clothes in them, are all in what seem to be living rooms. In the basement – which predates the great fire – is a tobacco shop, preserved as it was.

The rest of the museums (all June–Aug daily noon–5pm, Sept–May Mon–Fri 1–4pm) are all close together at the junction of Drottninggatan and Vinkelgatan. On the corner, the **Museum of Local History** (10kr) is in Smithska House, built in 1765 by Olof Berg, the town's richest man. Inside, there's the usual range of exhibits – old domestic furniture, marine odds and ends. Head instead into the old courtyard, around which are various buildings of more interest (though there's no English translation of the explanatory notes). You can wander up creaking stairs to authentic interiors, including a tobacco-processing works, where there's a collection of tobacco packages and the pervasive smell of the weed. The only other museum likely to fire enthusiasm is the **Punch Museum**, an intriguing place containing all the workings and contents of the Karlshamn Flaggpunch factory, which once blended the potent mixture of sugar, arrack and brandy (10kr, free with entry to local history museum). You can ask one of the guides to show you around, and even have a serving of the liquor (20kr). The factory was closed down in 1917, when a state monopoly over the trade and distribution of alcohol was begun. A non-alcoholic – and accordingly less celebrated – punch was made here until 1967.

Practicalities

Karlshamn is an hour's **train** ride from either Kristianstad or Karlskrona. A ten-minute walk from the station, the harbourside **tourist office** is on the corner of Ågatan and Ronnebygatan (mid-June to mid-Aug Mon–Fri 9am–7pm, Sat 10am–6pm, Sun noon–6pm; mid-Aug to mid-June Mon–Fri 9am–5pm; ☎0454/165 95, fax 842 45, *turistbyran@karlshamn.se*). They can book **private rooms** (100kr per person plus 40kr booking fee) and **private cottages** (3000kr per week for two) anywhere in the region. An STF **youth hostel** is next to the train station at Surbrunnsvägen 1C (☎0454/140 40; 130kr; May–Sept). The nearest **campsite** is at Kollevik, 3km out of town (☎0454/812 10; 450kr for four-person cabins; May–Sept); take bus #312 from next to the train station or from Stortorget. It's nicely positioned by the sea, with beaches and a swimming pool close by. Inland, another campsite is *Långasjönäs*, 10km north of town (☎0454/206 91; 360kr for four-person cabins; May–Sept); bus #310 gets you to within 3km of the site, from where you'll have to walk.

The cheapest central **hotel** is *Bode Hotel*, a plain, reasonable sort of place on Södra Fogdelyckegatan (☎0454/315 00; ①). For more luxury, there's the harbourfront *First Hotel Carlshamn*, Varvsgatan 1 (☎0454/890 00, fax 819 50; ⑤/②), with a grand atrium hall and a pleasant bistro.

Karlshamn has an extraordinarily good vegetarian **restaurant**, *Gourmet Grön* at Drottninggatan 61 (Mon–Sat noon–11pm), with massive bowls of food elegantly presented on its buffet table. Eating as much as you can manage costs a remarkable 65kr during the day, 115–185kr in the evening. There's an Italian menu, too, and some superb home-made desserts; even dedicated carnivores will be impressed. *Terrassen Restaurant*, Ronnebygatan 12 (daily 11am–midnight), has a wide range of fish and meat dishes, with outside seating. The most popular **café** is *Christin's* at Drottninggatan 65; though it's nothing special to look at, its location makes it a favourite local meeting place.

Ronneby

Much of **RONNEBY** has been ruined by development: as you arrive here by train, even the summer sun can't disguise the banality of the buildings ahead. There is, however, a tiny **old town**, a few minutes' walk up the hill to the left of the station, testimony to the fact that in the thirteenth century, this was Blekinge's biggest town and a centre for trading with the Hanseatic League. Only when the county became Swedish, four centuries later, did Ronneby fall behind neighbouring Karlskrona. Today, the main attraction is the beautifully preserved collection of spa houses, a couple of kilometres away at **Ronneby Brunnspark** (see p.270); you might also want to consider a trip out to the offshore island of **Käron** (see box, p.267).

In the town itself, walk uphill to the left of the train station, and turn left again onto the main street, Kungsgatan. There is nothing much of interest here until you reach **Helga Korskyrkan** (Church of the Holy Cross). With its whitewashed walls, blocked-in arched windows and red-tiled roof, the church looks like a

Greek chapel presiding over the surrounding modern apartment buildings. Dating originally from the twelfth century, this Romanesque church took quite a bashing during the Seven Years' War (1563–70) against the Danes. On the night of what is known as the **Ronneby Blood Bath** in September 1564, all those who had taken refuge in the church were slaughtered – gashes made in the north walls' heavy oak door during the violence can still be seen. The seventeenth-century wood carvings on the pulpit and altar are impressive. If you peer carefully at the south wall through the gloom, you'll see a partly damaged *Dance with Death* wall painting, each person depicted having a skeleton as a dancing partner.

Ronneby Brunnspark

In 1775, the waters here were found to be rich in iron, and Ronneby soon became one of Sweden's principal spa towns. The centre of this activity was **Ronneby Brunnspark**, fifteen minutes' walk from the train station up the hill and over the river (or take bus #211). Today, the park's houses stand proudly amid blazing rhododendrons and azaleas; one such property is now a fine STF youth hostel (see below). The neighbouring building is the wonderful café-bar **Wiener Café**, with bare floorboards and hand-painted abstract designs on the walls. Built in 1862 as a doctor's home, it was occupied by Danish resistance fighters during World War II. There are pleasant **walks** through the beautifully kept park, past the pond and into the wooded hills behind, picking up part of the **Blekingeleden** walking trail. Also through the trees are some unexpected gardens, including a Japanese Garden. Another of the old spa houses contains **Blekinge Naturum** (June–Aug 11am–6pm), which can advise on the best walking in the surrounding countryside. The park is also the site of a giant **flea market** every Sunday morning (May–Sept), where genuine Swedish antiques can be picked up amid general tat. Tours of the area run every Sunday from June to August – ask at the tourist office for details.

Practicalities

From Karlshamn, there are frequent **trains** (journey time 34min) and **buses** to Ronneby. The **tourist office** is in the Kulturcentrum, close to the church in the tiny old town area (June–Aug Mon–Fri 9am–7pm, Sat 10am–4pm, Sun noon–4pm; Sept–May Mon, Wed & Fri 9am–5pm, Tues & Thurs 9am–7pm; ☎0457/176 50, fax 174 44). You can rent **bikes** here for 40kr per day.

Without a doubt, the best place to stay is the STF **youth hostel** in Ronneby Brunnspark (☎ & fax 0457/263 00; 100kr; closed Dec to early Jan); you can eat alfresco on its balcony. In town, the owners of the hostel also run the inaptly named *Grand Hotel*, Järnvägsgatan 11 (☎0457/268 80, fax 268 84; ②), an adequate place in a modern apartment building opposite the train station. Less central, but better placed for Ronneby Brunnspark, is *Strandgården*, Nedre Brunnsvägen 25 (☎0457/661 36; ①), a small, family-run **pension** that's past the youth hostel on your right as you head out of town.

For **eating and drinking** in town, try *Nya Wienerbageriet* on Västra Torgatan, off the main square. An old bakery converted into a bar and café, with outside tables, it serves wholesome lunches, including a daily pasta dish, for 50kr. At the back is a stylish new **bar** (Thurs–Sat 7pm till late) with occasional live music, mostly blues or jazz. Just off Stortorget is the best *konditori*, the *Continental*; this well-stocked bakery is the only place to sit and have a coffee on a Sunday morning. There are also a few places near the station: *Restaurant & Pub Piaff*, on

Karlskronagatan, is an established pizza restaurant, with tables outside on the verandah; a few steps away is an intimate, traditional pub, *Jojjes Pub Bar*; and on the ground floor of the *Grand Hotel* is a cheap pizza restaurant, *Pizzeria Milano*, selling basic pizzas at 30kr. *Wiener Café* in Ronneby Brunnspark has live music, and is the place most people go to drink (Tues 6.30–11pm, Wed–Fri 6pm–midnight, Sat noon–1am, Sun noon–4pm).

Karlskrona and around

Set on the largest link in a chain of breezy islands, **KARLSKRONA**, the capital of Blekinge, is the county's most appealing destination. Founded by Karl XI in 1680, who chose the site as a base for his Baltic fleet because the seas here are ice-free in winter, the town still revolves around its maritime heritage today. Built to accommodate the king's naval parades, the town's wide avenues and stately squares survive intact, a fact which has earned Karlskrona a place on UNESCO's World Heritage list. Today, cadets in uniform still career around its streets, many of which are named after Swedish admirals and battleships; the town's biggest museum is, unsurprisingly, dedicated to maritime history (see p.273). Don't despair, though, if you're not a fan of things naval, for Karlskrona has plenty more to offer: a picturesque **old quarter**, around the once-busy fishing port at Fisktorget; and good **swimming** off the nearby island of Dragsö (see below), or, without braving the sea, at the fine pool opposite the train station.

Arrival, information and accommodation

The **train** and **bus stations** are opposite each other, 200m north of Hoylands Park. From either station, the **tourist office**, at Stortorget 2, just behind the Frederikskyrkan (June & Aug Mon–Fri 9am–6pm, Sat 10am–2pm; July Mon–Fri 9am–7pm, Sat 10am–4pm, Sun 10am–6pm; Sept–May Mon–Fri 10am–5pm, Sat 10am–1pm; ☎0455/30 34 90, fax 30 34 94, *turistbyran@karlskrona.se*), is an eight-minute stroll away: head south up Landbrogatan, with the park on your left, then proceed along Rådhusgatan to Stortorget. They can book **private rooms** for around 125kr per person and rent green military **bikes** for 25kr a day (especially useful if you intend to visit Kristianopel; see p.275). A better choice for bikes, however, is the Q8 petrol station, at Järnvägstorget near the train station (☎0455/819 93; Mon–Sat 7am–9pm, Sun from 9am–8pm), where new multispeed bikes can be rented for 50kr a day.

Accommodation

The STF **youth hostel** at Bredgatan 16 (☎ & fax 0455/100 20; 100kr; mid-June to mid-Aug) is very central, and has en-suite rooms. A newer STF hostel close by is *Trossö Vandrarhem*, Drottninggatan 39 (same number as Bredgatan hostel), which doesn't have en-suite facilities but does have the advantage of being open all year. You can **camp** out on Dragsö island, around 2.5km away (☎0455/153 54); bus #7 leaves from the bus station to Saltö, the island before Dragsö, from where it's a one-kilometre walk across the bridge.

The most glamorous **hotel** in town is *Hotel Carlskrona*, Skeppsbrokajen (☎0455/196 30, fax 259 90, ④/②), in a striking contemporary building right next to the Fisktorget ferry terminal. The price here includes a huge buffet breakfast, available to non-residents (55kr). For luxury with a traditional flavour, there's the 1890 *Statt Hotel* at Ronnebygatan 37–39 (☎0455/192 50, fax 169 09; ⑤/②), on the main shopping street. A really good choice is the very central *Hotel First Express*, Borgmästaregatan 13 (☎0455/270 00, fax 127 00), which even has a 24-hour bistro; choose a room facing the courtyard to avoid noise on the street front. Its lobby has the informality of someone's living room, with free coffee and cake from Mondays to Thursdays.

There are three cheaper, more basic places: *Hotel Conrad* on Västra Köpmangatan, halfway up the hill from the station towards Stortorget (☎0455/823 35; ③/①), is plain and reasonable; owned by the same people is the still more central, slightly brighter *Hotel Aston*, Landbrogatan 1 (☎0455/194 70; ③/①; closed weekends in summer); while *Hotel Siesta*, Borgmästaregatan 5, just off Stortorget (☎0455/801 80, fax 801 82; ②), is the ugliest and most central of the three.

The Town

Arriving by train or bus offers an encouraging first glimpse of the island network. The first island you'll pass on the way in is **Hästö**, once home to Karlskrona's wealthiest residents. It's just a few minutes further from Hästö to the centre on the island of **Trossö**, connected to the mainland by the main road, Österleden (the E22). Climb uphill past Hoglands Park, named after an eighteenth-century

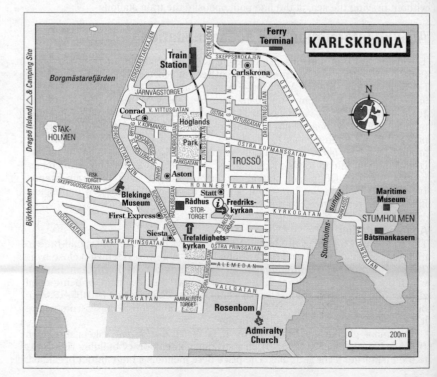

battle, to the main square, **Stortorget**, at the highest point and geographical centre of the island. It's a vast and beautiful square, dominated by two complementary **churches**; both were designed by Tessin the Younger and are stuccoed in burnt orange with dove-grey stone colonades. The more interesting of the churches is the circular, domed **Trefaldighetskyrkan** (Mon–Fri 11am–3pm, Sat 9.30am–2pm; guided tours can be requested here). Built for the town's German merchant community in 1709, its most remarkable feature is its domed ceiling, painted with hundreds of rosettes. The altar is also distinctive, golden angelic faces peering out of a gilded meringue of clouds. In the crypt are the remains of two of Karlskrona's most revered men, Count Hans Wachtmeister, responsible for much of the building of the town in the late seventeenth century; and Johan Törnström, who made most of the fabulous ship figureheads on show at the Maritime Museum (see below). **Fredrikskyrkan**, a few steps away, is an elegant, light-flooded church with towers, but holds fewer surprises inside (Mon–Fri 11am–3pm, Sat 9.30am–2pm).

The Admiralty Church

From Stortorget, head between the churches and walk past the pseudo-medieval castellated waterworks down Södra Kungsgatan. The wide, cobbled street is divided down the centre by the boulder-like stone walls of a tunnel, where a train line (disused) runs from the main station up to the harbour. The leafy square ahead is **Amiralitets Torget**; perched at its centre is the huge, peeling wooden bell tower of the Admiralty Church. To see the church itself (signposted "Kungliga Amiralitetskyrkan"), head down Vallgatan on the left of the square, passing the symmetrical austerity of the Marine Officers' School; just before you reach the harbour, the beautifully proportioned, entirely wooden **Admiralty Church** is up on the right. This simple elegant structure, Sweden's biggest wooden church, was built in 1685. Outside the entrance, take a look at one of the city's best-known landmarks: the wooden statue of **Rosenbom**, around which hangs a sorrowful tale. Mats Rosenbom, one of the first settlers on Trossö island, lived nearby with his family and earned his keep in the shipyard. However, after a fever killed six of his children and left him and his wife too ill to work, he applied for, and was granted, a beggar's licence. One New Year's Eve, while begging at the homes of leading townspeople, he became somewhat drunk from the festive wine on offer and forgot to raise his hat to thank the wealthy German figurehead carver, Fritz Kolbe. When admonished for this, Rosenbom retorted, "If you want thanks for your crumbs to the poor, you can take my hat off yourself!" Enraged, Kolbe struck him between the eyes and sent him away, but the beggar, unable to make it home, froze stiff and died in a snow drift by the church. Next morning, Kolbe found the beggar frozen to death and, filled with remorse, carved a figure of Rosenbom which stands at the spot where he died. Its design is such that you have to raise his hat yourself to give some money.

Stumholmen: The Maritime Museum and Båtsmanskasern Art Gallery

The best museum Karlskrona has is set on the island of **Stumholmen**, connected to the mainland by road and just five minutes' walk east of Stortorget, down Kyrkogatan. If you prefer, you can take a boat from Fisktorget, but this takes longer. As soon as you cross the bridge onto Stumholmen, there's a large sign indicating all the buildings of interest here. To the left, the worthwhile **Maritime**

Museum (mid-May to mid-Sept daily 10am–6pm, Thurs till 9pm; mid-Sept to mid-May Tues, Wed & Fri–Sun 11am–5pm, Thurs 11am–9pm; 40kr) has a facade like a futuristic Greek temple. A portrait of Carl XI, who had the Navy moved from Stockholm to Karlskrona in 1680, features in the hallway, a pet lion at his feet gazing up at the king's most unappealing, bloated face. Down a spiral staircase from here is a transparent underwater tunnel offering a view of hundreds of fish in the murky depths. The best room here, though, contains the great **figureheads** designed and made by the Royal Sculptor to the Navy, Johan Törnström. King Gustav III declared that ships of the line should be named after manly virtues, and so have male figureheads, while frigates have female ones. Among the finest is one made for the ship *Försiktigheten* (1784) – a metre-long foot, complete with toe nails and perfectly proportioned. There's a pleasant café here too, serving light meals for around 55 kr.

Just a couple of minutes' walk away is an **art gallery** (Tues–Fri noon–4pm, Wed 11am– 7pm, Sat & Sun noon–5pm; free), set in the splendid old Seamen's Barracks ("Båtamanskasern"). The building dates from 1842, and was once used to simulate life on the seas during the training of young would-be sailors – the wooden floor is slightly arched to appear like a ship's deck, and the apprentice seamen would have slept here in hammocks, as they did at sea. While the temporary exhibitions downstairs are usually of a good standard, it's well worth heading up to the first floor, where there's permanent exhibition of the work of the late Erik Langemark. Born in Karlskrona in 1915, he was the best known of those who chronicled the city in art. His paintings of Karlskrona are accompanied here by up-to-date photographs of the places depicted, showing how the city has changed; compare his *Gamla Teatern* (Old Theatre), painted in 1971, with the scene today – only the huge tree now remains.

The harbour and Fisktorget

From the waterside, at the end of Vallgatan, the divide between the picturesque town and the continuing military presence is most apparent: to the left are the old white lighthouse and the archipelago, and the pink- and white-stuccoed county governor's residence; to the right, however, mud-coloured military vessels fill the old quayside, and "Forbidden to Enter" signs abound. For more of a feel of old Karlskrona, wander west past the military hardware towards the **Björkholmen** area. Here, a couple of early eighteenth-century wooden houses survive, homes that the first craftsmen at the then new naval yard built for themselves. All the streets running north–south are named after types of ships, while those from west to east are named after admirals. Nearby **Fisktorget**, once the site of a fish market, is pleasant for a stroll. Nowadays the boats here are mainly pleasure yachts, and there are a couple of pleasant cafés. You'll also find the dull **Blekinge Museum** at the harbourfront (Tues & Thurs–Sun 11am–5pm, Wed till 7pm; 20kr), housed in the 1705 wooden home built for Count Wachtmeister – the pleasant summertime café is more appealing than the exhibits on shipbuilding and the like.

Eating and drinking

Several of the town's **konditori** stand out from the rest. *Café Tre G* on Landbrogatan, opposite Hoglands Park, serves baked potatoes, cakes and sandwiches in pleasant surroundings. At *Systrarna Lindkvists Café,* Borgmästaregatan 3, across from the tourist office, the coffee comes in fine old gilded china cups, with silver teaspoons and sugar tongs. Karlskrona is not without an *Espresso House*: located at Ronnebygatan 30 (Mon–Thurs 11am–10pm, Fri & Sat 11am–midnight, Sun 1–10pm), serving an exceptional range of well-prepared food. A very pleasant deli and café is *Börje Olssons Skafferiet* at Rådhusgatan 9 (Mon–Fri 10am–7pm, Sat 10am–3pm). Here, you can buy luscious olives, meats, cheeses and exotic pickles for picnics as well as filled baguettes, croissants, great coffees and the best hot chocolate in town.

The majority of Karlskrona's **restaurants** are along central Ronnebygatan. None is outstanding, but the best of the bunch is the Italian-style *Ristorante Michelangelo* at no. 29. A few metres up, *Red Light* serves kebabs and light meals; next door is a traditional pub, the *Old Cave Bar*. For British-style pub fare, locals go to the *Kings Crown*, on Stortorget. A newer addition is the Greek restaurant *Taverna Santorini*, Rådhusgatan 11 (☎0455/30 02 02; Mon–Thurs 3–11pm, Fri 3pm–midnight, Sat 2pm–midnight, Sun 2–10pm), serving a wide choice of dishes including several vegetarian options; no dish here is over 100kr. A popular and strikingly stylish steakhouse and bar is *Niva*, opposite the churches on Stortorget (Mon–Thurs noon–1am, Fri noon–2am, Sun 1pm–midnight).

Kristianopel

Arriving by road at the idyllic hamlet of **KRISTIANOPEL**, 30km northeast of Karlskrona (take either the E22 or the coast road to get here), there isn't the slightest hint that this village of just 38 inhabitants was once a strategically positioned fortification with a bloody history. Neither is it obvious – unless you're here during that time – that every July, the place packs out with holiday-makers and acquires an atmosphere of summer revelry that's seldom found elsewhere in Sweden. Only when you've walked past the minute, pristine cottages all the way to the tiny harbour do you see the three kilometres of three-metre-thick **fortification walls** that surround the settlement. The low, squat walls are actually a 1970s reconstruction, built on the foundations of the original fortifications. Erected in 1600 by the Danish king Christian IV to protect against Swedish aggression, the original walls were finally razed by the Swedes after the little town had spent 77 years changing hands with alarming regularity. The only other sight worth a look is the **church**, near the village shop; inside is an eye-catching altar, decorated with vividly drawn trees. The present church replaced a medieval one, whose site, located near the campsite (see p.276), is just a grassy mound today. In 1605, the former church was the scene of great bloodshed: it was burnt to the ground, killing all the women, children and elderly of the village who were huddled inside for what they imagined was protection. They mistakenly believed that the then sixteen-year-old King Gustav II Adolf would respect it as a place of God.

Though a charming place to visit at any time, Kristianopel is at its very best during summer, when the population jumps to around two thousand. Many of the visitors stay at the tiny ten-bed hostel and adjacent campsite, tucked inside the low walls and overlooking the sea. Every July, the restaurant here is the focus for a wide range of **music** and **night-time entertainment**, ranging from Eurovision Song Contest favourites to folk music. Even if the music doesn't grab you, the bonhomie and the wonderful setting make this a great social event that's well worth dipping into.

Practicalities

Hitching is easier here than in most places in Sweden – which is just as well, as getting to Kristianopel can be tricky by public transport. **Bus #122** from Karlskrona stops at Kristianopel, but runs only during school terms; throughout the year, you can use bus #120, which runs to Kalmar from Karlskrona along the E22. However, the closest to town you can get on this bus is Fågelmara, 6km from the village; luckily, you can cover the rest of the distance on a **bike**, which you can take on the bus at no extra cost. Though the signposting on the way can be confusingly ambiguous, cycling here from Karlskrona (around 45km) is an enjoyable experience. You don't need to use the relatively busy E22: the prettiest route is to follow minor roads first to Lyckeby, then tracks which lead through cornfields and flowering meadows to Ramdala and the little town of Jämjö. From here, the most appealing way is to cut to the coast (follow signs to Konungshamn), from where Kristianopel is straight up north.

For accommodation in the village, there's the **youth hostel** (☎ or fax 0455/36 61 30; 110kr), with a **campsite** attached (same phone number); at the campsite you can rent a **rowing boat** (20kr an hour) or – for those who prefer to shoot at wildlife rather than just admire it – go on **seabird hunting trips** to the local islands (Sept–Jan). The village's one **hotel**, a mellow eighteenth-century farmhouse called *Gästgiferi* (☎ or fax 0455/36 60 30; ①; April–Sept), is set in beautiful gardens and found to the left of the main road into the village. The *Sjöstugan* restaurant (see below) also has some bed-and-breakfast rooms (☎0455/36 60 88; ②); outside summer, you'll need to book two days in advance or they may shut. Just outside Fågelmara, on the road leading to Kristianopel, an old wooden farmhouse has rooms with a basic kitchen (☎0455/643 06). It has a rather unusual atmosphere, with hens and horses, not to mention the household's four children, but it's fun, and very cheap at 100kr per person for up to six people. Guests can also arrange **horse riding** here.

For **provisions**, there are a couple of shops on the campsite, and another near the church (Mon–Fri 9am–6pm, Sat & Sun 9.30am–noon). There are three **restaurants** in the village: the *Gästgiferi*, with its charming, authentic old farmhouse decor, tends to appeal to an older crowd; main courses here start from 95kr. The other two eateries are run by two very amicable brothers, Hans and Per. Hans presides over the campsite's wooden *Värdshuset Pålsgården* (Fri 6–9pm, Sat noon–9pm, Sun noon–6pm), serving tasty food in cosy surroundings; in July it opens late every night as a pub. A few minutes up the road, Per runs the *Restaurant Sjöstugan* (☎0455/36 60 88; daily noon–10pm), with a fine menu of fish, meat and pasta dishes, and good desserts too; try such delights as basil parfait with raspberry sauce, the basil marinated in Cointreau. Main courses here are between 100kr and 165kr each; on a Wednesday evening, you can try their grill buffet (7–10pm; 140kr). With glorious views of the islands off this lovely stretch of coast, it's also a great spot just for a drink.

travel details

Express trains

Daily express trains operate throughout the region, in particular **Oslo–Copenhagen** (via Gothenburg, Varberg, Halmstad and Helsingborg) and **Stockholm–Copenhagen** (via Helsingborg). Both routes have a branch service through to Malmö. Despite complicated timetabling, the service is frequent and regular north or south between Gothenburg and Helsingborg/Malmö.

Trains

Helsingborg to: Gothenburg (11 daily; 2hr 40min); Lund/Malmö (Mon–Fri 12 daily, Sat & Sun 10 daily; 40–50min).

Karlskrona to: Emmaboda for connections to Växjö, Stockholm & Kalmar (1–2 hourly; 40min).

Kristianstad to: Karlshamn (hourly; 50min); Karlskrona (hourly; 1hr 50min); Ronneby (hourly; 1hr 20min); Malmö (Mon–Fri hourly, Sat & Sun every two hours; 1hr 10min).

Malmö to: Gothenburg (8–10 daily; 3hr 45min); Karlskrona (hourly; 3hr 15min); Kristianstad (4 daily; 1hr 10min); Lund (3 hourly; 13min); Ystad (Mon–Fri hourly, Sat & Sun 5 daily; 50min).

Buses

Ängelholm to: Torekov (3–5 daily; 45min).

Båstad to: Torekov (5 daily; 30min).

Helsingborg to: Båstad (16 daily; 55min); Halmstad (6 daily; 1hr 50min).

Karlskrona to: Stockholm (Fri & Sun; 7hr 30min).

Kristianstad to: Kalmar (1 daily; 3hr); Lund/Malmö (1 daily; 2hr 30min/2hr 45min).

Malmö to: Gothenburg (Mon–Thurs 1 daily, Fri & Sun 3 daily; 4hr 25min); Halmstad/ Falkenberg/Varberg (Fri & Sun 2 daily; 2hr 25min/2hr 55min/3hr 20min); Helsingborg (Mon–Thurs 1 daily, Fri & Sun 6 daily; 1hr 5min); Jönköping (Mon–Thurs 1 daily, Fri & Sun 3 dily; 4hr 30min); Kristianstad/Kalmar (1 daily; 2hr/5hr 30min); Lund (hourly; 20min); Mellbystrand (Fri & Sun 1 daily; 2hr); Stockholm (Mon–Thurs 1 daily, Fri & Sun 3 daily; 9hr); Trelleborg (hourly; 35min).

Ystad to: Kristianstad (Mon–Fri 5–6 daily, Sat & Sun 3 daily; 1hr 55min); Lund (Mon–Fri 5; 1hr 10min); Malmö (3 daily; 1hr); Simrishamn (Mon–Fri 3 daily, Sat & Sun 1 daily; 50min); Smygehamn (Mon–Fri 5 daily, Sat & Sun 2 daily; 30min).

International ferries, hydrofoils and catamarans

All the following services are to towns in Denmark.

Halmstad to: Grenå (2 daily; 4hr).

Helsingborg to: Helsingør (3 hourly; 25min).

Malmö to: Copenhagen (hourly, 45min).

Simrishamn to: Allinge on Bornholm (summer-only catamaran 3–4 daily).

Trelleborg to: Rostock (3 daily; 6hr); Sassnitz (5 daily; 3hr 45min); Travämunde (2 daily; 7–9hr).

Varberg to: Grenå (2 daily; 3hr 45min).

Ystad to: Rönne on Bornholm (3–5 daily; 2hr 30min).

CHAPTER FOUR

THE SOUTHEAST

A lthough a less obvious target than the coastal cities and resorts of the southwest, Sweden's **southeast** certainly repays a visit. You'll find impressive castles, ancient lakeside sites, and numerous glassworks amid the forests of the so-called "Glass Kingdom", while off the east coast, Sweden's largest Baltic islands offer beautifully preserved medieval towns and fairy-tale landscapes. Train transport, especially between the towns close to the eastern shore of Lake Vättern and Stockholm, is good; speedy, regular services mean that you could see some places on a day-trip from Stockholm.

Småland county in the south encompasses a varied geography and some stridently different towns. **Kalmar** is a very likeable stop; a glorious historic fortress town, it deserves more time than its tag as a jumping-off point for the island of Öland suggests. Inland, great swathes of dense forest are rescued from monotony by the many **glass factories** that continue the county's tradition of glass production, famous the world over for its design and quality, though today drowning in its own marketing hyperbole. In **Växjö**, the largest town in the south, two superb museums deal with the art of glass-making and the history of Swedish emigration. At the northern edge of the county and perched on the southernmost tip of Lake Vättern, **Jönköping** is known as Sweden's Jerusalem for its remarkable number of Free Churches; it is also a great base for exploring the beautiful eastern shore of Vättern. In the middle of the lake is the island of **Visingsö**, rich in royal history and natural beauty.

The idyllic pastoral landscape of **Östergotland** borders the eastern shores of the lake and reaches as far east as the Baltic. One of its highlights, and popular with domestic tourists, is the small lakeside town of **Vadstena**, its medieval streets dwarfed by austere monastic edifices, a Renaissance palace and an imposing abbey, brought into being by the zealous determination of Sweden's first female saint,

---

ACCOMMODATION PRICES

The pensions and hotels listed in the guide have been price-graded according to the scale given below; the price category given against each establishment indicates the cost of the least expensive double rooms there. Many hotels offer considerable reductions at weekends all year round, and during the summer holiday period (mid-June to mid-Aug); in these cases the reduction is either noted in the text or, where a discount brings a hotel into another price band, given after the number for the full price. Single rooms, where available, usually cost between 60 and 80 percent of a double. Where hostels have double rooms, we've given price codes for them also.

① under 500kr   ③ 700–900kr   ⑤ 1200–1500kr
② 500–700kr   ④ 900–1200kr   ⑥ over 1500kr

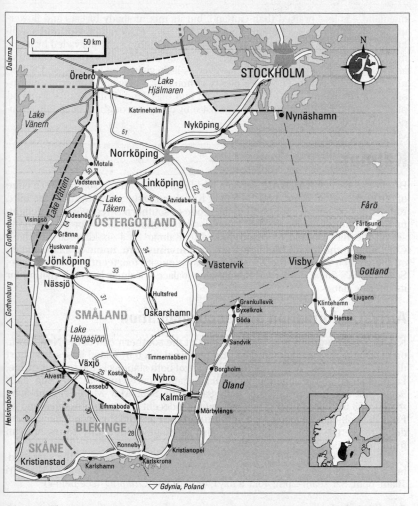

Birgitta. The **Göta Canal** wends its way through the northern part of the county to the Baltic, a number of fine towns lining the route. These include **Linköping**, with its strange open-air museum where people live and work in a re-created nineteenth-century environment. Just to the north, **Norrköping**, a bustling and youthful town, grew up around the textile industry; today it boasts Europe's best collection of preserved, and extremely handsome, red-brick and stuccoed factories.

Outside the fragmented archipelagos of the east and west coasts, Sweden's only two sizeable islands are in the Baltic: Öland and Gotland, adjacent slithers of land with unusually temperate climates for their latitudes. They were domestic tourist havens for years, but now an increasing number of foreigners are discovering their charms – lots of summer sun, delectable beaches and some impressive historic (and prehistoric) sights. **Öland** – the smaller island and closer to the mainland – is less praised than Gotland, but its mix of shady forests and flowering meadows makes it a tranquil spot for a few days' exploration. **Gotland**'s well-known highlight is its Hanseatic medieval capital, **Visby**, a city pervaded by a carnival atmosphere in summer when ferry-loads of young Swedes come to sunbathe and party. The rest of the island, however, is little visited by tourists, and all the more magical for that. There are plenty of hotels in Visby and numerous **campsites** dotted around the rest of the island and on Öland. Both islands are good places to exercise *Allemansrätten* (see p.48) by camping rough; they are also wonderful cycling country.

Kalmar

Bright and breezy **KALMAR**, set on a huddle of islands at the southeastern edge of the county of Småland, has the feel of Karlskrona (see p.271) without the hills. Kalmar has treasures enough to make it one of southern Sweden's most delightful towns (though, sadly, this fact is overlooked by most visitors here, their sights set on the Baltic island of Öland, linked to Kalmar by a six-kilometre bridge). Chief among the town's highlights are its **Lansmuseum**, home to an exhibition on the sunken warship, the *Kronan*, and an exquisite fourteenth-century **castle**, Scandinavia's finest preserved Renaissance palace – Kalmar is worth visiting for its interior alone.

Arrival, information and accommodation

Kalmar's **train station** is at Stationsgatan, at the southern end of the New Town, on the island of Kvarnholmen. The **bus terminal**, used by Öland buses, is a short distance to the west. Within spitting distance of both stations is the **tourist office**, Larmgatan 6, at the junction with Ölandsgatan (early June & late Aug daily 9am–7pm; mid-June to mid-Aug daily 9am–8pm; Sept–May Mon–Fri 9am–5pm; ☎0480/153 50, fax 174 53). They can supply a decent free map of Kalmar and an English booklet, with maps, for a **self-guided tour** around the town (30kr), worth doing to see the old sites. In July English-language **guided city tours** are run from the tourist office at 6pm (40kr).

Kalmar can be explored easily enough on foot. To strike out into the surrounding countryside, you can rent a **bike** from Team Sportia, Södravägen 2 (Mon–Fri 10am–6pm, Sat 10am–2pm; 40kr a day), or at *Stensö Camping* (see below).

Accommodation

The tourist office arranges **private rooms**, costing from 190kr per person or 300kr for a double, plus a 50kr booking fee. More popular are the **cottages** which the tourist office rents out by the week (from 1800kr for two people). The STF **youth hostel** is at Rappegatan 1c (☎0480/129 28, fax 882 93; 140kr), on the island of **Ängö**, a pleasant ten-minute walk north of the centre; it's well equipped, with laundry facilities and a shop for basic provisions. *Sjöfartsklubben*, Ölandsgatan 45, which provides accommodation for naval cadets, makes its rooms available to the public from June to August (①; book through the tourist office). The nearest **camping** is on Stensö island (☎0480/888 03), 3km from the centre, where you can rent cheap cabins and also **canoes**. Local buses head out this way; check with the tourist office.

There are several really attractive central **hotels** with good summer discounts. The 1906 *Stadshotel*, Stortorget 14 (☎0480/49 69 00, fax 49 69 10; ⑤/③), is in a lovely old building with a stuccoed facade; the price includes an excellent buffet breakfast (available to non-residents at 55kr). Another fine place, on the popular Larmtorget, is *Frimurarehotellet* (☎0480/152 30, fax 858 87; ③/②), in a castle-like building owned by the Freemasons. Breakfast for non-residents is 50kr here. The prettiest, most costly and most regal of Kalmar's hotels is the old *Slottshotellet* at Slottsvägen 7 (☎0480/882 60, fax 882 66; ⑤), which overlooks the castle across the bridge. The authentic interior is grand and extremely tasteful, with a charming conservatory area; guests can use their sauna and solarium. At the other end of the scale is the perfectly adequate *Hotel Svarnen*, next door to the youth hostel and run by the same management (same number as hotel; ①).

The Town

Kalmar's seventeenth-century **New Town** sits on the island of Kvarnholmen. The district is surrounded by fragments of ancient fortified walls, the cobbled streets and lively squares of its centre lined with some lovely old buildings. Kalmar was

rebuilt here after a devastating fire in the 1640s; to the west is the **Gamla Stan** (Old Town), which still retains some winding old streets that are worth a look. Reaching the **castle** from the centre entails a walk through the peaceful **Stadspark**, a few minutes' walk west of the train and bus stations; it was laid out by local businessman Johan Jeansson, whose bust stands at its centre.

Kalmar Slott

Beautifully set on its own island, just south of Stadspark, is the castle, **Kalmar Slott** (April–Sept daily 10am–6pm; Oct–March, second weekend of each month 10am–6pm; guided tours in English 11.30am & 2.30pm; 60kr). Its foundations were probably laid in the twelfth century; a century later, it became the best defended castle in Sweden under King Magnus Ladulås. Today, if the castle doesn't appear to be defending anything in particular, that's because a devastating fire in the 1640s laid waste to the Old Town, after which Kalmar was moved to its present site.

The most significant event to take place within its walls was when the Danish Queen Margareta instigated the **Union of Kalmar** in 1397, which made her ruler over all Scandinavia. With such hatred between the Swedes and Danes, the union didn't stand much change of long-term success. The castle was subject to eleven **sieges** as the Swedes and the Danes took power in turn; surprisingly, it remained almost unscathed. By the time Gustav Vasa became king of Sweden in 1523, Kalmar Slott was beginning to show signs of wear and tear, and so the king set about rebuilding it, while his sons, who later became Eric XIV and Johan III, took care of decorating the interior. The result, a fine **Renaissance palace**, is still preserved in fantastic detail today, and well illustrates the Vasa family's concern to maintain Sweden's prestige in the eyes of foreign powers and dignitaries.

Unlike many other southern Swedish castles, this one is storybook accurate, boasting turrets, ramparts, a moat and drawbridge, and a dungeon. The castle's fully furnished interior – reached by crossing an authentically reconstructed wooden **drawbridge** and through a stone arched tunnel beneath the grassy ramparts – is great fun to wander through. Among the many highlights is King Johan's bedroom, known as the **Grey Hall**. His bed, which was stolen from Denmark, is decorated with carved faces on the posts, but all their noses have been chopped off – he believed that the nose contained the soul and didn't want the avenging souls of the rightful owners coming to haunt him. The **King's Chamber** (King Eric's bedroom) is the most visually exciting – the wall frieze is a riot of vividly painted animals and shows a wild boar attacking Eric and another man saving him. Eric apparently suffered from paranoia, believing his younger brother Johan wanted to kill him. To this end, he had a secret door, which you can see, cut into the extravagantly inlaid wall panels, with escape routes to the roof in event of fraternal attack. As it happened, Eric didn't live that long – Johan is widely believed by historians to have poisoned him with arsenic in 1569.

The adjoining **Golden Room**, with its magnificent ceiling, should have been Johan's bedroom, but sibling hatred meant he didn't sleep here while Eric lived. Here you'll find a couple of huge and intriguing portraits: though Gustav Vasa was already of an advanced age when his was painted, he appears young-looking in his picture, with unseemly muscular legs – the royal artist had been ordered to seek out the soldier with the best legs and paint those, before attempting a sympathetic portrayal of Vasa's face. The portrait next to his is of Queen Margareta, her ghostly white countenance achieved in real life through the daily application of lead and arsenic. Isolated on another wall is King Eric's portrait, measuring less than one metre square and hung much higher up than the others: his family believed that the mental illness from which he supposedly suffered could be caught by looking into his eyes – even images of them.

The tour guides will tell you that the place is rattling with Renaissance-era ghosts, but for more tangible evidence of life during the Vasa period, the kitchen fireplace is good enough; it was built to accommodate the simultaneous roasting of three cows.

Around Kalmar Slott: Södra Kyrkogården and the Art Museum

A wander through Stadspark with the castle on your left leads you to the tranquil cemetery, **Södra Kyrkogården**. The most poignant section, labelled on city maps as **Mosaiska Kyrkogården**, is hidden away at its extreme southwest corner, where the city's now defunct Jewish community is buried. The saddest sight is a memorial to those who perished in the Nazi holocaust – surrounded by twenty square granite tablets commemorating Eastern European Jews, all in their teens and 20s, who were brought to Kalmar after surviving the concentration camps. Weak and ill after their ordeal, and without sufficient medical backup, most died on Swedish soil during their first months of liberation.

On the north side of the cemetery, Kalmar's **Konstmuseum** has changing exhibitions of contemporary art (early May to early Sept Mon–Fri 10am–5pm, Sat & Sun noon–5pm; early Sept to May Mon–Fri 10am–5pm & 7–9pm, Sat & Sun 11am–5pm; 30kr, under-16s free), with the emphasis on abstract Expressionist work painted by Swedish artists in the 1940s and 1950s. The top floor contains one largish gallery of nineteenth- and twentieth-century Swedish nude and landscape paintings, include some fine works by Anders Zorn and Carl Larsson.

Gamla Stan

For a feel of Kalmar's quaint **Gamla Stan** (Old Town), it's best to head into the small warren of cobbled lanes west of the *Slottshotellet*, which overlooks the Stadspark and is only a minute's walk along Slottsvågen from the Södra Kyrkogården. The old wooden cottages, painted egg-yolk yellow and wisteria blue, are at their prettiest on Gamla Kungsgatan and Västerlångatan. These little streets surround the **Old Churchyard**, a surprisingly poorly maintained place where some of the seventeenth- and eighteenth-century gravestones lie in pieces.

The Domkyrkan

The elegantly gridded Renaissance New Town is laid out around the grand **Domkyrkan** in Stortorget (daily 9am–6pm); to get here from the Old Town, head back east along Södravägen across the river, then carry on through Larmtorget and along Storgatan. Designed in 1660 by Nicodemus Tessin the Elder (as was the nearby Rådhus), after a visit to Rome, this vast and airy church in Italian Renassaince style is today a complete misnomer: Kalmar has no bishop and the church no dome. Inside, the altar, designed by Tessin the Younger, shimmers with gold, as do the *Faith* and *Mercy* sculptures around it. The massive painting beneath the altar rather unusually depicts the practical details of Jesus being taken down from the Cross by men on ladders, his lifeless form winched down with ropes. The pulpit is also worth a look; its roof is a three-tiered confection crowned with a statue of Christ surrounded by gnome-like sleeping soldiers, below which angels brandish instruments of torture, while on the "most inferior" level, a file of women symbolize such qualities as maternal love and erudition.

The Kronan Exhibition

From Stortorget, it's a few minutes' walk south down Östrasjögatan and then left into Skeppsbrongatan to the awe-inspiring **Kronan Exhibition**, housed in a refurbished steam mill. The exhibition is the main attraction of the **Länsmuseum**, Kalmar's county museum (daily: mid-June to mid-Aug 10am–6pm; mid-Aug to mid-June 10am–4pm; 50kr). Built by the British designer Francis Sheldon, the royal ship *Kronan* was once one of the world's three largest vessels; it had three complete decks and was twice the size of the *Vasa*, which sank off Stockholm in 1628 (see p.82).

The *Kronan* itself went down, fully manned, in 1676, resulting in the loss of 800 of its 842 crew. Its captain, Admiral Creutz, had received a royal order to attack and recapture the Baltic island of Gotland. Pursued by the Danish, Creutz, who had remarkably little naval experience – just one week at sea – was eager to impress his king and engage in combat. To this end, he ignored pleas from his crew and ordered the *Kronan* to turn and face the enemy. A gale caused the ship to heave, and water gushed into her open gun ports, knocking over a lantern, which ignited the entire gun-powder magazine. Within seconds, there was an explosion that ripped the mammoth ship apart.

It wasn't until 1980 that the whereabouts of the ship's remains were detected, 26m down off the coast of Öland, using super-sensitive scanning equipment. A salvage operation began, led by the great-great-great-great-grandson of the ship's captain; the Kronan exhibition displays the resulting finds as part of an imaginative **walk-through reconstruction** of the gun decks and admiral's cabin, complete with the sound of cannon fire and screeching gulls. The ship's **treasure trove** of gold coins is displayed at the end of the exhibition, but it's the incredibly preserved **clothing** – hats, jackets, buckled leather shoes and even silk bows and cuff links – which bring this exceptional show to life. The moments leading up to the disaster have been pieced together brilliantly.

Eating, drinking and nightlife

There's a wide range of places to eat in Kalmar. The liveliest night-time area is **Larmtorget**, with restaurants, cafés and pubs serving Swedish, Indonesian, Chinese, Greek, Italian and English food. For daytime snacks, *Kullzenska caféet*, Kaggensgatan 26 (Mon–Fri 10am–6.30pm, Sat 10am–3pm, Sun noon–4.30pm), is a charming **konditori**, containing a rather striking portrait of the Swedish Queen Victoria (worth a glance especially if you're heading to Borgholm to see the monarch who most hated Sweden; see p.289). Most people while their evenings away in the restaurant bars; this isn't a place for nightclubs. Kalmar's RFSL (☎0480/855 95 – to avoid recorded message, try Thurs 8–10pm) runs a small **gay** pub and disco at Bergavik, the football club house one kilometre north of the centre (first Sat of each month). To get there, head east from the Domkyrkan and then north, out of the city, along Lanshovdingegatan; the club house will be on your left, opposite a sign saying "Bergaviks Idrottsplats".

Restaurants and bars

Calmar Hamnkrog, Skeppsbrogatan 30 (☎0480/411020). Built right by the water on squat stilts, this place offers such delights as catfish, duck or lamb with classy sauces for 200kr.

Ernesto Spaghetti & Cocktail Bar, on Lärmtorget, opposite *Krögers*. This very popular place serves a huge range of very good pizzas (60–80kr) and pastas (60–70kr), as well as traditional Italian salads, antipasti and meat courses (120kr). Daily 11am–midnight, Wed, Fri & Sat till 2am.

Ernesto Steakhouse, at the harbour. In a building similar in style to its Italian sister restaurant, this one serves more substantial and expensive meat and fish meals. The *Dagens Rätt* is reasonable, though, at 55kr. Daily 11am–2pm & 5–11pm.

Helen & Jörgens Restaurant, Olof Palmes gata. Just off Larmtorget (☎0480/288 30). An upmarket Swedish/European eatery, with frighteningly bad (though amusing) paintings. Main courses cost 110–180kr; there's a range of tempting desserts (50–70kr). Their set meals aren't really better value than à la carte. Mon–Fri 11am–2pm & 6–10pm, Sat 6–10pm.

Krögers, on Lärmtorget. Light Swedish meals like *kottbullesmörgäs* (meatball sandwiches; 40kr) are served here alongside the rather less Swedish fish and chips (66kr). Once the most popular pub/restaurant in town, this place isn't quite as full now that they've stopped putting on live music. June–Aug Mon–Sat noon–1am, Sun 4pm–1am; Sept–May daily 4pm–1am.

Lodbroks Café & Pub (☎0480/288 82). In the same building as *Kullzenska Cafeet* (see opposite); entered from Norra Långgatan 20. Specializes in home-made pies, with an excellent-value pie- and-salad buffet: eat as much as you want, including coffee and cake, for 60kr.

Ming Palace, Fiskeragatan 7 (☎0480/166 86). The best Chinese restaurant in town, with a lunch special at 50–60kr. Mon–Thurs 11am–10.30pm, Fri 11am–11pm, Sat noon–11pm, Sun 1pm–10.30pm.

O'Keefe's, part of the *Stadshotel*. A pub with a good atmosphere outside of Larmtorget, it's full of bicycles and other oddities hanging from the ceiling. Sept–May Wed–Sat 9pm–2am.

Oscar Bar & Brasserie, Lärmgatan. A friendly, informal Greek-inspired place serving a three-course meal for 135kr and pan pizzas from 60kr; there's also a well-stocked bar. Summer daily 1pm till late, Fri & Sat till 2am; rest of year Mon–Thurs 4pm–1am, Fri & Sat 4pm–2am.

Peking Restaurant, at the train station (☎0480/105 33). A good spot for Indonesian and Chinese food, and cheaper than *Ming Palace*, though not quite as good. Mon–Thurs 11am–10.30pm, Fri 11am–11pm, Sat noon–11pm, Sun 1–10.30pm.

Pub Stocken, connected to the *Bamboo Restaurant* on Larmtorget. A regular bar offering light snacks and baked potatoes (30–50kr). Daily 5pm–1am.

T & T, Unionsgatan 20 (☎0480/235 36). Kalmar's hippest eaterie and becoming hugely popular, the place serves unusual (and delicious) pizzas – like banana, onion, curry and pineapple – for 55–75kr, and meat and poultry dishes, sold by weight. It has a good range of wines and some great desserts, like the chocolate tart (28kr). Mon–Thurs 11am–midnight, Fri & Sat noon–1am, Sun noon–midnight.

Öland

Linked to mainland Sweden by a six-kilometre-long bridge, the island of **ÖLAND**, with its unspoilt beaches, mysterious forests, pretty meadows and wooden cottages, has been drawing Swedes in droves for over a century. Now popular with visitors from abroad, too, the island is visited by 55,000 people every July and August. Despite this onslaught, which can clog the road from the bridge north to the main town, **Borgholm**, this long, splinter-shaped island retains a very likeable old-fashioned-holiday atmosphere. The bathing opportunities here are among the best in Sweden, and the island's attractions include numerous ruined castles, Bronze and Iron Age burial cairns, runic stones and forts, all set amid rich and varied fauna and flora and striking geography. Labyrinthine **walking trails** and **bicycle routes** wend their way past more than four hundred old wooden **windmills**, which give Öland a peculiarly Dutch air.

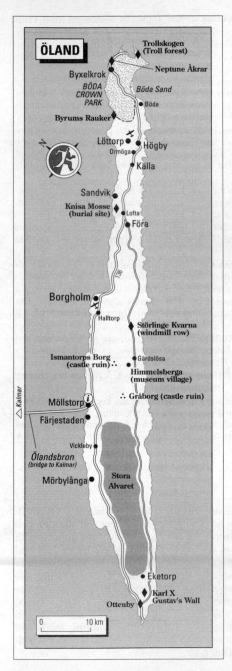

A royal hunting ground from the mid-sixteenth century until 1801, Öland was ruled with scant regard for its native population. Peasants were forbidden from chopping wood, owning dogs or weapons, or selling their produce on the open market. While protected wild animals did their worst to the farmers' fields, Kalmar's tradesmen exploited the restrictions on the islanders' trade to force them to sell at low prices. Danish attacks on Öland (and a ten-month occupation in 1612) made matters worse, with seven hundred farms being destroyed. A succession of disastrous harvests in the mid-nineteenth century was the last straw, causing a quarter of the population to pack their bags for a new life in America. This century, mainland Sweden has become the new magnet for Öland's young, and, by 1970, the island's inhabitants had declined to just twenty thousand.

The geology of the island varies dramatically due to the crushing movement of ice during the last Ice Age, and the effects of the subsequent melting process, which took place 10,000 years ago. To the south is a massive **limestone** plain known as the **Alvaret**; indeed, limestone has been used here for thousands of years to build runic monuments, dry-stone walls and churches. the northern coastline is craggy and irregular, peppered with dramatic-looking *rauker* – stone pillars, weathered by the waves into jagged shapes. Among the island's **flora** are plants that are rare in the region, like the delicate rock rose and the cream-coloured wool-butter flower, both native to southeast Asia and found in the south of the island. Further north, in the romantically named **Trolls Forest**, you'll find twisted, misshapen pine sand oaks. As regards **fauna**, the south contains a sensational **bird reserve**, where skylarks and lapwings join sea birds, waders and millions of migrating birds in spring and early autumn.

Travel practicalities

Öland's main **tourist office** is in a large pink building in **Möllstorp**, next to the end of the bridge (April & May Mon–Fri 9am–6pm, Sat 10am–5pm, Sun 10am–4pm; June, Aug & Sept Mon–Fri 9am–7pm, Sat 10am–6pm, Sun 10am–4pm; July Mon–Sat 9am–7pm, Sun 10am–6pm; Oct–March Mon–Fri 9am–5pm; ☎0485/390 00, fax 390 10). Here you can pick up a bus **timetable** (but don't expect an explanation) and the *Öland Karten*, a really good map with clear road routes (49kr). In the same building is the nature centre, Naturum, where a model of the island lights up to show all the areas of interest.

Bike rental is available in Kalmar and Borgholm; at most of the campsites and hostels, and the odd farm with a sign outside. All outlets charge around 50kr a day, 200kr a week, and it's not hard to find tandems (80kr) or child seats. In Färjestaden, you can rent a bike at Storgatan 67 (☎0485/300 74).

Orientation for drivers could not be simpler. There is only one big road, the Route 136 that runs from the lighthouse at the island's northernmost tip to the lighthouse in the far south. Route 136 is picked up directly from the bridge and runs parallel with the west coast, until it reaches Källa, where it swings to the east, before twisting west to run directly through to Byxelkrok. A smaller (unnumbered) road runs off Route 136 down the east of the island south from Föra.

The **bus** network connects most places in Öland, but the service, though efficient, is infrequent, and you have to be prepared for a lot of waiting around, particularly in the south – time trips carefully to avoid being stranded. **Hitching** is possible in the south and easiest when you are heading north across the plain.

An exciting, if short-lived, introduction to Öland is to take one of the **around-the-island flights** (15min; 150kr, children 100kr) from one of two tiny airfields, one a kilometre south of Borgholm (☎0485/104 00), the other at Ölanda Airfield, in a forest clearing near Löttorp (☎0485/281 41 or 0707/48 74 72). The tiny planes (they carry a maximum of three passengers each) also make flights to Visby on Gotland (500kr one-way, 700kr return).

GETTING TO ÖLAND

The **bus** timetable, available from Kalmar's bus or train station and tourist office, is almost impossible to decipher – a fact not helped by bus numbers changing with the season. Buses #101 and #106 are safe bets, however, and run pretty well every hour from Kalmar bus station to Borgholm (50min; 35kr). The evening service is more erratic, but continues in some form until 2am in summer. If you don't want to go to Borgholm, ask at the bus station for the buses that stop at **Färjestaden**, the bus network hub, a couple of kilometres south of Möllstorp. Heading to Öland by road, take the Ängö link road to Svinö (clearly signposted), just outside Kalmar, from where the bridge takes you across to **Möllstorp** on Öland.

A rule forbidding **bikes** to be cycled over the bridge has something of a silver lining: there is a free bus from Svinö especially for cyclists, which stops outside the island's main tourist office in Möllstorp. (If you're **hitching**, you can try your luck with the free bus, too, citing the bridge's lack of a footpath as the reason to take a free trip.)

Borgholm and around

As you walk the simple square grid of streets that makes up **Borgholm**, Öland's "capital", it becomes clear that tourism is the lifeblood of this small town. Though swamped each July by tens of thousands of visitors, Borgholm is in no way the tacky resort it could be. Encircled by the flaking, turretted and verandahed villas, once the pride of the town during its first period as a holiday resort in the nineteenth century, most of the centre is a friendly, if bland, network of shops and restaurants lining the roads that lead down to the very pleasant harbour.

Arrival, information and accommodation

Buses here terminate at Sandgatan, where you'll find Borgholm's **tourist office** (☎0485/890 00), tucked away out of the hubbub at no. 25. The only place to **rent a bike** in the town is *Hallbergs Hojar,* Köpmangatan 10 (Mon–Sat 9.30am–6.30pm; ☎0485/890 00; 50kr a day).

Set in quiet, park-like gardens, the fine, stately STF **youth hostel** at Rosenfors is a kilometre east of the town centre (☎0485/107 56; 140kr; May to mid-Aug); ask the bus driver to stop at Q8 filling station just before Borgholm proper, from where the hostel is just 100m away. Its dormitories and large kitchen are housed in old stone outbuildings. The tourist office will book **private rooms** over the counter only, from 150kr per person, plus a booking fee of 25kr. The local **campsite**, *Kapelludden's Camping* (☎0485/101 78, fax 129 44), is on a small peninsula five minutes' walk from the centre. As with the rest of the island, there's no shortage of beautiful spots to camp rough.

Of the **hotels** in town, the best choice for a central yet tranquil place is *Villa Sol,* Slottsgatan 30 (☎0485/562552; ①), a charming pale-yellow house with stripped wooden floors and old tiled fireplaces. Also central is *Hotel Borgholm*, Trådgårdsgatan 15 (☎0485/770 60, fax 12 466; ③), with smart rooms and pleasant gardens. Straddling one side of the harbour is the vast *Strand Hotel,* Villagatan 4 (☎0485/888 88, fax 888 99; ④). Blandly styled like a modern Spanish seaside hotel, its massive interior includes a small shopping mall, a disco and nightclub. Guests can use the indoor pool, sauna (free) and solarium (30kr). Eight kilometres south of Borgholm on Route 136 is one of the few really fine hotels on the island, *Halltorps Gästgiveri* (☎0485/850 00, fax 850 01; ④), based in a beautiful eighteenth-century manor house. The breakfasts, included in the price, are superb, and there's an excellent gourmet restaurant; weekend packages, including meals, are available. Buses #101 or #106 stop outside the hotel every thirty minutes on their way to Borgholm.

The Town

The only real attraction here is **Borgholms Slotts**, several hundred metres southwest of the centre (May–Aug 10am–6pm; free). A colossal stone fortification with rows of huge arches and corridors open to the skies, it is reached either through a nature reserve, signposted from the town centre, or from the first exit south off Route 136. Built in the twelfth century, the castle was fortified four hundred years later by King Johan III, and given its present shape – with a tower at each corner – in the seventeenth century. Regularly attacked, it eventually fell into disrepair, and when the town was founded in 1816, the castle was already a ruin; it did, however, give the town its name (*borg* means "castle").

Just a few hundred metres to the south of the castle is the present royal family's summer residence, **Solliden Park**, an Italian-style villa built to a design specified by the Swedish Queen Victoria (the present king's great-grandmother) in 1903; a huge, austere red-granite bust of her rises out of the trees at the entrance to the car park. Of Austrian stock, Victoria loathed Sweden, and demanded the bust face Italy, the country she most loved. The villa itself is not open to the public, but the formal gardens can be visited (mid-May to mid-Sept 1–6pm; 40kr): there's a very ordered Italian Garden, a colourful Dutch Garden and a simple English-style one. Alternatively, you could just head for the delightful café, *Kaffetorpet* (same hours as the garden), near the car park; irises and berrying bushes actually grow on the café's thatched roof. Here you can have light lunches, cakes, ice cream and waffles at reasonable prices.

The only other minor diversion in Borgholm is the **Stats Museet** (sometimes still called Forngård), Köpmangatan 23 (mid-May to Aug Mon–Sat 11am–5pm, daily in July; 20kr), a museum of Öland life, set in a fine 1840s house boasting a crumbling, though still impressive, glazed porchway. The ground-floor exhibits include bits of ancient skulls, some Viking glass, Bronze Age jewellery and grave finds. Upstairs there are some attractive period rooms, while the outbuildings all contain quaint seventeenth- and eighteenth-century peasant interiors; there's a café here too. The museum is best seen at the end of your visit to Öland, as the treasures on display are taken from the historical sites around the island.

To see what the town looked like before the likes of the *Strand Hotel* (see p.288) were built, head along Villagatan, the road to the left of the *Strand* as you face out to sea; the street is lined with classic wooden villas, their porches and eaves all fancy fretwork. At the end of Villagatan is a nature reserve. You can't drive along the street without authorization, though, as this is the route used by the king and queen to reach their summer home, just beyond the reserve.

Just to the north of the town centre is Öland's largest Bronze Age cairn, **Blå Rör**, a huge mound of stones excavated when a coffin was discovered in 1849. People have been turning up artefacts from time to time ever since: in the 1920s, burnt bones, indicating a cremation site, were found, along with bronze swords and tweezers – common items in such tombs. The tourist office promotes it as a major site, but there's not really a lot to see.

Eating, drinking and nightlife

There is a pronounced summer-holiday feel to the town's **restaurants** and bars. Pizza places abound around Stortorget and down towards the harbour, cashing in on the summer influx of tourists by charging relatively high prices (65–85kr per pizza). *Mama Rosa*, right at the harbour on Södra Långgatan (mid-May to mid-Aug daily noon–1am), is smarter than most and has a more varied menu. As well as pizzas (66kr), they offer classic Italian dishes and a decent wine list. On the north side of the harbour, *Skeppet* (☎0485/772 15; May–Sept daily noon–11pm) is a jolly little Italian restaurant, hidden behind 1940s industrial silos. Their special, a pizza with just about all the ingredients of their other pizzas, is a good choice at 70kr. For the finest food – with prices to match – head for *Backfickan* at *Hotel Borgholm* (daily 6–10.30pm); main courses here come at a hefty 200kr. One unpublicized treasure is the lunchtime **vegetarian** restaurant *Villa Harmoni*, on Storgatan (☎0485/100 41; Wed–Fri 11am–2pm). Tucked away at the back of *Ölands GlasCafé*, an unremarkable ice cream parlour, it doesn't have a fixed menu, but does serve delicious food. Just out of town to the north is a good place for carnivores, *Monica's Krog*, Postvägen 2 (☎0485/725 72), at the northernmost end of the village of Köpingsvik, off Route 136. Locals come for the steaks, served on wooden planks (110kr), and the warm service; pizzas are served too.

Although Borgholm's **café** life is limited, it has a couple of excellent places for a relaxed caffeine fix and a light bite. *Coffee House,* on Storgatan next to *Pubben* (see below), is the only place for a really good coffee, not to mention bagels, baguettes and great cakes and brownies. For absolutely delectable cakes and pies, though, there's no beating *Ebba's Café* on Storgatan. Set in one of the only old wooden houses on this main street, they serve a superb lunchtime buffet of savoury pies (try the delicate salmon), the price including bread and coffee (75kr). Lasagne, crepes, ciabattas and baked potatoes are also on offer here, at 50–70kr each. For **drinking**, *Pubben*, Storgatan 18 (daily 3pm–1am), is a cosy pub with old radios and crystal sets for decor. As well as lager, stout and bitter, this popular bar specializes in whisky – 46 varieties of malts and blends.

One **nightclub** worth checking out is *2001* (daily 6pm–2am), on Södralånggatan, 500m from the harbour. Built originally as a hospital for venereal diseases, and later used as a church, the place features R&B and house music, and occasional live bands. The spacious *O'Keefe's* bar and nightclub, on Storgatan (daily 11am–11pm), fills up nightly throughout summer (nightclub entrance 50kr); this is the place for cheap beer and cider as well as a wide range of food. A raucous young crowd invariably swarms into the *Strand disco* in the *Strand Hotel* every evening, turning it into a sort of Baltic Ibiza throughout the summer nights.

Around Borgholm

Cutting eastwards from Borgholm (take bus #102), following signs to **Räpplinge**, leads to **Störlinge Kvarna**, a row of seven windmills by the roadside. A sign tells you this is the island's longest line of windmills, but as you'll probably have already seen several windmills by then, there's no real inducement to stop. A couple of kilometres south, **Gärdslösa** has the island's best-preserved medieval church. The exterior has been so well maintained that it's almost too pristine; the interior is worth a look, particularly for its pulpit, completed in 1666, and the thirteenth-century ceiling paintings, whitewashed over in 1781 but uncovered in 1950.

The preserved village of **Himmelsberga**, about 3km further south, is an **open-air museum** in an idyllic setting (early May to early Sept daily 10am–6pm; 40kr). Since the decline of farming in the middle of this century, most of Öland's thatched farmhouses have been rather brutally modernized. Himmelsberga escaped this, however, and in the 1950s, two of its original farms were opened as museums. Subsequently, centuries-old buildings were brought here from all over the island, and the place now boasts a smithy, a windmill and an extensive collection of crofters' farmhouses. Due to a lack of timber on Öland – islanders were forbidden to cut their own lest it spoil the royal hunting – the peasants had to buy entire oak houses from the mainland and reassemble them on the island; you can see several of these here. There's also a **café** in the village, where tea and coffee are served in bright copper pots.

Dating from around 450 AD, **Ismantorps Borg**, an ancient castle ruin signposted a few kilometres east from Himmelsberga, is a huge ring of stones. Inside are the remnants of the walls and floors of 88 rooms – which you can attempt to pick out. **Gråborg**, 10km south on the route of bus #102, is Öland's largest ancient castle ruin, with walls totalling 640m in length. Built around 500 AD and occupied through the Middle Ages, when the Gothic entrance arch was built, today the walls encircle little more than a handful of hardy sheep.

Öland windmill

Ales Stennar, with some bovine visitors

Morning dip at Kalmar, with Öland bridge in the background

Cowhide-covered battering ram outside Visby city walls, Gotland

Kalmar Slott

Lake scene near Tärnaby, Lapland

Altarpiece at Vadstena church

Sledging across Padjelanta National Park, Lapland

Chapel at *Ice Hotel*, Jukkasjärvi

North Öland

The most varied and interesting landscape on the island is to be found towards the north, with no shortage of idyllic villages, dark woods and flowery meadows as you head up from Borgholm along the main road, **Route 136**. There are some interesting diversions along the route too. Though there aren't many in the way of proper hotels north of the Borgholm area, **campsites** of a high standard abound, marked every couple of kilometres off the road; most of these places are close to a beach. Public transport here is limited to **buses** heading up Route 136 towards Byxelkrok; the road is safe for **cycling** along too – ideal for exploring the tracks that lead off the main drag.

Föra to Sandvik

At **Föra**, a village about 20km north of Borgholm, there's a good example of a typical Öland **church**, built in the medieval era (the font is the oldest bit here, dating from 1250). It doubled as a fortress, and was capable of accommodating a considerable garrison in times of war. The windows are low enough to peer in at its medieval interior (though you shouldn't need to, as it'll usually be open during the daytime in summer). Just north of Föra is **Lofta**, where *Värdshuset Briggen Treliljor* offers a paradoxical combination of surprisingly expensive **eating** and good-value **accommodation** (☎0485/264 00; ②; May–Dec). The bar and elegant restaurant are open from 6pm (late June to Aug daily, Sept to late June Sat & Sun only), with starters like tomato soup with basil ice cream at 85kr, and main courses from 115kr and up. The English translation of the menu lists, among other items, "two centilitres of facile punsch" and one course called "plain food".

One kilometre north, a sign to **Knisa Mosse** leads to a peaceful nature reserve, centred on a shimmering lake, and to some Bronze Age burial mounds; there's not much to see at the burial area itself. To see a feat of nineteenth-century engineering, it's well worth stopping at **SANDVIK**, dominated by Scandinavia's largest **windmill**, built in the 1850s. A Dutch-style construction, with eight floors and ingenious wooden workings, it was a working mill until 1955; today, it's home to a cosy pizza restaurant. Sandvik's economy is still based around its stone-cutting, one of the few surviving traditional industries. Next door to the stone-cutters, the café and pizza **restaurant** (daily noon–11pm) has benefited from its neighbour; inside the benches, bar and tables are made of slabs of white marble cut at angles. It's not a bad place for pizza, lasagne and steaks (around 85kr each), and has daily specials (59kr); there's a range of beers and spirits too. From the mill, it's just 200m down to the peaceful **harbour**, where the *Hamn Cafe* does good simple meals, cheap coffee and a wide variety of teas.

Källa and around

Two kilometres outside the village of **KÄLLA** and about 7km north of Sandvik, proud, forlorn **Källa kyrka** sits in splendid isolation (it's not to be confused with the current church, by the sign for Källa). Surrounded by brightly flowering meadows, this tall, dull-white medieval church, empty since 1888, is bounded by dry-stone walls, its grounds littered with ancient, weathered tombs. Inside, the lofty interior has seen plenty of action: built in 1130 of limestone, to replace an earlier tiny stave church, Källa kyrka was regularly attacked by heathens from over the Baltic seas. It was modernized in the fourteenth century, when Källa was a relatively important harbour and trading centre, and stripped of its furnishings in the nineteenth century; inside, a row of six models of the church at various stages of its history is the only thing left to see. The only other building close by is home to a fish smokery.

Just over the main road, a low deep-thatched cluster of early eighteenth-century thatched farmhouses contains a restaurant, *Källagården* (daily 11am–11pm). It serves good-value lunch specials at 50kr and, on Tuesdays, a *räk buffe* – as many prawns as you can eat (7–10pm; 85kr). For an authentically Öland culinary experience, it's essential to try the island's speciality, **kroppkakor**, and the finest place to do so is undoubtedly *Nini's Kroppskaksbod*, reached by turning left off the main road at Källabygdegård (☎0485/273 00; June–Aug daily 11am–6pm; Sept–May Tues, Wed & Sat 11am–6pm). Their name translating unappetizingly as "body cakes", these delicacies (each 15kr, or 10kr to take away) are made with boiled and raw potato filled with lightly smoked and boiled pork. At *Nini's*, they're made in small batches, for which islanders willingly travel, and served with cream and lingonberries, and a glass of cold milk. They won't become everyone's favourite, but are quite delicious eaten in Nini's garden.

One of the most unexpected sights around here is an unsignposted **camel and llama farm**, 14km north of Borgholm at **Ormöga**. Bengt and Christen Erlingsson operate camel rides (☎0485/700 27; from 6pm during the summer; 50kr) in this most unlikely setting, while the llamas are for sale. A sign states reassuringly that although the llamas do spit at each other, they seldom spit at people. Even if you don't feel tempted to make a purchase, they're interesting animals to observe in this pastoral, Baltic island setting.

Högby to Böda Sand

Högby, a few kilometres on, has the only remaining tied church houses on the island, relics of the medieval Högby kyrka nearby; there's not a lot to see though. For a most unusual, though somewhat pricey, dining experience, head for the village of **Löttorp**, off Route 136, and follow the signs east for 4km down country lanes to the *Lammet & Grisen* restaurant, housed in a building like a Spanish hacienda (☎0485/203 50; daily 5.30pm–midnight). The only dishes on the menu are salmon and spit-roasted lamb and pork (hence the restaurant's name), served with baked potatoes, flavoured butters and sauces. You can eat all the meat you want for 210kr, or everything but the meat and salmon for 110kr – which isn't worth it.

Continuing north and west off Route 136, following signs for Byrums Sandvik and Raukområde, you come to **Byrums Rauker**, a striking sight: solitary limestone pillars formed by the eroding action of the sea, at the edge of a sandy beach. The best **beaches** are along the east coast; starting at Böda Sand, the most popular stretch is a couple of kilometres north at **Lyckesand**, with a nudist beach just to the north, the start of which is marked simply by a large boulder in the sea. Small east coast roads run to the beaches, and the many campsites signposted off Route 136 also lead on to the beaches.

The most extensive **campsite** in the north of the island is *Krono Camping* at Böda Sand (☎0485/222 00, fax 223 76), 50km north of Borgholm and 2km off the Route 136 at the southern end of the beach. It has cabins for rent, costing from 3000kr per week for four people, and a range of facilities, including shops, a bakery, and **restaurants** complete with balladeers for entertainment. Just south of Böda's campsite is an STF **youth hostel**, *Vandrarhem Böda*, at Mellböda (☎0485/220 38, fax 221 98; 100kr). A large, well-equipped hostel, it has a cosy kitchen and some single rooms. For an unusual alternative, you could stay at the nearby *Bödabaden Öland Square Dance Centre* (☎0485/220 12 or 220 85, fax 220 07), Europe's only square-dancing theme park, offering courses and the chance to take part in tournaments. Their cabins, all en suite, are quite upmarket and more like basic hotel rooms (①). They also have a good pub, decked out as an American saloon.

North of Böda Sand: the Trolls Forest and Byxelkrok

There are some gorgeous areas of natural beauty in the far north of the island. Some excellent walking is to be had at the island's northeastern tip, within the nature reserve of **Trollskogen** ("Trolls' Forest") – so named because it's exactly the kind of place you would imagine trolls to inhabit, with twisted, gnarled trunks of ancient oaks all shrouded in ivy. Around the western edge of the northern coast, the waters lapping against the rocky beaches are of the purest blue. On a tiny island at the very northern tip of Öland stands **Långe Eric Lighthouse**, a handsome obelisk built in 1845, and a good target for a walk or cycle ride. **Neptune Åkrar**, 3km south on the western coast, is covered with *blå jungfrun*, lupin-like flowers whose brilliant blue rivals the sea beyond. The name, which was given them by Carl von Linné (see p.116), means "Neptune's Ploughland" – the ridged land formation here looks like ploughed fields.

The only town in this region is **BYXELKROK**, a quiet place with an attractive harbour, where **ferries** from Oskarshamn, on the mainland, dock. You can **rent bikes** here from David Andersson (☎0485/281 09; 40kr a day). *Solö Värdhus* is a pleasant enough **hotel**, on the town's main road (☎0485/283 70; ②). What **nightlife** there is mostly happens here at *Sjöstugan* (April noon–5pm, May noon–8pm, June–Aug noon–2am), a restaurant, pub and disco, right by the shore. They specialize in salmon (100kr) and flounder (80kr), and also serve pizzas (55–85kr) and a vegetarian dish (70kr). Troubadours sing downstairs every day in June, while Swedish dance bands are their thing in July; there are discos every Thursday to Saturday all year.

South Öland

Dominated by **Stora Alvaret**, the giant limestone plain on which no trees can grow, the south of Öland is sparsely populated, its main town the rather dull **Mörbylånga**. Despite references in the tourist literature to "exposed rock", the landscape here consists of flat meadows which boast, among other unusual plant life, some rare alpine species that have stoically clung to life since the Ice Age. **Buses** run so infrequently here, you'll need to double-check times at Färjestaden (reachable from Borgholm on #101), just south of the bridge, where the few buses south (#101, #103 head to Mörbylånga) start their journey. **Hitching** is feasible – probably because drivers know that without their help, chances are you'll be stranded for long periods of time. Shops and other facilities are sparser than in the north, so if you don't have a car, it's worth stocking up on provisions before you head off. Despite the difficulties, the great advantage of travelling through the south is that the summer crowds elsewhere thin out here, allowing you to explore peacefully the most untouched parts of the island – and visit Öland's most interesting **fort**, at Eketorp.

Vickleby

The prettiest village south of Borgholm on Route 136 is **VICKLEBY**, a quaint place halfway between Färjestaden to the north and Mörbylånga to the south. It's where a remarkable art and design school, **Capella Gården**, was set up by Carl Malmsten early this century. A furniture designer and idealist, Malmsten struck out against the traditional system of teaching: his dream was to create a school that stimulated mind, body and soul – a sort of educational utopia that was criticized as unworkable by a shocked Stockholm society. In 1959, he bought a range of picturesque farmhouses at Vickleby, turning them into an art and design school for adults that's still in operation today. Capella Garden isn't for everybody – the atmosphere is more than a little intense – but its courses do attract people from all over the world, who live for a few weeks in a commune environment, brushing up on their textile weaving and pottery, among other skills. The results, including some lovely ceramic and wood pieces, are put on sale during their annual exhibition, held in summer. It's best to call ahead to arrange a visit (☎0485/361 32).

Eketorp and Ottenby bird station

Of all the forts on Öland, the one most worth a visit is at the village of **EKETORP** (May to mid-Sept daily 10am–5pm; guided tours in English at 1pm; 50kr, under 14s free). The site, reachable by bus #114 from Mörbylånga, is where three settlements were discovered during a major excavation in the 1970s; these included a marketplace from the fourth century and an agricultural community dating from 1000. Actual physical evidence being thin on the ground, what one sees today is a wonderful achievement in popular archeology: an encircling wall has been constructed on the plain, and pigs, sheep and geese – the same animals that were once reared here (their presence identified by examining food waste in bone fragments found at the site) – wander around. The best of the finds, such as jewellery and weapons, are on show in the adjacent museum, and there's also a workshop where, if you feel inclined, you can have a go at leatherwork or "authentic" ancient cookery.

South of here, a stone wall cuts straight across the island. Called **Karl X Gustav's Wall**, it was built in 1650 to fence off deer and so improve the hunting. A herd of 150 fallow deer still roam about today at **Ottenby**, Öland's largest private estate, in the far south of the island. Built in 1804, this is now a bird-watcher's paradise, boasting a huge nature reserve and the Ottenby **bird station**, which, since 1946, has been Sweden's largest sanctuary for migrating birds. There are also two protected observation towers and a bird museum. You have to be keen on our feathered friends, who trill in their millions, for the area to hold much appeal – there's absolutely nothing else here.

Practicalities

The main **tourist office** at Möllstorp (see p.287) will book **private rooms** from 150kr per person per night, with a 25kr booking fee. *Mörby Youth Hostel* (☎ & fax 0485/493 93; 150kr, ①), 15km south of the bridge to Kalmar, has some hotel-class double rooms with sheets and breakfast provided (②); bus #105 drops you off outside. Ten kilometres south of the bridge at Haga Park is the *Haga Park* (☎0485/360 30; ①), offering no-frills B&B in an oldish wooden house. There are four-bed family rooms with a kitchen and bathroom (650kr per night) and the most basic of dormitory accommodation (110kr). Nearby is a **campsite**; the beach here is a centre for windsurfing. For a regular **hotel**, try *Hotel Kajutan* (☎0485/408 10; ③), a pleasant old place built in 1860; it's at the harbour behind the bus station in Mörbylånga. At Vickleby, a more attractive location, *Hotel Bo Pensionat* (☎0485/360 01; ③), in a traditional row of village houses, is very popular; it's worth booking ahead in high season. A good, cheap evening **restaurant** can be found at the *Haga Park* hotel, where meals like salmon and potatoes go for 60kr.

Into Småland: the Glass Kingdom

Back on the mainland, **Småland county**, thickly forested and studded with lakes, makes up the southeastern wedge of Sweden. Although the scenery is appealing at first, the uniformity of the landscape means it's easy to become blasé about its natural beauty. Småland is often somewhere people travel through rather than to – from Stockholm to the southwest, or from Gothenburg to the Baltic coast. It does, however, have a few vital spots of interest of its own, such as **Kalmar** (already covered on p.280), alongside opportunities for hiking, trekking, fishing and cycling.

Historically, Småland has had it tough. The simple, rustic charm of the pretty painted cottages belie the intense misery endured by generations of local peasants: in the nineteenth century, subsistence farming failed, and the people were starving; consequently a fifth of Sweden's population left the country for America

---

GLASS-MAKING AND BUYING IN GLASRIKET

The **glass-making process** can be mesmerizing to watch. The process involves a glass plug being fished out of a shimmering, molten lake (at 1200°C) and then turned and blown into a graphite or steel mould. With wine glasses, a foot is added during the few seconds when the temperature is just right – if the glass is too hot, the would-be stem will slide off or sink right through; if too cold, it won't stick. The piece is then annealed – heated and then slowly cooled – for several hours. It all looks deceptively simple and mistakes are rare, but it nevertheless takes years to become a *servitor* (glass-maker's assistant), working up through the ranks of stem-maker and bowl-gatherer (in the smaller glassworks, all these roles are the responsibility of one person). It's an amazing sight to see the bowl-gatherer fetching the glowing gob for the master blower, who then skilfully rolls and shapes the syrupy substance.

The glassware is marketed with a vengeance in Småland – take a look at the often absurd hyberbole in the widely available *Kingdom of Crystal* magazine. If you want to buy glassware, don't feel compelled to snap up the first things you see: the same types of design appear at most of the glassworks, testimony to the fact that Kosta Boda and Orrefors are the main players nowadays; many of the smaller works have been swallowed up, even though they retain their own names. This makes price comparison easier, but don't expect many bargains; the best pieces go for thousands of *kronor*. Generally, Orrefors is much less experimental in its designs than Kosta. You may find it useful to see the glassware exhibition in Växjö's Smålands Museum first, to get an idea of the various styles and where you can find them (see p.299).

– most of them from Småland. While their plight is vividly retold at the **House of Emigrants** exhibition in **Växjö** (see p.300), which makes an excellent base from which to explore the region, the county's main tourist attractions are its myriad **glass factories** hidden in forest clearings. The bulk of these celebrated glass-works lie within the dense birch and pine forests that, together with a thread of lakes, make up the largely unbroken landscape between Kalmar and Växjö. Consequently, the area is dubbed **GLASRIKET**, or the "Glass Kingdom", with each glassworks signposted clearly from the spidery main roads.

This very picturesque setting for the industry is no coincidence. Glass-making in Sweden was pioneered by King Gustav Vasa, who'd been impressed by the glass he saw on a trip to Italy in the mid-sixteenth century. He initially set up a glassworks in Stockholm; however, it was Småland's forests that could provide the vast amounts of fuel needed to feed the furnaces, and so a glass factory was set up in the county in 1742. Called Kosta, after its founders, Koskull and Stael von Hostein, it is the largest glassworks in Småland today.

Visiting the glassworks

Of the twenty or so glassworks still in operation in Småland, thirteen of them have captivating **glass-blowing** demonstrations on weekdays, several have permanent exhibitions of either contemporary glasswork or pieces from their history, and all have a shop. **Bus** services to the glassworks, or to points within easy walking distance of them, are extremely limited, and without your own transport it is almost impossible to see more than a couple in a day (though this will satisfy most people). While each glassworks has its individual design characteristics, **Kosta Boda** (easiest to reach from Växjö; see p.298) and **Orrefors** (its main rival and closer to Kalmar) works have extensive displays and give the best picture of what's available. To get to Orrefors (June to mid-Aug: glass-blowing Mon–Fri 8am–3.30pm, Sat 10am–3pm, Sun 11am–3pm; exhibition Mon–Fri 9am–3pm, Sat 9am–4pm, Sun 11am–4pm), you first need to get to Nybro; you can do this on Route 25 from Kalmar, or by train from Kalmar or Växjö. You can then drive to the factory on Route 31, or catch bus #138, #139 or #140.

Kosta Boda glassworks

The **Kosta Boda** and **Åfors** glassworks are both operated by the same team. While two of Kosta's most celebrated designers, Bertil Vallien and Ulrica Hydman Vallien, have their studios at Åfors, the bigger glassworks is at Kosta (glass-blowing June to mid-Aug Mon–Fri 10am–4pm, Sat 10am–3pm, Sun 11am–4pm). The **historical exhibition** here (June to mid-Aug Mon–Fri 9am–6pm, Sat 9am–4pm, Sun 11am–4pm) contains some of the most delicate turn-of-the-century glass-ware, designed by Karl Lindeberg; for contemporary simplicity, Anna Ehrener's bowls and vases are the most elegant. Among the most brilliantly innovative works are those by Göran Wärff – examples of his expressive work can also be found in Växjö's Cathedral. Current design trends tend more towards what the Kosta blurb insists is "playful disrespect for conventional form – a rhapsody of sensuality", which in reality means colourful and rather graceless high kitsch. Ulrica Hydman Vallien's newest designs are very overrated and commercialized, involving painted-on faces with glass noses stuck on. Nonetheless, new designer-sculptural pieces can go for astoundingly high prices. In the adjacent shop (Mon–Fri 9am–7pm, Sat 10am–4pm, Sun noon–4pm) you can buy large vases by her for around 2000kr, and dishes for 1058kr; for a single, traditional *akvavit* glass, however, you're looking at paying something like 115kr.

To get to Kosta from Växjö, take Route 23 in the direction of Oskarshamn, then Route 31 southeast and turn onto Route 28. Heading here from Kalmar, you first take Route 25 west to Nybro, turning onto Route 31 northwest, and then left along Route 28. You can do a day-trip here by public transport from Växjö – take bus #218 from Växjö bus station, changing at Lessebo.

Other glassworks

Strömbergshyttan glassworks near Hovmantorp is the best bet for a local trip from Växjö (June to mid-Aug; shop only Mon–Fri 9am–6pm, Sat 9am–4pm, Sun 11am–4pm); with displays of both Kosta and Orrefors merchandise, it's more comprehensive than nearby **Sandvik**, an Orrefors company. Strömbergshyttan is south down Route 30 from Växjö, or take bus #218 (40min), which runs more frequently here than to Kosta. The simple and distinctive blue-rimmed glassware popular all over Sweden can be seen at **Bergdala**, 6km north of Hovmantorp (mid-June to mid-Aug: glass-blowing Mon–Fri 9am–2.30pm, Sat 10am–3pm, Sun noon–4pm; shop Mon–Fri 9am–7pm, Sat 10am–4pm, Sun noon–4pm); there's no public transport there. A small, traditional factory, it offers a more intimate look at the glassblowing process.

Signposted to the north, **Rosdala** is unusual in that it only produces glass for lampshades (mid-June to mid-Aug; glass-blowing Mon–Fri 8am–3pm, though closed most of July). It's not too exciting, though, as most of the designs are staid floral patterns painted on globes; its **museum** displays some of the ugliest 1970s designs (Mon–Fri 9am–6pm, Sat 10am–4pm, Sun 11am–4pm). The shop isn't bad value, with the smallest lampshades from 170kr (Mon–Fri 9am–6pm, Sat 10am–4pm, Sun 11am–4pm). A few kilometres further north on Route 30, the 1905-founded **Lindshammar** works has mostly quite ordinary glassware, and some real tat, too; the few really good vases cost 3200kr. From Växjö, take Route 23 to Norrhult-Klavreström, then Route 31 north; there's no public transport to *Rosdala*.

Johansfors, to the south of the region, is a small factory set by a lake, and specializing in wine goblets (exhibitions Mon–Fri 9am–6pm, Sat 10am–4pm, Sun noon–4pm; shop daily 9am–6pm). To get there, take Route 28 from Kosta; there's no bus service here. Nearby **Skruf** has the most basic, jam-jar style collection, which is also about the cheapest, but is one of the few to charge entry to its museum (5kr).

Practicalities

All the glassworks have simple **cafés**. There's often local **accommodation** available, particularly at the bigger glassworks; check availability with tourist offices at Kalmar or Växjö. One of the most enjoyable, though costly, eating experiences here – and one that really can claim to be a Småland original – is **hyttsill**, an evening meal of herrings baked in the factory glass furnaces at 300°C. Five of the glassworks – Kosta, Orrefors, Sandvik, Bergdala and Lindshammar – cook up *hyttsill*, each on a different night but always at 7pm (240kr; check days with the tourist office). The herring is served with furnace-baked potatoes, Småland curd cake (a rich local cheesecake), coffee and beer. To sample one of these meals, it's important to reserve a place a day or two in advance (Bergdala ☎0478/316 50; Kosta ☎0478/508 35 or 345 00; Lindshammar ☎0383/210 25; Orrefors ☎0481/300 59; Sandvik ☎0478/405 15).

Växjö and around

Founded by Saint Sigfrid in the eleventh century, **VÄXJÖ** (pronounced "veh-quer"), deep in the heart of Småland county (110km from Kalmar), is by far the handiest place to base yourself if you are interested in the distinctive **glassware** produced in the region. Though its centre is fairly bland, Växjö, whose name derives from *väg sjö*, or "way to the lake", enjoys some beautifully tranquil lake scenery a few kilometres away. The town itself offers a couple of great **museums**.

Arrival, information and accommodation

The **train** (hourly from Kalmar; 1hr 30min) and **bus stations** are side by side in the middle of town. Växjö's **tourist office** is in the train station building at Norra Järnvägsgatan (mid-June to mid-Aug Mon–Fri 9.30am–6.30pm, Sat 10am–2pm, Sun 10am–2pm; mid-Aug to mid-June Mon–Thurs 9.30am–4.30pm, Fri 9.30am–3pm; ☎0470/414 10, fax 478 14). **Bikes** – useful for visiting the countryside around Växjö (see p.301) – can be rented from Smålands Cykel, Västra Esplanaden 15 (Mon–Fri 8am–6pm, Sat 10am–2pm, Sun 1–2pm; ☎0470/475 48; 60kr a day).

Accommodation

The helpful tourist office will book **private rooms** from 130kr, plus a 50kr booking fee. Växjö's splendid STF **youth hostel** (☎0470/630 70, fax 632 16; 130kr) at **Evedal**, 5km north of the centre, is among the most civilized and beautifully maintained in the country; even if you normally don't stay in hostels, try this one. Set in parkland by a lake, tranquil Helgasjön, boasting its own beach, this eighteenth-century house was once a society hotel. Today they serve a good breakfast (45kr) and have laundry facilities (40kr). To get there, take Linnégatan north, following signs for Evedal, or take either bus #1C from the Växjö bus terminal to the end of the route (last bus is at 4.15pm, 3.15pm on Sat), or bus #1A; the latter drops you 1500m from the hostel, but has the utility of running daily till 8.15pm. Next to the hostel, and also by the lake, is a **campsite**, *Evedal Camping* (☎0470/630 34, fax 631 22), which has a decent shop for stocking up on food. Tents can be pitched for 130kr, plus 25kr for electricity; four-person cabins are 450kr, including electricity, kitchen and shower.

Växjö has several reasonable central **hotels**, listed below. One good place to stay outside town is the **Tofta Strand Hotel**, Lenhovdavägen 72, in Sandsbro, 4km away (☎0470/652 90, fax 614 02; ③). Its delightful gardens lead down to Lake Toft, which you can head out on using the hotel's bizarre motorized raft. To get to Sandsbro, take Route 23 in the direction of Oskarshamn, or hop on bus #5 from Växjö bus station; the hotel is 400m further on the right from where you leave the bus.

Esplanad, Norra Esplanaden 21A (☎0470/225 80, fax 262 26). A reasonable, central hotel room with no frills. ②/①.

SAS Radisson Royal Corner, Liedbergsgatan 11 (☎0470/414 80). Central, comfortable and featureless, this is nonetheless a popular choice for good service. ④/②.

Statt, Kungsgatan 6 (☎0470/134 00, fax 448 37). The usual executive-class hotchpotch of shiny marble, potted palms and terrible carpets, this hotel serves a generous buffet breakfast. Within the hotel is an Irish pub, *O'Keefe's*, and a summertime restaurant, the *Lagerlunden* (Mon–Thurs 6pm–1am, Fri & Sat 6pm–2am). ④/②.

Teaterpark, Nygatan (☎0470/399 00, fax 475 77). In the central Concert Hall building. Visually striking, this ultra-stylish, Functionalist hotel also has special bedrooms designed for disabled guests. There are also special allergy-free rooms. ⑤/③.

Värend, Kungsgatan 27 (☎0470/104 85, fax 362 61). Another standard hotel, this one also does good-value triple rooms. ①.

The Town

Växjö boasts two superb museums: the newly renovated and extensive **Smålands Museum**, notable for being home to the **Swedish Glass Museum**; and the **House of Emigrants**, which explores the subject of mass emigration from Sweden in the nineteenth and early twentieth centuries. There's also a particularly romantic **castle ruin** 4km north of town, and a **cathedral** that has been renovated almost as many times as it is centuries old – eight.

Smålands Museum

The enlarged and renovated **Smålands Museum**, behind the train station (June–Aug Mon–Fri 10am–5pm, Sat & Sun 11am–5pm; Sept–May Tues–Fri 10am–5pm, Sat & Sun 11am–5pm; 40kr), includes two permanent exhibitions: a history of Småland's manufacturing industries, and the more interesting "500 Years of Swedish Glass". The latter shows sixteenth-century place settings, eighteenth- and nineteenth-century etched glass, and stylish Art-Nouveau-inspired pieces, with subtle floral motifs. Most visually appealing among the displays are those of contemporary glass in the museum's extension. The range of exhibits is vast, with brash pop-art glass and other pieces that show just how inventive the glass-blower's rod can be in trained hands. The exhibition also explains how many

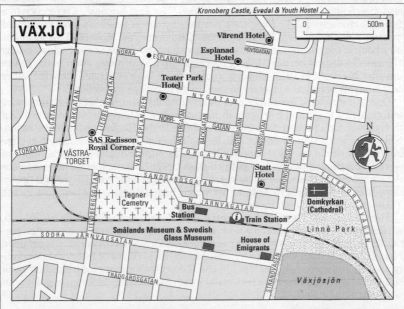

of the smaller glassworks have been taken over or squeezed out by the giant Kosta and Orrefors companies (see p.295).

House of Emigrants

Directly in front of the Småland Museum, and signposted "Utvandrarnas Hus", a plain building is home to the inspired **House of Emigrants** (June–Aug Mon–Fri 9am–6pm, Sat & Sun 11am–4pm; Sept–May Mon–Fri 9am–4pm; 30kr), with its moving "Dream of America" exhibition. The museum presents a living picture of the intense hardship faced by the Småland peasant population from the mid-nineteenth century. Due to the agricultural reforms that denied the peasants access to village common land, and a series of bad harvests, more than a million Swedes – a sixth of the population – emigrated to America between 1860 and 1930; most of them came from Småland. By 1910, Chicago had a higher population of Swedes than Gothenburg.

The museum's displays, which include English-language translations and audio narratives, trace the lives of individual emigrants and recount the story of the industry that grew up around emigration fever. Most boats used by the emigrants left from Gothenburg and, until 1915, were British-operated sailings to Hull, from where passengers crossed to Liverpool by train to board the transatlantic ships. Conditions on board were usually dire: the steamer *Hero* left Gothenburg in 1866 with five hundred emigrants, nearly four hundred oxen and nine hundred pigs, calves and sheep sharing the accommodation. Walking through the exhibition, past models of crofters' huts in Småland and a sizeable replica of the deck of an emigrant ship, you are led on to displays on emigré life in America. One man who gets a special mention was known as Lucky Swede; he became America's most successful gold prospector in the Klondike before losing it all to his chorus-girl wife. There is also a section on **women emigrants**, entitled "Not Just Kristina", a reference to a fictitious character in *The Emigrants*, a trilogy by one of Sweden's most celebrated writers, Wilhem Möberg. Upon publication, it became the most-read Swedish history book in the country, and was made into a film starring Max von Sydow and Liv Ullman. On display here is Möberg's writing cabin, which was given to the museum after his death in 1973. Möberg would himself have emigrated, only his father sold a farrow of piglets to pay for his son to go to college in Sweden.

One of the saddest tales here is of Mauritz Ådahl, who, like a fifth of those who left, returned to try and live again in his native land. Money pressure forced him to emigrate for a second time in 1912, and due to the English coal-miners' strike, which meant his ship could not sail, he took the much-publicized maiden voyage on the *Titanic*. Of the 1500 people killed in the *Titanic* disaster, several hundred were Swedish emigrants who, as third-class ticket holders, had no access to the deck until the lifeboats had all been taken. When his body was discovered twelve days later in the sub-zero waters, his watch had stopped at 2.34am, just as the *Titanic* vanished beneath the waves.

The museum's **Research Centre** (Mon–Fri 9am–4pm; ☎0470/201 20, *www.svenskaemigrantinstitutet.g.se*) charges 100kr per day to help interested parties trace their family roots, using passenger lists from ten harbours, microfilmed church records from all Swedish parishes and the archives of Swedish community assocations abroad. If you want to use the centre's services during their peak season (May to mid-Aug), it's especially worth booking ahead for an appointment with one of their staff.

The Domkyrkan

In the centre, on Linnégatan, the very distinctive **Domkyrkan**, with its unusual twin green towers and apricot-pink facade (daily 8am–8pm; free; guided tours June–Aug 9am–5pm), is worth a quick look. The combined impact of regular restorations, the most recent in 1995, together with a catalogue of disasters such as sixteenth-century fires and a 1775 lightning strike have left little of note except an organ. There are, however, some brilliant new glass ornaments by one of the best-known of the contemporary Glass Kingdom designers, Göran Wärff, including a wacky alternative church font. The cathedral is set in **Linné Park**, named after Carl von Linné (see p.116), who was educated at the handsome school very nearby.

Tegner Cemetery and the Xperiment House

Just one block west of the train station, and a five-minute walk from the Domkyrkan, **The Tegner Cemetery** is named after the town's most famous nineteenth-century resident, the poet and Bishop of Växjö, Esaias Tegner. It's a pretty, well-kept spot today, its strangest aspect being that the sepulchral monuments seem not to reflect the social position of the deceased: Tegner himself, buried here in 1846, is remembered with a very plain white marble tomb along the far wall. Larger and far more lavish is the granite mausoleum built here for the nineteenth-century opera singer Christina Nilsson, who was born in the locality. Her name is embossed in the intricate copper door; a peep through the keyhole reveals her bronze sarcophagus standing proud in the middle.

Travellers with **children** might wish to drop in at the **Xperiment House**, Lokstallarna (June–Aug Mon–Fri 10am–4pm, Sat 11am–4pm; Sept–May closed Mon; 55kr, children 30kr), a hands-on science centre. It's just a couple of minutes from the tourist office.

Out from the centre

Two castles, one a ruin just north of the centre, the other a nineteenth-century affair just to the south, make for delightful excursions of a couple of hours' duration. On the other hand, you could easily spend a whole day exploring the countryside surrounding Växjö, which is riddled with forest **hiking routes**; the tourist office can supply information and maps. **Cycling** is very popular, though the terrain is by no means flat and the forest lanes are often pretty rough. There are numerous **canoeing** opportunities on the still waters of the lakes, with special designated routes you can row along. Among the many places to rent canoes is Evedals Kanotuthyrning (☎0470/639 93), next to the youth hostel (see p.298); they provide not only equipment but also useful advice on where to go and what activities would suit children.

Kronoberg Castle

The ruin of **Kronoberg Castle** has a beautiful and uncommercialized setting, on a tiny island in a lake, Helgasjön, 4km north of the centre. Heading there by car, follow signs for Evedal, and the castle will be signposted off the road; or take bus #1B from Växjö bus station (Mon–Fri hourly, less frequent on Sat). Though the bishops of Växjö had erected a wooden fortress here in the eleventh century, the present stone structure was built by Gustav Vasa in 1540. Entered over an old wooden bridge set at a narrow spot in the lake, the ruin, complete with a rounded tower and lookouts set deep in the walls, leans precariously; some new brick archways and a couple of reinforced roofs, added in the 1970s, stop the whole thing collapsing.

The grass-roofed centuries-old **café** *Ryttmästargården*, directly opposite the castle and by the jetty, is a great place to have Italian pastries (see p.303). The jetty is used by the old **paddle steamer** *Thor*, which makes regular excursions from here around Helgasjön and up to another lake, Asasjön – a delightful way to see the pretty lakeland scenery (book tours at the café). You can go on the so-called "**sluice trip**" along the canal from Helgasjön to Asasjön. For a glamorous evening excursion (300kr), take the tour across Lake Asasjön to Asa Herregård, a country mansion, where you'll be served dinner (included in the price of the trip); alternatively, try the grill-dinner trip to the sluice gates between the lakes for 240kr (3hr 30min return); both these trips can be booked at Smålands Museum (☎0470/451 45).

Teleborgs Slott

Just five minutes' drive south of the town centre, the stunning castle of **Teleborgs Slott** is well worth a trip (mid-June to mid-Aug mandatory guided tours Wed 5pm & 6pm; 30kr). Standing on a peninsula jutting into Lake Trummen, this 1895 structure is a peculiar and winning concoction, looking like a Renaissance knight's castle in Rhineland but with National Romantic details, such as the beaten copper door handles. A stone staircase of more than fifty steps leads to the main entrance at the side of the castle (there is a lift too round the back). The castle was created as a gift from Count Fredrik Bonde to his new wife Anna Koskull, the idea being to offer her a castle comparable to what he imagined his Småland ancestors called home during the Middle Ages. At the time, the poverty-stricken locals, tinged with jealousy, are reported to have jeered, "what a peasant won't do for the sake of a cow" – a pun on the couple's names (*bonde* meaning "peasant", *ko* meaning "cow"). Today, the ground floor of the castle is used by the fledgling **Växjö University** as a research centre.

Eating and drinking

One of the pleasures of Växjö and its surroundings is the wealth of really good **eating** opportunities. Traditional **Småland cuisine** shows the influence of the forests and the poverty associated with the region, and is based around woodland berries, potatoes and game. Among local specialities are **isterband**, a flavoursome, spicy sausage usually served with potatoes and a dill sauce, and **krösamos**, potato pancakes with lingonberry sauce. The classic local dessert is a rich curd-cheese cake with warm cloudberry sauce. Växjö restaurants charge high prices for elk steaks, hare and venison; for cheaper fare, there's a glut of pizza and Chinese restaurants, and a *McDonald's*. **Drinking** in Växjö is mostly done in restaurant bars, as there are few actual pubs in town. This being an inland town, the local population migrates to the coasts in July and part of August, when some of the restaurants shut.

Cafés

Broqvists, Kronobergsgatan 14, just off Stortorget. Good cakes in this Växjö institution; it can get smoky though. Mon–Fri 8.30am–8pm, Sat 8am–7pm, Sun 8.30am–3pm.

Espresso Cafe, Bäckgatan. Off Storgatan, and opposite the *Cardinal Hotel*. The only stylish place within the bland grid of shopping streets.

Momento, in Smålands Museum. The best of the daytime cafés, serving *panini* and ciabatta, superb Italian pastries (35kr) and decadent desserts, to the sound of world music playing in the background. The proprietors also run *Café Ryttmästargården* and *PM & Friends*; see below. Mon–Fri 11am–6pm, Sat & Sun 11am–5pm.

Ryttmästargården, at Kronoberg Castle. Similar food to what's served at *Café Momento*, in an eighteenth-century cottage with an idyllic lakeside setting; summer mosquitoes can be a menace, though. July daily 11am–8pm; Aug Mon–Fri 11am–8pm, Sat & Sun 11am–6pm.

Tomas Skåres, Kungsgatan 13. A popular central *konditori* with coffee-and-cake specials for 22kr. Mon–Fri 7.30am–7pm, Sat 7.30am–5pm, Sun 10am–6pm. Closed Sundays in July.

Restaurants

Evedal Vardhus, next door to the youth hostel on Lake Helgasjön (☎0470/630 03). The best food in Växjö is served in this eighteenth-century lakeside restaurant. Its Swedish specialities include roast pike with crayfish, fresh from the local lake. Two courses 260kr; lunches 59kr. Daily 11.30am–2.30pm & 6–9.30pm; July closed Mon.

PM & Friends, Västra Esplanaden 9. Popular and stylish – though it doesn't look like much from the outside. This fine, modern European restaurant uses fish from the local lakes, and organic vegetables from local farms. Lunch specials are 56kr; there's an extensive wine list. Daily Mon–Thurs 11.30am–2pm & 6pm–midnight, Fri till 1am, Sat 6pm–1am. Closed lunchtime in July.

Spisen, Norra Järnvägsgatan 8. Another gourmet choice, but only for real money spenders; lunch at 59kr will give a taster of the food. Daily 11.30am–2.30pm & 6–11pm. Closed second half of July.

Teaterpark, connected to *Hotel Teaterpark* in the Concert Hall building. This beautiful restaurant has a good-value summertime menu of grills – shark, salmon or meat – at 100–150kr (Mon–Sat 5–11pm). In winter, when it opens for lunch, there's a pricier, more wide-ranging menu.

South of Växjö: Huseby Bruk

Taking Route 23 southwest out of Växjö for a distance of around 20km brings you to **Huseby Bruk**, a rather splendid estate, complete with an ironworks museum, mill, café, restaurant and a not very inspiring electricity museum. The real draw in this picturesque little "village", though, is the **manor house** itself. It's only possible to see round the interior on tours (April, May & Sept, Sat & Sun 1pm; June & Aug daily 1pm, July Mon 1pm, Tues–Sun 11pm–4pm every 30min; 60kr, under-15s free); these are conducted in Swedish only, although there is a massively over-detailed (and comically badly translated) sheaf of information in English to lead you through all the impressive rooms.

The manor's most recent owner was Miss Florence Stephens, who died here aged 97 in 1979; her father, who emigrated here from England, bought the estate from the Hamiltons, a Scottish family who owned the manor in the seventeenth century. From the outside, you're immediately struck by the contrast between the yellow Neoclassical facade and its black balustrades and Ionic columns, all made of cast iron. Inside, it can take well over an hour to drift through all the rooms, which sport decor and furnishings from the past four centuries. Among the highlights are the **study**, with its ceiling-high tiled stove decorated with blue sphinxes; the rather grand **Royal Bedroom**, with its grape purple walls, plum curtains and great canopied bed where King Oscar II slept occasionally; and the yellow **drawing room**, where the oil painting *Rape of the Sabine Women* hangs.

IKEA

Among Swedish exports, only Volvo and ABBA spring to mind as readily as the furniture store **IKEA**, the letters standing for the name of its founder – **Ingvar Kamprad** – and his birthplace – Elmtaryd, a farm in the hamlet of Agunnaryd. Outside Sweden, the identity of IKEA's originator is played down, and the firm is known for simple, innovative design lines and prices that appeal to a mass market. Every item of furniture IKEA produces is assigned a Swedish place name; the styles of certain items are drawn from particular areas of the country, and bear the relevant name.

Founded in 1943 at **Älmhult**, a small town 20km from Agunnaryd, as a mail-order company, IKEA began producing furniture based on **folk designs**, which Kamprad had simplified to appeal to a market he was determined would be forward-looking. In the 1950s, Sweden's existing furniture makers were sufficiently irritated by what they regarded as an upstart that they tried to pressure IKEA's suppliers into boycotting the company. Kamprad responded by importing furniture from abroad.

In his 1976 book, *Testament of a Furniture Dealer*, Kamprad wrote that from the outset, he wanted to promote **"constructive fantasies"**: to change the world's view of design, rather than produce what people already believed they wanted. Having opened in Denmark in 1969, the company began expanding around the world, though it didn't enter the US market until 1985 or the UK until 1987.

Since the publication of three biographies on the man, one of which (*The History of IKEA*) was authorized, Swedes have been made aware of Kamprad's Nazi sympathies during World War II. He has responded to these revelations by blaming his former political leanings on the folly of youth.

Today, if you pass through Älmhult, you'll be able to see the original IKEA store, built in 1958; the street on which it stands is called, appropriately enough, Ikeagatan. Ironically, IKEA's headquarters aren't in Sweden, but in Denmark, and Kamprad himself has chosen to live in London.

Down the drive is a simple **café**; for a grander lunch, the Värdshus, a restaurant on the approach to the manor, does daily **lunch specials** at 65kr (11.30am–2pm) alongside more expensive à la carte options.

Some 30km further southwest along Route 23 is the town of Älmhult, its claim to fame being that it was where one of Sweden's most famous companies, IKEA, was founded (see box, above).

North of Växjö: Dädsjö

Heading northeast out of Växjö on Route 23 en route for the Kosta Boda glassworks (see p.296), after 20km you come to a sign for **Dädsjö**, a tiny hamlet a further 3km away on the right. Here stands Gamla Kirke, a remarkable thirteenth-century **church** (don't confuse it with the nineteenth-century pile you reach first) with what are regarded as the best-preserved ceiling paintings from this period in Northern Europe . A simple, squat building set in idyllic surroundings, the church looks more like a grain store – which is what it was used as after being abandoned in the 1790s, and why its ancient wall and ceiling paintings were preserved. Though the walls have been whitewashed, and the patterns on it show through ghostly pale, the thirteenth-century ceiling, attributed to the revered Master Sigmunder, reveals some amazingly fresh reds and blues. There are no pews; the only relics in the dark interior are the original stone benches running around its perimeter, and a 700-year-old icon depicting Virgin Mary with St Olaf, a benign-looking early-Gothic figure. In the neat **graveyard**, look for an old iron crucifix grave-marker in the corner, to the left of the entrance gate as you face the church. Believed to date from the 1770s, the cross has been engulfed by an ancient, massive linden tree. Locals believe a curse will befall anyone who attacked the tree, and so leave it in this peculiar, photogenic state.

Just a few metres from the church, a path leads to a lovely old wooden cottage with intricate wooden gingerbreading. There's a café with a verandah here, where you can munch on cheesecake with jam and cream, waffles or cinnamon buns with coffee, each for 30kr.

Jönköping

Perched at the southernmost tip of Lake Vättern, one of the oldest medieval trading centres in the country, **JÖNKÖPING** (pronounced "Yun-shurp-ing") won its town charter in 1284. Today, it is famous for being the home of the matchstick, the nineteenth-century manufacture and worldwide distribution of which made the town a wealthy place (see box, p.306). Despite Jönköping's plum position on the lakeshore, its excess of high-rise offices and bland, central buildings ruin what could be a pleasant town. It does, however, have good accommodation and some excellent restaurants and bars, making the place a viable, if not so pretty, lakeside base. Jönköpingers themselves head for the coast during the summer months, so if you are here between June and August you'll find it fairly quiet.

Arrival, information and accommodation

The **train** and **bus stations** are next to each other on the lake's edge. Just over the bridge, a couple of minutes' walk away, is the **tourist office**, in the Djurläkartoget shopping centre (mid-June to mid-Aug Mon–Fri 8am–7pm, Sat 10am–2pm, Sun 11am–2pm; mid-Aug to mid-June Mon–Fri 8am–6pm Sat 9am–1pm; ☎036/10 50 50, fax 12 83 00, *turist@sfk.jonkoping.se*). **Bikes** can be rented from Renbergs Cykel Och Sport at Södra Strandgatan 1 (☎036/16 05 06; 115kr a day or 400kr a week).

Accommodation

The tourist office has a very limited number of **private rooms** at 200–250kr per person. The town's **youth hostel** is in the Kulturhuset, a short distance west of the train station (☎036/19 05 85; 100kr; mid-June to mid-Aug). Outside of summer, the nearest youth hostel is 6km east in **Huskvarna** (see p.309); to get there, take bus #1 from outside Jönköping's tourist office. There's a **campsite** at Rosenlund (☎036/12 28 63), right on the lakeshore, 3km from Jönköping, with several buses heading out that way, the most frequent being bus #1.

Most of the main **hotels** slash their prices in summer by up to a half. The best hotel in terms of style, atmosphere and value for money is the excellent *Hotel Victoria*, F.E. Elmgrensgatan 5, two blocks south of the tourist office (☎036/71 28 00, fax 71 50 50; ⑤/②). The price includes afternoon tea and an excellent buffet supper all evening in the appealing atrium dining area. Most prestigious of the hotels is the *Stora*, at Hotellplan (☎036/10 00 00, fax 71 93 20; ⑤/②); built in the

1860s, this imposing place overlooks the lake, and has rooms decorated in Gustavian-style pastels. For a rather stylish, yet surprisingly inexpensive place, try the 1904 *Grand Hotel* at Hovrättstorget, a short distance east of the *Stora* (☎036/71 96 00, fax 71 96 05; ②/①). The very central *Familian Ericcson City Hotel*, Västra Storgatan 25 (☎036/71 92 80, fax 71 88 48; ③/②), is just three minutes' walk south from the train station.

The Town

Jönköping's restored historical core is the most interesting part of town to explore. At its heart, in a quaint cobbled courtyard, is the **Tändsticksmuséet**, Tändsticksgränd 27 (Match Museum; June–Aug Mon–Fri 10am–5pm, Sat & Sun 11am–3pm; Sept–may Tues–Thurs noon–4pm, Sat & Sun 11am–3pm; 25kr), in what was the main building of the town's first match factory (see box). It's not all that thrilling a museum though, being not much more than a collection of matchbox labels and match-making machines. Opposite, at Tandstickgränd 16, is the **Erik E. Karlson Radio Museum** (daily Tues–Fri 10am–5pm, Sat 10am–1pm, June to mid-Aug also Mon 10am–5pm & Sun 11am–3pm). Hailing from nearby Huskvarna, Karlson built his first radio receiver aged 16, and later opened Sweden's first radio store. The museum that bears his name contains seemingly every type of radio, from early crystal sets to Walkmans.

The only other museum here worth bothering with is the **Länsmuseum** on Dag Hammarskjölds Plats, on the east side of the canal between lakes Vättern and Munksjön (daily 11am–5pm, Wed till 8pm; 20kr, under-18s free). A mishmash of oddities, its exhibits ranging from posters showing Swedish support for Che Guevara through garden chairs throughout the ages to samovars and doll's houses, the place is like a well-stocked junk shop; there's no English labelling, though that won't detract much from the fun. The best part is the well-lit collection of paintings and drawings by **John Bauer**, a local artist who enthralled generations of Swedes with his Tolkienesque representations of gnomes and trolls in the *Bland Tomtar och Troll*, a well-known series of Swedish children's books. Upstairs is a constantly changing **art gallery** collection; attached to the Länsmuseum is a library, worth a peek for its wide range of foreign-language **newspapers**.

THE RISE AND FALL OF THE SWEDISH MATCHSTICK

It was in Jönköping, in 1844, that Professor Gustav Pasch invented the **safety match**. Hot on his heels, the Lundström brothers opened the first safety-match factory here the following year; its main building is now the Match Museum. Twenty years after, one Alexander Lagerman designed the world's first machine for churning out matches, transforming the process from a craft into a mechanized industry. The various Swedish match firms which sprang up over the following decades were amalgamated into the Swedish Match Company in 1917, all under the control of **Ivar Kreugar**, to whom the industry's subsequent downfall is largely attributed. Jönköping's most notorious twentieth-century figure, he lent vast amounts of money he didn't have to countries with large national debts, in exchange for a monopoly on their match sales. For a time one of Sweden's wealthiest men, in 1932, rather than become a bankrupt, he shot himself in Paris, an act which signalled the start of his industry's decline; match-making limped on in Sweden until 1971, when it was extinguished by cheaper competition from abroad.

ASTRID LINDGREN – CREATOR OF PIPPI LONGSTOCKING

Some 90km east of Jönköping on Route 33 is **Vimmerby**, near where one of Sweden's most popular children's authors, **Astrid Lindgren**, was born in 1907. Her most endearing character, **Pippi Longstocking** (in Swedish, Pippi Långstrump), burst upon the world in 1945. Pippi had red hair and long thin legs on which she wore non-matching stockings. Wealthy and energetic, she could do as she pleased, and her adventures have appealed hugely to children everywhere.

Lindgren's face has appeared on a Swedish 6kr stamp; her eighty books have, in total, sold more than 80 million copies worldwide. Yet her writing hasn't simply been about lighthearted adventures: her cleverly conceived tale, *Bröderna Lejonhjärta* ("The Lionheart Brothers"), tries to explain the concept of death to children. In recent years, she has become a Swedish Brigitte Bardot figure, campaigning on animal-rights issues. She is also involved with children's rights: aged 90, she campaigned vigorously against the deportation of an 11-year-old girl from Sweden. Today, Vimmerby is home to Astrid Lindgren World, a theme park where actors take on the roles of her most famous characters.

Back in the centre, a few metres away from the Match Museum, and set in another old match factory, is **Kulturhuset** on Tändsticksgränd, west of the train station. A sort of trendy arts centre, it has rooms for band rehearsals, an alternative bookshop (Mon–Fri 5–7pm), and a good, cheap café (see p.308). The centre becomes a private youth hostel in summer (see p.305); from September to May, there's a bustling early-morning Saturday market on the street outside. Next door is Bio, a stylish art-house cinema.

Although there's little else to see in the town centre, it is remarkable for the sheer number of **Free Churches** – 23 in the immediate vicinity; consequently, Jönköping has been dubbed "Sweden's Jerusalem". As the traditional Church watches its congregations diminish, people are turning instead to these independent and fundamentalist churches. You may see a white #777 bus parked around town – it's a mobile café belonging to the Pingst, or Pentecostal church, into which people are invited to sip coffee and listen.

Eating, drinking and nightlife

Jönköping has plenty of good, lively places to **eat** and **drink**. However, some close for the summer when many of their regulars are away on the coast, while others are – inexplicably – closed on Fridays and Sundays. For a taste of a local food speciality, go for the **vätter Röding** (Arctic char) from the little fish shop down by the harbour, or at any of the better restaurants. The char is brought here from Vättern, an unusually cold and deep lake which can thereby sustain fish normally found in the Baltic Sea.

The town's trendiest **nightclub** is the stylish *Millennium* (50kr cover charge), in a former match factory by the Match Museum. With a big dance floor and more relaxed bar area, it's packed on Friday and Saturday nights, mainly playing host to an 18- to 23-year-old age group.

Cafés and restaurants

Anna-Gretas Matsal, Västra Torget (☎036/71 25 75). Once the oldest café in town, when it would have served market traders from daybreak, this lovely place is now an excellent-value restaurant with a friendly atmosphere and an eclectic, frequently changing menu. Tues–Sat 5–11pm.

Båten, at the harbour (☎036/12 53 53). This old boat restaurant appeals to many Swedes, as it's the very one featured in the long-running Swedish children's television programme Saltkråkan, still being produced today. The lower deck has a bar (from 3pm), and the top a restaurant (from 6 pm). A simple and popular place. Open later all year.

Koppar Och Bagels, Smedjegatan 38. A laid-back café-bar being entirely renovated at the time of writing, but destined to come back as a cool, relaxed hang-out as it has been before.

Mäster Gudmunds Källare, Kappellgatan 2. A vaulted cellar restaurant serving good, traditional Swedish fare. Mon–Fri 11.30am–10pm, Sat noon–10pm, Sun & holidays noon–5pm; summer closed Sun.

Nyfiket Cafe, in the Kulturhuset. A friendly, studenty place serving generous filled rolls (25–30kr) and an excellent daily lunch special (40kr). Mon–Fri 10am–9pm, Sat 9am–2pm & 5–9pm, Sun 5–9pm.

Svarta Börsen, Kyrkogatan 4 (☎036/71 22 22). The best restaurant in town, in one of the few remaining classic buildings on the west side of the centre. Expensive and excellent – it's best to book. Mon–Thurs 11.30am–2pm & 6–11pm, Fri 11.30am–2pm, Sat 6–11pm.

Taj Mahal, Kappellgatan 15 (☎036/12 82 55). One of the best Indian restaurants in town, specializing in tandoori and grill dishes. Lunch comes at 50kr, including coffee; most à la carte dishes cost 60–130kr. Mon–Thurs 11am–11pm, Fri & Sat 11am–midnight, Sun 1–10pm.

Trottoaren Restaurant, next to the *Stora Hotell* at Hotellplan. A wacky American-style diner, its decor including a pink Vespa, US number plates and filling-station pumps. In contrast, the tables have crisp linen and silver candlesticks. Full meals from 198kr. Mon–Sat 6pm–midnight, Sun till 11am.

Bars

Balzar's Bar & Brasserie, which is part of *Hotel Klosterkungen*, Klostergatan 28. A quiet, pleasant place for a meal or a beer, with main courses at 100–150kr or light meals at 65kr. There's occasional live music, a mix of pop and old tunes (Friday and Saturday). Happy hour 5–7pm.

Hemma, Smedjegatan 36. The town's most popular venue for laid-back live music, with very friendly service and a very pleasant terrace garden. There's also very good eating here with a summer menu of salmon, chicken and veal dishes from 95–175kr, and a wider range of choices during the rest of the year. Tues–Sat 6pm–midnight, Fri & Sat till 1am.

Karlsonns Salonger, Västra Storgatan 9. This bar gets very busy. Also does good food. Mon & Tues 5pm–midnight, Wed–Sat 5pm–2am.

Rignes, attached to the *Hotel Savoy* at Brunnsgatan 13–15. A candle-lit pub, serving Norwegian beer. The music, most of which is live, comprises blues and rock and roll. There's an inexpensive all-day set menu, mainly offering meat dishes, and a lunch menu (75kr). Mon–Thurs till midnight, Fri & Sat till 2am (30kr cover charge on Fri & Sat).

Solde Bar, next door to the *Trottoaren* restaurant (see above). This bar, part of *Stora Hotell*, is packed all through summer. Foodwise, it offers baguettes, tortillas and salads for 50–75kr each. It's a favourite with a young crowd, who come here to imbibe lots of cider and beer.

Along the shore of Lake Vättern to Vadstena

The eastern shores of **Lake Vättern** offer the most spectacular scenery and delightful historical towns in the region. Jönköping can be used as a base for excursions, but there are plenty of places to eat and stay along the way to Vadstena (see p.314), including some idyllic, little-known hotels. This part of Sweden is perfect for **trekking**, too, with lots of hiking trails to try.

From Jönköping to Gränna

Leaving Jönköping, head out along Östra Storgatan, which soon becomes the E4, towards **HUSKVARNA**, 6km to the east; you can also get there by bus (10min). The little town was named after the 1689 arms factory Husquarna; the company still exists, though today it produces sewing machines and motorbikes. Huskvarna may at first seem very industrial, but some quaint wooden cottages are still to be found in its old quarter and in the preserved smith's village called **Smedbyn**. Nearby, there's a town museum in the old powder house, **Kruthuset** (May–Aug Sat & Sun 2–5pm; 15kr), and a museum of local industry, **Husqvarna Fabriksmuseum** (April, May & Sept–Nov Sat & Sun 1–4pm; June–Aug Mon–Fri 10am–5pm, Sat & Sun 1–4pm; 20kr), based in the company's nineteenth-century musket-barrel factory.

For a place to **stay**, there's Huskvarna's **youth hostel**, at Odengatan 10 (☎036/14 88 70, fax 14 88 40; 130kr), 100m from its bus station. But unless you're particularly interested in the town's history, it's altogether more rewarding to continue north, up either the E4 or the more picturesque Grännavagen (the old E4). **Buses** #120 and #121 make the trip from here to Gränna in around an hour (stopping at Hakarp and Röttle on the way), and there are quicker express buses twice a day, too; there are no trains, though.

A few minutes on from Huskvarna, the crashing waterfalls that used to power the town's industry come into view as Grännavagen winds. A couple of kilometres further is the village of **Hakarp**, whose **church**'s interior is a riot of paintings that were clearly designed to terrify the peasant parishioners (daily 9am–4pm; June–Aug till 6pm). The ceiling bears graphic depictions of hell, with demons stabbing and torturing naked women. Also on the ceiling are interesting paintings of both the present church, built in 1694, and the medieval church that preceded it, together with an interpretation of New Jerusalem, with more naked women climbing from their graves. Note, too, the pew-backs, which are original – despite being painted with leopard-skin spots, which look more like something out of the 1970s than 1770s. Bus #15 runs infrequently from Huskvarna to Hakarp church.

Röttle and around

One of the most idyllic goals for a few hours' wandering, just south of Gränna, is the hamlet of **RÖTTLE**, its name deriving from words meaning "roaring torrent". Industry existed here as early as 1297, when Rytlofors Mill was granted the right to mill flour by the king. The Jerusalem Mill, one of the oldest built here, still stands; it was given by King Magnus to the Bishop of Linköping in 1330. The village was once owned by Per Brahe, one of Sweden's most prominent aristocrats, at a time when the professions here included glove-makers, coppersmiths and sword-cleaners. Today, the antiquated wooden cottages that sit snugly amid emerald-green grassland and stands of silver birch are picturesque rather than industrial, and the sound of the water is only a gentle gurgle.

Röttle's tiny harbour is a popular bathing spot during the summer. A couple of minutes' walk from Röttle is **Västanå Nature Reserve**, which runs all the way to the lake and is carpeted with heathers, cowberries and delicate yellow, blue, and white wood anemones in late spring. A splendid **walking trail** to take is the John Bauerleden, which wends its way from Huskvarna northwards for 50km; you can easily pick it up at Röttle (it's signposted).

Gränna

Forty kilometres north of Jönköping, the lakeside town of **GRÄNNA** is associated with the unlikely combination of pears, striped rock candy (see box, below) and a gung-ho nineteenth-century Swedish balloonist (see below). In late spring, the hills around Gränna are a confetti of pear blossom, Per Brahe (see p.312) having encouraged the planting of pear orchards hereabouts – the Gränna pear is one of the best-known varieties in the country today. Approaching from the south, the beautiful Gränna Valley sweeps down to your left, with the hills to the right, most notably the crest of Grännaberget, which provides a majestic foil to some superb views over Lake Vättern and its island, Visingsö (see p.311). On a hot summer's day, the trip here from Jönköping has something of the atmosphere of the French Riviera, evoked in particular by the winding roads, red-tiled roofs and the profusion of flowers in the old cottage gardens – not to mention the equal profusion of Porsches and Mercedes cars.

Per Brahe, one of Sweden's first counts (see p.312), built the town in the mid-seventeenth century, using the symmetry, regularity and spaciousness of planning that he had learnt while governor of Finland. The lively main street, **Brahegatan**, was subsequently widened and remodelled, allowing the houses fronting it to have gardens, while the other main roads were designed so Brahe could look straight down them as he stood at the windows of his now-ruined castle, **Brahehus**. The gardens along Brahegatan remain mostly intact, and until the 1920s, there were no additions to the original street layout. Even now, there's very much a village feel to the little town. The best starting point for a great view is to head up behind the market square, containing a statue of Brahe, to *Café Stugan* (see p.311). It's easy to while away a whole afternoon in Gränna's cafés, and there are a couple of really fine, historic hotels at which to stay.

S. A. Andree Museum

Next to the tourist office on Brahegatan is the fascinating **S.A. Andree museum** (same hours as the tourist office, where you buy your ticket; 30kr), dedicated to Salomon August Andree, the Gränna-born **balloonist** who led a doomed attempt to reach the North Pole by balloon in 1897. Born at Brahegatan 37, Andree was fired by the European obsession of the day to explore and conquer unknown areas; with no real way of directing his balloon, however, his trip was destined for disaster from the start. After a flight lasting only three days, during which time it flew more than 800km in different directions, the balloon made a forced landing on ice just 470km from its departure point. The crew of three attempted to walk to civilization, but the movement of the ice floes they were on meant they made

---

GRÄNNA ROCK

Gränna has been known for striped rock candy, called **polkagris**, ever since Amalia Eriksson, a penniless widow, began ekeing out a living by producing the red-and-white sugar tubes in the mid-nineteenth century. It's fun to watch it being produced, which you can do at one of the small factories, **Cabbe Polkagrisfabrik**, 3km south of Gränna, just opposite the *Hotel Gyllene Uttern*. Behind the counter, displaying a hundred colours and flavours of the sweet, you can watch as the ingredients (99 percent sugar, a little colouring and a drop of peppermint) are heated to 150°C, melted, poured, twisted, hardened and cut into the sweets.

no progress; after six weeks' trekking, they set up camp on a floe drifting rapidly southwards. Sadly, the ice cracked and their shelter collapsed, and with it their hopes. Finally they died from the effects of cold, starvation and trichinosis, caught after they ate the raw meat of a polar bear they had managed to spear. It would be another 33 years before their frozen, preserved bodies and their equipment were discovered by a Norwegian sailing ship. They were reburied in Stockholm at a funeral attended by a crowd of forty thousand. The museum exhibition poignantly includes a diary kept by one of the crew and film taken by the team, which makes for pitiful viewing: the men are seen with the polar bear they'd hunted, and other sequences show the three hopelessly pulling their sledges across the ice sheets.

Practicalities

Buses will drop you off on the main road, Brahegatan. The **tourist office** is on Brahegatan itself (May to mid-June daily 10am–5pm; mid-June to July daily 10am–7pm; Aug & Sept daily noon–4pm, Oct–April Mon–Fri & Sun noon–4pm; ☎0390/410 10, fax 102 75, *turism@grm.se*); they can book **private rooms** from 120kr, plus a booking fee of 50kr. Gränna has two **youth hostels**: *Gränna Vandrarhem*, along the same street as the tourist office (book through tourist office; 120kr; mid-June to early Aug), and another hostel right on the beach near where the ferry to Visingsjö puts in (☎0390/107 06; 125kr; May–Sept).

For a charming **hotel**, there's the *Gästgiveri Ribbagården*, just off Brahegatan (☎ & fax 0390/108 20; ③/②), a former farm converted into a hotel in 1922, and full of antiques. The other notable hotel hereabouts is *Hotel Gyllene Uttern*, or "Golden Otter" (☎0390/108 00, fax 418 80; ④), 3km south of town close to the main road. Built in the 1930s, it looks like a medieval German castle, with stone castellations and a Baronial interior; there is something a bit contrived about the place though. The rooms in the annexe are cheaper, but lack the glamour of those in the main building.

There are several excellent **cafés** in Gränna, all of which are on Brahegatan, except for *Café Stugan* (May 10am–9pm; June–Aug 10am–10pm), which should not be missed – though there's a climb of 243 steep steps to reach it: from the market square, walk across to the church then on for 200m to the steps in the hillside to the left. You can drive up, but this way you'll miss out on the ever-improving views as you head up the steps. Outside seating at the café affords a fabulous vista over the lake. The best café in town is *Café Fiket*, their speciality a rich almond pastry tart. *Café Amalia*, just a few steps down Brahegatan (daily: June–Aug 8am–9pm; Sept–May 10am–6pm), is named after the queen of Gränna rock (see p.310). Here you can buy superb lingonberry ice cream and eat it on a spacious terrace overlooking the rooftops and lake. A little further up the same road is *Haglunds Konditori,* with a wide selection of delicious cakes and breads. *Café Hjorten*, also on Brahegatan, is a very pleasing **restaurant** and bar, also featuring a beer garden and pizza parlour. Proper meals from 75kr are served on the sunny terrace, while you can eat cheap pizzas downstairs.

Visingsö

From Gränna, a twenty-minute **ferry** crossing drops you on the island of **Visingsö**, just 12km by 3km wide (June–Aug every 30min, Sept–May hourly; passengers 38kr; car and driver 150kr return). In the mid-sixteenth century, Eric XIV decided that Sweden should follow the example of Continental monarchies by bestowing titles and privileges on deserving noblemen. He created the title of Count of Visingsborg, whose lands included the island, and awarded it to Per Brahe the Elder. Brahe's son enjoyed a spate of castle building, and one of his creations was the **Visingsborg Slott**, on the east shore of the island, by the ferry terminal. After Brahe the Younger's death in 1680, the Crown took back much of the estate, including the island; his castle is an empty shell today, its roof having been burned off in 1718 by Russian prisoners celebrating the death of Karl XII, who'd taken them prisoner during his abortive march on Russia.

Visingsö is entirely flat, and so the whole island can be covered without strenuous exercise. Even less effort is needed to sit in a *remmalag*, a horse and trap. These make trips (50–65kr return) along the quiet lanes to the twelfth-century **Kumlaby** church, the oldest relic on the island, with a beautifully painted ceiling and walls. The church's truncated tower is the result of astronomy classes organized by Brahe the Younger, whose elementary school was the first in the region to accept women. The most intriguing aspect of the church is the extremely narrow, pitch-dark stone spiral in the tower which opens up as you climb (June–Aug 9am–8pm), the steep, wooden steps smelling strongly of ancient pine. From the top, you can see right across the island.

The only other sight here is the ruin of **Näs castle**, at the southern tip of the island. This was once a major power centre in Sweden, though today it's just battlements, showing little sign of its erstwhile glory. The journey to it on the perimeter road is a pleasure, through forest and corn fields, and past well-kept old cottages, some with fancy porches and verandahs.

For some summer **swimming**, there's a lagoon at the harbour; the water here is warmer than the much deeper waters of the surrounding Lake Vättern.

Practicalities

Arriving at the dock, you'll find the **tourist office** to your right (mid-May to late June & Aug daily 10am–5pm; late June & July daily 10am–7pm; Sept to mid-May Mon–Fri 8am–2pm; ☎0390/401 93, *visingsoturist@grm.se*); they **rent bikes** at 40kr for three hours, or 65kr for a day. There are plenty of places for **refreshment** on the island. A couple of cafés at the harbour serve lunches, pizzas and coffees, and all around the island are charming wooden houses with signs indicating they're offering home-made cake and cheesecake. There's also a fine smoked-fish shop opposite the dock, selling mackerel, whitefish and salmon smoked with brandy.

Lake Tåkern and around

The E4 runs from Gränna north to **Ödeshög**, crossing into the province of **Östergotland**. From Ödeshog you have a choice of routes: stay on the E4 and you'll be heading east towards Linköping (see p.323); or take Route 50 to continues north to Vadstena. Ten kilometres to the south of Vadstena is **Lake Tåkern**, formed around 7000 BC when the inland ice receded from Östergotland's plains. The lake is surrounded by some beautiful open landscapes, with excellent walking trails, a sprinkling of medieval churches and the substantial remains of a twelfth-century monastery; also here is one of the country's best bird sanctuaries, on the lake itself (see box, p.313). All these sites are probably best visited as day-trips from one of the main towns nearby, such as Vadstena and Motala, which can be

BIRDWATCHING ON LAKE TÅKERN

Not impressive in size, Lake Tåkern is one of the best in the country for **birdwatching**, with 260 species to be seen here in the space of a year. There are also several walking trails for a tranquil half-day meander; indeed from April 1 to June 30, you are restricted to trails clearly marked on signs all over the area. There's a **birdwatching tower** close to the car park, where the Tåkern Canal spills out of the lake; in late summer, thousands of wading birds rest on the mud banks in front. Large flocks of geese fill the air in autumn, when up to 45,000 bean geese migrate from Russia and Finland, using Tåkern as their resting point; still later in the year, golden and sea eagles appear, too. There's another tower for birdwatching, with disabled access, at Hor on the lake's eastern shore.

Approaching the lake from the north, take the sign for Strå, 7km off Route 50, for 2km and turn off just past the canal in order to reach the northern visiting area. For the other visiting area, take the E4, turning off at the sign for the tiny village of Kyleberg, then left at Kyleberg. To get to the birdwatching tower to the east, take Route 944 off the E4 and continue for 6km north of Väderstad.

reached on **bus** #610 from Ödeshög (Mon–Fri 7 daily, Sat & Sun 2 daily). Also useful is the express bus #840 between Gränna and Vadstena, though it doesn't stop along the way as many times as the #610. There's a handy **youth hostel** at Ödeshög, called *Hernbygdsgården*, at Södra Vägen 63 (☎0144/107 00; 120kr).

Omberg and the Alvastra Monastery

Omberg is a ten-kilometre stretch of forested hill country, 10km north of Ödeshög, with several walking trails. From its highest point, Hjässan, there are spectacular views over Vättern and the plains to the east. The **Naturum** (Nature Centre), near the southern end of Omberg, can provide general tourist information.

The ruins of **Alvastra Monastery**, just 2km off Route 50 at the southern tip of Omberg, are set amid unspoilt countryside, which in early to mid-summer is alive with colour: yellow rape and bluish, underripe cornfields against the duller blue of Vättern to the west. On the way to the ruins, you'll pass the **Sverker Stone** commemorating Sverker the Elder, king of Östergotland. Founded in 1143, when King Sverker invited a group of French Cistercian monks to Sweden, the monastery went on to become a centre of considerable power, at one point owning nearly five-hundred local farms. The monastery was destroyed by Gustav Vasa in the sixteenth century; Vasa used its stones to help build his castle at Vadstena. Midnight **concerts** of rock or classical music are staged here in summer, with lighting effects that play against the arches; they're worth catching, though you'll need your own transport to get here (for programme details, ask at Vadstena's tourist office; see p.314).

There's **accommodation** in the village of **ALVASTRA**, about 3km away. Its comfortable, genteel *Ombergs Turist Hotel* has been in operation since 1912 (☎0144/330 02, fax 330 90; ②); it has some family rooms, sleeping four, for the price of a double. With your own transport, the hotel makes an especially good alternative to the more expensive places to stay in Vadstena. It's worth checking out the hotel **restaurant** (Tues–Sun 11am–6pm), where you can eat fish fresh from Lake Vättern, with lunch at 85kr and à la carte meals costing 100–150kr. There's an STF **youth hostel** in the Omberg region at **Stocklycke** (April–Sept; ☎0144/330 44; 110kr), with cabins for two to six people, a café and sauna.

Rökstenen

About 8km east of Alvastra, off Route 50, stands **Rökstenen** (buses #664 and #665 head here from Alvastra Monastery; 10min), regarded as the most remarkable of all Sweden's two thousand or so **rune stones**. Dating from the ninth century, the four-ton granite lump of granite that is the **Rök Stone** stands beneath a specially made protective canopy next to an isolated church, Rök kyrka. The stone bears the world's longest continuous runic inscription, with over eight-hundred runes engraved into its surface. Written by a father, Varin, in memory of his son, Vaemod, it makes for some pretty incomprehensible reading, beginning: "I tell the tale which the two war booties were, twelve times, both together from man to man". . . The inscription is seen as providing the greatest insight into Swedish literature in times of antiquity, and the accompanying signboards explain all about the stanzas, narrative, metre and rhythm.

Vadstena

With its beautiful lakeside setting, **VADSTENA**, which once served as a royal seat and important monastic centre, is the most evocative town in Östergotland and a fine place for a day or two's stay. Sixty kilometres north of Gränna and just 16km southwest of Motala (see p.318), the town's main attraction is its moated **castle**, planned in the sixteenth century by Gustav Vasa as part of his defensive ring protecting the Swedish heartland around Stockholm. The cobbled, twisting streets, lined with cottages covered in climbing roses, also contain an impressive abbey, whose existence is the result of the passionate work of fourteenth-century **Birgitta**, Sweden's first female saint (see box, p.316).

Arrival, information and accommodation

Express **bus** #840 (the Jönköping express) runs to Vadstena (Mon–Fri 2 daily; Sun 1 daily; 90min from Jönköping; 50min from Gränna). Bus #610 runs regularly from Motala to Vadstena. The main **bus stop** is in the centre of town, between the castle and the abbey. By car, it's a straight run here along the E4 and Route 50 north from Gränna or southwest on Route 50 from Motala. There are no train services into town, apart from an old steam or diesel train which does **sightseeing tours** to and from **Fågelstra** to the east; the trains arrive at the old station by the castle (late May & June at weekends only; 2 daily in July; 50kr).

The **tourist office** is in the castle itself (May daily 9am–5pm; June & early Aug to end Aug daily 9am–7pm; July & early Aug daily 9am–8pm; Sept Mon–Fri 9am–5pm, Sat 10am–2pm, Oct–April Mon–Fri 9am–5pm; ☎0143/315 70, fax 315 79, *info@tourist.vadstena.se*). You can also buy a **Vadstena Card** here for 75kr for free entry to the castle, the hospital museum, Mårtens House and a sightseeing tour; it's only worth it if you intend to see the lot. Vadstena itself is easily walkable; for striking out into the Östergotland countryside, **bikes** can be rented from Sport Hörnen at Storgatan, by Rådhustorget (Mon–Fri 9.30am–6pm, Sat 9.30am–1pm; ☎0143/103 62).

Accommodation

The tourist office will book **private rooms** for a 50kr fee. Vadstena's STF **youth hostel** at Skänningegatan 20 (☎0143/103 02, fax 104 04; 130kr) is close to the lake, just up from the abbey. Advance booking here is essential outside the mid-June to mid-August period.

Set in converted historic buildings and catering for glamorous tastes, the town's main **hotels** are fairly expensive. The *Vadstena Kloster Hotel*, (☎0143/315 30, fax 136 48; ④), in the 1369 nunnery next to the abbey, is still very atmospheric, though some of its rooms are extremely dated and plain. It serves breakfasts, available to non-residents, in its old Kings Hall – part of the original Bjällbo palace (see p.316). Opposite the castle is the imposing *Vadstena Slottshotel,* Ayslen (☎014/103 25; ④), within a late nineteenth-century hospital building. A pleasant and cheaper choice, especially if you have your own transport, is *Ombergs Turist Hotel,* 10km south at Alvastra (see p.313).

The Town

While Vadstena boasts numerous ancient sites and buildings, each with an information plate (in English) – such as Sweden's oldest courthouse, the fifteenth-century Rådhus at Rådhustorget – the two outstanding attractions here are the **castle** and the **abbey**. Vadstena also makes for the most romantic evening strolls, with wonderful lakeside sunsets and evocative streets of the strangely shaped, irregularly built houses.

Vadstena Slott

Those who've visited the castle at Kalmar will be familiar with the antics of Gustav Vasa and his troubled family, whose saga continues at **Vadstena Slott** (same hours as the tourist office). With four round towers, each with a diameter of 7m, and a grand moat, it was originally built as a fortification to defend against Danish attacks in 1545, but was then prettified to serve as a home to Vasa's mentally-ill third son, Magnus. His elder brother, Johan III, was responsible for its lavish decorations, but fire destroyed them all just before their refurbishment was completed, and to save money they simply painted fittings and other decor on the walls, including swagged curtains that can still be seen today.

The castle's last resident was Hedvig Eleanor, the widowed queen of Karl X; after she died, the castle was regarded as hopelessly unfashionable, and so no royal would consider living there. At the end of the seventeenth century, the building fell into decay and was used as a grain store; the original hand-painted wooden ceilings were chopped up and turned into grain boxes. As a result, there hasn't been much to see inside, though a recent drive here to buy up period furniture from all over Europe has re-created something of the atmosphere. The place has also been crammed with **portraits** of the Vasa family, some very unhappy and ugly faces making for entertaining viewing. It's worth joining the regular English-language tours, which are mandatory if you want to see inside, to hear all the Vasa family gossip (late May to late June 2 daily; late June to early Aug 3 daily; 45kr, 10kr for children).

The most interesting areas of the castle are its dark, vaulted towers, which were able to accommodate 150 soldiers. Each summer, a **play** (entertaining enough even if you don't understand the dialogue) is performed in one of the towers (ask at reception for times), recounting the story of Gustav Vasa's daughter, Catarine. While Catarine was honeymooning at the castle, her sister Cecilia, famed for her beauty and defiance, chose to begin an affair with Caterine's husband's brother. The couple were discovered at an indelicate moment, and Cecilia's lover was carted off to prison, with the promise that when released he would never show interest in women again. According to contemporary records, he never did.

Opposite the castle is Vadstena's **glassworks**, Vas Vitreum (glass-blowing Mon–Fri 8am–4pm; shop Mon–Fri 9am–5pm, Sat noon–3pm). Founded in 1985, it produces some refreshingly simple designs, along with more traditional pieces. The seconds shop, in one of the two old wooden grain stores outside the castle, has the same items as the factory's shop at forty percent less.

The abbey

Saint Birgitta specified that the **abbey** church (daily: May 9am–5pm; June & Aug 9am–7pm; July 9am–8pm), easily reached by walking towards the lake from the castle, should be "of plain construction, humble and strong". Wide, grey and sombre, the lakeside abbey, consecrated in 1430, certainly fulfills her criteria from the outside; inside it has been embellished with a celebrated collection of medieval artwork. More memorable than its crypt, containing the tombs of various royals, is the statue of Birgitta, now devoid of hands, "in a state of ecstasy" – as its title puts it. To the right, the rather sad "Door of Grace and Honour" was where each Birgittine nun entered the abbey after being professed – the next time she would use the door would be on her funeral day. Birgitta's bones are encased in a red velvet box, decorated with silver and gilt medallions, in a glass case down stone steps in the monks' choir stalls.

The **altarpiece** here is worth a glance, too: another handless Birgitta, looking rather less than ecstatic, is portrayed dictating her revelations to a band of monks, nuns and acolytes, while around her, representations of hell and purgatory depict finely sculpted faces of woe disappearing into the bloody mouth of what looks like a hippopotamus. Other than Birgitta's, a tomb to note inside the abbey is that of Gustav Vasa's mentally retarded son Magnus. His grand, raised tomb is flanked at each corner by obese, glum-faced cherubs, two of which rest against skulls; most impressive of the tomb's features are the remarkably life-like hands on the likeness of Magnus on the top, which are raised in prayer.

Although now housing the *Vadstena Kloster* hotel (see p.315), the **monastery** and **nunnery** on either side of the abbey are open for tours; the nunnery, in what was the thirteenth-century Bjälbo Palace, is more evocative of times past. A minute is all it takes to see it; the most interesting part is the King's Hall, originally used for banquets, with an elegant lofty ceiling. On its conversion to a con-

---

ST BIRGITTA

Birgitta (1303–73) came to the village of Vadstena as a lady-in-waiting to King Magnus Eriksson and his wife, Blanche of Namur, who lived at Bjälbo Palace. Married at thirteen, she gave birth to eight children, and subsequently had her first of many visions while living at the palace. Such was the force of her personality, she persuaded her royal employers (to whom she was vaguely related) to give her the palace in order to start a convent and a monastery. To obtain papal approval for the monastery, she set off for Rome in 1362, but luck was against her – the pope was in Avignon, France. She spent the next twelve years in Rome, having more visions, pressing for his return, only to die before ever returning to Vadstena. She was canonized in 1391, a final vision having already told her this would be the case. Her daughter, Katarina, carried on her work and brought about the building of the monastery and abbey; she too became a saint.

vent, Birgitta had the ceiling lowered to what she considered a more appropriate level for the nuns – it remains thus today.

The Mental Hospital Museum

Just beyond the gates of the abbey graveyard, the **Mental Hospital Museum** is based in what was Sweden's oldest mental hospital (June–Aug daily 1–3pm; 25kr), dating from 1757 and once called Stora Dårhuset ("Large Mad House"). The display of terrifying contraptions used to control and "cure" the inmates includes a spinning chair, into which difficult patients were tightly strapped and spun until they vomited; an iron bath, in which patients were tied and then scalded; and a tub, used until 1880, in which patients were held down among electric eels. The most poignant displays on the first floor are the patients' own excellently drawn pictures, depicting the tortures inflicted on them. Also on display are moving photographs of inmates from the nineteenth century (extensive research having first been carried out to ensure that the people shown have no surviving relatives).

Gottfried Larsson Museum

A collection of powerful human figures by **Gottfried Larsson**, an underrated contemporary of Sweden's best-known contemporary sculptor, Carl Milles (see p.80), can be seen at the **Gottfried Larsson Museum**, Skänningegatan 9, around 300m from the abbey (Tues–Fri 1–5pm, Sat 1–3pm; 10kr). The sculptures, some of which are set in the gardens behind the seventeenth-century museum building, are mostly studies of naked male manual workers, along with some fine, female heads. The museum also plays host to temporary exhibitions of other modern sculpture.

Eating and drinking

Vadstena's **eating** places are mostly expensive and not particularly trendy. The best **café**, where you can eat well and relatively cheaply, is *Mi Casa*, on Storgatan (Mon–Fri 10am–7pm, Sat 10am–6pm, Sun noon–6pm); it serves pies, baguettes, ciabatta and cakes, and a lunch special (Mon–Fri 11am–2pm; 50kr). The busy *Gamla Konditori*, on the other side of Storgatan (Mon–Fri 9am–7pm, Sat 9am–6pm, Sun 11am–6pm), is another fine, more traditional choice, with great cakes and sandwiches. Next door is the best **restaurant** in town, *Vadstena Valven*, Storgatan 18 (summer daily 11.30am–10pm; rest of year Mon–Sat 11.30am–2pm & 6–10pm, Sun noon–2pm & 6–10pm), with a lunch special (65kr) and fine dinners. Their speciality is Vättern char in white wine sauce, but you won't find it on the menu – the fish is only in supply when the waters are warm enough. The stylish restaurant at *Vadstena Kloster Hotel*, in the monastery by the abbey (Mon–Fri 11.30am–11pm, Sat noon–11pm, Sun noon–10pm) is not at all what Saint Birgitta ordered. Not only does it serve beautifully cooked and presented meat and fish dishes, such as smoked deer, at around 185kr a course, it also has a superb wine cellar. More informal is *Restaurant Rådhus Källeren,* in the cosy cellars of the sixteenth-century courthouse on Rådhustorget (Mon–Wed & Fri noon–11pm, Thurs & Sat noon–midnight, Sun 1–10pm); their smoked whitefish, from Vättern, costs 129kr. The place is also a **pub** where Vadstena locals hang out, particularly on Thursday and Saturday evenings. For a good pizza, try *Pub No 1,* at Storgatan 13 (Mon–Wed 11am–11pm, Thurs & Fri 11am–1am, Sat noon–1am, Sun noon–10pm), which also passes for a bar and nightclub. A younger crowd heads for the bar and disco at *Sjömagasinet*, Lilla Hamnarmen, on the far side of the castle relative to the centre; it's the liveliest place in this otherwise staid town.

Motala

At **Motala**, 16km north of Vadstena, the Göta Canal tumbles into Lake Vättern through a flight of five locks. One of the most popular spots on the canal, Motala was designed by the waterway's progenitor, Baltzar Von Platen; his grave is beside his statue on the canal-side walk. There's very little to keep you occupied here, other than the impressive Motor Museum (see below); it's better to base yourself at Linköping to the east (see p.323) or Vadstena to the south (see p.314).

A promenade cuts a smooth arc around the bay where lake and canal meet, making for pleasant lakeside strolls. The best thing to do in Motala, however, is cruise down a stretch of the canal, something that's easiest during the peak summer season (mid-June to mid-Aug). In summer, **boats** run along the canal to Borensburg, 20km east, leaving Motala at 10.30am (5hr; 180kr return, lunch on board 110kr); tickets can be bought at the tourist office (see below). In June, a fourteen-thousand-strong field takes part in what is claimed to be the world's biggest friendly **cycle race**, around the lake.

One place of interest in this rather bland town is the **Motor Museum**, at the harbour edge (June–Aug daily 10am–8pm, May & Sept 10am–6pm, Oct–April 10am–3pm; 40kr). Much more entertaining than its name implies, this is really a museum of style, and great fun even if you have no particular interest in cars. Each of the unusual, rare and wacky motors – ranging from 1950s American classics to old Jaguars and the occasional Rolls Royce – is displayed in context, with music of the appropriate era blaring from radio sets.

Just up from the Motor Museum is the **Canal and Navigation Museum** (May, June & Aug Mon–Fri 9am–5pm; July daily 9am–6pm; 20kr), which details the canal's construction and demonstrates the operation of a lock. Just outside, at the point where the lake and canal meet, a plaque and maps show the striking similarities between the Göta Canal and its official "twin", Scotland's Caledonian Canal. Both waterways linked the east and west of their respective countries, and the men behind them, Von Platen in Sweden and Thomas Telford in Scotland, were contemporaries.

On the hill behind the town, 1500m from the centre, is a small **Radio Museum** at Radiovägen (June–Aug daily 11am–6pm; 25kr), recalling the days when "Stockholm Motala. . . Stockholm Motala" was as evocative to Swedes as "This is London" is to avid BBC World Service listeners. The place has crystal sets of various eras and enthusiastic staff who'll give you the lowdown on all the exhibits. A little further out, **Varamon beach**, with a kilometre of golden sand, lies just 3km west of the centre. It has the warmest waters in Lake Vättern, as Varamon bay is the most shallow area of the lake; swimming apart, the waters are also popular for windsurfing.

Practicalities

Trains pull in parallel with the canal about a kilometre from the centre. For the **tourist office** at Folkets Hus (June to mid-Aug daily 10am–7pm; mid-Aug to May Mon–Fri 10am–5pm; ☎0141/22 52 54, fax 521 03, *turistbyran@motala.se*), turn left along Östermalmsgatan, right along Vadstenavägen and left into Repslagaregatan. This will lead you past the central Storatorget and the **bus station**; the tourist office is on the right, close to the harbour. You can **rent a bike** – the twenty-kilometre ride east to Borensburg is worth considering – from Velosipede, at the harbour (☎ 0141/521 11; 95kr a day).

Private rooms can be booked at the tourist office (250kr). The STF **youth hostel**, with its own summer café, is at Varamon, right on the beach (☎ & fax 0141/22 52 85; 100kr) – take bus #301 from Storatorget. At the beach also is a well-equipped **campsite**, *Z-Parkens Camping* (☎0141/21 11 42), boasting what it calls *Varamon Chalet Colony* – pretty wooden cabins overlooking the lake, which should be booked through the tourist office.

An economical place to stay is *Park Hotel*, a **bed and breakfast** at Platersgatan 27, by the train station (☎0141/535 00; ②; June–Aug). Among the better town-centre **hotels**, *Stadshotellet* on Storatorget has big, worn-looking rooms (☎0141/21 64 00, fax 21 46 05; ④/③); *Palace Hotel,* Kungsgatan 1, just off Storatorget (☎0141/21 66 60, fax 57 221; ④/③) is much the same.

Most of Motala's **restaurants** are nondescript places grouped around Storatorget; they do daily lunches at around 50kr. A really good alternative for food and drink is *Hallen* (☎0141/21 91 00; daily 11am–2pm & 6pm–10pm, Sat 6–10pm), a bar-restaurant just off Storatorget near the *Stadshotellet*. Built in 1924 as a food market, it retains its original glazed brick interior, and the serving area and bar are designed like the original market stalls. Their daily lunch offers a choice of fish or meat (55kr); the evening menu is more extensive, specializing in Vättern fish. Fifty varieties of beer, mostly British and German, are available. It's busiest on Tuesday, Friday and Saturday nights, when the *Stadshotellet* has dancing with a strict 23-plus age limit.

North of Vättern: Örebro

North of Motala, there are no decent-sized towns until you reach **ÖREBRO**, 90km away. Its light industrial hinterland promises little, and even Örebro's proudest statistics are anticlimactic: it's Sweden's sixth most populous city, lying on the shores of the country's fourth largest lake, Hjälmaren. Örebro's development was dictated by its important strategic position: the former main route from southwest Sweden to Stockholm, King Eric's Way, ran right through the centre, where a build-up of gravel made the river fordable (Örebro means "gravel bridge"). Nowadays, the E20 links the southwest with the capital – and bypasses the town.

Arrival, information and accommodation

Örebro is just three hours from Stockholm on the main east-west **train** line and straight up Route 50 from Motala by **car**. The **train station** is on Järnvägsgatan, north of the castle; the **bus station**, where the regular buses from Stockholm and Motala stop, is close by in the recently renovated Resecentrum. The very helpful and knowledgeable **tourist office** is inside the castle (June–Aug Mon–Fri 9am–7pm, Sat & Sun 10am–5pm; Sept–May Mon–Fri 9am–5pm, Sat & Sun 11am–3pm; ☎019/21 21 21, fax 10 60 70, *www.orebro.se*); to reach it, turn right from the train station, left from the bus station, walk a few metres along Östra Bangatan, and a crescent of elegant apartments with wrought-iron balconies opens out to the right. Follow this around, and the castle is immediately ahead, sitting four-square on its island.

The town centre is easy to see on foot. To get a flavour of the surrounding countryside, it's a good idea to rent a **bike**; you can do this at the kiosk on

Hamnplatsen (☎019/21 19 09; Mon–Fri 9am–6pm, Sat & Sun 10am–5pm; 40kr a day), outside *Harry's Bar*.

Accommodation

The tourist office can book **private rooms** for 135kr per person, plus a 25kr booking fee. The STF **youth hostel** at Fanjunkarevägen 5 (☎019/31 02 40, fax 31 02 56; 130kr; ①), is in a surprisingly pretty nineteenth-century army barracks to the north of town; take bus #31 to Rynninge, getting off one stop before the end of the line. The nearest **campsite** is 2km south of town at Gustavsvik (☎019/19 69 50, fax 19 69 90; May to mid-Sept).

Of Örebrö's mostly rather uninspiring **hotels**, the best is the central *Stora Hotellet*, Drottninggatan 1 (☎019/15 69 00, fax 15 69 50; ⑤/③). The oldest hotel in town, built in 1858, it is supposed to be haunted by the ghost of a young woman and her mother; late in the nineteenth century, the girl hanged herself here because her mother forced her into an unrewarding marriage. Its suites and rooms are extremely attractive, the best being the ones on the top floor of the annexe. The *City Hotel*, Kungsgatan 24 (☎019/601 42 00, fax 601 42 09; ④/②), and *Hotel Continental*, opposite the train station at Järnvägsgatan 2 (☎019/611 95 60, fax 611 73 10; ④/②), are very similar mid-range hotels; while *Hotel Gullvivan*, Järnvägsgatan 20 (☎019/611 90 35, fax 18 94 50; ③/②), has been recently renovated and looks better inside than out. The cheapest hotel is the quite adequate *Hotel Linden*, Köpmangatan 5 (☎019/611 78 11, fax 13 34 11; ①, 100kr summer discount).

The Town

The heart of Örebro comes as a pleasant surprise, its much-fortified thirteenth-century **castle** forming a magnificent backdrop to the water-lily-studded **River Svatån**. Aside from the town-centre attractions, **Lake Tysslingen**, a few kilometres west, makes for a good half-day excursion by bike (follow signs for "Garphyttan"). In spring, several thousand whooper swans settle here on their way to Finland and make spectacular viewing from the lakeside observation towers.

You might want to consider taking a **boat trip** around Lake Hjälmaren on *M/S Linnea* or *M/S Gustav Lagerbjelke* (2hr trips 70kr; buy tickets at tourist office). Also popular are **canal tours** from Örebro to Kungsör, a village 45km to the east; tickets can be booked at the tourist office. A one-way tour lasting six hours costs 450kr including food and sightseeing, while special trains make the return trip for a further 150kr.

Örebro Castle

The town's first defensive fort was built after a band of German merchants settled here in the thirteenth century, attracted by rich iron-mining. It was enlarged in the fourteenth century by King Magnus Eriksson, who lived here; Gustav Vasa's son Karl IX added fortifications and then, following in the footsteps of Vasa's other sons, turned it into a splendid Renaissance castle, raising all the walls to the height of the medieval towers and plastering them in cream-coloured stucco. When the Danes were no longer a threat, the town lost its importance, and **Örebro Castle** fell into disuse and subsequently became a storehouse and a prison. Prisoners of war were locked up here: you can still see, in the former **prison** on the fourth floor, words scratched into the walls by Russian inmates. Another room was used to hold suspected witches and was furnished by King Karl as a well-

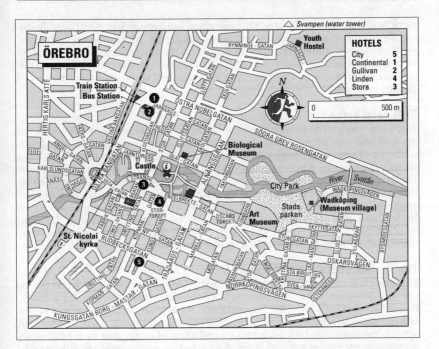

equipped **torture chamber**: at the time, fear of witchcraft was reaching fever pitch, and over four hundred women lost their heads (after surviving attempts to drown them in the nearby river). Today, the torture chamber serves as a rather macabre theme restaurant (see p.323).

The fairy-tale exterior you see today is the result of renovation in the 1890s. Influenced by the National Romanticism of the day, the architects carefully restored the castle to reflect both its medieval and Renaissance grandeur. The same cannot be said for the interior, where the valiant guides face a real challenge: there's no original furniture left, and many of the rooms are used for conferences. The mandatory **tours** sell the place as a "living castle" to make up for what it lacks (tours May–Sept 6 daily, in English at 2pm; 45kr); naturally, it's said to be riddled with ghosts, ranging from that of Magnus Eriksson's wife Blanka, who is said to be in torment for having murdered her son, to Engelbrecht, who had his head lopped off two years after he stormed the castle in 1434 and led a riot on behalf of farmers oppressed by harsh taxes. Among the few features of interest are some fine doors and floors, dating from as recently as the 1920s, the inlays depicting historical events at Örebro, and a large **family portrait** of Karl XI and his family, their faces painted to look similar; all have popping eyes, the result of the people depicted using arsenic to whiten their faces.

The Biological Museum

By the castle, in the grand old Karolinska School, is the charmingly dilapidated **Biological Museum** (mid-June to mid-Aug daily 11am–2pm; 25kr). It's interesting for the fact that its musty and fearsome occupants – stuffed polar bears, ostriches, bison and lynx – aren't behind glass, but instead lean over the walkway – a throwback to nineteenth-century museum design. Most unusual is the vast number of badly stuffed sparrows on display; in the late nineteenth century, they were the Swedish equivalent of an apple for the teacher. The gallery floor, up the original spiral staircase, has more stuffed fauna and some gruesome bottles of pickled marine life.

St Nicolai kyrka

Just a few hundred metres south of the castle, **St Nicolai kyrka**, at the top of the very oblong Stortorget, dates from 1260. Extensive restoration in the 1860s robbed it of most of its medieval character, though recent renovations have tried to undo the damage. It was here in 1810 that the relatively unknown figure of Jean Baptiste Bernadotte, Napoleon's marshal, was elected successor to the Swedish throne. The descendants of the new King Karl Johan, who never spoke a word of Swedish, are the current royal family. Engelbrecht was also supposed to be buried here after his execution, but when his coffin was exhumed in the eighteenth century, it was empty, and his bones have never been recovered. Today, the church is home to exhibitions of contemporary art.

The Art Museum and Wadköping

Following the river eastwards from the castle for about a kilometre leads you to the **Art Museum**, Engelbrektsgatan 3 (daily 11am–5pm, Wed till 9pm; 25kr), housed in what used to be the Länsmuseum. It has a surprisingly spacious series of galleries, with temporary and permanent collections, though much of what's on show is mediocre, the best work being a collection of landscapes by the late nineteenth-century local artist Axel Borg. A little further up the river, past the appealing Stadspark, stands an open-air museum, **Wadköping** (May–Aug 11am–5pm, Sept–April 11am–4pm; free; shops and exhibitions closed on Mon). An entire village of centuries-old wooden cottages and shops brought to the site, it's all extremely pretty but rather staged. Some of the cottages are now residences again, and the twee little shops sell pastel-coloured wooden knick-knacks. There's a very good bakery and café; the delicious smell from the former is enough to make your visit worthwhile.

Eating and drinking

There are plenty of atmospheric **cafés** and **restaurants** around town, together with some popular **pubs**. In July, expect some of the smaller restaurants to be shut for the holidays, though the best of these, *Stallyktan*, stays open. For a fine café in beautiful surroundings, head for *Café Stadsträdgården* in the greenhouses at the entrance to Stadspark (daily 11am–5pm); the place isn't to be confused with the newer restaurant next door which is not nearly so appealing. The café's delicious cakes, pies and sandwiches are home-made, using organic ingredients, and there's plenty for vegetarians. For a very scenic afternoon tea, head 1500m north of town to the 58-metre-high mushroom-shaped water tower, **Svampen**; buses #11 or #21 head here from Järntorget. There are sweeping views from the top of the surrounding plain and Lake Hjälmaren, and it has a reasonable café and restaurant inside. The boats which do trips on the lake also play host to popular prawn-eating evenings (200kr, drinks extra; advance bookings on ☎019/18 23 51 for *M/S Linnea* or ☎019/10 71 91 on *M/S Lagerbjelke*).

Restaurants and bars

Babar, Kungsgatan 4 (☎019/10 19 00), directly opposite *Bjornstugan*. The hippest bar-restaurant in town, with a vast oblong bar. They serve European food, with a meat-weighted menu.

Bishop's Arms, next door to the *Slottskällaren*. Hugely popular for outdoor drinking; serves the likes of fish and chips for 55kr.

Björnstugan, on Kungsgatan (☎019/13 58 90). Still very popular, though it has lost its position of trendiest bar in town to *Babar*.

Drängen, Oskarstorget 9 (☎019/32 32 96). A compact restaurant with an intriguing farm-style decor (*drängen* means "farm boy"), this unpretentious place is one of the finer gourmet spots. Main courses 100–150kr.

Harry's Bar, on the riverside, a minute's walk east of the castle, in the old red-brick technical museum building. They have a big fish menu (try the three salmons – smoked, salted and gravadlax – at 110kr for a serving of all three), and also serve light dishes at 60–70kr. Daily 4pm–2.30am.

Medeltidspuben, Drottning Blanka, in the old torture chamber at the castle (☎019/14 38 85). Its name translating as *Queen Blanka's Medieval Pub*, this fun place serves dishes such as wild boar and spare ribs, accompanied by stone flagons of mead. Main courses and a drink cost around 100kr; desserts include almond pie and a rather disappointing rose-flavoured blancmange.

September, Ringgatan 30. About ten minutes' walk west from the castle. A pleasant enough tapas bar, though not quite as hip as one might hope.

Slottskrogen Restaurant, in the castle, above *Queen Blanka's Medieval Pub* (☎019/13 42 69). Rather commercialized, and always packed out in summer. Pikeperch is the restaurant's speciality; there's also a cheap grill menu. The best value light dish is the *brännvinbord* – herring, sausage and cheese (evenings only; 60kr); bring your own schnapps. June–Aug daily 10.30am–2am.

Slottskällaren Restaurant & Bar, opposite the castle in the *Stora Hotellet* building (☎019/15 69 60). Its name means "castle-cellar", though it's neither of these. A long-established, popular restaurant, it serves main courses costing upwards of 150kr, and there are also cheaper, light meals like the classic *pytt i panna* for 59kr. Daily 6pm–midnight.

Stallyktan, Södra Strandgatan 3B (☎019/10 33 23). This excellent, rustic pub is a better choice for a quiet drink and dinner than most of the bigger venues. Their freshly cooked chicken, salmon or steak dishes go for a very reasonable 89kr. The shelves of giant flagons above the bar each have regulars' names printed beneath.

Wärdshuset Gyllene Oxen, Ringgatan 19. An upmarket meat and pasta place; try the "special" pizza, seemingly with every topping you can imagine, at 59kr. Mon–Fri 11am–2am, Sat & Sun noon–2am.

East of Vättern: Linköping and around

Sixty kilometres east of Lake Vättern, **LINKÖPING**, in the county of Östergötland, has an appealing character, its 900-year-old history apparent in a range of pleasing buildings; surprisingly, it's not an especially popular holiday destination for Swedes. The architectural highlights are the remarkable **Domkyrkan**, and an entire living village a few kilometres to the west, **Gamla Linköping**, caught in a late nineteenth-century time-warp. Linköping's best-kept secret, however, missed by all but a handful of visitors, is a little-known collection of **pictures** by the Oslo-born artist Peter Dahl, which reveals more about eighteenth-century Swedish society than any number of preserved dwellings could hope to do. The town has one other hidden treasure: the basement excavations at the often-overlooked twelfth-century St Lars kyrka.

Linköping and its sister town Norrköping (see p.328), to the east, have a relationship not dissimilar to that between Lund and Malmö in the west of Sweden. Linköping – like Lund – is essentially a middle-class university town, albeit with relatively recent academic credentials, whereas Norrköping – like Malmö – is staunchly working-class.

Arrival, information and accommodation

Linköping is easy to walk around, and the Domkyrkan spire is rarely out of sight, a useful point of reference in the unlikely eventuality that you lose your way. All **trains** and **buses** arrive at and leave from **Resecentrum** (travel centre) in the north of the town centre, at Järnvägsgatan. To get to the **tourist office** from here, cross over to Järnvägsavenyn, from where you turn into Klostergatan and head to its southern end; the tourist office is at no. 68, in the *Ekoxen Hotel* (open 24hr all year; ☎013/20 68 35, fax 12 19 03, *info@ekoxen.se*).

Though the tourist office doesn't book **private rooms**, it provides a free listing, with phone numbers, of the ones on offer. The STF **youth hostel** (☎013/14 90 90, fax 14 83 00; ①, 140kr) is very central and well appointed; every room is en suite and has its own kitchenette. For a good, modern **campsite**, with four-bed cabins, *Glyttinge Camping* is 3km east of town at Berggårdsvägen (☎013/17 49 28; mid-April to Sept); bus #201 from Resecentrum brings you right to the site. As regards the town's **hotels**, listed below, several of the smaller establishments close in July; of those that stay open, some will drop their prices dramatically then.

Du Nord, Repslagaregatan 5 (☎013/12 98 95; fax 14 52 91). Just 200m from Resecentrum, this pink detached house is prettier outside than inside, though its rooms are modern and have en-suite facilities and satellite TV. ③/② at weekends. Closed July.

Frimürarehotellet, St Larsgatan 14 (☎013/12 91 80, fax 13 95 44). With a grand, National Romantic facade from 1912 and elegant columns in its dining hall, this hotel is only spoiled by the 1970s interiors. ⑥/③.

Park, Järnvägsgatan 6 (☎013/12 90 05, fax 10 04 18). Dating from the turn of the century, this place serves a good buffet breakfast. ③/①.

Quality Ekoxen, Klostergatan 68 (☎013/25 26 00, fax 12 19 03). A good, well-equipped hotel, with a sauna, swimming pool, solarium, and massage and gym facilities. There's also a 24hr delicatessen and a bistro with an international menu. ⑤/②.

Stora Hotellet, Stortorget 9 (☎013/12 96 30, fax 13 37 69). A plush pile right in the centre of town. ⑤.

Östergyllen, Hamngatan 2 (☎013/10 20 75, fax 12 59 02). The cheapest and best-value hotel in town, Östergyllen includes a good breakfast in the price. The hotel also operates packages, with bike or canoe rental, such as three nights in a double room including bike rental and route maps for 890kr per person. Discounts at weekends. ②.

The town and around

The elegant **Domkyrkan**, with its soaring, 107-metre-high spire, is set in a swathe of greenery, Domkyrkoparken, just west of Storatorget (June & July Mon–Sat 9am–7pm, Sun 9am–6pm; Aug–May 9am–6pm, Sun 10am–6pm). It dates from 1232 – though the bulk of the present, sober building was completed in around 1520 – and is built entirely of local hand-carved limestone. Stonemasons from all over Europe worked on the well-proportioned building and, with a belfry and the west facade added as late as 1885, it incorporates a number of styles from

Romanesque to Gothic. Of particular note is the restored south portal, with carved biblical scenes above its Moorish-influenced, geometrically worked doors. The venerable old buildings around the Domkyrkan include the much rebuilt thirteenth-century **castle** which, like so many others in the south of Sweden, was fortified by Gustav Vasa and beautified by his son Johan III.

Just one block east on St Larsgatan, **St Lars kyrka** (Mon–Thurs 11am–4pm, Fri 11am–3pm, Sat 11am–1pm) is often bypassed as it stands within a few metres of the great Domkyrkan. The church was consecrated by Bishop Kol in 1170, and the present interior has had too many face-lifts to show many signs of its great age. Work undertaken as part of a ground reinforcement plan led to the discovery of twelfth-century engraved stone and wood coffins. Beneath the church, in the half-light of candles, are some complete twelfth-century skeletons – including one without a head – lying in new glass coffins, alongside remarkably preserved wood coffins and the exposed remains of the original church, rebuilt in the 1730s. There are no signs to direct you; to see it all, just ask whoever is selling postcards to unlock the door leading to the basement - no one will offer to show you.

Five minutes' wander down Ågatan in the direction of the Stångån river, the town's most unexpected cultural diversion is in the unlikely setting of the **Labourers' Educational Association** (ABF) at Snickaregatan 22 (closed Jul). On the fourth floor is a collection of 85 brilliantly executed pictures, some shot through with vibrant colour, others fine sepia sketches, depicting all the **Epistles of Bellman**. Carl Michael Bellman was an eighteenth-century poet and songwriter who exposed the hypocrisies of Swedish society of the time; his epistles tell of life in pubs: of prostitutes and of the wild and drunken sexual meanderings of high society, set against fear of the Church and final damnation. The pictures are the work of the Oslo-born artist Peter Dahl, a former head of the Stockholm Art School, who's been adopted by Swedes as one of their own. Though this collection is much admired by those who have seen it, you won't find many who know of its existence in Linköping.

Gamla Linköping

Just 3km west of Linköping proper is a real must, **Gamla Linköping**, a living open-air museum (Mon–Fri 10am–5.30pm, Sat & Sun noon–4pm; free). An entire town of houses, shops and businesses has been brought here from the centre of Linköping, along with street lighting, fences, signs and even trees, to re-create the town as an identical copy of its nineteenth-century incarnation; even the street plan is exactly the same. Fifty people actually live here, and there's a massive waiting list for eager new tenants, despite the drawbacks of not being allowed to alter the properties and the fact that tourists trundle through year round. Craftsmen work at nineteenth-century trades, and most shops are open every day, including a small chocolate factory, gold- and silversmiths, a woodwind workshop and linen shops. An eighteenth-century farm house from southern Östergotland is now a very pleasant cafeteria, and there's an open-air theatre, with performances throughout the summer. Buses #203 and #205 run there (Sept–May; every 20min) from Resecentrum.

Canal and lock trips

Linköping is riddled with waterways and offers the chance to see a lot of locks in close proximity. The most obvious one to choose is the **Göta Canal**, which wends its way from Motala through Borensberg to the seven-sluice Carl Johan

Lock at Berg, just north of Linköping, where it meets Lake Roxen. South of the city, the less well-known **Kinda Canal** has a manually operated triple lock at Tannefors, from where you can head south for 35km through a mix of canal and river to Rimforsa. There are endless combinations of canal and river trips, from a basic Göta Canal trip for two adults or an adult and two children for 295kr (245kr one-way), to a more glamorous spree to Söderköping (35km east) and back in a 1915 steamer, the *M/S Nya Skärgården* (bookings ☎070/637 17 00). For a less ambitious trip, boats also head down the Kinda Canal/Stångån river to a pleasant outdoor café at Tannefors. The least expensive canal experience – and probably just as enjoyable as the rest – is cycling along the old towpath at *Hotel Östergyllen* (see p.324).

Eating and drinking

Linköping is a likeable spot to spend an evening. The liveliest and most appealing places to **eat** and **drink** after dark are mostly on **Ågatan** running up to the Domkyrkan. Some of these are open during the daytime, too. The more traditional **café-konditori** around Storatorget serve great cakes and sandwiches: *Lind's*, on the edge of the square, is better than its neighbouring rivals, while *Gyllen* on Lilla Torget is very popular, with outside seating. A friendly **gay** café is the RFSL-run *Joy Café*, Nygatan 58 (Tuesdays 7–10pm; closed July). To get into the RFSL's popular pub (alternate Fridays 9pm–1am) and Saturday night discos (10pm–2.30am on alternate weeks to the pub nights), both at the *Joy Café*, you have to be an RFSL member; for information, call the RFSL (☎013/13 20 22; 9am–4pm).

Restaurants and bars

Amore Mio, corner of Ågatan and Snickaregatan. This ultra-plain place is where to get very cheap pasta dishes and pizza. Mon–Thurs 11am–10pm, Fri 11am–1am, Sat noon–1am, Sun 1–10pm.

B.K. (Bar & Kök), Ågatan. A cosy, stylish place with a huge cocktail bar and a small, elegant restaurant, serving unusual and well-presented dishes, mostly based on meat, with one fish and one vegetarian option.

Cafe & Restaurant Lindeman, inside the Concert Hall. With a bright, lofty, modern interior, *Lindeman* serves up good daily lunch specials – the likes of pasta, steak, prawn salad or vegetarian pizza for 45–52kr, including salad, a soft drink and coffee. There's also a healthy salad bar. Mon–Fri 9am–3pm.

Chiccolatta, Stortorget. A very popular Italian café beneath the *Good Evening Hotel*. The place to come for good, strong coffee. Mon–Sat 11am–10pm, Sun noon–10pm.

Gula Huset, Ågatan 19. With a long tradition of serving an extensive vegetarian buffet until 3pm (5pm on Sat; 55kr), and big portions of Swedish dishes and pan pizzas (84kr) later on, this place is justifiably popular. The beer is the cheapest in town. Daily 11am–midnight, Sat & Sun till 1am.

Harry's Bar & Restaurant, Ågatan. A couple of doors down from *B.K.* This ever-popular chain restaurant-bar is always crowded. Mon & Tues 11am–11pm, Wed–Fri 11am–1am, Sat 1pm–1am, Sun 1pm–11pm.

Metropole Beer Bar and Barbeque, St Larsgatan 14, at the *Frimürarehotellet*. Serves good-value steaks, ribs and baked potatoes in summer; at other times, there's a pricier à la carte menu. Open Thurs–Sat.

People's Cafe, Platengatan 5. With a very friendly, young crowd, wacky LP covers on the walls and Edith Piaf playing in the background, this is a great place for generously filled baguettes. Mon–Sat 11am–10pm, Sun noon–10pm.

PM & Co, where the Kinda Canal meets the River Stånga (☎013/31 21 00). The trendiest hangout for food and drink, in the only pleasant building in sight at the Kinda Canal guest harbour. Early Aug–June Mon 11.30am–2pm, Tues–Fri 11.30am–2pm & 6pm–midnight, Sat 6pm–midnight.

Safari, in the Concert Hall. Next to *Café Lindeman*. Song and dance shows (Wed & Thurs) accompany the meals at this restaurant, owned by the same people who run *PM & Co*. On Saturdays it's a nightclub too. Closed summer.

Steve's Cafe, Ågatan. Next to the Filmstaden cinema. This hugely popular and laid-back bar is big on beer, cider and a very tempting range of dips. The food includes big slices of quiche, and freshly made baguettes and bagels. Mon–Thurs 11am–10pm, Fri & Sat 11am–11pm, Sun noon–9pm.

Verandon Restaurant and Benny Hill pub, Storatorget 9, at *Stora Hotellet*. The menu boasts such over-stated dishes as "*carpaccio* of ostrich with pears, pistachio and cognac", which comes as a starter for 69kr. Open daily.

Överste Mörne, Storatorget, next door to *Stora Hotellet*. There's busy drinking at this traditional, spacious, candle-lit pub.

Around Linköping: Ekenäs Castle and Åtvidaberg

A rewarding excursion from Linköping is the old copper-mining town of **Åtvidaberg**, 35km southeast on Route 35, set in charming countryside and boasting a particularly good lakeside restaurant. On the way there, after 15km you'll come to **Ekenäs Castle** (May, June & Aug Sat & Sun 1–5pm; July Tues–Sun 1–5pm; guided tours hourly; to arrange English-language tours call ☎013/771 46), built in the early seventeenth century. One of the best-preserved Renaissance castles in Sweden, Ekanäs is a plainish, white building topped with three beautiful shingle towers. Its moated surround and proximity to cliffs make its strategic importance clear, even though the lake which it overlooks has been drained. The interiors, though not exceptional, have been preserved as they were during the seventeenth to nineteenth centuries. In summer the castle plays host to re-enactments of medieval **jousting** and a range of **concerts**, from classical to jazz. There's a charming café here too, serving ice cream and home-made bread. To get to the castle by **bus**, take bus #530 from Linköping to Björksätter, which is within 2km of the castle.

A few kilometres further along Route 35 at the hamlet of **Grebo** is an odd sight, a red, black and white **stone phallus** in the middle of a field to the right. Legend has it that if the farmer on whose land it stands fails to repaint it in these colours every year, his farm will burn down. So far, no farmer has had the guts to risk testing this out, and so the phallus is always sparkling.

Åtvidaberg

It's only a few kilometres further down Route 35 to the small and dying copper mining town of **ÅTVIDABERG**, by **Lake Bysjö**; **buses** #530, #531 and 532 head directly here from Linköping. The mines are signposted on the approach road, but no mining is carried out any more – all that's here is a coppersmith's selling its wares. On the shores of the picturesque lake is a manor house (follow the signs marked "Musikbåten" to get here), a splendid, fairy-tale villa with shingle roofs on numerous levels and a black-and-white Tudor-style facade. Close by is a tower looking out on the lake, inside which is a cannon. At midday, an eccentric group, the **Solkanon Klubben** (Sun Cannon Club) meets here, using a lens above the cannon to concentrate the sunlight onto gunpowder; the resulting daily explosion can be heard all over town. You can pay to ignite the cannon yourself at other times, and become the proud owner of a certificate to that effect.

The real draw of this otherwise unexceptional little town is *Bysjökrog*, a great **restaurant and bar** built into the old laundry of the manor house (☎0120/145 40; June–Sept Mon–Fri 11.30am–2pm & 6–10pm, Sat noon–10pm, Sun noon–8pm; pub open Mon–Thurs till 11pm, Fri & Sat till 1am); follow the signs for Musikbåten (a sort of covered raft on which bands play, moored near to the restaurant). The varied menu includes such delights as gazpacho with avocado and ginger salad, and main courses like home-made burgers and a delicate seafood casserole; desserts here are a treat – try the pistachio *crème brûlée* with white chocolate. There's also a considerable wine list, and live music (Mon & Wed evenings). A popular practice is to take your food in a picnic basket and head out into the middle of the lake on the Musikbåten (ask at the restaurant how to arrange this); on a summer's evening the sunsets here are like Monet paintings. For cheaper refreshments, there's the summertime *Cafe Villan*, in a back room at the manor (Mon–Fri 1.30–8pm, Sat & Sun noon–5pm).

Norrköping and around

It is with good reason that the dynamic, youth-oriented town of **NORRKÖPING** calls itself Sweden's Manchester. Like its British counterpart, Norrköping's wealth came from its textile industry, which built up in the eighteenth and nineteenth centuries – such are the parallels between the two towns that the Swedish for corduroy is "Manchester". The legacy from this period is the town's most appealing feature: it has one of Europe's best-preserved urban industrial landscapes, with handsome red-brick and stuccoed mills reflecting in the waters of its river, Motala Ström. Textiles kept Norrköping booming until the 1950s, when foreign competition began to undermine the town's share of the market. The last big textile mill here closed its doors in 1992.

Norrköping has one of the highest immigrant populations in Sweden. The first to come were the Jews, who came here from Germany and Holland after 1782, when Gustav III granted them the right to settle, hoping they would bring new manufacturing techniques into Sweden. Today's immigrant communities are mostly from Asian and Arabic countries, and in the past few years the most noticeable influx has been from the former Yugoslavia.

Arrival, information and accommodation

The **train** and **bus stations** are opposite each other on Norra Promenaden at the northern end of the centre. From here, walk south down Drottninggatan for five minutes, then head one block across to the right towards the Concert Hall (see p.330). The helpful **tourist office** is housed in an old cotton warehouse opposite the gates of the paper mill at Dalsgatan 16 (June to mid-Aug daily 10am–7pm, Sat 10am–5pm, Sun 10am–2pm; mid-Aug to May Mon–Fri 10am–6pm, Sat 10am–2pm; ☎011/15 50 00, fax 15 50 74, *www.norrkoping.se*). Among other things, they'll be able to explain routes and times for the 1902 **vintage tram**, which circles around on a sightseeing tour during summer. The town's ordinary, yellow **trams** run on two lines all over the town centre, costing a flat 15kr, including any tram changes within the space of an hour.

Accommodation

The tourist office will book **cottages** all over the county. In high season, a secluded cottage, sleeping five, in the countryside 30km away will cost around 1600kr a week including the booking fee, while one more central to Norrköping and sleeping up to eight would cost 3520kr per week. There's an STF **youth hostel**, *Turistgården*, at Ingelstadsgatan 31 (☎011/10 11 60, fax 18 68 63; 120kr), just a few hundred metres behind the train station; a much more picturesque hostel can be found at Abborreberg, 5km east of town (see p.333). The closest **campsite** by the rock carvings at Himmelstalund, is *City Camp* on Utställningsvägen (☎011/17 11 90, fax 17 09 87). To get there, either walk west from the centre along the river, or take bus #115 from the bus station, or tram #3, which brings you closer than the bus.

The cheapest central **hotel**, *Hotel Centric,* Gamla Rådstugugatan 18–20 (☎011/12 90 30, fax 18 07 28; ③/①), 500m south of the train station, is quite reasonable; at its reception is a striking wall fresco by Gothenburg artist Lars Gillies, depicting all Norrköping's central areas. More upmarket is the classic, turn-of-the-century *Grand Hotel*, Tyska Torget 2, bang in the centre (☎011/36 41 00, fax 18 11 83; ⑤/③). The *President Hotel*, just as central and next door to the fine theatre at Vattengränd 11 (☎011/12 95 20, fax 10 07 10; ⑤/③), has secure parking and is very comfortable; its very small, French-style *Teater Bar* restaurant is renowned for its pepper steaks. A calm and pleasant alternative is *Södra Hotellet*, in a sympathetically renovated 1920s house at Södra Promenaden 142 (☎011/25 35 00, fax 12 46 96; ④/②), once a favoured residential street for the textile mill owners.

The Town

Running south from the train station, **Drottninggatan** is a straight north–south central artery, crossing Motala Ström, the small, rushing river that attracted the Dutch industrialist Louis De Geer to the town in the early seventeenth century. He was known as the father of Swedish industry, and his paper mill, which still runs today, became the biggest factory in town. The mill's construction was followed by the creation of many wool, silk and linen factories here. Today many of Norrköping's buildings are painted a tortilla-chip yellow, as are the trams – De Geer favoured the colour, which has become symbolic of the town.

Drottninggatan and around

Just a few steps down from the station, the compact **Carl Johans Park** has 25,000 cacti, which are formally arranged in thematic patterns, interspersed with brilliantly coloured flowers and palm trees. Glance to the right from here (with the station behind you) down Teatergatan, and you'll see the splendid 1906 city **theatre**, with its Art Nouveau curves and double Ionic columns. Over the river, following the tram lines up cobbled Drottninggatan brings you to a right turn into Repslagaregatan for **Gamla Torget**, overlooked by a charismatic Carl Milles sculpture of Louis De Geer with a bale of cloth slung over his shoulder.

At the southernmost tip of Drottninggatan is Norrköping's **Konstmuseum** (Art Museum; May–Aug Tues–Sun noon–4pm, Wed till 8pm; Sept–April Tues & Thurs 11am–8pm, Wed & Fri–Sun 11am–5pm; 30kr), full of some of the country's best-known modernist works. Founded by a local snuff manufacturer at the turn of the century, the galleries offer a fine, well-balanced progression from seventeenth-

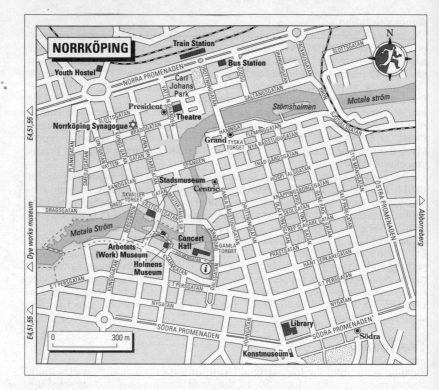

century Baroque through to up-to-the-minute twentieth-century paintings. As you head back north from the art museum, the bunker-like, concrete building to the right is the town **library**; more user-friendly than most, it has a big range of newspapers from all over the world and offers free use of the Internet.

West of Gamle Torget

Back at Gamle Torget, to the west lies the modern and stylish riverside **Concert Hall**, fronted by trees, providing a lovely setting for the café, *Kråkholmen Louis De Geer* (see p.332). It's worth stepping inside the Concert Hall for a moment, as its apparent modernity belies the fact that this was once one of De Geer's paper factories. Continuing west from the Concert Hall, go through the impressive, eighteenth-century paper mill gates to the left, across a wooden bridge behind the hall, and you'll pass the new **Norrköping campus** of Linköping University. Next door is the small **Holmens Museum** (Tues & Thurs 9am–12.30pm; free), depicting life in the town's paper mills. It's run on a voluntary basis by retired paper-mill workers; sadly, though, the exhibits aren't labelled in English. The best known of the mills, Holmens, is still functioning just a few metres away.

West along the river on your right is the exceptionally well presented **Arbetets Museum** (Museum of Work; daily 11am–5pm; free), housed in a triangular, yellow-stuccoed factory built in 1917. Known as "The Iron" – though its shape and colour are more reminiscent of a wedge of Cheddar cheese – the building was described by Carl Milles as Europe's most beautiful factory. The museum has seven floors of exhibitions on living conditions, workers' rights and day-to-day life in the mills. In the spring and autumn, there are jazz and blues evenings on the first floor (Tues only). Next door and over another little bridge is the excellent **Stadsmuseum** (Tues, Wed & Fri 10am–4pm, Thurs 10am–8pm, Sat & Sun 11am–5pm; free), set in an interconnecting (and confusing) network of old industrial properties. The most rewarding of its permanent exhibitions is a street showing various trades: there are workshops of a milliner, confectioner, chimney sweep and, in a back yard, a carriage maker. All are cleverly designed and worth wandering through.

Following the river bank further west for ten minutes leads to the **Färgargården**, an open-air dyeworks museum (May Sat & Sun noon–4pm, June–Aug Tues–Sun noon–4pm; free), in a huddle of wooden nineteenth-century houses. A better reason to come here than the exhibitions and garden, with herbs and plants for dyeing, is the outdoor **café**, open whenever the weather is good during summer.

The synagogue

Three hundred metres north of the Stadmuseum stands the architectural and cultural gem of Norrköping's **synagogue**, on Bråddgatan (pre-booked tours mandatory; the tourist office can make arrangements). The present synagogue, the city's third, was built in 1858, and has recently been beautifully restored; highlights include the enormous central chandelier; the pulpit, finely painted in blues, reds and yellows; and a magnificent ark, with a superb, hand-painted everlasting light, representing the "eternal flame" that's kept lit in all synagogues. There are only around thirty synagogue members now living in Östergotland; services are held by rabbis visiting from Stockholm and Malmö, as Norrköping has not had its own rabbi since 1890.

Eating and drinking

There is a fair selection of **eating places** in Norrköping, most of which double as **bars**. It's a town custom to drink at home before heading out, so the town only starts coming alive from 11pm; but from then onwards, it gets very busy.

In the past couple of decades, Norrköping has become a nucleus for music-inspired youth culture. Made fashionable in the 1970s and 1980s by one of Sweden's most famous singer-songwriters, Ulf Lundell, who hails from Norrköping, the town was also home to the country's best-known working-class rock band, Eldkvarn.

Restaurants and bars

Bishop's Arms Pub, at the *Grand Hotel*, Tyska Torget 2. Just up Drottninggatan from the station, this is a long-standing, traditional-English-style pub.

Café Curiosa, Hörngatan 6. An old-fashioned café in the town centre, serving home-made cakes, savoury pies and ice cream. Pie and salad costs 35kr. Mon–Fri 10am–6pm, Sat 10am–3pm.

Cromwell House, Kungsgatan. More upmarket than the *Wasa*, it serves light meals for around 85kr. The best main course dish is perch fillet; the ice cream with warm cloudberry and punch is a delight at 52kr. Closed July. Mon–Thurs 11.30am–2pm & 5–11pm, Fri & Sat 11.30am–2pm & 5pm–1am, Sun 11.30am–2pm.

Guskelov, Dalsgatan 13 (☎011/13 44 00). Next door to the Concert Hall, this Art-Deco-style restaurant specializes in fish dishes; try the seafood chowder with aïoli (95kr). The restaurant's name translates as "Thank God", a common Östergötland exclamation. Mon–Fri 11.30am–2.30pm & 5.30pm–11.30pm, Sat 5.30pm–11.30pm.

Källaren Bacchus, Gamla Torget 4 (☎011/10 07 40). The cellar restaurant of *Trädgården* (see below), serving warm grills or light eats, and a long list of cocktails, whiskies and beers. Its garden is a perfect spot for cold beer and a bite.

Kråkholmen Louis De Geer, outside the Concert Hall (enter through the hall, or round the back). Eat here against the backdrop of Motala Ström's crashing waters; the daily lunch menu features the likes of beef casserole at 45kr. Daily 11am–4.30pm.

Laxholmen Restaurant, sixth floor of the Arbetets Museum. Their menu, which changes daily, includes the likes of fish soup, apple pancakes, and baked potato with tuna filling. They also do warm, filled baguettes for 35kr. Daily 11am–4pm.

O'Leary's, Drottninggatan 60 (☎011/10 51 07). American and Mexican classics such as black bean soup and cajun chicken. Service can be slow.

Palace, Bråddgatan 13. On the ground floor of a hideous 1960s office block, this nightclub and restaurant with its red neon and flashing lights is where the tourist office invariably send anyone asking about dinner and evening entertainment. There's a big grill menu – nothing for vegetarians though – and the standard of cooking is mediocre.

Pappa Grappa, Gamla Rådstugugatan 24 (☎ 011/18 00 14). A terrific Italian restaurant, not to be missed for inventive combinations of fresh ingredients, served up in a mellow atmosphere. Try raw marinated angler fish, fig cream with amaretto or the fabulous sorbet of peach grappa. The drinks list is also remarkably varied. Tues–Sat from 6pm.

Pub Wasa, Gamla Rådstugugatan 33 (☎ 011/18 26 25). The upstairs is all done up like a ship's interior (hence the name) with little cannons pointing out of the windows. The cheap food at this friendly place includes *pytt i panna* (58kr), pasta and – a popular choice – a bowl of prawns for four people (120kr). There's live music from 11pm. Tue & Wed 8pm–1am, Thurs–Sun 8pm–3am.

Restaurant La Mansion, Södra Promenaden 116. A sedate and charming place for lunch or dinner, in the preserved former home of a textile mill manager. Dinner menus, like venison and wild mushrooms, and salmon and seafood mousse, are 150kr. The two-course lunch is a steep 135kr. Mon–Fri 11.30am–2.30pm & 5.30–11pm, Sat noon–midnight; shorter hours in July.

Tegelvalvet Bar, Gamla Rådstugugatan. In the basement, beneath *Pub Wasa*, with live music in the form of live bands (Friday and Saturday). Closed Jul. Fri & Sat 8pm–1am.

Trädgården, Prästgatan 3 (☎011/10 07 40). The entrance is beneath an iron sign marked "VIP Paraden". This bar and grill is very popular, especially for outdoor eating in summer. Daily from 5pm.

Around Norrköping: Abborreberg, Löfstad Manor and Kolmården Djurpark

Close to the centre are the rock carvings at **Himmelstalund**, a couple of kilometres west of the centre. Norrköping's present appearance belies its far more ancient origins; these carvings date from around 1500 BC and show with unusual clarity ships, weapons, animals and men. Some burial mounds at the site, though nothing much to look at, attest to Iron Age and Viking settlements in the area. To get there, take bus #118 from the centre. Further out from town are several places, including a manor house and an unusual zoo complex, that make for easy and worthwhile excursions from Norrköping.

Abborreberg

The splendid old wooden villas at **ABBORREBERG**, 5km east of Norrköping, are weathered but charmingly authentic early nineteenth-century summer residences and make a delightful lakeside setting for coffee and cake. Passing through the affluent suburb of Lindö, Abborreberg looks out onto Lindö Bay from a forested setting. The collection of small, verandahed villas and cottages all retain their lived-in look, but the drawing room of the main Seaside Villa should be the target of your visit. Although the views from the lovely old windows are fine enough, it's the wallpaper that takes the limelight. Hand-printed and brought from Paris in the 1870s, it is one of only four such papers and depicts in gloriously unrealistic detail a panoramic scene called "The Banks of the Bosporus". If you ask at the **café**, they will unlock the larger villa which has a wonderful atmosphere of faded gentility, with fancy woodwork and old furnishings; today it's used for weddings. Another of the old residences is now an STF **youth hostel** (☎011/31 91 41, fax 31 91 48; 105kr; mid-June to mid-Aug). To reach Abborreberg, take **bus** #111 from outside the Domino Store on Repslagaregatan, just off Drottninggatan in the town centre, to Lindö; ask the driver for the nearest stop to *STF Vandrarhem*. After 6pm, take bus #101 from outside the library.

Löfstad Manor

Just 10km southwest of town, **Löfstad Manor** (May Sat & Sun only; June to Aug daily; mandatory tours hourly noon–4pm on the hour, in late Aug, last tour is at 2pm; ☎011/33 50 67; 40kr) is a fine country home dating from the 1650s, though it was rebuilt a hundred years on after a fire left it a shell. Bus #481 runs from Norrköping bus terminal to Löfstad (ask for Löfstad Slott). Getting back to town on the infrequent buses can be a problem without your own transport, especially on weekend afternoons.

The same family owned Löfstad until 1926, when Emily Piper, who died unmarried, bequeathed the whole estate to the Museum of Östergötland. The house contains a splendid collection of eighteenth- and nineteenth-century Baroque and Rococo furniture and pictures, though presented in a rather more stiff and formal way than the billing "as she left it" implies. The areas with the most authentic, lived-in feel are the original kitchen and servants' quarters; a bathroom in the latter later became Emily Piper's, with her ancient bathrobe still hanging from the door. In the scullery there's an elaborate candle-making gadget and a machine for twisting metal into bed springs (the house was meant to be as self-sufficient as possible). It's best to ask about English commentary before the tour gets underway, as the busy tour guides sometimes have to cope with large groups and don't like to be hassled once the tour's underway. During the summer, the house plays host to a **cultural programme** ranging from classical and jazz concerts to Swedish poetry recitations.

There's a pleasant **restaurant** in one wing of the house, *Löfstad Värdhus* (11am–10pm), which serves traditional Swedish food; their *Dagens Rätt* costs 65kr. For a less formal and very enjoyable cold lunch, a **café** in the stables does delicious smoked beef with mounds of potato salad for 55kr (11am–5pm).

Kolmården Djurpark

One of Sweden's biggest attractions, **Kolmården Djurpark**, lies 28km northeast of Norrköping. A combined zoo, safari park and dolphinarium, it's understandably popular with children, for whom there's a special section. If your views on zoos are negative, it's just about possible to be convinced that this one is different. There are no cages; instead sunken enclosures, rock barriers and moats prevent the animals from feasting on their captors. There's certainly no shortage of things to do either: there's a cable-car ride over the safari park, a tropical house, a working farm and dolphin shows.

If you're interested in just one or two specific attractions in the park, it might be as well to confirm those are open before you visit (call ☎011/24 90 00); the safari park only opens when the weather is calm and the temperature above -10°C. Generally, though, most things are open daily (10am until around 4–6pm); the dolphinarium has between one and four shows a day for most of the year. The entrance price varies according to what you want to see, but a combined ticket for everything runs from 195kr to 235kr, depending on the season. If you don't have your own transport, take bus #432 here from Norrköping bus terminal (hourly; 50min). There's an expensive hotel, the *Vidmarkshotellet* (☎011/15 71 00, fax 39 50 84; ④), at the park; alternatively, you can **camp** at *Kolmården Camping* (☎011/39 82 50, fax 39 70 81).

Nyköping and around

Heading northeast from Norrköping, after 30km or so you enter the county of **Södermanland** – known as Sörmland. Its capital, the very small historic town of **NYKÖPING**, has seen a lively past, but today is used by most visitors simply as a springboard for the picturesque coastal islands to the east. This is a pity, as its underrated charms include an excellent museum, in and around the ruins of its thirteenth-century **castle**, and a harbour – a regular target for the Stockholm yachting set – that bustles with life in summer.

Arrival, information and accommodation

The train station and, 500m to the south, the bus station are ten minutes' walk west of the winding Nyköping river. Conveniently, all the sights lie between the stations and the river, or by the river itself. The harbour is at the other end of town from the stations, but the distance is easily walkable. The central and enthusiastic **tourist office** is in the Rådhus, the only hideous building on the otherwise graceful Storatorget (June to mid-Aug Mon–Fri 8am–6pm, Sat & Sun 10am–5pm; mid-Aug to May Mon–Fri 8am–5pm; ☎0155/24 82 00, fax 24 81 36, *turism@nykoping.se*). They **rent bikes** (40kr a day or 200kr a week), useful for several excursions, such as a trip to the islands closest to town (see p.336).

Accommodation

Set in the castle grounds, the delightful **youth hostel** is at Brunnsgatan 2 (☎0155/21 18 10; ①, 90kr), in an eighteenth-century former hospital and overlooking the King's Tower. You can get here from the train station by heading south down Järnvägsgatan, then cutting east along Västra Kvarngatan; Brunnsgatan is the third right off this street. The closer of the town's two campsites is *Oppeby Camping* (☎0155/21 13 02; May–Sept), 2km northwest of the centre near the E4, with cheap cabins; the other site is *Strandstuvikens*, 6km south on the Baltic coast (☎0155/978 10; mid-May to mid-Sept). **Private rooms** can be booked at the tourist office (from 125kr, no booking fee).

The most stylish and well-positioned **hotel** is the excellent-value *Kompaniet* on Folkungavägen, near the harbour (☎0155/28 80 20, fax 28 16 73; ⑤/③); the price includes breakfast, afternoon tea and a buffet dinner. The cheap and basic *Hotel Wictoria*, Fruängsgatan 21 (☎0155/21 75 80, fax 21 44 47; ②, 150kr summer discount), is quite adequate and close to the town's picturesque theatre. Out of town, off the E4, the *Blommenhof Hotel*, Blommenhovsvägen, has private saunas, a heated pool and a stylish restaurant (☎0155/20 20 60, fax 26 84 94; ④/②).

The Town

It's convenient to start your tour of the town at the tourist office, just opposite which is the vast **St Nicolai Church**, with its white, vaulted ceiling. The building dates from the 1260s, although most of what you see is the result of sixteenth-century refurbishment. The pillars here are adorned with dozens of beautiful, heavily moulded silver candle sconces. It's the pulpit, though, that's the highlight of the church; crafted in Norrköping, it was modelled on the one in the Storkyrkan in Stockholm. Outside, standing proudly on a nearby rocky outcrop, is the red 1692 bell tower, the only wooden building not destroyed in 1719 when the town's worst fire struck.

The castle

From the tourist office, it's just a couple of minutes' wander south, down Slottsgatan with the river to your left, to Kungsgatan. Here you'll see the museum complex and beyond it, the King's Tower. A late twelfth-century defensive tower, built to protect the trading port at the estuary of the Nyköping river, it was subsequently converted into a **fortress** by King Magnus Ladulås. It was here in 1317 that the infamous **Nyköping Banquet** took place: One of Magnus's three sons, Birger, invited his brothers Erik and Valdemar to celebrate Christmas at Nyköping and provided a grand banquet. Once the meal was complete, and the visiting brothers had retired to bed, Birger had them thrown in the castle's dungeon, threw the key into the river and left them to starve to death. In the nineteenth century, a key was found by a boy fishing in the river; whether the rusting item he found, now on display in the museum, really is the one last touched by Birger, no one knows.

In the sixteenth century, Gustav Vasa fortified the castle with gun towers; his son Karl, who became Duke of Södermanland, converted the place into one of Sweden's grandest Renaissance palaces. A fire here in the 1660s reduced all lesser buildings to ash and gutted the castle. With no money forthcoming from the national coffers, it was never rebuilt; only the King's Tower was saved from demolition and became used as a granary. Today, the riverside tower and the adjoining early eighteenth-century house built for the county governor form a **museum complex** (July daily noon–4pm; Aug–June closed Mon; 20kr). Wandering through the original gatehouse beneath Karl's heraldic shield, you reach the extensively restored **King's Tower**. On the way up to the first floor you'll pass carefully stacked bits and pieces excavated from Karl's palace, most notably some spectacular Ionic columns. On the first floor, a stylish job has been done of rebuilding the graceful archways that lead into the Guard Room. Here a model of the fortress, fronted by a dashboard of buttons, allows you to follow the events of the Nyköping

Banquet – complete with gory detail. The top floor has some evocative exhibits, too, including a bizarre three-dimensional diorama depicting the dead King Gustav II Adolf, his body brought here after he was killed at the Battle of Lützen; his widow, twisted in misery, is also shown, as is six-year-old Queen Kristina.

It's the old **Governor's Residence**, however, that has the most exquisite collections. Downstairs is the original kitchen, with shiny copper pots and utensils, and a surprisingly tasteful souvenir shop, selling expensive medieval-style clothes for both sexes. Climb the stairs, lined with menacing portraits, to gain access to an exceptional run of magnificently decorated rooms from each stylistic period in Sweden. Among the many highlights are the red-silk bed in the Baroque room, a copper steam bath in a nineteenth-century bedroom, and best of all, the *Jugendstil* room – about the finest example you'll see in the country. Amid the stylish finery are some splendid early-twentieth-century portraits by twin brothers Bernard and Emil Österman, who were famous for their passionate and sensual style. There's also a modern museum building next door, with temporary art installations.

Eating and drinking

Most of the **eating** and **drinking** is, unsurprisingly, done at the harbour, but for the best daytime **café** by far, head for *Café Hellmans* on Västra Trädgårdgatan 24 (Mon–Fri 7.30am–6pm, Sat 9am–4pm, Sun 10am–4pm), just off Storatorget (head down Västra Storgatan from the square, then left). In a converted grain warehouse with a back courtyard (open in summer), it attracts a young, relaxed crowd and serves great sandwiches, fruit flans, the gooiest chocolate cakes and large mugs of good coffee; there's also a great breakfast buffet (40kr). Close to the harbour, *Tova Stugen*, behind the castle (Mon–Fri 11am–5pm, Sat & Sun noon–5pm), serves light sandwich meals – try the cold fried fish and sour cream sandwich, called *inlagd strömming* (35kr) – in low, grass-roofed fifteenth-century cottages brought here from around Södermanland, one of which has medieval wall paintings. One place a few kilometres out of town that's worth trying is *Åstugan*, a café and antique shop with a riverside setting on the old E4, past Svarta (mid-June to mid-Aug daily noon–8pm; mid-Sept to mid-June Sat & Sun noon–8pm); it offers fine pastries and a relaxed atmosphere.

For a bright and fun **restaurant** and **bar** scene head for the old wooden storage buildings along the harbourside. The first warehouse you'll see when you arrive, a handsome eighteenth-century grain store, is home to the *Kapten Krook Bistro* (☎0155/269 29 20). With a range of beers, whiskies and schnapps, it serves food ranging from Cajun shrimp to more traditional gravadlax; steaks and seafood cost 120–170kr. A couple of big red wooden storehouses on is the popular and more economical *Cafe Aktersnurran*, with lots of outside eating. The most laid-back place here for a young, casual crowd, and worth pressing on for, is *Lotsen* (daily 11am–2pm), in a picturesque wooden house serving similar food to *Kapten Krook*, at lower prices. On cooler summer nights, the stylishly nautical, candle-lit interior is a pleasant place to drink and listen to regular live music.

The islands around Nyköping

There are hundreds of **islands** that are accessible from Nyköping, with regular boat trips from town. The most popular of these excursions is to the nature reserve on **Stendörren**, around 30km east of town; once there, it's possible to enjoy some fine walks to other islands via connecting footbridges. Another pleasant destination is **Trosa**, 40km northeast of town along the E4, with tranquil riverside walks, forested trails and picture-perfect red, wooden cottages around the old centre.

M/S Labrador leaves the dock at Nyköping for Trosa, via Stendörren, at 9am; the return boat leaves Trosa at 2pm (mid-June to mid-Aug Tues & Thurs; to Stendorren 80kr; to Trosa 120kr; ☎0155/26 71 00). You can stay on Trosa in the STF **youth hostel** (June to mid-Aug; ☎0156/53 2100; 120kr), based in an old school. To head back to Stockholm instead of Nyköping, take bus #702 from Trosa bus terminal to Liljeholmen (1hr), where you connect with public transport to Stockholm. **Camping** near Trosa is possible at *Sandviks Camping* (☎0156/410 09; mid-April to mid-Oct); there's only one cabin, so it's worth booking well in advance if you want to use it. A rather bigger site is *Trosa Havsbaden* (☎0156/124 94) which has nine cottages, bookable through Trosa's **tourist office** (☎0156/522 22.)

Ringsö

The archipelago of **Ringsö**, reached by following the coast road east of town, is a natural haven of primeval forest riddled with paths and windy shores in between the sea-smoothed outcrops. One appealing activity here is a gentle **Icelandic-horse safari** (book on ☎0155/26 16 30 or 26 16 14). Boats leave from Studsviks quay (reached on Route 219 from Nyköping – follow the road to Studsviks brygga) and arrive on the eastern shore of Ringsö at 9.15 am, with breakfast served on Ringsö itself. The safari runs to Södra Udden, the most southerly point of the island, and boats arrive back at Studsvik at 5pm, though if you want to stay longer, you can book accommodation in an old crofter's cottage, close to the sea, when you book the safari. A full day trek costs 580kr, including breakfast.

Gotland

Tales of good times on **GOTLAND** are rife. Wherever you are in Sweden, one mention of this ancient Baltic island will elicit a typical Swedish sigh, followed by an anecdote about what a great place it is. You'll hear that the short summer season is an exciting time to visit; that the place is hot, fun and lively. These claims are largely true: the island has a distinct youthful feel, with young, mobile Stockholmers deserting the capital in summer for a boisterous time on its beaches. The flower-power era makes its presence felt with a smattering of elderly VW camper vans lurching off the ferries, but shiny Saabs outnumber them fifty to one. During summer, the bars, restaurants and campsites are packed, the streets swarm with revellers, and the sands are awash with bodies. It's not everyone's cup of tea: to avoid the hectic summer altogether, come in late May or September when, depending on your level of bravado, you might still manage to swim in the waters around the island. To experience the setting at its most frenetic, come in August during Medieval Week (see p.347), when people put a huge effort into dressing the part, the only vestige of modern life among the tunics, chain mail and velvet robes being the participants' mobile phones.

Visby, Gotland's capital, has always been the scene of frenetic activity of some kind. Its temperate climate and position attracted the Vikings as early as the sixth century, and the lucrative trade routes they opened, from here through to

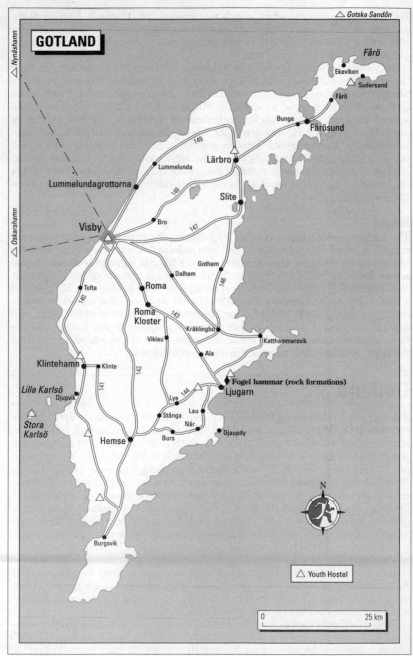

△ Gotska Sandön

GOTLAND

△ Nynäshamn

△ Oskarshamn

Fårö

Ekeviken
△ Sudersand

Fårö

Bunge
Fårösund

149

Lärbro

Lummelunda

Lummelundagrottorna

148

Slite

Bro

147

Visby

Gothem

Dalhem

146

Tofta

Roma

140

Roma
Kloster

143

Kräklingbo

Viklau

Katthammarsvik

Klintehamn   Klinte

Ala

Lilla Karlsö

Djupvik

142

Fogel hammar (rock formations)

Ljugarn

△
*Stora
Karlsö*

141

Lye   144

Lau

Stånga

När

Djaupdy

Hemse

Burs

Burgsvik

N

△ Youth Hostel

0   25 km

Byzantium and western Asia, guaranteed the island its prosperity. With the ending of Viking domination, a "golden age" followed, with Gotland's inhabitants maintaining trading posts abroad and signing treaties as equals with European and Asian leaders. However, by the late twelfth century their autonomy had been undermined by the growing power of the **Hanseatic League**. Under its influence, Visby became one of the great cities of medieval Europe, as important as London or Paris, famed for its wealth and strategic power. A contemporary ballad had it that "The Gotlanders weigh their gold with twenty-pound weights. The pigs eat out of silver troughs and the women spin with golden distaffs." Today, all the revelry which keeps Visby buzzing from late June to the end of August takes place amid the spectacular backdrop of its medieval architecture; two hundred or so Hanseatic warehouses are dotted among stone and wooden houses, the whole lot nestled within its ancient walls.

Nowhere else in Scandinavia is there such a concentration of unspoilt **medieval country churches**, all built before the end of the fourteenth century. Today 93 of them are still in use, displaying a unique Baltic Gothic style and providing the most permanent reminder of Gotland's ancient wealth.

There is a real charm to the **rest of Gotland** – rolling green countryside, forest-lined roads, fine beaches and small fishing villages. Everywhere the rural skyline is dominated by churches, the remnants of medieval settlements destroyed in the Danish invasion. Yet – perhaps because of Visby's magnetic pull – very few people bother to explore the island; consequently, the main roads here are pleasingly free of traffic and minor roads positively deserted – cycling is a joy. As you travel, keep an eye out for the waymarkers erected in the 1780s to indicate the distance from Wisby (the old spelling of the town's name), calculated in Swedish miles – one of which equivalent to about 10km.

Travel practicalities

You can **reach Gotland** by plane or ferry. Competition between the two airlines serving the island has made **flying** a competitive option compared to ferry sailings, though flying is still only really worthwhile if you're entitled to under-26 stand-by fares. The cheaper of the two airlines is Flying Enterprise, with flights to Visby from Stockholm's Bromma airport (under-26 fare 270kr one-way, 540kr return; 26-and-over 1233kr return; book on ☎020/95 95 00); Skyways' fares from Arlanda airport cost about ten percent more (book on ☎0498/75 00 00). Most people visiting Gotland, however, get there by **ferry** from **Nynäshamn**, the nearest port to Stockholm, or **Oskarshamn**, more convenient if you're heading to Gotland from Gothenburg or the south; a succession of local and national train links means you can get from Gothenburg to Oskarshamn in little over six hours.

Ferries to Gotland

Ferry services to Gotland are numerous and, in summer, packed, so try and book well ahead. Destination Gotland runs a range of **ferries** to the island (to reserve a seat, call ☎0498/20 10 20 or fax 20 13 90 in Visby itself; ☎08/20 10 20 for the Stockholm office). Another option is to try Gotland City at Kungsgatan 57 in Stockholm (☎08/406 15 00, fax 406 15 90), which can provide plenty of information and sell advance tickets. Daytime sailings to Gotland from Nynäshamn take four hours; from Oskarhamn, five hours. **Night crossings** allow you to stay on the boat until morning proper; they're packed out in summer, so you may well think it worthwhile to book one of the very comfortable, en-suite cabins (④, including a return ticket for two to Oskarshamn). Without a cabin, one-way fares cost around 135kr during high season (June to mid-Aug), 195kr on Friday, Saturday and Sunday. Taking a bicycle on board costs 35kr. See "Travel details", p.354, for a full run-through of ferry schedules and frequencies.

There are also very comfortable **high-speed ferries** to Gotland from Oskarshman and Nynashamn, which make the crossing in just two and a half hours (from 205kr to 430kr depending on the time of year). The price list is confusing in the extreme, though during the high season of mid-June to mid-August it roughly divides into three categories: blue (cheapest), green (standard) and yellow (most expensive). Return prices are simply double that of single. There are discounts for children aged 6–18; students receive a reduction of around 60kr.

Transport on Gotland

For **getting around** the island, it's hard to resist the temptation to **rent a bike**, given the flat terrain and empty roads. Most ferry arrivals at Visby are plagued by people hustling bikes outside the terminal; there are outlets in town where you can rent bikes too (see p.342). Handily for striking out into the countryside beyond Visby (a real joy that's little visited by most of the young summer crowd), bikes can easily be rented at various towns to the south of Visby, less so further north. As for Gotland's **buses**, services are pretty sparse; outside Visby, buses tend to run only twice daily – morning and evening. **Hitching**, however, is an accepted means of transport; unless you have a specific destination, the general attractiveness of the countryside, especially in the south, means it's often just as well to go wherever the driver is heading.

CYCLING AROUND GOTLAND

- Gotland is flat but even so, cycling can get tiring, and so it's worth renting a bike with gears.
- **Luggage** can usually be left at the bike rental office, although paying a few *kronor* more gets you baskets or bicycle trolleys to take your gear with you as you cycle.
- Most bike rental outlets offer **bike insurance** (around 25kr a day). The built-in rear wheel lock should be enough to deter most joyriders, but if you're not satisfied with that level of security, buy an extra chain and padlock. Be warned, though, that if your machine goes walkabout when insured, you'll still be liable for the first 200kr of a claim.
- Most rental places are down by the ferry terminals, and it's fairly standard practice – ask about this – for them to let you keep the bike overnight to ride down to the harbour the next morning. In the unlikely event you have to return your bike the same day you rented it, you may well need to take a long hike from your hostel the next morning if you want to catch an early ferry.
- You can take bikes on the island's buses for a flat fee of 20kr.
- A cycle route circumnavigates almost the entire island, signposted out of Visby. You can pick up a free route map from the tourist office.

Visby

VISBY is much older than its medieval trappings – which include a magnificent defensive **wall** – suggest: its name comes from *vi*, "the sacred place", and *by*, "the settlement", a derivation that reflects its status as a Stone Age sacrificial site. After the Gotlanders had founded their trading houses in the eleventh and twelfth centuries, the Hansa or Hanseatic League was created, comprising a group of towns who formed a federation to assert their interests and protect their sea-borne commerce. Visby became the place where all lines of Baltic trade met. Following the foundation of Lübeck in the 1150s, German merchants began to expand into the eastern Baltic area in order to gain access to the coveted Russian market. A trading agreement between Gotlanders and the League in 1161 gave Gotlanders the right to trade freely throughout the whole Saxon area, while Germans were able to settle in Visby, which became the principal centre of the Hanseatic League. As Visby metamorphosed from Gotlandic village to international city, it was the Germans who led the way in form and architecture, building warehouses up to six storeys high with hoists facing the street, still apparent today.

In 1350 the **Black Death** swept through Gotland, creating ghost towns of whole parishes and leaving more than eight thousand people dead. Eleven years later, during the power struggle between Denmark and Sweden, the Danish king, Valdemar III, took Gotland by force and advanced on Visby. The burghers and traders of the city, well aware of the wealth here, shut the gates and sat through the slaughter which was taking place outside, surrendering when it was over. Hostilities and piracy were the hallmarks of the following two centuries. In 1525, an army from Lübeck stormed the much weakened Visby, torching the northern parts of the town. With the arrival of the Reformation and the weakness of the local economy, the churches could no longer be maintained, and Visby's era of greatness clanged to a close.

Undoubtedly the finest approach to **Visby** today is by ship, seeing the old trading centre as it should be seen – from the sea. If you sail on one of the busy summer night-time crossings, it's good to get out on deck for the early sunrise. By 5am the sun is above the city, silhouetting the towers of the cathedral and the old wall turrets.The heady experience of gliding in on the morning tide is – much as it must have been for thirteenth-century traders – welcoming and reassuring.

Arrival and information

Visby **airport** is 3km from town, a five-minute ride on the airport bus (30kr). A **taxi** into the centre will cost around 75kr while a mini-cab will cost 65kr. All the **ferries** serving Visby dock at the same terminal, just outside the city walls. Just turn left out of the terminal and keep walking for the centre, a five-minute stroll.

The main **tourist office** is within the city walls at Hamngatan 4, conveniently en route between the ferries and the old city (mid-April to May Mon–Fri 8am–5pm, Sat & Sun 10am–4pm; June to mid-Aug Mon–Fri 7am–7pm, Sat & Sun 10am–7pm; mid-Aug to mid-April Mon–Fri 9am–4pm; ☎0498/20 17 00, fax 20 17 17). Here you can buy the excellent *Turistkarta Gotland* (25kr), a map marking and describing all the points of interest on the island, or take one of the free Visby guides – though you'll need to fork out 35kr for the best guide, entitled *Visby On Your Own*. There's also a selection of **tours** available here, one of which, the walking tour of Visby (May–Aug daily at 11.30am; 70kr), is worth considering especially if time is short.

Visby's main square, **Storatorget**, is signposted from most places. The town is best **walked** around; despite its warren-like appearance, it's a simple matter to get 'the hang of the narrow, crisscrossing cobbled streets. Modern Visby has spread beyond the limits defined by its old city walls, and today the new town gently sprawls from beyond **Österport** (East Gate), a few minutes' walk up the hill from Storatorget. Here, in **Östercentrum**, is the **bus terminal**, used by buses serving the rest of the island; the tourist office has free timetables.

Bikes can be rented just outside the ferry terminal (gearless bikes 50kr a day, bikes with up to seven gears 70kr a day; tandems 110kr a day). Bike rental is also possible at several outlets on Korsgatan. Most charge around 50kr a day; to secure a tandem, it's best to arrive early as they are popular.

ACCOMMODATION

Finding **accommodation** in Visby should seldom be a problem. There are plenty of hotels (though few are particularly cheap), several nearby campsites and cabins, and a youth hostel. This is an island where summer is everything, so there are sharp price reductions outside the high season of July and August. The Gotlandsresor office at Färjeleden 3, a short way to the right along the harbourfront from the ferry terminal (daily 8am–7pm; ☎0498/20 12 60, fax 20 12 70), and the town's tourist office can book **private rooms** (285kr for a single or 425kr for a double within the city walls, cheaper outside) and **cottages**. More information and help is available at Gotlands Turist Service at Österport (Mon–Fri 9am–6pm; ☎0498/20 33 00, fax 20 33 90), which has better access to accommodation information than the tourist office. Gotlandsresor also owns **Gula Villan,** a block of eight apartments located in front of *Hamn Hotellet* (②, summer ③).

Of Visby's several **youth hostels**, the two most central are *Visby Jernvagshotell*, Adelsgatan 9 (☎0498/27 17 07 or 21 98 32; 190kr), and the more interesting and well-placed *Fängelset Sjumastarn* (☎0498/20 60 50 or 070/426 57 60; 150kr, ①), near the harbour and just opposite the ferry terminal; within the former prison building, the latter hostel has its own café and sauna, and boasts individual rooms. The town's only **STF hostel** changes venue regularly; to track it down, call Visby Vandrarhem (☎0498/26 98 42; fax 20 42 90). Further out, 3km from Visby's centre, is the *Gotlands Ice Hockey Federation Youth Hostel* (☎0498/24 82 02, fax 24 82 70; 150kr), behind the city's ice hockey hall, Ishallen. Set in forest surroundings, this big, well-equipped place has chalets and rooms, with laundry facilities and a huge TV lounge.

Chiefly, though, Gotland is a place for **camping**. After the success of Ulf Lundell's youth-culture novel *Jack* (after Kerouac), which extolled the simple pleasure of getting wasted on a beach, Gotland became the place to go for wild summer parties: at many campsites, the most exercise you'll get is cycling to and from the Systembolaget. The closest campsite, *Nordenstrands* (☎0498/21 21 57; May–Sept), is 1km outside the city walls – follow the cycle path that runs through the Botanical Gardens along the seafront. Though the city is well supplied with **hotels**, a selection of which appears below, it's advisable to book in advance to stay here in July and August.

Donnersplats, Donnersplats 6 (☎0498/21 49 45, fax 21 49 44). A popular, central hotel that also has economical two- to three-bed apartments for 950kr, and suites for six people for 1800kr. Pleasant enough. It's essential to book in July and August, especially during Medieval Week. ③.

Gute, Mellangatan 29 (☎0498/24 80 80, fax 24 80 89). A very central, comfortable hotel with the possibility of reduced rates if you turn up at the last minute. ③, summer ④.

Hamn Hotellet, Färjeleden 3 (☎0498/20 12 50, fax 20 12 70). Opposite the harbour, this hotel is owned by Gotlandsresor and shares its reception. It's by far the most convenient hotel for early-morning ferries back to the mainland. The rather plain, en-suite rooms are perfectly comfortable. ①, summer ②.

Solhem, Solhemsgatan 3 (☎0498/27 90 70, fax 21 95 23). Just outside the city walls at Skansporten, this large, comfortable hotel has its own sauna, and the advantage of being considerably quieter than more downtown hotels. ④.

Strand, Strandgatan 34 (☎0498/25 88 00, fax 25 88 11). A rather glamorous place in a delightful street in the heart of town, with a sauna, steam bath, indoor pool. ⑤.

Villa Borgen, Adelsgatan 11 (☎0498/27 99 00, fax 24 93 00). An attractive family hotel with lovely, peaceful gardens. All rooms are en suite; there's a sauna and solarium. ④.

Wisby, Strandgatan 6 (☎0498/25 75 00, fax 25 75 50). The loveliest hotel in town, this splendid, centrally located place is housed in a building dating back to the Middle Ages. Mellow rooms and fine breakfasts (non-residents 65kr). ⑥.

The Town

The old **Hanseatic harbour** at Almedalen is now a public park; none of the town's attractions are much more than a few minutes' walk from here. Pretty **Packhusplan**, the oldest square in the city, is bisected by curving Strandgatan, which runs southwards to the fragmentary ruins of **Visborg Castle**, overlooking the harbour. Built in the fifteenth century by Erik of Pomerania, the castle was blown up by the Danes in the seventeenth century. In the opposite direction, Strandgatan runs northwest towards the sea and the lush **Botanical Gardens**, just beyond which is the **Jungfrutornet** (Maiden's Tower), where a local goldsmith's daughter was walled up alive – reputedly for betraying the city to the Danes. Today, you can climb the tower for the nice view.

Strolling around the twisting streets and atmospheric walls is not something that palls quickly, but if you need a focus, aim for **Norra Murgatan**, above the cathedral, once one of Visby's poorest areas. At the end nearest Norderport is the best view of the walls and city rooftops, and there's a rare opportunity to climb up onto the ramparts. The dark, atmospheric tower on Strandgatan, **Kruttornet** (June–Aug daily 10am–6pm), affords more grand views; while the roof of the **Helge And** church ruin (May–Sept daily 10am–6pm), which has been reinforced to allow access to the second floor, provides another central vantage point. Or head for the water's edge, where **Studentallén** is a popular late-evening haunt and the sunsets are magnificent – brilliant fiery reds, glinting mirrored waters and bobbing sailing boats in the distance.

Strandgatan itself is the best place to view the impressive **merchants' houses** looming over the narrow streets, with storerooms above the living quarters and cellars below; most notable among these properties is the clearly signposted **Burmeisterska house**, which is attractive and in good condition (June–Aug 11am–6pm; free). One of the most picturesque buildings on the street is the old pharmacy nearby, **Gamla Apoteket** (June–Aug Mon–Fri 2–6pm, Sat 10am–1pm; 10kr), a lofty old place with gloriously higgledy-piggledy windows.

GOTLANDS FORNSAL MUSEUM

At Strandgatan 14 is the fine **Gotlands Fornsal Museum** (May to mid-Sept daily 10am–5pm, mid-Sept to April Tues–Sun noon–4pm; 40kr). Housed in a mid-

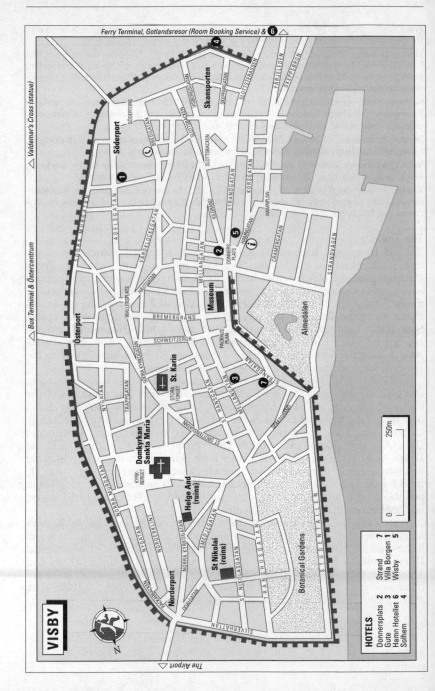

VISBY

△ Valdemar's Cross (statue)

△ Bus Terminal & Östercentrum

▽ The Airport

Ferry Terminal, Gotlandsresor (Room Booking Service) & **6** △

N

Söderport

Österport

Norderport

Skansporten

SÖDERTORG

BREDGATAN

SÖDRA MURGATAN

ADELSGATAN

VÄRDKLOCKEGATAN

HÄSTGATAN

WALLERSPLATS

SÖDRA KYRKOGATAN

NYGATAN

TRAPPGATAN

NORRA MURGATAN

NYGATAN

NORDERKLINT

NORRA KYRKOGATAN

PACKARE...

SILVERHÄTTAN

S:T DROTTNINGGATAN

ST NIKOLAIGATAN

SMEDJEGATAN

ST HANSGATAN

S:T HANSGATAN

MELLANGATAN

MELLANGATAN

PADHUS PLAN

SCHWEITZERGR

BREMERGRÄND

STORA TORGET

DONNERS PLATS

KILGRÄND

VISBYSCKEN

SLOTTSBACKEN

SLOTTSTERRASSEN

SKEPPSGATAN

FÄRJELEDEN

SKEPPSBRON

STRANDGATAN

KORSGATAN

HAMNPLAN

CRAMERGATAN

STRANDVÄGEN

STRANDGATAN

HAMNGATAN

STUDENTALLEN

TRANSHUSGATAN

SKANSGRÄND

KYRK-BERGET

Museum

St. Karin

Domkyrkan Sankta Maria

Helge And (ruins)

St Nikolai (ruins)

Botanical Gardens

Almedalen

1
2
3
5
7
4
ⅰ

0   250m

HOTELS

Donnersplats	**2**	Strand	**7**
Gute	**3**	Villa Borgen	**1**
Hamn Hotellet	**6**	Wisby	**5**
Solhem	**4**		

eighteenth century distillery, it comprises five storeys of exhibition halls covering eight thousand years of history, plus a good café and bookstore. Among the most impressive of the exhibitions is the **Hall of Picture Stones** in Room 1. Dating mostly from the fifth to seventh centuries, these large, keyhole-shaped stones are richly ornamented. The earlier ones are covered in runic inscriptions and are more intriguing, with vivid depictions of people, animals, ships and houses. The **Hall of Prehistoric Graves** is also fascinating; here skeletons dating back six thousand years are displayed in glass cases. The occupant of one was killed by a flint arrowhead lodged in his hip (the site of the wound is indicated by red arrows); another case contains the body of a 20-year-old woman from 2500 BC, alongside whom are the decorative pins she once used to fix her hair. Rooms 9 to 13 trace the history of **medieval Visby**; in room 9, you can see an actual trading booth, the sort of place where the burghers of Visby and foreign merchants would have dealt in commodities – furs, lime, wax, honey and tar – brought from all over northern Europe.

The years **1500 to 1900** are cleverly represented in a series of **tableaux**, starting with one on Eric of Pomerania, the first resident of Visborg Castle, and leading on through the years of Danish rule to the Peace of Brömsebro, when Gotland was ceded to Sweden. The central feature of the eighteenth-century section is a depiction of **Linnaeus**, later knighted von Linné, who explored the remarkable flora and fauna on the island (see p.116). In the same section is a wax model of Anna Margareta Donner, a member of the Visby-based **Donner** family who ran one of Sweden's largest trading houses of the time. The Donner name can still be seen all over the centre of the city, notably the square in which the tourist office stands.

VISBY ART MUSEUM

A couple of streets up on St Hansgatan, **Visby Art Museum** at no. 21 (May to mid-Sept 10am–5pm; 30kr) has some very innovative temporary exhibitions of contemporary painting and sculpture, and installations which really tease the eye. Though for the most part much less exciting, the permanent work on the top floor is given over to twentieth-century Gotlandic art, and among the few notable classics is Axel Lindman's 1917 oil of Visby from the beach, showing brilliant dabs of sun before a storm. The eye is also drawn to a stunning picture by William Blair Bruce of his wife, the sculptress Carolina. The painting from 1891 shows her working on a sculpture, and the lifelike qualities of the style are remarkable.

THE TOWN WALL AND VALDEMAR'S CROSS

The oldest of the towers in Visby's town wall is the **Gunpowder Tower**, built in the eleventh century to protect the old harbour. The **wall** itself, a three-kilometre circuit enclosing the entire settlement, was built around the end of the thirteenth century for a rather different purpose: it was actually aimed at isolating the city's foreign traders from the locals.

Valdemar's Cross, a few hundred metres east of Söderport (South Gate), marks the mass grave, excavated in the twentieth century, of two thousand people, more than half of them women, children and invalids; they were slaughtered when the Danish King Valdemar attacked the town in 1361. Erected by the survivors of the carnage, it reads pathetically: "In 1361 on the third day after St James, the Goths fell into the hands of the Danes. Here they lie. Pray for them."

A section of the wall near Söderport was broken down to allow Valdemar to ride through as conqueror. **Valdemar's Breach** is recognizable by its thirteen crenellations representing, so the story goes, the thirteen knights who rode through with the Danish king. Valdemar soon left, in possession of booty and trade agreements, and Visby continued to prosper while the countryside around it stagnated, its people and wealth destroyed.

VISBY'S CHURCHES

At the height of its power, Visby maintained more **churches** than any other town in Sweden – sixteen in all, most of which are dramatic ruins today. However, one, the **Domkyrkan Sankta Maria** (Cathedral of St Mary; Mon–Fri & Sun 8am–9pm, Sat 8am–6.30pm), is still in use. Constructed between 1190 and 1225, it was built for visiting Germans, becoming the German Parish Church when they settled in the city. In 1300, a large Gothic chapel was built to the south, the eastern tower was elevated, and the nave was raised to create storage space; this was where the burghers kept their money, papers and records. It's been heavily restored, and about the only original fixture left is the thirteenth-century sandstone font inside. Most striking are its **towers**, a square one at the western front end and two slimmer eastern ones, standing sentry over the surrounding buildings. Originally each had spires, but following an eighteenth-century fire, they were crowned with fancy Baroque cupolas, giving them the appearance of inverted ice-cream cones. Inside, have a look beneath the pulpit, decorated with a fringe of unusually ugly angels' faces.

Seventeenth- and eighteenth-century builders and decorators found the smaller churches in the city to be an excellent source of free limestone, tiles and fittings – which accounts for the fact that most are ruins today. Considering the number of tourists clambering about them, it's surprising that the smaller church ruins manage to retain a proud yet abandoned look. Best of what's left is the great **St Nicolai** ruin, just down the road from the Domkyrkan. Destroyed in 1525, its part-Gothic, part-Romanesque shell hosts a week-long **chamber music festival**, starting at the end of July; tickets range from 150kr to 300kr and are available from the tourist office. One of the loveliest ruins to view at night is **St. Karin's** (St. Catherine's; mid June to mid-Aug daily 10am–6pm; 10kr) on Storatorget; its Gothic interior is one of the finest here, having belonged to one of Visby's first Franciscan monasteries founded in 1233. This church was built in 1250; at night its glorious arches, lit creamy yellow, frame the blue-black sky.

The tourist office gives away a reasonably informative English-language **guide**, *The Key to all of Gotland's Churches*, which lists the key features of all 92 churches on the island in alphabetical order. These are also found near the entrance of most of the churches themselves.

Eating, drinking and nightlife

Adelsgatan is lined with cafés and snack bars. At lunchtime, the eating places at Wallersplats, the square at Adelsgatan's northern end, and Hästgatan, the street leading off the square to the southwest, are particularly busy; Strandgatan is the focus of Visby dining in the evening (Hästgatan also boasts a number of evening restaurants). For good, cheap food all day, try *Saluhallen,* the **market** opposite the old harbour. Here you can buy freshly baked bread, fish and fruit, and eat at

---

MEDIEVAL WEEK

During the second week of August, Visby becomes the backdrop for a boisterous re-enactment of the conquest of the island by the Danes in 1361. **Medieval Week** sees music in the streets, medieval food on sale in the restaurants (no potatoes – they hadn't yet been brought to Europe) and on the Sunday a procession re-enacting Valdemar's triumphant entry through Söderport to Storatorget. Here, people in the role of burghers are stripped of their wealth, and then the procession moves on to the Maiden's Tower. Locals and visitors alike really get into the spirit of this festival, with a good fifty percent of everyone all dressed up and on the streets.

---

tables overlooking the water. For inexpensive fare at night, the lively **Donnersplats** has lots of stalls selling takeaway food.

Youthful **nightlife** is to be had down at the harbour. The unmarked *Anton's Pub*, at the northern end, is filled with old rock hits and folk music, both live and on record; *Skeppet*, next door, is a lively place too. A couple of boats are also bars: *Graceland* is popular with a 35-plus crowd, its *Priscilla Bar* pouring out Elvis hits (noon–2am). Many of Visby's discos and clubs open in the late afternoon (around 4pm onwards) for people to have cheap beer, post-beach.

Gotlanders enjoy a unique licence from the state to brew their own **beer**, the recipe differing from household to household. Though it's never for sale, summer parties are awash with the stuff – be warned that it's extremely strong and murky.

CAFÉS

Café Björkstugan, Späksgränd. In a lush garden on the prettiest central cobbled street, this little café only serves savoury and sweet pies, and coffees. Daily 11.30am–10pm.

Café Lupo, Hästgatan, just inside the city walls and near Österport. Nothing special to look at, this place is good for strong coffee and superb, fruity muffins (try pear, raspberry and cardamom). Daily 9am–6pm.

Café Ryska Gården, Storatorget. Amid fine rustic decor, you can sample a local speciality, *saffranspanskakka*, a saffron-yellow rice pie – rather more winning in colour than taste – which is served along with Gotland's own salmberry (a sweet, hybrid berry) jam and cream. Also serves sumptuous pies. Mon–Sat 10am–11pm, Sun 11am–11pm.

Gula Huset, Tranhusgatan 2, near the Botanical Gardens. This is where the locals come – a cosy place serving delightful home-baked port-wine cake and concoctions of almonds, chocolate and fruit, in an unspoiled garden setting. Summer daily noon–5pm, autumn Sun noon–4pm.

Kafé Strandporten, just outside Almedalen park, near the harbour and looking onto Strandgatan. A candle-lit, splendidly rustic place, it serves *saffranspanskakka*, superb fruit pies, as well as good-value light savoury dishes. June–Aug daily 9am–10pm.

Skafferiet, Adelsgatan. In a lovely eighteenth-century house, with a lush garden at the back, this café is full of character. Serves baked potatoes and great cakes.

Vinäger Cafe Bar, Hästgatan 3 (☎0498/21 11 60). A great place for giant muffins, terrific cakes and pies and a relaxed, mellow atmosphere; also good for massive filled baguettes and plates of healthy, filling salads. Daily 10am–9pm.

RESTAURANTS AND BARS

Acacia Restaurant, on Strandgatan, opposite Fornsal Museum. Not the most sophisticated of places, this very popular café and kebab joint caters to a young, chatty crowd.

Bakfickan, corner St Katarinegatan and Storatorget (☎0498/27 18 07). A quiet, relaxed little restaurant, with a tiled interior. It's a good place for a drink and seafood. Daily 11am–11pm.

Barbeque Garden, Strandgatan 15. This is a huge pizza restaurant, with indoor and extensive outdoor seating. Lots of cocktails.

Boråslagret, St Hansgatan 35 (☎0498/27 19 81). At the back of *Munk Källaren*. The eclectic menu at this mellow place includes a wide choice of mezes.

Burmeister, Strandgatan. A full à la carte menu with starters at around 80kr, pasta (90kr) and main courses at 160kr. Pizzas can also be had for a pricey 90–100kr.

Café Boheme, Hästgatan 9. Young and lively without being frenetic, this place serves inexpensive salads, sandwiches and pizzas and lots of cakes, including a rather good *chokkladdkaka* (a gooey chocolate pie). Also try the Swedish speciality, rose-hip soup – unusual, healthy and cheap at 28kr. June–Aug Mon–Sat 11am–11pm; Sept–May shorter hours.

Clematis Medeltidskrogen, Strandgatan 20. By far Visby's most brilliantly atmospheric restaurant, in the vaulted half-cellars of a thirteenth-century house; the place packs out in summer. Mead is served in flagons here, while the food comes in rough ceramic bowls. A veritable banquet costs 225kr. The place is only open July and during Medieval Week at the start of August; at other times, group bookings can be made through the Fornsal Museum.

Friheten, Donnersplats. A lively pub attached to *Wisby Hotel*. The sound of loud, live bands reverberates here on Friday and Saturday evenings. Daily 11.30am–2am.

Gutekällaren, Lilla Torggränd, just a couple of steps up from *Boråslagret* (see above) and fronting onto Stora Torget. Less frenetic than the other Stora Torg restaurants, this one has excellent, quite costly food, with main courses from 140–190kr.

Kors & Tvars, St Hansgatan 51 (☎0498/28 28 28). This very good restaurant specializes in superb home-made pasta dishes and very little else – a good choice for vegetarians and lovers of lots of fresh herbs and spices. Open all year.

Munk Källeren, Lilla Torggränd, opposite *Gutekällaren*. Massively popular, this is *the* place to be seen. There's an extensive à la carte menu, all in English.

Nunnan Restaurant and Pub, Storatorget. A lively, crowded, sit-down eating place attracting a mixed-age group spilling out onto this bustling square.

Trädgårn, Hästgatan. Has a pleasant terrace eating with lots of salads, light meals at 78kr and more costly mains. Noon–midnight.

Wallers Krog, Wallers Plats (☎0498/24 99 88). Well regarded by locals for its good food, this restaurant has a menu mostly given over to meat dishes. The speciality three-course meal at 267kr comprises salmon, lamb and saffron pancake.

Listings

Banks and exchange Östercentrum has the largest concentration of branches for changing money; the tourist office also has fairly good rates and charges no fee.

Car rental Avis, Donnersplats 2 (☎0498/21 98 10, fax 21 84 20); Hertz, at the airport (☎0498/248550).

Ferries Buy tickets down at the terminal buildings or at the travel agency on Södertorg.

Market Fruit, veg and souvenirs in Storatorget. Open Mon–Fri all year, and Sat also in summer.

Post office Norra Hansegatan 2 (Mon–Fri 9am–6pm, Sat 10am–noon).

Systembolaget In Storatorget and at Östervägen 3.

Central Gotland: Roma, Romakloster and around

Heading straight down Route 143 southeast of Visby leads after 15km to **ROMA**; bus #11 from Visby's bus station runs here three times each morning and 3–4 times in the afternoon. Nothing to do with Rome, this small settlement gleans its name from "room" or "open space", as this was the original location of ancient Gotland's courthouse. The place looks something of a ghost town as its century-old sugar-beet factory, to the right of the main road as you approach from Visby, has recently closed, and the early twentieth-century cottages fronting Route 143 are also deserted (they can't be demolished, though, as they're perceived as having rarity value). The church here, dating from 1215, is large and pretty; its three-aisled nave gives it a surprisingly Romanesque appearance, and because of this the church is known as the False Basilica.

Just 1km further down the road, the Cistercian cloister ruins, **Romakloster**, are the real draw of the area; take a left down a long avenue of beech trees. The crumbling Roma monastery, dating from 1164, lacks both apse and tower, being Romanesque in design; it would once have comprised a church with three wings built around a rectangular cloister. What is left is sturdy stuff – big arches of grey stone blocks so regular they could be breeze block. The multitude of spotlights set in the ground here make it very dramatic as a backdrop for night-time **theatre**, with Shakespeare being performed here every summer, though they detract from the site's timeless character by day. The ruin is not the isolated site one might expect, as it's behind the cream-stucco **manor house** built in the 1730s for the county governor. Part of the monastery was in fact destroyed by the Danish crown during the Reformation of the early sixteenth century, and it was further ruined when the governor used materials from it in the building of the house. Temporary art exhibitions are held within (20kr), and there's a **café** here serving delicious sweet pies.

Practicalities

For cheap and basic **accommodation**, the guide Peter Doolk provides rooms in his manor-house home at the hamlet of Viklau (☎0498/512 12; 100kr). *Konstnärsgården* (☎0498/550 55) is a complex of art galleries south of Roma, just off Route 143; the main reason to come here, though, is to **eat** at the appealing and popular **restaurant** round the back, serving filling meals including excellent fish and meat dishes for 78kr, and a special children's menu (53kr). It's open daily in summer (noon–9pm). There's also a café here, offering the usual baguettes and cakes.

The south of Gotland: Hemse to Ljugarn

The so-called "capital" of the south, **HEMSE**, around 50km from Visby (buses come here along Route 142), is little more than a main street. The **bus station**, parallel with Storgatan (head down Ronevägen for one block and turn left), is oddly located in a boarded-up and vandalized house. Hemse does have a couple of banks and a good local café and bakery, *Bageri & Conditori Johansson* on Storgatan – this is where to stock up with food and provisions. You can rent **bikes** from two places on Ronevägen, off Storgatan: Hemse Krog and, next door, Ondrell's, which is the cheapest place in town (☎0498/48 03 33; 40kr per for the first day, 20kr on each subsequent day after or 160kr per week); it also rents trailers. There's not a lot else to Hemse, except for a swimming pool (June–Aug Mon–Thurs 2–8pm, Fri 5–8pm; 35kr, solarium 40kr), signposted "*simhall*", off Storgatan at the north end of the town.

Taking Route 144 east, signposted for Burs, you'll find the countryside is a glorious mix of meadows, ancient farms and dark, mysterious forest. At **Flors**, you'll come across Studioglass Ronny Carlsson, a small glass and ceramics works where you can watch the experts blowing simple semi-opaque blue glassware. One of the most charming villages just a couple of kilometres further on, **BURS** has a gorgeous thirteenth-century saddle church, so-called because of its low nave and high tower and chancel. There's a fabulously decorated ceiling, medieval stained-glass windows and ornately painted pews. For a really friendly, locals' café, the nearby *Burs Café* (June–Aug daily noon–10pm; Sept–May Tues–Sun 4–9pm) serves cheap, filling meals like beef stroganoff, or hamburgers made with Gotland beef for just 30kr (25kr to takeaway).

När and Lau

Heading east from Burs, following signs to the pretty, tranquil hamlet of När, you encounter a paradise of wild, flowering meadows and medieval farm holdings, untouched by the centuries, with ancient windows and carved wooden portals. **När** itself is notable for its church, set in an immaculate churchyard. The tower originally served as a fortification in the thirteenth century; more arresting are the bizarre portraits painted on the pew-ends right the way up the left-side of the church. All depict women with demented expressions and bare, oddly placed breasts. A couple of kilometres north and just beyond the village of **LAU**, *Garde* **youth hostel** (☎0498/49 11 81, fax 49 11 81; 95kr; pre-book outside summer) provides accommodation in a cluster of buildings situated right by the local football pitch. There's a food shop (daily 9am–7pm) around the corner from the hostel reception. For a delightful daytime café, art gallery and evening bar, try *Svinhuset* (Tues–Sun 11am–6pm; pub June–Aug till 9pm, Sept–May Sat & Sun only), set in lovely countryside. The pub's mascot, a pot-bellied pig, wanders around the place while you drink.

Ljugarn

For beaches, and the nearest thing Gotland has to a resort, the lively and charming town of **LJUGARN** makes a good base. You can get here from Roma by heading straight down Route 143; from Lau, just head north following the signs for Ljugarn. The **tourist office** (daily: May & mid-Aug to mid-Sept 11am–4pm; June 9am–6pm, July to mid-Aug 9am–7pm) is just off the main road as you approach town, and has plenty of information about the southeast of the island. Ljugarn, though full of restaurants and obviously aimed at tourists, retains an authentic feel; it's famous for its *rauker* – tall limestone pillars rising up from the sea.

Claudelinska Huset, on Storgatan (the main street) opposite *Kräkan* restaurant (see below), is an **art gallery** (open 2–6pm; free) in the rather fine drawing room of a private house, complete with old Gustavian furniture and Indian silk carpets on sloping wooden floors; it's these that appeal, though the temporary exhibitions can be worth a view too. It's only 100m to the popular beaches from here. A delightful cycle or stroll down Strandvägen follows the coastline through woods and clearings carpeted in *blåeld,* the electric-blue flowers for which the area is known. The *rauker* along the route stand like ancient hunched men, their feet lapped by the waves.

The **tourist office** at Hallute backe (☎0498/49 34 60, 49 30 60) will book **private rooms** from 125kr (plus 10 percent booking fee). Ljugarn has a range of eating places and accommodation to suit most tastes. Rooms ("*Rums*") are advertised in appealing-looking cottages all over the little town, and Ljugarn's STF **youth hostel** (☎0498/49 31 84; 105kr; May–Aug), on Strandridaregården, has two- to six-bed rooms. Just off this street is Gotland's oldest **B&B**, *Badpensionatet*

(☎0498/49 32 05; ②); it opened its doors in 1921. All the rooms here have toilet, shower and telephone; there's also a restaurant (daily noon–10pm), with lunch at 55kr and evening meals with two or three courses for 138–160kr. Cheap but perfectly functional rooms are available at *Storvägen 91*, its name being its address (☎0498/49 34 16; ①); **bike rental** here costs 35kr per day.

For a splendid **café**, *Café Espegards* on Storvägen is a must (daily 9am–8pm). Serving some of the best cakes you could find anywhere in Sweden – try their lemon-iced tart – it's very popular, so expect a queue. Further down Storvägen, on the corner of Claudelinsvägen, is *Kräkan*, the best fish **restaurant** in town (daily 5pm–1am), with main courses at 130–240kr. A lovely, relaxed place, it also has plenty of meat options and a decent wine list. A few steps further down the street is *Brunna Dorren* (Mon–Thurs & Sun noon–midnight, Fri & Sat noon–1am), a pizza place in a pleasant old stuccoed house (pizzas 60kr, other light meals 35–65kr). A surprisingly genteel place for a tasty snack is *Strandcafé*, located on the beach itself (daily 10am–10pm); it's done up like a country kitchen and has luscious cakes, as well as salads, hamburgers, pies.

Stånga

Heading back west from Ljugarn, Route 144 passes through **Lye**, a charming if sleepy hamlet. Just a few kilometres on is the village of **STÅNGA**, home to a fourteenth-century church that's worth visiting for the extremely unusual sculptured wall tablets running down the facade; these are attributed to Egypticus, a sculptor whose exact identity has never been discovered, but who shows strong Egyptian influences. Inside this atmospheric church, which has little in the way of windows, is a single, heavily carved stone pillar decorated with a grotesque gargoyle. Likewise, the twelfth-century font has fanged monsters devouring frog-like creatures around its base.

By the golf course outside is a fine **place to stay** at a very reasonable price, *Gumbalda Golf* (☎0498/48 28 80, fax 48 28 84; ①). A beautiful wooden hotel occupying old stables, it's a perfect base for exploring the south.

The north of Gotland: from Visby to Slite

Thirteen kilometres north of Visby are the **Lummelundagrotta**, limestone caves, stalagmites and stalactites that are a disappointingly dull and damp stop (daily: May to late June & mid- to late Aug 9am–4pm; late June to mid-Aug 9am–6pm; late Aug to mid-Sept 10am–2pm; 45kr). There's a more interesting natural phenomenon 10km to the north, where you'll see the highest of Gotland's coastal *rauker* (see opposite). The remnants of reefs formed over four hundred million years ago, the fact that the stacks are now well above the tide line is proof that sea levels were once much higher. This particular stack, 11.5m high and known as **Jungfruklint**, is said to look like the Virgin and Child – something you'll need a fair bit of imagination to discern.

Instead of taking the coastal road from Visby, you could head inland towards the village of **BRO**, which has one of the island's most beautiful churches. Several different stages of construction are evident from the Romanesque and Gothic windows in its tower. The most unusual aspect is the south wall, with its flat-relief picture stones, carved mostly with animals, that were incorporated from a previous church that once stood on the site. On the whole, though, it's better to press on further into the eminently picturesque north, where many of the secluded cottages are summer holiday homes for urban Swedes. The peninsula north of **Lärbro** is no longer prohibited to foreign tourists now the army has left. At the village of **BUNGE**, it's worth visiting the bright fourteenth-century fortified church, and the open-air museum of seventeenth- to nineteenth-century buildings (mid-May to mid-Aug daily 10am–6pm; 30kr). **SLITE**, just to the south of Lärbro, is the island's only really ugly place – the day-trip buses pass right by its cement factories, quarries and monumentally dull architecture. Beyond, though, Slite has a sandy beach and good swimming; its **campsite** (☎22 08 30; May–Sept), right on the beach, is a reasonable place to stay.

The islands around Gotland

The two islands of **Stora Karlsö** and **Lilla Karlsö**, lying over 6km off the southwest coast, have been declared nature reserves: both have **bird sanctuaries** where razorbills, guillemots, falcons and eider duck breed relatively undisturbed. On Lilla Karlso you'll also see the unique horned Gute sheep. It's possible to reach Stora Karlsö from Klintehamn some 30km south of Visby on Route 140; tickets are available from the harbour office for sailings at 9am and 11am (200kr return; 45min). There are also daily tours from Visby (May–Aug, a few in Sept; book on ☎0498/24 05 00; 250kr per person). Lilla Karlsö is reached from Djupvik (120kr return; tickets from the harbour office or book on ☎0498/48 52 48), 7km south of Klintehamn (no buses). You can stay in hostel-style accommodation, near the pier (☎0498/24 11 39; 100kr).

The only **accommodation** on Stora Karlsö is at the STF **youth hostel**, which puts guests up in tiny fishermen's huts sleeping up to four people (☎0498/24 05 00, fax 24 52 60; 200–280kr per night for a hut); as picturesque as it sounds, it's also extremely basic, with no showers. There are restaurant facilities for breakfast and dinner. Any other kind of camping is not allowed on the islands.

Fårö

Most of **Fårö** island is flat limestone heath, with shallow lakes and stunted pines much in evidence. In winter (and sometimes in summer, too) the wind whips over the Baltic, justifying the existence of the local windmills – and of the sheep shelters, with their steeply pitched reed roofs, modelled on traditional Fårö houses. Examples of both line the road as you leave the ferry.

The best place to head for is the five-kilometre arc of white sand at **Sudersandsviken**; much of the rest of the swimming is done at **Ekeviken**, on the other side of the isthmus. The rest of the coastline is rocky, spectacularly so at **Lauterhorn** and, particularly, **Langhammars**, where limestone stacks (see p.350) are grouped together on the beach. At Lauterhorn you can follow the signs for Digerhuvud, a long line of stacks leading to the tiny fishing hamlet of **Helgumannen**, which is no more than a dozen shacks on the beach, now used as holiday homes. There are fine **diving** opportunities here. Continuing along the same rough track brings you to a junction; right runs back to the township of Fårö; left, a two-kilometre dead-end road leads to Langhammars.

You can get to Fårö by taking a bus from Visby to the town of **Fårösund** and making the ferry crossing from there (daily every 15min; 30min; free). There's a down-at-heel but surprisingly good **café** in town, *Fårösund Grill*, which serves

INGMAR BERGMAN

Since the mid-1960s, Sweden's best known film director and screenwriter, **Ingmar Bergman**, has lived for much of the time on Fårö. He was born in 1918, the son of a Lutheran pastor. The combination of his harsh upbringing, his interest in the religious art of old churches, and the works of August Strindberg inspired Bergman constantly to consider the spiritual and psychological conflicts of life in his films. The results – he made forty feature films between 1946 and 1983 – are certainly dark, and for many, deeply distressing and/or depressing. He made his first breakthrough at the Cannes Film Festival in 1944, winning the Grand Prix for his film *Hets* (*Persecution*), based on his school life. Among his best-known movies are the *The Seventh Seal*, starring Max von Sydow, and *Wild Strawberries*. The two most prevalent themes in his films were marriage and the motives for marital infidelity, and the divide between sanity and madness. One of his finest films, *Fanny and Alexander* (1983), portrays bourgeois life in Scandinavia at the turn of the twentieth century; it's actually based on the lives of his own maternal grandparents and was to be the last major film he made.

Bergman married five times (divorcing all but the last of his wives, who died in 1995). One of his eight children, Lin, wasn't the result of marriage – her mother is the actress Liv Ullman.

excellent sandwiches (25kr), a moist almond tart (10kr), and good, cheap coffee. Just opposite is *Bungehallen*, a very well-stocked supermarket (daily till 10pm).

Gotska Sandön

To experience real solitude, head for the untouched island of **Gotska Sandön**, 38km north of Fårö. The most isolated island in the Baltic, this nine-kilometre-long blob of land boasts 30km of deep, sandy beaches. Bronze needles and buckles, indicating the presence of ancient settlements, have been found all around the island. Traditionally, this is where Fårö residents came to kill seals. In the early to mid-nineteenth century, a hundred people lived here (it was also said to be a base for pirates at the time); nowadays, the only human residents on the island are lighthouse personnel.

Wildlife here is limited – certainly more so than on the southern islands of Stora and Lilla Karlsö (see opposite). The bird population includes parrot crossbills, which nest here in early spring, and mountain hares, a fairly common sight as they have no natural enemies here. Other **rare birds** are willow warblers and red-breasted flycatchers. The long horned beetle is also in attendance; at over 8cm in length, it causes visitors who have come to look for it great excitement. In terms of **fauna**, there's a good possibility of seeing lots of **orchids** and heathers, and stately clusters of red hellebore.

There's an **information point** for Gotska Sandön (call ☎0498/22 59 14 or fax 22 59 17). **Tours** here run in summer from Fårö and from Nynäshamn, with visitors being put ashore one to four kilometres from the island's **campsite**. However, if winds are unfavourable, you may be dropped up to 9km away. Your baggage can be taken to the campsite by tractor, but you'll have to get there on foot. Once at the site, you can either stay in your own tent or in a cottage; though there's drinking water, you'll need to bring your own food as there are no shops. Limited first aid and a telephone are available at the site.

travel details

Trains

Jönköping to: Falköping (change for Stockholm & Gothenburg; hourly; 45min); Nässjo (change for Stockholm & Malmö; hourly; 35min).

Kalmar to: Gothenburg (5 daily; 4hr 15min) plus more frequent local trains from Emmaboda and Växjo; Malmö (8 daily; 3hr 40min); Stockholm (5 daily; 6hr 30min); Växjo (10 daily; 1hr 15min).

Motala to: Hallsberg (for Örebro, Stockholm & Gothenburg; 6 daily; 45min); Mjöbly (for Malmö & Stockholm; 2 daily; 15min).

Norrköping to: Linköping (1 or 2 hourly; 25min); Malmö (11 daily; 3hr 15min); Nyköping (5 daily; 40min); Stockholm (hourly; 1hr 40min).

Oskarshamn to: Gothenburg (3 daily; 5hr 30min); Nässjo (3 daily; 2hr 25min); Jönköping (3 daily; 3hr 20min).

Växjo to: Kalmar (6 daily; 1hr 40min); Karlskrona (2 daily; 1hr 30min).

Örebro to: Gävle (6 daily; 3–4hr); Hallsberg (change for Stockholm & Gothenburg; 1 or 2 hourly; 20min); Motala (6 daily; 1hr 30min); Stockholm (7 daily; 3hr 10min).

Buses

Jönköping to: Gothenburg (Mon–Fri 2, Sun 3; 2hr 15min); Gränna/Vadstena/Motala/Örebro (up to 2 daily; 30min/1hr 20min/1hr 40min/3hr 5min); Växjo (Fri & Sun 1; 1hr 20min).

Kalmar to: Gothenburg (1 daily; 6hr); Lund/Malmö (1 daily; 5hr 30min/5hr 45min); Oskarshamn/Västervik/Stockholm (3 daily; 1hr 25min/2hr 35min/6hr 50min).

Motala to: Norrköping/Stockholm (Fri & Sun 2; 1hr 35min/3hr 25min).

Norrköping to: Kalmar (5 daily; 4hr 15min); Linköping/Jönköping/Gothenburg (6 daily; 30min/2hr 40min/4hr 55min); Löfstad Manor (every 2hr; 20min); Stockholm (5 daily; 2hr 10min).

Växjo to: Jönköping/Linköping/Norrköping/Stockholm/Uppsala (Fri & Sun 1; 1hr 20min/3hr 30min/4hr/6hr 30min/7hr 30min).

Ferries

Nynäshamn to: Visby (mid-June to mid-Aug 3 daily; 5hr day, 6hr night).

Oskarshamn to: Byxelkrok (3 daily, mid-June to mid-Aug); Visby (mid-June to mid-Aug 1 daily; 4hr day, 6hr night).

Timmernabben to: Borgholm (3 daily, mid-June to mid-Aug).

Plus **fast ferries**

Oskarshamn to: Visby 1 daily 2 hours 30 min, **Nynashamn** to: Visby two to three daily, 3 hours. No night time crossings on fast ferries.

Throughout the rest of the year, the service between Visby and Nynäshamn or Oskarshamn is usually night boats only and is much less frequent.

CHAPTER FIVE

THE BOTHNIAN COAST: GÄVLE TO HAPARANDA

S weden's east coast forms one edge of the **Gulf of Bothnia** (Bottenhavet), a corridor of land that, with its jumble of erstwhile fishing towns and squeaky-clean contemporary urban planning, is quite unlike the rest of the north of the country. The Bothnian coast is dominated by towns and cities; the forest, so apparent in other parts of the north, has been felled here to make room for settlements. Almost the entire coastline is dotted with towns and villages that reveal a faded history. Some, like **Gävle** and **Hudiksvall**, still have their share of old wooden houses, promoting evocative images of the past, though much was lost during the Russian incursions of the eighteenth century. Today, though, cities like **Sundsvall**, **Umeå** and **Luleå** are more typical of the region – modern, bright and airy metropolises that rank as some of Sweden's liveliest and most likeable destinations.

Throughout the north you'll find traces of the religious fervour that swept the region in centuries past; **Skellefteå**, **Piteå** and particularly **Luleå** (included on the UNESCO World Heritage List) all boast excellently preserved *kyrkstäder* or parish villages, clusters of old wooden cottages dating from the early eighteenth century, where villagers from outlying districts would spend the night after making the lengthy journey to church in the nearest town. Working your way up the coast, perhaps on the long train ride to **Lapland**, it's worth breaking your trip at one or two of these places.

The highlight of the Bothnian coast is undoubtedly the stretch known as the **Höga Kusten**, or the High Coast (see p.375), between Härnösand and Örn-

---

ACCOMMODATION PRICES

The pensions and hotels listed in the guide have been price-graded according to the scale given below; the price category given against each establishment indicates the cost of the least expensive double rooms there. Many hotels offer considerable reductions at weekends all year round, and during the summer holiday period (mid-June to mid-Aug); in these cases the reduction is either noted in the text or, where a discount brings a hotel into another price band, given after the number for the full price. Single rooms, where available, usually cost between 60 and 80 percent of a double. Where hostels have double rooms, we've given price codes for them also.

① under 500kr	③ 700–900kr	⑤ 1200–1500kr
② 500–700kr	④ 900–1200kr	⑥ over 1500kr

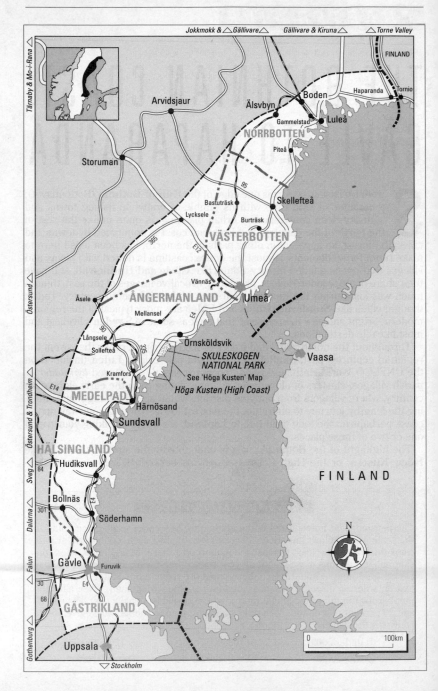

Jokkmokk & △Gällivare△   Gällivare & Kiruna△   △Torne Valley

FINLAND

Tärnaby & Mo-i-Rana

Arvidsjaur

Boden

Haparanda   Tornio

Älsvbyn

Gammelstad   Luleå

NORRBOTTEN

Storuman

Piteå

95

Bastuträsk   Skellefteå

Lycksele   Burträsk

VÄSTERBOTTEN

Östersund

E12

365

Vännäs

Åsele   ÅNGERMANLAND   Umeå

Mellansel

Vaasa

E4

Långsele

335

Sollefteå   Örnsköldsvik

Kramfors   SKULESKOGEN
NATIONAL PARK

E14   See 'Höga Kusten' Map

Östersund & Trondheim

MEDELPAD   Höga Kusten (High Coast)

Härnösand

Sundsvall

HÄLSINGLAND

FINLAND

Sveg

84   Hudiksvall

Bollnäs

Dalarna

301   E4

Söderhamn

N

Falun

Gävle   Furuvik

30

68   E4

Gothenburg

GÄSTRIKLAND

Uppsala

0   100km

▽ Stockholm

sköldsvik – for peace and quiet, this is easily the most idyllic part of the Swedish east coast. Its indented coastline is best seen from the sea, with shimmering fjords that reach deep inland, tall cliffs and a string of pine-clad islands that make it possible to island-hop up the coast. There's also good **hiking** to be had here in the **Skuleskogen National Park** (see p.382). The weather along this stretch of coast may not be as reliable as further south, but you're guaranteed clean beaches (which you'll often have to yourself), crystal clear waters and some of the finest countryside for walking.

Travel practicalities

The **train** route north from Uppsala hugs the coast from Gävle until just beyond Härnösand, where InterCity services terminate. From here, a branch line swings inland, joining up in Långsele with the **main line to Lapland** and on to the Norwegian port of Narvik. To head north along the High Coast from Härnösand, you'll need to catch one of the **buses** through Örnsköldsvik and Umeå to Luleå, where you can connect back onto the train. There are also several bus services running inland from Örnsköldsvik, Umeå and Skellefteå, which can whisk you up into the mountains.

Regular train services between **Stockholm** and **Sundsvall** stop at Gävle, Söderhamn and Hudiksvall; from Sundsvall, there are a handful of trains on to **Härnösand**, some of which are through services from Stockholm. There's also a handy train and bus connection to Sundsvall from the inland town of Östersund (see p.438). After Härnösand things get more tricky; just two trains a day run to **Långsele** via Kramfors and Sollefteå (there are also three buses plying this route that accept train tickets and passes). At Långsele, you can connect onto the night train up to **Boden**, **Luleå**, **Gällivare** and **Kiruna**, but not Umeå; the best option to get to **Umeå** is to take the direct night train from Stockholm or Gävle (only bus connections are available from Söderhamn and Hudiksvall) which runs via Vännäs.

Along the High Coast, island-hopping between Härnösand and Örnsköldsvik – via Högbonden, Ulvön and Trysunda (see p.375) – is a wonderful way to make your way north and to take in one of northern Sweden's most beautiful regions at the same time. Ferry tickets here are good value; see p.377 for details. From Örnsköldsvik north, there are frequent **Norrlandskusten** bus services (see p.408) to Luleå via Umeå, Skellefteå and Piteå.

From Luleå, it's quite possible to travel **south** by **bus** to Härnösand (as above but in reverse), taking in the High Coast if you wish; you'll be able to pick up train services again in Härnösand. Heading south from Luleå or Lapland by **train**, you can get to Östersund by changing at Bräcke, or Sundsvall by changing at Ånge. There's also a handy night train from Umeå to **Stockholm**.

Gävle

It's only one and a half hours north by train from Stockholm to **GÄVLE** (pronounced "Yev-luh", and confusingly similar to a much used Swedish swearword), capital of the county of Gästrikland. Gävle is also the southernmost city of **Norrland**, the region – comprising two-thirds of Sweden – which represents wilderness territory in the thinking of most Swedes. To all intents and purposes, Norrland means everything north of Uppsala; crossing into here from Svealand (as the rest of the country is sometimes called) is – as far as the Swedish psyche is concerned – like leaving civilization behind.

Gävle's town charter was granted as long ago as 1446, a fact that's at variance with the modernity of the centre's large squares, broad avenues and proud monumental buildings. The city was almost completely rebuilt after a devastating fire in 1869, and its docks and warehouses reflect the heady success of its late nineteenth-century industry, when Gävle was the export centre for locally produced iron and timber. Today, the city is more famous as the home of **Gevalia coffee** ("Gevalia" being the old Latinized name for the town), which you'll no doubt taste during your time in Sweden. If you're heading north for Höga Kusten only, Gävle makes a good, brief, stop; if you're travelling all the way into Lapland, you'd do better to break your journey further north than Gävle, in Sundsvall or Umeå, say.

Arrival, information and accommodation

The city centre is concentrated in the grid of streets spreading southwest from the **train station** on Stora Esplanadgatan. You'll find left-luggage lockers (15kr) on the main platform. The **bus station** is linked to the train station by the subway that goes under the train tracks. A two-minute walk from the train station is the **tourist office** at Drottninggatan 37 (June–Aug Mon–Fri 9am–6pm, Sat 9am–2pm, Sun 11am–4pm; Sept–May Mon–Fri 9am–5pm; ☎026/14 74 30, *www.gavle.se*). They will book private **apartments** from 345kr per person per night (cheaper by the week or month). Gävle has two **youth hostels**, one of which is superbly located in the old quarter at Södra Rådmansgatan 1 (☎026/62 17 45, fax 61 59 90; 120kr). The other is on the coast at Bönavägen 118 in **Engeltofta**, 6km northeast of the city (☎026/961 60, fax 960 55; 120kr; May–Aug); to get there, take bus #5 from Rådhuset (12 daily). Gävle's **campsite**, which has cabins for rent, (☎026/980 28) is by the amusement park out at Furuvik (see p.361), a bus ride away on either #821, #838 or #832, which leave roughly every half-hour. It's much better to make use of *Allemansrätt* and camp rough somewhere on the outskirts of town. The town has a number of decent **hotels**, listed below.

Aveny, Södra Kungsgatan 31 (☎026/61 55 90, fax 65 15 55). A small and comfortable family-run hotel south of the river, offering a small breakfast buffet. ③/②.

Boulogne, Byggmästargatan 1 (☎026/12 63 52, fax 12 63 52). Cosy, basic hotel, with breakfast brought to each room on a tray. Close to Boulognerskogen park. ①.

Grand Central, Nygatan 45 (☎026/12 90 60, fax 12 44 99). One of the smartest hotels in town, with old-fashioned en-suite rooms. ④/②.

Nya Järnvägshotellet, Centralplan 3 (☎026/12 09 90, fax 10 62 42). The cheapest hotel in Gävle; quite okay, though rooms aren't en suite. ②/①.

Winn, Norra Slottsgatan 9 (☎026/64 70 00, fax 10 59 60). Another smart hotel, with its own pool, sauna and sunbeds. ⑤/③.

The city and around

The modern city lies north of the river, its broad streets and avenues designed to prevent fires from spreading. A slice through the middle of the centre is comprised of parks, tree-lined spaces and fountains, running north from the spire-like **Rådhus** to the beautiful nineteenth-century theatre. All the main banks, shops and stores are in the grid of streets on either side of Norra Kungsgatan and Norra Rådmansgatan; the train and bus stations are about 700m to the east.

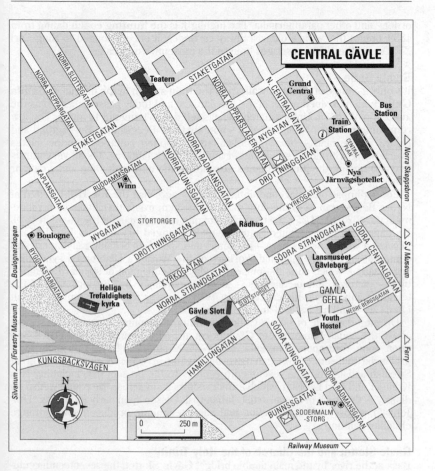

CENTRAL GÄVLE

Teatern
STAKETGATAN
NORRA SLOTTSGATAN
NORRA SKEPPARGATAN
Grand
Central
N CENTRALGATAN
Bus
Station
Norra Skeppsbron
STAKETGATAN
NORRA KOPPARSLAGERGATAN
NYGATAN
Train
Station
KAPLANSGATAN
RUDDAMMSGATAN
NORRA RADMANSGATAN
NORRA KUNGSGATAN
DROTTNINGGATAN
CENTRALPLAN
Nya
Järnvägshotellet
S J Museum
Winn
KYRKOGATAN
STORTORGET
Boulogne
NYGATAN
Rådhus
BYGGMÄSTARGATAN
Boulognerskogen
DROTTNINGGATAN
KYRKOGATAN
NORRA STRANDGATAN
SÖDRA STRANDGATAN
Lansmuséet
Gävleborg
SÖDRA CENTRALGATAN
Heliga
Trefaldighets
kyrka
GAMLA
GEFLE
NEDRE BERGSGATAN
Silvanum (Forestry Museum)
SLOTTSTORGET
Gävle Slott
Youth
Hostel
Ferry
KUNGSBÄCKSVÄGEN
HAMILTONGATAN
SÖDRA KUNGSGATAN
SÖDRA RADMANSGATAN
N
0   250 m
BUNNSGATAN
Aveny
SÖDERMALM
-STORG

Railway Museum

Around the train station

From the train station, look across the tracks, beyond the bus station, and you'll see the beginnings of an industrial area. Home to a number of old dock-side **warehouses**, off Norra Skeppsbron just by the river, it's a reminder of the days when ships unloaded coffee and spices in the centre of Gävle. To get to the warehouses, use the subway in front of the train station to head under the railway tracks, and walk past the bus station to the riverside. Today, with the company names emblazoned on the red, wooden fronts of the empty buildings, the area feels more like a Hollywood movie set than a Swedish town.

Especially on a rainy day, you may find yourself contemplating the **Sveriges Järnvägsmuseum**, Swedish Railways' museum at Rälsgatan 1 (June–Aug daily 10am–4pm; Sept–May Tues–Sun 10am–4pm; 30kr, free with InterRail) – reached from the station along Muréngatan. In what used to be Gävle's engine shed, it's a train enthusiast's paradise, stuffed to the gills with about fifty locomotives – sixteen of these are over one hundred years old, and five are still in full working order – and other paraphernalia. The highlight is the **hunting coach** dating from 1859, one of the world's oldest railway carriages; it once belonged to King Carl XV. One of the 1950s' carriages houses the museum's own café.

Gamla Gefle

It's only a couple of minutes' walk from the train station to the district of **Gamla Gefle**, which escaped much of the fire damage and today passes itself off as the authentic old town. Unfortunately, what's left doesn't amount to much. The few remaining narrow cobbled streets – notably Övre Bergsgatan, Bergsgränd and Nedre Bergsgränd – boast pastel-coloured wooden cottages, window boxes overflowing with flowers in summer and old black lanterns. It's all very attractive and quaint; the jumbled lanes now house the odd craft shop and a café or two.

For a glimpse of social conditions a century ago, visit the **Joe Hill-Gården** at Nedre Bergsgatan 28 (June–Aug daily 11am–3pm; free; other times by arrangement on ☎026/61 34 25), the birthplace of one Johan Emanuel Hägglund in 1879. He emigrated to the United States in 1902, changed his name to Joe Hill, and became a working-class hero – his songs and speeches became rallying cries to comrades in the International Workers of the World, a Utah-based syndicalist organization, which runs the museum today. Its collection of standard memorabilia – pictures and belongings – is given piquancy by the inclusion of the telegram announcing his execution in 1915 – he was framed for murder in Salt Lake City – and his last will and testament.

On the other side of Gamla Gefle is a thoughtful county museum that's a cut above the usual, **Länsmuséet Gävleborg**, at Södra Strandgatan 20 (Tues–Sun noon–4pm, Wed noon–9pm; 25kr, under-20s & students free). Unusually for a provincial museum, it has extensive displays of artwork by most of the great Swedish artists from the seventeenth century to the present day, including Nils Kreuger and Carl Larsson, which attract visitors from across the country. Also on display is the work of a local artist, Johan-Erik Olsson (popularly known as "Lim-Johan"), whose vivid imagination and naive technique produced some strange childlike paintings.

Gävle Slottet and the Church of the Holy Trinity

Back at the river by the main double bridge, **Gävle Slottet**, the seventeenth-century residence of the county governor, lost its ramparts and towers years ago and now lurks behind a row of trees like some minor country house. It's not possible to get inside for a poke around, although you can ask the tourist office to arrange a visit to the **Fängelsemuseum** (Prison Museum), on the premises. Housed in what was the county's first prison, dating from the seventeenth century, the museum gives some idea of how jails were back then. From Gävle Slottet, a short walk west following the river leads to a wooden bridge, across which is Kaplansgatan and the **Heliga Trefaldighets kyrka**, the Church of the Holy Trinity, a seventeenth-century masterpiece of decoration with **woodcarving**: check out the pulpit, towering altarpiece and screen – each the superb work of a German craftsman, Ewardt Friis.

Silvanum and Boulognerskogen

Crossing back over the river and taking a fifteen-minute stroll down picturesque Kungsbäcksvägen, a narrow street lined with brightly painted wooden houses, you'll arrive at northern Europe's largest forestry museum, **Silvanum** (Tues,

Thurs & Fri 10am–4pm, Wed 10am–7pm, Sat & Sun 1–5pm; free), at Kungsbäcksvägen 32. It's interesting only if you're keen to learn more about the unforgiving forest that you'll soon become well acquainted with as you travel further north. Continue along Kungsbäcksvägen and you'll come to the rambling park, **Boulognerskogen**. Opened in the mid-nineteenth century, it provides an oasis of trees, water and flowers just outside the city centre – a good place for a picnic and a spot of sunbathing. Among its attractions are music pavilions, mini-golf, an open-air **café** and a sculpture, by Carl Milles, of five angels playing musical instruments.

Out from the centre: the beaches, Limön and the Furuvik amusement park

If the sun's shining, you'll find locals catching the rays at the nearby sandy beach of **Rullsand**, which stretches for about 3km northeast of town. The beaches at **Engeltofta** or **Engesberga**, a few kilometres further on, can be reached on bus #5 from the Rådhus. From Engesberga, the bus continues to **Bönan**, where an old lighthouse marks a spot where good swimming can be had. Other enjoyable beaches are on the island of **Limön**, reached by a summer ferry from Skeppsbron (3 daily; 30kr), with one service calling at Engeltofta on the way. Limön is a pleasant place for some gentle walks, with paths crisscrossing the island.

In the other direction from town is the **Furuvik amusement park** (May to late June Mon–Fri 10am–4pm, Sat & Sun 10am–5pm; July daily 10am–6pm; early Aug daily 10am–5pm; 95kr, children 55kr); buses #821, #832 and #838 leave for here roughly every half-hour from Gävle's bus station. The place boasts a zoo, fairground, parks and playgrounds; you can buy coupons for individual rides (12–24kr) or a pass for everything (Åkband, 95 kr).

Eating, drinking and nightlife

The roomy Stortorget, just west of the central esplanade, has an open-air **market** that's worth visiting for its fruit and veg (Mon–Sat 9am–4pm). There's a fair choice of **eating places** in Gävle, with the best options in the central grid of streets around Stortorget and up and down the streets running from Rådhus to the theatre. Nearly all cafés and restaurants double as **bars**. For dancing, *Heartbreak Hotel* and *O'Leary's* are fun and always very busy. There are two **cinemas** on Norra Slottsgatan, Filmstaden and Sandrew.

Cafés, restaurants and bars

Café Artist, Norra Slottsgatan 9. A trendy hang-out offering fish and meat dishes for around 150kr; smaller dishes such as *pytt i panna* for 62kr. In the evenings, this is a relaxed place for a beer or two on cosy sofas.

Bali Garden, corner of Nygatan and Norra Kopparslagergatan. Good Indonesian food with meat dishes from 85kr.

Brända Bocken, Storatorget. Young and fashionable, with outdoor seating in summer. Beef and pork dishes, hamburgers and salmon, each for around 80kr. Lunch for 63kr. Also a popular place for a drink.

Heartbreak Hotel, Norra Strandgatan 15. A pub, bistro-style bar and nightclub, this attracts a 35-plus crowd – worth checking out.

Herman, opposite the Rådhus on Norra Kungsgatan. This trendy eatery is a good place for lunch (59kr); it also does a variety of snacks (40–60kr) and meat dishes from 120kr.

Kungshallen, Norra Kungsgatan 17. Serves mammoth pizzas for 44–60kr; also has cheap beer.

O'Leary's, Södra Kungsgatan 31. A 20min walk from the centre, this incredibly busy bar caters for a 20- to 30-something crowd – *the* place to do your boozing and boogieing. Closed Mon.

Skeppet, in the *Grand Central Hotel* at Nygatan 45. Amid maritime decor, here you can enjoy fine fish and seafood dishes – with prices to match: main courses start from 150kr.

Tennstoppet, Nygatan 38. Cheap and cheerful hamburger restaurant close to the station, with sausage and chips, egg and bacon and a mixed grill.

Österns Pärla, Ruddammsgatan 23. Fairly standard Chinese restaurant, serving the usual favourites for 80–90kr each.

Listings

Banks Förenings Sparbanken and Handelsbanken are both on Nygatan, west of Norra Kungsgatan; Nordbanken, Norra Kungsgatan 3–5.

Bus information Local buses operated by XTrafik (☎020/91 01 09); long-distance buses to Bollnäs, Uppsala and Stockholm operated by Swebus (☎0200/21 82 18).

Car rental Budget (☎026/65 40 00); Europcar (☎020/78 11 80); Hertz (☎026/51 18 19); Statoil (☎020/25 25 25).

Pharmacy Drottninggatan 12 (Mon–Fri 9am–6pm, Sat 9am–2pm, Sun 11am–3pm; ☎026/14 92 01).

Police Södra Centralgatan 1 (☎026/65 50 00).

Post office Drottninggatan 16 (☎026/12 13 90).

Systembolaget at Södra Kungsgatan near Gävle Slottet; also at Nygatan 13. Mon–Thurs 10am–6pm, Fri 9.30am–6pm.

Taxi Gävle Taxi (☎026/12 90 00 or 10 70 00).

Travel agent Ticket, Drottninggatan 27. Mon–Fri 9am–6pm, Sat 10am–1pm.

Söderhamn and Hudiksvall

On the first leg of the coastal journey further into Norrland, train services, including the X2000, are reasonably frequent. Along this stretch of coast, **Söderhamn** and **Hudiksvall** both make for a leisurely stop en route to the bigger towns and tourist centres further north. Hudiksvall's wood-panelled architecture gives it the edge over sleepy Söderhamn; a few hours at most is all you'll need to get to grips with either place. Out of the main tourist season, it's best to avoid arriving on Sundays, when you'll probably be the only person in the streets.

Söderhamn and around

It's easy to see that **SÖDERHAMN**, founded in 1620, was once much more important than it is today. The seventeenth-century **Ulrika Eleonora kyrka** that towers over the Rådhus gives hints of the wealth that once accrued to the city, primarily from fishing. Relics from an earlier church that stood on the same spot are kept in **Söderhamns Museum** (late June to early Aug Tues–Sun noon–5pm; free), halfway up Oxtorgsgatan from Rådhustorget, the main square. The museum is housed in what was once a rifle-manufacturing workshop, a reminder of

Söderhamn's seventeenth-century role as supplier of the weapons that helped Sweden dominate northern Europe.

A number of devastating fires took their toll on the town; the largest, on July 22, 1876, destroyed virtually everything in its path. As a result, the modern town is built on a grid pattern, with space for central parks and green spaces. The familiar Swedish mix of pedestrianized shopping streets and parkland gives the town a likeable air, one that's inviting enough to while away some time at a pavement café. However, the wide open spaces in the centre of town don't give a true impression of the surrounding area, as a climb up the white, 23-metre-tall **Oskarsborg tower** will demonstrate; there's a path to it signposted from down by the train tracks. From the top, the surrounding forests that hem the town in stretch away as far as the eye can see. You can easily take a **walk** out into the countryside: head up Kyrkogatan, from under the railway bridge near Rådhustorget, and continue up the hill onto the footpath; turn left into Krongatan and on towards the hospital past the helipad, then head right along any one of a series of paths into the forest.

Another diversion here is a **boat trip** out into Söderhamn's **archipelago**, made up of about five hundred islands; the largest, **Storjungfrun** (literally, "The Great Virgin"), gave its name to the stretch of coast around Söderhamn and Hudiksvall – Jungfrukusten, "The Virgin Coast". The *M/S Sandskär* does a tour around the islands, lasting about three hours (mid-May to mid-Sept; 100kr; more information on ☎0270/122 54 or 070/667 23 74); it leaves from the opposite end of town to Rådhustorget – walk down the main street and along the canal for about fifteen minutes until you come to the jetty.

Practicalities

Söderhamn's **Resecentrum** ("Travel Centre") not only houses both the **train** and **bus stations** but also the town's **tourist office** (June to early Aug Mon–Fri 7am–7pm, Sat & Sun noon–5pm; early Aug to May Mon–Fri 7am–5pm; ☎0270/753 53, *www.soderhamn.se*). From here it's a ten-minute walk down Brädgårdsgatan, past the *First Hotel Statt*, into the main square, Rådhustorget. You won't exactly be overwhelmed with choice for a place to **stay** here. In town, the best of the bunch is the central and swanky *First Hotel Statt*, Oxtorgsgatan 17 (☎0270/414 10, fax 135 24; ③/②). The wonderfully situated **youth hostel** is at **Mohed**, 13km west of town, in a deep pine forest (☎0270/42 52 33, fax 42 53 26; 110kr; June–Aug). Right by a lake, the hostel occupies an old sanatorium, built here so that patients could benefit from Mohed's famous clean air; swimming, boat rental, fishing, horse-riding and mini-golf are all available in the vicinity. There's a year-round **campsite** here, too. To get to Mohed from Söderhamn, take the hourly buses #64 or #100 (the latter continues to **Bollnäs**, about thirty minutes' ride from Mohed, which is handy for catching the mainline trains north to **Lapland**).

Eating and **drinking** establishments in Söderhamn have come on in leaps and bounds in recent years, and there's now a fair number vying for your custom, though they're nothing spectacular. For **daytime** coffee and cake, try *TeWe's Konditori* on the main pedestrian street, Köpmangatan; it's open daily. Most restaurants are to be found along the same thoroughfare: at the Rådhus end of the street, *Mosquet Restaurant* has pizzas for 40–50kr, pasta for 55kr and fish dishes for 100–120kr. The Chinese restaurant, *Mandarin Palace*, in Köpmantorget, has a

Dagens Rätt for 53kr; they also do some Swedish dishes. À la carte eating starting at 100kr can be had at *Sportsbar* on Kungsgatan; upmarket food is also served at the *Stadsrestaurang*, inside the *First Hotel Statt* on Oxtorgsgatan. **Drinking** is best done at *Dino* at Oxtorgsgatan 17 (where half a litre of beer costs 29kr during happy hour), at the *King's Road Café* on Kungsgatan, or at *Memory* on Dammgatan.

Hudiksvall

Granted town status in 1582 and accordingly the second oldest town in Norrland, **HUDIKSVALL** has seen its fair share of excitement over the years. Though the original settlement was built around what had been the bay of Lillfjärden, at the mouth of the Hornån river, the harbour began to silt up, and so it was decided to move the town to its current location: the old bay is now a lake, connected to the sea by a small canal. The town has suffered no less than ten **fires**, the worst occurring in 1721 when Russian forces swept down the entire length of the Bothnian coast, burning and looting as they went. Then an important commercial and shipping centre, the town bore the brunt of the onslaught; only its church (still pockmarked with cannonball holes today) remained standing. A further blaze, east of Rådhustorget, in 1792 led to a rethink of the town's layout, following which the street plan which exists today was conceived.

The oldest part of the rebuilt town – the most interesting part of the city – is split into two main sections. Turn right out of the train station and cross the narrow canal, Strömmingssundet ("Herring Sound"), and you'll soon see the small old **harbour** on the right; this area is known as **Möljen**. Here the wharfside is flanked by a line of red, wooden fishermen's cottages and storehouses, all leaning into the water; it's a popular place for locals to while away a couple of hours in the summer sunshine, dangling their feet into the water. The back of the warehouses hides a run of boat-repair shops, handicraft studios and the tourist office (see p.365). More impressive and much larger than Möljen, **Fiskarstan** (Fishermen's Town), beyond *First Hotel Statt* down Storgatan, contains neat examples of the so-called "Imperial" wood-panel architecture of the late eighteenth and nineteenth centuries. It was in these tightly knit blocks of streets, lined with beautiful wooden houses and fenced-in plots of land, that the fishermen used to live in during the winter. Take a peek inside some of the little courtyards – all window boxes, summer flowers and cobblestones. The history of these buildings is put into context in the excellent **Hälsinglands Museum** on Storgatan (Tues, Thurs & Fri 9am–4pm, Wed 9am–8pm, Sat & Sun 11am–3pm; 20kr, free on Sat and for students and children), which traces the development of Hudiksvall as a harbour town since its foundation. Have a look at the paintings by **John Sten** upstairs: born near Hudiksvall in 1879, he produced work that veered strangely from Cubism to a more decorative fanciful style.

The best time to visit Hudiksvall is in the middle two weeks of July, when the town hosts the **Musik vid Dellen**, a multifarious cultural festival, including folk music and other traditional events (for more information, contact the tourist office). For a day-trip out of town, head out to the beautiful and unspoilt **Hornslandet peninsula** and its quaint fishing villages, **Hölick** and **Kuggörarna**. The whole area is rich in flora and fauna, as well as being ideal for swimming, fishing and walking. To get there, take bus #37, which runs from the bus station to both villages (mid-June to mid-August, 2 daily).

Practicalities

The **train** and **bus stations** are opposite each other on Stationsgatan. It takes two minutes to walk from either, along the main road, to the centre around Möljen. Close by, behind the old warehouses, is the **tourist office** (mid-June to mid-Aug Mon–Fri 9am–7pm, Sat & Sun 10am–5pm; mid-Aug to mid-June Mon–Fri 9am–4pm; ☎0650/191 00, *www.hudiksvall.se*).

The **youth hostel** (☎0650/13260; 140kr; June–Aug) is out at the Malnbaden **campsite**, 3km from town. Bus #5 runs there hourly in summer (10am–6pm); at other times you'll have get there by taxi (80kr one-way; there's a rank at the train station). Situated on the bay, the hostel overlooks a large sandy beach and jogging tracks on the opposite side of the road; there are also cottages for rent here, which can be booked through the tourist office. For **hotel** accommodation, there's *Hotell Temperance* (☎ and fax 0650/311 07; ②/①) a cheapish place at Håstagatan 16, near the train station. The swishest hotel in town is the 1878 *First Hotel Statt* at Storgatan 36 (☎0650/150 60, fax 960 95; ④/②). It was here that the barons of the timber industry did their best to live up to the town's nickname of "Glada Hudik" ("Happy Hudiksvall"), a phrase coined in the first half of the nineteenth century, when the people here became known for their lively social life and generous hospitality.

Today, oddly enough, Hudiksvall has fewer **eating and drinking** opportunities than smaller Söderhamn to the south. A popular restaurant is *Bolaget* at Storgatan 49, where main dishes cost around 85kr and pizzas 45kr. Alternatively, try the smarter *Le Bistro* on Hamngatan, which has happy hours for both food and drink (3–10pm). The poshest place in town is *Stadts Bar o Kök*, the restaurant attached to *First Hotel Statt* on Storgatan; fresh seafood is a speciality here (from 200kr) and you'll need to dress smartly if you want to blend in. The one and only bar is the *Pub Tre Bockar* at Bankgränd, opposite the fishermen's warehouses at Möljen, with occasionally evening jazz. **Nightlife** is to be found at the club and bar *Bruns* on Storgatan, though don't get your hopes up too high.

Sundsvall and around

The capital of the tiny province of Medelpad, **SUNDSVALL**, is often referred to as "Stone City", for the reason that its buildings are mostly of stone – a fact that distinguishes it immediately from other coastal towns here. Once home to a rapidly expanding nineteenth-century sawmill industry, the whole city burned to the ground the day after Midsummer in June 1888. A spark from the wood-burning steamboat *Selånger* (promptly dubbed "The Arsonist") set fire to a nearby brewery and the rest, as they say, is history – so much so that the remark "that hasn't happened since the town burned down" is now an established Sundsvall saying. Nine thousand people lost their homes in the resulting blaze. The work of rebuilding the city began at once, and within ten years a new centre had been constructed, entirely of **stone**. The result is a living document of turn-of-the-century urban architecture, designed and crafted by architects who were involved in rebuilding Stockholm's residential areas at the same time. Wide streets and esplanades that would serve as firebreaks in the event of another fire formed the backbone of their work. These thoroughfares are home to 573 residential buildings, all of which went up in four years; the centrepiece is the house that dominates the main square, Storatorget.

The reconstruction, however, was achieved at a price: the workers who had laboured on the city's refurbishment became the victims of their own success. They were shifted from their old homes in the centre and moved out south to a run-down suburb – the glaring contrast between the wealth of the new centre and the poverty of the surrounding districts was only too obvious. When **Nils Holgersson**, a character created by the children's author Selma Lagerlöf (see p.420), looked down from the back of his flying goose (see the picture on 20kr notes), he remarked: "There was something funny about it when you saw it from above, because in the middle there was a group of high stone houses, so impressive that they hardly had their equal in Stockholm. Around the stone houses was an empty space, and then there was a circle of wooden houses, which were pleasantly scattered in little gardens, but which seemed to carry an awareness of being of lesser value than the stone houses and therefore dared not come too close."

Arrival, information and accommodation

From the **train station**, it's a five-minute walk to the city centre; turn left and go through the subway. The helpful **tourist office** is in the main square, Storatorget (June to Aug Mon–Fri 10m–6pm, Sat & Sun 10am–3pm; Sept–May Mon–Fri 11am–4pm; ☎060/67 18 00). North of the square is the **bus station**, at the bottom of Esplanaden. The **airport**, 24km north of town on the way to Härnösand, is linked to Sundsvall by an airport bus (60kr), timed to coincide with flights to and from Stockholm, and by taxi (245kr).

Rooms in Sundsvall, even in summer, are plentiful, and so finding somewhere to stay is unlikely to be a problem. The **youth hostel** is roughly a half-hour walk out of town at Norra Stadsberget, the mountain overlooking the city (☎060/61 21 19, fax 61 78 01; 110, ①); to get there, take any bus for Norra Berget from the bus station. With accommodation in minuscule cabins, the hostel is a bit shabby; you're better off going for one of the low-budget central **hotels** in the list below.

Baltic, Sjögatan 5 (☎060/15 59 35, fax 12 45 60). Centrally located near the Kulturmagasinet and the harbour, with perfectly adequate rooms. ④/②.

Continental Hotell, Rådhusgatan 13 (☎060/15 00 60, fax 15 75 90). A fairly cheap hotel, centrally located, with all rooms en suite; also has a sun terrace and cable TV. ③/②.

First Hotel Strand, Strandgatan 10 (☎060/12 18 00, fax 61 92 02). The smartest hotel in town, with two hundred rooms, an indoor pool and a superb breakfast buffet. ⑤/③.

Good Morning Hotel, Trädgårdsgatan 31–33 (☎060/15 06 00, fax 12 70 80). All rooms are en suite here, and some have actual baths. Worth trying especially if the cheaper hotels are full. ②/①.

Grand, Nybrogatan 13 (☎060/64 65 60, fax 64 65 65). The basement sauna and jacuzzi suite are excellent; the rooms, however, are on the small side, with rather worn furnishings. ④/②.

Lilla Hotellet, Rådhusgatan 15 (☎060/61 35 87). One of the cheapest hotels in town with just eight rooms, all of which are en suite and have cable TV. ②/①.

Prize, Sjögatan 11 (☎060/15 07 20). A middle-of-the-range hotel where each room is named after a particular village in the province of Medelpad. ③/②.

Scandic Hotel Sundsvall City, Esplanaden 29 (☎060/17 16 00, fax 12 20 32). This hotel boasts eight cinemas, saunas, sunbeds and a golf simulator, with prices to match the opulence. ⑤/③.

Svea Hotell, Rådhusgatan 11 (☎060/61 16 05). The ten rooms at this, the cheapest hotel in Sundsvall, soon fill up in summer. Doubles in summer and weekends all year for just 350kr. ②/①.

Södra Berget, on the southern hill from which the hotel takes its name (☎060/67 10 00, fax 67 10 10). With fantastic views, this hotel is popular in winter for skiing; a solarium, steamroom and jacuzzi are also available here. ⑤/②.

The City

As you walk in from the train stations, the sheer scale of the rebuilding here after the 1888 fire is clear to see. The style of the buildings is simple, utilizing limestone and brick, their dimensions often overwhelming: the four- and five-storey houses are palatial structures. As you stroll the streets, you can't help but be amazed by

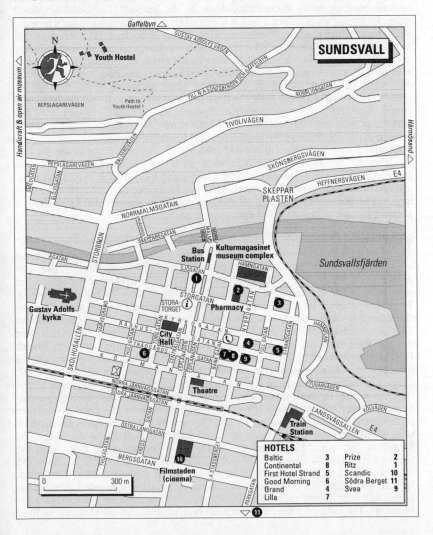

HOTELS

Baltic	3	Prize	2
Continental	8	Ritz	1
First Hotel Strand	5	Scandic	10
Good Morning	6	Södra Berget	11
Grand	4	Svea	9
Lilla	7		

the tremendous amount of open space that surrounds you, even in the heart of the city; Sundsvall is unique among Swedish cities in this respect, yet it's the most densely populated metropolis in northern Sweden. **Esplanaden**, the wide central avenue, cuts the grid of streets in two; towards its northern end it's crossed by **Storgatan**, the widest road in town. **Storatorget**, the central square, is a delightfully roomy shopping and commercial centre, home to the city hall, various impromptu exhibitions and displays, as well as a fresh fruit and veg market (Mon–Sat from 9.30am).

Several of the buildings in the centre are worth a second look, not least the sturdy bourgeois exterior of Sundsvalls Museum, housed within four late-nineteenth-century warehouses on Hamngatan, down by the harbour. The buildings stood empty for twenty years before a decision was taken to turn them into what's now the **Kulturmagasinet** (Culture Warehouse; Mon–Thurs 10am–7pm, Fri 10am–6pm, Sat & Sun 11am–4pm; June–Aug 20kr, rest of year free), comprising museum, library and café. The museum is actually built over an old street, Magasinsgatan, complete with its train tracks running between the warehouses, providing a glimpse of the days when coffee and rice were transported along its length to the harbour for export. Deserving of a quick look, the museum does its best to depict the history of Sundsvall and the province of Medelpad. Upstairs, the art exhibition warrants a few minutes of your time: the works of twentieth-century Swedish artists are on show here, in particular, those of the local artist Carl Frisendahl.

Continue west along the main pedestrian street, Storgatan, and at the far end you'll come across a soaring red-brick structure, **Gustav Adolfs kyrka** (June–Aug daily 11am–4pm; Sept–May 11am–2pm; free), which marks the western end of the new town. The church's interior looks like a large Lego set, its pillars, vaults and window frames all constructed from smooth bricks, making a pleasing picture of order for the eye.

Gaffelbyn

The most attractive diversion in Sundsvall is the three-kilometre climb to the top of **Gaffelbyn**, the 140-metre-high northern hill that overlooks the city; the view gives a fresh perspective on the city, not only of its planned layout but also of the restrictive nature of its situation, hemmed in on three sides by hills and the sea. To get to Gaffelbyn, head up Storgatan, cross over the main bridge and follow the signs for the youth hostel, which is also up here; the walk takes about half an hour. Alternatively, take any bus for Norra Berget from the bus station. On a clear day the view from the top is fantastic; you can see straight across to **Södra Berget**, the southern hill, with its winter ski slopes. The best views can be gained from the top of the **viewing tower** which has stood on this spot since 1897. Originally made entirely from wood, the tower fell victim over the years to the Swedish winter. By the 1930s it was in such poor condition that during one particularly severe autumn storm, the entire tower blew down; the present concrete replacement, 22m high, dates from 1954. The nearby **Norra Bergets Hantverks och Friluftsmuseum** is an open-air handicrafts museum (June–Aug Mon–Fri 9am–4pm, Sat & Sun 11am–3pm; Sept–May Mon–Fri 9am–4pm; free), with the usual selection of old wooden huts and assorted knick-knacks. It does, however, offer you the chance to try your hand at baking some *tunnbröd*, the thin bread, looking something like pitta bread, that's typical of northern Sweden. The idea is to roll out your dough extra thin, brush off as much flour as you can, slip the bread into the oven on a big, wooden pizza-type paddle, and count slowly to five.

Eating, drinking and nightlife

Restaurants have mushroomed in Sundsval over the last couple of years, and there's a good choice of places to eat and cuisines to choose from, including unusual options such as Vietnamese and Spanish – something you may want to make the most of if you're heading further north, as culinary options up there are limited. There are a handful of inexpensive pizza places and restaurants on Storgatan, most offering daily lunches. **Bars** in the city generally have a good atmosphere, and there are several places serving cheap beer. **Nightclubs** are a bit thin on the ground; the best one to head for is *Seaport* at the *First Hotel Strand*, Strandgatan 10, where over-23s gather to shake their stuff to the latest sounds.

Cafés

Café Charm, Storgatan 34 and in Världshuset shopping centre on Sjögatan. A good choice for coffee and cake, with free refills and naughty-but-nice cream concoctions. Mon–Fri 10am–6pm, Sat & Sun 10am–4pm.

Coffee House, on Storgatan, opposite *O'Leary's*. Small and agreeable modern café with Swedish coffee, tea, sandwiches, and newspapers.

Svenssons Café & Bar, Torggatan 8. Always busy at lunchtime, thanks to its central location in the main square. Has a *Dagens Rätt* that changes daily.

Ullas Skafferi, Rådhusgatan 15. A right-on café serving vegetarian and vegan food, with main courses, salads and pies.

Wayne's Coffee, Storgatan 13. *The* coffeehouse in Sundsvall, located in an atmospheric old building on the main drag. Dozens of varieties of coffees and excellent sandwiches and cakes.

Restaurants

Athena, Köpmangatan 7. Run by a Moroccan football star who ended up in Sundsvall. This place has all your Greek favourites, from tzatziki to souvlaki, as well as good pizzas. Main courses 100kr.

Cactus, Trädgårdsgatan 17, just off Esplanaden. An authentic Mexican place, serving the likes of chicken enchiladas and nachos from 100kr.

China Restaurant, Esplanaden, near bus station. Chicken (72kr), meat (76kr) and duck (93kr) dishes to eat-in, or take away.

La Spezia, Sjögatan 6. Serves decent bargain-basement pizzas 35kr; also has a takeaway service.

Saigon Palace, Trädgårdsgatan 5. Vietnamese and Chinese restaurant with some good-value dishes – try the chicken in peanut sauce for 89kr. Lunch costs 50kr.

Seaport, Strandgatan 10, in the *First Hotel Strand*. A chi-chi international brasserie, with gourmet dishes and accompanying clientele. Reckon on at least 200kr for a two-course meal.

Sevilla, Rådhusgatan 7. A Spanish restaurant whose fare includes a reasonable selection of tapas, all at moderate prices.

Skeppsbrokällaren, next to *Hotell Baltic* on Sjögatan. Limited choice of meat or fish dishes plus a strong beer, for 100kr.

Åhlénsrestaurangen, inside the Åhléns department store on Storgatan. Offers a good lunchtime vegetarian buffet (60kr).

Bars

Dublin, Nybrogatan 16. This Irish pub has a broad selection of beers, including Cafferys and Kilkennys, plus Irish food, music – and darts.

Hoagy's, Strandgatan 10. In the *First Hotel Strand*. A tasteful piano bar, where well-oiled locals can be found rounding off an evening's boozing. Cheap beer is available during happy hour (8–11pm). Daily 6pm–3am.

JOP's, Trädgårdsgatan 35. A popular place for a mid-evening tipple; darts is available.

Marley's, Sjögatan 25. Playing reggae sounds on disc, this place attracts a 20-plus crowd.

Mercat Cross, Esplanaden 27. Part of the Filmstaden complex, at the southern end of Esplanaden. This Scottish pub, with staff in kilts, serves just about every variety of whisky you can think of.

O'Bar, Bankgatan 11. A good, lively bar; try the excellent, pricey cocktails (100kr and up). The staff are happy to make up any concoction you throw at them.

O'Leary's, Storgatan 40. A sports-oriented pub with a good choice of beer, and pub food with a Tex-Mex flavour. Big screens show the latest football and hockey matches.

Spegelbaren, Nybrogatan 10. One of the biggest bars in Norrland, this is a good place to start the evening off. Large glass mirrors, glass ceilings and nineteenth-century paintings add to the lively atmosphere. It's unusual for Swedes to go out for a drink after work – but people do just that here.

Listings

Airlines SAS ☎060/18 80 00; Skyways ☎060/18 80 10.

Airport Information on ☎060/608 80 10.

Banks Handelsbanken, Storgatan 23; Nordbanken, Kyrkogatan 15; SEB, Storgatan 19.

Buses For information or advance tickets for the daily express bus south to Stockholm, north to Umeå, or inland to Östersund, visit Y-Bussen at Sjögatan 7 (☎060/17 19 60). For the express bus to Gothenburg via Gävle, Västerås and Örebro, contact Sundsvallarn at Sjögatan 8 (☎060/15 10 99). For other bus information, including departures on the Norrlandskusten buses, which operate between Sundsvall and Luleå, contact the tourist office.

Car rental Bilbolaget, Bultgatan 1 (☎060/18 08 00); Budget, at the airport (☎060/57 80 06).

Cinema Filmstaden, at the southern end of Esplanaden.

Hospital Lasarettsvägen 19 (☎060/18 10 00).

Pharmacy Storgatan 18 (Mon–Fri 9.30am–6pm, Sat 10am–3pm; ☎060/18 11 17).

Police Storgatan 37 (☎060/18 00 00).

Post office Köpmangatan 19 (☎060/19 60 00).

Systembolaget Torggatan 1 (Mon–Wed 10am–6pm, Thurs 10am–7pm, Fri 9.30am–6pm; ☎060/61 36 69).

Taxi Taxi Sundsvall (☎060/19 90 00)

Train station Parkgatan (☎060/18 30 00).

Travel agent Ticket, on the corner of Rådhusgatan and Esplanaden (Mon–Fri 9am–6pm, Sat 10am–1pm).

Around Sundsvall: Alnö

The island of **Alnö** is within easy striking distance of Sundsvall and makes for a good day-trip. Alnö's empty roads and tranquil scenery are particularly popular with **cyclists** (ask at Sundsvall tourist office for bike rental information), who come to navigate the narrow country lanes that wind their way past pine forests, sandy coves and the odd farmstead. The main place to head for here is the tiny, pretty fishing village of **SPIKARNA** in the southeast corner of the island. Its red, wooden fishermen's cottages, snuggled round a tiny bay for pro-

MOVING ON FROM SUNDSVALL

Regular **direct trains** run west from Sundsvall to Östersund, for connections inland; and south to Stockholm via Hudiksvall, Söderhamn, Gävle, Uppsala and Arlanda airport. There are also limited services north to Härnösand. To continue further north to **Lapland**, you'll have to time your departure carefully, since there's just one daily evening service (not Sat) leaving Sundsvall for Ånge, where there's a change of train and an hour's wait for the night train for Narvik in Norway, via Boden, Luleå, Gällivare and Kiruna.

To get to the **High Coast** or any of the **coastal towns** between Sundsvall and Luleå, it's a much better idea to travel by **bus**. **Norrlandskusten** services, bound for Luleå, begin their trek north at Sundsvall's bus station four times daily, with stops en route including Härnösand, Örnsköldsvik and Umeå. For more on getting to the High Coast, see p.377.

tection from the wind and snow that sweeps in from the Gulf of Bothnia, are evidence of a long fishing tradition, still going strong today: you'll see nets laid out to dry on frames all around the village. To get into what passes for a centre, cross the wooden bridge from the spot where the bus drops you, and continue along the footpath for just a couple of minutes. In summer, you can buy smoked whitefish from small huts by the side of the path, while to the right there's a cluster of rocks that are good for sunbathing. Once a week in summer there are jazz evenings, held by the side of the fishermen's cottages – a wonderful way to enjoy the light nights.

To get to Alnö, take the frequent bus #1 from Sundsvall's bus station over the arched Alnöbron bridge. The bus will stop at the main village, Vi, from where you can get to Spikarna on the bus for Södra Alnö. In summer a special bus, Badbussen, runs directly to Spikarna from Sundsvall's bus station – ask at Sundsvall's tourist office for departure times; in winter, the water in the channel below freezes, allowing people with their own snow scooters to nip across. For a **place to stay** in Spikarna, the tourist office back in Sundsvall has **cottages** for rent, which get snapped up very quickly (2000–2500kr a week); alternatively, you could always camp rough.

Härnösand and Sollefteå

Full of architectural delights, including a number of old wooden cottages from the 1730s, the town of **Härnösand** is definitely worth a stop on the way north. An hour's train trip along the coast from Sundsvall, Härnösand marks the beginning of the stunningly beautiful county of **Ångermanland** – one of the few areas in Sweden where the countryside resembles that of neighbouring Norway. The coast here, north from Härnösand to Örnsköldsvik, is known as **Höga Kusten** (the High Coast, see p.375), with craggy coastlines, long fjords that reach far inland and low mountains. This is the most scenic coastal stretch in northern Sweden and a wonderful route further north from Härnösand. Alternatively, you can go inland to **Sollefteå** and on to **Långsele** (see p.374) to connect up with the main-line train north to Lapland.

Härnösand

A pleasant little place at the mouth of the Ångerman river, **HÄRNÖSAND** – the centre is on the island of **Härnön**, from which the town takes its name – was founded in 1585 by King Johan III. In 1647, the town was selected as the capital of the second most northerly diocese in Sweden and, accordingly, the new bishop decreed that the old stone church, which already stood in the town, be enlarged into a cathedral. The town has since had more than its fair share of disasters: in 1710, flames tore through the town after drunken churchgoers accidentally set fire to a boathouse; just four years after, Härnösand fell victim to a second great fire, started by a group of school students. Newly rebuilt, the town fell victim to a third blaze in 1721 when invading Russian forces burnt every house to the ground – bar one (see p.373).

Arrival, information and accommodation

The closest **airport**, with regular flights from Stockholm, is 34km south of Härnösand; you can get to the centre by airport bus (80kr) and taxi (around 335kr). Trains from Sundsvall and Långsele arrive at the **train station** on Järnvägsgatan, from where the **tourist office** is a couple of minutes' walk down the road at no. 2 (June–Aug Mon–Fri 8am–6pm, Sat & Sun 10am–2pm; Sept–May Mon–Fri 8am–5pm; ☎0611/881 40, *www.turism.harnosand.se*), inside the building marked "Spiran". It has free maps, bus times and accommodation details for the town and further afield in Ångermanland, in particular, up the High Coast. The **bus station** is east along Nybrogatan from the small roundabout in front of the train station.

The cheapest place to stay in town is the **youth hostel**, a fifteen-minute walk from the centre of town up Nybrogatan and then left (☎0611/104 46; 100kr; mid-June to early Aug); it's located in a student village, *Statens Skola För Vuxna*, at Volontären 14. Staying here gets you a flat to yourself, complete with kitchen and bathroom; there's also a non-STF hostel in Murberget (see p.373). The **campsite**, *Sälstens Camping* (☎0611/181 50), has a small selection of four-bed cabins for 250kr per person per night. It's around 2km northeast of the town centre, next to a string of pebble beaches; to get there, take Storgatan off Nybrogatan and follow the road as it swings eastwards along the coast. Of the town's three **hotels**, *Hotell Royal*, close to the train station at Strandgatan 12 (☎0611/204 55; ③/②) is the cheapest; *Hotell City* at Storgatan 28 (☎0611/277 00, fax 167 03; ③/①) is only marginally more expensive. Much bigger and a lot plusher than either is the *First Hotell Härnösand* at Skeppsbron 9 (☎0611/105 10; ⑤/②).

The Town

For a small, provincial place, Härnösand reeks of grandeur and self-importance, each of its proud civic buildings a marker of the confidence the town exudes. From the main square, **Stora Torget** (once declared by local worthies as the most beautiful in Sweden), take a stroll up Västra Kyrkogatan to the heights of the Neoclassical **Domkyrkan** (daily 10am–4pm), the smallest – and only white – cathedral in the country. Dating from the 1840s, it incorporates elements from earlier churches on the site; the Baroque altar is from the eighteenth century, as are the VIP boxes in the nave.

From the Domkyrkan, turn right and follow the road round and back down the hill until you come to the narrow old street of Östanbäcksgatan, with its pretty painted wooden houses from the 1730s. In one of the oldest parts of town, Östanbäcken, the houses here were among the first to be built after the Russian incursions. For a further taste of the town's architectural splendour, take a walk up the hilly main street, Nybrogatan: the Neoclassical yellow **Rådhuset** here, complete with white semi-circular portico, originally served as a school and home to the diocesan governors; while opposite at no. 15, the headquarters of the county administration is particularly beautiful, in a Neo-Baroque and Art Nouveau building with a pastel orange facade. You'll doubtless notice many other public buildings as you stroll around: being the capital of the administrative region of Västernorrland (which encompasses much of Ångermanland and neighbouring Medelpad), Härnösand is home to the county court and prison, among other institutions. From the top of Nybrogatan, there are good **views** back over the town and the water.

Out from the centre: the beaches and Murberget

The long sandy **beaches** in nearby **Smitingen**, 5km to the southeast, are generally regarded as some of the best in Norrland; to get there, take **bus #14** from the bus station (4 daily; 15min), straight ahead along Nybrogatan from the train station and just before the bridge across to the town. There are also pebble beaches near the Sälsten campsite, within walking distance of the town centre.

If you continue walking along the coast from here for about half an hour, you'll reach the impressive **open-air museum** (June–Aug daily 11am–5pm; free) at **MURBERGET**, which is the second biggest in Sweden after Skansen in Stockholm. You can also take bus #2 here from in front of the Rådhuset in Nybrogatan. The first building to take up its location here was a bell tower, which was moved from the village of Ullånger (further north) to its current position in 1913. There are around eighty other buildings, most notably traditional Ångermanland farmhouses and the old Murberget church, once a popular venue for local weddings. Look out for the Rysstugan, the one and only wooden building to escape the devastating fire caused by the Russians in 1721. The nineteenth-century *Spjute Inn* here is still home to a restaurant, and also contains a skittle alley, dating from 1910, where you can have a game. In the nearby **Länsmuseum** (County Museum; daily 11am–5pm; free), there are worthy exhibitions showing how people settled the area two thousand years ago, as well as very dull displays of birds' feet, old silver goblets and spectacles from more modern times. Those with an interest in weaponry are in luck, though: the museum has a collection of weapons used by huntsmen, peasants and the military from the seventeenth, eighteenth and nineteenth centuries. To **stay** at Murberget, there's a simple non-STF hostel at Murbergsvägen 32 (☎0611/220 80; 150kr).

Eating, drinking and nightlife

The most popular **restaurant**, also a pub, is *Kajutan*, on the pedestrianized Storgatan, which links Stora Torget and Nybrogatan. It has special eat-as-much-as-you-can lunch deals for 89kr; otherwise reckon on 90kr for pasta, 140kr for something more meaty; in summer the price of a beer can drop to 30kr. A good place to **drink** and grab a bite to eat is *Highlander* at Nybrogatan 5 – a Scottish theme pub (Tues–Sat from 6pm). To splash out, *Restaurang Apothequet*, Nybrogatan 3, is the place: its two-course set meals cost 179kr, three courses 209kr. The restaurant is in an old pharmacy, which dates from 1909; on the ground floor there's also a bar, where locals ask for a glass of "medicine" at what was the pharmacist's counter. Other places to eat include the neighbouring *Restaurang Nybrokällaren*; the popular pizzeria, *Matverkstaden*, at Storgatan 5 (to

---

MOVING ON FROM HÄRNÖSAND

At Härnösand, the coastal train line swings inland to **Långsele**, where you can change onto the main Gothenburg–Luleå line. You'll have to time your departure for Långsele carefully, as there are only two daily northbound train services from Härnösand; three daily buses also cover the route and their times are posted up at the train station. A much more picturesque way of heading for Långsele is to take a **boat** trip; departing from Skeppsbron, the *M/S Ådalen III* sails up the Ångerman river as far as **Sollefteå** (late June to mid-Aug; single trip 120kr; for information call ☎0612/505 41 or contact the tourist office), from where there are buses and trains the short distance to Långsele. Once at Långsele you can catch the night train north via Boden to Luleå, Gällivare and Kiruna. To head west or south from Härnösand, there are regular local trains (Mittlinjen; rail passes accepted) and buses to Sundsvall, for connections inland; and through services from Härnösand to Stockholm. You can also fly to Stockholm from the Midlanda airport, 34km south of town, reachable by airport bus (80kr) and taxi (335kr).

To reach the beauty of the **High Coast** there are two options: one is to take the daily 9am Norrlandskusten express bus bound for Luleå; it passes through the tiny village of Docksta, from where a ferry sails for the island of Ulvön (see p.379). The bus also skirts round the Skuleskogen National Park with its excellent **hiking** opportunities. Much better, though, is island-hopping up the coast (see p.377). All Norrlandskusten services leave from the bus station and operate daily via the High Coast to the coastal towns of Örnsköldsvik, Umeå, Skellefteå, Piteå and Luleå.

---

get there, walk along Storgatan away from the town centre and cross two bridges heading for the Landsting council buildings); and *New China Restaurant*, in the centre of town at Storgatan 34, with Chinese and Indonesian dishes from about 80kr each.

For a cup of coffee or good lunchtime dishes, head for the *Rutiga Dukan Café* at Västra Kyrkogatan 1, near the cathedral; here lunch goes for 60kr, and good home-baked pastries and apple pie are also on the menu. In summer, a refreshing place to sit with a coffee or a beer is *Café Skeppet & Restaurang*, a small wooden house which has a terrace overlooking the water; it's on Skeppsbron, by the bridge over to the train station. For **nightlife**, try the discos at *Kajutan* at Storgatan 28 or at *Nybrokällaren,* in Nybrogatan, next to the *Highlander* pub at Nybrogatan 5. The Saga **cinema**, at the junction of Storgatan and Nybrogatan, is your best bet for films.

Inland to Sollefteå

The train line swings inland after Härnösand, winding its way 80km northwest to **SOLLEFTEÅ** (you can also get here by boat; see box). An appealingly peaceful little town, it's beautifully sited on the banks of the Ångerman river, which was once the main transport artery of the region, carrying logs from the great inland forests down to the sawmills on the coast. Sollefteå is not only the home of one of Sweden's best beers, Zeunerts, but also one of its most famous – and infamous – politicians, Mona Sahlin. Once Deputy Prime Minister, she resigned amid a scandal linking use of her government credit card to the private purchase of nappies and chocolates for her young children.

However, once you've walked the one main pedestrianized street, Storgatan, and seen its parks and gardens, there's not much left to do. It's an easy fifteen-minute stroll from the main square, along Storgatan and then right into Kyrkogatan, to the single attraction, the unassuming **Sollefteå kyrka** (June–Aug daily 7am–4.30pm; Sept–May daily 8am–dusk), on a small hill overlooking the river just outside town. This eighteenth-century church encompasses bits of the original medieval building within its shell; inside you'll find an eighteenth-century Rococo pulpit and a carved altarpiece. The separate wedding-cake bell tower is a later addition. Across the main road from here, the curious **Regiment Museum** (July daily noon–3pm & Tues 6–8pm; rest of year Mon–Fri noon–3pm; free) contains, among other more mundane exhibits, a stuffed regimental horse.

Practicalities

On the pedestrianized main street, the **tourist office**, at Storgatan 49 (June to mid-Aug Mon–Fri 9am–7pm, Sat 10am–3pm, Sun noon–6pm; mid-Aug to May Mon–Fri 8am–4pm; ☎0620/68 29 00, *www.sollefteা.se/turism*), has useful information on local hiking trails and the whole province of Ångermanland. You can get to the tourist office from the adjacent **train** and **bus stations** by following Kungsgatan downhill to its junction with Storgatan. Arriving by **boat**, take Djupevägen up from the jetty until it becomes Järnvägsgatan; this road continues to the main square. The **airport**, served by daily Skyways flights from Stockholm, is 30km southeast of the town, from where there are taxis into the centre (200kr) but no buses.

The **youth hostel** (☎0620/158 17; 110kr) shares its management with the adjacent **hotel**, the *Björklunden* (☎0620/158 17; ①). To get to either, turn right out of the train station and follow the road, crossing the train tracks and turning left at the next T-junction; it's about a two-kilometre walk. The tourist office itself has a few rooms and cabins for rent – ask there for the latest details and prices. Back in town, the cheapest place to stay is *Hotell Appelberg* at Storgatan 51, which represents excellent value for money with its traditional-style rooms (☎0620/121 30; ②/①). More upmarket accommodation is nearby at *City Hotell*, Storgatan 47, with en-suite rooms and cable TV in every room (☎0620/167 00; ③/①). The town's campsite is the beautifully situated *Sollefteå Camping* (☎0620/68 25 42 or 68 25 43; reduced rates with a train pass), right on the river; there are water slides and outdoor heated swimming pools on site. It has twelve four-bed cabins for rent at around 300kr per cabin. To get there, head down Kungsgatan, cross the river and head right.

There's a rash of pizzerias in the centre of town around Storgatan; for good pizza here at reasonable prices, try *La Betola*. At lunchtime, the best deals on this street are to be had at *Appelbergs* **restaurant**, in the hotel of the same name; its *Dagens Rätt* goes for around 50kr, and it also has a good buffet for slightly more. The **pub** and restaurant, *Old House,* also on Storgatan, is worth checking out for its agreeable atmosphere; while you're here, remember to try the local beer, Zeunerts.

Höga Kusten – the High Coast

HÖGA KUSTEN, or the High Coast, is the highlight of any trip up the Bothnian Coast. This stretch of coastline between Härnösand and Örnsköldsvik is of striking elemental beauty: rolling mountains and verdant valleys plunge precipitously into the Gulf of Bothnia, and the rugged shoreline is composed of sheer cliffs and craggy outcrops, as well as gently undulating sandy coves. It's possible to walk along virtually the entire length of the coast on the **Höga Kusten Leden**, a long-

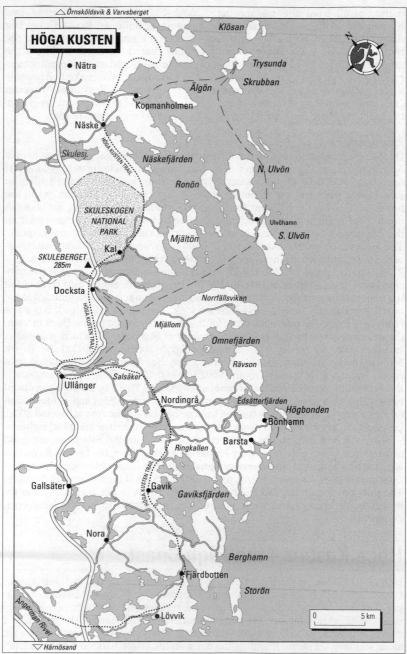

distance hiking path that stretches 130km north from the new bridge over the Ångerman river (see below); we cover this trail on pp.382-383.

Off the Höga Kusten are dozens of islands, some no more than a few metres square in size, others much larger and covered with dense pine forest. It was on these islands that the tradition of preparing the foul-smelling *surströmming* is thought to have begun (see p.379). A trip here is a must for anyone travelling up or down the Bothnian coast; from out at sea, you'll get the best view possible of the coastal cliffs which (as the very name High Coast suggests) are the tallest in the country. The islands themselves are havens of peace and tranquility, offering the chance to get away from it all. Among the most beautiful in the chain are, from south to north, **Högbonden**, **Ulvön** and **Trysunda**; we've covered them in this order, although without your own car, visiting all three will probably require a different sequence, as public transport doesn't allow you to complete a journey between Högbonden and Ulvön on the same day. Each of these islands can be visited using a combination of buses and boats; before setting off, make sure you've understood the boat timetables, which are in Swedish only and can be confusing.

Travel practicalities

The boats that serve the islands here operate only in summer, except for the *M/S Ulvön*, which sails for Ulvön all year round. For the latest bus and ferry times, contact the local transport operator, Din Tur (☎020/511 513, *www.dintur.se*). If you're visiting more than one of the islands, you can save money by buying the **Båtluffarkort**, available at tourist offices or on the boats themselves (late June to mid-Aug; 250kr adults, 125kr children). Containing four boat and three bus tickets, the card covers all the boat routes within the Höga Kusten area except the Bönhamn–Högbonden service; it's also valid on the *M/S Ådalen III*, sailing between Härnösand and Sollefteå (see p.374).

If you're reliant on public transport and want to visit the three islands we cover, the best northbound route is to start at Högbonden, then visit Trysunda, and finally double back south to Ulvön, from where you can connect directly to Örnsköldsvik on the mainland to continue your journey; heading south, make straight for Ulvön on the once-daily boat from Örnsköldsvik, then backtrack north to Trysunda, after which you can get the morning boat across to Köpmanholmen on the mainland and continue south by bus to Bönhamn for the boat across to Högbonden. You can take bicycles on any of the boats, but you should leave your car behind on the mainland as there are hardly any roads on the islands.

Travelling between Härnösand and Örnsköldsvik along the E4 will involve crossing over the Ångerman river via the stunning High Coast **bridge** (no tolls), opened in 1997. The seventh longest suspension bridge in the world, with a span of 1210m, it has dramatically shortened the journey by cutting out a lengthy detour upriver to the old bridge between Lunde and Klockestrand (though this route is still used by some buses). The new bridge is Sweden's tallest construction, reaching a height of 180m above the water; its length is only 70m less than that of its inspiration, San Francisco's Golden Gate Bridge, which it closely resembles.

Högbonden

After a mere ten-minute boat ride from the mainland, the steep sides of the tiny island of **Högbonden** rise up in front of you. Though the island can feel a little overcrowded in peak season, as dozens of people come over from the mainland for the day, at its best, the place is a wonderfully deserted, peaceful haven. There are no shops – so bring any provisions you'll need with you – and no hotels on the island; in fact the only building here is a former lighthouse, now converted into a youth hostel (see below). It's situated on a rocky plateau at the island's highest point, where the pine and spruce trees, so prominent elsewhere on the island, have been unable to get a foothold; Högbonden's flora also includes rowan, sallow, aspen and birch trees, as well as various mosses that compete for space with wild bilberries.

You'll only get to know the special charm of Högbonden if you stay a couple of nights and take time to explore: a narrow gorge runs north–south across the island, and there are also forested hillsides and a shoreline where eider ducks glide by with their young. The **views** out across the Gulf of Bothnia are stunning; on a sunny day you could easily imagine you're in the middle of the Mediterranean. At any time, you can head for the traditional **wood-burning sauna** down by the sea, two minutes' walk from the jetty (it's signposted "*bastu*" off the island's one and only path); you'll need to book your slot with the youth hostel staff, who keep the sauna's key. The logs, which fuel the fire, are piled behind the sauna; if it's been raining, you'll need to pick out some of the driest ones from underneath. If no one's used the sauna for several hours, you may need to restart the fire: matches will start it off, and putting some newspaper in the burner will help get it going. Afterwards, you can take a quick skinny-dip in the cool waters of the Gulf of Bothnia. The sunsets, seen from the boardwalk in front of the sauna, are truly idyllic.

Practicalities

Sailing from the mainland village of **Bönhamn**, the *M/F Högbonden* makes the ten-minute trip out to Högbonden (mid-June to mid-Aug daily 10am–6pm; every 2hr; 60kr return). To get to Bönhamn by car, turn off the E4 at Gallsäter onto the minor road leading there via Nordingrå. The ferry doesn't take cars, so you'll need to leave your vehicle in Bönhamn. To get to Bönhamn on public transport **from Härnösand**, take the 11.55am Norrlandskusten bus to Gallsäter (40min), where you change for a connection at 1.05pm to Nordingrå; once there, you catch the once-daily connecting bus to Bönhamn (mid-June to mid-Aug weekdays only). Tell the bus driver you're taking the boat over to Högbonden, and he'll ring the skipper to ask him to wait for the bus; on the trip back to the mainland, you can ask the ferry man to let the bus driver know of your impending arrival. To head straight for Högbonden **from Stockholm**, take the 6.25am X2000 train to Sundsvall, where you change for Kramfors, arriving at around 11.45am. Head to the bus station (5min on foot from the train station; ask locally for directions) for the bus to Nordingrå, which leaves around 12.20pm. At Nordingrå, you can catch the bus to Bönhamn mentioned earlier. Heading for Högbonden **from Trysunda**, take the 9.15am boat to Köpmanholmen arriving at 10am, then travel on the midday Örnsköldsvik bus as far as Bjästa, where there's a connection at 12.15pm for Ullånger. Change again here for the 1pm service to Nordingrå, where you finally connect on to the bus to Bönhamn.

Högbonden's **youth hostel**, with thirty beds, is in what was its lighthouse (☎0613/230 05; 160kr; mid-May to end-Sept; group bookings only outside mid-June to mid-Aug), reached by means of several sets of steep wooden steps from the path which begins at the jetty.

Ulvön

ULVÖN, 20km northeast of Högbonden and 12km southwest of Trysunda, is really two islands, Norra and Södra Ulvön, their combined area making it the largest in the High Coast archipelago. The southern island is uninhabited, separated from its northern neighbour by a narrow channel, Ulvösund, which provides a well-protected harbour. During the seventeenth and eighteenth centuries, Ulvön became home to the High Coast's biggest fishing community, as fishermen from Gävle came here to exploit the rich fishing grounds off the island; in subsequent centuries, though, many islanders moved to the mainland, especially after World War II, when the industry started to decline. Today, there are only around fifty permanent residents.

Ulvön is famous for its production of **surströmming**, fermented Baltic herring (see below); two of the firms involved, Söderbergs Fisk and Ruben Madsén, are based in the main village of Ulvöhamn (see p.380). It's possible to buy the locally produced stuff in the island's shops.

Travel practicalities

To reach Ulvön **from Härnösand**, take the 9am bus to the village of **Docksta**. There's an **STF hostel** here, 3km south of the village (✆0613/130 64, fax 403 91; 100kr; mandatory advance bookings Sept to mid-May), though you probably won't need to use it; the bus will drop you by the Docksta jetty, from where the *M/S Kusttrafik* leaves at 10.15am (June–Aug daily; ✆0613/105 50, *www.hkship.se*; 135kr return), arriving in **Ulvöhamn**, on Ulvön, at 11.30am, heading back to the mainland at 3pm. Ulvön is easily reached all year round **from Trysunda**, via Köpmanholmen, on the *M/F Ulvön* (✆070/651 92 65; 2hr 30min; 40kr one-way). Sailings are roughly twice daily on weekdays, at 9.15am and 6.20pm, and once daily at weekends. Better and faster is the once-daily

---

SURSTRÖMMING

Mention the word **surströmming** to most Swedes and they'll turn up their noses in disgust. It's best translated as "fermented Baltic herring" – though to the non-connoisseur, the description "rotten" would seem more appropriate. The tradition of eating the foul-smelling stuff began on Ulvön sometime during the sixteenth century when salt was very expensive; as a result just a little was used in preserving the fish, a decision which inadvertently allowed it to ferment.

The number of **salthouses** producing the herring has dwindled from several hundred early in the twentieth century to around twenty to thirty manufacturers now. Today, *surströmming* is made in flat tins containing a weak salt solution. Over the course of the four- to ten-week fermentation process, the tins blow up into the shape of a soccer ball under the pressure of the odious gases produced inside. Restaurants refuse to open the tins on the premises because of the lingering stink that's exuded, not unlike an open sewer; the unpleasant job has to be done outside in the fresh air.

The **season** for eating *surströmming* begins on the third Thursday in August, ending around two to three weeks later, when supplies run out. The fish can accompanied with the yellow, almond-shaped variety of northern Swedish potatoes and washed down with beer or *akvavit*; alternatively it's put into a sandwich, perhaps with onion or tomato, all rolled up in a piece of *tunnbröd*, the thin unleavened bread traditional in this part of the country.

direct service on the *M/F Otilia II*, which takes an hour to reach Ulvön from Trysunda; it departs **from Örnsköldsvik** for Sandviken and Ulvöhamn, via Bockviken on Trysunda (late June to early Aug daily; 2hr 30min; ☎0660/22 34 31; 70kr one-way). The boat leaves Örnsköldsvik at 9.30am, returning from Ulvöhamn at 3pm.

Ulvöhamn

All boats to the island dock at the main village, **ULVÖHAMN**, a picturesque one-street affair with red and white cottages and tiny boathouses on stilts snuggling up to each other eave to eave. Walking along the waterfront, you'll pass the pretty fishermen's chapel, dating from 1622 and now the oldest wooden building in Ångermanland (June–Aug daily 1.45–2.15pm); inside, its walls are covered with flamboyant eighteenth-century murals. The church was established by Gävle fishermen who began summer fishing forays up the Baltic coast in the sixteenth century. Its detached bell tower was once used to signal that it was time to assemble for the daily fishing trip. To get to the **beaches**, follow the sign marked "Strandpromenaden" from the village shop (see below); it's about ten minutes by bike past small sandy coves to the harbour entrance and a promontory of red rocks, Rödharen, beyond which lie several pebbly stretches. The unusual red rock here, which occurs infrequently around the Gulf of Bothnia, is a granite known locally as *rappakivi*.

The **tourist office** is in a tiny wooden hut (mid-June to mid-Aug daily 11am–3.30pm; ☎0660/23 40 93), a short distance from the quay where the *M/S Kusttrafik* from Docksta puts in. You can **rent bikes** here (30kr for 4hr) and pick up information about the *Ulvön Regatta*, an annual gathering for ostentatious yachting types that takes place in July. The island's only **hotel**, *Ulvö Skärgårdshotell*, is just to the right of the quay as you come off the boat (☎0660/22 40 09, fax 22 40 78; ③; May to mid-Oct); it has cosy, modern rooms with good views of the sea. At the other end of the road from the hotel is the jetty where the *M/S Otilia II* puts in; the village **shop** is here too. To get to the non-STF **youth hostel**, about 2km from the harbour, take the road, just beyond the chapel midway between the jetties, that leads uphill to the right (☎0660/22 41 90; 120kr; June to mid-Aug). Pine **cabins** with cooking facilities can be rented on the island (☎0660/22 40 14 or 22 41 57; June–Aug 640kr for one night, 3840kr per week; Sept–May 410kr for one night, 2550kr per week); there are four four-bed cabins at Fiskeläget, just by the village shop, with fantastic views out over the harbour and the bay; and ten four-bed cabins, at Fäbodvallen, a ten-minute walk up the hill behind the harbour. Residents at the latter set of cabins can use its *hälsohus*, a small health spa, containing a sauna, jacuzzi and solarium.

For **eating**, there's the *Almagränd* restaurant, with its limited menu, near the tourist office; and the excellent restaurant at *Ulvö Skärgårdshotell*, with main courses from 100kr; or, for light snacks, *Café Måsen* (11am–3pm only). You may well find it preferable not to eat out but to buy your own **provisions** from the village shop, at the southern end of Ulvöhamn's main street. There's a **pub** below the hotel called *Fred & Barney's*, where a *storstark* costs around 45kr. The place buzzes in summer and is great for making new friends.

Sandviken

To get to the island's second village, **SANDVIKEN**, take the road to the youth hostel and continue on out of town; you'll soon pass Ulvön's cemetery on a tiny island in the middle of a lake. About 5km further from the hostel, over a few hills, lies Sandviken, a fishing village for over three hundred years, now restored to its seventeenth-century prime, its unpainted wooden cabins standing in a row. You can also get here on *M/S Otilia II*, which puts in at Sandviken fifteen minutes after sailing from Ulvöhamn for Örnsköldsvik; the same boat, heading from Örnsköldsvik, can take you back to the main village. With its long, peaceful beach, Sandviken is certainly the place to come if you want to get away from it all.

For a place to **stay**, there are fourteen small cottages (300kr a night, 1750kr a week) and eight boathouses (300kr a night, 1900kr a week) on the beach which function as a sort of tiny holiday resort for about six weeks from the end of June. Running water, toilets, showers and a wood-burning sauna are found in the service building on site; also here the small kiosk sells limited provisions and also rents out **cycles**. To book accommodation here, call ☎0660/752 23 or 22 40 33.

Trysunda

The charming fishing village of **TRYSUNDA**, on the tiny island of the same name, is the best-preserved in Ångermanland, hemmed in around a narrow U-shaped harbour, with forty or so red and white houses right on the waterfront. The village's wooden chapel, which is usually unlocked, is one of the oldest on the Bothnian coast, dating from around 1655. Like the church on neighbouring Ulvön, it is decorated with some colourful murals inside.

Trysunda is crisscrossed with plenty of walking paths, leading through the forests of dwarf pine that cover the island – many of which have become gnarled and twisted under the force of the wind. The island's gently sloping rocks make it ideal for bathing, and you'll find plenty of secluded spots where you can do so. There's a **sandy beach** at **Björnviken**, a bay on the eastern part of the island, and some smooth rocks – ideal for sunbathing – on the north coast, just to the east of **Bockviken**, where *M/S Otilia* from Örnsköldsvik puts in. An easily walked path from the village will take you to both beaches and round the entire island. To continue east from Björnviken, don't be tempted to strike off round the headland, as the rocks there are impassable; instead, stay on the path, which cuts inland, and follow the signs for Storviken.

As you approach or leave the island, you might be lucky enough to catch a glimpse of the elk on the neighbouring island, the volcanic and uninhabited **Skrubban**. Although the island has been a nature reserve since 1940, every year some hunting is allowed to take place here to kill some of the animals and prevent unnecessary suffering from starvation, a practice followed elsewhere in Sweden too.

Practicalities

The *M/S Otilia II* sails here **from Ulvön** (summer 1 daily; 60kr). Heading here **from Örnsköldsvik** or **Högbonden**, you'll need to get to **Köpmanholmen**, from where you can either catch the *Otilia II* or the twice-daily ferry to Trysunda. Coming from Örnsköldsvik, take one of the regular buses from the town to Köpmanholmen (for bus information call ☎0660/844 55). From Högbonden, take the 1.45 pm bus from Bönhamn to Nordingrå (Mon–Fri), where you change for the bus to Gallsäter. At 2.35pm there's a connection north to Bjästa; after about half an hour, the bus will drop you on the E4 motorway at the Bjästa turning. The only landmark on the fifteen-minute walk in to Bjästa is a school; you'll want to be at the station to catch the bus to Köpmanholmen (3.30pm and 4.35pm; 10min), from where the ferry leaves for Trysunda at 5.40pm (30kr; 50min). The journey isn't as complicated as it may sound; in fact every bus on your route will know you're coming because each driver is informed by radio of connecting passengers.

For **accommodation** on Trysunda, seven simple **rooms** are available in the service building of the small marina at the harbour entrance (June–Sept only); three rooms have four beds (360kr per room per night, 2160kr per week), another three have three beds (290kr per night, 1740kr per week), and the remaining room sleeps two (200kr per night, 1200kr per week). There's a kitchen and a sauna in the same building. There are also two **cabins** for rent: one, with a kitchen and hot and cold water, is located close to the village shop by the marina and sleeps six (400kr per night, 2400kr per week); the other, which has no electricity or running water, stands by itself in one of island's bays and also sleeps six in one room (200kr per night, 1200kr per week). Both the rooms and the cabins can be booked at the village shop (Mon–Sat 9am–8pm, Sun 10am–6pm; ☎0660/430 11 or 430 38), where you can also buy the bare necessities, including fresh and smoked fish, and the dreaded *surströmming*. Ask at the shop for their free map of the island.

The High Coast Trail and Skuleskogen National Park

It's possible to walk the entire length of the High Coast along **Höga Kusten Leden**, or High Coast Trail, which stretches 130km from the High Coast bridge at the mouth of the Ångerman river to **Varvsberget**, virtually in the centre of Örnsköldsvik. The trail is divided into thirteen stages, which vary in difficulty and length (all are between 7km and 15km long); see p.383 for details. There's accommodation at each break between stages, mostly in the form of cabins. The buses between Härnösand and Örnsköldsvik stop very close to several stages along the way: Lappudden, Ullånger, Skoved, Skule Naturum (for Skuleberget) and Köpmanholmen. For more **information** on the trail, contact the tourist offices in Härnösand or Örnsköldsvik (see p.372 and p.384), both of which sell the excellent *Small Map Book for the High Coast*, which includes not only good maps of the region but also detailed descriptions of the trail (40kr). For more general guidance on the dos and don'ts of hiking in Sweden, see p.471.

Skuleskogen National Park

The High Coast Trail takes in the eastern edge of the magnificent, 26-square-kilometre **Skuleskogen National Park**, noted for its dense evergreen forests, coastal panoramas and deep ravines. Its main sight is the gorge known as Slåtterdalsskrevan, located at the eastern edge close to the coast; though only 200m long and 7m wide, it's 40m deep.

The park is home to a rich mix of **flora and fauna**, including many varieties of bird. Woodpeckers thrive here, with the grey-headed, black, three-toed, lesser spotted, greater spotted and even the rare whitebacked woodpecker among the types you might see. All four of Sweden's forest game birds, namely the capercaillie, hazelhen, black grouse and willow grouse, are also found here, along with other birds such as the wren, coal tit and crested tit. Among the numerous forest animals in the park are elk, roe deer, lynx, fox, gopher, stoat,

STAGES IN THE HIGH COAST TRAIL

Below, we list the thirteen sections of the High Coast Trail, with accommodation details for each. Most parts of the trail can be easily covered by most people, but where we've described a section as "demanding", you'll need to be pretty fit in order to complete it. Further details of each stage are given in the booklet *Walking Guide The High Coast Path* (30kr), available in both English and Swedish at tourist offices.

HIGH COAST BRIDGE–SÖR-LÖVVIK (9.3km; demanding). Cabins with kitchen at Sjöbodviken.

LÖVVIK–FJÄRDBOTTEN (9.6km; moderate). Four wooden cabins at Fjärdbotten by the promontory at Häggnäset.

FJÄRDBOTTEN–GAVIK (12.8km; demanding). Cabin Nipstugan Lidnipan for a maximum of five or six people.

GAVIK–LAPPUDDEN (11.5km; easy). Six cabins available in Lappudden on the edge of the Vågfjärden.

LAPPUDDEN–ULLÅNGER (15km; demanding). *Hotell Erikslund* (☎0613/104 75).

ULLÅNGER–SKOVED (10.5km; average). Cabins on the beach at Lake Mäjasjön; no cooking facilities.

SKOVED–SKULE NATURUM (6.8km; easy). Youth hostel in Docksta at Dockstavägen 47 (open all year, Sept to mid-May advance bookings only; ☎0613/130 64, fax 403 91; 100kr) complete with sauna.

SKULE NATURUM–KÄL (9.2km; moderate). Cabins at Bergsbodarna, 5km north of Skuleberget mountain; a path leads there from Skule Naturum.

KÄL–NÄSKE (8.5km; demanding). Passes through wilderness. Simple hut by Lake Tärnettvattnet in Skuleskogen National Park.

NÄSKE–KÖPMANHOLMEN (7km; easy). Youth hostel in Köpmanholmen by the ferry quay (☎0660/22 34 96; 100kr; May–Sept; rest of year book in advance on ☎0660/22 37 64).

KÖPMANHOLMEN–SANDLÅGAN (12.3km; demanding). One cabin at Bodviken in the Balesudden nature reserve.

SANDLÅGAN–SVEDJEHOLMEN (12km; moderate). Restored farm storehouse at Småtjärnarna.

SVEDJEHOLMEN–VARVSBERGET (5.5km; easy). Accommodation in Örnsköldsvik (see p.384).

pine marten, mink, mountain hare and red squirrel. Spruce is the dominant tree here; some of the large, mature specimens have regenerated naturally after logging ended one hundred years ago. Half of the park consists of bare stone outcrops home only to a few gnarled and stunted pines – some of these trees are over five hundred years old. You'll also see the slow-growing long beard lichen *(Usnea longissima)*, which is entirely dependent on old spruce trees, on whose branches it's found.

Leading inland through the park are a number of well-marked paths off the High Coast trail that take you past some wonderful, if very steep, countryside. You can also go **mountain climbing** in Skuleskogen; trails up **Skuleberget** (285m), near Docksta, afford stunning views from the top, and anyone in normal shape can make it safely to the summit. For some serious climbing, you can rent equipment at Skule Naturum nature centre (see below) at the foot of the mountain and get sound advice from experts.

Örnsköldsvik

About 75km beyond the northern edge of the High Coast, and about 110km north of Härnösand, lies the port of **ÖRNSKÖLDSVIK** (usually shortened to Ö-vik, pronounced Urr-veek). A busy, modern place stacked behind a superbly sheltered deep-water harbour, Örnsköldsvik began life as a market town in 1842 (when it was known as Köping), becoming a city in 1894. The town's present name comes from that the county governor, Per Abraham Örnsköld; the ending *-vik* simply means "bay". Try not to get stuck in Örnsköldsvik, since a night spent here can be a pretty depressing experience: bars and restaurants are thin on the ground, and there isn't even a cinema. Much better is to head 100km north to buzzing Umeå, or south to the beautiful High Coast or the architectural delights of Härnösand.

Arrival, information and accommodation

The **bus station** is on Strandgatan, right in the centre. **Boats** to and from Trysunda and Ulvön dock at the Arken quay, in front of the bus station. The nearest **train station** is about 30km to the northwest in **Mellansel**, on the main line from Stockholm to Lapland; to get into town, get a Tågtaxi (train-taxi), which you can either hail at the station or book by calling ☎020/75 75 75. The **airport** is 24km northeast of town, from where you can catch a bus (70kr) or taxi (170kr) into the centre. A ten-minute walk from the bus station is the **tourist office** at Nygatan 18 (mid-June to mid-Aug Mon–Fri 9am–7pm, Sat 9am–3pm, Sun 10am–3pm; mid-Aug to mid-June Mon–Fri 10am–5pm; ☎0660/125 37 or 880 15, *www.ovik.se*), where you can get free town maps, bus and boat schedules and accommodation information for both the city and the Höga Kusten islands. It's a ten-minute walk to the tourist office from the bus station: head up the steps by the side of the terminal building, following the sign marked "Turistbyrå"; then cross Lasarettsgatan into Fabriksgatan, which you head down until the junction with Nygatan, where you turn right.

Among the most central of Örnsköldsvik's **hotels** is *Strand City Hotell,* a cheap and cheerful hostel-like establishment at Nygatan 2 (☎0660/106 10, fax 21 13 05; ③/①). Another inexpensive option is the small *Hotell Park* at Örnsköldsgatan 7, just to the north of the bus station (☎0660/103 60, fax 21 17 79; ③/②). Don't be misled by the swanky exterior of the *First Hotell Statt* (☎0660/101 10, fax 837 91; ③/②) down the road at no. 2; its expensive rooms are down at heel and its fittings and decor seemingly Soviet-inspired. Best of all is the plain and functional *Hotell Focus* just up the hill, at Lasarettsgatan 9 (☎0660/821 00, fax 838 67; ④/②). The **youth hostel** is in Överhörnäs, 7km to the southwest (☎0660/702 44; 110kr); to get there, take the local bus for Köpmanholmen from the bus station, and tell the driver where you're going.

The City

A tour of the city will occupy you for no more than a couple of hours: Örnsköldsvik holds little of appeal. The city's only saving grace is its **museum** at Läroverksgatan 1 (mid-June to mid-Aug daily noon–4pm; mid-Aug to mid-June Tues–Sun noon–4pm; 10kr), five minutes from the tourist office. You can ignore its predictable collections of prehistoric finds and nineteenth-century furniture, and ask instead to be let into the adjacent workshop, which conceals a sparkling documentation of the work of **Bror Marklund**, a twentieth-century artist who was born locally. Most of his art was commissioned for public spaces and goes unnoticed by passers-by; for example, his *Thalia* – a sculpture of the goddess of the theatre – rests outside Malmö's City Theatre, and his figures adorn the facade of the Historical Museum in Stockholm. On his death in 1977, he left his plaster models and sketches to the local municipality; inside the workshop, look for the plaster casts used to make the jesters which now decorate the hospital in Sundsvall, brilliantly executed and one of Markland's most well-known works.

Close to the bus station, at Järnvägsgatan 10, is the **Kulturfabriken**, an art gallery and industrial museum (late June to early Aug daily noon–4pm; early–Aug to late June Tues–Fri noon–4pm, Sun noon–3pm; free); a visit here is a handy way to kill time before you leave Örnsköldsvik. It displays the work of local artists, alongside a potted history of the town's most important company, MoDo, one of Europe's biggest producers of paper, newsprint and pulp. To discover the strategic importance of the sawmill and forestry industries to Sweden and learn how paper is made, this is the place.

The liveliest part of town is the harbourside, a pleasant place to eat or drink. It's relaxing to stroll past the impressive culture and business centre, known as Arken, and the old warehouses. For further relaxation or some exercise, you might want to visit the indoor **swimming complex**, Paradisbadet, off Centralesplanaden behind the bus station, with a 25-metre pool, two massive water slides, jacuzzis, a steam room and a heated outdoor pool.

Eating, drinking and nightlife

There are several good **cafés** in Ö-vik. During the day, open sandwiches and cakes are available from *Café UH*, which is inside the *Hotell Focus* (see p.384). Rather better is *Café Brittas II*, in the pedestrianized Storgatan; with its homely feel and home-made cakes and bread, you could easily think you were in your own kitchen. For snacks, check out *Brittas Delikatessen* at Skolgatan 4, serving sandwiches and pies.

There are a number of pizza **restaurants** in the city centre: the best are *Il Padrino* on Läroverksgatan, a dark and dingy little place just off Stora Torget, with pizzas for around 60kr, pasta at 80kr and steaks from 135kr; and the much larger *Restaurangen Mamma Mia*, with outdoor seating on Storgatan and a yard where people play boules in summertime. Off Stora Torget, between Hemköp and the FöreningsSparbanken, is the *China Tower Restaurangen*, a Chinese restaurant that's also a pub; dishes here start at 110kr. For more stylish eating and drinking, head for the more lively harbourside, where restaurants with outdoor tables offer good views out over the water of Örnsköldsviksfjärden. To splash out and indulge yourself, try *StrandKaj 4*, which serves up local delicacies such as reindeer (89kr) and stag (189kr). Decked out as a wooden cabin, the nearby *Fina Fisken* is, appropriately for a place whose name means "fine fish", a seafood restaurant; it has an excellent fish buffet at lunchtime for 65kr, with evening fish dishes from 130kr.

You can buy alcohol at the Systembolaget in Fabriksgatan. Among the **drinking** holes is the brasserie-style place, *Arkenrestaurangen*, next to the harbour, which also offers a lunch deal, including soup, for 85kr and main dishes for around 120kr. Next door, *Puben Nr. 1* charges a reasonable price for beer. The best bar in town, though, is *O'Leary's* at Storgatan 24, an Irish-style pub with a similar menu to others in the chain. Örnsköldsvik's **nightlife** is severely limited; on the corner of Viktoriaesplanaden and Strandgatan there's *Hamncompaniet*, a bar and **disco** popular with 18- to 25-year-olds.

Umeå and around

UMEÅ (pronounced Oom-io) is the biggest city in the north of Sweden: 104,000 people currently reside in and around Umeå, which means that an astonishing one in ten of the population of Norrland (see p.357) live here. Demographically speaking, it's probably Sweden's youngest city, a notion borne out by taking a stroll round the airy modern centre: you'll form the impression that anyone who's not in a pushchair is pushing one, and that the cafés and city parks are full of teenagers. Indeed one in five people are in their twenties, figures that are partly due to the presence of Norrland University in this city. Its youthfulness may well be responsible for the fact that Umeå is the only town or city in northern Sweden where there's an air of dynamism: new restaurants and bars are opening all the time, there's a thriving cultural scene, and by 2006, a high-speed rail link to Stockholm should be completed, making it possible to reach the capital in just five and a half hours.

With its fast-flowing river – a feature no other Swedish coastal city enjoys – and wide, stylish boulevards, Umeå is an appealing metropolis. It would be no bad idea to spend a couple of days here, sampling some of its bars and restaurants – the variety of which you won't find anywhere else in Norrland.

Arrival, information and accommodation

Trains from Stockholm, Gothenburg and Lapland arrive at the **train station**, at the northern end of the city centre on Järnvägsallén. Directly opposite is the long-distance **bus station** used by services from Vilhelmina and Östersund, and by the Norrlandskusten buses. The city centre is a ten-minute walk south from here. Six kilometres from the city is Umeå's busy **airport**, with flights to and from Stockholm, Gothenburg, Luleå and Lapland; it's linked with the centre by airport buses (30kr) and taxis (90kr). Silja line ferries from Vaasa in Finland dock at Holmsund, 20km from Umeå, from where connecting buses run inland to Umeå's bus station.

The city centre is easy to get around on foot, and many of its streets are pedestrianized, including the main drag, Kungsgatan. Everything of interest is north of the River Ume. A good first stop is the **tourist office** in Renmarkstorget (mid-June to mid-Aug Mon–Fri 8am–7pm, Sat 10am–5pm, Sun 11am–5pm; mid-Aug to mid-June Mon–Fri 10am–6pm, Sat 10am–2pm; ☎090/16 16 16, *www.umea.se*), a concrete square whose ugliness is at odds with its romantic name, meaning "reindeer-country square". The helpful staff here dish out assorted literature, including a free multilingual newspaper, *Umeåguiden*, with detailed listings of local events. From the train and bus stations, it's a ten-minute walk down the main thoroughfare, Rådhusesplanden, to the square.

Accommodation

The tourist office will book **private rooms** from 150kr per night (booking fee 25kr). Umeå's bright and airy **youth hostel**, one of the best deals in town, is centrally located at Västra Esplanaden 10, just 450m from the stations (☎090/77 16 50, fax 77 16 95; 100kr). A hotel until 1975, its building then became a drop-in centre for alcoholics and unemployed people; subsequently, it was completely renovated and turned into a youth hostel in 1996, one of the best STF establishments. The nearest **campsite** is *Umeå Camping Stugby* (☎090/70 26 00, fax 70 26 10), 5km from town on the shore of a lake beside the E4 at **Nydala**. Open all year, it has **cabins** for four to six people (610kr a night, 3660kr a week), individual double rooms in other cabins (①) and *trätält* (tiny two-bed huts; ①); washing machines and **bike rental** are also available. To get there, take buses #2, #6, #7 or #82 (these services don't run on Sundays), get off at Nydala and walk for around five minutes towards Nydalabadet, which is signposted. Umeå has a good selection of central **hotels**, the like of which you won't experience anywhere north of here; in short, splash out and treat yourself.

Björken, Lasarettsbacken 10 (☎090/10 87 00). This place is used by patients who've travelled a long way to get to hospital appointments in the city, but don't let that put you off: the rooms here are all good. ④/②.

Comfort Home Hotel Uman, Storgatan 52 (☎090/12 72 20, fax 12 74 20). Home from home, with evening coffee and newspapers for all guests. Not recommended if you want to be left alone. ④/③.

First Hotel Grand, Storgatan 46 (☎090/77 88 70, fax 13 30 55). Newly renovated and quite chic, right in the heart of town overlooking the river. ④/③.

Pilen, Pilgatan 5 (☎090/14 14 60). One of the cheaper smaller hotels, with clean, basic rooms, and weekend and summer discounts. ③/②.

Provobis Umeå Plaza, Storgatan 40 (☎090/17 70 00, fax 17 70 50). This very smart place is where to treat yourself; it even boasts marble washbasins and loudspeakers in the bathrooms. There are superb views from the fourteenth-floor sauna suite, with free light beer, too. ④/③.

Royal, Skolgatan 64 (☎090/10 07 30). A good, centrally located hotel, with modern rooms, a sauna, jacuzzi and solarium. ④/②.

Strand, Västra Strandgatan 11 (☎090/70 40 00, fax 12 18 40). A perfectly adequate budget-class hotel. ③/②.

Tegs, Verkstadsgatan 5 (☎090/12 27 00, fax 13 49 90). The cheapest hotel in town but south of the river and some way from the action. ②/①.

Wasa, Vasagatan 12 (☎090/77 85 40, fax 77 85 49). A comfortable hotel with modern rooms, in a lively central location. ③/②.

Winn, Skolgatan 64 (☎090/71 11.11, fax 12 54 28). Close to the bus station, and good for nearby restaurants and bars. The traffic noise can be obtrusive. ④/②.

The City

The sound of the **rapids** along the River Ume gives the city its name: *uma* means "roar". Umeå is sometimes also referred to as the "City of Birch Trees", after the trees that were planted along every street after a devastating fire in 1888. Most of the city was burnt to the ground in the blaze, and two thirds of the town's three-thousand inhabitants lost their homes. In the rebuilding which soon began apace, two wide esplanades, one of which is Rådhusesplanaden, were constructed to act as fire breaks and help prevent such a disaster happening again. A decree was then handed down stating that the birch was the most suitable tree to add life to the town's newly reconstructed streets; even today, the city council places ads for free trees in the local papers and provides free birch saplings every spring to anyone who wants them.

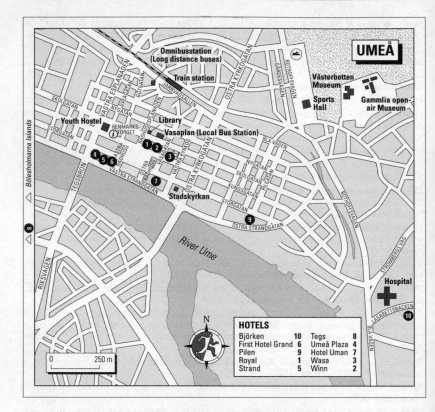

The river freezes over during the coldest winter months, when the *Plaza Hotel* runs **snow-scooter safaris** upriver. Reckon on 800kr per person (minimum five people) for a four-hour trip, which ends with a dip in a hot pot close to the river bank. Another wintertime attraction here is the **northern lights**; January and February are both good months for observing this phenomenon.

Gammlia open-air museum

The highlight of Umeå is undoubtedly its terrific museum complex, **Gammlia**, which merits a good half-day's exploration. It's a twenty-minute walk from the train or bus stations: head east along Järnvägsallén and turn left into Östra Kyrkogatan, crossing under the railway tracks. After the bridge, turn right into Hemvägen, which after its junction with Rothoffsvägen becomes Gammliavägen, leading to the museum.

Gammlia grew out of the **Friluftsmuseum** (late June to late Aug daily 10am–5pm; free), an open-air cluster of twenty regional buildings, the oldest of which is the seventeenth-century gatehouse you pass on the way in. The grounds are home to the customary farmyard animals – cows, pigs, geese and the like – and the people dressed in period costume that you'll meet are very willing to tell you about life in their mock town. It all goes towards creating the right rural ambience for you to wander around, past, among other buildings, a windmill, a church, two threshing floors and a smokehouse for pork. At the bakery, you'll see how the thin unleavened bread, *tunnbröd*, used to be baked in people's homes. You can also take a ride through the grounds in a horse-drawn carriage, an experience that's bound to entertain kids. The indoor **Västerbottens Museum** (late June to late Aug Mon–Fri 10am–5pm, Sat & Sun noon–5pm; late Aug to late June Tues–Fri 9am–4pm, Sat noon–4pm, Sun noon–5pm; free) houses Gammlia's main collection: three exhibitions that canter through the county's past, from prehistoric times (the section on this period contains the oldest ski in the world, over five thousand years old) to the Industrial Revolution. It's all good stuff, well laid out and complemented by an array of videos and recordings; a useful English guidebook is available at reception.

Part of the Västerbottens Museum is the **Bildmuseum** (late June to late Aug daily noon–5pm; late Aug to late June Tues–Sat noon–4pm, Sun noon–5pm; free), one of the country's best art museums outside Stockholm, housing Norrland University's collection. Contemporary Swedish works by artists such as Carl Larsson and Anders Zorn are highlighted here, and there's also a cobbled-together set of old masters. Back outside, you can resume your exploration of county history in the separate **Fiske och Sjöfartsmuseum** (Fishing and Maritime Museum; late June to late Aug daily noon–5pm; late Aug to late June Tues–Sat noon–4pm, Sun noon–5pm; free), which tries its best to be a regional maritime museum – its small hall is clogged with fishing boats.

Bölesholmarna and Norrfors

On the southern side of the river, following the **cycle path**, Umeleden, west from the centre leads you to **Bölesholmarna**, two islands in the river that are an ideal spot for picnics and barbecues. One island even contains a small lake where you can have a quick dip. It takes about twenty minutes to get here on foot from the centre; both the cycle path and the route to the islands are detailed on a free map available from the tourist office. By bike (see "Listings" for rental details), you can carry on further west along the cycle path to the rapids of **Norrfors**, with its five-thousand-year-old rock carvings in the former river bed; it takes about an hour to get here from the centre.

Eating, drinking and entertainment

Eating and **drinking** opportunities are varied and generally of a high standard in Umeå, partly because of the size of the city and partly due to the large student population. Most restaurants and cafés are centred around the central pedestrianized Kungsgatan or Rådhusesplanaden. For fresh fruit and vegetables try the daily market in the main square, Rådhustorget, outside the old Town Hall.

Cafés

Kafé Black, Magasinsgatan. Opposite the railway station. A popular hangout for students, teenagers and 20-somethings, this place serves coffee – in thermos flasks – and cheap snacks.

Konditori Mekka, Rådhusesplanaden 15, close to the train station. Has delicious pastries and cakes, and free coffee refills.

Rex, Rådhustorget. Located in the old town hall. A stylish place to sip coffee, with outdoor seating in summer.

Kafé Station, Östra Rådhusgatan 2L, next to the Filmstaden cinema. Rough brick walls, wooden floors and great coffee.

Vita Björn, in a boat moored off Västra Strandgatan, near the old Town Hall. Sit on deck and enjoy a view over the river.

Wayne's Coffee, Storgatan 50. Another branch of the highly successful chain sweeping Sweden. This one's stylish, elegant and, above all, has a fantastic range of excellent coffee.

Restaurants

Blå, corner of Rådhusesplanaden and Norrlandsgatan. Stylish evenings-only restaurant whose summer eat-until-you-drop smorgasbord (99kr) is popular with a young crowd.

Great Eastern, Magasinsgatan 17, close to the railway and bus stations. The best Chinese restaurant in Norrland. Lunch for 60kr, evening chicken and beef dishes from 86kr.

Il Fratello, corner of Nygatan and Rådhusesplanaden. Probably the priciest place in town: reindeer, duck, sole, lamb from 250kr per head.

K-A Svenssons kök och matsalar, Vasaplan. In an old, blue wooden building with 1960s decor and checked tablecloths. Small dishes for 79kr, fish, seafood or meat dishes for 100kr. The service and the quality of food can vary.

Lottas Krog, Nygatan 22. This pub-restaurant is a good place for lunch; the pub's menu includes a 75kr special of entrecote and potatoes. Also features some sixty different beers, and darts.

Primo Ciao Ciao Restaurant, in the basement of the *Grand Hotell* at Västra Rådhusgatan 1. Good quality local specialities under a vaulted ceiling, from 200kr a dish.

Rex Bar och Grill, Rådhustorget. The most popular – and stylish — place to eat in Umeå, it has everything from spaghetti bolognaise (69kr) to reindeer noisettes in madeira sauce (168kr).

Sjöbris, boat moored off Västra Strandgatan at Kajplats 10. An excellent fish restaurant on board an old white fishing boat. Fresh fish dishes from 100–160kr.

Skytten, Järnvägstorget. Near the train station. Two restaurants in one, an upmarket place with fine cooking, including good fish dishes, and a brasserie with simpler fare.

Teater Cafeet, Vasaplan. A bar-restaurant with grill specialities and light dishes. Lunch here costs 59kr, and there are often also two-course specials for 159kr. During the happy hours here (daily 3–6pm), the price of a beer comes down to 30kr. There's outdoor seating in summer.

V&R, inside the *Plaza Hotell* at Storgatan 40. Very smart and chi-chi; specializes in traditional Swedish dishes given an international flavour.

Bars and nightlife

Umeå buzzes at night, with plenty of stylish and friendly **bars** to choose from, most of them British-style pubs or brasseries. A lot of the **nightlife** revolves around the students, and Umeå is liveliest when they're in town; there are usually discos in the union building, Universum, on term-time weekends (best reached from the centre by taxi as it's a bit far to walk). Strictly, you need to be a student to get in, but you may be let in if you're accompanied by one of the students. For non-student **clubs**, head for the *Plaza Hotel* on Storgatan where there's late-night music and dancing on Friday and Saturday; in winter *Sportpuben Dragonen*, Västra Norlandsgatan 5, is also popular – note there's an age limit of 23 on Saturday nights only.

Blå, Rådhusesplanaden. Though meals can be had here, this place has the distinction of being *the* place to imbibe in town. Lots of glass and chrome, and people with attitude.

Brasseriet Skytten, Rådhusesplanaden 17. One of the most popular places to be seen and to do the seeing – always packed out.

Mucky Duck, Vasaplan. Around forty types of beer; attracts an older crowd.

Rex, Rådhustorget. The all-round establishment: café, pub and restaurant rolled into one. Attracting a trendy 20-something crowd, this place is definitely worth a visit.

Sportpuben Dragonen, Norrlandsgatan 5. A popular pub with large video screens showing various sports. Also has dancing on Friday and Saturday nights.

Listings

Airlines Braathens Malmö Aviation, at the airport (☎090/10 62 80); SAS, at the airport (☎090/18 30 08). For other airlines and general information, call the airport on ☎090/728 30 10.

Banks Föreningsbanken, Renmarkstorget 9; FöreningsSparbanken, Rådhustorget; Handelsbanken, Storgatan 48; Nordbanken, Rådhusesplanaden 3; SEB, Kungsgatan 52.

Beaches Nydala, at Umeå's campsite; Bettnesand, 20km south of town; Bölesholmarna, 15min walk west from the centre along the south bank of the river.

Bike rental Reckon on 50kr a day any of these places: Bike, Storgatan 38 (Mon–Fri 11am–6pm, Sat 11am–2pm); Cykel & Mopedhandlar'n, Kungsgatan 101 (Mon–Fri 9.30am–5.30pm, Sat 10am–1pm; ☎090/14 01 70); Oves Cykelservice, Storgatan 87 (Mon–Fri 8am–5pm, Sat 10am–2pm (☎090/12 61 91).

Buses Long-distance bus station, Järnvägstorget 2 (☎020/91 00 19, *www.lanstrafikeniac.se*). City buses at Vasaplan (☎090/16 22 50).

Cinemas Filmstaden, Östra Rådhusgatan 2D; Folkets Bio, Gärdesvägen 6; Royal, Skolgatan 68.

Ferry tickets Silja Line, in Renmarkstorget (Mon–Fri 9am–5pm;☎090/71 44 00, *www.silja.se*).

Pharmacy Renmarkstorget 6 (☎090/77 05 41).

Police Ridvägen 10 (☎090/15 20 00).

Post office Vasaplan (Mon–Fri 8am–6pm, Sat 10am–2pm; ☎090/15 05 00).

Swimming pools Indoor swimming at Umeå simhall, Rothoffsvägen 12 (☎090/16 16 40).

Systembolaget, Kungsgatan 50A (Mon–Thurs 10am–6pm, Fri 9.30am–6pm).

Taxi City Taxi (☎090/14 14 14); Taxi Umeorten (☎090/13 20 00); Umeå Taxi (☎090/77 00 00); Taxi Lillebil (☎090/441 44).

Train station Järnvägsallén 7 (☎090/15 58 00).

Travel agent Ticket, Kungsgatan 58 (Mon–Fri 9am–6pm, Sat 10am–3pm); Kilroy Travels, Kungsgatan (Mon–Fri 10am–6pm).

North from Umeå: Holmön

The Gulf of Bothnia is at its narrowest between **Holmön**, part of an island group 30km northeast of Umeå, and the Finnish island of Björkö. Consequently, the sea route between the two islands was for centuries used to transport goods, people, soldiers and mail. Sweden and Finland were one country until 1809, and there are still strong links between the respective island communities here; every summer, the **postrodden** (literally "mail row") is held, when a number of boats row and sail their way between Holmön and Björkö just as the mail boats used to do (the starting point alternates between Sweden and Finland from one year to the next). It's worth making the effort to get there for the event, which is usually held in early July; more details can be obtained from Umeå's tourist office. Other summer events worth checking out are the **Sea Jazz Festival**, in the middle of August, and the **Holmöns Visfestivalen**, a **song contest** held in late July, when people get up to sing traditional ditties at drinking parties.

To get to **Holmön**, take the bus from Umeå to the tiny port of **Norrfjärden** (1 daily from Vasagatan; 50min), the departure point for the free **ferry** to the islands (June–Aug 2 daily, Fri 3 daily; 40min; Sept–May Mon–Sat 2 daily, Sun 1 daily; more information on ☎070/346 48 19). The island's **tourist office** (June–Aug daily 10am–5pm; ☎090/552 20), which provides **maps** of the island and rents **bikes**, is a few metres from the jetty where the boat puts in. **Cycling** is a wonderful way to see the small farmsteads, flower meadows and pine forests that fill the landscape; conveniently, this part of Sweden is arguably the sunniest in the country, as has been borne out by 150 years' worth of records from the weather station here. On a bike, you'll also easily be able to find your own secluded little nook where you can swim, though for proper facilities, head to Holmö Havsbad. For a place to **stay**, there's *Bäckströms B&B*, not far from the tourist office (☎090/550 84; 250kr).

Skellefteå

There used to be a real religious fervour about the town **SKELLEFTEÅ** (pronounced Shell-eff-tee-oh), 140km northeast of Umeå. In 1324, an edict in the name of King Magnus Eriksson invited "all those who believed in Jesus Christ or wanted to turn to him" to settle between the Skellefte and Ume rivers. Many heeded the call, and parishes mushroomed on the banks of the Skellefte river. By the end of the eighteenth century, a devout township was centred around the town's monumental church, which stood out in stark contrast to the surrounding plains and wide river. Nowadays, though, more material occupations, including computer and electronics industries, and the mining of gold and silver, support the town. The tourist office makes the most of these metalworks, as well as being disarmingly honest in its attempts to sell the place – as its brochures state: "Don't go to Skellefteå because it seems remarkable – it isn't. The best part of Skellefteå is that it is nice and cosy."

Arrival, information and accommodation

The small centre is based around a modern paved square flanked by Kanalgatan and Nygatan; at the top of the square is the **bus station** and a summertime **tourist office** (end June to early Aug Mon–Fri 10am–7pm, Sat & Sun 10am–3pm; ☎0910/73 60 20, *www.skelleftea.se*), which will provide all the usual information and help with accommodation. The main **tourist office**, open all year, is in Mossgatan (Mon–Fri 8am–5pm; same number). The **airport** is 18km southeast of town, from where buses (40kr) and taxis (179kr) will bring you into the centre.

On the southern bank of the Skellefte river is the **youth hostel**, a yellow pastel building at Elevhemsgatan 13 (☎0910/372 83; 110kr; mid-June to mid-Aug). It's located half an hour's walk from the centre: head east on either Storgatan or Nygatan, turn right onto Viktoriagatan, cross the river over Viktoriabron and take the first left, Tubölegatan, to its end; finally, take the gravel path to its end, and the hostel is on the left. There are four central **hotels**; the cheapest is

Hotell Viktoria at Trädgårdsgatan 8 (☎0910/174 70; ②/①), a family-run establishment on the top floor of one of the buildings on the south side of the main square. Virtually next door at Torget 2, *Hotell Malmia* has perfectly adequate rooms (☎0910/77 7 300, fax 77 88 16; ④/②) and is the centre of Skellefteå's nightlife (see p.394). Nearby at Stationsgatan 8, *First Hotel Statt* has rather dark and dingy rooms, and a breakfast room to match (☎0910/141 40, fax 126 28; ④/②). The smartest hotel is *Scandic Hotel* (☎0910/383 00; ④/③) at Kanalgatan 75, next to the library, but despite its plush surroundings, it's not worth the money. For **campers**, *Skellefteå Campingplats* is about 1500m north of the centre on Mossgatan, just off the E4 (☎0910/188 55); you can rent four-bed **cabins** here for 250kr per night. Popular with dozens of holidaying Norwegians, who, quite inexplicably, drive hundreds of kilometres down the E95 to visit Skellefteå, the site also has a heated outdoor swimming pool, wave machine and jacuzzi.

The Town

There's little to see in the town centre; you should concentrate on the nearby **Bonnstan**, comprising Skellefteå's **church** and **kyrkstad** (parish village). The only museum in town that deserves a visit is the **Anna Nordlander Museum**, one of just three in the world dedicated to women artists; it's on Kanalgatan, inside the library. Born in 1843, Anna Nordlander made plain that art was her first love, showing a remarkable talent for painting in her childhood; she went on to become one of the few successful women artists of her time. The museum is exclusively devoted to her work, mostly landscapes and portraits.

A fifteen-minute walk west from the centre along Nygatan brings you to the **Nordanå Kulturcentrum**, a large and baffling assortment of buildings that's home to a theatre, an old-world grocer's store (labelled "Lanthandel" – the Swedish word for a country grocer's) and a dire **museum** (Mon noon–7pm, Tues–Thurs 10am–7pm, Fri–Sun noon–4pm; free), containing three floors of mind-numbing exhibitions on everything from the region's first settlers to swords. Tucked away to the side of the grocer's store is a pleasant restaurant, *Nordanå Gårdens Värdshus*, with outdoor seating in summer.

The church and parish village

Skellefteå's church and **parish village** are within easy striking distance of the centre: walk west along Nygatan and keep going for about fifteen minutes. An evocative sight, the **kyrkstad** (see box, p.394) here comprises five long rows of weather-beaten log houses, with battered wooden shutters. The houses are protected by law: any renovations, including the installation of electricity, are forbidden. You can take a peek inside, but bear in mind that these are privately owned summer houses today. Next to these cottages is the **kyrka** (daily: mid-June to Aug 10am–6pm; Sept to mid-June 10am–4pm; free), a proud white Neoclassical church which so enthused Leopold von Buch, a traveller who visited here in the nineteenth century, that he was moved to describe it as "the largest and most beautiful building in the entire north of Sweden, rising like a Palmyra's temple out of the desert". Its domed roof is supported by four mighty pillars along each of the four walls; inside, there's an outstanding series of medieval sculptures. Look out too for the 800-year-old *Virgin of Skellefteå*, a

---

SWEDEN'S PARISH VILLAGES

After the break with the Catholic Church in 1527, the Swedish clergy were determined to teach their parishoners the Lutheran fundamentals, with the result that, by 1681, church services had become compulsory. There was one problem with this requirement, though – the population in the north was spread over considerable distances, making weekly attendance impossible. The clergy and the parishes agreed a compromise: it was decreed that those living within 10km of the church should attend every Sunday; those between 10km and 20km away, every fortnight; and those 20–30km away, every three weeks. The scheme worked, and within a decade, **parish villages (kyrkstäder)** had appeared throughout the region to provide the travelling faithful with somewhere to spend the night after a day of praying and listening to powerful sermons.

Of the 71 parish villages Sweden originally had, only eighteen are left today, predominantly in the provinces of **Västerbotten** and **Norrbotten**. Each *kyrkstad* consists of rows of simple wooden houses grouped tightly around the church. The biggest and most impressive, at **Gammelstad** near Luleå (see p.401), is included in the UNESCO World Heritage List; another good example, aside from the one in Skellefteå, is at **Öjebyn**, near Piteå (see p.396). Today, they are no longer used in the traditional way, though people still live in the old houses, especially in summer, and sometimes even rent them out to tourists.

---

walnut woodcarving near the altar – it's one of the few remaining Romanesque images of the Virgin in the world. Nearby, on the River Skellefte, is a pretty place to sit and while away an hour or two: the islet of **Kyrkholmen**, reached by a small wooden bridge. It's home to an outdoor **café** that's handy for a cup of coffee and simple sandwiches (late May to Aug).

From the church you have two walking routes back to the centre: either take Strandpromenaden along the river's edge, interrupted by barbecue sites and grassy stretches; or cross **Lejonströmsbron**, the longest wooden bridge in Sweden, beneath the hill where the church stands. Dating from 1737, the bridge was the scene of mass slaughter when Russian and Swedish forces clashed there during the war that started in 1741. Once on the south side of the river, you can stroll back to Parksbron, past the occasional boat and silent fisherman.

Eating, drinking and nightlife

For all its contemporary go-ahead industry, modern Skellefteå is quiet and retiring; its restaurants will barely whet your appetite, and there are few interesting bars. For **cafés**, try *Café Carl Viktor* at Nygatan 40, or the popular *Lilla Mari* at Köpmangatan 13, both good for an afternoon break. The **restaurant** on the verandah at the *Scandic Hotel* offers northern Swedish food for around 150kr; it's the place to try reindeer and cloudberries. In the main square, *Fosters* is a restaurant where **lunch** goes for 60kr; you're better off at *Urkraft*, at the corner of Nygatan and Tjärhovsgatan (Mon & Sun 11am–1pm; Tues–Thurs 11am–1pm & 4–10pm; Fri & Sat 11am–1pm & 6pm–midnight); with a young, friendly clientele, it too serves a *Dagens Rätt* for 60kr. There are two decent pizzerias in town: *Pizzeria Pompeii* at Kanalgatan 43 serves pizzas (60kr) and meat dishes (80–90kr), and *Pizzeria Dallas* at Köpmangatan 9 has fourteen different pizzas (each 35kr).

MOVING ON FROM SKELLEFTEÅ

The easiest way to continue **north** from Skellefteå is by one of the frequent **Norrlandskusten buses** which stop in Piteå, before terminating in Luleå. The nearest **train station** is at Bastuträsk, which is on the main line; you can get there by bus (4 daily; 50min). For **Lapland**, take the 7.15am bus to Bastuträsk to connect with the northbound train to Boden and Luleå; change at Boden for Gällivare, Kiruna and Abisko. To travel **south** by train, take either the 6pm or 10.45pm bus to Bastuträsk, where you can connect onto the night train south to both Stockholm and Gothenburg (the later bus though only connects with the train to Stockholm). Skellefteå is also connected by **air** to Sundsvall, Umeå and Stockholm. Airport buses (40kr) call at *First Hotel Statt* on Stationsgatan and *Scandic Hotel* on Kanalgatan about an hour before Stockholm planes depart; a taxi will cost approximately 179kr. For airport information call ☎0910/68 32 10.

Drinking is best done at *MB* at *Hotell Malmia* in the main square, where a beer is just 24kr during happy hour. It has outdoor seating in summer, when people gather here to listen to pop music on disc and catch the last rays of the sun before it disappears behind the tall buildings on the other side of the square. Also worth a look nearby on Storgatan is the traditional-English-style *Old William's Pub*. The oddly named *Restaurant Etage*, inside the *Malmia* is actually the best **disco** in town; though in summer, *Mollys Nightclub*, at the same hotel, puts up stiff competition, staying open until 3am.

Into Norrbotten: Piteå and around

Located in Sweden's most northerly province, Norrbotten, the small town of **PITEÅ** has a history that goes back to the beginning of the fourteenth century, when the village was founded at **Öjebyn**, site of one of northern Sweden's oldest **parish villages** (see opposite). At the time of Piteå's being granted its town charter, in 1621, it was still situated 5km west of its current location, but a fire in 1666 destroyed much of the town, and it was decided to up sticks and move it to the coast. Tragically, the Russians burnt the new town to the ground in 1721. Piteå today is a mix of modern concrete buildings, pedestrianized shopping streets and anodyne squares, as well as being home to one of Sweden's biggest paper producers, AssiDomän. There's very little to do in Piteå itself; it's best to use the place as a base to see Öjebyn's *kyrkstad* and the beach resort of Pite Havsbad.

Pite Havsbad

Once you've had a quick look around town, it's best to escape the concrete grey of the centre and head out to the superb beaches and swimming complexes at **Pite Havsbad**, 10km to the southeast. You can get here easily from Piteå on **bus #1** (they'll display the destination "Pite Havsbad"; hourly until 8pm; 14kr); the Norrlandskusten bus also stops here on the way to and from Skellefteå. Now one of the most popular summer resorts in Sweden, Pite Havsbad is renowned for its long hours of summer sunshine, and for sandy beaches that are well looked after, friendly and not as crowded as you might expect. There's even a separate official

ÖJEBYN'S PARISH VILLAGE

Centred around a fifteenth-century medieval stone church on Kyrkovägen, the **kyrkstad** at **Öjebyn** is one party in an ongoing debate as to whether it's the oldest in Sweden, a title also claimed for the parish village at nearby Luleå. Inside the church, the 1706 carved pulpit is the work of a local craftsman, Nils Fluur, and the Baroque altar was brought from Stockholm at the start of the eighteenth century. The small wooden cottages here are privately owned and most of them still have no electricity. To get to Öjebyn from Piteå, take bus #1 from the bus station (hourly till 4.15pm).

nudist beach, quite a rarity in Sweden, given that you can sunbathe nude more or less anywhere you choose away from the crowds. To reach the nudist beach, follow the side of the main building of the swimming complex down to the sea, turn left along the beach and look out for a large rock, with the words "Naturist Bad" painted on, approximately where the caravan park ends; the beach runs as far as the wooden post marked "Här slutar naturistbad". Back at the swimming complex, you'll find open-air pools with water slides, and the indoor Tropical Bath, with its jacuzzis, saunas and decorative waterfalls.

Practicalities

Piteå's **bus station** is located at the end of the pedestrianized Prästgårdsgatan, the main street. The **tourist office**, at Noliagatan 1 (June–Aug Mon–Sat 9am–8pm, Sun noon–8pm; Sept–May Mon–Fri 8am–5pm; ☎0911/933 90, *www.pitea.se*), can fix up **private rooms** for around 300kr per person per night (there are also a couple available for just 100kr). The **youth hostel** is located in the old hospital, 2km out of town at Storgatan 3 (☎0911/158 80; 130kr): from the bus station, walk east to the junction with Trädgårdsgatan, where you turn right and continue on until you come to a path leading off to the left, which is actually the beginning of Storgatan. Of the town's two **hotels**, the comfortable *Stadshotellet* at Olof Palmes Gata 1 is the older (☎0911/197 00, fax 122 92; ④/③); its smart rooms have an old-world atmosphere, with grand furnishings. Cheaper is *Skoogs City Hotell* at Uddmansgatan 5, off the main square (☎0911/10 000, fax 10 001; ③/②); it's smaller and has less character. The **campsite** at Pite Havsbad, one of the largest in the country, has a variety of four-bed cabins, which can be rented for 690–1390kr per night (☎0911/327 00, fax 327 99). There's also a modern hotel here, *Hotell Pite Havsbad* (same tel & fax as campsite; ⑤/④).

Most **restaurants** in Piteå serve up **pitepalt**, a local speciality, akin to dumplings and eaten with butter; it's made from potato and flour rolled up into balls, stuffed with meat, then boiled. In the middle of July, there's a good chance they'll be served up for free along Storgatan – for no reason in particular. The range of **restaurants** in town (most of which serve *pitepalt*) is pretty limited; the best bet is *Pentryt* at Sundsgatan 29 (closed Fri), with lunch deals for around 50kr – it serves food until 8pm, when it turns into a bar and disco. Another reasonable choice is *Pigalle*, across the road at Sundsgatan 36, renowned for its big portions; a meat-based main dish will cost 100–200kr. The best pizzeria is *Angeln* at Källbogatan 2, with pizzas and pastas from 45kr. **Drinking** dens include the *Cockney Pub*, serving expensive beer downstairs at the *Stadshotellet*; and *Karls Källa*, where beer costs slightly less, in Sundsgatan.

MOVING ON FROM PITEÅ

Taking the **Norrlandskusten bus** to Luleå is the easiest way to continue your journey north. You can also use buses to connect with the Gothenburg–Lapland **train** line. To head north by train, take the Norrlandskusten service to Luleå and change there; to head south, take the 4.30pm bus from Piteå to Älvsbyn (50min), which connects with the sleeper to Gothenburg and Stockholm, or get the 7.20pm Älvsbyn bus (not Sat), which connects with the later train south to Stockholm.

Luleå and around

When **LULEÅ** (pronounced "loo-lee-o"), twenty-five minutes down the train line from Boden and 55km from Piteå up the E4, was founded in 1621, it had at its centre a parish village (see p.394) and medieval church. Numerous trading ships would load and unload their goods at its tiny harbour, reflecting the importance of trade with Stockholm even in those days. The harbour soon proved too small, thanks to the growth in business, and so, by royal command, the settlement was moved to its present site in 1649; only the church and parish village, today part of Luleå's **Gammelstad** (Old Town), remained in situ. Up until the end of the eighteenth century, Luleå was still little more than a handful of houses and storage huts; indeed Linnaeus, Sweden's famous botanist, who passed through here in 1732 on his journey to Lapland, described Luleå as a village. Though the town had started to become something of a shipbuilding centre in the nineteenth century, it wasn't until the construction in 1888 of the Malmbanan, the railway built to transport iron-ore from the Gulf of Bothnia for wintertime export at the ice-free Norwegian port of Narvik, that Luleå's fortunes really started to flourish. Luleå was at one end of the line, and its port was vital for lucrative iron exports (the main ironfields were – and are – around Kiruna and Malmberget).

Although shipping is still important today, in recent years Luleå has become the hi-tech centre of the north, specializing in metallurgy; it also has an important university. The town's wide streets and lively, friendly atmosphere make Luleå immediately likeable, and if you're heading north for the wilds of the Torne valley, Gällivare and Kiruna, or to the sparsely populated regions of Lapland, Luleå represents your last chance to enjoy a decent range of restaurants and bars before entering the forest and wilderness that spreads north and west from here. Be mindful of the weather, though: Luleå is built on a peninsula which takes the full brunt of the northerly winds.

Arrival, information and accommodation

The **train** and **bus stations**, five minutes' walk apart, are at the eastern end of the central grid of streets. A good ten-minute walk to the west is the **tourist office**, in the Kulturcentrum Ebeneser at Storgatan 43B (mid-June to mid-Aug Mon–Fri 9am–7pm, Sat & Sun 10am–4pm; mid-Aug to mid-June Mon–Fri 10am–6pm, Sat 10am–2pm; ☎0920/29 35 00 or 29 35 05, *www.norrbotten.se*). Kallax **airport** lies 10km from the city, with buses (40kr) and taxis (145kr) linking it with Luleå.

Private rooms – of which there are only about ten here – can be booked through the tourist office for about 200kr per person. The **youth hostel**, out at

Gäddvik (☎0920/25 23 25, fax 25 24 19; 100kr), unfortunately suffers from being close to the main E4 – the drone of heavy lorries penetrates the thin walls of the tiny cabins all through the night. To get there, take bus #6 from right outside the main door of the train station (hourly; 10–15min), and tell the bus driver where you want to go; get off at the stop just after the bridge over the Lule river, and take the riverside footpath. Once you have passed under the motorway bridge, cut up to the right through the trees to the red buildings of the hostel. Another five minutes' walk on from the youth hostel is Luleå's nearest **campsite** (☎0920/25 00 60). Below we give a selection of Luleå's **hotels**, most of which are modern and centrally located.

Amber, Stationsgatan 67 (☎0920/102 00, fax 879 06). A small and cosy family-run place in an old wooden building. Summer doubles for 600kr. ④/②.

Arctic, Sandviksgatan 80 (☎0920/109 80, fax 607 87). This smart little hotel, with en-suite rooms, is very handy for the train station. ⑤/②.

Aveny, Hermelinsgatan 10 (☎0920/22 18 20). Another compact, modern and comfortable hotel. ④/②.

Provobis Luleå Stads, Storgatan 15 (☎0920/670 00, fax 670 92). Right in the centre of town, this is the oldest and smartest of the city's hotels, with old-fashioned rooms, kitted out with drapes and large armchairs, and a huge breakfast buffet. ⑤/③.

Park, Kungsgatan 10 (☎0920/21 11 49). Without en-suite rooms, this basic place, the cheapest of Luleå's hotels, is perfectly acceptable. ③/①.

Radisson SAS Luleå, Storgatan 17 (☎0920/940 00). A modern hotel, done out in dark, heavy colours – a bit too sombre. ⑤/③.

The City

Just to the south of **Storgatan**, the main street, lies Luleå's main square, **Rådhustorget**, by the southeast corner of which is the **Domkyrkan** (Mon–Fri 10am–3pm; free), whose medieval incarnation disappeared centuries ago. The present cathedral, built in 1893 on the same spot as its predecessor, is a modern barrage of copper chandeliers hanging like Christmas decorations. Unusually for northern Sweden, it's built of brick in late Gothic style to the design of the architect Adolf Emil Melander. The interior was completely renewed in 1938 when the original wooden walls and fittings were removed, revealing the brickwork underneath which was then painted white. Southeast of the Domkyrkan, **Konstens Hus** at Smedjegatan 2 is worth a look, with interesting displays of work from modern Swedish artists and sculptors (Tues &Thurs-Fri 11am-6pm, Wed 11am-8pm, Sat & Sun noon-4pm; free); to get there, head east from the Domkyrkan until you reach Smedjegatan, when you turn right and walk about 200m south.

Back at the main square, walk 300m west along Köpmangatan, and you'll come to the **Norrbottens Museum** at Storgatan 2 (Mon–Fri 10am–4pm, Sat & Sun noon–4pm; free). Containing the usual, rather dull resumé of county history, it's worth a look mainly for the informative displays and exhibitions on *Sámi* life and culture that predominate northwest of Luleå (see p.456). The museum also has a pleasant **café**.

When the weather's good, it's worth heading to the oddly named **Gültzauudden**, a wooden promontory that has a great **beach**; it was named after the German shipbuilder, Christian Gültzau, who helped to make Luleå a shipbuilding centre. You can get there from the main square by heading north on Rådstugatan until you reach Norra Strandgatan, where you turn left and continue

for around 600m. On warm days, it can seem like Luleå's population have all come down to the beach.

Eating, drinking and nightlife

While the city often has a busy feel in summer, from a **cultural** standpoint Luleå is most busy when the university is in session. The best bet for music recitals and theatre productions all year round is the Kulturcentrum Ebeneser at Storgatan 43B; with a good café downstairs, this is the biggest concert hall in Luleå (contact the tourist office, in the same building, for information about events here). For concerts of all types, the small **theatre**, *Lillian*, is also worth trying; it's at Skeppsbrogatan 16 (☎0920/29 41 00). There are two **cinemas** in town: Filmstaden at Timmermansgatan 19 (☎0920/27 02 00) and Sandrews at Nygatan 1 (☎0920/21 10 15). During the second week of August, fiddle and accordion players travel from all across Sweden to perform at the **Svensk Folkmusikfestival**, which takes place at the Ebeneser Kulturcentrum (tickets from the tourist office; 120kr).

Drinking is generally done at the main restaurants listed, although a couple of British-style **pubs** have become inordinately popular. You can go **clubbing** at the raucous *Cleo Nightclub*, Storgatan 17; *Bryggeriet* on Västra Varvsgatan, popular with 20- to 25-year olds and known for its house and soul music; and, during the summer months, the very loud *Terrazzen*, inside the *Provobis Luleå Stads* hotel, on Skeppsbrogatan. The most lively and interesting **places to eat** are all found along Storgatan.

Restaurants and bars

Ankaret, Köpmangatan 16, near the Domkyrkan. Serving delicious fish dishes (from 100kr), this place is deservedly very popular.

Bryggan, inside *Stads Hotell* at Storgatan 15. Offers great views out over the northern harbour, and international fare, with main courses at around 150kr.

Cook's Krog, inside *Radisson SAS Luleå Hotel* at Storgatan 17. Intimate and cosy, this is the best place in Luleå for steak cooked over a charcoal grill, for around 200kr.

Corsica, Nygatan. The dark and dingy interior notwithstanding, this place offers a welcome change from Swedish fare, serving some traditional Corsican dishes as well as lots of steak and pizzas. Entrecôte for 98kr.

Fiskekyrkan, in Södra Hamnen. Walk down Nygatan, cross Sandviksgatan, and you'll see the seafront orange warehouse building housing this place. One of the cheaper restaurants in town, with pasta and other simple dishes for around 100kr, it's also a popular drinking hole in the evenings.

O'Leary's, Skomakargatan 22. Has Tex-Mex-style food for around 120kr, with a good choice of beer too. It's definitely *the* place to watch, from its adjoining terrace, the summer sun set over the northern harbour.

Oliver's Inn, Storgatan 11. Serving pub food and a good selection of beer, this bar is known for its 1970s and 1980s music, which attracts a large crowd at weekends.

Pasta Restaurangen, tucked away in a side street at Magasinsgatan 5. Serves hefty pizzas from around 60kr.

Pimpinella, Storgatan 40. This is the liveliest and trendiest bar in town, catering to a young crowd, with tables out in the street during summer. Good-value food can be ordered at the bar.

Tallkotten, inside the *Provobis Luleå Stads* hotel at Storgatan 15. A smart business person's restaurant, serving high quality, high-price dishes. Expense-account stuff.

Tegel, Storgatan 27. Wear your sharpest clothes, darkest shades and sip a chilled foreign beer before going clubbing here. The predictably stylish menu in its restaurant is surprisingly good value.

Waldorf, Storgatan 33. Inside the Wasa City shopping centre. Renowned for its pizzas, this restaurant also serves decent Chinese and Japanese food. Pizzas from 60kr upwards, more substantial dishes over 100kr.

Listings

Airlines SAS, Storgatan 61, close to the bus station (Mon–Fri 9am–6pm, Sat 10am–2pm; ☎0920/24 31 00).

Airport ☎0920/58 71 00.

Banks Handelsbanken, Storgatan, between the *Luleå Stads* hotel and tourist office; Nordbanken, Köpmangatan, near the pharmacy.

Buses City buses are operated by Kvarteret Loet (☎0920/24 11 00); long-distance bus information is on ☎020/47 00 47 and at *www.ltnbd.se*.

MOVING ON FROM LULEÅ

From Luleå, **trains** run northwest along the Malmbanan to Murjek (change here for bus connections to Jokkmokk, see p.462), Gällivare, Kiruna, Abisko, Riksgränsen and ultimately Narvik in Norway. Services along this route can be subject to lengthy delays, particularly in winter, so plan your journey with flexibility in mind. In the opposite direction there's a once daily service via Boden and Haparanda to Tornio in Finland (mid-June to mid-Aug only). **Buses** complement the train service in this part of Sweden; particularly useful routes from Luleå are bus #21 (for Älvsbyn and Arvidsjaur); bus #44 (for Jokkmokk and Gällivare); bus #10 (for Gällivare and Kiruna); bus #11 (for Haparanda); bus #55 (for Pajala); and bus #94 (for Kvikkjokk via Murjek and Jokkmokk). From Luleå airport there are short **flights** to Gällivare and Kiruna – with fantastic views of the extensive forest and tundra or northern Lapland.

Three **night trains** run **south** from Luleå; the first leaves at 4.45pm for Gothenburg, followed by trains for Stockholm at 5.05pm and 9pm. The Stockholm services operate via Boden, Gävle, Uppsala and Arlanda airport; the 4.45pm Gothenburg service provides the only train connection between Luleå and Umeå. By taking the 9pm train you can also reach Östersund (change in Bräcke at 5.30am) and Sundsvall (change in Ånge). There are four daily **Norrlandskusten buses** from Luleå to Sundsvall via the towns along the Bothnian Coast.

Car rental Avis, at the airport (☎0920/22 83 55); Budget, Robertviksgatan 3 (☎0920/131 11); Europcar, at the airport (☎0920/101 65); Englunds Hyrcenter, Hummergatan 8 (☎0920/24 44 74); Hertz, Gammelstadsvägen 23 (☎0920/873 44); Statoil, Stationsgatan 30 (☎0920/186 22).

Hospital Luleå Lasarett, Repslagaregatan 6–8 (☎0920/710 00).

Pharmacy Köpmangatan 36c (Mon–Fri 9am–6pm, Sat 9am–2pm, Sun –4pm; ☎0920/22 03 95).

Police Skeppsbrogatan 37 (☎0920/29 50 00).

Post office Storgatan 53 (Mon–Fri 8am–6pm, Sat 10am–2pm; ☎0920/841 21).

Swimming pool Pontusbadet, Bastugatan 6–8 (☎0920/29 32 72).

Systembolaget Corner of Nygatan and Storgatan (Mon–Wed & Fri 10am–6pm, Thurs 10am–7pm).

Taxi Taxi Luleå (☎0920/100 00); 6:ans Taxi (☎0920/666 66); Taxi Kurir (☎0920/22 26 66).

Trains For train times call ☎0920/22 23 33 or ☎0920/75 75 75.

Travel agent Ticket, Storgatan 27 (Mon–Fri 9am–6pm, Sat 10am–1pm).

Gammelstad

One of the most significant places of historical interest north of Uppsala, **GAMMELSTAD**, the original settlement of Luleå, is included on UNESCO's World Heritage List. The **church** here (June–Aug Mon–Fri 8am–5pm, Sat 8am–2pm, Sun 8am–5pm; Sept–May Mon–Fri 10am–2pm; free) was completed at the end of the fifteenth century; originally intended to be a cathedral, it's one of the largest churches in Norrland, and among the most impressive in the whole of Sweden. The building was worked on by artists from far and wide. On the outside are decorative brick and plaster gables and there's an opening above the south door through which boiling oil was poured over unwelcome visitors. The high altar, made in Antwerp, is adorned with finely carved biblical scenes; the decorated choir stalls and ornate triptych are other medieval originals. Have a close look at the sumptuous 1712 pulpit, too, a splendid example of Baroque extravagance, its details trimmed with gilt cherubs and red and gold bunches of grapes.

When Luleå was moved to the coast, a handful of the more religious among the townsfolk stayed behind to tend the church, and the attached **parish village**, the largest in Sweden, remained in use. It comprises over four hundred **cottages**, gathered around the church; these can only be occupied by people born in Gammelstad (even people from Luleå must marry a local to gain the right to live here).

Practicalities

Gammelstad, 10km northwest of the modern city centre, is readily reached by **bus** from Luleå: bus #32 operates during the summer months (Mon–Fri 2 hourly, reduced service at weekends), while outside the summer period buses #8 and #9 run here every half-hour. Services leave from Hermelinsparken, at the west end of Skeppsbrogatan; in summer the last one back is at 7.45pm Monday to Friday (5.40pm on Sat and 5.05pm on Sun); the journey takes 30min. The **tourist office** is right by the old church (mid-June to mid-Aug daily 9am–6pm; mid-Aug to mid-June Mon–Fri 11am–4pm; ☎0920/25 43 10, *worldheritage.gammelstad@lulea.se*); they organize guided walks around the village and have brochures telling you all about the historical significance of the place. Down the hill from the tourist office is **Friluftsmuséet Hägnan** (June to mid-Aug daily noon–5pm), an **open-air heritage park**, whose main exhibits are two old farmstead buildings from the eighteenth century. During summer, it plays host to displays of rural skills, such as sheep-rearing, the making of traditional wooden roof slates and the baking of northern Sweden's unleavened bread, *tunnbröd*. For a place to **eat**, there's *Margaretas Wärdshus*, in a beautiful old wooden house at Lulevägen 2, close to the old church; among the fine fare it serves up are Norrbotten delicacies like reindeer and arctic char.

Off the coast of Luleå: the archipelago

Luleå's **archipelago** is the only one in the world surrounded by brackish water (the Atlantic Ocean off the Norwegian port of Narvik contains ten times more salt than this part of the Gulf of Bothnia). Made up of over 1700 islands and skerries, most of which are uninhabited and unexploited, it's well worth a visit; the islands are renowned for rich birdlife and a profusion of wild berries: lingonberries, blueberries and raspberries are very common, with arctic raspberries, cloudberries, wild strawberries and sea buckthorns also found in large numbers. The **islands** mentioned below are among the most **popular** destinations in the archipelago; being served by once-daily boats from Luleå, they're also the most easily accessible.

The wildest and most beautiful of all the islands is **Brändöskär**. Located far out in the Gulf of Bothnia, the island can often by very windy; its best features are some terrific upland scenery and smooth rocks along the coast, ideal for sunbathing.

People have lived and worked on **Hindersön**, one of the bigger islands here, since the sixteenth century. Then, fishing, farming and catching seals were the main occupations; today, this is the only island north of Arholma in the Stockholm archipelago which is still farmed.

Kluntarna has a little of everything – small fishing villages, dense pine forest and thousands of seabirds – and is a good choice, especially if you've only time to visit one island. You can rent a simple **cottage** here (book at Luleå's tourist office; 150kr), and there's a sauna for your use as well.

South of Luleå in the outer archipelago is **Rödkallen**. Site of an important lighthouse, this tiny island offers fantastic sea and sky views; parts of it have been declared a nature reserve.

Klubbviken, a bay on the island of **Sandön**, is the place to come for good sandy beaches, and has the added advantage of regular boat connections to Luleå. Walking paths crisscross the island, taking in some terrific pine moorland scenery. **Cabins** on Klubbviken can be booked at the tourist office; reckon on 550kr for four people per night.

Småskär is characterized by virgin forest, flat cliff tops and countless small lakes. The island traces its history back to the seventeenth century, when it was a base for Luleå's fishermen. Its small chapel, dating from 1720, was the first to be built in the archipelago.

Travel practicalities

Three **boats** serve the various islands in the archipelago from June to August. From Luleå's northern harbour, *M/S Favourite* goes to **Brändöskär, Hindersön, Rödkallen, Altappen, Junkön, Småskär** and **Kluntarna**. You're most likely to find yourself on board this boat since it serves more islands than the other two; information on routes and times can be obtained from Luleå's tourist office or on ☎0920/11 06 85. The *M/S Laponia* sails, also from the northern harbour, to **Kluntarna, Småskär, Altappen** and **Brändöskär** (details of sailings on ☎0920/120 84 or 070/530 33 44, *www.laponia.net*). From the southern harbour, day trips out to the sandy beaches of **Klubbviken** on the island of **Sandön** are made by the *M/S Stella Marina* (details of sailings on ☎0920/22 38 90 or 010/225 07 61).

Boden

Roughly halfway along the coast of Norrbotten, at the narrowest bridging point along the Lule river, **BODEN** is a major transport junction for the entire north of the country; from here, trains run northwest to Gällivare and Kiruna and eventually on to Narvik in Norway, south to Stockholm, Gothenburg and Arlanda Airport, as well as east to Haparanda and Finland (see box, p.404, for details on getting to Finland by train). From the station, you simply head west along Kungsgatan to get to the town centre, a ten-minute walk. Although first impressions of Boden are of a drab northern town, things get considerably better around the **Överluleå kyrka** (mid-June to end-June & early July Aug daily 1–7pm; rest of the year daily 10am–2pm) and its **parish village**, which were founded in 1826. It's roughly a twenty-minute walk here from the station, turning right into Strandplan once you've crossed the Kungsbron bridge on Kungsgatan. Pleasant enough in itself, the church's appeal benefits considerably from its location, perched on a hillock, surrounded by whispering birch trees and overlooking the water. The surrounding cottages of the parish village once spread down the hill to the lake, Bodträsket, lining narrow little alleyways. Today, the cottages that remain are rented out as superior **hostel accommodation** during the summer (see p.405).

CROSSING INTO FINLAND BY TRAIN

Trains to and from **Finland** are meant to resume in the summer of 2000, after a break of several years. A service should run between Luleå and Tornio via Boden and Haparanda (mid-June to mid-Aug 1 daily), timed to provide connections in Boden with other north and southbound services (change in Tornio for Finnish trains to Kemi). Current train information can be obtained by calling ☎020/75 75 75 (or visiting *www.tagkompaniet.se*). Travellers heading for Haparanda outside the summer months can also make the journey by bus #27 to Börjeslandet, changing there to bus #11 (105kr; rail passes valid).

Boden happens to have the distinction of being Sweden's largest military town: everywhere you look, you'll see young men kitted out in camouflage gear and badly fitting black boots strutting purposefully (if somewhat ridiculously) up and down the streets; there are infantry, tank, artillery and air corps here. At the turn of the twentieth century, with the railway opening up the north, it was deemed necessary to defend the area against invasion. The first garrison was established in 1901, and by 1907, a fortress, **Svedjefortet**, had been constructed about 3km southeast of the centre (June–Aug daily 11am–5pm; 20kr). It's a forty-minute walk here from the train station: take Stationsgatan west, turn left into Garnisonsgatan, cross two sets of railway tracks before continuing straight on along Svedjebergsleden, from where you'll see the fort on the hilltop; a hiking path leads up to it from the main road. There is no public transport here. The fort, no longer in military use, offers good views of the town. Blasted out of the hill is a second fortress, a subterranean affair, where you can view old cannons made in 1894 and 1917, as well as a selection of military uniforms. For more military attire through the ages, head for the **Garnisonsmuseum** (Garrison Museum; June–Aug daily 11am–4pm; free, housing the largest collection of uniforms north of Stockholm. It's at the southwestern edge of town; bus #1 (direction Sävast; 13kr) comes here from the railway station.

Two places in Boden will almost certainly appeal to kids. Located in the town centre, roughly midway between the two military establishments, is Boden's fantastic **swimming complex**, Nord Poolen (mid-June to mid-Aug daily 9am–6pm; mid-Aug to mid-June Mon–Fri 9am–9pm; ☎0921/624 00), at Garnisonsgatan 1. One of the best in northern Sweden, it boasts indoor and outdoor pools (all edged with tropical palms), two water slides, jacuzzis and saunas; a swim here will cost you 55kr. The complex is a ten-minute walk south on Lulevägen from the Kungsbron bridge on Kungsgatan. For a taste of the Wild West, head out to **Western Farm** (June–Aug Tues–Sun 11am–6pm; 50kr), a theme park 3km from town in the village of **Buddbyn** (reached by bus #8 from the train station; 13kr). Here, you can see a recreation of an American frontier town (the year is supposedly 1879) and watch re-enactions of cowboys and Indians fighting it out, all unfolding on the edge of the Arctic Circle.

Practicalities

The **train station**, on Stationsgatan, is at the eastern edge of town; buses leave from in front of the station). The **tourist office** is handily located at the train station (June–Aug daily 8am–9pm; Sept–May Mon–Fri 9am–5pm; ☎0921/624 10, *www.boden.se*); just as handily, the **youth hostel** is 100m from the train station at

Fabriksgatan 6 (☎0921/133 35; 100kr). One of the most convenient **hotels** for the station is the cheap and cheerful *Hotell Standard* at Stationsgatan 5 (☎0921/160 55, fax 175 58; ①; dorm beds available at 100kr); it's the first thing you'll see when coming out of the station building. For more comfort and style, there's *Hotell Bodensia*, in the centre of town at Kungsgatan 47 (☎0921/177 10, fax 192 82; ③/②). The **campsite** is at Björkans (☎0921/624 07), a few minutes' walk from the church following the path along the lakeside. It has six-bed cabins for 700kr per night or 4500kr per week, and four-bed cottages for 450kr per night, 3000kr per week; **canoes** (30kr an hour, 150kr a day) and **bikes** can also be rented here (50kr a day), and there's a heated outdoor pool too. You might want to consider staying in one of Boden's **parish cottages** (to rent one, call ☎0921/198 70; ①), though it's worth noting that these usually get booked up months in advance, particularly for July.

Eating in Boden is plain and simple. Of the very few **restaurants** in town, the best of the bunch is the excellent and unexpectedly chic *Pär och Mickes Kök* at Kungsgatan 20 (at the station end of the street), where fine food is served up every evening. Opposite is another restaurant, the unpretentious *Panelen*, in an old wooden building; orders are taken at its counter, with meat dishes here starting at 80kr. For pizza, head for *Restaurang Romeo* on Drottninggatan in the pedestrianized centre, with pizzas from 58kr and meat dishes starting at 100kr. Your best bet for a good lunch is *Café Ollé* at Drottninggatan 4 (opposite *Restaurang Romeo*), where the *Dagens Rätt* goes for 50kr; this place is also good for open sandwiches. Chinese dishes can be had for about 100kr each at *Ming Palace* in the square on Drottninggatan. As for **drinking**, a battle rages between *Olivers Inn* just before Kungsbron bridge on Kungsgatan where a beer in summer can go for as little as 30kr and the oddly-named *Puben med stort P* (its name means "Pub with a capital P") at Kungsgatan 23 as to who has the cheapest beer; at the last count the P's had it with 29kr. Alternatively, you can buy drink at the local Systembolaget at Drottninggatan 8 (Mon–Wed & Fri 9.30am–6pm, Thurs 9.30am–7pm).

Haparanda and around

Right by the Finnish border, at the very northern end of the Gulf of Bothnia, **HAPARANDA** is hard to get to like. The signpost near the bus station reinforces the fact that the town is a very long way from anywhere significant: it mentions Stockholm, 1100km away; the North Cape in Norway, 800km away; and Timbuktu – 8386km distant. The train station, eerily empty today, only serves to reinforce the town's backwater status. A grand-looking building, it was the result of Haparanda's aspirations to be a major trading centre after World War I. The hoped-for take-off never happened, and walking up and down the streets around the main square, Torget, is a pretty depressing experience.

The key to Haparanda's grimness is the neighbouring Finnish town of Tornio. Finland was part of Sweden from 1105 until 1809, with Tornio an important trading centre, serving markets across northern Scandinavia. Things began to unravel when Russia attacked and occupied Finland in 1807; the Treaty of Hamina followed, forcing Sweden to cede Finland to Russia in 1809 – thereby losing Tornio. It was decided that Tornio had to be replaced, and so in 1821, the trading centre of Haparanda was founded – on the Swedish side of the new border, which ran along the Torne river. However, the new town was never more than a minor upstart compared to its neighbour across the water – until recently. With both Sweden and Finland now members of the European Union, Haparanda and **Tornio** have declared themselves a **Eurocity** – one city made up of two towns from different countries. A regional council, the Provincia Bothiensis (a neutral name – neither Swedish nor Finnish) has been set up to foster co-operation between the towns. The inhabitants of Haparanda and Tornio are bilingual and use both Finnish and Swedish currencies; roughly half of the children in Haparanda have either a Finnish mother or father. Services are also shared between the two: everything from central heating to post delivery is centrally co-ordinated. If a fire breaks out in Tornio, for example, Swedish fire crews from Haparanda will cross the border to help put out the flames.

There are only two real sights in town. The **train station**, built in 1918, dominates the suburban streets of southern Haparanda. Constructed from red brick and reached by a flight of steps leading up from the grassy square, complete with stone tower and lantern on Järnvägsgatan, it provides Sweden's only rail link to Finland. From the platforms, you'll be able to discern two widths of track – Finnish trains run on the wider, Russian, gauge. The empty sidings, overgrown with weeds and bushes, backed by the towering station building, with its vast roof of black tiles and chimneys, give the place a strangely forlorn air. The only other place worthy of some attention is the peculiar copper-coloured **Haparanda kyrka** on Östra Kyrkogatan, a monstrous modern construction that looks like a cross between an aircraft hangar and an apartment building. When the church was finished in 1963, its design caused a public outcry: it even won the prize for being the ugliest church in Sweden.

Practicalities

A daily passenger train service between Luleå and Tornio resumes in June 2000 after an eight-year break. From the **train station**, you can reach the centre of town by heading west along Järnvägsgatan, then turning left into the main street, Storgatan, which runs parallel to the Torne river (the buildings you can see here across the river are in Finland). Storgatan leads to the main square, Torget, the **bus station**, the bridge over to Tornio and the **tourist office** (June to mid-Aug Mon–Fri 8am–8pm, Sat & Sun 10am–8pm; mid-Aug to May Mon–Fri 8am–4pm; ☎0922/120 10, *www.haparanda.se*), actually in Finland in the Green Line Welcome Center. There are no border formalities, and so you can simply walk over the bridge to Finland and wander back whenever you like. From June to August it's also possible to get basic information from the *Stadshotel* in the main square. The cheapest beds in town are to be had at Haparanda's **youth hostel**, a smart riverside place at Strandgatan 26 (☎0922/611 71; 110kr), affording good views across to Finland. Another inexpensive place is the cheap and cheerful pension, *Resandehem*, in the centre of town at Storgatan 65B (☎0922/120 68); it charges 150kr for you're travelling on your own, 250kr for a group of two, and 300kr for three. *Haparanda Stadshotel* is the only **hotel** in town, at Torget 7 (☎0922/614 90, fax 102 23; ⑤/②); though rather dark and stuffy, it's reasonable value in summer. The **campsite**, *Sundholmens Camping* (☎0922/618 01) is at the opposite end of town from the youth hostel at Järnvägsgatan 1 – walk along the river down Strandgatan, take a right onto Storgatan, cross the train lines and follow the signs. There are four-bed cabins here for 270kr per day.

As far as eating, drinking and nightlife go, you're better off in Tornio in every respect. Friday nights there are wild, the streets full of people trying to negotiate the return leg over the bridge; meanwhile, Haparanda sleeps undisturbed. It used to be the case that Tornio was much cheaper than Haparanda, but prices are now roughly the same, although drinking is still a little less expensive in Finland. It's worth remembering that Finnish time is one hour ahead of Swedish time and that Haparanda and Tornio have different names in Swedish (Haparanda and Torneå) and Finnish (Haaparanta and Tornio).

For **eating** without trekking over to Finland, there are several options: the lunches at the plastic-looking *Prix Restaurant* at Norra Esplanaden 8 are OK, though not particularly inspiring (50kr). The youth hostel has its own restaurant that does a *Dagens Rätt* (55kr); however, your best bet is *El Paso Pizzeria* at Storgatan 88, close to Torget, which has lunch for 43kr. As well as a range of Chinese and Thai dishes, the local Chinese restaurant, *Lei-Lane* at Köpmangatan 15, also does pizzas; lunch here is 61kr. *Nya Konditoriet* on Storgatan is good for coffee and cakes; for open sandwiches and baguettes try *Café Rosa*, in the Gallerian shopping centre on Storgatan. For **drinking** in Haparanda, head for the *Ponderosa* pub at Storgatan 82, where during happy hour (8–9pm) you can have a beer for 20kr, or alternatively, try the *Gulasch Baronen* pub, attached to the *Stadshotel*, which serves strong beer for around 30kr.

Around Haparanda

Haparanda is a handy base for several side trips. Twenty-four kilometres to the southwest, reachable by bus from town, you'll find the sandy island of **Seskarö**, a favourite refuge for windsurfers and swimmers. There's a **campsite** here (☎0922/201 50), with cabins for 4–6 people available (490kr), as well as cycle and boat rental. South of Seskarö is the start of the Haparanda **archipelago**, which extends into the Baltic's northernmost arm; the two main islands, **Seskar-Furö** and the larger **Sandskär**, were declared a national park in 1995 and contain important fauna and flora, including the razorbill and little tern, as well as the lesser butterfly orchid. A boat leaves for Sandskär from the quay on Strandgatan, 400m south of the youth hostel (July Wed & Thurs only; boat information on ☎0922/133 95 and at *www.bosmina.bd.se*). You can also get **bus** #322 to the island (Mon–Fri 4 daily; 28kr).

Fifteen kilometres north of town, reached on buses #53 and #54 to Pajala, the impressive rapids at **Kukkolaforsen** (pictured on the front cover of this book) are best visited during the *Sikfesten* ("Whitefish Festival"), held on the last week-

---

MOVING ON FROM HAPARANDA

Two **bus** routes head north on the Swedish side of the border through the beautiful Torne valley: #54 runs to Pajala (Mon–Thurs 3 daily, 4 daily on Fri, 1 daily on Sun; 130kr), whereas #53 makes the eight-hour journey via Pajala and Vittangi to Kiruna (Mon–Thurs & Sun 1 daily, 2 buses on Fri; 220kr). Connections can be made in Vittangi for bus #50 to Karesuando. To head west take bus #11 to Luleå (Mon–Fri 12 daily, Sat & Sun 5 daily). Finnish-operated buses connect Haparanda with Tornio and Kemi every hour; times are posted up at the bus station in Haparanda. There's also a once-daily direct afternoon bus from Haparanda to Rovaniemi (Mon–Fri; journey time 3hr). It's possible to change buses in Finland and reach Rovaniemi – ask at the tourist office for further information.

end in July. The **whitefish**, a local delicacy grilled on large open fires, are caught in nets at the end of long poles, fishermen dredging the fast, white water and scooping the fish out onto the bank. The festival celebrates a sort of fisherman's harvest, centuries old, although it's now largely an excuse to get drunk at the beer tent, with evening gigs and dancing the order of the day. It costs 100kr to get in on the Saturday, 60kr on the Sunday; if you're staying in the adjacent **campsite** (☎0922/310 00), which has four-berth cabins for 420kr per night or larger cottages at 660kr per night, you should be able to sneak in for free. Also worth checking out is the local **Fiskemuseum** (mid-June to mid-Aug daily 10am–6pm; free), which gives accounts of local fishing activities; there's also a freshwater aquarium, a working nineteenth-century mill and enormous salmon.

The Swedish Sauna Academy has rated the **sauna** at Kukkolaforsen the country's finest; after you've sweated to your heart's content here, you can breathe the crisp air on the verandah, heavy with the scent of pine, and look across the river to Finland with the sound of the rapids in the background. To get out onto the water, **river rafting** down the rapids can be arranged through the tourist office in Haparanda or at the campsite at Kukkolaforsen – 180kr rents the gear, specifically helmet and life jacket, pays for a short trip down river, and gets you a certificate at the end.

travel details

Trains

Boden to: Gothenburg (1 daily; 16hr); Gällivare (3 daily; 2hr); Gävle (2 daily; 11hr 30min); Haparanda (mid-June to mid-Aug 1 daily; Kiruna (3 daily; 3hr); Luleå (5 daily; 25min); Narvik (2 daily; 6hr); Stockholm (2 daily; 13hr); Uppsala (2 daily; 12hr).

Gävle to: Boden (2 daily; 11hr); Gällivare (2 daily; 13hr 30min); Falun (4 daily; 1hr); Hudiksvall (9 daily; 1hr 20min); Härnösand (2 daily; 3hr); Kiruna (2 daily; 15hr); Luleå (2 daily; 12hr); Stockholm (hourly; 1hr 30min); Sundsvall (9 daily; 2hr); Söderhamn (9 daily; 40min); Umeå (1 daily; 9hr); Uppsala (hourly; 45min); Örebro (6 daily; 3hr); Östersund (4 daily; 4hr).

Hudiksvall to: Gävle (8 daily; 1hr 15min); Härnösand (2 daily; 2hr); Stockholm (8 daily; 2hr 30min); Sundsvall (9 daily; 45min); Söderhamn (8 daily; 30min); Uppsala (8 daily; 2hr).

Härnösand to: Långsele (2 daily; 1hr 45min); Sollefteå (2 daily; 1hr 30min); Stockholm (3 daily; 4hr 30min); Sundsvall (3 daily; 1hr).

Luleå to: Boden (5 daily; 25min); Gothenburg (1 daily; 16hr 45min); Gällivare (3 daily; 2hr 30min); Haparanda (mid-June to mid-Aug 1 daily;

Kiruna (3 daily; 3hr 30min); Narvik (2 daily; 6hr 30min); Stockholm (2 daily; 14hr); Umeå (1 daily; 4hr 15min); Uppsala (2 daily; 13hr).

Sundsvall to: Gävle (8 daily; 2hr); Hudiksvall (8 daily; 45min); Härnösand (3 daily; 1hr); Stockholm (8 daily; 3hr 30min); Söderhamn (8 daily; 1hr 30min); Östersund (5 daily; 2hr 20min).

Söderhamn to: Gävle (8 daily; 40min); Hudiksvall (8 daily; 30min); Härnösand (2 daily; 2hr 30min); Stockholm (8 daily; 2hr); Sundsvall (9 daily; 1hr 30min); Uppsala (8 daily; 1hr 30min).

Umeå to: Gothenburg (1 daily; 13hr 30min); Gävle (1 daily; 9hr 20min); Luleå (1 daily; 4hr 20min); Stockholm (1 daily; 11hr 15min); Uppsala (1 daily; 10hr 30min).

Buses

The reliable **Norrlandskusten** buses run four times daily between Sundsvall and Luleå, generally connecting with trains to and from Sundsvall. Tickets should be bought from the bus driver when boarding. The buses have toilets on board. From Sundsvall, the buses call at Härnösand (45min); Gallsäter (1hr 35min) and Docksta (1hr 50min; for connections to the

High Coast); Örnsköldsvik (2hr 30min); Umeå (4hr); Skellefteå (6hr 15min); Piteå (7hr 30min) and Luleå (8hr 30min).

Other bus services run from the coast into central northern Sweden, often linking up with the Inlandsbanan. Key routes are:

Boden to: Luleå (43 daily, Sat & Sun 9 daily; 50min); Haparanda (Mon–Fri 6 daily, Sat 4 daily, Sun 5 daily; 3hr).

Hudiksvall to: Sveg (Mon–Fri 2 daily, Sat & Sun 1 daily; 3hr)

Luleå to: Arvidsjaur (Mon–Fri 2 daily, Sat & Sun 1 daily; 3hr); Boden (Mon–Fri 43 daily, Sat & Sun 9 daily; 50min); Gällivare (Mon–Thurs 2 daily, Fri & Sun 3 daily, Sat 1 daily; 3hr 15min); Haparanda (Mon–Fri 11 daily, Sat & Sun 5 daily); Jokkmokk (Mon–Fri 3 daily, Sat 1 daily, Sun 2 daily; 2hr 45min); Kiruna (Mon–Thurs 2 daily, Fri & Sun 3 daily, Sat 1 daily; 5hr); Pajala (Mon–Fri & Sun 2 daily, Sat 1 daily; 3hr 30min).

Piteå to: Arvidsjaur (Mon-Fri & Sun 1 daily; 2hr).

Skellefteå to: Arjeplog (3hr15min), Arvidsjaur (2hr), Jäckvik (4hr) and Vuoggatjålme (5hr), Mon–Fri & Sun 1 bus; also continuing to Fauske and Bodø in Norway.

Sollefteå to: Örnsköldsvik (Mon–Fri 2 daily, Sat & Sun 1 daily; 1hr 45min); Östersund (Mon–Fri 3 daily, Sat & Sun 1 daily; 3hr).

Umeå to Dorotea (2 daily; 3hr); Vilhelmina (Mon-Fri 3 daily, Sat & Sun 2 daily; 3hr 30min); Storuman and Tärnaby/Hemavan (Mon–Thurs & Sat 3 daily, 4 buses on Fri, 1 bus on Sun; 3hr 40min to Storuman, 6hr to Tärnaby/Hemavan; 1 daily continuing to Mo-i-Rana Norway).

Örnsköldsvik to: Dorotea (Mon-Sat 2 daily, Sun 1 daily; 5hr); Sollefteå (Mon–Fri 2 daily, Sat & Sun 1 daily; 1hr 50min); and Östersund (Mon–Fri 2 daily, Sat & Sun 1 daily; 4hr 30min).

Haparanda to: Boden (Mon–Fri 6 daily, Sat 4 daily, Sun 5 daily; 3hr); Kiruna (Mon–Thurs & Sun 1 daily, Fri 2 daily; 6hr); Luleå (Mon–Fri 12 daily, Sat & Sun 5 daily; 2hr 30min); Pajala (Mon–Thurs 3 daily, Fri 4 daily, Sun 1 daily; 3hr 30min).

For the latest information on buses leaving Hudiksvall, Örnsköldsvik and Sollefteå call ☎020/511 513 or visit *www.dintur.se*; for details on buses from Umeå and Skellefteå, call ☎020/91 00 19 or visit *www.lanstrafikeniac.se*; from Boden, Piteå, Luleå and Haparanda call ☎020/47 00 47 or visit *www.ltnbd.se*.

International ferries

Umeå to: Vaasa (July to mid-Aug 2 daily; mid-Aug to June 1–2 daily; 3hr 30min).

CHAPTER SIX

CENTRAL AND NORTHERN SWEDEN

I n many ways, the long wedge of land that comprises **central and northern Sweden** – from the shores of the third largest lake in Europe, **Lake Vänern**, up to the Finnish border north of the **Arctic Circle** – encompasses all that is most typical of the country. This vast area of land is really one great forest, broken only by the odd village or town. Rural and underpopulated, it epitomizes the image most people have of Sweden: lakes, pine forests, wooden cabins and reindeer. Until just one or two generations ago, Swedes across the country lived in this sort of setting, taking their cue from the people of these central lands and forest, who were the first to rise against the Danes in the sixteenth century and who shared their land, uneasily, with the *Sámi*, earliest settlers of the wild lands in the far north of the country.

At the extreme southwest of the region, the province of **Värmland**, with its shimmering lakeside capital, **Karlstad**, is best known for sweeping forests, fertile farmland and lazy rivers, once used to float timber into Lake Vänern and now the best means of seeing this most peaceful part of central Sweden, through one of the trips downstream on ready-built pontoon rafts. Just to the northeast, **Dalarna** province, centred around **Lake Siljan**, is an intensely picturesque – and touristy – region, its inhabitants maintaining a cultural heritage (echoed in contemporary handicrafts and traditions) that goes back to the Middle Ages. You won't need to brave the crowds of visitors for too long, as even a quick tour around one or two of the more accessible places here gives an impression of the whole: red cottages with white door and window frames, sweeping green countryside, water that's

---

ACCOMMODATION PRICES

The pensions and hotels listed in the guide have been price-graded according to the scale given below; the price category given against each establishment indicates the cost of the least expensive double rooms there. Many hotels offer considerable reductions at weekends all year round, and during the summer holiday period (mid-June to mid-Aug); in these cases the reduction is either noted in the text or, where a discount brings a hotel into another price band, given after the number for the full price. Single rooms, where available, usually cost between 60 and 80 percent of a double. Where hostels have double rooms, we've given price codes for them also.

① under 500kr	③ 700–900kr	⑤ 1200–1500kr
② 500–700kr	④ 900–1200kr	⑥ over 1500kr

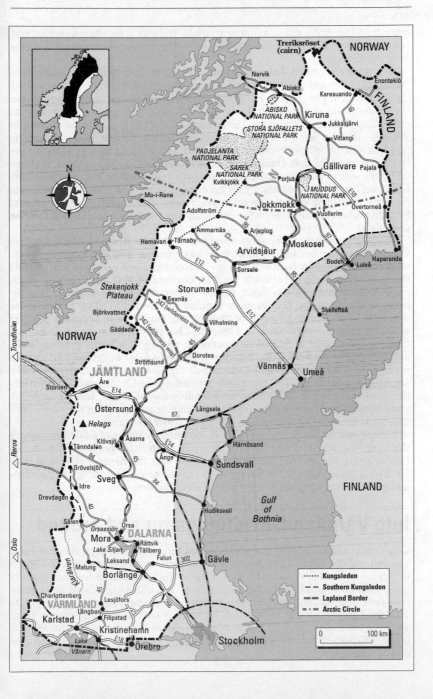

bluer than blue and a riot of summer festivals. Dalarna is *the* place to spend midsummer, particularly Midsummer's Eve, when the whole region erupts in a frenzy of celebration.

The privately owned **Inlandsbanan**, the great Inland Railway, cuts right through central and northern Sweden and links virtually all the towns and villages covered in this chapter. Running from **Mora** in Dalarna to **Gällivare**, above the Arctic Circle, it ranks with the best of European train journeys, covering an enthralling 1067km in two days. Buses connect the rail line with the **mountain villages** that lie alongside the Norwegian border, where the surrounding Swedish *fjäll*, or fells, offer some spectacular and unspoilt hiking. Marking the halfway point of the line, **Östersund**, the only town of any size along it, is situated by the side of Storsjön, the great lake that's reputed to be home to the country's own Loch Ness monster. From here trains head in all directions: west into Norway through Sweden's premier ski resort, **Åre**, south to Dalarna and Stockholm, east to Sundsvall on the Bothnian coast and north into the wild terrain of Lapland.

The heartland of the indigenous **Sámi** people, **Lapland** begins 200km north of Östersund and makes for the most fascinating trip in northern Sweden. A constant reminder of how far north you are, the omnipresent **reindeer** still provide the basis of the livelihood of many families, but the enduring *Sámi* culture, which once defined much of this land, is now under threat. Centuries of mistrust between the *Sámi* and the Swedish population have led to today's often tense standoff; *Sámi* accusing Swede of stealing his land, Swede accusing *Sámi* of scrounging off the state. Back in 1986, the Chernobyl nuclear accident led to a fundamental change in *Sámi* living patterns: the fallout affected grazing lands, and even today the lichen (the reindeer's favourite food) in certain parts of the north is unfit for consumption, a fact which the *Sámi*, perhaps understandably, are keen to play down. The escalating problems posed by tourism – principally the erosion of grazing land under the pounding feet of hikers, and the inconsiderate behaviour of some tourists during the calving and branding seasons – have also made the *Sámi*'s traditional existence increasingly uncertain.

Moving further north, around the iron-ore mining centres of **Gällivare** (where the Inlandsbanan ends) and **Kiruna**, the rugged **national parks** offer a chance to hike and commune with nature like nowhere else: the **Kungsleden trail** runs for 500km through the last wilderness in Europe to the tiny village of Abisko – oddly, yet reassuringly, the driest place in all of Sweden.

Into Värmland: Kristinehamn and around

Connected to Stockholm by fast and frequent trains, the northern shore of **Lake Vänern** and the adjoining province of **Värmland** are two of the easiest regions of central Sweden to reach, with direct trains from the capital passing south of Lake Mälaren bound for here, via Katrineholm and Hallsberg. The latter, a major transport hub for this part of the country, is where you change to get to Värmland from Lapland, Östersund, Dalarna, Västerås or Gothenburg. Once you've arrived in the vicinity of the lake, the places to seek out are the shy and retiring Kristinehamn and the much livelier and more enjoyable **Karlstad** (see p.415), both at the lakeside.

The Inlandsbanan (see p.421) once began in **KRISTINEHAMN**, a pretty harbour town on the northeastern fringes of Lake Vänern. Today, though, this inland train route starts 300km to the north, sparing peaceful Kristinehamn the attentions of hordes of Lapland-bound backpackers, who are forced to start their trip on the line in Mora instead. Kristinehamn's main attraction is its pleasant setting directly on the lakeside, which for views of the water, gives it the edge over nearby Karlstad (see p.415). However, once you've taken in Kristinehamn's most famous piece of artwork (see below), there's precious little else to do here other than use it as a convenient base from which to see the Nobel museum in nearby Karlskoga (see p.414).

Kristinehamn has been a significant trading centre since the fourteenth century, and soon also became the point of export for iron ore from Sweden's upland mining area, Bergslagen, a role that was further strengthened with the arrival of the railway here in the middle of the nineteenth century. A quick walk around the prosperous town soon confirms its strategic importance to Swedish industry: rail and lake transport have made Kristinehamn the compact industrial and maritime centre that it is today. However, apart from the handful of old wooden houses nestled together around central Trädgårdsgatan, and the town hall from 1798, there's little else of note in the centre. Having got a flavour of the place, it's much better to make for the lakeside, where the towering 15-metre high **sculpture**, of which the folk of Kristinehamn are justifiably proud, stands guard where the river that runs through town enters the lake. A sandblasted concrete pillar, the striking piece is one of the *Les Dames des Mougins* series, based on Picasso's wife, Jaqueline, and was realized and decorated by the Swedish artist Carl Nesjar. He was working from a photograph, provided by Picasso, of a model of the sculpture; seeing as Picasso never even set foot in Sweden, the tag "Picasso sculpture" – as the work is generally referred to – is a little unfair to Nesjar. The statue is 6km from the centre: heading there from the train station, take Karlstadsvägen west until its junction with Västra Ringvägen; turn left into this street and carry on until the right-hand turning, Presterudsvägen; the sculpture is signposted from here.

Practicalities

The **train station** is only a short distance from the large main square, Södra Torget, reached by turning left out of the station and walking straight ahead for about five minutes. The **tourist office** is close to the square, at Västerlånggatan 22 (June & Aug Mon–Sat 9am–6pm, Sun noon–6pm; July Mon–Fri 9am–8pm, Sat 9am–6pm, Sun noon–6pm; Aug–May Mon–Fri 9am–4pm; ☎0550/881 87 and 881 83, *www.kristinehamn.se*); you can book **private rooms** here (from 120kr). On the same site, the **youth hostel** (☎0550/881 95; 100kr; mid-May to Aug) and **campsite** (same number as hostel) are in the village of Kvarndammen. You can drive there by taking the E18 east in the direction of Örebro; alternatively, take bus #1 from the train station. The campsite **rents bikes** at 55kr a day, 20kr cheaper than the tourist office. The biggest **hotel** in town is *Stadshotellet* on Södra Torget (☎0550/150 30, fax 41 12 35; ④/②), in a lovely turn-of-the-century building with modern rooms and a restaurant. A cheaper alternative is *Hotel Fröding*, at Kungsgatan 44 (☎0550/151 80, fax 101 30; ③/②). At either hotel, you'll need to book two days before arrival if you want to claim their summer discount rate.

For **food**, *Restaurant Sjöjungfrun*, at Vålösundsvägen 117 (June–Aug), has top-quality fish and meat dishes; it's right by the Picasso statue. A good cheap choice for lunch is *Roma Restaurant*, a busy pizzeria at Skaraborgsvägen 13, with pizzas for 50–60kr; it's also open in the evenings. The most popular place for a **drink**, *Restaurang Varvet*, is at Hamnbrogatan 18.

East of Kristinehamn: the Alfred Nobel Museum in Karlskoga

A half-hour bus ride east of Kristinehamn, **Karlskoga** is an ugly industrial town that's home to the Swedish armaments manufacturer, Bofors. Yet it has one saving grace: the **Alfred Nobel Museum** (June–Aug daily 10.30am–4.30pm; Sept–May advance booking required on ☎0586/818 94), situated in the Karlskoga house and laboratory, Björkborn Herrgård, that Nobel once owned (see box, below, for more on his life). There are four sections to the museum, including one that contains his original **laboratory equipment**, and another that's an experimental workshop for children.

There are direct buses from Kristinehamn to Karlskoga (3 daily, two of which leave around 7am); alternatively, take the train to Degerfors (10 daily; 20min) and then the frequent buses from there to Karlskoga (25min). It's not possible to get to the museum by public transport; from Karlskoga's train and bus stations, which are together, it's a forty-minute walk there. You begin by heading east along Järnvägsgatan, continuing from the road's end onto the footpath which leads into Centralplan square. From here, continue east along Kungsvägen to the main square, Torget, from where you head north along a road called, at various stages along the route, Stadshusgatan, Bergmansgatan or Björkbornsvägen. The last of these becomes a cycle path, which you follow under the busy Norrleden and then right, over the canal, where the road picks up again and leads to the museum.

ALFRED NOBEL AND THE NOBEL PRIZES

Born in Stockholm in 1833, **Alfred Nobel** is known across the globe as the inventor of **dynamite**, the explosive which played such a central role in the industrial development of the world. Yet by his death in 1896, Nobel held the patent for not only dynamite but 354 other inventions, ranging from safety fuses to smokeless gunpowder. The immense fortune he amassed during his life, roughly thirty million *kronor* at the time (equivalent to 1.5 billion *kronor* today), came mostly from his industrial activities in Sweden and several other European countries.

Nobel stipulated in his will that the income from his estate be divided annually into five equal parts and distributed "in the form of prizes to those who during the preceding year have conferred the greatest benefit on mankind". Upon his death, his wealth was used to establish the **Nobel Foundation**, which still administers the award of these prices today. In selecting the five fields for his **prizes** – physics, chemistry, physiology or medicine, literature and peace – Nobel emphasized that "no consideration shall be given to the nationality of the candidates . . . the most worthy shall receive the prize, whether he is a Scandinavian or not".

All the prizes, except the one for peace, are presented to the recipients by the Swedish king at a **ceremony** held in Stockholm Concert Hall on December 10, the anniversary of Nobel's death in Italy in 1896; the peace prize presentation takes place on the same day at Oslo City Hall. Nobel gave no reason why he selected Norway as a venue, but it wasn't a separate country during his lifetime, as the union between Sweden and Norway was only dissolved in 1905.

Karlstad and around

"Wherever I look I see fire – fire in the houses, fire in the air, fire everywhere. The whole world is burning. There is thundering, crackling, shouting, hissing and howling."

The recollections of Karlstad's most famous son, the poet Gustaf Fröding, on the Great Fire of 1865.

Sitting elegantly on Lake Vänern, **KARLSTAD**, capital of the province of Värmland, is named after King Karl IX, who granted the place its town charter in 1584. Since then, the town has been beset by several disasters, devastating **fires** having ripped through the centre in 1616 and 1729; but it was in 1865, when fire broke out in a bakery on the corner of Östra Torggatan and Drottninggatan, that Karlstad suffered its worst calamity: virtually the entire town, including the Cathedral, burned to the ground – giving rise to the local saying "the bishop swore and doused the flames whilst the governor wept and prayed". Of 241 buildings that made up the town then, only seven survived the flames. Sweden had not experienced such a catastrophe in living memory, and a national emergency fund was immediately set up to help pay for reconstruction. Building began apace, with an emphasis on wide streets and large open squares to act as firebreaks and so prevent another tragedy. The result is an elegant and thoroughly likeable town, full of life, which makes an altogether more agreeable base from which to tour the surrounding country and lakeside than nearby Kristinehamn.

Karlstad is served by InterCity **trains** between Stockholm and Oslo (it's roughly halfway between the two), as well as the faster X2000 service from Stockholm. Direct train services also run along the western side of the lake from Gothenburg. Heading here from southeastern Sweden, Västerås and towns in Norrland, you'll need to change in Hallsberg. From Dalarna it's quickest to get here by **bus**, with a handy Swebus Express service, the #800 (2 daily; 3hr 30min; 140kr), making the trip from Falun and Borlänge to Karlstad (and on to Gothenburg); leaving from Mora, Rättvik or Leksand, you can change onto this bus in Borlänge. Karlstad is also linked with Stockholm by SAS **flights**.

Arrival, information and accommodation

The modern centre of Karlstad is built upon the island of **Tingvalla**. The **bus station** is located at the western end of Drottninggatan; close by is the **train station** on Hamngatan. Karlstad's **airport**, 18km from the centre, is served by buses (40kr) and taxis (200kr). At the opposite end of the town centre from the stations is the **tourist office**, located in the Carlstad Conference Centre on Tage Erlandergatan 10D (June–Aug Mon–Fri 9am–7pm, Sat 10am–7pm, Sun 11am–4pm; Sept–May Mon–Fri 9am–5pm; ☎054/22 21 40, *www.karlstad.se/turist/eng/*). It's a good place to pick up general information and make bookings for river rafting trips on the Klarälven river (see p.420); they also have timetables for buses throughout Värmland, which can help you plan a trip elsewhere in the province.

Karlstad's **youth hostel** is located 3km from the centre in Ulleberg (☎054/56 68 40, 110kr), spread over three floors in a rambling old house; it's reached on buses

#11, #21 or #32 in the direction of Bellevue. The nearest **campsites** are a nine-kilo-metre drive west out of the town along the E18: *Skutbergets camping* is open all year (☎054/53 51 39), whereas *Bomstad Badens camping* next door (☎054/53 50 68), beautifully situated on the lakeshore, is only open from June to August. The daily Badbussen, bus #18 (mid-June to mid-Aug hourly 10.30am–5.30pm; 25min) runs from Stora Torget via Drottninggatan to the beaches at Bomstad; ask at the tourist office for information on getting to the campsites by public transport at other times of the year. To claim the **summer discount** offered by all Karlstad's **hotels** – 550kr for a double room – you must book at least two days in advance.

Hotels

Carlton, Järnvägsgatan 8 (☎054/21 55 40, fax 18 95 20). The cheapest hotel in Karlstad, located in the pedestrianized centre. ②.

Drott, Järnvägsgatan 1 (☎054/10 10 10, fax 18 99 30). Just 50m from the train station. Built in 1980, this is a smart, elegant hotel, next to a busy main road. ④/②.

First Hotel Plaza, Västra Torggatan 2 (☎054/10 02 00, fax 10 02 24). Large, modern, plush hotel, with a fantastic sauna offering panoramic views over the city. ⑤/②.

Freden, Fredsgatan 1A (☎054/21 65 82). Cheap and cheerful place, close to the bus and train stations. ②.

Good Morning Hotel Karlstad City, Västra Torggatan 20 (☎054/21 51 40, fax 21 94 43). Good-value hotel in the centre of town, boasting a large breakfast buffet and free evening parking for guests. ②.

Nya Solsta Hotell, Drottninggatan 13 (☎054/15 68 45). Central hotel with cable TV and some rooms adapted for the disabled. A good choice. ②.

Stadshotellet, Kungsgatan 22 (☎054/21 52 20, fax 18 82 11). Beautifully located next to the river, with well-appointed rooms and good views. This place also boasts a men's sauna with a plunge pool, and a women's sauna with solarium and spa. ⑤/②.

The Town

It's best to start your wanderings around town in the large and airy main square, Stora Torget, one of the largest market squares in the country. The Neoclassical **town hall**, on the square's western side, was the object of much local admiration upon its completion in 1867, just two years after the great fire; local worthies were particularly pleased with the two stone Värmland eagles that adorn the building's roof, no doubt hoping the birds would help ward off another devastating blaze. In front of the town hall, the rather austere **Peace Monument** commemorates the peaceful dissolution of the union between Sweden and Norway in 1905, which was negotiated in Karlstad. Unveiled fifty years later, it portrays an angry woman madly waving a broken sword whilst planting her right foot firmly atop a soldier's severed head; "feuds feed folk hatred, peace promotes people's understanding" reads the inscription. Across Östra Torggatan, the nearby **Cathedral** was consecrated in 1730, although only its arches and walls survived the flames of 1865. Its most interesting features are the altar, made from Gotland limestone with a cross of Orrefors crystal, and the font, also of crystal. The site where the Cathedral stands, Lagberget on Kungsgatan, was only selected after previous churches located by the river on the island of Tingvalla (now the modern centre of Karlstad) were destroyed by various fire.

Continuing east along Kungsgatan and over the narrow Pråmkanalen, the road swings left and changes its name to Nygatan ahead of the longest arched **stone**

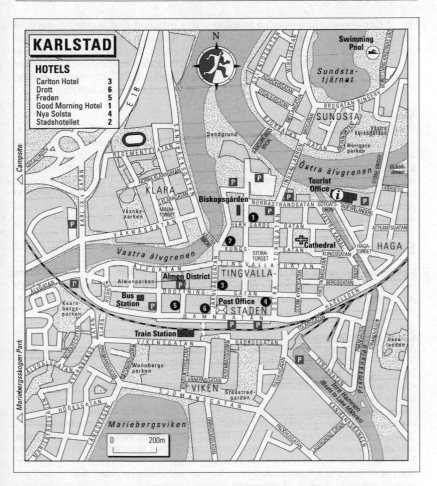

bridge in Sweden, Östra Bron. Completed in 1811, this massive construction is made up of twelve arches and spans 168m across the eastern branch of the Klarälven river. It's claimed the bridge's builder, Anders Jacobsson, threw himself off the bridge and drowned himself, afraid the achievement of his life would collapse; his name is engraved on a memorial stone tablet in the centre of the bridge. On sunny days, the nearby wooded island of **Gubbholmen**, reached by crossing the stone bridge and turning right, is a popular place for soaking up the rays; if you head there, take a picnic with you. Heading back towards town, turn right into Tage Errlandergatan from the stone bridge, and carry on until you reach the old bathhouse, **Gamla Badhuset**, on Norra Strandgatan; the building is worth a quick look for its impressive red stonework. Used as a spa and swimming baths until 1978, it today houses occasional temporary art exhibitions. Nearby, at the junction of Norra Strandgatan and Västra Torggatan, the Bishop's Residence, **Biskopsgården**, dates from 1781 and, as such, is one of the handful which was not destroyed in the great fire. A two-storey yellow wooden building with a mansard roof, it owes its survival to the massive elm trees on its south side, which formed a natural firebreak, and to the sterling firefighting efforts of the bishop of the time, alluded to in the phrase on p.415. The only other houses which survived are located in the Almen district of town, next to the river at Älvgatan; though their facades are all nineteenth century, the oldest parts of these wooden buildings date from the century before.

Mariebergsskogen park

Originally based on the Skansen open-air museum in Stockholm, **Mariebergsskogen**, 2km southwest of the centre, was established in 1920 when a number of old wooden buildings from across Värmland, including a smoking house, windmill and storehouse were relocated here. Today, as well the original open-air museum, the **leisure park** (June–Aug daily 7am–10pm) has a funfair and children's animal park. From the train or bus stations, head west to Klaraborgsgatan, which becomes Jungmansgatan a bit further south; turn right off this street into Hööksgatan and carry on until you reach the park.

Eating, drinking and nightlife

Eating and **drinking** in Karlstad is a joy. There's a good selection of **restaurants** here, specializing in everything from Spanish to vegetarian dishes. **Bars** are thick on the ground for a Swedish town; the *Bishops Arms* and the *Woolpack Inn* are particularly popular and recommended.

Cafés and restaurants

Ankdammen, Magasin 1, Tynäsgatan, in the Inner Harbour. Open-air restaurant with a large wooden jetty which catches the afternoon sun. A nice place for coffee and a snack. Open mid-June to mid-Aug only.

Casa Antonio, Drottninggatan 7. Good Spanish restaurant with tapas from 30kr and paella for two for 190kr.

Glada Ankan, Kungsgatan 12. A lively first-floor restaurant with a balcony overlooking the main square, this place serves mostly Swedish dishes from around 129kr. Nice place for coffee.

Gröna Trädgården, Västra Torggatan 9. With a small balcony overlooking the pedestrianized street below, this first-floor vegetarian restaurant has a large salad buffet, and serves home-made bread with all meals. Open lunchtimes only.

Harrys, Kungsgatan 16. An American-style bar, café and restaurant in the main square, with open-air seating in summer. Main courses, including burgers, from 75kr. The evening bar is pretty popular.

Jäger, Västra Torggatan 8. There's always a choice of two lunches here, one for 59kr and another at 79kr. This restaurant buzzes in the evening, when it's open till 2am.

Kebab House, Västra Torggatan 7. Small but pleasant pizza and kebab place with outdoor seating in summer. Snacks from 40kr.

La Baguette, Kungsgatan 14. Has baguettes with every imaginable filling for 35kr; also does coffee. A good choice for a quick bite at lunchtime, this café has outdoor seating in summer.

Munken, Västra Torggatan 17. Just off the main square. A cosy little restaurant, with stained-glass windows and a vaulted roof. Imaginative menu with fine food from 160kr.

Pråmen, Älvgatan 4. A café on a boat moored close to the main square, with good views over the river and the centre. Serving uncomplicated Swedish home cooking, it's also a great place for a cup of coffee out on deck.

Rådhuscafeet, Tingvallagatan 8. Elegant café in the town hall, entered from the left side of the building.

Bars and clubs

Bishops Arms, Kungsgatan 22. Classic British-style pub enjoying a great location overlooking the river, with outdoor seating in summer and a wide range of beers.

Glada Ankan, Kungsgatan 12. With seats out in the main square, this place is known for its wide choice of beers and lively evening atmosphere.

Harrys, Kungsgatan 16. Good-sized American-style bar, with a wooden interior.

Jäger, Västra Torggatan 8. A trendy nightspot, with live rock and pop music most evenings until 2am.

N.Y. Nightclub, Västra Torggatan 2. Inside the *First Hotel Plaza*. Definitely *the* in place for anyone over 23, with late night dancing – and much drinking. Fri & Sat evenings only.

Woolpack Inn, Järnvägsgatan 1. Just across the road from the train station. Very popular, this is one a few pubs in town doing its best to create a traditional-British-style drinking establishment.

Listings

Airline SAS at the airport on ☎054/55 50 00.

Banks FöreningsSparbanken, Kungsgatan 10; Handelsbanken, Tingvallagatan 17; Nordbanken, Tingvallagatan 11-13; S-E Banken, Drottninggatan 24.

Beaches Sundstatjärnet, at the swimming pool on Drottning Kristinas väg; Mariebergsviken, across the bay from Mariebergsskogen (bus #20 or #31 head here); Bomstad, at the campsite southwest of Karlstad (#18).

Buses Information on buses in Värmland on ☎020/22 50 80 or at *www.kollplatsen.com*

Car rental Avis, Hamngatan 24 (☎054/15 26 60); Budget, Gjuterigatan 26 (☎054/85 35 50); Hertz, Körkarlsvägen 7 (☎054/56 15 00).

Cinemas Arenan, Västra Torggatan 26 (☎054/29 58 45); Filmstaden, Drottninggatan 33A (☎054/770 40 00); Sandrews, Östra Torggatan 9 (☎054/18 47 00).

Police Drottninggatan 4 (☎054/14 50 00).

Post Office Järnvägsgatan 2 (Mon–Fri 8am–6.30pm, Sat 10am–2pm).

Swimming pool Sundsta Bad-och Idrottshus, Drottning Kristinas väg, reached by crossing Tingvallbron from Tingvall (☎054/29 68 71).

Systembolaget Drottninggatan 26 (Mon–Thurs 10am–6pm, Fri 8am–6pm).

Taxis Karlstad Taxi (☎054/15 02 00); Taxi Kurir (☎054/10 11 01).

Trains For information call ☎054/14 33 50 or ☎020/75 75 75.

Travel agent Ticket, opposite the cinema on Drottninggatan (Mon–Fri 9am–6pm, Sat 10am–2pm).

Around Karlstad

Karlstad's importance as an inland port is in no small measure due to the sheer scale of **Lake Vänern**. The city makes an ideal base from which to explore the northern reaches of the lake and see the twenty-two thousand islands and skerries off Karlstad, which comprise the largest freshwater **archipelago** in Europe. You can do both by taking a ride on the *M/S Lindön II* (☎0500/41 26 00, *www.chrissman.se*), which sails from Karlstad's Inre Hamnen (July to early Aug, 3–4 weekly) out into the archipelago, as well as across to Kristinehamn; trips costs 120kr one-way. Karlstad's also a good place from which to sail down one of the longest waterways in Scandinavia, the **Klarälven river**. An interesting day trip from Karlstad is a visit to the house, at nearby Mårbacka, where the

Nobel-prize-winning author **Selma Lagerlöf** once lived, and where she wrote many of her books.

Rafting on the Klarälven river

The **Klarälven river** begins over the border in Norway near Lake Femunden, entering Sweden at Långflon in the north of Värmland. One of the longest rivers on the Scandinavian peninsula, with a length of 500km (slightly over half of which lies within Sweden), the Klarälven was one of the last Swedish rivers where timber was floated downstream to sawmills; the practice only ceased in 1991 here. Two companies, Sverigeflotten (☎0564/402 27) and Vildmark i Värmland (☎0560/140 40, *www.vildmark.se*), now operate **trips** along the river on sixteen-square-metre **timber rafts**, each of which takes two people. A three-day trip with either company costs around 2000kr. Travelling with Vildmark i Värmland, you must even build the raft yourself, supervised by one of their staff, using the three-metre-long logs and the rope provided; no other materials are allowed. Once you're underway, you'll find the water flows at around 2km per hour, which gives you time to swim, fish and study the countryside and animals along the river (beavers and elk are plentiful, and there are also wolverine, wolf, lynx, marten and bears out in the forest). At night, you sleep in a tent either on the raft, which is moored, or on the riverbank. Both companies begin their trips in at Branäsberget, near **Likenäs**; to **get there**, take bus #304 from Karlstad bus station and tell the driver you're going to the rafts (Mon–Thurs & Sun 2 daily, Sat 1 daily; 3hr); you'll be let off in Ransby, from where you can easily walk to Likenäs. Sverigeflotten's trips end 90km south of Branäsberget at *Byns Camping*, near Ekshärad; with Vildmark i Värmland, you'll end up a little further downriver at Gunnerud. You can get back to Karlstad on bus #304, which stops in Ekshärad and Edebäck, the latter close to Gunnerud.

Mårbacka: the home of Selma Lagerlöf

Just a short ride north of Karlstad by train and bus is **Mårbacka**, the house where the author, **Selma Lagerlöf**, was born and died. The first woman winner of the Nobel Prize for Literature, in 1909, Lagerlöf is arguably Sweden's best known author of her generation, familiar to every Swede. Her fantastical prose was seen as a revolt against the social realism of late nineteenth-century writing. Commissioned to write a geography book for Swedish children, Lagerlöf came up with *The Wonderful Adventures of Nils*, a saga of myth and legend, infused with affection for the Swedish countryside; the book became compulsory reading at every school in Sweden. Lagerlöf never married; she had a long-term relationship with another woman, though the fact wasn't generally acknowledged until their love letters were published some fifty years after Lagerlöf's death. The first woman to gain membership of the Swedish Literary Academy, her hatted face now appears on 20kr notes, which Swedes affectionately refer to as "Selmas".

The house, complete with portico supporting a wonderfully long balcony, was completely rebuilt after Lagerlöf won the Nobel Prize. Upstairs is her **study**, much as she left it, along with a panelled library and an extensive collection of her work. Mårbacka is reached by taking the train to **Sunne**, from where you can connect onto bus #345 (usually this service is operated by a taxi, charging bus fares). There's just one weekday connection, which allows you to spend a couple of hours at Mårbacka before returning.

Dalarna

A sizeable province, **DALARNA** takes in not only the area around **Lake Siljan** (see p.426) but also the ski resorts of **Sälen** (see p.431) and **Idre** (see p.432), close to the Norwegian border. Dalarna holds a special misty-eyed place in the Swedish psyche and should certainly be seen, although not to the exclusion of places further north. Verdant pastures, gentle rolling meadows sweet with the smell of summer flowers, and tiny rural villages make up most of the county, backed by the land to the northwest of Lake Siljan, which rises slowly to meet the chain of mountains that forms the border with Norway. One small lakeside town can look pretty much like another, so if time is short, restrict yourself to visiting just one or two: **Leksand** (see p.426) and **Mora** (see p.429) are the best options. If you're staying in the area for a few days or more and tire of the lakeside area's predominantly folksy character and tourist crowds, the nearby industrial towns of **Borlänge** (see p.422) and **Falun** (see p.423) can provide light relief. North of Mora, the county becomes more mountainous and less populous, the only place of note here being **Orsa**, with its fascinating **bear park** (see p.435). There's no need to worry about lack of **accommodation** in the province: there are numerous hotels, hostels and campsites around.

Travel practicalities

SJ-operated **trains** call at Borlänge – where you can get a connection to Falun – and at all the towns around Lake Siljan, terminating in Mora; north of here, the privately operated **Inlandsbanan**, the great Inland Railway that links Dalarna with Lapland, takes over (see box, below, for practical information on using the

---

THE INLANDSBANAN – PRACTICAL DETAILS

The Inland Railway is now only operated as a tourist venture in summer, generally from mid-June to late August. **Timetables** are only approximate, and the train will stop whenever the driver feels like it – perhaps for a spot of wild-strawberry picking or to watch a beaver damming a stream. Generally there are daily trains north from Mora at around 7.30am, but this can change from year to year. Done in one go, the whole journey (Mora–Gällivare, 1067km) lasts two days, with an overnight stop in Östersund. Take it at a more relaxed pace, with a couple of stops along the route (you can break your journey as many times as you like on one ticket), and you'll get much more out of it. More details of Inlandsbanan services are given in the text and in "Travel Details", p.486.

Short trips cost 50kr per 100km, with tickets bought on the train; Mora–Östersund, for example, would cost 160kr and take around six hours. InterRail pass holders travel for free, whereas those with ScanRail passes don't get a discount on individual journeys but do get 25 percent off the price of an **Inland Railway Card** (normal price 700kr), which gives unlimited travel on the entire stretch of the railway for fourteen days. Seat reservations are best made at least 24 hours in advance and cost 50kr per seat. Two children under 16 can travel free if accompanied by an adult; otherwise they pay half price. Bicycles can be carried on board at a cost of 35kr. For **train times**, contact Inlandståget AB, Kyrkgatan 56, S-831 34 Östersund (☎063/12 76 95, fax 51 99 80, *www.inlandsbanan.se* or *www.ief.se*).

line). With special guides on board the trains to provide commentaries and information about places along the route, it's certainly a fascinating way to reach the far north of the country, though the Inlandsbanan today is a mere shadow of its former self. Spiralling costs and low passenger numbers forced SJ to sell the line, and the last state-run trains trundled down the single-line track in the autumn of 1992. Trains on the southern section between Mora and Kristinehamn had ceased running several years earlier, and part of the track there has been dismantled. The railway was then sold to the fifteen municipalities that the route passes through, and a private company, Inlandståget AB, was launched to keep the line going.

Paradoxically, in summer, when Dalarna is inundated with visitors, its **bus** system is down to a skeleton service; buses to some places, like Idre and Sälen, are reduced to one bus a day then. It's worth picking up a timetable from the tourist office and organizing your route before you go, otherwise you could find yourself facing a very long wait for your next connection. Mora is one of the main interchanges in Dalarna's bus network; the only way to get to Sälen or Idre by public transport is by bus from Mora, and if you want to visit both, you'll be forced to retrace your steps back to Mora to get from one village to the other, adding about five hours to your journey. A good way to get about locally, especially around Lake Siljan, is to rent a **bike** from one of the tourist offices.

Borlänge

The biggest town in Dalarna, **BORLÄNGE** developed into a centre for the steel and papermill industries, which still dominate the town today. Luckily the place has a few saving graces, most of which lie in the centre. The **Jussi Björling Muséet**, at Borganäsvägen 25 (mid-May to mid-Sept Mon–Fri 11am–6pm, Sat 10am–2pm, Sun noon–5pm; mid-Sept to mid-May Tues–Fri noon–5pm; 20kr), not far from the tourist office, commemorates the life and career of the world-renowned tenor, Borlänge's most famous son; in its listening rooms, you can have Jussi sing for you at the flick of a button. It's a toss-up as to which of the town's other two museums is the more interesting: the **Geologiska Muséet** at Floragatan 6 has mind-numbing displays of rocks, minerals and fossils (Mon–Fri 11am–2pm, Sat 11am–5pm; 10kr), whereas at **Framtidsmuséet**, Jussi Björlingsvägen 25 (Museum of the Future; Mon 1–5pm, Tues–Fri 10am–5pm, Sat & Sun noon–5pm; 25kr), the best section is the planetarium.

You could well pass up the museums in favour of a stroll along the river. A pleasant trail starts at the open-air **Gammelgården** craft village, with its small collection of old wooden houses on Stenhålsgatan. From here, head away from the main road bridge to the left and follow the riverside path as far as the impressive power station built across the river; you can get across to the opposite bank here and retrace your steps. All in all, it's a pleasant walk of around an hour or so, with plenty of places to stop for a picnic. To get to Gammelgården itself, take the footbridge over the main road, Siljansvägen, which begins just beyond Svea Torget, and follow it till you get to Kontorsvägen.

Practicalities

Direct InterCity and X2000 trains run daily to Borlänge from Stockholm. The Swebus Express #800 bus service comes here twice daily from Karlstad, with a stop at Filipstad for the connecting #401 from Kristinehamn. Borlänge's **bus** and

train stations are centrally located at Ovanbrogatan, from where it's a five-minute walk past the green Liljekvistska parken to the **tourist office** on Borganäsvägen (mid-June to mid-Aug daily 9am–7pm; mid-Aug to mid-June Mon–Fri 10am–6pm; ☎0243/665 66, *www.borlange.se*). One place to **stay** within easy walking distance of the centre is the **youth hostel** at Kornstigen 23A (☎0243/22 76 15; 110kr). The town's several central, very similar **hotels** cater mainly to business people, and offer modern, well-decorated rooms. There's little to choose between the four hotels in the centre of town. At Stationsgatan 21–23, *Scandic Hotel Borlänge* has the largest and most modern rooms (☎0243/22 81 20, fax 22 81 96; ④/③). The *Hotel Galaxen* at Jussi Björlingsvägen is more dated, looking a bit 1970s (☎0243/800 10, fax 162 30; ④/③); its bright, en-suite rooms are quite adequate. The second best place, after the *Scandic*, is *Hotel Brage* at Stationsgatan 1 (☎0243/22 41 50, fax 871 00; ④/③). Only *Hotel Gustaf Wasa*, at Tunagatan 1, has actual bathtubs (☎0243/810 00, fax 806 00; ④/③). Smaller and cheaper than the rest is *Hotell Saga* (☎0243/21 18 40; ③) at Borganäsvägen 28. The **campsite**, *Mellsta Camping*, is beautifully located by the river at **Mellstavägen**, a bit of a trek from the centre; take bus #58 there.

When it comes to **restaurants**, Borlänge holds the record (so says its tourist office) for the greatest number of pizzerias in any small Swedish town – 26; the best of these is the romantic *La Pizza* on Tunagatan. For Greek specialities, head to *Akropolis* on Vattugatan – try their lamb cutlets with garlic for 89kr. Chinese food is best enjoyed at *Le Mandarin* in Svea Torget, with dishes from 80kr; and for Mexican and Cajun delights at around 100kr, check out *Broken Dreams* inside *Hotel Gustaf Wasa*. The very best food, though, is served up in the smart *Stationsgatan 1*, the restaurant inside *Hotel Brage* – their flounder is legendary. Inside the *Scandic Hotel Borlänge*, the *Tuna Krog* is well-reputed for its home-style cooking (around 130kr for a main meal). The most popular **pubs** in town, though they're nothing exceptional, are the *Flying Scotsman*, in the same building as the Framtidsmuseet on Jussi Björlingsvägen, and *Rockfickan* inside *Hotel Brage*.

Falun and around

Northeast of Börlange, **FALUN** is essentially an industrial town – a pleasant one at that – known for copper mining, which began here as early as the eleventh century; today, the mines, which closed as recently as 1992, can be visited on hour-long guided tours (see p.424). Falun is also known for a much more sobering event: in 1994, the town witnessed Sweden's worst case of mass murder, when a young soldier, inflamed with jealousy after seeing his girlfriend with another man, ran amok and shot dead seven local people.

Arrival, information and accommodation
Falun is easily reached by train from Börlange (7 daily; 20min). The **train** and **bus stations** are to the east of the centre; if you walk through the bus station, then take the underpass below the main road and head towards the shops in the distance, you'll soon come to Falun's **tourist office**, in Trotzgatan opposite the *First Hotel Grand* (mid-June to mid-Aug Mon–Sat 9am–7pm, Sun 11am–5pm; mid-Aug to mid-June Mon–Fri 9am–6pm, Sat 10am–2pm; ☎023/830 50, *www.welcome.falun.se*).

The nearest **youth hostel** is at Hälsinggårdsvägen 7 in **Haraldsbo**, a small town about 3km away (bus #701 or #704 from the centre; ☎023/105 60; 120kr). Housed in a couple of long, low-rise modern buildings, the hostel is close to Lake

Runn, and so is an ideal place to swim. Up at Lungnet hill is Falun's best **hotel**, *Scandic Hotell Falun*, at Svärdsjögatan 51 (☎023/669 22 00, fax 669 22 11; ④/②), which has fantastic views down over the town, as well as ultra-modern rooms and a basement pool and sauna complex. The biggest hotel in town is the swanky, central *First Hotel Grand* at Trotzgatan 9–11 (☎023/79 48 80, fax 141 43; ④/②), whose rooms are sumptuous to say the least. For a more homely feel, try *Hotell Winn* at Bergskolegränd 7, near the train station (☎023/636 00, fax 225 24; ④/②). It's also worth considering *Pensionat Solliden*, 6km away in **Hosjö** at Centralvägen 36 (☎023/325 90, fax 331 31; ③/②); a pleasant boarding house, it has its own restaurant and sauna. The nearest **campsite** (☎023/835 63) is up at Lungnet by the National Ski Stadium.

The town and around

Falun grew in importance during the seventeenth and eighteenth centuries, when its **copper mines** produced two-thirds of the world's copper ore. Commensurate with its status then as Sweden's second largest town, the town acquired grand buildings and an air of prosperity. The few old, wooden houses that survive in the town (in 1761, two fires wiped out virtually all of central Falun) are worth seeking out to gain an idea of the cramped conditions mine workers had to live in; you'll find these buildings in the districts of Elsborg (southwest of the centre), Gamla Herrgården and Östanfors (both north of the centre).

By far the most interesting attraction in Falun are its **mines**, reached from the centre along Gruvgatan – head along this street right to the far end, about a kilometre away (March, April & Sept to mid-Nov Sat & Sun 12.30–4.30pm; May–Aug daily 10am–4.30pm; 60kr). Mandatory **guided tours** (English commentary available) lasting around an hour are organized on the site, beginning with an elevator ride 55m down to a network of old mine roads and drifts. The temperature down below is only around 6–7°C, so make sure you bring warm clothing; try also to wear old shoes, as your footwear is likely to come out tinged red. The site has a worthy **museum** (May–Aug daily 10am–4.30pm, Sept–April 12.30–4.30pm; 10kr), recounting the history of Falun's copper production. Conditions below ground in the mines were appalling, said by the botanist Carl von Linné to be as dreadful as hell itself. One of the most dangerous aspects of eighteenth-century copper mining was the presence everywhere in the mines of **vitriol** gases, which are strong preservatives. It's recorded that the body of a young man known as *Fet Mats* (Fat Mats) was found in the mines in 1719; though he'd died 49 years previously in an accident, his corpse was so well preserved when discovered that his erstwhile fiancée, by then an old woman, recognized him immediately.

Be sure not to miss peering into the **Great Pit** (Stora Stöten), just nearby, which is 100m deep and 300–400m wide. It suddenly appeared on Midsummer Day in 1687, when the entire pit caved in – the result of extensive mining and the unsystematic driving of galleries and shafts.

Back in the centre, the riverside **Dalarnas Museum** at Stigaregatan 2–4 makes for a worthwhile visit (May–Aug Mon–Thurs 10am–5pm, Fri–Sun noon–5pm; Sept–May Mon, Tues & Thurs 10am–5pm, Wed 10am–9pm; Fri–Sun noon–5pm; 20kr). Containing sections on the county's folk art, dresses and music, it includes among its exhibits a reconstruction of the study where the author Selma Lagerlöf worked when she moved to Falun in 1897 (for more on Lagerlöf, see p.420).

THE NATIONAL SKI STADIUM AND THE BEACHES
In fine weather, it's well worth getting out of the centre and heading up Svärdsjögatan to **Lungnet** (a 25min walk), the hill overlooking the town, where you'll find Sweden's **National Ski Stadium** (*Riksskidsstadion*). You can take a lift 90m up to the top of the ski jump for great views of the town and the surroundings. Close to the ski arena are a couple of free outdoor **swimming pools** and a **nature reserve**, where you can sit undisturbed in a carpet of blue harebells in July.

If you want to take a dip, you should head out north from the centre along Slaggatan for the **beach** at **Kålgårdsparken**, near the area of wooden houses at Östanfors; or take bus #101 to **Sandviken**, where there are good sandy beaches. There's also a pleasant bathing area at **Uddnäs**, which can be reached from the centre by bus #20.

Eating, drinking and nightlife
The variety and quality of the places to **eat** and **drink** in Falun, all of them in or around the main square, far outstrips the selection in the other towns around Lake Siljan. The most popular is the trendy *Banken Bar & Brasserie* at Åsgatan 41, which, as the name suggests, is housed in what used to be a bank (old notes adorn the walls today). The excellent Swedish home cooking here isn't cheap – burgers come at 80kr and up, other meat dishes from 150kr; try their delicious salmon at 100kr. Next door is the slightly less expensive *Två rum och kök*, a restaurant whose cosy feel is like eating in a friend's dining room. Another busy spot is *Rådhuskällaren*, under the Rådhus in Stora Torget, in what looks to be a wine cellar; here you can indulge in delicious, if somewhat pricey, food – the cheapest bottle of wine will set you back around 200kr. Good Greek fare can be had at the *Akropolis* restaurant, opposite Dalarnas Museum. One of *the* places to be seen, as far as Falun's young and trendy are concerned, is the *Firefly* **bar** and restaurant, next door to *Rådhuskällaren*. Other drinking establishments include the excellent *Pub Engelbrekt*, Stigaregatan 1, with its old wooden benches; and the British-style *King's Arms* at Falugatan 3, merely so-so.

Without doubt the best time to be here is during the annual **International Folk Music Festival** (generally July 10–13), when the streets come alive to the sound of panpipes, bagpipes and every other type of pipes. The tourist office can provide details of the festival programme and how to get tickets.

Out from Falun: Sundborn
The delightful **Carl Larsson-gården** (May–Sept daily 10am–5pm; 65kr), once the home of the artist **Carl Larsson**, lies in the nearby village of **SUNDBORN**, 13km from Falun; to get there, take bus #64 from Falun's train station (Mon–Fri 5 daily). One of Sweden's most visited tourist attractions, the cottage was at first the summer dwelling of Carl and his wife Karin, later becoming their permanent home. The artist's own murals and portraits of his children form part of the decor, as do the embroidery and tapestries of his wife; at the start of the twentieth century, when the Larssons had done the place up, the house represented an entirely new decorative style for Sweden, its bright, warm interior quite unlike the dark and sober colours used until that time. Other paintings by Carl Larsson are displayed in the village church, the artist being buried outside in the churchyard.

Around Lake Siljan

Things have changed since Baedeker, writing in 1889, observed that "Lake Siljan owes much of its interest to the inhabitants of its banks, who have preserved many of their primitive characteristics. . . In their idea of cleanliness they are somewhat behind the age." Today it's not the people who draw your attention but the setting: **Lake Siljan**, created millions of years ago when a meteorite crashed into the earth, is what many people come to Sweden for, its gently rolling surroundings, traditions and local handicrafts weaving a subtle spell on the visitor. There's a lush feel to much of the region, the charm of the forest heightened by its proximity to the lake, all of which adds a pleasing dimension to the low-profile towns and villages that interrupt the rural scenery. Only Mora (see p.429) stands out as being bigger and busier, with the hustle and bustle of holidaymakers and countless caravans crowding the place in summer.

Leksand

Perhaps the most popular and traditional of the Dalarna villages, **LEKSAND**, 43km northwest of Börlange, is certainly worth making the effort to reach at midsummer, when it stages festivals recalling age-old dances performed around the **Maypole** (unlike the practice in most other European countries, Sweden's maypoles are erected in June – in May the trees here are still bare and the ground can be covered with snow). The celebrations culminate in the **church boat races**, a waterborne procession of sleek wooden longboats, which the locals once rowed to church every Sunday. Starting on Midsummer's Day in nearby **Siljansnäs** – take bus #84 from Leksand (Mon-Fri only) – and continuing for ten days at different locations around the lake, the races hit Leksand on the first Saturday in July and Tällberg on the first Tuesday after Midsummer's Day. Leksand's tourist office will have details of the arrangements for each summer's races.

Another event you should try to catch is **Musik vid Siljan** (Music by Lake Siljan), nine days of musical performances in lakeside churches and at various locations out in the surrounding forest. The range of music covered is pretty wide, including chamber music, jazz, traditional folk songs, and danceband music. It all takes place during the first week of July, with proceedings starting in the early morning and carrying on until late evening every day.

There's little else to do in Leksand other than take it easy for a while. A relaxing stroll along the riverside brings you to **Leksands kyrka** (daily 9.30am–3pm), one of Sweden's biggest village churches; it's existed in its present form since 1715, although the oldest parts of the building date back to the thirteenth century. The church enjoys one of the most stunning locations of any in the land, its peaceful churchyard lined with whispering spruce trees and looking out over the lake to the distant shore. Next door are a few old wooden buildings which make a passable attempt at an open-air homestead museum.

PRACTICALITIES

There are seven **trains** a day between Mora and Börlange in both directions, all of which stop at Leksand. The **tourist office** is in the station building (mid-June to mid-Aug Mon–Fri 9am–8pm, Sat & Sun 10am–7pm; mid-Aug to mid-June Mon–Fri 9am–5pm, Sat 10am–1pm; ☎0247/803 00, *www.siljan-dalarna.com*). The centre of town is a five-minute walk up Villagatan, the street opposite the station.

Leksand's cosy **youth hostel**, one of the oldest in Sweden, is around 2.5km from the train station, over the river at Parkgården (☎0247/152 50; 100kr). There are two **campsites**: *Leksands Camping* at Orsandbaden, a twenty-minute walk from the tourist office along Tällbergsvägen (☎0247/803 13 or 803 12); and 6km from the village at Västanvik, across the bay (☎0247/342 01). Four-bed **cabins** in the vicinity of Leksand are available (450–500kr a night); you can book these at the tourist office, which is also where to head in the afternoon for any last-minute **hotel** deals. Comfortable rooms in log cabins are to be found at *Hotell Moskogen*, Insjövägen 50 (☎0247/146 00, fax 144 30; ③). By the far the best place to stay in Leksand is *Hotell Korstäppen* at Hjortnäsvägen 33 (☎0247/123 10, fax 141 78; ③), a wonderful hotel tastefully decked out in traditional Dalarna colours. Its sitting room looks out over the lake, whose lapping waters can be reached by a path behind the hotel.

A good place to **eat** is *Siljans Konditori & Bageri*, in the main square; their summer terrace is a wonderful place from which to watch the world go by while sipping a cup of coffee. They serve up sandwiches with fantastic home-made bread, and salads and pies; make this place your first choice for lunch (they're not open in the evenings). Alternatively, try *Bosporen* in the tiny pedestrianized centre of town; the village's main restaurant, it serves pizzas from 60kr as well as meat and fish dishes from 115kr. In the same vein is the nearby *Bella Pizza* at Norsgatan 34. Chinese food can be had at *Lucky House*, in the main square, with the usual array of dishes from 98kr. Down at the station, *Rallaren Wärdshus & Pub* serves up lunch and dinner and is a good place for a **drink** when evening comes; there's outdoor seating here in summer. Alternatively, try the bar and disco in the *Bosporen*.

Tällberg

If you believe the tourist blurb, then **TÄLLBERG** (pronounced "tell-berry"), all lakeside log cabins amid rolling hills, *is* Dalarna. A folksy hillside village between Rättvik and Leksand, its wooden cottages draped with flowers in summer, Tällberg first became famous in 1850, when the Danish writer Hans Christian Andersen paid it a visit; on his return to Copenhagen, he wrote that everyone should experience Tällberg's peace and tranquility, and marvel at its wonderful lake views. Ever since, hordes of tourists have flooded into the tiny village to see what all the fuss was about – prepare yourself for the crowds that unfortunately take the shine off what is otherwise quite a pretty little place. Tällberg today is also a prime destination for wealthy middle-aged Swedes, who come to enjoy the good life for a few days, savour the delicious food dished up by the village's seven hotels, and admire the fantastic views out over Lake Siljan. To escape the crowds, walk down the steep hill of Sjögattu, past the campsite, to the calm lapping water of the lake and a small sandy beach; keep going through the trees to find quieter spots for nude bathing.

Tällberg is on the main **train** line round Lake Siljan; the **station** is a ten- to- fifteen minute walk from the village. The Rättvik–Borlänge **bus**, #58, stops every two to three hours in the village itself. There's no tourist office here. For **accommodation**, avoid the expensive hotels and walk down Sjögattu to *Siljansgården* (☎0247/500 40), a wonderful old wooden farm building with a cobbled courtyard and a fountain. Its rooms, not en suite, are comparable to those in youth hostels; prices fluctuate, but reckon on around 200kr per night – one of the best deals in Dalarna. Alternatively, head for the **campsite** (☎0247/503 01), a little further along from *Siljansgården* – head down to the lakeshore and turn left.

Rättvik

On the eastern bulge of the lake, **RÄTTVIK** (pronounced "Rett-veek"), 8km from Tällberg and 37km from Mora, comprises one tiny shopping street, a jetty out into the lake, an outdoor swimming pool, and not much else. What the town lacks in the way of sights it makes up for by way of being set in plenty of wonderful countryside. Get out of the village as soon as you can, and head up to the **viewing point** at **Vidablick** – it's about an hour's walk and quite a climb, but the view is worth the effort. From the top, you'll be able to survey the surrounding forest-covered hillsides, with the occasional small farm interrupting the greenery, and get a view of virtually all of Lake Siljan, even all the way to Mora. There's a small café and a shop at Vidablick. To get to the viewing point, walk along one of the marked **trails** through the forests above Rättvik. The most appealing route there is the well-signposted walk that begins at Bockgatan: head down the road towards *Hotell Lerdalshöjden* (see below), then follow the signs for Tolvåsstugan by walking right along Märgatan and then right again up Werkmästargatan – take another right into the forest at the sign for Fäbodarstigen. Right here there are a couple of information boards showing the different onward trails. The quickest way back to Rättvik from Vidablick is to take the steep road down the hill (there are a couple of them, so ask the staff in the shop to point out the right one), go left at the end onto Wallenkampfvägen and then right along Mårsåkervägen towards Lerdal again, all the time coming down the hill. As you head back along this route, you'll see some of the most beautifully situated homes in Dalarna – all log cabins, gardens and views out over the lake.

PRACTICALITIES

Rättvik's **train station** contains the **tourist office** (mid-June to mid-Aug Mon–Fri 9am–8pm, Sat & Sun 10am–7pm; mid-Aug to mid-June Mon–Fri 9am–5pm, Sat 10am–1pm; ☎0248/702 00, *www.siljan-dalarna.com*). The best place to stay in Rättvik is the **youth hostel** at Centralgatan (☎0248/105 66; 110kr), its buildings constructed using large pine logs, in the old Dalarna style. To get there, take either Järnvägsgatan and Vasagatan (which run either side of the square outside the station) northeast to their junction with Centralgatan, where you turn right and walk another 200m. There's not much variety here when it comes to **hotels**; the closest to the centre is *Hotell Lerdalshöjden*, on Bockgatan (☎0248/511 50, fax 511 77; ③), with good views of the lake, though the rooms are pretty average. The only other hotel worth considering is *Hotell Vidablick* (☎0248/302 50, fax 306 60; ②), with pine cabins that have been converted into comfortable rustic apartments; it's about 3km out of Rättvik and can be reached by heading south from the station along Faluvägen. There are two **campsites** in town: one is across the road from the youth hostel, close to Rättviksparken (☎0248/561 10); the other, *Siljansbadet* (☎0248/516 91), has its own swimming pool – it's 200m from the station, right on the lakeside behind the train lines.

Rättvik has a dearth of good places to **eat and drink**; indeed, things are so bad that the local youth take off to Leksand and Mora of an evening in search of a decent pub or restaurant. The best of the bunch here is the cosy *Restaurant Anna* at Vasagatan 3, with a *Dagens Rätt* and pricey evening meals; they specialize in local dishes – elk and reindeer casserole will set you back 138kr. The main alternative is *Krögar'n*, on the pedestrianized shopping street, Storgatan, serving burgers and meat dishes at good prices; during the evening happy hour here, a *storstark* costs around 30kr. For cheap pizzas, head for *Bella Pizza* at Ågatan 11; good home-made bread, cakes, sandwiches and pies can be had at *Fricks Konditori*, in the main square.

Mora and around

At the northwestern corner of the lake, **MORA** (pronounced "Moo-ra") is as good a place as any around the lake to head for, handy for onward trains on the Inlandsbanan (see p.421) and for moving on to the ski resorts of Idre (see p.432) and Sälen (see p.431). Mora's main draw is its excellent **Zorn Museum** at Vasagatan 36 (mid-June to mid-Sept Mon–Sat 9am–5pm, Sun 11am–5pm; mid-Sept to mid-June Mon–Sat noon–5pm, Sun 1pm–5pm; 30kr), showcasing the work of Sweden's best-known painter, **Anders Zorn** (1860–1920). Most successful as a portrait painter (he even went to the United States to paint American presidents Cleveland, Theodore Roosevelt and Taft), Zorn came to live in Mora in 1896. At the museum, look out for his self-portrait and the especially pleasing *Midnatt* (Midnight) from 1891, which depicts a woman rowing on Lake Siljan, her hands blue from the cold night air. You might also want to wander across the museum lawn and take in his home, **Zorngården**, where he lived with his wife, Emma (mid-June to mid-Sept Mon–Sat 10am–4pm, Sun 11am–4pm; mid-Sept to mid-June Mon–Sat noon–3pm, Sun 1–5pm; 35kr). The other museum in town worth considering is the **Vasaloppsmuséet** (mid-Jun to mid-Aug daily 10am–5pm; mid-Aug to mid-June Mon–Fri 10am–5pm; 30kr), telling the history of the ski race, Vasaloppet (see p.431); it's east of the Zorn Museum, on the other side of Vasagatan.

PRACTICALITIES

You should leave the **train** at the central Mora Strand station (which consists of little more than a platform), rather than at the main Mora station which is further out; the latter is where you'll catch the Inlandsbanan and obtain SJ train information. The bus office is at Moragatan, close to Mora Strand. The **tourist office**, actually in Mora Strand station (mid-June to mid-Aug Mon–Fri 9am–8pm, Sat & Sun 10am–7pm; mid-Aug to mid-June Mon–Fri 9am–5pm, Sat 10am–1pm; ☎0250/56 76 00, *www.siljan-dalarna.com*), has all the usual literature, including a map of the Vasaloppsleden hiking route, which you can follow north from Mora to Sälen (see p.431).

By the finishing line for the Vasaloppet is the **youth hostel**, at the corner of Fredsgatan and Prostgatan, 100m off the main Vasagatan (☎0250/381 96; 130kr). From Mora station, turn left and keep walking for about five minutes along Vasagatan; from Mora Strand station, turn right and head northeast on Strandgatan, turning left at the junction with Fredsgatan. The biggest and best **hotel** is the *First Resort Mora*, opposite Mora Strand station at Strandgatan 12 (☎0250/717 50, fax 189 81; ③/②), with modern and old-fashioned rooms. A small and sweet little place, *Hotell St Mikael* at Fridhemsgatan 15 (☎0250/159 00, fax 380 70; ②) has tasteful rooms; it's five minutes' walk from Mora Strand (turn left out of the station into Strandgatan, then take the first right). Close to the main station, *Hotell Kung Gösta* (☎0250/150 70, fax 170 78; ③/②), is handy for those early-morning departures on the Inlandsbanan; the hotel also has a decent annexe where the rooms are about 100kr cheaper. Travelling with children, your best bet is *Mora Parkens Hotell* at Parkvägen 1 (☎0250/178 00, fax 185 83; ②), which has a playground nearby; it's a ten-minute walk from the centre along Hantverkaregatan, which begins near the bus station. Nearby is the **campsite**, *Mora Camping* (☎0250/153 52), with a good beach as well as a lake for swimming.

In summer, coffee and cakes can be enjoyed outside at two **cafés**, *Helmers Konditori* and *Mora Kaffestugan*, which are virtually next door to each other on the main shopping street, Kyrkogatan. For more substantial **eating**, all the hotels serve up a decent *Dagens Rätt*, with little to choose between them. Among the town's **restaurants**, *Pizzeria Primo* in Fridhemplan, off Fridhemsgatan, and *Pizzeria Torino* at Älvgatan 73, serve up virtually any pizza you can imagine at reasonable prices; for bland Chinese *Dagens Rätt* or evening meals (three-dish set menu 129kr), try *China House*, at the corner of Hamngatan and Moragatan near the church. The most popular place to eat is *Wasastugan*, a huge log building at Tingnäsvägen, between the main train station and the tourist office. Here you can have reasonably priced lunch and dinner (good meat and fish dishes from 80kr); at night, it's also a lively place to drink, with regular live music. It tends to attract a young crowd, especially to its disco evenings. Inside the *First Resort Mora* on Strandgatan is *Terassen* **bar**, one of the town's other lively evening places.

AROUND MORA

It's worth taking one of the **cruises** on Lake Siljan on board the lovely old steamship *M/S Gustaf Wasa*, which leaves from the quay by Mora Strand station (timetables vary; check sailing times with the tourist office or call ☎010/252 32 92). The excursions include a round trip to Leksand and back, which takes anything from two to five hours as routes vary from day to day (120kr), or a two-hour lunch cruise round a bit of the lake (80kr including food). Another trip you might want to consider is a visit to **Nusnäs**, just east of Mora on the lakeside, where you'll find the **workshop** of the Olsson brothers (mid-June to mid-Aug Mon–Fri 8am–6pm, Sat & Sun 9am–5pm; mid-Aug to mid-June Mon–Fri 8am–5pm, Sat & Sun 10am–2pm; free), creators of Sweden's much-loved **Dala horses** (see box, below). There'll, you see skilled craftsmen carving the horses out of wood from the pine forests around Lake Siljan; the horses are then hand-painted and varnished. You can get to Nusnäs from Mora on bus #108 (Mon–Fri 4 daily; 20min). The wonderful **bear park** near Orsa is also worth a visit (see p.435); to get there, take bus #118 (1hr).

THE DALA HORSE

No matter where you travel in Sweden, you'll come across small wooden figurines known as **Dala horses** (*dalahästar*). Their bright red colour, stumpy legs and garish floral decorations are, for many foreigners, high kitsch and rather ugly; the Swedes, however, adore bright colours (the redder the better) and so love the little horses – it's virtually an unwritten rule that every household in the country should have a couple on display. Two brothers from the town of **Nusnäs**, **Nils** and **Jannes Olsson**, began carving the horses in the family baking shed in 1928, when they were just teenagers. Though they were simply interested in selling their work to help their cash-strapped parents make ends meet, somehow the wooden horses started catching on – Swedes are at a loss to explain why – and soon were appearing across the country as a symbol of rural life.

Northwest of Mora: from Sälen to Grövelsjön

The area to the northwest of Mora offers travellers approaching from the south a first taste of what northern Sweden is really all about. The villages in this remote part of Dalarna lie few and far between, separated by great swathes of **coniferous forest** which thrives on the hills and **mountains** which predominate here. On its way to the Norwegian border, **Route 70**, the main artery through this part of the province, slowly climbs up the eastern side of a river valley, Österdalälven. After the tiny village of Åsen, the road leaves the river behind and strikes further inland towards the mountains which mark the border between Sweden and Norway. Buses to Särna, Idre and Grövelsjön follow this route, whereas services to Sälen only travel as far as Älvdalen before heading west towards Route 297.

Sälen

Considered as one entity, **SÄLEN** and the surrounding resorts of Lindvallen, Högfjället, Tandådalen, Hundfjället, Rörbäcksnäs and Stöten constitute the biggest **ski centre** in the Nordic area, with over a hundred pistes and guaranteed snow from November to May. It isn't unreasonable to lump all these places together, as each of the minor resorts, despite having its own ski slope, is dependent on Sälen for shops (not least its Systembolaget) and services. Novice skiers can take advantage of Sälen's special lifts and nursery slopes, with tuition available; there are also plenty of intermediate runs through the densely forested hillsides and, for advanced skiers, twenty testing runs as well as an off-piste area. To get the best value for money, it's really worth buying a package rather than trying to book individual nights at local hotels; prices are high and in season they're

---

HIKES AROUND SÄLEN

The **Vasaloppsleden** from Sälen to **Mora** (90km) is the route taken by skiers on the first Sunday in March during the annual **Vasaloppet race**. The event commemorates King Gustav Vasa's return to Mora after he escaped from the Danes on skis; two men from Mora caught up with him and persuaded him to come back to their town, where they gave him refuge. The path starts just outside Sälen, in **Berga**, and first runs uphill to Smågan, then downhill all the way to Mora via Mångsbodarna, Risberg, Evertsberg, Oxberg, Hökberg and Eldris. For **accommodation**, there are eight **cabins**, each equipped with a stove and unmade beds, along the route; it's also possible to stay in a number of the hamlets on the way – look out for *rum* or *logi* signs. A detailed map of the route is available from the tourist offices in Sälen and Mora.

Another hike to consider is the little-known **southern Kungsleden** (for the main Kungsleden, see pp.478-482). It starts at the *Högfjällshotellet* on **Högfjället**, one of the slopes near Sälen, and leads to **Drevdagen**, a thirty-minute drive west of Idre off Route 70 (there is no public transport to or from Drevdagen), where it continues to Grövelsjön and all the way north to **Storlien**. Although it's an easy path to walk, it doesn't pass through particularly beautiful scenery, and so is best suited to serious walkers who are not averse to covering large distances. As there's no accommodation on the Högfjället–Drevdagen stretch, you're better off opting for the Vasaloppsleden from Sälen to Mora.

packed to capacity. During the **summer**, Sälen specializes in assorted **outdoor activities** – fishing, canoeing and beaver safaris are all available, and the hills, lakes and rivers around the town will keep you busy for several days. There's also some fantastic **hiking** to be had in the immediate vicinity (see box, p.431).

Bus #95 heads from Mora to Sälen (mid-June to mid-Aug 1 daily; mid-Aug to mid-June 2 daily; 1hr 40min). Heading here from Borlänge, take the train to **Malung**, from where bus #157 takes just an hour to reach Sälen. The bus calls at each resort in turn, terminating at Stöten. Annoyingly, to get to **Idre** by public transport (see below), you'll need to backtrack to Mora and set out from there as there's no transport to Idre from Sälen. By car it's much more straightforward; take Route 297 north from Sälen to Särna, from where you head northwest on Route 70 to Idre.

Sälen's **tourist office** is on the straggly main street that runs through the village (late April to late June & mid-Aug to Dec Mon–Fri 9am–6pm; late June to mid-Aug & Dec to late April Mon–Fri 9am–6pm, Sat & Sun 10am–4pm; ☎0280/202 50, *www.salen.nu*). **Accommodation** is best had at the wonderfully situated *Högfjällshotellet* at Högfjället (4 buses daily from Sälen; ☎0280/870 00, fax 211 61; ④/②), just on the tree line; it has a restaurant and a bar with large windows offering fantastic panoramic views over the surrounding hills. There's also a superb sauna suite in the basement, and a swimming pool with whirlpool and jet streams. To be out in the wilds, head for the **youth hostel** at Gräsheden, near Stöten (☎0280/820 40; 100kr); call before you set off so that the hostel staff will know to pick you up in Stöten. Meals can be ordered in advance here; there's also a kitchen, laundry facilities room and a sauna.

Idre

The twice-daily bus from Mora follows the densely forested valley of the Österdalälven on its three-hour journey to **IDRE** – one of Sweden's main **ski resorts** and home to its southernmost community of reindeer-herding *Sámi*. However, if you're expecting wooden huts and reindeer herders dressed in traditional dress, you'll be disappointed – the remaining six herding families live in conventional houses in the area around Idre and dress like everyone else.

The continental climate here – Idre is located at one of the wider points of the Scandinavian peninsula, and thus isn't prone to the warming influence of the Atlantic – means that the summers are relatively dry; consequently Idre, like its fellow ski resort, Sälen (see above), offers plenty of **outdoor activities** to pursue. Its tourist office can help arrange fishing trips, horse riding, mountain biking, tennis, climbing and golf. There are some good sandy beaches along the western shore of **Idresjön**, a lake that's a kilometre east of town; to go canoeing, you can rent a boat through the tourist office.

Advice about local hiking routes is available at the tourist office. By far the best hiking hereabouts is to be had around **Grövelsjön**, 3km northwest of Idre and reachable by bus from Idre (Mon–Fri 2 daily; Sun 1 daily). The area is renowned throughout Sweden for its stark, beautiful mountain scenery and is well worth making the extra effort to reach; see p.434.

Continuing up the mountain (take the twice-daily local bus; 20min), you'll come to the ski slopes at **Idrefjäll**, one of the most reliable places for snow in the entire country, with particularly cold winters. Although not quite on the scale of Sälen, Idre's ski resort manages to be Sweden's third largest and one of the most important in the Nordic area, with 32 lifts and thirty slopes. In winter the place is buzzing – not only with skiers but also with reindeer, who wander down the main street at will hoping to be able to lick the salt on the roads for minerals. Unfortunately for them, though, Route 70 is not salted north of Mora, which means you should be especially carefully if you're driving here in winter.

PRACTICALITIES

Idre is a tiny one-street affair; if you come in summer, it's where you should stay, rather than up at Idrefjäll. The main street, where the bus drops you, is where you'll find everything of any significance here, including a supermarket, bank and post office. The **tourist office** is at the far end of the main street when approaching from Mora (mid-June to mid-Aug Mon–Fri 8am–7pm, Sat 8.30am–7pm, Sun 9am–7pm; mid-Aug to mid-June Mon–Fri 9am–5pm, Sat & Sun 10am–2pm; ☎0253/207 10). For **accommodation** in the village itself, try the small and comfortable *Hotell Idregården* on the main road just as you come in from Mora (☎0253/200 10, fax 206 76; ③/①). When it comes to **eating**, there's precious little choice: you can either go to the *Idregården*'s restaurant, which is famous for its ostrich and wild game, or *Kopparleden*, right at the other end of town near the tourist office, which does simple fry-ups. The **bar** at the hotel is the most popular spot at weekends. On Friday and Saturday evenings, you could try *Garaget*, which is attached to the *Kopparleden*.

Idrefjäll consists of one **hotel**, *Idre Fjäll* (☎0253/410 00, fax 401 58; ⑤/③), and the surrounding ski slopes and lifts. The place also boasts snowboard areas, indoor swimming pools, saunas, five hotel restaurants and a sports hall. All other facilities, such as banks, are down in the town. Room prices are fiendishly complicated and vary almost week to week through the season, depending on when Stockholmers take their holiday (don't just turn up here in winter and expect to find a room – you won't). You can get a much better rate if you book a package for a week or so; contact the tourist office down in the village for details.

AROUND IDRE: THE NJUPESKÄR WATERFALL

From Idre, it's well worth a trip to **Särna**, 30km away, to see the impressive **Njupeskär waterfall**, Sweden's highest, with a drop of 125m. In winter, **ice climbers**, in particular, will want to head here, as the waterfall freezes then. An easy, circular **walking route** is clearly signposted from the car park to the waterfall and back, making for a good, two-hour hike. There's no public transport from Idre; by **car**, take the main road to Särna, then turn right following signs for Mörkret and later for Njupeskärsvattenfall.

Grövelsjön

Surrounded by nature reserves and national parks, **Grövelsjön**, reachable by bus #95 from Mora via Idre (Mon–Fri 2 daily, Sun 1 daily), is where the road ends and the mountains and wilderness really start. The area is renowned throughout Sweden for its stark, beautiful mountain scenery; in summer, the pasture around here is home to hundreds of grazing reindeer. Virtually the only building here is the STF **fell station**, with a variety of rooms and prices depending on the season (☎0253/230 90; 230–610kr; closed May to mid-June and Oct–Jan except Christmas & New Year); it boasts a sauna, massage room and solarium. The fell station makes an ideal base for **hikes** out into the surroundings, with a variety of

HIKING THE SOUTHERN KUNGSLEDEN FROM GRÖVELSJÖN

From Grövelsjön, the **southern Kungsleden** goes over the reindeer-grazing slopes of Långfjället, skirts round Töfsingdalens National Park, crosses the provincial border from Dalarna to Härjedalen to the east of Slagufjället and continues northwards (the stretch around Tännäs is especially scenic), passing Sweden's southernmost glacier on **Helagsfjället** on the way (the stretch from Grövelsjön to Helagsfjället is 124km). The trail ends at **Storlien** (see p.446), from where there are trains to Trondheim in Norway and to Stockholm and Gothenburg via Östersund.

The stretch from Grövelsjön to Tänndalen makes an excellent hike, taking three to four days to complete (76km). For much of the time the route passes through sparse pine forest relatively untouched by modern forestry; an eight-kilometre stretch also runs alongside Lake Rogen, known for its rich birdlife and unusual moraine formations. Between the lake and Tänndalen, you might be lucky enough to see the only herd of **musk oxen** in Sweden. They spend the winter in the mountain area between Storvålen and Brattriet before nipping over the border into Norway's Femundsmarka national park (close to the western edge of Lake Rogen) for the summer months. It's wise to keep your distance should you come across them, as musk oxen can be ferocious creatures; also bear in mind they're one of the few animals which can run faster uphill than downhill!

This hike takes in three STF **cabins**, each within around 20 beds and selling provisions, at: Storrödtjärn (22km from Grövelsjön; closed May, June & mid-Aug to mid-March), Rogen (16km from Storrödtjärn; closed early May to end June & end Aug to mid-Feb) and Skedbro (17km from Rogen; closed end April to end June and end Aug to mid-March). At the end of the hike, in **Tänndalen** (21km from Skedbro), there's an STF **youth hostel** (☎0684/221 11; 115kr). From here, there are also buses to Funäsdalen (Mon–Fri 3 daily), where connections can be made east to Östersund via Klövsjö and Åsarna (for the Inlandsbanan) or south to Sveg (also on the Inlandsbanan).

routes available, some lasting a day, others several days; an excellent three- to four-day hike is the stretch of the **southern Kungsleden** from Grövelsjön to Tänndalen (see box, above).

Among the established **day-hikes** is the clearly marked route (16km round-trip) from the fell station up to Storvätteshågnen (1183m), with its fantastic views over the surrounding peaks and across the border into Norway. Another worthwhile hike starts with a short walk from the fell station to Sjöstugan on Lake Grövelsjön (roughly 1500m away), from where you take the morning boat to the northern (Norwegian) end of the lake. You can now return along the lake shore to the fell station (9km) by way of the Linné path, following in the footsteps of the famous botanist who walked this route in 1734. It's possible to do the whole route in the opposite direction, heading out along the Linné path in the morning and returning by boat in the late afternoon; ask at the fell station for details of boat departure times. A third option is to strike out along the path leading northwest from Sjöstugan, heading for the Norwegian border and Salsfjellet (1281m) on the other side of it (16km round-trip). There's no need to take your passport with you as the border is all but invisible; people wander back and forth across it quite freely.

North of Mora: Orsa

The first stop for the Inlandsbanan on its long journey north from Mora (see p.429) is the tiny town of **ORSA** (pronounced "Ush-a", 21km from Mora. Step off the train here and you're entering bear country – it's reckoned that there are a good few hundred huge brown bears roaming the dense forests around the town. Despite their steadily increasing numbers, few sightings of the bears are made in the wild, except by hunters who cull the population each year.

Appropriately, the main attraction in Orsa is the nearby **Orsa Grönklitt björnpark**, the biggest **bear park** in Europe (mid-May to late June & Aug to early Sept daily 10am–3pm; late June & July 10am–5pm; 65kr). Whatever your reservations about such places, think again: the bears here aren't tamed or caged, but wander around the nine hundred square kilometres of the forested park at will, hunting and living as they would in the wild. It's the human visitors who are confined, having to clamber up viewing towers and along covered walkways.

Watching the bears will put paid to any preconceptions you may have had about them: their behaviour is amusing, and they're gentle and vegetarian for the most part (though occasionally, they're fed the odd dead reindeer or elk that's been killed on the roads). The king of the park is the enormous male bear called Micke, who weighs in at a staggering 450 kilos; he's become something of a celebrity in recent years, after his teeth were fixed live on Swedish TV. Trying hard not to be upstaged by the bears are two lynx and a couple of wolves – although you'll be lucky to see them; in fact, it's a good idea to bring along a pair of binoculars to help you pick out any rustlings in the undergrowth.

The bear park is located 13km from Orsa, and can be reached by taking the twice-daily bus #118 from outside the train station (or from Mora, where the bus starts). From late autumn to early spring the park closes, when the bears hibernate in specially constructed lairs, monitored by closed-circuit television cameras.

Practicalities

Orsa's **train station**, outside which buses stop, is in the centre on Järnvägsgatan. The **tourist office** is directly opposite at Centralgatan 3 (mid-June to mid-Aug Mon–Fri 9am–8pm, Sat & Sun 10am–7pm; mid-Aug to mid-June Mon–Fri 9am–5pm, Sat 10am–1pm; ☎0250/55 21 63). Half a kilometre from the station is the *Strandvillan* **hotel**, Älvgatan 6 (☎0250/408 73, fax 435 30; ③/②), a very small place with modern rooms. There's a beautifully located **youth hostel** by the side of Lake Orsa just 1km east of the centre on Moravägen, near the ice stadium (☎0250/421 70; 110kr, ①; closed late April to mid-May & Nov). It offers fine twin-bedded rooms, plus breakfast, TV and a kitchen. Watch what you eat, though, in the nearby *Fyrksås Restaurang* – if it looks like pink roast beef, it's really bear meat (sometimes an excess number of bears in the park means that one or two have to be killed – and end up being served up here).

Härjedalen

An excellent area for walking, **Härjedalen** province is a sparsely populated fell region, stretching north and west to the Norwegian border. The region belonged to Norway until 1645, and the Norse influence is still evident today in the local dialect. Härjedalen got its name from the unfortunate Härjulf Hornbreaker, a servant to the Norwegian king, who mistakenly killed two of the king's men and was banished from the court. He fled to Uppsala, where he sought protection from King Amund, but after falling in love with Amund's cousin, Helga, and arousing the king's fury, he was forced to make another hasty exit. It was then he came across a desolate valley in which he settled and which he named after himself: Härjulf's dale, or Härjedalen as it's known today.

The main towns of **Sveg** (see below) and **Åsarna** (see p.437) make good bases from which to go walking (the latter is also a popular ski centre), while **Klövsjö** (see p.437), set amid exceptionally pretty forested hillsides, is among the most enchanting places in all Sweden. Indeed, Härjedalen contains some of the best scenery in the country, with more than thirty mountains of above 1000m, affording some great views. The highest of these peaks is **Helags** (1797m), whose icy slopes support Sweden's southernmost glacier. Härjedalen is also home to the largest population of bears in the country, as well as a handful of shaggy musk oxen that have wandered over the border from Norway.

Sveg

The main town in Härjedalen – and the first main stop on the Inlandsbanan after Orsa – is **SVEG** (pronounced "Svay-gg"), with a tiny population of just four thousand. Back in 1273, it was the site of a parliament assembled to hammer out a border treaty between Sweden and Norway. Things have quietened down considerably since then, and even on a Friday night in the height of summer you'll be pushed to find anyone in the streets. Though there's not an awful lot to do here, Sveg's a pretty enough place: the wide streets are lined with grand old wooden houses, and a beautiful and very graceful river runs right through the centre of town. When the weather's fine, the walk along the bank is particularly delightful, and right at the end, you can cross the road and train bridge at the end of Fjällvägen and head right over a little stream into the forest, towards the river's edge. Hidden from the road by the trees is a wonderful sweet-smelling open flower meadow, a gorgeous place for a picnic and a spot of skinny-dipping in the river – but don't forget your mosquito repellent (the countryside around Sveg is made up of vast tracts of uninhabited marshland and countless small lakes, ideal breeding grounds for the insect).

Practicalities

The **train** and **bus stations** are on Järnvägsgatan. The **tourist office** at Ljusnegatan 1 (☎0680/107 75, *www.haerjedalen.se*), within the *Folkets Hus* building in the town centre, has leaflets about local hiking routes, useful for their maps even if you don't understand Swedish.

For a place to **stay**, try the ramshackle and very welcoming **youth hostel** (☎0680/103 38; 100kr; bookings mandatory Oct–May), a ten- to fifteen-minute walk from the station at Vallervägen 11, near the main square. It's run by Svea af Trampe, who unfortunately is rather hard of hearing. Next door, in the same building, is *Hotell Härjedalen* (same number; ①), with rather shabby rooms. More upmarket and just the other side of Torget at the corner of Fjällvägen and Dalagatan is the smart *Hotell Mysoxen* (☎0680/71 12 60, fax 100 62; ③/②). The campsite (☎0680/130 25) is by the riverside, a stone's throw from the tourist office.

Most of the town's **eating places** seem pretty deserted. One that isn't is the *Knuten* pizzeria, in the main square, serving OK pizzas for around 50kr. For bargain-basement meals, try the greasy spoon *Inlandskrogen*, next to the train and bus stations, which offers fry-ups, burgers and pizzas; the fare may not be excellent but there's a sporting chance you'll find people in there. Finer food can be had at the restaurant in the *Hotell Mysoxen*. All the places mentioned above serve *Dagens Rätt* for around 50–60kr.

North from Sveg: Åsarna and Klövsjö

From Sveg, the Inlandsbanan veers eastwards in order to get around the vast area of marshland north and east of the town. The train line finally swings west at Överhögdal, where the Viking Age tapestries now on display in Östersund were discovered (see p.441), before continuing north to **ÅSARNA**. Here, four of the region's many skiing champions – Tomas Wassberg, Torgny Mogren, Jan Ottosson and Hans Persson – have clubbed together and set up an all-year **ski centre**, which organizes skiing and provides advice on hiking. You may want to check out its **ski museum** (daily: June–Aug 8am–9pm; Sept–May 8am–7pm; 15kr), which has worthy displays of the Åsarna ski club's Olympic and World Championship medals and equipment, as well as photographs of famous Swedish skiers and a couple of video exhibits. The centre is on the one and only main road, a few minutes from the train station.

Much more interesting is the peculiar **Utedassmuséet**, or Outside Loo Museum, which is behind the main ski centre – entrance is free for this illuminating array of the alfresco pots and bowls graced by countless Swedish bottoms over the years. For an evening stroll or an afternoon picnic in summer, wander past the campsite cabins (visible from the ski centre) down to the river, turn right, and follow the age-old Kärleksstigen, Lover's Lane, along the water's edge; you can cross the river over an old stone bridge, further upstream by the rapids, and return on the opposite bank along a minor road. The smooth, low rocks by the bridge make an ideal spot at which to fish or catch a few rays of sunshine.

The village has a post office, a filling station and a branch of *Sparbanken* – and little else. Its **tourist office** is housed in the ski centre complex (daily: June–Aug 8am–9pm; Sept–May 8am–7pm; ☎0687/301 93). While it's virtually impossible to **stay** in Åsarna in winter without an advance booking, in summer you can just turn up and find a room. The ski centre's **youth hostel** (☎0687/302 30; 100kr) and **campsite** (☎0687/302 30, fax 303 60) are down by the river's edge, with a small bathing pool and a sauna. Three non-STF four-berth **cabins** are available to rent here from 490kr per day. The *Åsarna Hotell* (☎0687/300 04; ②), opposite the train station, has smarter rooms than the hostel's, and a proper restaurant and bar. To get away from conventional roof-over-head type accommodation, why not try a *Sámi kåta*, or tent, in the grounds, complete with wood for your evening fire and reindeer skins to sleep on, for just 50kr. The ski centre **restaurant** is hard to beat for cheap meals (closes around 9pm), with breakfast for 35kr, *Dagens Rätt* for 55kr and evening meals around the 75kr mark. When the Inlandsbanan is running, a northbound **train** for Östersund generally leaves around midday, while the southbound service to Sveg and Mora doesn't go until around 4pm.

Klövsjö

Åsarna is well placed for a quick jaunt out to **KLÖVSJÖ** (4 daily buses from Åsarna; 20min). A thoroughly charming place, its log cabins set in rolling verdant pastures, the village has gained the reputation of being Sweden's most beautiful village, with some justification: the distant lake and the forested hills that enclose Klövsjö on all sides give it a special, other-worldly feeling. In and around the village itself, the flower meadows, trickling streams, wooden barns and the smell of freshly mown hay drying on frames in the afternoon sun cast a wonderful spell on all who pass through.

The ten farms here work the land in much the same way as in medieval times: ancient grazing rights, still in force, mean that horses and cows are free to roam through the village. Once you've taken a look at **Tomtangården** (July to mid-Aug daily; free), a preserved seventeenth-century farm estate, there's not much else to do except breathe the biting, clean air and admire the beauty. Unfortunately there's nowhere to stay in the village, but the **tourist office** on the main road (mid-June to mid-Aug Mon–Sat 9am–7pm, Sun noon–7pm; mid-Aug to mid-June Mon–Fri 9am–5pm; ☎0682/212 50) has cabins to rent in the vicinity (375–500kr a day). The bus that arrives from Åsarna continues to **Funäsdalen** (where you can change here for **Tänndalen** and hike along the southern Kungsleden, see p.434), passing within fifteen minutes' walk of *Katarina Wärdshus* (tell the driver if you wish to go here), a guesthouse which has **cabins** for rent (☎0682/212 77, fax 212 72; ①); they're popular in winter with the skiers who make the most of the thirteen ski slopes nearby. It's worth noting that the #164 bus from Funäsdalen back to Åsarna, via Klövsjö, continues on to Östersund (3 daily).

Into Jämtland: Östersund

Having reached **ÖSTERSUND**, which sits gracefully on the eastern shore of the mighty **Storsjön** (Great Lake), it's worth stopping at what is the only large town along the Inlandsbanan until Gällivare inside the Arctic Circle. The town (and the surrounding province of Jämtland) has only been Swedish since 1645, before when it was part of Norway. The people here have a strong sense of regional identity and, in recent years, have even called (albeit rather half-heartedly) for independence from Sweden. Östersund was only given its charter two hundred years ago by King Gustavus III, and it took another century for the town's growth to really begin, heralded by the arrival of the railway from Sundsvall. Today, the town is a major **transport hub**: the E14 runs through town on its way to the Norwegian border; the Inlandsbanan stops here (the town is 90min north of Åsarna by this line); and other trains run west to Åre and Storlien (with connections in Storlien to Trondheim in Norway), east to Sundsvall (a very beautiful run which hugs lakeshore and riverbank the entire way) and south to both Stockholm and Gothenburg, through some of Sweden's most stunning primeval forest. Coming from Lapland, train connections can be made for Östersund in nearby Bräcke.

Arrival, information and accommodation

From the **train station**, on Strandgatan, it's a five-minute walk north to the town centre; the **bus station**, on Gustav IIIs Torg, is more central. The town's **airport** is on Frösön, an island 11km from town, from where buses (45kr) and taxis (130kr) run to the centre. A couple of blocks north of the bus station is the **tourist office** at Rådhusgatan 44 (June and early to mid-Aug Mon–Sun 9am–7pm; July Mon–Sat 9am–9pm, Sun 9am–7pm; mid-Aug to May Mon–Fri 9am–5pm; ☎063/14

40 01, *www.ostersund.se/turist*), opposite the minaret-topped Rådhus. Here you can obtain the **Storsjökortet** (valid mid-May to mid-Aug; 110kr), a nine-day pass giving free bus rides, museum entry and fifty percent discounts on bus and boat sightseeing trips in and around the town.

Accommodation

For a place to **stay**, the modern and central STF **youth hostel** is at Södra Gröngatan 36, a few minutes' walk south from the tourist office (☎063/13 91 00; 130kr; late-June to early Aug). More atmospheric, though, is a night spent inside *Jämtli*, a wonderful hostel set in the old buildings at the museum (☎063/10 59 84; 130kr); you should be guaranteed free entry to the museum if you smile politely. Campers can stay either at *Östersunds Camping* (☎063/14 46 15), a couple of kilometres south down Rådhusgatan and handy for the fantastic indoor swimming complex, Storsjöbadet; or over on Frösön at *Frösö Camping* (☎063/14 46 15; June–Aug), reached by bus #3 or #4 from the centre. Unlike many other places in central northern Sweden, Östersund has good quality **hotels** at reasonable prices, listed below. You won't find their like north of here until Gällivare.

Asken, Storgatan 53 (☎063/51 74 50). Only has eight rooms (all en suite and rather plain and simple), one of which is for the use of people with allergies. ③/①.

Aston, Köpmangatan 40 (☎063/51 08 51). Entrance in Postgränd. This small place is cheapest hotel in town, with plain rooms, some of which are en suite. ②/①.

Emma, Prästgatan 26 (☎063/51 78 40). Nineteen tiny garishly decorated rooms, mostly en suite. ④/②.

Gamla Teatern, Thoméegränd 20 (☎063/51 16 00, fax 13 14 99). This is without doubt the best hotel in town, housed in an atmospheric turn-of-the-century theatre with sweeping wooden staircases; the rooms are disappointingly plain though. ⑤/③.

Jämteborg, Storgatan 54 (☎063/51 01 01). Tasteless, drab and miserable – and inexpensive. ②/①.

Linden, Storgatan 64 (☎063/51 73 35). Cramped and basic rooms, all with en-suite facilities. ③/①.

Nya Pensionatet, Prästgatan 65 (☎063/51 24 98). Near the train station, this tastefully decorated house, dating from around 1900, has just eight rooms, none of which are en-suite. ①.

Pensionat Svea, Storgatan 49 (☎063/51 29 01). Seven tweely decorated rooms, not en suite. Discounted rates are available for long-term stays. ①.

Zäta, Prästgatan 32 (☎063/51 78 60). This simple, plain and comfortable place has cable TV and a sauna. ④/②.

Älgen, Storgatan 61 (☎063/51 75 25). Handy for the train station, this is yet another of the town's small central hotels, with plain and comfortable en-suite rooms. There are also thirteen smaller hostel-style rooms for 180kr per person. ③/②.

Östersund, Kyrkgatan 70 (☎063/57 57 00, fax 57 57 11). A massive modern hotel with 126 rooms; high on quality, with carpeted rooms and leather chairs, but low on charm. ③/②.

The town and around

Östersund's **lakeside** position lends it a seaside-holiday atmosphere, unusual this far inland, and it's an instantly likeable place in which to fetch up. The town has a number of interesting museums and, so it's said, a **monster** resident in the lake, rivalling that of Loch Ness (see p.440). Östersund is also a centre for the engineering and electronics industries – as well as the Swedish armed forces, who maintain several regiments here (witness the numerous military aircraft flying overhead).

STORSJÖODJURET – THE "GREAT LAKE MONSTER"

The people of Östersund are in no doubt: **Storsjöodjuret** (pronounced "stoor-shur-ooo-yoor-et) is out there, in their lake. Eyewitness accounts – there are hundreds of people who claim to have seen it – speak of a creature, with a head like a dog, long pointed ears and bulging eyes, that sweeps gracefully through the water, sometimes making a hissing or clucking sound, often several hundred metres away from the shore; every summer come new reports of sightings. Although several explanations have been given that dispel the myth – a floating tree trunk, a row of swimming elk, the wake from a passing boat, a series of rising water bubbles, the monster's existence is taken so seriously that a protection order has now been slapped on it, using the provisions of paragraph fourteen of Sweden's Nature Conservation Act. For most people, though, the monster will be at its most tangible not in the lake, but on the Web (*www.storsjoodjuret.jamtland.se*).

In 1894, the hunt for this sinister presence began in earnest, when King Oscar II founded a special organization to try to catch it. Norwegian whalers were hired to do so, but the rather unorthodox methods they chose proved unsuccessful: a dead pig gripped in a metal clasp was dangled into the water as bait; and large, specially manufactured pincers were on hand to grip the creature and pull it ashore. Their tackle is on display in the Länsmuséet, together with photographs claimed to be of the creature.

If you fancy a bit of monster spotting, consider taking a **steamboat cruise** on the lake on board *S/S Thomée*, a creaking 1875 wooden steamship. Routes and timetables vary, but in general the boat does a two-hour trip (65kr) round the lake leaving from the harbour in town. Also available are three-hour trips out to the island of **Andersön**, with its nature reserve and virgin forests (75kr); five-hour trips to **Verkön**, where there's a turn-of-the-century castle (85kr); as well as one-hour trips across the water towards **Sandviken** and back (55kr); for more information, contact the tourist office.

A stroll through the pedestrianized centre reveals an air of contented calm about the place – take time out to sip a coffee around the wide open space of the main square, Stortorget, and watch Swedish provincial life go by while you're at it, or amble along one of the many side streets that slope down to the still, deep waters of the lake. In winter, though, temperatures here regularly plummet to -15°C; the modern apartment buildings you'll see lining the town's gridded streets are fitted with quadruple-glazed windows to keep the winter freeze at bay.

The main thing to do in Östersund is visit **Jämtli Historieland**, an impressive **open-air museum**, a quarter of an hour's walk north of the centre along Rådhusgatan (late June to mid-Aug daily 11am–5pm; 80kr, under-17s free when accompanied by an adult). You'll find the first few minutes a bit bewildering, as it's full of people milling around in traditional country costume, farming and milking much as their ancestors did. (They're not just acting the part as a day job – they actually live here throughout the summer.) Everyone else is encouraged to join in – baking, tree felling, grass cutting, and so on. The place is ideal for children, and adults would have to be pretty hard bitten not to enjoy the enthusiastic atmosphere. Intensive work has been done on getting the settings right: the restored and working interiors are authentically gloomy and dirty, and the local store, Lanthandel, among the wooden buildings around the square near the entrance, is suitably old-fashioned. In the woodman's cottage (presided over by a bearded

lumberjack, who makes pancakes for the visitors), shoeless and scruffy young-sters snooze contentedly in the wooden cots. Outside, even the roaming cattle and the crop varieties are accurate to the period.

On the same site, the **Länsmuséet** is a rambling houseful of local exhibits, including monster-catching gear devised by lakeside worthies in the nineteenth century (late June to mid-Aug 11am–5pm; mid-Aug to late June Tues–Sun 11am–5pm; 50kr, under-17s free when with an adult). The museum's prize exhibits are the awe-inspiring Viking **Överhögdal tapestries**, crowded with brightly coloured pictures of horses, reindeer, elk and dogs, and different types of dwellings. Dating from the ninth to tenth centuries, most of the tapestries were discovered by accident in an outhouse here in 1910. One piece was rescued after being used as a doll's blanket – rumour has it the child had to be pacified with a 2kr reward to hand it over.

There's nothing much else to see back in the town centre, apart from the **Stadsmuseum** on Rådhusgatan (Mon–Fri noon–4pm, Sat & Sun 1–4pm; free), housing a crowded two hundred years of town history in a building the size of a shoebox. The **harbour**, where a fleet of tiny boats bobs about on the clean water, is a better bet for a place to head. Immediately to the north of the harbour is the tiny **Badhusparken**, an extremely popular sunbathing spot in summer; in winter it's the place for a quick dip in the invigorating waters of Lake Storsjön – a hole in the ice is kept open here for this purpose. Once you're out of water, though, head straight for the nearby sauna or you'll be covered in frost faster than you can say "Storsjöodjuret", the name of Östersund's lake monster.

Frösön

Take the foot bridge across the lake from Badhusparken, or the road bridge a little further north, and you'll come to the island of **Frösön**. People have lived here since prehistoric times; the island's name comes from the original Viking settlement here, which was associated with the pagan god of fertility, Frö. There's plenty of good walking on Frösön, as well as a couple of historical sights. Just over the bridges, in front of the red-brick offices, look for the eleventh-century **rune stone** telling of Östmadur (East Man), son of Gudfast, the first Christian missionary to the area. From here, you can clamber up the nearby hill of Öneberget to the fourth-century settlement of **Mjälleborgen** – the most extensive remains of its type in northern Sweden.

Five kilometres west of the bridges along the island's main road, and up the main hill, is the beautiful **Frösö kyrka** (bus #3 from the centre comes here), an eleventh-century church with a detached bell tower. In 1984, archeologists digging under the altar came across a bit of old birch stump surrounded by animal bones – bears, pigs, deer and squirrels – evidence of the cult of ancient gods, who were known as the *æsir*. Today, the church is one of the most popular in Sweden for weddings – to tie the knot here at midsummer, you have to book years in advance.

From Frösön, there are fantastic **views** across the lake back to Östersund, which appears to tumble down the hill towards the water. In **winter,** when the trees hang heavy under the weight of snow and ice, and the town's streetlights cast a soft glow into the dark sky, the view across the frozen lake to the streets buried deep under a fresh snowfall is one of the most romantic and beautiful in Sweden.

Eating, drinking and nightlife

Gastronomically, there's more **choice** in Östersund than for a long way north, with good Swedish, Greek, and even Indonesian food. Most of the city's eating places, many of which double as bars, are to the south of Stortorget. For **breakfast** (and convenient for the several trains that leave early in the morning), the train-station café is good value and always busy. **Coffee and cakes** can be had at *Törners Konditori* at Storgatan 24, or better, *Wedemarks Konditori* at Prästgatan

27, where you can have sandwiches made to order. *Brunkullans Krog* restaurant (see below) also opens as a daytime café. **Nightlife** can be found at *G III* in *Hotell Östersund*, the most popular **club** in town, attracting a 20-something crowd; or at *Saga Night Club* at Prästgatan 50.

Restaurants and bars

Athena, Stortorget 3. Tucked away in one corner of Stortorget, this pompously decorated pizza restaurant serves tasty, authentic pizzas and pasta dishes, as well as steaks.

Brunkullans Krog, Postgränd 5. Östersund's premier eating place, this old-fashioned, home-from-home restaurant, with polished lanterns and a heavy wooden interior, offers traditional Swedish dishes as well as more international fish and meat dishes. It's expensive, although in summer a cheaper menu can be had at tables in the garden at the rear.

Captain Cook, Hamngatan 9. This moderately priced place has a selection of delicious Australian-style fish-and-grill delights that really draws in the crowds; it's also one of the most popular places for a drink, with its extensive beer and whisky selection.

En Liten Röd, Brogränd 19. A cosy, somewhat expensive, neighbourhood restaurant with a good choice of meat dishes from 200kr; vegetarian main courses cost around 120kr.

Kvarterskrogen, Storgatan 54. A linen tablecloth place, with high prices to match, serving lamb, entrecôte, beef and sole as well as northern Swedish delicacies from 160kr.

Ming Palace, Storgatan 15. The town's best Chinese restaurant, with the usual dishes at moderate prices.

O'Leary's, Storgatan 28. A popular Irish-style pub, offering a large selection of beer and a Tex-Mex-inspired menu.

Paviljon Thai, Prästgatan 50B. Next to the *Saga* nightclub, this is the only Indonesian/Thai restaurant in central northern Sweden – make the most of it. Excellent green curry and tiger prawn soup. Dishes around 95kr; lunch for 65kr.

Restaurang G III/Pub Köket, both inside the Hotel Östersund, Kyrkgatan 70. A standard, fairly expensive à la carte restaurant, but right beside one of the town's popular drinking holes, *Pub Köket*.

Restaurang Volos, Prästgatan 38. Cheap pizzas and a few authentic Greek dishes. Look out for special offers on beer, which sometimes goes for around 30kr.

Simon & Viktor, Prästgatan 19. At the top end of the main square. An English-style pub with upmarket pub food.

Listings

Airlines Airborne (☎0680/100 95); SAS, at the airport (☎063/635 10 10); Swedeways (☎063/15 10 10).

Airport ☎063/635 1000.

Banks FöreningsSparbanken, Handelsbanken and Sparbanken are all on Prästgatan.

Bike rental Cykelogen at Kyrkogatan 45 (Mon–Sat 10am–6pm; ☎063/12 20 80), has mountain bikes from about 100kr per day.

Buses Information on all buses on ☎020/61 62 63, or visit *www.lanstrafiken-z.se*.

Car rental Avis at the airport (☎063/448 70) or at Bangårdsgatan 9 (☎063/10 12 50); Budget, Köpmangatan 25 (☎063/10 44 10); Europcar, Hofvallsgränd 1 (☎063/57 47 50); Hertz, Köpmangatan 25 (☎063/10 21 12); Statoil, Krondikesvägen 97 (☎020/75 75 75).

Cinemas Filmstaden 1-6, Biblioteksgatan 14; Filmstaden 7-8, corner of Tullgatan and Prästgatan.

Doctor Health Centre Z-gränd (Mon–Fri 8am–5pm; ☎063/14 20 00).

Left luggage Lockers at the train station for 15kr.

MOVING ON FROM ÖSTERSUND

Direct **trains** from Östersund include services **south** to Stockholm, Arlanda airport and Gothenburg, **east** to Sundsvall and Gävle, and **west** to Åre and Storlien. By changing in Bräcke it's possible to travel by night train to Boden, Luleå and northern **Lapland**. For the **Bothnian Coast**, take the train to Sundsvall, then change to the Norrlandskusten bus services up the coast. **Inlandsbanan** services (late June to mid-Aug) operate north to Gällivare and south to Mora. The **Inlandsexpressen bus** (#45) covers the same route as the Inlandsbanan and operates year round. Other key bus services include the #40 to Sollefteå and Örnsköldsvik and the #164 to Tännas and Funäsdalen via Åsarna and Klövsjö. There's also a daily direct express bus to Stockholm with Y-Bussen.

Pharmacy Prästgatan 51 (Mon–Fri 9am–6pm, Sat 9am–4pm, Sun 11am–4pm).

Police ☎063/15 25 00.

Post office Kyrkgatan.

Systembolaget Prästgatan 18 (Mon–Fri 10am–6pm).

Taxi Taxi Östersund (☎063/51 72 00).

Trains Information from the station on Strandgatan (also on ☎020/75 75 75).

Travel agents Ticket, Kyrkgatan (Mon–Fri 9am–6pm, Sat 10am–1pm); Z-Resor, opposite McDonald's on Prästgatan (Mon–Fri 9.30am–5.30pm).

West from Ostersund: Åre and Storlien

Heading west from Östersund, the **E14** and the **train** line follow the course trudged by medieval pilgrims on their way to Nidaros (now Trondheim in Norway) over the border, a twisting route that threads its way through sharp-edged mountains rising high above a bevy of fast-flowing streams and deep, cold lakes. Time and again, the eastern Vikings assembled their armies beside the holy Storsjön lake to begin the long march west, most famously in 1030 when King Olaf of Norway collected his mercenaries for the campaign that led to his death at the Battle of Stiklestad. Today – although the scenery is splendid – there are no real attractions en route, other than the winter skiing and summer walking centres of Åre and **Storlien**.

Åre

The alpine village of **Åre** (pronounced "Or-ruh") is Sweden's most prestigious ski resort, with 44 lifts and guaranteed snow between December and May; it can be reached from Östersund either by **train** (4 daily; 1hr 45min) or on the late-afternoon **bus** (#155, 1hr 30min). During the skiing season, rooms here are like gold dust and prices sky high: book accommodation for this period well in advance through the tourist office or, better yet, take a package trip. Equipment isn't that expensive to rent (details of where to do so can be obtained at the tourist office): downhill and cross-country gear costs 100–150kr per day.

In summer, the village is a quiet, likeable haven for ramblers, sandwiched as it is between the Aresjön lake and a range of craggy hills that's overshadowed by the mighty **Åreskutan** mountain (1420m). A network of tracks crisscrosses the hills; the tourist office here has endless information about **hiking routes** in the nearby mountains and further afield – ask them for the excellent *Hiking in Åre-fjällen* booklet, which will tell you all you need to know, with detailed mountain maps. A popular route is the **Jämttriangle** from Sylarna via Blåhammaren to Storulvån, which takes in fantastic wilderness scenery close to the Norwegian border and involves two overnight stays in STF fell stations.

A cable car, the **Kabinbanan** (80kr return), whisks you from just behind Storlien's main square to the viewing platform and *Stormköket* restaurant, some way up Åreskutan. The ride takes just seven minutes, and it'll take you a further thirty minutes to clamber to the summit. Take sensible shoes with you and warm clothes, as the low temperatures are intensified by the wind, and it can be decidedly nippy even in summer. From the top the view is stunning – on a clear day you can see over to the border with Norway and a good way back to Östersund. There's a tiny wooden café at the summit, serving coffee and extortionately priced sandwiches. Even the shortest route back down to Åre (2hr) requires stamina; other, longer, paths lead more circuitously back down to the village. One word of warning: there are phenomenal numbers of **mosquitoes** and other insects up here in July and August, so make sure you are protected by repellent. The mountains around Åre are also as good a place as any to go **mountain biking**; the tourist office can help sort out a bike for you.

Back in the centre, Åre's **kyrka** (use the key hanging on a hook outside the door to get in), just above the campsite, is a marvellous thirteenth-century stone building: inside, the simple blue decoration and the smell of burning candles create a peaceful ambience.

PRACTICALITIES

The **tourist office** is in the square (May to late June and late Aug to mid-Dec Mon–Fri 9am–3pm; late June to late Aug & mid-Dec to April daily 9am–6pm; ☎0647/177 20), 100m up the steps opposite the train station building. **Accommodation** in the village, of which there's plenty, is packed in winter; in summer however, there'll be room to spare, when it's worth asking the tourist office about fixing up a **private room** (from around 125kr per person), almost all of which will have a kitchen, shower and TV. The cheapest place to stay is the unofficial **youth hostel**, known as *Åre Backpackers Inn*, in the park below the square (☎0647/177 31; 150kr). Alternatively there's the **campsite** (☎0647/136 00; closed Sept–Nov), five minutes' walk from the station. The nearest STF hostel is at Brattlandsgården in **Brattland**, 8km to the east (☎0647/301 38; 110kr; booking mandatory Sept to mid-June and groups only Oct–Dec). It's a four-kilometre hike from the train station at Undersåker, a stop on the train line from Östersund to Åre; you can also get to the hostel on the weekday buses from Åre.

Åre's not up to much in terms of **food**, but there are several cheap eating places around the square: try the pie or sandwich lunches served at *Café Bubblan*, or the more substantial dishes at *Werséns*. At the bottom of the cable car, *Bykrogen* serves lunches at 60kr and reasonably priced main meals, but note the early closing time of 7pm. More palatable but very expensive fare can be sampled at *Villa Tottebo*, down by the train station, which cooks up local meat and fish for 200–250kr. Two winter-only restaurants are the upmarket *Bakfickan* at Åregården, and *Broken Dreams* in the main square.

Storlien

Just six kilometres from the Norwegian border, **STORLIEN** is an excellent place to stop if you're into hiking, surrounded as it is by rugged, scenic terrain. The southern stretch of the **Kungsleden** (see box) starts here and winds its way south via Sweden's southernmost glacier on the slopes of Helagsfjället, continuing on to Tänndalen and Grövelsjön, terminating on the hills above Sälen. Storlien is also prime berry-picking territory (the rare cloudberry grows here); mushrooms can also be found in great number hereabouts, in particular the delicious chanterelle.

There are regular **trains** here from Åre (4 daily; 1hr). The **tourist office** is in an old train carriage at the station (June–Aug daily 10am–5pm; Sept–May takes enquiries on ☎0647/701 70). Aside from this, Storlien is little more than a couple of hotels and a supermarket amid open countryside. The **youth hostel** is a four-kilometre walk across the tracks to the E14 and then left down the main road to Storvallen (☎0647/700 50; 100kr; closed mid-June to mid-July). There's also a youth hostel in **Ånn**, halfway between Åre and Storlien (☎0647/710 70; 100kr); it's right by from the station, which is served by all trains Östersund–Storlien trains. Of the **hotels**, *Hotell Storlien*, right by the station (☎0647/701 51, fax 705 22; ①), has very cheap rooms in summer – 95kr per person in a double room. **Apartments** can be rented at *Fjäl-lyor* (☎0647/701 70; 350kr for four people), just to the right of the station; there's also a youth hostel-style section here, with beds at 125kr per night. Ten minutes away, *Storliens Högfjällshotell* is a luxury affair (☎0647/701 70, fax 70 446; ③), with nearly two hundred well-appointed modern rooms, 35 cottages and its own swimming pool.

HIKING THE SOUTHERN KUNGSLEDEN FROM STORLIEN

The southern stretch of the **Kungsleden** begins in Storlien and stretches over 160 km to Högfjället, just outside Sälen in Dalarna. Generally speaking, the countryside at the northern end of the path is more rugged and mountainous than at the southern end, which tends to be rather flat and uninspiring. The **Storlien–Tänndalen** part of the route passes Sweden's southernmost **glacier**, on the mountain of Helags, at an altitude of 1796m. The nearest town to the mountain is **Ljungdalen**, reached by bus #613 from Åsarna (Mon–Fri 2 daily, Sat & Sun 1 daily; 2hr), which terminates at the *Dunsjögården* **youth hostel** (☎0687/202 85; 110kr). This is a good base from which to climb the mountain: a strenuous hiking path leads northwest from the village through the hamlet of Skrallån, past a small group of cottages at Kesuvallen to the STF mountain cabin at Helags. The glacier, on the mountain top above the cabin, is disappointingly small, only a couple of square kilometres in size.

There are several place for overnight **accommodation** on this stretch of the southern Kungsleden, with prices varying according to season: Blåhammaren fell station at 1086m, 14km from Storvallen youth hostel (☎0647/701 20; 220–340kr; late Feb to May & July–Sept); Sylarna fell station, 19km from Blåhammaren (☎0647/750 10; 155–330kr; late Feb to May & July–Sept;); Helags cabin at the foot of the glacier, 19km from Sylarna, with 78 beds, a sauna and sale of provisions (☎0687/201 50; March to early May, late June to late Sept); Fältjägaren cabin, 12km from Helags, with twenty beds and sale of food (Feb to late April & June–Sept); and Tänndalen youth hostel (☎0684/221 11; 110kr). The **Tänndalen–Grövelsjön** section of the path is covered on p.434.

Eating and **drinking** opportunities in Storlien are very limited. The best bet is *Le Ski* restaurant, nightclub and bar at the station, which has cheapish eats for lunch and dinner (but beer will cost you 43kr); or try *Café Storliengården* (Tues–Sun 9am–5pm), a two-minute walk left out of the station, which serves coffee, waffles and sandwiches all year round.

Moving on from Storlien, two trains operated by Norwegian railways leave Storlien daily for Trondheim. In the opposite direction, there are through trains to Stockholm and Gothenburg via Östersund, with sleeper services to both these destinations.

North from Östersund to Lapland

North of Östersund, the **Inlandsbanan** slowly snakes its way across the remote Swedish hinterland, a vast and scarcely populated region where the train often has to stop so that elk and reindeer – and occasionally bears – can be cleared from the tracks. Otherwise, it'll come to a halt – when no station's in sight – for a spot of berry picking, or for the guard to point out a beaver damming a nearby stream; the train also stops at least once by a lake for everyone to take a quick dip at Tandsjöborg (2hr north of Mora) or at Varjisträsk (4hr south of Gällivare). At the **Arctic Circle** it stops again, so that everyone can jump off and take some photos. The train terminates in Gällivare, 100km north of the Arctic Circle, where mainline train connections can be made.

Route 45, the **Inlandsvägen**, is the best road north from Östersund, sticking close to the train line on its way to Gällivare. It's easy to drive and well surfaced for the most part, although watch out for reindeer with a death wish – once they spot a car hurtling towards them they seem to do their utmost to throw themselves in front of it. You could drive from Östersund to Gällivare in a day if you left very early and put your foot down, but you are better off taking it in stages. The **Inlandsexpressen**, the daily bus service that runs from Östersund to Gällivare, follows Route 45; it's not as much fun as the train, but is faster and very comfortable (see p.486).

Strömsund

The first stop of any significance north along the Inlandsbanan from Östersund is the small waterside town of **STRÖMSUND**, an hour and a half up the line. There's no actual train station here; you'll need to get off at nearby Ulriksfors and walk the 3km or so into Strömsund. The Inlandsexpressen **bus** stops in the town itself.

Strömsund is a centre for **canoeing** along **Ströms Vattudal**, an extensive network of **waterways** that stretches northwest of here, and its **tourist office**, in the Kommunhuset on Storgatan (late June to mid-Aug daily 9am–6pm; mid-Aug to late June Mon–Fri 8am–4pm; ☎0670/164 00), can fix you up with canoes (25kr an hour, 125kr a day). The tourist office can also provide information (plus maps, walking routes and details of places to stay) on the road known as the **Wilderness Way** (see p.448), which starts here and leads through some wonderful scenery. Worth making an effort to get to are the **Stone Age rock paintings**, the Hällmålningar, at **Brattfors**, around 45km southeast of Strömsund; bus #421 runs here (June–Aug 1 daily; Sept–May Mon, Wed & Fri 1 daily) on its way to Backe. Once at Brattfors, you can reach the site using the map which the tourist office provides. The paintings, created by hunter-gatherers around 2500BC, were a plea to their gods for plentiful hunting.

For a **place to stay**, there's a simple **youth hostel** 4km south of the town in Tullingsås (☎0670/300 88; 100kr) which can be reached by the Inlandsexpressen bus. The **campsite** is just outside town, on the way to Östersund (☎0670/164 10). Good **hotel** accommodation is available at *Hotell Vattudalen* at Ramselevägen 6 (☎0670/61 10 00, fax 133 70; ④/③).

Route 342 from Strömsund: The Wilderness Way

From Strömsund, **Route 342**, the Wilderness Way, strikes out northwest towards the mountains at Gäddede, before hugging the Norwegian border and crossing the barren treeless Stekenjokk plateau. It then swings inland again, rejoining Route 45 at Vilhelmina. The route has to rank as one of the most beautiful and dramatic in Sweden, passing through great swathes of **virgin forest**, tiny forgotten villages and true wilderness, where the forces of nature have been left undisturbed. It's also the part of Sweden with the densest population of **bears**. If you're driving, stop wherever you can, turn off the engine and listen to the deep silence broken only by the calls of the birds and the whisper of the forest. There are also plenty of **lakes** along the way ideal for **nude bathing** – you can choose whichever one you want to make your own; there'll be nobody else there. One of the best stretches of rocky beach is just south of the tiny village of Alanäs on the beautiful Flåsjön lake, before you get to Gäddede.

If you have your own transport (for information on travelling the route by bus, see box, p.449), you should turn left at **Bågede** and follow the minor, very rocky road along the southern shore of **Lake Fågelsjön** to reach **Hällsingsåfallet**, an impressive **waterfall**. Sweden's answer to Niagara Falls, it has an 800-metre-long canyon, into which the falls plummet, that's getting longer every year due to the continuing erosion of the rock by the water.

The only town along the route is **Gäddede** (pronounced "Yedd-aye-de"), whose name means "the spot where the northern pike can no longer go upstream". The name may be cute but the place certainly isn't; give it a miss and instead turn off the main road and follow the road signed "Riksgränsen" (National Border) for a few kilometres to the long and empty sandy beach of **Lake Murusjöen**, right on the border with Norway (the beach is in Sweden, the water in Norway). You'll be hard pushed to find a more idyllic spot: the silence is total, the deep blue water still and calm, and the mountains in the distance dark and brooding.

Heading back towards Gäddede, take the left turn for **BJÖRKVATTNET**, a tiny village reached by a twenty-kilometre road that hasn't even one building along its entire length. On the edge of the village is the **youth hostel** (☎0672/230 24; 110kr; groups only mid-Nov to mid-Feb). Complete with a sauna, the hostel has information on some good local **hiking** trails and a local bus that runs to Gäddede, where there's a **tourist office** (June–Aug; ☎0672/105 00, *gaddede.turistbyra@stromsund.se*) and a **campsite** (☎0672/100 35) on the lake shore. From Björkvattnet, it's possible to rejoin the Wilderness Way by nipping briefly over the border into Norway, driving along the northern shore of **Lake Kvarnbergsvattnet** and taking a poorly surfaced minor road through dense forest to Jormlien and on to Åsarna (a different village to the one covered on p.437).

Lake Stora Blåsjön, a lake to the north of Gäddede, is surrounded by blue mountains; the village of Stora Blåsjon is where the road starts to climb above the tree line to cross the desolate, boulder-strewn **Stekenjokk plateau** into the province of Lappland. Just outside Stora Blåsjön, look out for the minor road

THE WILDERNESS WAY BY BUS

The #425 **bus** runs from **Strömsund** to **Gäddede**. On weekdays there are two daily services, one in the afternoon and another in the evening; on Saturdays and Sundays there's one service daily, in the morning and evening respectively. Travelling on a weekday, you can stock up with picnic delights in Strömsund, catch the earlier of the two buses, get off wherever you like (just tell the driver to stop), and spend the afternoon and early evening walking or chilling out by the side of a lake. You can then catch the evening bus on to Gäddede; unfortunately there's no connection from Gäddede over the Stekenjokk plateau to **Klimpfjäll**, from where bus #420 runs down to Saxnäs and Vilhelmina (Mon–Fri 3 daily, Sat 2 daily, Sun 1 daily); on weekdays the last bus from Klimpfjäll goes at 3.30pm. It may be possible to **hitch** between the two places – there are a lot of German and Dutch campervans on this stretch of the road who may be able to help out with a lift over the plateau.

leading to **Ankarede**, an age-old meeting place for the local *Sámi*; even today families from Sweden and Norway get together here at midsummer and again in the autumn. Its old wooden **church** dates from 1896 and is located by the lake, between the two rivers. In addition there are around twenty *Sámi* circular wooden huts, *kåtor*, close by. The Stekenjokk plateau is the temporary summer home of several *Sámi* families, who tend their reindeer on the surrounding slopes, including those of the magnificent peak of **Sipmeke** (1424m) to the west of the road. After dropping into the minuscule village of **Klimpfjäll** (the stretch of road over the plateau between Leipikvattnet, a lake, and Klimpfjäll is open mid-June to mid-Oct only), the Way continues east. Taking the first turn to the left, you'll reach **Fatmomakke**, a fascinating **Sámi parish village** made up of dozens of *kåtor*, gathered neatly around the church. The first church on the site was built in 1790, but the *Sámi* met together here long before that for special religious celebrations. The huts are made out of birch wood, with a hole in the roof to let the smoke out, and birch twigs on the floor to sit on. Everything inside is orderly, the fireplace in the middle, the cooking area at the back; there's a strict code of behaviour as well – you must first wait in the entrance before being invited to enter. Look out for the *visningskåta* (signposted), the "show house" near the church, and have a peek inside.

Nearby **SAXNÄS** has a **youth hostel** at Kultsjögården on the main road (☎0940/700 44; March–Sept 110kr, Oct–Feb 75kr), next door to a luxury **hotel** complex, *Saxnäsgården* (☎0940/377 00, fax 377 01; March, April and late June to Sept ④; Oct–Feb except Christmas & New Year & May to late June ③). The hostel has lakeside **cabins** for rent, each sleeping up to eight people, with open fireplaces and a sauna (May to late June & Oct–Feb 595kr, other times 805kr for 1–4 people, higher prices apply for large groups). The place also doubles up as a **health complex**: surrounded by water and situated at the foot of the Marsfjällen mountains, it is quite literally an oasis in the surrounding wilderness and a wonderful place to pamper yourself for a day. This alcohol-free place boasts divine 34°C saltwater swimming pool, herbal health baths, massage facilities, saunas, fitness centre and sports hall. It also **rents** out mountain **bikes**, **canoes, fishing tackle** and **motor boats**. In summer the hotel runs a boat service to the Fatmomakke *Sámi* village as well as a **seaplane** up into the mountains for **hiking**. A second seaplane, Fjällturen, links Saxnäs with Borgafjäll (350kr), Tärnaby (500kr), Ammarnäs (500kr), Adolfström (650kr) and Jäkkvik (800kr); information on ☎0940/310 80 or 710 68 or at *www.slit.net/flygtjanst*. In winter, **dog-sledge** trips can be arranged through the hotel, which also has **snow scooters** for hire.

Lapland

The word **LAPLAND** means different things to different people. Mention it to a Swede (the Swedish spelling is Lappland) and they'll immediately think of the northern province of the same name which begins just south of Dorotea, runs up to the Norwegian and Finnish borders in the north, and stretches east towards (but doesn't include) the Bothnian Coast. For the original inhabitants of the north, the *Sámi*, the area they call *Sápmi* (the indigenous name for Lapland) extends from Norway through Sweden and Finland to the Russian Kola peninsula, an area where they've traditionally lived a semi-nomadic life, following their reindeer from fell top to valley bottom. Most foreigners have but a hazy idea of where Lapland is; for the sake of this book, we've assumed Swedish Lapland (the English spelling) to be located within the borders of the administrative province of Lappland.

Vilhelmina

Route 45 enters the province of Lappland just south of the tiny and insignificant town of **Dorotea**, before reaching the pretty little town of **VILHELMINA**, once an important forestry centre. Today the timber business has moved out of town and the main source of employment is a telephone booking centre for Swedish Railways and the package tour company, Fritidsresor. The town, a quiet little place with just one main street, is named after the wife of King Gustav IV Adolf, Fredrika Dorotea Vilhelmina (as is its southerly neighbour Dorotea). Its principal attraction is the **parish village**, nestling between Storgatan and Ljusminnesgatan, whose thirty-odd wooden cottages date back to 1792, when the first church was consecrated. It's since been restored, and the cottages can be rented out via the tourist office (from 150kr per night).

The **tourist office** is on the main Volgsjövägen (mid-June to mid-Aug Mon–Fri 8am–8pm, Sat & Sun noon–6pm; mid-Aug to mid-June Mon–Fri 8am–5pm; ☎0940/152 70, *www.vilhelmina.se*), a five-minute walk up Postgatan from the **train station**, which also serves as the **bus** arrival and departure point. The airport, with handy flights to and from Stockholm, is just 12km away, from where a taxi into Vilhelmina will cost around 130kr. There are two **hotels** in town; the posh and showy *Hotell Wilhelmina* at Volgsjövägen 16 (☎0940/554 20, fax 101 56; ④/②), and the simpler and friendly *Lilla Hotellet* at Granvägen 1 (☎0940/150 59; ②). The **campsite**, *Rasten Saiva Camping* (☎0940/107 60), has two- to six-berth cabins for rent (250–525kr depending on size) and a great sandy **beach**; to get there, walk down Volgsjövägen from the centre and take the first left after the youth hostel – allow about ten minutes. **Eating** and **drinking** doesn't exactly throw up a multitude of options: try the à la carte restaurant at *Hotell Wilhelmina* for traditional northern Swedish dishes, and *Dagens Rätt* for 60kr, or the plain *Pizzeria Quinto*, Volgsjövägen 27, for cheap pizzas. *Kyrkstadens Café & Data*, next to the parish village, serves coffee and sandwiches and has a reasonably priced lunch menu, as well as Internet access. In the evenings, locals gravitate towards *Krogen Besk*, in the main square, for a **drink** or two.

Storuman

In 1741, the first settler arrived in what was to become **STORUMAN**. His first neighbours didn't appear until forty years later and even by the time of World War I, Storuman, then called Luspen (the Swedish name for a river which emerges from a lake) numbered barely forty inhabitatants working just eight farms. Things changed, though, with the arrival of the railway in the 1920s; today Storuman is an important centre for the generation of hydroelectric power. That said, there's not much to the town: the centre consists of one tiny street that supports a couple of shops and banks. You can head off into the mountains west of here for some good **hiking** and **fishing** (ask at the tourist office for maps and information).

An hour by the Inlandsbanan from Vilhelmina, Storuman is a **transport hub** for this part of southern Lapland. From here, **buses** run northwest up to E12, skirting the Tärnafjällen mountains to Tärnaby and Hemavan, before wriggling through to Mo-i-Rana in Norway; in the opposite direction, the road leads down to Umeå via Lycksele, from where there are bus connections to Vindeln and Vännäs on the main coastal train line. A direct bus, **Lapplandspilen**, links Storuman with Stockholm. Skyways also operate twice-daily flights (Mon–Fri & Sun) to Stockholm and Arvidsjaur.

The **tourist office** is on Järnvägsgatan, 50m to the right of the **train station** (mid-June to mid-Aug 8am–8pm; mid-Aug to mid-June Mon–Fri 9am–5pm; ☎0951/333 70), and can supply a handy map of town and a few brochures; **buses** (3 daily from Vilhemina; 50min) stop outside the station. While you're here, check out the wonderful old **railway hotel**, across from the tourist office, which now houses the library; built in association with the Inlandsbanan, the wide-planked wooden exterior hides an ornate interior that's well worth a look.

The **youth hostel** is just 200m from the station (☎0951/777 00; 130kr; June to Aug), and is attached to the luxurious **hotel**, *Hotell Toppen* (☎0951/777 00, fax 121 57; ④/②), with pine and birchwood rooms; to get here, walk up the hill from the station to Blå Vägen 238. In the middle of the local **campsite** at Vallnäsvägen (☎0951/106 96) is a church built in the style of a *kåta*, a traditional *Sámi* hut. The **restaurant** at *Hotell Toppen* should be your first choice for **food**, with a 60kr lunch buffet; alternatively, the basic *Cleo Bar* in the main square serves cheap *Dagens Rätt* and pizzas. *Restaurang Storuman*, opposite the station, has Chinese food, pizzas and lunch for much the same prices. For good Greek food, it's a twenty-minute walk to *Grill 79*: take on the E12 road towards Tärnaby and head underneath the railway bridge.

Northwest from Storuman on the E12: Tärnaby and Hemavan

Buses (Mon–Fri 4 daily, Sat 3 daily, Sun 1 daily) make the two-hour drive northwest from Storuman to the tiny mountain village of **TÄRNABY**, the birthplace of Sweden's greatest skier, Ingemar Stenmark. (A double Olympic gold medallist, he occasionally spiced up his training with a spot of tightrope walking and monocycling.) It's a pretty place: yellow flower-decked meadows run to the edge of the mountain forests, the trees felled to leave great empty swathes that accommodate World Cup ski slopes. At the eastern edge of the village as you approach from Storuman, the **Samegården** (end June to mid-Aug daily 10am–4pm; 10kr) is a pleasant introduction to *Sámi* history, culture and customs. Among other things, the museum recalls a practice in older times when, after a kill in a bear hunt, the gall bladder was cut open and the fluid drunk by the hunters. A popular **walk** here leads across the nearby mountain, **Laxfjället**, with its fantastic views down over the village – it can be reached by chair lift from either of the two hotels listed below.

The **tourist office**, on the one main road (mid-June to mid-Aug daily 9am–8pm; mid-Aug to mid-June Mon–Fri 8.30am–5pm; ☎0954/104 50, *www.tarnaby.se*), can supply advice about local **fishing**, which is reputed to be excellent, and information on **hiking trails** in the surrounding mountains. When it's sunny, head for the beach at **Lake Laisan**, where the water is often warm enough to swim – to get there, take the footpath that branches off right from Sandviksvägen past the campsite (☎0954/100 09). There are several other inexpensive places to stay, including *Tärnaby Fjällhotell*, Östra Strandvägen 16 (☎0954/104 20, fax 106 27; ②/①), which also has four-bed apartments for 445kr per day; and *Fjällvindens Hus* (☎0954/104 25, fax 106 80; ②/①) on Skyttevägen, which rents out two- to six-berth cabins for 545kr per day.

Hemavan

Buses continue on to **HEMAVAN**, also reachable from Stockholm on direct Skyways flights (information on ☎0951/400 60, *www.hemavansflygplats.ans.se*; journey time 1hr 45min). The village marks the beginning and the end of the five-hundred-kilometre the Kungsleden trail (for more information on the trail and hiking in general, see "Hiking: some practical information", p.471). The main road from Tärnaby into the village, Blå Vägen, is where you'll find the **youth hostel**, *FBU-Gården* (☎0954/305 10; 115kr; mid-June to Sept); it's always busy with hikers, so its pays to book ahead. With your own transport, you may want to continue along the E12 for around fifteen minutes towards Norway, to reach the tiny village of Klippen and the gay-friendly *Hotell Sånninggården* (☎0954/330 00, fax 330 06; ①). Dramatically located next to a range of craggy mountains, the hotel is renowned for its excellent **food**, particularly game dishes; its restaurant has been voted one of the very best in Sweden. The hotel is the last stop for the Lapplandspilen bus to and from Stockholm.

North of Storuman: Sorsele

The next major stop on the Inlandsbanan north of Storuman (also served by three daily buses from Storuman; 1hr), **SORSELE** (pronounced "Sosh-ay-le") is a pint-sized, dreary town on the **Vindelälven** (Vindel river). The town became a *cause célèbre* among conservationists in Sweden when activists forced the government to abandon its plans to build a hydroelectric power station, which would have regulated the river's flow. Consequently, the river remains in its natural state today – seething with rapids – and is one of only four in the entire country that hasn't been tampered with in some way or other. During the last week in July, the river makes its presence felt with the **Vindelälvsloppet**, a long-distance race that sees hundreds of competitors cover, in stages, over 350km from nearby Ammarnäs (see p.453) down to Vännäsby near Umeå. It's quite a spectacle – needless to say accommodation at this time is booked up months in advance. The other big event here is the **Vindelälvsdraget**, a dog-sleigh race held over the same course in the third week of March.

Sorsele is an ideal base for **fly-fishing**: the Vindelälven and the other local river, Laisälven, are teeming with grayling and brown trout, and there are a number of local lakes stocked with char. Information on fishing can be obtained at the **tourist office** (end June to Aug Mon–Fri 9am–6pm, Sat & Sun 10am–6pm; end Aug to end June Mon–Fri 8.30am–11.30am; ☎0952/140 90) at the **train station** on Stationsgatan; **buses** stop outside. In the same building is a small **museum** (same opening times as the tourist office; 20kr) detailing the life and times of the Inlandsbanan; the labelling here is in Swedish only. For **accommodation**, there are **cabins** at the riverside **campsite** (☎0952/101 24; 285–550kr a day), as well as a small **youth hostel** at Torggatan 1–2 (☎0952/100 48; 110kr; 140kr in a cabin; mid-June to end-Aug), just 500m from the station. The only **hotel** in town is *Hotell Gästis*, a plain and rather drab affair at Hotellgatan 2 (☎0952/100 10; ②). **Eating** choices in Sorsele are scant, although what food's on offer is cheap, with few dishes costing more than 60kr. At lunchtime, head for the hotel, which has simple fare, or the drab pizzeria *La Spezia* on Vindelvägen. Other than these, you're left with *Grillhörnan*, near the station, with its burgers and pizzas; there's a bakery in the same building for fresh bread. As with many of the villages in this part of Sweden, there are no **bars** here, but expensive beer can be found at all the restaurants. The **Systembolaget** is over the river from the train station on the main shopping street.

Northwest from Sorsele: Ammarnäs

The tiny mountain village of **AMMARNÄS**, with a population of just two hundred and fifty, lies ninety minutes' bus ride northwest of Sorsele. Set in a wide river valley by the side of the **Gautsträsk lake** and at the foot of the towering **Ammarfjället mountains**, the village offers peace and tranquillity of the first order. This is **reindeer** country (one-third of the villagers here are reindeer herders), and for hundreds of years the local *Sámi* are known to have migrated with their animals from the coast to the surrounding fells for summer pasture.

HIKES AROUND AMMARNÄS

There's some excellent **hiking** to be had around Ammarnäs, not least along the Kungsleden (see p.454), which passes through the village. For the less adventurous, **Mount Kaissats** (984m) is ideal for a day spent in the mountains; to get there, take the road at the western end of the village that leads to the lake of **Stora Tjulträsk**, from where a marked trail for Kaissats (not particularly difficult) leads off to the right (2hr). Least strenuous is taking a **chair lift** from the village and up **Näsberget**, from where trails lead back down into Ammarnäs. Yet another hiking possibility is along the road up to the village of **Kraipe**; this small turning, to your left before you reach Ammarnäs on Route 363, is one of the steepest in Sweden. From Kraipe you can easily reach the surrounding summits, and if you take this route in September you may well encounter the marking and slaughtering of reindeer at Kraipe corrals. From any of these bare mountain tops, the spectacular views look out over some of the last remaining wilderness in Europe – mountains and dense forest as far as the eye can see.

The first settlement began here in 1821 when two *Sámi* brothers, Måns and Abraham Sjulsson, were granted permission to set up home at Övre Gautsträsk. When they failed to keep the terms of their agreement a new tenant, Nils Johansson, took over. He eked out an existence by cultivating the land and is responsible for *Potatisbacken* or Potato Hill, by the river at the eastern end of the village, where the northern Swedish potato (a sweet, yellow variety), is grown – unusual for a location so far north. With the founding of a postal station in 1895, the village changed its name from Gautsträsk (a *Sámi* word meaning "bowl" – an accurate description of its valley-bottom location) to Ammarnäs – the foreland between the Tjulån and Vindelälven rivers.

The **Sámi parish village**, near the hill on Nolsivägen, was built in 1850, moving to its present site in 1911. The dozen or so square wooden huts, which are perched on horizontal logs to help keep them dry, are still used today. Three times a year *Sami* families gather here, much as they did in days gone by, to celebrate important **festivals**: the *Sámi* festival (Sunday before midsummer), Vårböndagshelgen (spring intercession day, on the first Sunday in July) and Höstböndagshelgen (autumn intercession day, on September 30). The nearby **Samegården** on Strandvägen has a simple display of *Sámi* history and traditions (Mon–Thurs 9am–2pm). At **Vinkas Sameviste**, at the edge of town, you can obtain a much better insight into local culture; this is the place to come face to face with **reindeer**, try your hand at a spot of lassoing and learn about the traditional methods of building a wooden *kåta*.

Adjoining the tourist office on Tjulträskvägen is the **Naturum Vindelfjällen** (mid-June to mid-Aug Mon–Fri 9am–7pm, Sat & Sun 1–6pm), which has information about the local geology, flora and fauna, and an unflattering selection of stuffed animals, including a lynx. It also shows a 1940s film of bears in the woods along the Vindelälven – just ask them to put it on. Look out also for their model of the surrounding peaks, which will give you an idea of just how isolated Ammarnäs is, locked in on three sides by mountains.

Practicalities

Buses take an hour to reach here from Sorsele (Mon–Sat 2 daily), and will drop you along the main road, Tjulträskvägen, where you'll find the **tourist office** (mid-June to mid-Aug Mon-Fri 9am–7pm, Sat & Sun 1–6pm; ☎0952/600 00). They have plenty of maps and brochures on the surrounding countryside and useful information on hiking, and can also help with the renting of **Icelandic ponies**, **dog sledges** and **snow mobiles** in winter. To rent canoes, mountain bikes, fishing and camping equipment, head for the shop, Vägvisaren, on the hill beside the ICA supermarket.

Virtually opposite the tourist office is the **youth hostel** (☎0952/600 45; 140kr; advance booking required Sept–May); it's in an annex to *Jonsstugan*, a small and simple pension (☎0952/600 45, fax 602 51; 210kr per person). Another very cheap alternative is *Fridas Stugor*, also on the main street, with small wooden four-bed **cabins** (☎0952/600 36; 250kr per cabin). The only **hotel** is the busy and popular *Hotell Ammarnäsgården* (☎0952/600 03, fax 601 43; ①), on the main road, which has rather simple en-suite rooms aimed at hikers walking the Kungsleden; its fabulous sauna and pool complex in the basement makes up for the lack of creature comforts in the rooms. For **eating** and **drinking**, your only option is the hotel's bar and restaurant; it's much cheaper to bring some beer with you from the nearest Systembolaget, 90km away in Sorsele.

Travelling on from Ammarnäs is quite tricky – all connections are via Sorsele. The best way to reach Stockholm is to take a bus to Sorsele, change for a connection to Östersund and change again for the train to Stockholm. On Saturdays, there's a direct afternoon bus from Ammarnäs to Vännäs, which connects with the Stockholm night train (more information on ☎020/91 00 19 or at *www.lanstrafikeniac.se*). There's also a **seaplane** that heads elsewhere in the mountains (see p.460).

Arvidsjaur and around

An hour and a quarter north of Sorsele by Inlandsbanan, **ARVIDSJAUR** (pronounced "Ar-veeds-yowr") was for centuries where the region's **Sámi** gathered to trade and debate. Their presence was of interest to Protestant missionaries, who established the first church here in 1606. The success of this Swedish settlement was secured when silver was discovered in the nearby mountains, and the town flourished as a staging point and supply depot. While these developments unfolded, the *Sámi* continued to assemble on market days and during religious festivals. At the end of the eighteenth century, they built their own parish village of simple wooden huts, which you can visit. Today, out of a total population of five thousand, there are still twenty *Sámi* families in Arvisdjaur who make their living from reindeer husbandry, and the town is one of the best places in northern Sweden to get a real hands-on experience of *Sámi* life.

Arrival, information and accommodation

The **train station** is on Järnvägsgatan. Just off the main street, Storgatan, is the **tourist office** at Garvaregatan 4; it's five minutes' walk up Lundavägen from the train station (mid-June to mid-Aug daily 8.30am–6.30pm; mid-Aug to mid-June Mon–Fri 9am–5pm; ☎0960/175 00, *www.arvidsjaururturism.se*). The **bus station** is at Gökstigen, off Stationsgatan, from where you simply walk south down Stationsgatan, across Storgatan, and then take the first left into Garvaregatan to get to the tourist office. Flights from Storuman and Stockholm's Arlanda airport land at the modern **airport** terminal, 15km from town, which has been designed to resemble a *Sámi* wooden *kåta*; you can get from here to the centre by bus (25kr) or taxi (95kr).

The tourist office will fix you up with a **private room** for around 110kr, plus a booking fee of 25kr. By far the best place to **stay** in Arvidsjaur, though, is *Rallaren* (☎0960/216 02; 100kr; June–Aug), a wonderful old wooden house which ranks as one of the best deals in northern Sweden. With just eight beds and a kitchen, it's been tastefully restored by a local artist, and now boasts stripped floorboards, painted walls and dried flowers. There's also a cosy private **youth hostel**, *Lappugglans Turistviste*, conveniently situated at Västra Skolgatan 9 (☎0960/124 13; 100kr; April–Oct). The **campsite**, *Camp Gielas* (☎0960/556 00), has **cabins** for 520kr with TV, shower and running water (or 375kr for a cabin without running water). It sits beside one of the town's dozen or so lakes, Tvätttjärn, with its bathing beaches; there's a sports hall here, too, as well as a gym, sauna, tennis courts and mini-golf. The site is a ten-minute walk from the tourist office (head south down Lundavägen, left along Strandvägen and left again into Järnvägsgatan). There's just one **hotel** in town: *Laponia Hotel* at Storgatan 45 (☎0960/555 00; ④/③), with comfortable, modern en-suite rooms and a swimming pool. Between October and April much of the accommodation will be full of test

---

A BRIEF LOOK AT THE SÁMI

Among the oldest people in Europe, the **Sámi** – better known (erroneously) to many as "Lapps" – are probably descended from the original, prehistoric inhabitants of much of Scandinavia and northern Russia. Today, there are around 58,000 *Sámi*, stretched across the whole of the northernmost regions of Norway, Sweden, Finland and Russia; traces of their nomadic culture have even been discovered as far south as Poland. Rather than Lapland, the *Sámi* name for their lands is *Sápmi*. In Sweden itself, they number around 17,000 (the population is declining, however), their domain extending over half the country, stretching up from the northern parts of Dalarna.

The *Sámi* **language** is a rich one, strongly influenced by their harmonious natural existence. There are no words for certain alien concepts (like "war"), but there are ninety different terms to express variations in snow conditions. One of the Finno-Ugric group of languages, which also contains Finnish and Hungarian, the *Sámi* language is divided into three dialects: Southern (spoken in southern parts of the *Sámi* region), Central and Eastern (both spoken only in Russia). In Sweden you'll come across two words for *Sámi*: the politically correct *Sámi* (as used by the *Sámi* themselves), and, more commonly, the Swedish corruption *Same* (plural *Samer*). Opposite is a brief glossary of some of the *Sámi* words, many related to snow and reindeer, that you may come across while travelling in northern Sweden.

Reindeer, of which there are estimated to be 238,000 in Sweden, have been at the centre of *Sámi* life and culture for thousands of years, with generations of families following the seasonal movements of the animals. Accordingly, the *Sámi* year is divided into eight separate seasons, ranging from early spring, when they traditionally bring the reindeer cows up to the calving areas in the hills, through to winter, when they return to the forests and the pastures.

In the past, what characterized the *Sámi* perhaps more than anything was that they didn't want their way of life to be disturbed by outsiders. Yet for centuries, Scandinavian adventurers treated them dreadfully: as early as the ninth century, a Norse emissary, Othere, boasted to Alfred the Great of his success in imposing a fur, feather and hide tax on his *Sámi* neighbours. In more recent times the *Sámi* fell victim for a time to the fervent religious teachings of **Lars Levi Laestadius**, who offered them acceptance into Swedish society and salvation in return for their abandoning the bottle (see p.484).

---

drivers from Europe's leading car companies, who come to the area to experience driving on the frozen lakes – book well in advance to secure a room during this period, especially in March.

The Town

Arvidsjaur's drab housing estates spread out either side of the nondescript main street, Storgatan. The best way to get to grips with the *Sámi* culture (which manifests itself more and more as you travel north from here) it to visit the **Lappstaden** (free; daily tours in July at 6pm, 25kr), reached by walking west along Storgatan and turning right into Lappstadsgatan. Although you probably won't meet any *Sámi* here, you will at least be able to see how they used to live in traditional huts or *kåtor*. About eighty of these huts in the eighteenth-century

The *Sámi* were dealt a grievous blow by the **Chernobyl** nuclear disaster of 1986, which contaminated not only the lichen that their reindeer feed on in winter, but also the game, fish, berries and fungi that supplement their own diet. Contamination of reindeer meat meant the collapse of exports of the product to southern Scandinavia, Germany, America and the Far East; promises of government compensation came late in the day and failed to address the fact that this disaster wasn't just on an economic level for the *Sámi*, their traditional culture being inseparably tied to reindeer herding. However, perhaps as a consequence of Chernobyl, there has been an expansion in other areas of *Sámi* culture. Traditional **arts and crafts** have become popular and are widely available in craft shops, and *Sámi* **music** (characterized by the rhythmic sounds of joik, a form of throat singing) is being given a hearing by fans of world music. On balance, it would appear that the *Sámi* are largely managing to retain their own culture and identity in modern Sweden.

A glossary of Sámi words

aahka	grandmother, old woman	*lopme*	storm
aajja	grandfather, old man	*lopme-aajma*	snow storm
aaltoe	reindeer cow	*lopmedahke*	surface of the snow in autumn
aehhtjie	father	*lopme-moekie*	snow shower
båtsuoj	reindeer	*miesie*	reindeer calf
daelvie	winter	*nejpie*	knife
geejmas	black reindeer	*ruvveske*	water on the surface of the ice in spring
giedtie	reindeer pasture		
gierehtse	sledge drawn by reindeer	*sarva*	reindeer bull
		saevrie	loose, heavy snow that you can't walk on
giesie	summer		
gijre	spring	*sahpah*	powdery wet snow that doesn't stick
gåetie	house, hut, tent		
jiengedahke	autumn frost	*sieble*	slush
klomhpedahke	sticky snow surface	*soehpenje*	lasso
klöösehke	grey and white reindeer	*tjakje*	autumn
kåta	tent	*tjidtjie*	mother
lijjesjidh	to snow lightly on bare (snowless) ground	*vielle*	brother
		åabpa	sister

Sámi **parish village** have survived, and are clumped unceremoniously next to a yellow, modern apartment building. The huts are still used today during the last weekend in August as a venue for a special **festival**, Storstämningshelgen.

The town's **reindeer enclosure**, off Järnvägsgatan, is an easy way of seeing these creatures close-up (late June to mid-Aug 5–7pm; 60kr). There are generally ten to forty animals in the enclosure, although numbers sometimes increase when hungry reindeer out in the forest drop in on an unexpected visit (for the free and easy food here). Smoked reindeer meat is also available for the tasting, along with some delicious locally caught and smoked fish. The enclosure is a twenty-minute walk from the centre; head along Järnvägsgatan towards the campsite, cross the railway lines opposite Sandbackaskolan and take the footpath through the trees towards Lillberget.

Eating and drinking

For snacks, coffee, fresh pastries and bread, try *Kaffestugan* at Storgatan 21, which also has cheap lunches, sandwiches (often filled with reindeer meat) and salads; there's outdoor seating here in summer. Arvidsjaur has a small selection of **restaurants**. You can sit down to Italian food at *Athena*, Storgatan 10, with averagely priced lunches, pizzas, meat and fish dishes; next door at Storgatan 8, *Cazba* serves up pizzas for the same price but has less atmosphere. For finer food and higher prices, head for the restaurant at the *Laponia Hotel*, where the delicious à la carte meals include local reindeer and other Lapland delicacies. The bar here is the place to be seen of an evening; be prepared to shell out at least 49kr for a beer. Another popular spot, particularly in winter when the car crews are in town, is *Stockis Pub* at Camp Gielas, Järnvägsgatan 111, where prices are much the same.

Around Arvidsjaur

To the west of Arvidsjaur, in the village of **GASA**, the **Båtsuoj Forest Sámi Center** (June–Aug daily noon–9pm; at other times book by calling ☎0960/610 26 or emailing *same-id@algonet.se*) is a good place to get to grips with the everyday life of the *Sámi*. Here, you'll not only come face to face with **reindeer** (*båtsuoj* in *Sámi*) but also meet real reindeer herders, who'll teach you about their religion and way of life, including the way to milk a reindeer and the tricks of baking their traditional bread; frozen reindeer meat is also available for purchase.

A half-day visit to Båtsuoj costs 390kr and includes dinner (of reindeer cooked over an open fire); a full day costs 590kr and adds an overnight stay in a *kåta* (tent); for children under twelve both trips are half price. From late June to early July you can go on **branding** trips here, which generally take place in the evenings (375kr). The centre also arranges **cloudberry-picking** expeditions with pack-bearing reindeer (Aug to mid-Sept; 600kr); these rare berries grow in the most inaccessible of northern Sweden's marshlands – hence the hefty price. To get here from Arvidsjaur, head west on Route 45 until the village of Slagnäs, from where you take the unnumbered minor road 19km north towards Arjeplog. Although you can reach Slagnäs by the Inlandsbanan, there's no public transport on to Gasa from there.

RIVER RAFTING

One of the other main attractions around Arvidsjaur is two-hour **rafting** trips on the Piteälven river, traversing some of the region's most exciting rapids – watch the video at the tourist office for an idea of how wet you can get on one of these jaunts. The trips, each requires a minimum of ten people, leave at 10am, 1pm and 3.30pm; the price includes rental of rain clothes, helmets, boots and life jackets as well as return transport from Arvidsjaur (July 260kr; all other times 350kr each; 10- to 15-year-olds 120kr; minimum age 10). Certificates are given to all those who complete the trips, **bookings** for which can be made at the Arvidsjaur tourist office; at the rafting centre, Forsfärd på Piteälven (☎0960/800 20 or ☎070/316 8299); or at the Jokkmokk tourist office (see p.462). After the trip, it's possible to continue north on the Inlandsbanan from nearby **Moskosel**, 54km north of Arvidsjaur.

STEAM TRAINS AND RAIL INSPECTION TROLLEYS

In July and early August, an incredibly popular **steam train**, pulling vintage coaches from the 1930s, runs from Arvidsjaur along sections of the Inlandsbanan.

The trips head west to **Slagnäs** on Fridays and north to **Moskosel** on Saturdays (130kr for either trip, under-16s free); en route to Slagnäs the train stops at Storavan beach for swimming and a sausage barbecue. Alternatively, you can strike out through the surrounding countryside under your own steam on a **rail inspection trolley** (a bike with train wheels), which can be booked through the tourist office (90kr for up to 5hr, 160kr for 24hr). Each trolley can carry two people, with camping gear provided. Thus equipped, you can cycle along the disused rail line from Arvidsjaur 75km southeast to **Jörn** – a stopping-off point for trains on the main coastal route.

Northwest from Arvidsjaur: Arjeplog and Route 95

The municipality of **ARJEPLOG**, roughly the size of Belgium, supports a population of just three and a half thousand – half of whom live in the eponymous lakeside town. It's one of the most beautiful parts of Sweden, with nearly nine thousand lakes and vast expanses of mountains and virgin forests. Here the air is clear and crisp, the rivers clean and deep and the winters mighty cold – in 1989 a temperature of -52°C was recorded; January and February, in particular, are bitter, dark and silent months. However, it's during winter that Arjeplog is at its busiest: hundreds of test drivers from Korea, Australia, Germany, Britain, Italy, America and France descend on the town to put cars through their paces in the freezing conditions, with brakes and road-holding being given a thorough examination on the frozen lakes. In summer, Arjeplog is a likeable little place away from the main inland road and rail routes, where **hiking**, **canoeing** and **fishing** are all popular activities, each offering the chance of blissful isolation, be it by the side of a secluded mountain tarn or in a clearing deep in the pine forest. In late July you can go **cloudberry picking** in the surrounding marshland, and in the autumn, you can hunt for lingonberries, blueberries and wild mushrooms.

In **Arjeplog town** itself, it's worth checking out the **Silvermuséet** (mid-June to mid-Aug daily 9am–6pm; mid-Aug to mid-June Mon–Fri 10am–4pm, Sat 10am–2pm; 40kr), in a yellow wooden building opposite the tourist office in the square. Founded by the Lapland doctor Einar Wallquist, it's home to fascinating collections of *Sámi* silver, including an ornate silver collar that was handed down from mother to daughter. If you're around in the first week of July, make sure you see the **Lapplands festspel** – an orgy of chamber music, folk and fiddle music and dancing.

Practicalities

There are daily buses here from Arvidsjaur (Mon–Fri 4 daily, Sat & Sun 2 daily; 1hr 10min). The **tourist office** is in the main square (mid-June to mid-Aug Mon–Fri 9am–7pm, Sat 10am–5pm, Sun noon–5pm; mid-Aug to mid-June Mon–Fri 9am–4pm; ☎0961/142 70, *www.turist.arjeplog.se*); they can help with local hiking trails, fishing (70kr will rent equipment for a day) and **bike rental** (50kr a day). The best-value **accommodation** is the central and palatial **youth hostel** on Silvervägen (☎0961/612 10; 130kr; May to late Nov), where every room sleeps a maximum of four and has en-suite facilities. The hostel is part of *Hotell Lyktan* (☎0961/612 10, fax 101 50; ③/②), which offers comfortable modern rooms of the highest standard. At *Arjeplog Hotel* (☎0961/107 70, fax 614 26; ④/③), 1500m up Öberget from the centre (a 30min walk), the accommodation is dowdy but perfectly okay, with fantastic views over the village and surrounding lake. Ten minutes' walk along Silvervägen, the lakeside **campsite** *Kraja* (☎0961/315 00, fax 315 99) has simple **cabins** for 220–775kr a day, the price depending on the size and the facilities included; there's also a swimming pool here which is open to non-residents (free). To get away from it all in your own private **cabin in the wilds**, speak to the tourist office: it has dozens for rent in **Jäkkvik** or **Adolfström** (both on the Kungsleden); for complete isolation at stunning **Vuoggatjålme**, tucked right up in the mountains close to the Norwegian border, see p.461. Bear in mind that in winter, accommodation hereabouts is often booked months in advance by major car manufacturers.

Eating and **drinking** in Arjeplog isn't a joy. There are two cut-price options: the basic *Mathörnan* on Drottninggatan, which serves up moderately priced reindeer, Arctic char and traditional Swedish home cooking amid hideously tacky decor; the other is *Pizzeria Verona* opposite, with an equally dingy 1970s interior, offering salads and pizzas at similar prices. The *Mathörnan's* downstair **bar**, *Källarn*, attracts the town's hardened drinkers who seem prepared to pay 45kr for a beer. For gourmet food head for *Kraja Wärdshus* at the campsite (summer lunch and dinner, winter dinner only), where you can tuck into fillet of elk or saddle of reindeer; there's also a pub and disco here on Fridays. Fine food, including Arctic char and salmon, is also served in the light and airy restaurant at the *Arjeplog Hotel*, complete with open fire. For a coffee in summer try the kiosk next to the tourist office, which has outdoor seating; or better the *Silverkoppen* on Storgatan, which serves up salads, soups, sandwiches – and cakes.

Beyond Arjeplog on Route 95

From Arjeplog, the **Silver Road** (Route 95) – so called because it cuts through the omnipresent birch forest – strikes out for the craggy chain of mountains which marks the border with Norway. The **views** on this stretch of the road are stunning – unlike in so many other parts of Lapland, the forest here is set back

---

THE KUNGSLEDEN IN ONE DAY: JÄKKVIK–ADOLFSTRÖM

From the shop in **Jäkkvik**, walk back along the main road to the sign for Kungsleden car parking. The trail begins at the car park, climbing first through mountain birch forest, before emerging on bare upland terrain dominated by **Mount Pieljekaise** (1138m), which is said to look like a large ear (hence its name, which means just that in *Sámi*). From here, the views over the surrounding mountains are truly spectacular. The trail winds round the mountain and descends below the tree line into virgin birch woodland, carpeted with stately flowers like the northern wolfsbane, alpine sow-thistle and angelica. Pieljekaise National Park is also home to elk, bear, arctic fox, wolverine, golden eagle and the gyrfalcon. It's a moderate 27km hike from Jäkkvik to Adolfström (all downhill after climbing out of Jäkkvik; allow 6–7 hours). Cabin **accommodation** can be rented in Adolfström at *Adolfströms Stugby* (☎0961/230 41, fax 230 44; from 350kr) and *Johanssons Fjällstugor* (☎0961/230 40, fax 230 23; from 230kr); there's an old-world village shop at the former. Buses (information on ☎020/47 00 47) only leave once daily at 10.20am from the post box on Mon, Wed & Fri for **Laisvall** (change here for Arjeplog), so time your hike carefully. Alternatively, a **seaplane** (Mon & Thurs at 12.30pm; ☎0940/310 80, *www.slit.net/flygtjanst*) heads to Jäkkvik to connect with the bus south to Skellefteå or north to Vuoggatjålme; at 2.30pm the plane leaves for Ammarnäs, Tärnaby and Saxnäs.

from the road, rising and falling over the surrounding hills, giving an awe-inspiring sense of the scale of the uninhabited territory you're passing through. The **Silverexpressen** bus #200, running between Skellefteå and Bodø in Norway, via Arvidsjaur and Arjeplog, is the only public transport on this section of the road (daily except Sat). Thirty minutes northwest of Arjeplog, the bus reaches the minuscule settlement of **JÄKKVIK**, little more than a cluster of houses dependent on the tiny shop and petrol station which doubles as the bus station. From here, one of the least walked sections of the Kungsleden trail (see box, p.460) heads across to **ADOLFSTRÖM**, a tiny village on Lake Gautosjön, where the summer air is sweet with the smell of freshly scythed hay. The route makes an ideal day's hike through the beauty of the **Pieljekaise national park**, containing the least disturbed flora and fauna in the entire Swedish mountains, just south of the Arctic Circle. There are **cabins** in Adolfström at the *Stugby* (☎0961/211 20, fax 210 62; from 350kr) or simple hostel rooms and a **campsite** at *Kyrkans Fjällgård* (☎0961/210 39).

To get away from it all, **VUOGGATJÅLME** (*Sámi* for "fish hook channel", pronounced "vwogg-a-chol-mi"), 45km from Jäkkvik, is the place to come. The Silverexpressen **bus** stops here on its way between Norway and Skellefteå; jump off at the petrol station, and walk around 2km following the sign for the village. Only two families live here, one of which comprises Björn and Monica Helamb who manage the **cabin accommodation** (☎0961/107 15, fax 613 57), while the other, Björn's relatives, run the petrol station and small food store across the main road. The cabins couldn't be better situated, with a view of Lake Vuoggatjålmejaure from one window, the majestic snowcapped Tjidtjak mountain from the other. From mid-June to end-Aug they cost 550kr or 635kr per night depending on size (the ones on the lakeshore have open fireplaces); in winter both types of cottage go for around 300kr per night. Bear in mind, though, if you're here out of season, that Vuoggatjålme proudly boasts one of the coldest temperatures ever recorded in Sweden (-53°C, in 1966), although the minimum here is generally -40°C.

The surrounding area offers superb **hiking** and a chance to commune with nature. Björn operates a **helicopter service** (1600kr per person) which can take you right up into the mountains, allowing you to establish a base from which to strike out, thus avoiding the hassle of getting up there with heavy packs. An excellent trip takes you by helicopter up to the **Pieskehaure cabins**, stunningly located in the Arjeplogsfjällen mountains, from where you can hike across to Kvikkjokk (64km, see p.481) and the Kungsleden in around three days. There's also good hiking closer to the cottages; ask Björn for advice. Before you leave, look carefully at the forest beside the main house – the eyes you might be lucky enough to see are likely to be those of elk, as there are dozens of them around the cottages.

Into the Arctic Circle: Jokkmokk and around

During his journey in Lapland, the botanist Carl von Linné said, "If not for the mosquitoes, this would be earth's paradise". His comments were made after journeying along the river valley of the Lilla Luleälven during the short summer weeks, when the mosquitoes are at their most active. Along this valley is the town of **JOKKMOKK**, its name deriving from one particular bend (*mokk* in *Sámi*) in the river (*jokk*); see the box on p.456 for more on *Sámi*. The densely forested

municipality through which the river runs is the size of Wales and has a minuscule population of 6500.

The town is a welcome oasis, although not an immediately appealing one. At one time winter quarters for the *Sámi*, by the beginning of the seventeenth century the site had a market (see p.464) and church, which heralded the start of a permanent settlement. Today, as well as being a well-known handicraft centre, the town functions as the capital of the *Sámi* and is home to Samernas Folkhögskola, the only further education college in Sweden using the *Sámi* language, teaching handicraft making, reindeer husbandry and ecology.

Arrival, information and accommodation

Coming up by train from Stockholm, get off at **Murjek**, from where bus #94 runs west to Jokkmokk (2 daily). It's a four-hour journey here on the Inlandsbanan from Arvidsjaur, or just over two hours on the Inlandsexpressen bus. Jokkmokk's **tourist office** is at Stortorget 4 (mid-June to mid-Aug daily 9am–7pm; mid-Aug to mid-June Thurs–Sat 8.30am–4pm; during the winter market 8am–6pm; ☎0971/121 40, *www.jokkmokk.se/turism*), five minutes' stroll from the train station along Stationsgatan; the walk takes you past some of the prettiest houses and shops in Jokkmokk, oddly reminiscent of small-town America. The tourist office has all sorts of literature, useful for planning a hike in the region.

Accommodation in town is plentiful enough, but staying here during the winter market will require booking a good year in advance. That said, in the autumn the tourist offices puts together a list of **private rooms** available for the forthcoming market; these should be booked directly, not through the tourist office (150kr). In a wonderful old house, the **youth hostel** at Åsgatan 20 (☎0971/559 77; 100kr) is especially delightful in winter, when the garden is deep with snow and the trees outside the windows are laden with ice. For a **hotel**, there's *Hotell Jokkmokk*, in an attractive and convenient lakeside setting at Solgatan 45 (☎0971/553 20, fax 556 25; ⑥/③); however its en-suite rooms are dull and the restaurant decor a 1970s nightmare. A much better choice is *Hotell Gästis*, at Herrevägen 1 (☎0971/100 12; ③/②), though its simple en-suite rooms with modern decor are nothing to write home about. By the Lule river, the **campsite**, *Jokkmokks Turistcenter* (☎0971/123 70), has **cabins** from 475kr; it's 3km southeast of town off Route 97. The best way to get here is to **rent a bike** from the tourist office for 50kr per day.

THE ARCTIC CIRCLE AND THE MIDNIGHT SUN

Just 7km south of Jokkmokk, the Inlandsbanan finally crosses the **Arctic Circle**, the imaginary line drawn around the earth at roughly 66°N, which links the northernmost points along which the sun can be seen on the shortest day of the year. Crossing into the Arctic is occasion enough for a bout of whistle-blowing by the train, as it pulls up to allow everyone to take photos. However, the painted white rocks that curve away over the hilly ground here, a crude delineation of the Circle, are completely inaccurate. Due to the earth's uneven orbit, the line is creeping northwards at a rate of about 14–15m every year; the real Arctic Circle is now around a kilometre further north than this line. It won't be for another ten- to twenty-thousand years that the northward movement will stop – by which time the Circle will have reached 68°N – and then start moving slowly south again.

Thanks to the refraction of sunlight in the atmosphere, the **midnight sun** can also be seen south of the Arctic Circle – Arvidsjaur marks the southernmost point in Sweden where this happens – for a few days each year. The further north you travel, the longer the period when the phenomenon is visible, and conversely the longer the polar winter. True midnight sun occurs when the entire sun is above the horizon at midnight. The following is a list of the main towns here and the dates when the midnight sun can be seen; remember, though, that even outside these periods, there is still 24-hour daylight in the north of Sweden in summer, since only part of the sun ever dips below the horizon.

Arvidsjaur and Haparanda	June 20 /21
Arjeplog	June 12 /13 to July 28 /29
Jokkmokk and Övertorneå	June 8 /9 to July 2 /3
Gällivare	June 4 /5 to July 6 /7
Kiruna	May 28 /29 to July 11 /12
Karesuando	May 26 /27 to July 15 /16
Treriksröset	May 22 /23 to July 17 /18

The Town

Jokkmokk's fascinating **Ájtte museum** (*ájtte* means storage hut) is the place to really mug up on the *Sámi* (mid-June to late Aug Mon–Fri 9am–7pm, Sat & Sun 11am–6pm; late Aug to mid-June Mon–Fri 9am–4pm, Sat & Sun noon–4pm; 40kr); it's a brief walk east of the centre on Kyrkogatan, which is off the main street, Storgatan. Its displays and exhibitions recount the tough existence of the original settlers of northern Scandinavia, and show how things have slowly improved over time – today the modern *Sámi* are more dependent on snow scooters and helicopters to herd their reindeer than on the age-old methods employed by their ancestors. The museum also has imaginative temporary exhibitions on *Sámi* culture and local flora and fauna; its staff can arrange day-trips into the surrounding marshes for a spot of mushroom picking.

Close to the museum on Lappstavägen, the **Alpine Garden** (late June to mid-Aug Mon–Fri 10am–7pm, Sat & Sun 10am–3pm; other times by arrangement on ☎0971/101 00; 25kr) is home to moor-king, mountain avens, glacier crowfoot and other vegetation that's found on the fells around Jokkmokk. Also worth a quick look is **Naturfoto**, at the main Klockartorget junction; it's an exhibition of work by the local wilderness photographer, Edvin Nilsson – a good place to pick up a few postcards or posters.

Have a look, too, at the **Lapp kyrka** (daily 8am–4pm), off Stortorget, a recent copy of the 1753 church on the site (the original burnt down in 1972). The octagonal design, curiously shaped tower and colours inside the church represent *Sámi* styles, but the surrounding graveyard wall is all improvisation: the space in between the coarsely hewn timbers was used to store coffins during winter, waiting for the thaw in May when the *Sámi* could go out and dig graves again (temperatures in this part of Sweden regularly plunge to -30°C and below).

During the summer, Talvatissjön, the lake behind *Hotel Jokkmokk*, is the preferred spot for catching Arctic char and rainbow trout. To **fish** here you'll need a **permit** (*fiskekort*), available from the tourist office. There's a barbecue on the lakeside behind the hotel, should you catch anything. It's also possible to go **white-water rafting** on the Pärlälven river just to the west of town. You can choose from two different routes, one for beginners and a more turbulent stretch of water for those who live life in the fast lane – safety equipment is included in the price; for more information and bookings, contact Vildmarkstjänst (☎0971/126 96; from 600kr).

THE WINTER MARKET

Known simply in Swedish as Jokkmokk's **marknad**, the town's 400-year-old **great winter market** traces its origins back to 1602, when King Karl IX decreed that a series of market sites should be set up in the north to help extend Swedish territory and increase taxes to fund his many wars. A chapel, a parsonage and a row of market sheds were built here, and the rest is history. Today the market is held on the first Thursday to Sunday of each February, when thirty thousand people force their way into town – ten times the normal population. It's the best (and coldest) time of year to be here; with lots of drunken stallholders trying to flog reindeer hides and other unwanted knick-knacks to even more drunken passers-by, there's a Wild West feeling in the air at this time. Held on the frozen Talvatissjön lake behind *Hotell Jokkmokk* (see below), the **reindeer races** run during the market can be a real spectacle, as man and beast battle it out on a specially marked-out ice track. The reindeer, however, often have other ideas and every now and then veer off with great alacrity into the crowd, sending spectators fleeing for cover. A smaller and less traditional autumn fair around August 25 is an easier, but poorer, option.

Eating and drinking

Jokkmokk has a limited number of **eating** and **drinking** possibilities. At the cheap and cheerful *Restaurang Milano*, on Berggatan, lunch is 50kr (pizzas cost 60kr at other times). The rather nicer *Restaurang Opera*, Storgatan 36, offers lunch and pizzas for the same prices; it also has the usual range of meat and fish à la carte dishes. For Swedish home cooking or burgers, head for *Smedjan* on Föreningsgatan, where lunch deals go for 60kr; avoid the overpriced restaurant at *Hotell Jokkmokk*. Traditional *Sámi* dishes can be savoured at the Ájtte museum's restaurant – the cloudberry and ice cream is simply divine. Perfectly decent meals, including pizza and pasta, are also served up at the restaurant out at the campsite. For pastries and a cup of coffee, try *City Konditoriet* at Storgatan 28, which also serves up good sandwiches. Your first choice for drinking should be *Restaurang Opera* (beer can cost just 35kr); failing that try *Restaurang Milano*, and of an evening the bar inside *Hotell Jokkmokk* – if you've drunk your way round Jokkmokk this far you won't mind the late-night drunken company here (but mind the prices, such as a totally outrageous 55kr for a *storstark*).

Around Jokkmokk: Vuollerim

Forty-five kilometres southeast of Jokkmokk on Route 97 to Boden and Luleå lies the tiny village of **VUOLLERIM**, site of a 6000-year-old **Stone Age winter settlement**. Archeological digs here have uncovered well-preserved remains of houses, storage pits, tool and weapon shards, rubbish dumps and drainage works. A small and excellent **museum** on the edge of the village (mid-June to mid-Aug Mon–Fri 9am–6pm; mid-Aug to mid-June Mon–Fri 9am–4pm; 50kr) covers the development of the various sites and finds, with a slide show that takes you on a journey through time, depicting how the inhabitants probably lived. The whole thing really comes alive when a minibus carts you off to the digs themselves, with archeologists providing a guided tour in English (without it, the whole thing would be nothing more than a mudbath to the untrained eye). To **get here** from Jokkmokk, you can take the #44 Boden–Luleå bus, and get off at the Statoil filling station, from where it's a one-kilometre walk up the road towards the village; or better, the #94 to Murjek, which goes via Vuollerim and right to the museum. The site is on a narrow, wooded promontory that juts out into the lake – a great place for a picnic.

North of Jokkmokk: to Gällivare

North of Jokkmokk, Route 45 and the Inlandsbanan pass through pretty **POR-JUS**, blighted only by the ugly hydroelectric power station constructed in the 1910s. Being sited on the fast-flowing Stora Luleälven river, the town was an obvious choice at which to site the power plant – usefully for Swedish State Railways, who required power for the electrification of the new line between Luleå and the Norwegian border. But the spot proved to be a disaster logistically: the nearest train station was then 50km away at Gällivare, and there was no road to Porjus.

For the first year until the inland rail stretch was complete, men carried loads of up to seventy kilos on their backs along planked paths all the way from Gällivare here. The **heritage park** at **Porjus Kraftbyggarland** (mid-June to mid-Aug Mon–Fri 10am–6pm, Sat & Sun noon–6pm; free), by the station, documents the power plant's history; another part of the park, **Porjus EXPO**, tells of the men who made the power plant a reality.

Following a brief halt at the Mosquito Museum in Avvakajjo (see p.468), the Inlandsbanan reaches its last stop, **GÄLLIVARE** (pronounced "Yelli-vaa-re"). The town is one of the most important areas for iron ore in Europe – if you have any interest in seeing a working mine, don't wait until Kiruna's tame "tourist tour" (see p.475); instead take a trip down the more evocative mines here. Gällivare is also a good starting point for walking in the national parks, which fill most of the northwestern corner of the country (see pp.471-473).

Arrival and information

The **train station** is on Lasarettsgatan, about five minutes' walk from the tourist office. Gällivare's **airport**, 10km from the town, is served by flights from Stockholm, Kiruna, Luleå and Umeå (the journey here from Stockholm takes 2hr by air, compared to 20hr by train); you can get into town from here by taxi (150kr). The very accommodating **tourist office**, at Storgatan 16 (June to mid-Aug Mon–Fri 9am–8pm, Sat & Sun 10am–6pm; mid-Aug to May Mon–Fri 9am–4pm; ☎0970/166 60, *www.gellivare.se*), has good free maps and hiking information; downstairs in the same building there's a café, and upstairs a simple museum dealing with *Sámi* history and forestry. Gällivare is an easy place to walk around, with nearly everything you could want located east of the train line, except the youth hostel, which is west of the tracks, and the one main sight, the mines (just outside town in Malmberget), to which you're ferried on a tourist office bus. **Bike rental** is available through the tourist office or the train station for 50kr a day (plus a 50kr deposit).

Accommodation

Advance bookings for places to **stay** in Gällivare are a good idea from mid-June to mid-August, when the town receives trainloads of backpackers – thanks to its strategic location at the junction to two major rail routes. The tourist office can fix you up with a **private room** for around 130kr per person, plus a booking fee of 10kr. The **youth hostel** (☎0970/143 80; June–Aug 75kr; Sept–May 120kr with bookings required at this time), behind the train station (cross the tracks by the metal bridge), offers a good sauna and accommodation in small cabins. It's a wonderful place to stay in winter when the Vassara träsk lake is frozen and snow scooters whizz up and down its length under the eerie northern lights, which are clearly visible in Gällivare. There's also a twenty-bed **private hostel**, Lapphärberget, (☎0970/125 34; 100kr) near the Lappkyrkan (see opposite), although be prepared for a less than warm welcome by the manager. The premier place to stay, however, is in the reconstructed shantytown up at Malmberget, **Kåkstan** (reached by bus #1; ☎0970/183 96 or book through the tourist office; 90kr; four-bed hut 360kr), where the iron miners once lived. You can rent one of the simple four-berth wooden huts here (toilets and showers are located across the unpaved road) and pretend you're back in 1888, when iron ore was first loaded onto trains at the beginning of the great iron-ore boom. The town's **campsite** is close to the centre, at Malmbergsvägen 2 (mid-May to mid-Sept; ☎0970/165 45), by the river and off Porjusvägen (Route 45 to Jokkmokk). Gällivare is one of the few places in northern Lapland to offer a good range of affordable **hotel** accommodation, a selection of which appears below.

Dundret, at the top of the Dundret mountain (☎0970/145 60, fax 148 27). Not to be confused with *Hotell Dundret* in the centre. You'll need your own transport to get to this, the best hotel hereabouts, with fantastic views over town. Take Route 45 south out of town and take the signed turning left up to Dundret; the hotel is just 1km from the main road. ⑤/③.

Hotell Dundret, Per Högströmsgatan 1 (☎0970/550 40). Actually a small pension, with just seven rooms (not en suite). ②/①.

Grand, Per Högströmsgatan 9 (☎0970/164 20, fax 164 25). The second best hotel in town, with decent rooms; it's handily situated for the *Kilkenny Inn*, which shares the same building. ③/②.

Gällivare Värdshus, Klockljungsvägen 2 (☎0970/162 00, fax 155 45). A cheap, central German-run place with small hostel-style rooms;, it looks dreadfully run-down on the outside but is perfectly OK inside. ②/①.

Malm, Torget 18, in Malmberget (☎0970/244 50). The rooms here are basic and not en suite, but reasonable enough. ①.

Nex, Lasarettsgatan 1 (☎0970/550 20, fax 154 75). The best of the bunch in the town centre, with smart, tastefully decorated rooms and good restaurant (see p.470); it's also handy for the station. ④/③.

The town and around

Though an industrial town, Gällivare is quite a pleasant place to fetch up after so long on the road; it's certainly a far cry from the small inland villages that predominate along the Inlandsbanan. If you've come here from the Bothnian Coast, the town's steely grey mesh of modern streets will, on the surface at least, appear familiar. Located just north of the 67th parallel, Gällivare has a pretty severe climate: as you stroll around the open centre of town, have a look at the double windows here, all heavily glazed and insulated to protect against the biting Arctic cold.

What makes Gällivare immediately different from other towns is its large *Sámi* population – this is, after all, the heart of Lapland. The site the town occupies was once that of a *Sámi* village, and one theory has it that the name Gällivare comes from the *Sámi* for "a crack or gorge *(djelli)* in the mountain *(vare)*". The *Sámi* church, **Lappkyrkan** (mid-June to late Aug 10am–3pm), down by the river near the train station, is a mid-eighteenth-century construction; it's known as the *Ettöreskyrkan* ("1 öre" church) after the sum Swedes were asked to contribute to the subscription drive that paid for its construction. To dip into *Sámi* culture – meet (and taste) reindeer, and see how the *Sámi* make their handicrafts and throw lassoes – you can visit a **Sámi camp** at **Repisvare**, 2.5km from the town centre (book through Vägvisaren-Samiska Upplevelser on ☎0970/555 60). A ninety-minute visit there costs 275kr excluding transport (you can pay a little extra to be driven there and back). You'll return smelling of wood smoke after sitting around an open fire inside a traditional *kåta*, so it may be wise not to wear your best gear on the trip.

THE TOWN'S MINES

Tucked away at **Malmberget**, one of the two hills that overlook the town, the modern mines and works are distant, dark blots down which the tourist office ferries relays of tourists in summer. There are two separate tours, both running from June to August: one of the underground **iron-ore mine** (Mon–Fri 9.30am & 1.30pm; 160kr), the other to the open-cast **copper mine** known as Aitik (Mon–Fri

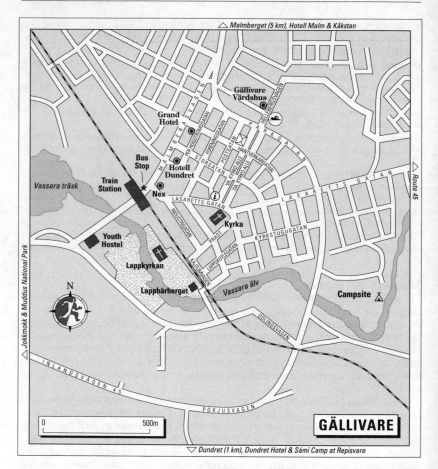

△ Malmberget (5 km), Hotell Malm & Kåkstan

Gällivare Värdshus

Grand Hotel

Bus Stop

Hotell Dundret

Train Station

Nex

Vassara träsk

Jokkmokk & Muddus National Park

△ Route 45

LASARETTS GATAN

i

Kyrka

KYRKSTUGUGATAN

Youth Hostel

Lappkyrkan

Lapphärberget

Vassara älv

Campsite △

N

ODLINGSVAGEN

INLANDSVAGEN 45

PORJUSVAGEN

0   500m

GÄLLIVARE

▽ Dundret (1 km), Dundret Hotel & Sámi Camp at Repisvare

2pm; 160kr), the largest of its kind in Europe (and also Sweden's biggest gold mine – the metal is recovered from the slag produced during the extraction of the copper). The ear-splitting noise produced from the mammoth-sized trucks (they're five times the height of a human being) in the iron-ore mine can be quite disconcerting in the confined darkness. On the copper-mine tour you'll visit **Kåkstan** on the way, the shantytown where the miners lived over a hundred years ago – today, you'll see rows of reconstructed wooden huts either side of an unpaved street (it's possible to stay here, see p.466).

THE MOSQUITO MUSEUM

The **Sjaunja Myggmuseum** (Mosquito Museum; free), the only one of its kind in the world, is within easy swatting distance of Gällivare at nearby Avvakajjo – a wayside halt on the Inlandsbanan. If you haven't been bitten yet by a **mosquito** (unlikely), the chances are you will be here; the museum is full of live specimens buzzing around at leisure waiting for their next free lunch. Just how important the

MUDDUS NATIONAL PARK

Recommended for novice hikers, **Muddus National Park** is a pine-forested and marshland park between Jokkmokk and Gällivare, hemmed in by the Inlandsbanan on one side and the train line from Boden to Gällivare on the other. Muddus is home to bears, lynx, martens, weasels, hares, elk and (in summer) also reindeer; among birds, the whooper swan is one of the most common sights. The park's western edges are skirted by Route 45; the easiest approach is to leave the highway at **Liggadammen** (there are also buses here from Gällivare) and then follow the small road to **Skaite**, where an easy hiking **trail** begins; two suggested routes are Skaite–Muddusfallet–Måskoskårså–Skaite (24km) or Skaite–Muddueluobbal–Manson–Skaite (44km). There are cabins along the trail (April–Sept; rest of the year keys can be obtained from Jokkmokk and Gällivare tourist offices), with a campsite at Muddus Falls. Distances between the various stages are as follows: Liggadammen to Skaite 13km; Skaite to Muddus Falls 7km; Muddus Falls to Muddusluobbal 9km; Muddusluobbal to Manson 5km; Sarkavare to Muddus Falls 14km; Solaure to Manson 7km. There are no outlets for buying food or provisions en route.

insects are for the Lapland countryside – they're responsible for pollinating the cloudberry bushes out in the surrounding marshes – is demonstrated by the exhibitions here. The only public transport to the museum is the Inlandsbanan: indeed the museum opens whenever a train arrives – you'll need to dash in and out again (and use your mosquito repellent). To get there from Gällivare you have to be keen: take the 6.45am Inlandsbanan, which stops for ten minutes at the museum, then get back on the train and disembark at Porjus, from where you can travel back to Gällivare on the 9am bus.

HIKING AROUND GÄLLIVARE

Though there's precious little else to see or do in Gällivare, the town is well positioned as a base for walking. For a fairly gentle walk, you can head up to the *Björnfällan* **restaurant** (the name means "bear trap"), a four-kilometre hike on a well-marked path up **Dundret** hill, from where the views are magnificent. Special buses, which head right to the top, are laid on for the midnight sun, making the journey from the train station to the end of the winding road up the hill (mid-June to mid-July daily at 11pm, returning 1am); tickets, available from the tourist office, cost 160kr return and include the ubiquitous Swedish waffle covered with cloudberries and cream. You can also explore the marshes and forests of one of the nearby national parks (see p.471), the nearest of which is **Muddus National Park** (see box, above).

Eating, drinking and entertainment

If you're arriving from one of the tiny villages on the Inlandsbanan, the wealth of **eating** possibilities in Gällivare will make you quite dizzy; if you're coming from Luleå, grit your teeth and bear it. As for **drinking**, the place to be seen is the *Kilkenny Inn* inside the Grand Hotel at Per Högströmsgatan 9, which has half-price beer for 22kr before 8pm in summer and 10pm in winter; there's also a **nightclub** here on Friday and Saturday (entrance 50–60kr) which has occasional live music, although their choice of artistes can leave a lot to be desired. *Pub Wassara* in the *Nex Hotell* is also a popular drinking hole.

CAFÉS AND RESTAURANTS

Björnfällan, at *Dundret* hotel out of town. Good northern Swedish food but at a price – nothing here is under 150kr.

Centralskolans Kafé, Storgatan 16. In the same building as the tourist office. This basement café is the best place in town for good sandwiches, coffee and cakes.

Kilkenny Inn, Per Högströmsgatan 9. With decent pub food, including burgers, and an Irish style atmosphere, this is a good place to meet other travellers and locals.

Pizzeria Dylan, Östra Kyrkogatan. In the Arkaden shopping centre. The best pizzeria in town, it also does takeaways. Open 10am–5pm.

Pub Wassara, Lasarettsgatan. In the *Nex Hotell*. Although a little pretentious and expensive, this bar-restaurant does a range of good lunches and serves excellent local delicacies such as Arctic char and reindeer.

Restaurang Peking, Storgatan 21 B. Serves reasonable Chinese food and pizzas. A good place for lunch.

Strandcafeet, Malmbergsvägen 2 at the campsite. Beautifully located café right by the graceful Vassara river. Open until 10pm, but shut outside summer.

Tre Kronor, Kaptensvägen 4 in Malmberget. Serving pizzas so big they're just about falling off the plates, this place is consequently very popular with locals.

Åhults Bageri & Café, Lasarettsgatan 19. Great for coffee and cakes.

Listings

Airport Information on ☎0970/780 00.

Banks FöreningsSparbanken, Storgatan 5; Handelsbanken, Storgatan 12; S-E Banken, Storgatan 21.

Buses For long distance bus information call ☎020/47 00 47.

Camping equipment Fjällsport, Järnvägsgatan in Malmberget.

Car rental Avis, Lasarettsgatan 1 at the *Nex Hotel* (☎0970/160 30); Statoil, Malmberget (☎0970/229 00).

Doctor Treatment available at the hospital at Källgatan 14 (☎0970/190 00).

Left luggage At the railway station (15kr).

Pharmacy Storgatan 15 (Mon–Fri 9am–6pm, Sat 10am–1pm).

Police Lasarettsgatan 20 (☎0970/551 65).

Post office Hantverkaregatan 15.

Swimming pool Hellebergs väg, near the post office, with an excellent sauna suite.

Systembolaget Kyrkallén 10.

Taxi Gällivare Taxi ☎0970/10 000.

Trains For information call ☎020/75 75 75.

MOVING ON FROM GÄLLIVARE

From Gällivare, **trains** run south daily at 6.45am in summer to Östersund on the Inlandsbanan; northwest to Kiruna and onto Narvik in Norway; and southeast to Boden, Luleå and then all points south. **Buses** run west to the **Laponia World Heritage Area** of Stora Sjöfallet National Park and Ritsem (see p.472), east to Pajala (see p.483) and northeast to Svappavaara, where connections can be made to Karesuando (see p.484); and from there via Finland to Treriksröset (see p.485) – the northernmost point in Sweden, where the country meets Norway and Finland. Especially handy when the Inlandsbanan isn't running are the year-round Inlandsexpressen buses, which run south via Jokkmokk and Arvidsjaur to Östersund.

Northwest of Gällivare: Northern Sweden's national parks

It's not a good idea to go **hiking in the national parks** of northern Sweden on a whim. Even for experienced walkers, the going can be tough and uncomfortable in parts, downright treacherous in others. **Mosquitoes** are a real problem: it's difficult to describe the utter misery of being covered in a blanket of insects, your eyes, ears and nose full of the creatures (for more on practicalities and safety guidelines see box, below). Yet the beautiful landscape here is one of the last wilderness areas left in Europe – it's one vast expanse of forest and mountains, where roads and human habitation are the exception rather than the norm.

HIKING: SOME PRACTICAL INFORMATION

The best time to go **hiking** in the Swedish mountains is from late June to September: during May and early June the ground is still very wet and boggy as a result of the rapid snow melt. Once the snow has gone, wild flowers burst into bloom, making the most of the short summer months. The weather is very changeable – one moment it can be hot and sunny, the next it can be cold and rainy – and snow showers are not uncommon in summer.

It's always wise to keep to the **designated trails**, which, for summer hikes, are worn paths marked here and there by stone cairns or ribbons on trees and poles (a red "X" on a pole marks a winter snow-scooter trail). Many routes cross large streams – bridges or rowing boats are provided. **Rest shelters** are always open but aren't intended for overnight stays; head instead for **mountain cabins** (*fjällstugor*) or **STF fell stations** (*fjällstationer*), which appear at intervals of roughly 15–20km. Only the fell stations can be booked in advance and offer bed and breakfast accommodation; at cabins you'll need your own sheets or sleeping bags. There are telephones in cabins and some rest shelters. Safety advice and some guidelines on how to reduce damage to the land are posted at the park entrances and on huts and cabins; these are worth reading and remembering. A few tips:

- Get decent **maps**, boots and proper advice before setting out.

- Bring several bottles of **mosquito repellent**.

- Take a good **sleeping bag**, and for longer treks a **tent**, as parts of some trails don't have overnight cabins.

- **Other essentials** for a day-hike pack include rain gear, scarf, gloves, cap, matches, a compass and a knife.

- When **fording streams** never wade in water above your knees; wade across where the stream is shallow and wide. Go one at a time and wear training shoes if possible. Unbuckle the hip belt and chest strap on your pack.

- Watch out for **snow bridges** across streams – take great care not to fall into the water, which is likely to be deep and cold.

- Never go on a **glacier** without a knowledgeable guide – concealed crevasses can be fatal.

For additional detailed information, advice and encouragement for all the routes and parks covered here, contact **Svenska Turistföreningen** (Swedish Touring Club; Box 25, 101 20, Stockholm; *info@stfturist.se*) or speak to any of the tourist offices in Ammarnäs, Arjeplog, Jokkmokk, Gällivare, Kiruna or Tärnaby.

Reindeer are a common sight, as the parks are their breeding grounds and summer pasture, and **Sámi** settlements are dotted throughout the region – notably at **Ritsem** and **Vaisaluokta**.

The five **national parks** here range in difficulty from moderately challenging to a positive assault course. Four of these lie about 120km northwest of Gällivare in the tract of Swedish wilderness edging Norway (the only national park not in this zone is the easy Muddus National Park, covered on p.469). The low fells, large lakes and moors of **Padjelanta** (see below), **Stora Sjöfallet** (see below) and **Abisko** (see p.478) parks act as the eyebrows to the sheer face of the mountainous and inhospitable **Sarek** park. Classed as "extremely difficult", Sarek (not covered in this book) has no tourist facilities, trails, cabins or bridges; the rivers are dangerous and the weather rotten – in short, you need good mountaineering experience to tackle it. For up-to-the-minute **information** on walking in the parks contact Fjällförvaltningen (Mountain Area Unit for Norrbotten) at Industrivägen 10, Jokkmokk (☎0971/127 80); the fell station at Saltoluokta (☎0973/410 10); or Kvikkjokk youth hostel (☎0971/210 22).

Padjelanta National Park

Padjelanta is the largest of Sweden's national parks; its name comes from the *Sámi* language and means "the higher country", an apt description for this plateau that lies almost exclusively above the tree line. The **Padjelanta trail** (150km) runs from **Vaisaluokta** through the **Laponia World Heritage Area** (see box, below) south to **Kvikkjokk**, and is suited to inexperienced walkers – allow at least a week to finish it. You can get to Vaisaluokta by taking a **bus** from Gällivare to Ritsem (which will take you through the beautiful **Stora Sjöfallet** national park with its luxuriant forests and sweeping vistas), from where a boat takes you across Lake Akkajaure to Vaisaluokta. To get to Kvikkjokk, hop on a bus in Jokkmokk (times can be obtained from Länstrafiken Norrbotten on ☎020/47 00 47, or from any tourist office in the area). For bus times, contact Länstrafiken Norrbotten (☎020/47 00 47) or any tourist office in the area. There's also a helicopter service, operated by Norrlandsflyg, between Kvikkjokk, Saltoluokta and Ritsem (daily late June to early Sept daily; 1225kr

---

THE LAPONIA WORLD HERITAGE AREA

"It is one of the last and unquestionably largest and best preserved examples of an area of transhumance, involving summer grazing by large reindeer herds", said the UNESCO World Heritage Committee when they established **Laponia** as a **heritage area** in 1996. Covering a vast area of 9,400 square kilometres, including the Padjelanta, Sarek and Stora Sjöfallet **national parks**, Laponia is the home and workplace of **Sámi** families from seven different villages, who still tend their reindeer here much as their ancestors did in prehistoric times. The population comprises the Forest *Sámi*, who move with their herds within the forests; and the Mountain *Sámi*. The latter follow their animals from the lichen rich forests, where they spend the winter, up to the tree line by the time spring comes, then on into the mountains for summer; in August they start making their way down. Come September, many animals will be slaughtered either at the **corrals** in Ruokto, on the road between Porjus and Kebnats, or at highland corrals between Ritsem and Sitasjaure.

per person over whole route, 680kr over part of route; ☎0970/140 65 or ☎0971/210 68).

For **accommodation**, there's an STF mountain cabin at Ritsem (☎0973/420 30; 120–145kr; late Feb to mid-May & late June to early Oct), an STF fell station at Saltoluokta (☎0973/410 10; 150–325kr; early March to early May & mid-June to mid-Sept), and a **youth hostel** at the end of the trail, in Kvikkjokk (☎0971/210 22; 140kr; late March to early May & late June to mid-Sept). **Cabins** can be found elsewhere along the route; distances between points where they're located are as follows: Ritsem to Vaisaluokta (by boat) 16km; Vaisaluokta to Kutjaure 18km; Kutjaure to Låddejokk 19km; Låddejokk to Arasluokta 12km; Arasluokta to Saltoluokta 10km; Saltoluokta to Tuottar 18km; Tuottar to Tarraluoppal 11km; Tarraluoppal to Såmmarlappa 15km; Såmmarlappa to Tarrekaise 13km; Tarrekaise to Njunjes 7km; Njunjes to Kvikkjokk 17km. The wardens at the cabins or fell stations can tell you the locations of the nearest **food** stores.

Kiruna

KIRUNA (the town's name comes from the *Sámi* word "Giron", meaning "ptarmigan") was the hub of the battle for the control of the iron-ore supply during World War II; ore was transported north from here by train to the great harbour at Narvik over the border in Norway. Much German firepower was expended in an attempt to interrupt the supply to the Allies and wrest control for the Axis. In the process, Narvik suffered grievously, whilst Kiruna – benefiting from supposed Swedish neutrality – made a packet selling to both sides. Today the train ride to Kiruna, 200km north of the Arctic Circle, rattles through sidings, slag heaps and ore works, a bitter contrast to the surrounding wilderness.

Arrival, information and accommodation

The **train** station is at Bangårdsvägen, from where it's a brisk ten-minute walk up the steep hill to the **tourist office** in Folkets Hus, in the central square off Mommagatan (mid-June to end Aug Mon–Fri 9am–8pm, Sat & Sun 9am–6pm; end Aug to mid-June Mon–Fri 9am–5pm; ☎0980/188 80, *www.lappland.se*). The **bus station**, where regular daily buses from Gällivare stop, is at the corner of Bibloteksgatan and Hjalmar Lundbohmsvägen; turn off the latter street and into Lars Janssonsgatan to get to the main square. Served by flights from Stockholm, Luleå and Umeå, the **airport**, 10km away, is linked to town by bus (40kr) and taxi (140kr). For a place to **stay**, the **youth hostel** is 900m from the train station at Bergmästaregatan 7 (☎0980/171 95; 120kr). Boasting its own sauna, it fills quickly in summer, as does the **campsite** (☎0980/131 00), with four-berth cabins (550kr) and an open-air swimming pool; it's on Campingvägen in the Högalid area of town, a twenty-minute walk north of the centre. Though the town has only a limited range of **hotels**, some of which are listed below, reservations are generally not required here.

Gullriset Lägenhetshotell, Bromsgatan 12 (☎0980/109 37, fax 103 04). Boasts apartments sleeping one to four people, costing 350–660kr depending on size.

Kebne, Konduktörsgatan 7 (☎0980/681 80). Good-quality rooms, wooden floors and marble bits here and there. ④/②.

Scandic Hotell Ferrum, Lars Jansongatan 17 (☎0980/39 86 00, fax 39 86 11). By far the most expensive hotel in town, best avoided with its characterless rooms and indifferent staff. ⑤/③.

Vinterpalatset, Järnvägsgatan 18 (☎0980/677 70, fax 130 50). A listed building with wooden floors, large double beds, and superb sauna and jacuzzi suite on the top floor. There are four cheaper, more basic rooms in the annex. ③/①.

Yellow House, Hantverkaregatan 25 (☎0980/137 50, fax 137 51). Budget hotel with dorm beds (120kr) and shared rooms for 2–4 people. Breakfast not included. ①.

The Town

When, in the early 1600s, Swedish pioneers first arrived in what is now Kiruna, they found the *Sámi* already in place here. Completely ignoring the indigenous population, the Swedes opened their first mine in 1647 nearby at Masugnsbyn ("Blast Furnace Village"), but it wasn't until the beginning of the following century that the **iron-ore** deposits in Kiruna itself were finally discovered. Exploratory drilling began in the 1880s, which nicely coincided with the building of the **Malmbanan**, the iron-ore railway between Luleå and Narvik in Norway, along which the first train laden with iron ore trundled out from Malmberget in Gällivare in March 1888. It wasn't until 1900 that the settlers braved their first winter in Kiruna, a year which is now regarded as the town's birthday.

Not surprisingly, most sights in town are firmly wedded to iron in one way or another. The tower of the **Rådhus** is a strident metal pillar, designed by Bror

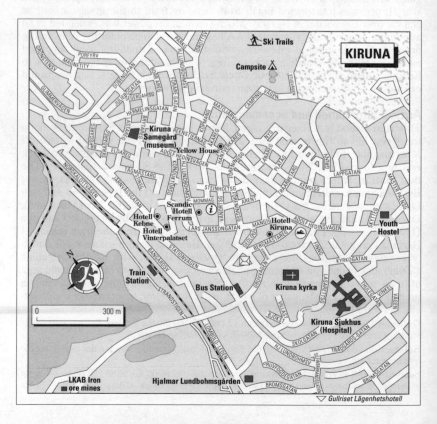

Marklund (see p.385) and harbouring an intricate latticework, clock face and sundry bells that chime raucously at noon; unbelievably, the Rådhus won an award in 1964 for being the most beautiful Swedish public building. Inside, there's a tolerable art collection and, in summer, displays of *Sámi* handicrafts.

The **mines**, ugly brooding reminders of Kiruna's prosperity, still dominate the town, much more depressingly so than in Gällivare (see p.466); despite its new central buildings and open parks, Kiruna retains a grubby industrial feel. The tourist office arranges **guided tours** around the mines (July to mid-Aug 3 daily; late June and mid- to late Aug 2 daily; 125kr; minimum age 6), on which visitors are bussed to a "tourist mine", a closed-off section of the rabbit warren of tunnels comprising a working mine. The rest of the mine contains facilities such as petrol stations and a workers' canteen; and mining paraphernalia, including trains for transporting ore and equipment, and mills for crushing the ore-bearing rock. Oddly enough, *shiitake* mushrooms are also grown here – at a depth of 540m – and can be sampled during the tour.

Back in town, **Kiruna kyrka**, on Kyrkogatan (July 11am–10pm, Aug–June 11am–5pm), causes a few raised eyebrows when people see it for the first time: built in the style of a *Sámi* hut, it's an origami-like creation of oak beams and rafters, the size of a small aircraft hangar. LKAB, the iron-ore company (and the town's main employer) which paid for its construction, was also responsible for the **Hjalmar Lundbohmsgården** at Ingenjörsgatan 1 (June–Aug daily 10am–5pm; Sept–May Mon–Fri 10am–4pm; 30kr), fifteen minutes' walk away (take Gruvvägen south, turn left at Hjalmar Lundbohmsvägen, then right into Ingenjörsgatan). The displays in this country house once used by the managing director of the company, who was the town's "founder", consist mostly of turn-of-the-century photographs featuring the man himself and assorted *Sámi* in their winter gear. Try to visit the house, in order to get a perspective on the town's history, before going down the mine; you'll be all the more aware afterwards how, without the mine, Kiruna would be a one-reindeer town instead of the thriving place it is today – quite a feat when you consider its location on the map (don't be surprised to see snow on the slag heaps in the middle of June).

For the most rewarding exhibition of *Sámi* culture in town, head for the handicraft centre, **Kiruna Samegård**, at Brytaregatan 14 (mid-June to Sept daily 10am–6pm; Oct to mid-June Mon–Fri 10am–4pm; 20kr). The handicrafts you'll see here may well be familiar by now; what probably won't be is its small but impressive display of *Sámi* art. It also has a café and a souvenir shop, where you can buy a piece of antler bone or reindeer skin.

Eating, drinking and nightlife

Eating and **drinking** in Kiruna is not a joy. Restaurants and bars are few and far between, and in summer you may even find several closed: frustratingly, the staff take their holidays just when the town is full of tourists. That said, Kiruna is a good place to try some traditional *Sámi* delicacies such as reindeer.

RESTAURANTS
Restaurang Lapplandia, Bergmästaregatan 7. Don't be deceived by the rather down-at-heel exterior – this place serves up the best food in Kiruna, with Lapland delicacies, such as different cuts of reindeer, a speciality. Main courses at 200kr.

Mats & Mums, Bergmästaregatan 10. An inordinately popular eatery with a window through to the adjacent swimming pool, making for an unusual setting. Burgers, meat, fish dishes and Arctic specialities are the order of the day here.

Nan King, Mangigatan 26. This dreary little place is the most northerly Chinese restaurant in Sweden, serving – besides the expected fare – pizza and spaghetti. Main dishes from 90kr.

Pizza & Pasta Plus, Mangigatan. Next door to *Nan King*. Serves a decent range of pizzas from 45kr.

CAFÉS AND BARS

Restaurang Arran, Föreningsgatan 9. A grotty drinking den offering the cheapest beer in town. Go in with a friend.

Brända Tomten, inside the Gallerian shopping centre at the corner of Mangigatan and Föreningsgatan. Decent coffee, cakes and sandwiches; a bit soulless.

Mommas, inside the *Scandic Hotell Ferrum* in the main square, by the tourist office. An American-style place with a dark and dingy interior, serving up burgers and the like.

Safari, Geologgatan. *The* place for tea and coffee with outdoor seating in summer and a wonderful continental feel.

3nd Baren, Föreningsgatan 11. A great old wooden building with coarsely hewn floorboards, attracting a trendy crowd during the evenings. There's outdoor seating under the trees at the rear. A good choice especially at lunchtime, when the place fills up.

Listings

Airport Information on ☎0980/28 48 00.

Banks Nordbanken, in the main square opposite the tourist office.

Buses For long distance bus information call ☎020/47 00 47.

Car rental Avis, at the airport (☎0980/130 80); Budget, Industrivägen 26 (☎0980/831 65).

Cinema There are weekly films inside Folkets Hus in the main square (☎0980/157 00).

Medical treatment At the hospital (☎0980/731 12).

Left luggage At the railway station (15kr).

Pharmacy Inside the Gallerian shopping centre on Föreningsgatan (Mon–Fri 9.30am–6pm, Sat 9.30am–1pm).

Police Lars Janssonsgatan (☎0980/744 00).

Post office Meschplan (Mon–Fri 9.30am–6pm, Sat 10am–1pm; ☎0980/100 55).

Swimming pool Simhallsbadet at Bergmästaregatan 10.

Systembolaget Föreningsgatan.

Taxi Taxi Kiruna (☎0980/202 50).

Trains For information call ☎020/75 75 75.

Travel agent Avanda, at the train station (☎0980/150 02).

East of Kiruna: Jukkasjärvi and the Ice Hotel

An obvious destination for any tourist travelling in Lapland in winter is the tiny village of **JUKKASJÄRVI** (known locally as simply "Jukkas"), 17km east of Kiruna. It's the site of what's effectively the world's largest igloo, the **Ice Hotel**, built every year by the side of the Torneälven river in late October, from when it stands proudly until it melts in May. Thirty thousand tons of snow and ten thousand tons of ice are used to make the igloo, whose exact shape and design changes from year to year; there's usually a bar in the entrance hall (don't leave your beer on the bar for too long, or it'll freeze), bedrooms for at least 120 people (the beds are made out of blocks of compact snow and covered with reindeer hides), an exhibition hall, a cinema, and a chapel where couples can **marry**. The temperature here in winter is generally around -20°C to -30°C, which makes for a temperature inside the igloo of around -5°C. Guests are provided with specially made, tried-and-tested, **sleeping bags** of a type used by the Swedish army, who have used the hotel for Arctic survival training; the bags are guaranteed to keep you warm in temperatures down to -35°C. In the morning, you can refresh yourself with a sauna at the *Wärdshus* restaurant across the road, and then have a hearty breakfast there.

The *Ice Hotel* is open from mid-December each year until it thaws. Unfortunately, the whole operation has become money-driven of late; prices have more than doubled in recent years as demand for rooms has surged, and even day visitors now have to pay an entrance fee (100kr). The double **rooms** here cost 1700kr, while a suite, decorated with ice carvings and ornaments, is 1250kr per person. There are also en-suite **cabins** for rent on the site, all with kitchens (May–Nov ④; Dec–April ⑤; four-bed cabins also available). Hotel rooms and cabins can be booked through Jukkas AB, on the main road at Marknadsvägen 63 (☎0980/668 00, fax 668 90, *www.icehotel.com*). **Activities** here – inordinately expensive – include a dog-sledging trip to see reindeer and meet some local *Sámi* (2 hr; minimum two people; from 875kr per person), and an accompanied drive on rented snow scooters down the Torne river and into the wintry forests (995kr; 4hr). In **summer** there's organized river rafting (a 6hr trip costs 550kr per person), fishing and hiking – details can be obtained from Jukkas AB. You can **eat** all meals across the road at *Jukkasjärvi Wärdshus* in winter (only open lunchtimes in summer); for **provisions**, there's a small supermarket in the village.

To get here from Kiruna, take bus #006 (Mon–Fri 1 daily). Undoubtedly the best way to arrive, though, is by **dog sledge** from Kiruna airport; for a hefty 3500kr you can be met at your plane and pulled all the way to your room.

Jukkasjärvi village

The **village** of Jukkasjärvi is very small. At the end of Marknadsvägen, a dead-end road, there's an old wooden *Sámi* **church** (June–Aug daily 8am–10pm; restricted hours in winter), parts of which date from 1608, making it the oldest surviving church in Lapland. Check out the richly decorated altarpiece by Uppsala artist, Bror Hjorth, depicting the revivalist preacher, **Lars Levi Laestadius** (see p.484), alongside the woman who inspired him to rid Lapland of alcohol, Maria of Åsele. The triptych was given to the church in 1958 by the mining company, LKAB, who were then celebrating their 350th anniversary. Under the floor are the mummified remains – not on public display – of villagers who died here in the eighteenth century. The sandy ground and frost are thought to have been responsible for keeping the bodies, including that of a woman dressed in white wedding dress and high-heel shoes, so remarkably well preserved. The organ above the door is made from reindeer horn (even the keys consist of the stuff) and birch wood; the artwork in the centre of the organ, suspended over the pipes, symbolizes the sun rising over the Lapporten, the two mountains tops near Abisko which have come to represent the gateway to Lapland. Across the road from the church, the wooden houses of the tedious Hembygdsgården **homestead museum** (daily 11am–4pm; 15kr) contain the usual suspects: a stuffed reindeer, an old sleigh, a rickety spinning wheel and other equally dull how-we-used-to-live paraphernalia.

Nikkaluokta and Kebnekaise

Nikkaluokta, 66km west of Kiruna and reached on the twice-daily bus, is the starting point for treks towards and up Sweden's highest mountain, **Kebnekaise** (2114m). From the village, a nineteen-kilometre trail leads to the **fell station** at Kebnekaise (early March to early May & mid-June to mid-Sept; ☎0980/550 00; 250–300kr) at the foot of the mountain. There's also a **helicopter** connection here; see opposite. The mountain was first conquered by a Frenchman, Charles Robot, in 1883; today it can be reached in 8–9 hours by anyone in decent physical condition. Two paths lead to the peak: the eastern route goes over Björling glacier, includes some climbing and is only recommended for experts; the western route is much longer and is the one most people opt for.

Northwest from Kiruna: Abisko and the Kungsleden

Leaving Kiruna, the most obvious route is **northwest into Norway** and on to Narvik, which can be covered by **train** (the line here is the last leg of the long run from Stockholm or Luleå) and also by road (see below). The train route from Luleå to Narvik, known as the **Malmbanan**, is Europe's northernmost line, and would never have been built had it not been for the rich deposits of iron ore around Gällivare and Malmberget. The idea to construct the line, which connects the Bothnian coast with the Atlantic coast (170km), passing through some of the remotest and most inhospitable parts of Europe, was talked about on and off throughout the nineteenth century, when the only means of transporting the ore was by reindeer and sleigh. Finally, in 1884, an English company was awarded the contract to build it; by 1888, the company was bankrupt, when the line had reached Gällivare from the Bothnian Coast. Ten years passed before the state took over the project; in July 1902, the navvies – who'd been subject to temperatures of below -30°C and conditions of great isolation – finally shovelled their way through deep snow at Riksgränsen to cross the Norwegian border. A year later, the line was officially opened by King Oscar II.

The much newer **Nordkalottvägen** road (North Calotte Highway, the E10) runs parallel to the train line on the Swedish side of the border, threading its way across barren plateaux (the lakes up here are still frozen in mid-June), before slicing through the mighty Norwegian mountains. By train or car, the journey here is an exhilarating run that passes the start of the Kungsleden trail at **Abisko** (see opposite). If you stop in Abisko, you can take the **cable car** (*linbanan*; 85kr return) 500m up Nuolja mountain (1169m) for fantastic views of the surrounding wilderness: the spectacular U-shaped mountain tops of Lapporten (used as landmark by the *Sámi* for guiding their reindeer between their summer and winter grazing land), the seventy-kilometre-long Torneträsk lake, and the vast wooded expanses of **Abisko National Park**. The mountain is a popular place from which to observe the midnight sun. From the café at the end of the cable car, an easy walking path (7km; allow 2–3hr) leads downhill to nearby **Björkliden**, comprising nothing more than a few houses gathered around the railway station. From here, the **Navvy Road** (Rallarvägen) leads to Rombaksbotn, near Narvik, in Norway; the road was built alongside the Malmbanan, then under construction, in order to transport materials needed for the line. Today it provides a walking or mountain-biking route between Abisko and Narvik – though it can be fairly narrow and rough going in parts.

ABISKO: THE KUNGSLEDEN TO HEMAVAN

The **Kungsleden** (literally "King's Trail") is the most famous and popular of the hiking routes in Sweden. A well-signposted, five-hundred-kilometre path from **Abisko** in the north to **Hemavan**, near Tärnaby (see p.451), it takes in Sweden's highest mountain, **Kebnekaise** (2114m), en route. If you're looking for splendid isolation, this isn't the trail for you; it's the busiest in the country (one of the least busy sections is between Jäkkvik and Adolfström, see p.460). A handy tip is to go against the flow: most people walk from Abisko down to Kebnekaise, so by walking the route in the opposite direction you won't need to keep overtaking people.

There are **cabins** along the entire route, and from Abisko to Saltoluokta, north of the Arctic Circle, and in the south between Ammarnäs and Hemavan, there are also STF **fell stations**. The ground is easy to walk, with bridges where it's necessary to ford streams; marshy ground has had wooden planks laid down to ease the going, and there are either boat services or rowing boats with which to get across several large lakes. The route, which passes through the national parks (see p.471), is traditionally split into the five segments given below. For the distances between the places mentioned on each segment, see the map on p.480; a good map to have of the area is Lantmäteriet Kartförlaget's *Norra Norrland* (scale 1:400,000), available in Gällivare.

ABISKO TO KEBNEKAISE – 6 DAYS, 105KM

The Kungsleden doesn't begin at Abisko Ö(stra) train station, which is in the village of Abisko; the actual starting point is the next stop along, **Abisko Turiststation**, whose **fell station** has a great sauna suite and bar, with panoram-

---

REACHING THE KUNGSLEDEN BY PUBLIC TRANSPORT

You can get to Abisko pretty easily by **train**; it's just before the Norwegian border on the Kiruna–Narvik run. The **Inlandsbanan** will get you to Jokkmokk, from where you can get a bus to Kvikkjokk, another point on the trail. A **helicopter** service, run by Norrlandsflyg, operates between Nikkaluokta and Kebnekaise (late June to mid-Sept; 390kr per person; information on ☎0970/140 65 or ☎0971/210 68).

There are also several useful **bus** routes that you can take to link up with the trail, listed below; most of these services are run by Länstrafiken Norrbotten (☎020/47 00 47), who produce a handy pocket timetable, entitled *Busstidtabell för Fjällinjerna*, for the mountain buses which they and Länstrafiken Västerbotten (☎020/91 00 19) run, and for the privately run connecting boats. The buses operate a *bussgods* service, which allows you to send your pack ahead to your destination or alternatively back to your starting point, sparing you the effort of lugging your stuff around; ask about this service at bus stations or on the bus.

#31: Hemavan to Umeå	#94: Murjek to Jokkmokk and Kvikkjokk
#92: Kiruna to Nikkaluokta (19km from Kebnekaise fell station)	#200: Arjeplog to Jäkkvik
#93: Gällivare to Ritsem (passes through Vakkotavare and Kebnats for the boat to Saltoluokta)	#303: Arjeplog to Laisval (change there for Adolfström)
	#341: Ammarnäs to Sorsele

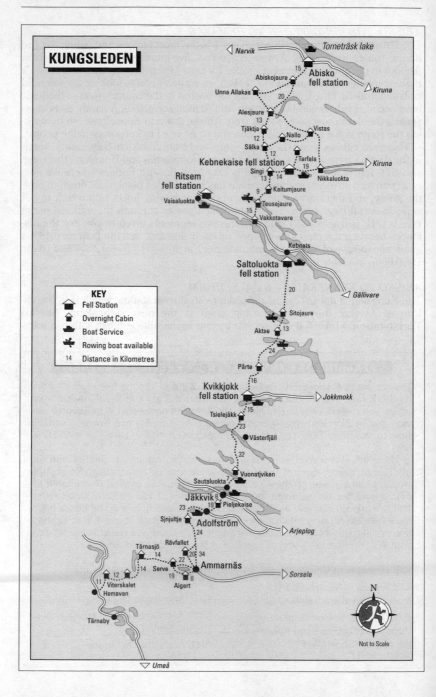

KUNGSLEDEN

◁ Narvik — Torneträsk lake

15 — Abisko fell station
Abiskojaure ◁ — ▷ Kiruna
Unna Allakas — 20

Alesjaure
13
Tjäktja — Vistas
12 — Nallo
Sälka — 12 — Tarfala
Kebnekaise fell station — 19 — ▷ Kiruna
Singi — 14
13 — Nikkaluokta
Kaitumjaure
Ritsem fell station — 9
Vaisaluokta — Teusajaure
15 — Vakkotavare

Kebnats

Saltoluokta fell station
20 — ▷ Gällivare

Sitojaure
Aktse — 13
24
Pårte
16
Kvikkjokk fell station — ▷ Jokkmokk
Tsielejåkk — 15
23
● Västerfjäll
32
Vuonatjviken
Sautaluokta
Jäkkvik — ● Pieljekaise
23 — 19
Sjnjultje — Adolfström
24 — ▷ Arjeplog
Rävfallet
Tärnasjö — 20 34
14 — 22 — Ammarnäs — ▷ Sorsele
Serve — 19
14 — 8
12 — Aigert
11 Viterskalet
Hemavan

Tärnaby

KEY
🏠 Fell Station
🏠 Overnight Cabin
⛴ Boat Service
🚣 Rowing boat available
14 Distance in Kilometres

N

Not to Scale

▽ Umeå

ic views out over the vast Torneträsk lake (☎0980/402 00; from 150kr; late Feb to early May & June to late Sept). At the start of the trail, the vegetation is lush and dense: beech forest stretches across the valley bottom. From the Alesjaure cabins, perched on a mountain ridge 35km from the start, you'll get a fantastic view over the open countryside below; there's a sauna here, too. The highest point on this segment is the Tjäktja pass (1105m), from where there are also wonderful views. There are **cabins** en route at Abiskojaure, Alesjaure, Tjäktja, Sälka and Singi. At the end of this section lies **Kebnekaise fell station** (14km from Singi; (☎0980/550 00; 250–300kr; early March to early May & mid-June to mid-Sept), from where it's possible to leave the main trail and head to Nikkaluokta, 19km away (served by buses to Kiruna). **Provisions** are available at Abisko, Alesjaure, Sälka and Kebnekaise.

KEBNEKAISE TO SALTOLUOKTA – 3 DAYS, 51KM
One of the quietest sections of the trail, this segment takes in beech forest, open fells and deep valleys. First of all you backtrack to **Singi**, before heading south again with an unobstructed view of the hills and glaciers of Sarek National Park. You then paddle across the river at **Teusajaure** and climb over a plateau, from where you drop steeply through more beech forest to **Vakkotavare**. Here a bus runs to the quay at Kebnats, and then a short boat trip brings you to **Saltoluokta fell station** (☎0973/410 10; 150–325kr; early March to early May & mid-June to mid-Sept) and the start of the next section. There are **cabins** en route at Singi, Kaitumjaure, Teusajaure and Vakkotavare. **Provisions** are available at all the cabins apart from Singi.

SALTOLUOKTA TO KVIKKJOKK – 4 DAYS, 73KM
This segment involves crossing two lakes and also passes through a bare landscape edged by pine and beech forests. A long uphill climb leads first to **Sitojaure** on a bare high fell. The shallow lake here, which you have to cross, is choppy in the strong wind; take the boat service operated by the cabin caretaker. You then cross the wetlands on the other side of the lake, making use of the wooden planks laid down here, to **Aktse**, where there's a vast field of yellow buttercups in summer. Row across **Lake Laitaure** for Kvikkjokk; as you approach you'll see pine forest. There are **cabins** en route at Sitojaure, Aktse, and Pårte; at **Kvikkjokk** there's a **youth hostel** (☎0971/210 39; 140kr; late March to early May & late June to mid-Sept). **Provisions** are available at Saltoluokta, Aktse and Kvikkjokk.

KVIKKJOKK TO AMMARNÄS – 8 DAYS, 166KM
Not recommended for novices, this is one of the most difficult stretches of the trail (distances between cabins can be long and there are four lakes to cross); it is, however, also one of the quietest. From **Kvikkjokk** you take the boat over Saggat lake and walk to the first cabin at **Tsielejåkk**. It's 55km to the next cabin at **Vuonatjviken**. You then take the boat across Riebnesjaure and walk to Hornavan for another boat across to the village of **Jäkkvik**; there are cabins available here (see p.460). It's a short hike to the next cabin, then on to the village of **Adolfström**, where once again there is accommodation (see p.460). Then you get another boat over Iraft lake and on to the cabins at **Sjnjultje**. From here there's a choice of routes: 34km direct to Ammarnäs, or 24km to Rävfallet and from there another 20km into Ammarnäs. **Accommodation** en route is at Tsielejåkk,

Vuonatjviken, Jäkkvik village, Pieljekaise, Adolfström village, Sjnjultje, Rävfallet and Ammarnäs. **Provisions** are available in Jäkkvik and Adolfström.

AMMARNÄS TO HEMAVAN – 4 DAYS, 78KM
This is the easiest part of the trail: on it you'll pass over low fells and heather-covered moors and through beech forests and wetlands, the horizon lined with impressive fell peaks. The only steep climb is between **Ammarnäs** and **Aigert**, where there's an imposing waterfall and a traditional steam sauna in the cabin. On the way to the **Syter** cabin, you'll pass a network of bridges, which cross the various lakes in what is called the **Tärnasjö archipelago**. There are no fell stations on this stretch of the trail; cabins en route are at Aigert, Serve, Tärnasjö, Syter, Viterskalet and Hemavan. **Provisions** are available at all the cabins apart from Hemavan (see also p.452).

From Abisko on to Norway

From Abisko and Björkliden, the train line and the E10 continue on to **RIKSGRÄNSEN**, a border settlement where it's possible to ski and snowboard until late June. There's a **hotel** here, *Hotell Riksgränsen* (☎0980/400 80, fax 431 25; ④/③) opposite the train station – but little else. Some great **fishing** and **hiking** can be had in these parts; the hotel can supply detailed information as well as rent **mountain bikes** to cycle along the Rallarvägen (see p.478) or **canoes** for use on the lake here (both cost 190kr a day). Bear in mind, though, that Riksgränsen is one of the wettest places in the entire country in summer (unlike neighbouring Abisko which is in a rain shadow).

While you're in Riksgränsen, be sure to check out the slide show of the fantastic **landscape and wildlife pictures** of the local photographer, Sven Hörnell, who lived up here for forty years (mid-June to mid-Sept daily at 3pm; 90min; 50kr). He made it his life's work to record the changing seasons in the Sarek national park and the Lofoten archipelago over the hills in Norway, with much of his output consisting of aerial photos taken while flying his own propeller plane across the wilds of Lapland.

The Torne Valley

Along the border with Finland, the lush, gentle slopes of the lush **TORNE VALLEY** (Tornedalen) are among the most welcoming sights in northern Sweden. Stretching over 500km from the mouth of the Gulf of Bothnia to Sweden's remote northern tip, the three rivers, Torne, Muonio and Könkämä, mark out the long border between Sweden and Finland. The valley is home to Swedes, Finns and *Sámi*, who all speak an archaic **dialect** of Finnish known, in Swedish at least, as *tornedalsfinska* ("Torne Valley Finnish"), though Swedish is understood by most people here and is the language of choice for the younger generation. Refreshingly different from the coast and from the heavily wooded inland regions of the country, the area is dotted with small villages, often no more than a couple of wooden cottages near a river, bordered by flower meadows that run down to the water's edge. To either side of Route 400, the main road along the valley, lie open fields providing much-needed grazing land for the farmers' livestock.

Arriving from the west, you can enter the valley by **bus** at its midway point, **Pajala**; take the #46 here from **Gällivare** (Mon–Fri 3 daily, Sat & Sun 1 daily; 2hr

30min), or the #51 or #53 from **Kiruna** (Mon–Thurs 2 daily, Fri 3 daily; Sun 1 daily; 3hr). From the north, bus #50 runs from Karesuando to Vittangi (Mon–Thurs 2 daily, Fri 3 daily; Sun 1 daily), where you change onto the #51 or #53 for Pajala. From the **Bothnian Coast**, buses run daily from Haparanda (see p.405) up the valley as far as **Pajala**. The main **bus** route through the Torne Valley (there are no trains here) is the #54 between Pajala and Haparanda (Mon–Thurs 3 daily, Fri 4 on Fri, Sun 1 daily; 3hr).

Pajala

The valley's main village is pretty **PAJALA** (pronounced "Py-allah"), a place that has earned itself a reputation and a half throughout Sweden. The predominance of heavy labouring jobs in the north of Sweden has produced a gender imbalance here – around three men to every woman (a fact which also explains the ridiculously macho behaviour that seems to prevail in these parts). So, to celebrate the village's recent four-hundredth anniversary, the local council placed advertisements in the national papers inviting women from the south of the country up to Lapland to take part in the birthday festivities. Journalists outside Sweden soon heard of the ads, and articles about the unusual invitation began to appear in newspapers across Europe. Before long, busloads of women from all over the continent were heading for the village. The anniversary festivities proved to be a drunken, debauched bash that tiny Pajala won't forget in a long time, but they did help to redress the gender problem: dozens of east European women lost their hearts to gruff Swedish lumberjacks, and began new lives north of the Arctic Circle. It remains to be seen whether these women will adapt to a lifetime of winters spent in darkness, in temperatures of -25°C.

Taking place in the third week in September, the **Römpäviiko** ("romp week") cultural festival, featuring live music and streets stalls selling food and handicrafts, is undoubtedly the liveliest time to be in the village. At any other time, Pajala is a great place to rest up in for a day or so – take a walk along the riverside, or head off in search of the great grey **owl** (*strix nebulosa*) that sweeps through the nearby forests. The huge wooden **model** of the bird in the bus station will give you an idea of its appearance: lichen grey, with long, slender tail feathers and a white crescent between its black and yellow eyes. Close by is the largest **sundial** in the world, a circular affair with a diameter of 38m.

While you're in Pajala, make an effort to visit the **grave** of the revivalist preacher, Lars Levi Laestadius (see p.484), who strived throughout his life to rid Lapland of alcohol abuse. He died in Pajala in 1861, and his grave is located in the middle section of the old graveyard next to Pajala kyrka on Kyrkallén.

PRACTICALITIES

The **bus station**, right in the centre of town, contains the **tourist office** (mid-June to Sept Mon–Fri 9am–6pm, Sat & Sun 11am–5pm; Oct to mid-June Mon–Fri 9am–5pm; ☎0978/100 15). For **accommodation**, the *Bykrogen Hotell*, close by at Soukolovägen 2 (☎0978/712 00, fax 714 64; ④/②) has cosy little rooms; *Hotell Smedjan*, Fridhemsvägen 1 (☎0978/108 15, fax 717 75; ④/②), has similar en-suite rooms. The best place to stay is right at the other end of the village at *Pajala Camping* (☎0978/718 80; May–Sept), with its stunning views over the lazy Torne river; there are simple **cabins** here with cold water only (nos. 1–16 have good river views; 285kr per person). For **eating** and **drinking**, the *Bykrogen Hotell* has *Dagens Rätt* for 60kr; count on at least double that for traditional northern

Swedish delicacies. At the weekends, there's a popular disco in its basement. Just around the corner is plain *Bykrogen*, a cheap and cheerful pizzeria.

South of Pajala: Övertorneå

The only sight in the tiny village of **ÖVERTORNEÅ**, some 70km south of Pajala, is the large wooden **Övertorneå kyrka**, dating from 1615, with its medieval wood carvings; the building was enlarged to its present crucifix shape in 1735. To experience what the Torne Valley is really all about, though, head out to one of the many local lakes shrouded in mist, where you can dangle your toes in the water and listen to the mooing of the cows and the whisper of the birch trees. You can get off the bus (#54) when you see a lake that appeals, and, provided you've timed it right, flag down the next bus a couple of hours later to head back or continue on.

Just off the main street, the **tourist office**, at Finlandsvägen 1 (mid-June to mid-Aug daily 9am–7pm; mid-Aug to mid-June Mon–Fri 9am–4pm; ☎0927/796 51, *www.arctic-circle.net*), can arrange cabin accommodation in the vicinity of the village. There's a pleasant enough modern **hotel** in town, *Hotell Tornedalia* (☎0927/790 60, fax 103 50; ④/②), which serves food. Alternatively, there's a **youth hostel** in the village of **Hedenäset**, 20km south of Övertorneå (☎0927/303 50; 130kr; June–Aug). Beautifully situated by a lake, it boasts views across to Finland.

North of Pajala: Karesuando and around

Sweden's northernmost village, **KARESUANDO**, is a surprisingly likeable little place which you can reach from Pajala by bus (Mon–Fri 2 daily, Sun 1 daily; change in Vittangi). This is as good a spot as any to take stock of just where you've reached: the Arctic Circle is 250km to the south, you're as far north as Canada's Baffin Island and the northern tip of Alaska, and the tree line slices through the edge of the village. **Winters** up here can be particularly severe; the first snow falls at the end of September or early October and stays on the ground until late May, when the Muonioälven, the river which curls around the village, also finally melts. Just a few centimetres beneath the surface, the ground is in the grip of **permafrost** all year round. Summer here is short and sweet – except that the region becomes a mosquito paradise then.

LAESTADIUS AND THE DEMON DRINK

No other man has made a greater impression on northern Scandinavia than **Lars Levi Laestadius**, the Swedish revivalist preacher who dedicated his life to saving people in three different countries from the perils of **alcoholism**. Born in Jäkkvik in 1800 and educated in Kvikkjokk, the young Laestadius soon developed a close relationship with the indigenous *Sámi*, many of whom had turned to drink to escape the harsh reality of their daily lives. It was while the priest was working in Karesuando (1826–49) that he met **Maria of Åsele**, the *Sámi* woman who inspired him to steer people towards a life of total purity. Following Laestadius's death in Pajala in 1861, the movement continued under the leadership of Juhani Raattamaa before splitting into two opposing branches: a conservative western group in Sweden and Norway, and a more liberal eastern one in Finland. Today tens of thousands of teetotal Swedes, Finns, Norwegians and *Sámi* across the Arctic area of Scandinavia still follow Laestadius's teachings; they're not allowed to have flowers or curtains in their homes, nor are they permitted to wear a tie, listen to the radio or watch TV. Drinking, of course, is totally out of the question.

TRERIKSRÖSET

Heading north for **Treriksröset** – the **three-nation marker post** where Sweden, Norway and Finland all meet – walk over the bridge to Kaaresuvanto in Finland, from where a bus leaves (June–Aug Mon–Fri at 4.30pm; remember Finland is an hour ahead of Sweden) for Tromsö in Norway via **Kilpisjärvi**. From here, there are two ways to get to Treriksröset. One of these is a hike of 11km down a track which passes through an area of dwarf woodland before running around a small lake to reach Sweden's northernmost point, marked by a yellow bell-shaped piece of concrete, suspended in a lake and surrounded by wooden walkways; don't forget your camera and mosquito repellent. The path then continues (14km) towards the **northernmost peak** in Sweden, **Pältsan** (1445m); the going here is rocky in parts. The STF **cabins** at the foot of the mountain, two of Sweden's most northerly buildings, boast thirty beds and a sauna (late March to early May & mid-July to mid-Sept). There's an easy hike (40km) from the Pältsa cabins back to **Keinovuopio** (see p.486), then across the river to the main E8 road in Finland, where you can catch the bus back towards Karesuando (Mon–Fri late morning).

Alternatively, you can reach Treriksröset from Kilpisjärvi by getting a **boat ride** across the lake on board *M/S Malla*, which shortens the hike to just 3km. The boat requires at least four passengers if it's to sail (July to mid-Aug 9am, 1pm & 5pm Swedish time; 20min; 80kr return); for boat information ask at the tourist office in Karesuando or call the Finnish number ☎00358/16 53 77 83.

Karesuando is right in the midst of *Sámi* heartland; reindeer husbandry, particularly in the nearby villages of Övre and Nedre Soppero, as well as in Idivuoma, where many herders live, is of primary importance to the local economy. Nevertheless unemployment here remains stubbornly high.

The only sight to speak of in Karesuando is beyond the tourist office: the wooden cabin here was once the rectory of **Lars Levi Laestadius**, the village's most famous son (see box, p.484). Complete with simple wooden pews, it was used as a meeting place while Laestadius was rector in Karesuando; the cabin is now used as a simple **museum** of Laestadius' life and works. Also worth a quick look, along the road to the campsite, is the **Sámiid Viessu**, a **photography** and **handicraft exhibition** (July to mid-Aug, daily 10am–7pm), which has some atmospheric black-and-white shots of *Sámi* gatherings from generations past; there's also a small café here serving up coffee and cakes. With your own transport, it's well worth the short drive south along Route 400 for fantastic **views** over the surrounding tundra: about ten minutes after leaving the village, take the right turn marked "Suijavaara" and continue past the lake, Suijajärvi (a good camping spot), whereupon the road begins to climb up past a TV mast and eventually ends in a small car park. On a clear day you can see for miles across the Swedish and Finnish tundra from up here. The vast tract of land you'll see stretching away to the northwest contains **Treriksröset**, the point where Sweden, Finland and Norway meet (see box, above).

PRACTICALITIES

National **borders** in northern Scandinavia carry little significance: people cross them without as much as a batting an eyelid as they go about their everyday duties. Since Finland is just a stone's throw away across the river, business in Karesuando is done in both Swedish *kronor* and Finnish *markka*.

The **tourist office** is located in the village school, to the left of the bridge across to Finland (mid-June to mid-Aug daily 10am–7pm; ☎0981/202 05). **Accommodation** is limited to *Karesuando Camping* (☎0981/201 39), a two-kilo-metre walk past the church, heading out of the village along the main road. A number of four-berth **cabins** are available at the campsite; those with a simple kitchen go for 375kr, those without are a little smaller and cost 275kr; there's a separate toilet and shower block. To get away from it all, there are **cabins** in the wilds at **Keinovuopio**, a tiny settlement that's home to just fifteen people, right on the river Konkämä; these can be booked through the tourist office for 250kr per day. To reach Keinovuopio, cross the river to **Kaaresuvanto** in Finland, and then take a Finnish bus towards **Kilpisjärvi**, from where there's a footbridge back over the river to Swedish Keinovuopio. Alternatively, there's a **youth hostel** across the river in Finnish Kaaresuvanto (☎00358/167 77 71). There's just one **eating** place in Karesuando, a greasy-spoon grill-restaurant between the Statoil and OK filling stations, and at the opposite end of the village to the campsite. Both these stations have limited supplies of food for sale, but a better option for **provisions** is the ICA shop opposite Statoil.

travel details

Trains

The **Inlandsbanan** runs from Mora to Gällivare via Östersund from late June to mid-Aug. **Northbound** trains leave Mora daily at 7.35 am, calling at Orsa, Sveg and many other wayside halts en route for Östersund. Northbound trains leave Östersund daily for Gällivare at 7.05am calling at Ulriksfors (for Strömsund), Dorotea, Vilhelmina, Storuman, Sorsele, Arvidsjaur, the Arctic Circle, Jokkmokk and Gällivare. **Southbound** trains leave Gällivare daily at 6.45am for stations to Östersund. From Östersund a train leaves at 2.45pm daily for Mora.

Borlänge to: Gävle (4 daily; 1hr 30min); Falun (11 daily; 15min); Malung (3 daily; 2hr); Mora (7 daily; 1hr 20min); Stockholm (8 daily; 2hr 20min); Uppsala (8 daily; 1hr 45min); Örebro (4 daily; 2hr).

Falun to: Borlänge (11 daily; 15min); Gävle (4 daily; 1hr); Stockholm (10 daily; 2hr 40min); Uppsala (10 daily; 2hr 20min); Örebro (4 daily; 2hr 30min).

Gällivare to: Boden (3 daily; 2hr); Gothenburg (1 daily; 19hr 30min); Gävle (2 daily; 14hr); Kiruna (3 daily; 1hr); Luleå (3 daily; 2hr 20min); Stockholm (2 daily; 16hr 30min); Umeå (1 daily; 7hr); Uppsala (2 daily; 15hr 30min).

Karlstad to: Hallsberg (6 daily; 1hr 15min); Kristinehamn (11 daily; 20min); Oslo (2 daily; 3hr); Stockholm (5 daily; 2hr 40min).

Kiruna to: Abisko (3 daily; 1hr 20min); Boden (3 daily; 3hr); Gothenburg (1 daily; 20hr 30min); Luleå (3 daily; 3hr 20min); Narvik (3 daily; 3hr); Riksgränsen (3 daily; 2hr); Stockholm (2 daily; 17hr 30min); Uppsala (2 daily; 16hr 30min).

Kristinehamn to: Karlstad (12 daily; 20min); Oslo (2 daily; 3hr 30min); Stockholm (5 daily; 2hr 40min).

Mora to: Borlänge (8 daily; 1hr 20min); Leksand (8 daily; 40min); Rättvik (8 daily; 25min); Stockholm (6 daily; 4hr); Tällberg (8 daily; 30min); Uppsala (8 daily; 3hr 40min).

Östersund to: Gothenburg (1 daily; 11hr); Stockholm (6 daily; 6hr); Storlien (4 daily; 3hr); Sundsvall (5 daily; 2hr 15min); Trondheim (3 daily; 5hr 30min); Uppsala (6 daily; 5hr 40min); Åre (4 daily; 1hr 45min).

Buses

The **Inlandsexpressen** (#45) runs **north** from Mora to Gällivare via Orsa, Sveg, Åsarna, Östersund, Strömsund, Dorotea, Vilhelmina, Storuman, Sorsele, Arvidsjaur, Moskosel, Jokkmokk and Porjus. It operates daily all year round, leaving **Mora** at 8am and 2pm for Östersund, and leaving from **Östersund** at 7am for Gällivare, at 1.40pm for Arvidsjaur and at 4.55pm for Storuman. **Southbound**, a bus leaves Gällivare at 9.30am for Östersund, from Arvidsjaur at 8.35am for Östersund and from Storuman at 7.10am for Östersund. From Östersund two buses operate to Mora at 6.50m and 12.30pm.

Swebus Express (☎0200/218 218, *www.express.swebus.se*) operates a long-distance service from Falun and Borlänge to Stockholm (#890) via Uppsala. Another service (#800) runs from Falun via Borlänge and Karlstad to Gothenburg. From Karlstad and Kristinehamn, service #845 runs west to Oslo and east to Stockholm via Karlskoga and Örebro. The **Lapplandspilen** express runs overnight from Stockholm to Hemavan via Arlanda airport, Uppsala, Gävle, Söderhamn, Hudiksvall, Sundsvall, Härnösand. Kramfors, Vilhelmina, Storuman and Tärnaby. Northbound services leave Stockholm on Wed and Fri, southbound services return from Hemavan on Thurs and Sun. For information call ☎0951/333 70 or 08/440 8570.

Ammarnäs to: Sorsele (2 daily; 1hr 20min).

Arjeplog to: Arvidsjaur (4 daily; 1hr 15min).

Arvidsjaur to: Arjeplog (4 daily; 1hr).

Gällivare to: Jokkmokk (5 daily; 1hr 30min); Kiruna (4 daily; 2hr); Luleå (4 daily; 3hr 15min); Pajala (3 daily; 2hr 20min); Ritsem (3 daily; 3hr 30min).

Jokkmokk to: Gällivare (5 daily; 1hr 30min); Kvikkjokk (2 daily; 1hr 50min); Murjek (3 daily; 1hr).

Kiruna to: Gällivare (3 daily; 2hr); Karesuando (2 daily; 3hr); Luleå (2 daily; 4hr 45min); Pajala (2 daily; 3hr 15min); Nikkaluokta (3 daily; 1hr 10min).

Kvikkjokk to: Jokkmokk (2 daily; 1hr 50min).

Mora to: Grönklitt bear peak (2 daily; 45min); Idre (2 daily; 2hr 30min); Malung (2 daily; 1hr); Orsa (26 daily; 20min); Sälen (daily; 2hr 30min); Särna (4 daily; 1hr 50min).

Sorsele to: Ammarnäs (3 daily; 1hr 30min).

Storuman to: Tärnaby (4 daily; 2hr); Hemavan (3 daily; 2hr 20min).

Åsarna to: Klövsjö (3 daily; 15min); Östersund (5 daily; 1hr 20min).

Östersund to: Umeå (2 daily; 6hr).

PART THREE

THE

CONTEXTS

A BRIEF HISTORY OF SWEDEN

Sweden has one of Europe's longest documented histories, but for all the upheavals of the Viking times and the warring of the Middle Ages, the country has, in modern times, seemed to delight in taking a historical back seat. For one brief period, when Prime Minister Olof Palme was shot dead in 1986, Sweden was thrust into the limelight. Since then, however, the country has regained some of its equilibrium, though the current situation is fraught. Political infighting and domestic disharmony are threatening the one thing that the Swedes have always been proud of and that other countries aspire to: the politics of consensus, the potential passing of which is arguably of far greater importance than even the assassination of their prime minister.

EARLY CIVILIZATIONS

It was not until around 6000 BC that the **first settlers** roamed north and east into Sweden, living as nomadic reindeer hunters and herders. By 3000 BC people had settled in the south of the country and were established as farmers; from 2000 BC there are indications of a development in burial practices, with **dolmens** and **passage graves** found throughout the southern Swedish provinces. Traces also remain of the **Boat Axe People**, named after their char-

acteristic tool/weapon, shaped like a boat. The earliest horse riders in Scandinavia, they quickly held sway over the whole of southern Sweden.

During the **Bronze Age** (1500–500 BC) the Boat Axe People traded furs and amber for southern European copper and tin. Large finds of finished ornaments and weapons show a comparatively rich culture. This was emphasized by elaborate burial rites, the dead laid in single graves under mounds of earth and stone.

The deterioration of the Scandinavian climate in the last millennium before Christ coincided with the advance across Europe of the Celts, which halted the flourishing trade of the Swedish settlers. With the new millennium, Sweden made its first mark upon the Classical world. In the *Historia Naturalis*, Pliny the Elder (23–79 AD) mentioned the "island of Scatinavia" far to the north. Tacitus was more specific: in 98 AD he mentioned a powerful people who were strong in men, weapons and ships, the *Suinoes* – a reference to the **Svear**, who were to form the nucleus of an emergent Swedish kingdom by the sixth century.

The Svear settled in the rich land around Lake Mälaren and became rulers of the most of the territory comprising modern Sweden, except the south. They gave Sweden its modern name: *Sverige* in Swedish or *Svear rik*, the kingdom of the Svear. More importantly, their first dynastic leaders had a taste for expansion, trading with Gotland and holding suzerainty over the Åland Islands.

THE VIKING PERIOD

The Vikings – raiders and warriors who dominated the political and economic life of Europe and beyond from the ninth to the eleventh centuries – came from all parts of southern Scandinavia. But there is evidence that the **Swedish Vikings** were among the first to leave home, the impetus being rapid population growth, domestic unrest and a desire for new lands. Sweden being located on the eastern part of the Scandinavian peninsula, the raiders turned their attention largely eastwards, in the knowledge that the Svear had already reached the Baltic. By the ninth century, the trade routes were well established, with Swedes reaching the Black and Caspian seas and making valuable trading contact with the **Byzantine Empire**. Although more commercially inclined than their Danish and Norwegian counterparts, Swedish Vikings were quick to use force if profits were slow to materialize. From 860 onwards Greek and Muslim records relate a series of raids across the Black Sea against Byzantium, and across the Caspian into northeast Iran.

The Vikings were settlers as well as traders and exploiters, and their long-term influence was marked. Embattled Slavs to the east gave them the name **Rus**, and their creeping colonization gave one area in which the Vikings settled its modern name, Russia. Russian names today – Oleg, Igor, Vladimir – can be derived from the Swedish – Helgi, Ingvar, Valdemar.

Domestically, **paganism** was at its height; dynastic leaders would claim descent from Freyr, "God of the World". It was a bloody time: nine **human sacrifices** were offered at the celebrations held every nine years at Uppsala. Adam of Bremen recorded that the great shrine there was adjoined by a sacred grove where "every tree is believed divine because of the death and putrefaction of the victims hanging there".

Viking **law** was based on the *Thing*, an assembly of free men to which the king's power was subject. Each largely autonomous province had its own assembly and its own leaders: where several provinces united, the approval of each *Thing* was needed for any choice of leader. For centuries in Sweden, each newly elected king had to make a formal tour to receive the homage of each province.

THE ARRIVAL OF CHRISTIANITY AND THE EARLY MIDDLE AGES

Christianity was slow to take root in Sweden. Whereas Denmark and Norway had accepted the faith by the turn of the eleventh century, the Swedes remained largely heathen. Missionaries met with limited success: no Swedish king was converted until 1008, when **Olof Skötonung** was baptized. He was the first known king of both Swedes and Goths (that is, ruler of the two major provinces of Västergötland and Östergötland), and his successors were all Christians. Nevertheless, paganism retained a grip on Swedish affairs, and as late as the 1080s the Svear banished the then king, Inge, when he refused to take part in the pagan celebrations at Uppsala. By the end of the eleventh century, though, the temple at Uppsala had gone and a Christian church was built on its site. In the

1130s, Sigtuna – original centre of the Swedish Christian faith– was replaced by Uppsala as the main episcopal seat, and in 1164 Stephen, an English monk, was made the first archbishop.

The whole of the early Middle Ages in Sweden was characterized by a succession of struggles for control of a growing central power. Principally two families, the Sverkers and the Eriks, waged battle against each other throughout the twelfth century. **King Erik** was the first Sverker king to make his mark: in 1157 he led a crusade to heathen Finland, but was killed in 1160 at Uppsala by a Danish pretender to his throne. Within 100 years he was to be recognized as patron saint of Sweden, and his remains interred in the new Uppsala Cathedral.

Erik was succeeded by his son **Knut**, whose stable reign lasted until 1196, a period marked by commercial treaties and strengthened defences. Following his death, virtual civil war weakened royal power. As a result, the king's chief ministers, or **Jarls**, assumed much of the executive responsibility for running the country, so much so that when Erik Eriksson (last of the Eriks) was deposed in 1229, his administrator **Birger Jarl** assumed power. With papal support for his crusading policies he confirmed the Swedish grip on the southwest of Finland. His son, Valdemar, succeeded him but proved a weak ruler and didn't survive the family feuding after Birger Jarl's death.

In 1275, Valdemar's brother, **Magnus Ladulås**, assumed power. He earned his nickname "Ladulås", or "Barn-lock", from his having prevented the nobility from claiming maintenance at the expense of the peasantry, who travelled from estate to estate. Magnus's reign represented a peak of Swedish royal might not to be repeated for 300 years. While he was king, his enemies dissipated; he forbade the nobility to meet without his consent, and began to issue his own authoritative decrees. He also began to reap the benefits of conversion: the clergy became an educated class upon whom the monarch could rely for diplomatic and administrative duties. By the thirteenth century, there were ambitious Swedish clerics in Paris and Bologna, and the first stone churches were appearing in Sweden, the most monumental of which is the early Gothic **cathedral** built at Uppsala.

Meanwhile, the nobility had come to constitute a military class, exempt from taxation on the understanding that they would defend the crown. In the country the standard of living was still low, although an increasing population stimulated new cultivation. The forests of Norrland were pushed back, more southern heathland turned into pasture, and crop rotation introduced. Noticeable, too, was the increasing **German influence** within Sweden as the Hansa traders spread. Their first merchants settled in Visby and, by the mid-thirteenth century, in Stockholm.

THE FOURTEENTH CENTURY – TOWARDS UNITY

Magnus died in 1290, power shifting to a cabal of magnates led by **Torgil Knutsson**. As marshal of Sweden, he pursued an energetic foreign policy, conquering western Karelia to gain control of the Gulf of Finland, and building the fortress at Viborg, only lost with the collapse of the Swedish Empire in the eighteenth century.

Magnus's son Birger came of age in 1302 and soon quarrelled with his brothers Erik and Valdemar, who had Torgil Knutsson executed. They then rounded on Birger, who was forced to divide up Sweden among the three of them. An unhappy arrangement, it lasted until 1317 when Birger had his brothers arrested and starved to death in prison – an act that prompted a shocked nobility to rise against Birger and force his exile to Denmark. The Swedish nobles restored the principle of elective monarchy by calling on the three-year-old **Magnus** (son of a Swedish duke and already declared Norwegian king) to take the Swedish crown. During his minority, a treaty was concluded in 1323 with Novgorod in Russia to define the frontiers in eastern and northern Finland. This left virtually the whole of the Scandinavian peninsula (except the Danish provinces in the south) under one ruler.

Yet Sweden was still anything but prosperous. The **Black Death** reached the country in 1350, wiping out whole parishes and killing perhaps a third of the population. Subsequent labour shortages and troubled estates meant that the nobility found it difficult to maintain their positions. German merchants had driven the Swedes from their most lucrative trade routes: even the copper and iron-ore **mining** that began around this time in Bergslagen and Dalarna relied on German capital.

Magnus soon ran into trouble and was threatened further by the accession of Valdemar

Atterdag to the Danish throne in 1340. Squabbles concerning sovereignty over the Danish provinces of Skåne and Blekinge led to Danish incursions into Sweden; in 1361, Valdemar landed on Gotland and sacked **Visby**. The Gotlanders were massacred outside the city walls, refused refuge by the Hansa merchants.

Magnus was forced to negotiate and his son **Håkon** – now king of Norway – was married to Valdemar's daughter Margaret. When Magnus was later deposed, power fell into the hands of the magnates who shared out the country. Chief of the ruling nobles was the Steward **Bo Jonsson Grip**, who controlled virtually all Finland and central and southeast Sweden. Yet on his death, the nobility turned to Håkon's wife **Margaret**, already regent in Norway (for her son Olof) and in Denmark since the death of her father, Valdemar. The nobles were anxious for union across Scandinavia, to safeguard those who owned frontier estates and strengthen the crown against any further German influence. In 1388 she was proclaimed "First Lady" of Sweden and, in return, confirmed all the privileges of the Swedish nobility. Called upon to choose a male king, Margaret nominated her nephew, **Erik of Pomerania**, who was duly elected king of Sweden in 1396. As he had already been elected to the Danish and Norwegian thrones, Scandinavian unity seemed assured.

THE KALMAR UNION

Erik was crowned king of Denmark, Norway and Sweden in 1397 at a ceremony in **Kalmar**. Nominally, the three kingdoms were now in union but, despite Erik's kingship, real power remained in the hands of Margaret until her death in 1412.

Erik was at war with the Hanseatic League throughout his reign. He was vilified in popular Swedish history as an evil and grasping ruler, and the taxes he raised went on a war that was never fought on Swedish soil. He spent his time instead in Denmark, directing operations, leaving his queen Philippa (sister to Henry V of England) behind. Erik was deposed in 1439 and the nobility turned to **Christopher of Bavaria**, whose early death in 1448 led to the first major breach in the union.

No one candidate could fill the three kingships satisfactorily, and separate elections in Denmark and Sweden signalled a renewal of the infighting that had plagued the previous century. Within Sweden, unionists and nationalists skirmished, the powerful unionist **Oxenstierna** family opposing the claims of the nationalist **Sture** family, until 1470 when **Sten Sture** (the Elder) became "Guardian of the Realm". His victory over the unionists at the **Battle of Brunkeberg** (1471) – in the centre of what's now modern Stockholm – was complete, gaining symbolic artistic expression in the **statue of St George and the Dragon** that still adorns the Great Church in Stockholm.

Sten Sture's primacy fostered a new cultural atmosphere. The first **university** in Scandinavia was founded in Uppsala in 1477, with Sweden's first printing press appearing six years later. Artistically, German and Dutch influences were great, traits seen in the decorative art of the great Swedish medieval churches. Only remote **Dalarna** kept alive a native folk art tradition.

Belief in the union still existed though, particularly outside Sweden, and successive kings had to fend off almost constant attacks and blockades emanating from Denmark. With the accession of **Christian II** to the Danish throne in 1513, the unionist movement found a leader capable of turning the tide. Under the guise of a crusade to free Sweden's imprisoned archbishop Gustav Trolle, Christian attacked Sweden and killed Sture. After Christian's coronation, Trolle urged the prosecution of his Swedish adversaries (who had been gathered together under the pretext of an amnesty) and they were found guilty of heresy. Eighty-two nobles and burghers of Stockholm were executed, their bodies burned in what became known as the **Stockholm Blood Bath**. A vicious persecution of Sture's followers throughout Sweden ensued, a move that led to widespread reaction and, ultimately, the downfall of the union.

GUSTAV VASA AND HIS SONS

Opposition to Christian II was vague and disorganized until the appearance of the young **Gustav Vasa**. Initially unable to stir the locals of the Dalecarlia region into open revolt, he was on his way to Norway, and exile, when he was chased on skis and recalled, the people having had a change of heart. The chase is celebrated still in the **Vasaloppet** race, run each year by thousands of Swedish skiers.

Gustav Vasa's army grew rapidly. In 1521 he was elected regent, and subsequently, with the capture of Stockholm in 1523, king. Christian had been deposed in Denmark and the new Danish king, Frederick I, recognized Sweden's de facto withdrawal from the union. Short of cash, Gustav found it prudent to support the movement for religious reform propagated by Swedish Lutherans. More of a political than a religious **Reformation**, the result was a handover of church lands to the crown and the subordination of church to state. It's a relationship that is still largely in force today, the clergy being civil servants paid by the state.

In 1541 the first edition of the Bible in the vernacular appeared. Suppressing revolt at home, Gustav Vasa strengthened his hand with a centralization of trade and government. On his death in 1560, Sweden was united, prosperous and independent.

Gustav Vasa's heir, his eldest son **Erik**, faced a difficult time, not least because the Vasa lands and wealth had been divided among him and his brothers Johan, Magnus and Karl (an uncharacteristically imprudent action of Gustav's before his death). The Danes, too, pressed hard, reasserting their claim to the Swedish throne in the inconclusive **Northern Seven Years' War**, which began in 1563. Erik was deposed in 1569 by his brother who became **Johan III**, his first act being to end the war by the **Peace of Stettin** treaty. At home, Johan ruled more or less with the goodwill of the nobility, but matters were upset by his Catholic sympathies: he introduced Catholic liturgy and the Catholic-influenced *Red Book*. On Johan's death in 1592, his son and heir, Sigismund (who was Catholic king of Poland) agreed to rule Sweden in accordance with Lutheran practice, but failed to do so. When Sigismund returned to Poland the way was clear for Duke Karl (Johan's brother) to assume the regency, a role he filled until declared king **Karl IX** in 1603.

Karl, the last of Vasa's sons, had ambitions eastwards but was routed by the Poles and staved off by the Russians. He suffered a stroke in 1610 and died the year after. His heir was the seventeen-year-old Gustav II, better known as **Gustav II Adolf**.

The rule of Vasa and his sons made Sweden a nation, culturally as well as politically. The courts were filled with and influenced by men of learning; art and sculpture flourished. The **Renaissance** style appeared for the first time in Sweden, with royal castles remodelled – Kalmar being a fine example. Economically, Sweden remained mostly self-sufficient, its few imports being luxuries like cloth, wine and spices. With around eight thousand inhabitants, Stockholm was its most important city, although **Gothenburg** was founded in 1607 to promote trade to the west.

GUSTAV II ADOLF AND THE RISE OF THE SWEDISH EMPIRE

Sweden became a European power during the reign of **Gustav II Adolf**. Though still in his youth he was considered able enough to rule, and proved so by concluding peace treaties with Denmark (1613) and Russia (1617), the latter pact isolating Russia from the Baltic and allowing the Swedes control of the eastern trade routes into Europe.

In 1618, the **Thirty Years' War** broke out. It was vital for Gustavus that Germany should not become Catholic, given the Polish king's continuing pretensions to the Swedish crown and the possible threat it could pose to Sweden's growing influence in the Baltic. In 1629, the Altmark treaty with a defeated Poland gave Gustav control of Livonia and four Prussian sea ports, and the income this generated financed his entry into the war in 1630 on the Protestant side. After several convincing victories, Gustav pushed on through Germany, delaying an assault upon undefended Vienna. The decision cost him his life: Gustav was killed at the **Battle of Lützen** in 1632, his body stripped and battered by the enemy's soldiers. The war dragged on until the **Peace of Westphalia** in 1648.

With Gustav away at war for much of his reign, Sweden ran smoothly under the guidance of his friend and chancellor, **Axel Oxenstierna**. Together they founded a new Supreme Court in Stockholm (and did the same for Finland and the conquered Baltic provinces); reorganized the national assembly into four Estates of nobility, clergy, burghers and peasantry (1626); extended the university at Uppsala (and founded one at Åbo – modern Turku in Finland); and fostered the mining and other industries that provided much of the country's wealth. Gustav had many other accomplishments, too: he spoke five languages and

designed a new light cannon, which assisted in his routs of the enemy.

THE CAROLEANS

The Swedish empire reached its territorial peak under the **Caroleans**. Yet the reign of the last of them was to see Sweden crumble.

Following Gustav II Adolf's death and the later abdication of his daughter Christina, **Karl X** succeeded to the throne. War against Poland (1655) led to some early successes and, with Denmark espousing the Polish cause, gave Karl the opportunity to march into Jutland (1657). From there his armies marched across the frozen sea to threaten Copenhagen; the subsequent **Treaty of Roskilde** (1658) broke Denmark and gave the Swedish empire its widest territorial extent.

However, the long regency of his son and heir, **Karl XI**, did little to safeguard Sweden's vulnerable position, so extensive were its borders. On assuming power in 1672, Karl was almost immediately dragged into war: beaten by a smaller Prussian army at Brandenberg in 1675, Sweden was suddenly faced with war against both the Danes and Dutch. Karl rallied, though, to drive out the Danish invaders, and the war ended in 1679 with the reconquest of Skåne and the restoration of most of Sweden's German provinces.

In 1682, Karl XI became **absolute monarch** and was given full control over legislation and *reduktion* – the resumption of estates previously alienated by the crown to the nobility. The armed forces were reorganized too: by 1700, the Swedish army had 25,000 soldiers and twelve regiments of cavalry; the naval fleet had expanded to 38 ships and a new base had been built at **Karlskrona** (which was nearer to the likely trouble spots than Stockholm).

Culturally, Sweden began to benefit from the innovations of Gustav II Adolf. *Gymnasia* (grammar schools) continued to expand, and a second university was established at **Lund** in 1668. A national **literature** emerged, helped by the efforts of **George Stiernhielm**, father of modern Swedish poetry. **Olof Rudbeck** (1630–1702) was a Nordic polymath whose scientific reputation lasted longer than his attempt to identify the ancient Goth settlement at Uppsala as Atlantis. Architecturally, this was the age of **Tessin**, both father and son. Tessin the Elder was responsible for the glorious palace at **Drottningholm**, work on which began in 1662, as well as the cathedral at **Kalmar**. His son, Tessin the Younger, succeeded him as royal architect and was to create the new royal palace at Stockholm.

In 1697, the fifteen-year-old **Karl XII** succeeded to the throne; under him, the empire collapsed. Faced with a defensive alliance of Saxony, Denmark and Russia, there was little the king could have done to avoid eventual defeat. However, he remains a revered figure for his valiant (often suicidal) efforts to take on the rest of Europe. Initial victories against Peter the Great and Saxony led him to march on Russia, where he was defeated and the bulk of his army destroyed. Escaping to Turkey, where he remained as guest and then prisoner for four years, Karl watched the empire disintegrate. With Poland reconquered by Augustus of Saxony, and Finland by Peter the Great, he returned to Sweden only to have England declare war on him.

Eventually, splits in the enemy alliance led Swedish diplomats to attempt peace talks with Russia. Karl, though, was keen to exploit these differences in a more direct fashion. Wanting to strike at Denmark, but lacking a fleet, he besieged Fredrikshald in Norway (then united with Denmark) in 1718 — and was killed by a sniper's bullet. In the power vacuum thus created, Russia became the leading Baltic force, receiving Livonia, Estonia, Ingria and most of Karelia from Sweden.

THE AGE OF FREEDOM

The eighteenth century saw absolutism discredited in Sweden. A new constitution vested power in the Estates, who reduced the new king **Frederick I**'s role to that of nominal head of state. The chancellor wielded the real power, and under **Arvid Horn** the country found a period of stability. His party, nicknamed the "Caps", was opposed by the hawkish "Hats". The latter forced war with Russia in 1741, a disaster in which Sweden lost all of Finland and had its whole east coast burned and bombed. Most of Finland was returned with the agreement that **Adolphus Frederick** (a relation of the crown prince of Russia) would be elected to the Swedish throne on Frederick I's death. This duly occurred in 1751.

During his reign, Adolphus repeatedly tried to reassert royal power, but found that the con-

stitution was only strengthened against him. The Estates' power was such that when Adolphus refused to sign any bills, they simply utilized a stamp bearing his name. The resurrected "Hats" forced entry into the **Seven Years' War** in 1757 on the French side, another disastrous venture, as the Prussians were able to repel every Swedish attack.

The aristocratic parties were in a state of constant flux. Although elections of sorts were held to provide delegates for the *Riksdag* (parliament), foreign sympathies, bribery and bickering were hardly conducive to democratic administration. Cabals continued to rule Sweden, the economy was stagnant, and reform delayed. It was, however, an age of **intellectual and scientific advance**, surprising in a country that had lost much of its cultural impetus. **Carl von Linné**, the botanist whose classification of plants is still used, was professor at Uppsala from 1741 to 1778; **Anders Celsius** initiated the use of the centigrade temperature scale; **Carl Scheele** discovered chlorine. A royal decree of 1748 organized Europe's first full-scale **census**, a five-yearly event by 1775. Other fields flourished, too. The mystical works of **Emmanuel Swedenborg**, the philosopher who died in 1772, encouraged new theological sects; and the period encompassed the life of **Carl Michael Bellman** (1740–95), the celebrated Swedish poet (see also p.325) whose work did much to identify and foster a popular nationalism.

With the accession of **Gustav III** in 1771, the crown began to regain the ascendancy. A new constitution was forced upon a divided *Riksdag* and proved a watershed between earlier absolutism and the later aristocratic squabbles. A popular king, Gustav founded hospitals, granted freedom of worship and removed many of the state controls over the economy. His determination to conduct a successful foreign policy led to further conflict with Russia (1788–90) in which, to everyone's surprise, he managed to more than hold his own. But with the French Revolution polarizing opposition throughout Europe, the Swedish nobility began to entertain thoughts of conspiracy against a king whose growing powers they now saw as those of a tyrant. In 1792, at a masked ball in Stockholm Opera House, the king was shot by an assassin hired by the disaffected aristocracy. Gustav died two weeks later and was succeeded by his son

Gustav IV, with the country being led by a regency during his minority.

The wars waged by revolutionary France were at first studiously avoided in Sweden but, pulled into the conflict by the British, Gustav IV entered the **Napoleonic Wars** in 1805. However, Napoleon's victory at Austerlitz two years later broke the coalition and Sweden found itself isolated. Attacked by Russia the following year, Gustav was later arrested and deposed, and his uncle was elected king.

A constitution of 1809 established a liberal monarchy in Sweden, responsible to the elected *Riksdag*. Under this constitution **Karl XIII** was a mere caretaker, his heir a Danish prince who would bring Norway back to Sweden – some compensation for finally losing Finland and the Åland Islands to Russia (1809) after 500 years of Swedish rule. On the prince's sudden death, however, Marshal Bernadotte (one of Napoleon's generals) was invited to become heir. Taking the name of **Karl Johan**, he took his chance in 1812 and joined Britain and Russia to fight Napoleon. Following Napoleon's first defeat at the Battle of Leipzig in 1813, Sweden compelled Denmark (France's ally) to exchange Norway for Swedish Pomerania.

By 1814 Sweden and Norway had formed an uneasy union. Norway retained its own government and certain autonomous measures. Sweden decided foreign policy, appointed a viceroy and retained a suspensive (but not absolute) veto over the Norwegian parliament's legislation.

THE NINETEENTH CENTURY

Union under Karl Johan, or **Karl XIV** as he became in 1818, could have been disastrous. He spoke no Swedish and just a few years previously had never visited either kingdom. However, under Karl and his successor **Oscar I**, prosperity ensued. The **Göta Canal** (1832) helped commercially, and liberal measures by both monarchs helped politically. In 1845 daughters were given an equal right of inheritance. A Poor Law was introduced in 1847, restrictive craft guilds reformed, and an Education Act passed.

The 1848 revolution throughout Europe cooled Oscar's reforming ardour, and his attention turned to reviving **Scandinavianism**. It was still a hope, in certain quarters, that closer co-operation between Denmark and Sweden–Norway could lead to some sort of revived Kalmar Union. Expectations were raised with the **Crimean War** of 1854: Russia as a future threat could be neutralized. But peace was declared too quickly (at least for Sweden) and there was still no real guarantee that Sweden would be sufficiently protected from Russia in the future. With Oscar's death, talk of political union faded.

His son **Karl XV** presided over a reform of the *Riksdag* that put an end to the Swedish system of personal monarchy. The Four Estates were replaced by a representative two-house parliament along European lines. This, together with the end of political Scandinavianism (following the Prussian attack on Denmark in 1864 in which Sweden stood by), marked Sweden's entry into modern Europe.

Industrialization was slow to take root in Sweden. No real industrial revolution occurred, and development – mechanization, introduction of railways, etc – was piecemeal. One result was widespread **emigration** amongst the rural poor, who had been hard hit by famine in 1867 and 1868. Between 1860 and 1910 over one million people left for America (in 1860 the Swedish population was only four million). Given huge farms to settle, the emigrants headed for land similar to that they had left behind – to the Midwest, Kansas and Nebraska.

At home, Swedish **trade unionism** emerged to campaign for better conditions. Dealt with severely, the unions formed a confederation (1898) but largely failed to make headway. Even peaceful picketing carried a two-year prison sentence. Hand in hand with the fight for workers' rights went the **temperance movement**. The level of alcohol consumption was alarming and various abstinence programmes attempted to educate the drinkers and, if necessary, eradicate the stills. Some towns made the selling of spirits a municipal monopoly – not a big step from the state monopoly that exists today.

With the accession of **Oscar II** in 1872, Sweden continued on an even, if uneventful, keel. Keeping out of further European conflict (the Austro-Prussian War, Franco-Prussian War and various Balkan crises), the country's only worry was growing dissatisfaction in Norway with the union. Demanding a separate consular service, and objecting to the Swedish king's veto on constitutional matters, the Norwegians brought things to a head, and in 1905 declared the union invalid. The Karlstad Convention confirmed the break and Norway became independent for the first time since 1380.

The late nineteenth century was a happier time for Swedish culture. **August Strindberg** enjoyed great critical success and artists like **Anders Zorn** and **Prince Eugene** made their mark abroad. The historian **Artur Hazelius** founded the Nordic and Skansen museums in Stockholm; and the chemist, industrialist and dynamite inventor **Alfred Nobel** left his fortune to finance the Nobel Prizes. It's an instructive tale: Nobel hoped that the knowledge of his invention would help eradicate war, optimistically believing that humankind would never dare unleash the destructive forces of dynamite.

THE TWO WORLD WARS

Sweden declared strict neutrality on the outbreak of **World War I**, influenced by much sympathy within the country for Germany, stemming from the longstanding linguistic, trade and cultural links. It was a policy agreed with the other Scandinavian monarchs, but a difficult one to pursue. Faced with British demands to enforce a blockade of Germany and with the blacklisting and eventual seizure of Swedish goods at sea, the economy suffered grievously; rationing and inflation mushroomed. The **Russian Revolution** in 1917 brought further problems to Sweden. The Finns immediately declared independence, waging civil war against the Bolsheviks, and Swedish volunteers enlisted in the White Army. But a conflict of interest arose when the Swedish-speaking Åland Islands wanted a return to Swedish rule rather than stay under the victorious Finns. The League of Nations overturned this claim, granting the islands to Finland.

After the war, a Liberal–Socialist coalition remained in power until 1920, when **Branting** became the first socialist prime minister. By the time of his death in 1924, franchise had been extended to all men and women over 23, and the state-controlled alcohol system (Systembolaget) set up. Following the Depression of the late 1920s and early 1930s, conditions began to improve after a Social Democratic government took office for the fourth time in 1932. A **welfare state** was rapidly established, offering unemployment benefit, higher old-age pensions, family allowances and paid holidays. The

Saltsjöbaden Agreement of 1938 drew up a contract between trade unions and employers to help eliminate strikes and lockouts. With war again looming, all parties agreed that Sweden should remain neutral in any struggle, and so the country's rearmament was negligible, despite Hitler's apparent intentions.

World War II was slow to affect Sweden. Unlike in 1914, there was little sympathy in the country for Germany, but Sweden again declared neutrality. The Russian invasion of Finland in 1939 brought Sweden into the picture, with the Swedes providing weapons, volunteers and refuge for the Finns. Regular Swedish troops were refused though, the Swedes fearing intervention from either the Germans (then Russia's ally) or the Allies. Economically, the country remained sound – less dependent on imports than in World War I and with no serious shortages. The position became stickier in 1940 when the Nazis marched into Denmark and Norway, isolating Sweden. Concessions were made – German troop transit allowed, iron ore exports continued – until 1943–44, when Allied pressure had become more convincing than the failing German war machine.

Sweden became the recipient of countless refugees from the rest of Scandinavia and the Baltic. Instrumental in this process was **Raoul Wallenberg**, who rescued Hungarian Jews from the SS and persuaded the Swedish government to give him diplomatic status in 1944. Anything up to 35,000 Jews in Hungary were sheltered in "neutral houses" (flying the Swedish flag), and fed and clothed by Wallenberg. But when Soviet troops liberated Budapest in 1945, Wallenberg was arrested as a suspected spy and disappeared; he was later reported to have died in prison in Moscow in 1947. However, unconfirmed accounts had him alive in a Soviet prison as late as 1975; in 1989 some of his surviving relatives flew to Moscow in an unsuccessful attempt to discover the truth about his fate.

The end of the war was to engender a serious crisis of conscience in the country. Though physically unscathed, Sweden was now vulnerable to **Cold War** politics. The Finns had agreed to let Soviet troops march unhindered through Finland, and in 1949 this led neighbouring Sweden to refuse to follow the other Scandinavian countries into **NATO**. The country did, however, much to Conservative disquiet, return into Stalin's hands most of the Baltic and German refugees who had fought against Russia during the war – their fate is not difficult to guess.

POSTWAR POLITICS

The wartime coalition quickly gave way to a purely Social Democratic government committed to welfare provision and increased defence expenditure – now non-participation in military alliances did not mean a throwing-down of weapons.

Tax increases and a trade slump lost the Social Democrats seats in the 1948 general election, and by 1951 they needed to enter into a coalition with the Agrarian (later the Centre) Party to survive. This coalition lasted until 1957, when disputes over the form of a proposed extension to the pension system brought it down. An inconclusive referendum and the withdrawal of the Centre Party from government forced an election. Although the Centre gained seats and the Conservatives replaced the Liberals as the main opposition party, the Social Democrats retained a (slim) majority.

Sweden regained much of its international moral respect (lost directly after World War II) through the election of **Dag Hammarskjöld** as Secretary-General of the United Nations in 1953. His strong leadership greatly enhanced the prestige (and effectiveness) of the organization, which under his guidance participated in the solution of the 1956 Suez crisis and the 1958 Lebanon–Jordan affair. He was killed in an air crash in 1961, towards the end of his second five-year term.

Domestic reform continued unabated throughout the 1950s and 1960s. It was during these years that the country laid the foundations of its much-vaunted social security system, although at the time it didn't always bear close scrutiny. A **National Health Service** gave free hospital treatment, but only allowed for small refunds on doctor's fees and the costs of medicines and dental treatment – hardly as far-reaching as the British system introduced immediately after the war.

The Social Democrats stayed in power until 1976, when a **non-Social-Democrat coalition** (Centre–Liberal–Moderate) finally unseated them. In the 44 years since 1932, the Socialists had been an integral part of govern-ment in Sweden, their role tempered only during periods of war and coalition. It was a remarkable record, made more so by the fact that modern politics in Sweden has never been about ideology so much as detail. Socialists and non-Socialists alike share a broad consensus on foreign policy and defence matters, even on the need for the social welfare system. The argument in Sweden has instead been about economics, a manifestation of which is the issue of **nuclear power**. A second non-Socialist coalition, formed in 1979, presided over a referendum on nuclear power (1980); the pro-nuclear lobby secured victory, with the result being an immediate expansion of nuclear power generation.

OLOF PALME

The Social Democrats regained power in 1982, subsequently devaluing the *krona*, introducing a freeze on prices and cutting back on public expenditure. They lost their majority in 1985, having to rely on Communist support to get their bills through. Presiding over the party since 1969, and prime minister for nearly as long, was **Olof Palme**. He was assassinated in February 1986, and his death threw Sweden into modern European politics like no other event. Proud of their open society (Palme had been returning home unguarded from the cinema), Swedes were shocked by the gunning down of a respected politician, diplomat and pacifist. The country's social system was placed in the spotlight, and shock turned to anger and then ridicule as the months passed without his killer being caught. Police bungling was criticized and despite the theories – Kurdish extremists, right-wing terror groups – no one was charged with the murder.

Then the police came up with **Christer Pettersson**, who – despite having no apparent motive – was identified by Palme's wife as the man who had fired the shot that night. Despite pleading his innocence, claiming he was else-where at the time of the murder, Pettersson was convicted of Palme's murder and jailed. There was great disquiet about the verdict, however, both at home and abroad. Pettersson was eventually acquitted on appeal; it was believed that Palme's wife couldn't possibly be sure that the man who fired the shot was Pettersson, given that she had only seen the murderer once, on the dark night in question, and then only very briefly. The police appear to believe they had the right man all along, but in recent years some convincing evidence of the involvement of the South African secret services has come to light (Palme having been an outspoken critic of apartheid).

CARLSSON AND BILDT

Ingvar Carlsson was elected prime minister after Palme's murder, a position confirmed by the **1988 General Election** when the Social Democrats – for the first time in years – scored more seats than the three non-socialist parties combined. However, Carlsson's was a minority government, the Social Democrats requiring the support of the Communists to command an overall majority – support that had usually been forthcoming but, after the arrival of the **Green Party** into parliament in 1988, could no longer be taken for granted. The Greens and Communists jockeyed for position as protectors of the Swedish environment, and any Social Democrat measure seen to be anti-environment cost them Communist support. Perhaps more worryingly for the government, a series of **scandals** swept the country, leading to open speculation about a marked decline in public morality. The Swedish **Bofors** arms company was discovered to be involved in illegal sales to the Middle East, and early in 1990 the Indian police charged the company with paying kickbacks to politicians to secure arms contracts. In addition, there was insider dealing at the stock exchange, and the country's Ombudsman resigned over charges of personal corruption.

The real problem for the Social Democrats, though, was the economy. With a background of rising inflation and slow economic growth, the government announced an **austerity package** in January 1990. This included a two-year ban on strike action, and a wage, price and rent freeze – strong measures which astounded most Swedes, used to living in a liberal, consensus-style society. The Greens and Communists would have none of it and the Social Democrat government resigned a month later. Although the Social Democrats were soon back in charge of a minority government, having agreed to drop the most draconian measures of their programme, the problems didn't go away. The **General Election of 1991** merely confirmed that the consensus model had finally

broken down. A four-party centre-right coalition came to power, led by **Carl Bildt**, which promised tax cuts and economic regeneration, but the recession sweeping western Europe did not pass Sweden by. Unemployment hit a postwar record and in autumn 1992 – as the British pound and Italian *lira* collapsed on the international money markets – the *krona* came under severe pressure. Savage austerity measures did little to help: VAT on food was increased, statutory holiday allowances cut, welfare budgets slashed, and – after a period of intense currency speculation – short-term marginal interest rates raised to a staggering 500 percent. In a final attempt to steady nerves, Prime Minister Bildt and Carlsson, leader of the Social Democratic opposition, made the astonishing announcement that they would ignore party lines and work together for the good of Sweden – and then proceeded with drastic **public expenditure cuts**.

The fat was trimmed off the welfare state – benefits were cut, health care was opened up to private competition and education was given a painful shake-up. But it was too little too late. Sweden was gripped by its worst **recession** since the 1930s and unemployment had reached record levels of fourteen percent – the days of a jobless rate of one or two percent were well and truly gone. Poor economic growth coupled with generous welfare benefits, runaway speculation by Swedish firms on foreign real estate and the world recession all contributed to Sweden's economic woes. With the budget deficit growing faster than that of any other western industrialized country, Sweden also decided it was time to tighten up its asylum laws – in a controversial step it introduced visas for Bosnians, to try to stem the flood of refugees from the Bosnian War.

THE RETURN OF THE SOCIAL DEMOCRATS

A feeling of nostalgia for the good old days of Social Democracy swept through the country in September of 1994, and Carl Bildt's minority conservative government was booted out. Swedes voted in massive numbers to return the country's biggest party to power, headed by **Ingvar Carlsson**. He formed a government of whom half the ministers were women. Two ministers subsequently decided they no longer wanted to work in Stockholm – the Minister for

Culture upped sticks and moved her office out to Lake Vänern to be with her family, while the Minister for Employment thought he could be closer to the people by working from home in Piteå, up in the far north. Social Democracy, with all its quirks and foibles, was back.

During 1994, negotiations on Sweden's planned **membership of the European Union** were completed and the issue was put to a referendum, which succeeded in splitting Swedish public opinion right down the middle. The *Ja till EU* lobby argued that little Sweden would have a bigger voice in Europe and would be able to influence pan-European decisions if it joined. *Nej till EU* warned that Sweden would be forced to lower its standards to those of other EU countries, unemployment would rise, drug trafficking would increase, and democracy would be watered down; they also argued that the additive-free Swedish food market would be swamped with cheap additive-packed Eurosausages. But in November of that year, the Swedes followed the Austrians and the Finns in voting for membership from 1 January 1995 – by the narrowest of margins, just five percent.

In 1995, Sweden allowed **gay couples** effectively to marry, adopting a law on registered partnerships similar to that already in force in neighbouring Denmark and Norway. Same-sex couples won virtually the same rights as straight couples, the exceptions being that gay couples aren't allowed to adopt children, lesbians can't apply for artificial insemination, and gay partnership ceremonies can't be carried out in a church.

The Swedish authorities also faced the seemingly impossible task of stopping the smuggling of refugees into the country by organized gangs based, in particular, in Iraq, Afghanistan and Pakistan. However, the influx of illegal refugees was overshadowed by the problem of how to get the massive **state debt** under control. The *krona* fell to new lows as money-market fears grew that the minority government wouldn't be able to persuade parliament to approve cuts in state spending. However, the cuts were duly introduced – the welfare state was trimmed back further and new taxes were announced to try to rein in the spiralling debt. Unemployment benefit was cut to 75 percent of previous earnings, benefits for sick leave were reduced, and lower state pension payments also came into force; a new tax

was also slapped on newspapers. To try to keep public support on his side, Finance Minister **Göran Persson** reduced the tax on food from a staggering 21 percent to just 12 percent.

Just when everything appeared under control, Carlsson announced his resignation – he was retiring to spend more time with his family, a very Swedish way of bowing out. He was replaced by the bossy Persson, known to friends and enemies alike as HSB – short for *han som bestämmer*, he who decides. Following elections in September 1998, marked by a drift to the far left and the traditional right, Persson clung on to power by the skin of his teeth, remaining Prime Minister of a coalition government but with a much-reduced majority. He currently depends on support from the formerly communist Left Party, and the anti-European Greens, to push his legislation through parliament. The election was a disaster for the Social Democrats, who recorded their worst result since World War II after losing support to the far left. Many voters complained that the SPD had slashed the welfare state too far in an effort to revive the flagging economy.

INTO THE TWENTY-FIRST CENTURY

Sweden enters the new millennium with the government facing the prospect of compensating the victims of a **forcible sterilization** programme. Uncovered by the daily newspaper *Dagens Nyheter* in 1998, the Nazi-like policy had been carried out on anyone the Swedish authorities considered socially unfit: minors, the mentally retarded, the mentally ill, epileptics and alcoholics. Some operations were performed as a prerequisite for release from prison, to qualify for certain welfare benefits, or to avoid losing custody of children. It's thought that 63,000 people were subjected to the policy between 1936 and 1976; investigators have now proposed that the victims be compensated to the tune of $22,000 each.

Another issue that's very much in the public eye is that of **race relations**, with some Swedes blaming their economic troubles on the rise in the **immigrant** population (Sweden has one million immigrants in a total population of nearly nine million). Tension began to surface in the early 1990s when refugee housing centres were set on fire and immigrants in Stockholm lived in fear of the "laser man", who shot dead several dark-skinned foreigners with a laser-sighted gun. The government has done little to stamp out the violence, and neo-Nazi groups are on the rise – attacks and even murders have become all too frequent, and it's no longer unusual to hear of foreigners being forced from their homes by racial abuse and violence. As the cradle-to-grave pattern of welfare is abandoned and the gap between rich and poor widens, racial tension will continue to pose a major threat to social order. Only renewed economic prosperity is likely to bring about a change in public opinion.

The planned decommissioning of the country's four **nuclear power** stations, whose dozen reactors produce half of Sweden's energy, is set to become a focus for debate. Following the Three Mile Island incident, Swedes voted in a referendum to close all nuclear plants by 2010, but already the government is trying to wriggle out of this commitment, in view of the vast cost of making up the energy shortfall.

Sweden remained on the sidelines at the launch of the **European single currency** in January 1999. It was one of four EU countries which chose not to take part in the venture: a lack of public support for the Euro had persuaded the Swedish government that the time was not yet right to sign up. The ruling Social Democratic party has long been split over the issue, and it's likely that a referendum will have to be held before any final commitment is made. A pathetic voter turnout of just 36 percent in the European Parliamentary elections of June 1999 was further proof of the Swedish people's ambivalence towards their membership of the EU. As the new century begins, debate is likely to continue over the pros and cons of Sweden's membership of the European Union. Opinion polls now consistently show that a majority of Swedes would like to leave the EU.

SWEDISH ARCHITECTURE

PREHISTORIC BUILDINGS

Discussion of **Prehistoric** building in Sweden is mostly a matter of conjecture, for the only structures to have survived from before 1100 are ruined or fragmentary. The most impressive structures of **Bronze Age** Sweden are the numerous grassy burial barrows and the coastal burial sites (particularly apparent on the island of Gotland) that feature huge boulders cut into the shapes of a prow and stern. One of the best known of the latter type is at **Ales Stennar** on the South Skåne coast – a Swedish Stonehenge set above windy cliffs.

More substantial are the **Iron Age** dwellings from the **Celtic** period (c. 500 BC to 800 AD). The best example of a fortification from this era is at **Ismantorp** on the Baltic island of Öland. Dating from the fifth century AD, this remarkable site has limestone walls up to fifteen feet high and some eighty foundations arranged into quarters, with streets radiating like spokes of a wheel.

From the remnants of pre-Christian era houses a number of dwelling types can be identified. The open-hearth hall, for example, was a square house with an opening in the roof ridge by which light entered and smoke exited. The two-storey gallery house had an open upper loft reached via an exterior stair, while the post larder was a house on stilts allowing for ventilation and protection from vermin.

ROMANESQUE TO GOTHIC

The Christianization of Sweden is dated from 1008, the year Saint Sigfrid is said to have baptized King Olof. In the eleventh and twelfth centuries the Church and the monastic orders were the driving force behind the most significant building projects, with the most splendid example of Romanesque architecture being **Lund Cathedral**. Consecrated in 1145, when Lund was the largest town in Scandinavia and the archiepiscopal see, this monumental building was designed as a basilica with twin western towers, and boasts some tremendously rich carvings in the apsidal choir and vast crypt. The chief centre of Romanesque church building, however, was the royal town of **Sigtuna** to the northwest of Stockholm. Apart from boasting Sweden's oldest street, Sigtuna has the ruins of three eleventh-century churches – one of which, St Peter's, features the country's oldest groin vault.

Round arches, a distinctive feature of Romanesque architecture, flourished wherever limestone and sandstone were found – principally in regions of southern and central Sweden, such as Västergötland, Östergötland and Närke as well as Skåne. An easy supply of both types of stone was to be found on the Baltic island of Gotland, from where numerous baptismal fonts and richly carved sandstone decorations were exported to the mainland both to the west (Sweden proper) and the east (Swedish-controlled Finland).

Of the great monastic ruins of this period, the finest is **Alvastra Monastery** (1143), just south of Vadstena near the eastern shores of Lake Vättern. A portion of the huge barrel-vaults can still be seen, though much of the graceful structure was carted off by Vasa to build his castle at Vadstena.

Gothic architecture emerged in the thirteenth century, one of the finest early examples being the **Maria Church** in Sigtuna (1237), which with its red-brick step gables is markedly unlike the austere grey stone churches of a century earlier. The cathedral at **Strängnäs**, due east of Stockholm, is another superb piece of Gothic brick architecture, while in Sweden's third city of Malmö, the German-inspired **St Peter's Church** survives as a fine example of brick Gothic, a style often known as the Hanseatic Style. The cathedral at Uppsala (the largest in Scandinavia) is another intriguing specimen, designed by Parisian builders as a limestone structure to a French High Gothic plan, but eventually built in brick in a simpler, **Baltic Gothic** form. A good example of late Gothic is **Vadstena Convent Church**; begun in 1384, this austere limestone and brick hall was built exactly as decreed by Saint Birgitta, the founder of the church, and is flanked by her monastery and nunnery. However, the most rewarding place to explore Sweden's Gothic architecture is **Gotland** – the countryside is peppered with almost one hundred richly sculpted medieval churches, while the island's capital, the magnificently preserved Hanseatic seat of **Visby**, is replete with excellent domestic as well as ecclesiastical Gothic.

Few examples of the castles and fortifications of this period exist today. One of the best examples, **Varberg's Fortress** in Halland, just south of Gothenburg, was built by the Danes, while the best Swedish-built medieval fortifications are in Finland, a Swedish province until the early nineteenth century. One stark and beautifully unmolested example of a fortification in Danish-controlled Skåne is the castle of Glimmingehus; dating from around 1500, it was built by Adam van Duren, who also supervised the completion of the cathedral of Lund.

RENAISSANCE AND BAROQUE ARCHITECTURE

Gustav Vasa (1523–60) could not have had a more pronounced an effect on Swedish architecture. In 1527, with his reformation of the Church, Catholic properties were confiscated, and in many instances the fabric of monasteries and churches was used to build and convert castles into resplendent palaces. Wonderful examples of such Renaissance palaces are **Kalmar Castle**, in the south of Småland, and **Vadstena's Castle** – though unlike Kalmar, the latter's interior has been stripped of its original furnishings. Another magnificent Vasa palace, a glorious ruin since a nineteenth-century fire, is **Borgholm Castle** on the Baltic island of Öland.

While few churches built in this period enjoyed much prominence, one of outstanding elegance is the **Trefaldighetskyrkan** (Trinity Church) in Kristianstad, Danish king Christian IV's model Renaissance city in Skåne. With its tall windows, slender granite pillars and square

bays, it is the epitome of sophistication and simplicity.

By the time Gustav II Adolf (Gustavus Adolphus) ascended the throne in 1611, a greater opulence was becoming prevalent in domestic architecture. This tendency became even more marked in the **Baroque** area, which in Sweden commenced with the reign of Queen Kristina, art-loving and extravagant daughter of Gustav II Adolf. The first wave of Baroque, so-called Roman Baroque, was largely introduced by the German Nicodemus Tessin the Elder, who had spent much time in Italy.

The most glorious of palatial buildings from this era is **Drottningholm** outside Stockholm, a Baroque masterpiece created by Tessin for the Dowager Queen Hedvig Eleonora. Tessin's other masterpiece was **Kalmar Cathedral**, the finest church of the era and a truly beautiful vision of Italian Baroque. Nicodemus Tessin the Younger followed his father as court architect. He designed in Baroque style the new **Royal Palace at Stockholm** following the city's great fire of 1697 and the two contrasting **Karlskrona** churches: the domed rotunda of the Trefaldighetskyrkan (Trinity Church) and the barrel-vaulted basilica of the Fredrikskyrkan (Fredrik's Church). Karlskrona, like **Gothenburg**, is a fine example of regulated town planning, a discipline that came into being with the Baroque era.

THE EIGHTEENTH CENTURY

In the eighteenth century **Rococo** emerged as the style favoured by the increasingly affluent Swedish middle class, who looked to France for their models. This lightening of architectural style paved the way for the Neoclassical elegance which would follow with the reign of Gustav III, who was greatly impressed by the architecture of classical antiquity. Good examples of this clear Neoclassical mode are the **Inventariekammaren** (Inventory Chambers) at Karlskrona, and the **King's Pavilion at Haga**, designed for Gustav III by Olof Temelman, complete with Pompeiian interiors by the painter Louis Masreliez.

Another, and quite distinct aspect of late eighteenth-century taste, was the fascination with **chinoiserie**, due in large measure to the power and influence of the Gothenburg-based Swedish East India Company, founded in 1731. The culmination of this trend was the **Kina**

Slott (Chinese Pavilion) at Drottningholm, a tiny Palladian villa built in 1763 and now beautifully restored.

THE NINETEENTH CENTURY

Two vast projects dominated the Swedish architectural scene at the beginning of the nineteenth century: the remarkable **Göta Canal**, a 190-kilometre waterway linking the great lakes of Vänern and Vättern, Gothenburg and the Baltic; and the **Karlsborg Fortress** on the western shores of Vättern, designed to be an inland retreat for the royal family and the gold stocks, but abandoned ninety years later in 1909.

By the mid-nineteenth century, a new style was emerging, based on Neoclassicism but flavoured by the French-born king's taste. This **Empire Style** (sometimes referred to as the Karl Johan Style) is most closely associated with the architect **Fredrik Blom** of Karlskrona, whose most famous building is the elegant pleasure palace **Rosendal** on Djurgården, Stockholm.

During the reign of Oskar I (1844–59), while the buildings of Britain's manufacturing centres provided models for Sweden's industrial towns, the styles of the past couple of centuries began to reappear, particularly Renaissance and Gothic. One of the most glamorous examples of late nineteenth-century neo-Gothic splendour is **Helsingborg Town Hall**, built around 1890 as a riot of fairy-tale red-brick detail. The names which crop up most often in this era include Fredrik Scholander, who designed the elaborate **Stockholm Synagogue** in 1861, and Helgo Zetterwall, whose churches of the 1870s and 1880s bear a resemblance to neo-Gothic buildings in Britain and Germany.

THE TWENTIETH CENTURY

Some of the most gorgeous buildings in Sweden's cities are the result of a movement germinated in the final, resurgent years of the nineteenth century – **National Romanticism**, a movement that set out to simplify architecture and use local materials to create a distinctive Swedish style. The finest example of this new style, which was much influenced by the Arts and Crafts movement in Britain, is **Stockholm City Hall**, built in 1923 from plain brick, dressed stone and rustic timber, a combination that created a feeling of natural power. Another luscious example is Lars Israel Wahlmann's **Tjolöholm Castle**, just south of Gothenburg – a city in which some of the finest apartment buildings are those produced in the associated **Art Nouveau** style. One beautifully renovated building in full-blown Art Nouveau form is the theatre in Tivoli Park in **Kristianstad,** a town otherwise known for its Renaissance buildings.

In the second quarter of the century a new movement – **Functionalism** – burst onto the scene, making great use of "industrial" materials such as stainless steel and concrete. The leading architect of his generation was **Gunnar Asplund**, famed for Stockholm City Library (mid-1920s) and his contribution to many other buildings – his interior of the law courts in **Gothenburg's Rådhus** is a Mecca for architecture students and enthusiasts today, with its flowing laminates and curving glass and steel elevators. Asplund was also responsible for the famed **Woodland Cemetery** in Stockholm, a magnificent project that also involved another designer, **Sigmund Lewerentz**.

The creation of the welfare state went hand in hand with the ascendancy of a functionalist approach to architecture which rejected many of the individualistic features of traditional Swedish design. By the 1960s, the faceless International Style had gained dominance in Sweden, as town planning gave way to insensitive clearance of old houses and their replacement with bland high-rises. Since the late 1980s, however, restoration has become the order of the day (despite one-offs like Ralph Erskine's playful **Utkiken** office block in Gothenburg), and areas that had been left to decay – such as the old working-class area of **Haga** in Gothenburg – have been gentrified and preserved. For now, this forward-looking country is concentrating on its rear-view mirror.

SWEDISH GEOGRAPHY AND WILDLIFE

GEOGRAPHY

The appearance of Sweden's terrain owes most to the last **Ice Age**, which chafed the landscape for 80,000 years before finally melting away 9000 years ago. Grinding ice masses polished the mountains to their present form, a process particularly evident in scooped-out U-shaped mountain valleys such as **Lapporten** (The Lapp Gateway) near Abisko, in the extreme north of the country. Subsequent to the thaw, the land-mass rose, so that former coastlines are now to be seen many kilometres inland, manifested in the form of huge plains of rubble, while the plains of Sweden were created by the deposition of vast quantities of silt by the meltwater.

The northwest of the country is dominated by **mountains**, which rise well above the timber line. Deciduous trees are most prevalent, except in the most southerly regions, where coniferous forest predominates. Sweden also boasts some of Europe's most impressive **archipelagos**, such as the dramatically rugged Bohuslän Coast on the west, and Stockholm's own archipelago of 25,000 islands, many covered in meadows and forest, on the east.

The country is also known for its **lakes**, which number more than 100,000. These support rich aquatic life, mostly salmon and salmon trout, although the coastlines are where most of the country's fishing takes place.

THE NORTH

Sweden's mountainous north is home to many of the country's national parks. The mountains here are part of the **Caledonian range**, the remains of which are also to be found further south in Europe, notably in Scotland and Ireland. Formed around 400 million years ago, the range is at its highest at **Kebnekaise** and **Sarek**, both above 2000m, in the extreme northwest of Sweden. Ancient spruce, pine and birch forest extends continuously along most of the 1000-kilometre range, providing an unspoilt habitat for birds such as the golden eagle. The tree line here lies at around 800m above sea level; higher up are great expanses of bare rockface and heathland, the latter often covered in wild orchids. In addition to eagles, the bird life in these raw mountain areas includes snow bunting, golden plovers and snowy owls, while the woodlands support willow grouse and bluethroat, among other species.

CENTRAL SWEDEN

The most extensive of Sweden's plains is in the **central Swedish lowlands**, a broad belt spanning from the Bohuslän Coast in the west to Uppland and Södermanland on the east. Divided by steep ridges of rock, this former seabed was transformed by volcanic eruptions that created rocky plateaux such as Ålleberg and **Kinnekulle** (Flowering Mountain) to the west of Lidköping. The latter is Sweden's most varied natural site, comprising deciduous and evergreen woodland, meadows and pastures, and treeless limestone flats. Particularly notable among the flora here are cowslips, lady's-slipper orchids, wild cherry trees and, in early summer, the unusual and intensely fragrant bear-garlic.

Stretching some 160km north from Gothenburg up to the Norwegian border, the rough and windswept **Bohuslän Coast** possesses a considerable **archipelago** of around three thousand islands. Most of these are devoid of trees – any which existed were cut down to make into boats and houses during the great fishing era of the eighteenth century. This low coastal landscape is peppered with deeply indented bays and fjords, interspersed with islands and peninsulas. To the north of the region, the waves have weathered the pink and reddish granite, and the resulting large, smooth stone slabs with their distinctive cracks are characteristic of the province. Inland from this stretch of coast are steep hills and plateaux which are separated from one another by deep valleys, the inland continuations of the fjords. Long, narrow lakes have developed here, the Bullaren lakes being the largest. Until around a thousand years ago, these comprised a journeyable waterway from Norway to the Gota river.

One of the region's most splendid areas of virgin forest is **Tiveden National Park**, around 50km northeast of Karlsborg and just to the northwest of **Lake Vättern**, one of the two enormous lakes in this part of Sweden. The other, **Lake Vänern**, is home to nesting seabirds such as the turnstone, water pipit and Caspian tern. Fishing being a major sport in Sweden, Vänern and Vättern attract thousands each year who wish to try their luck each year. Around 1300 tonnes of fish are taken from Vänern alone each year, with commercial fisheries accounting for around eighty percent of the catch. The lake's waters were once the most productive for salmon in Sweden, but the construction of hydroelectric dams ruined the spawning grounds, and by the 1970s salmon was almost extinct here. In an effort to complement natural reproduction, salmon and brown trout have been raised in hatcheries and released into the lake with considerable success, though stocks are still not high.

The plains of central Sweden are dotted with lakes, and many wetland and migratory birds shelter here. **Kvismaren**, near Örebro, is an area of reed marsh and open waters where geese and ducks live in their thousands. **Lake Tysslingen**, just to the west of Örebro, is also well worth heading for, especially during March and April, when as many as 2500 whooper swans gather here. Just east of Vättern is **Lake Tåkern**, one of northern Europe's finest bird habitats. Like Kvismaren, it was largely drained in the nineteenth century and has an average depth of just a metre. Some 250 bird species spend time here, particularly huge flocks of geese in autumntime.

Sweden's most famous lowland lake is **Hornborgasjön**, southeast of Lidköping, which boasts 120 species of wetland birds. Every April, thousands of cranes briefly settle in the potato fields just to the south of the lake on their migration to the northern marshes.

THE SOUTH

The southernmost third of Sweden, the country's most highly populated and industrialized region, is a mixture of highlands (in the north), forests, lakes and cultivated plains. In southeastern Sweden, the forests of **Småland** have kept the furnaces of the province's glass factories alight since the seventeenth century. In the south, where the highlands give way to a gently undulating landscape, the combination of pastures and fields of rape and poppy makes for some glorious summertime scenery in **Skåne**. Though this province has a reputation for being monotonous and agricultural (true of much of its southwest), it also boasts tracts of conifers, a dramatic coastline and lush forests of beech, best seen in the first weeks of May. The province also boasts dramatic natural rock formations at **Hovs Hallar**, a stunning castellation of red rock sea-stacks on the northern coast of the Bjäre peninsula.

To the east of Skåne, the **Stenshuvud National Park** has rocky coastal hills surrounded by woods of hornbeam, alder and moorlands full of juniper. Animals untypical of Sweden live here, such as tree frogs, sand lizards and dormice.

ÖLAND AND GOTLAND

Sweden's two largest islands, **Gotland** and **Öland**, lying in the Baltic Sea to the east of the mainland, have excited botanists and geologists for centuries. When Carl von Linné first arrived in Öland in the mid-eighteenth century, he noted that the terrain was "of an entirely different countenance" from the rest of the country, and indeed the island's limestone plateaux – known as *alvar* – are unique in Sweden. In southern Öland, **Stora Alvaret** (Great Limestone Plain) is a thin-soiled heathland with vividly colourful flora in spring and summer – Öland rockrose, red kidney vetch and blue globe daisy are among the unusual flowers which grow here. Birdlife is also rich and varied on Öland. The **Öland goose**, one of the oldest domesticated breeds in the country, originated here from interbreeding with wild geese. **Ottenby**, on the island's southern point, is Öland's largest nature reserve, supporting golden oriole as well as fallow deer, which have lived here since the time when the entire island was a royal hunting ground.

Gotland is the more dramatic of the two great islands, thanks to its tall sea-stacks, the remains of old coral reefs which loom like craggy ghosts along the island's shoreline. Like Öland, Gotland sustains rich floral life, including at least 35 species of orchid. This is also the home of the **Gotland sheep**, an ancient (and now rare) breed characterized by a dark, shaggy coat and powerful, bow-shaped horns. Nearby, off Gotland's western shores, is **Stora Karlsö**, an island breeding ground for guillemot and razorbill.

FAUNA

Stretching over two thousand kilometres from the northern temperate zone into the Arctic Circle, Sweden is unsurprisingly home to a considerable diversity of flora and **fauna**. To see endangered species from Sweden in conditions approaching those in the wild, it's worth visiting **Nordens Ark**, near Lysekil on the Bohuslän coast. A not-for-profit breeding park, it is home to wolves, wolverines and lynxes, as well as to lesser pandas and snow leopards from the Himalayas.

Sweden's attitude to wild animals is in marked contrast to that of, say, Britain, in that Swedes deeply concerned with animal rights will often also be in support of **hunting**, regarding the practice as working hand in hand with nature conservation. Elk, bear, deer, fox and grouse are all hunted during specified seasons.

MAMMALS

The animal with the highest profile in Sweden is the **reindeer**: "reindeer crossing" signs are common all over Sweden, as is serious damage to vehicles involved in collisions with them. Throughout the year, reindeer are to be seen not just on mountainsides but also in the wooded valleys and lowlands throughout the country, except for Gotland and in the far north.

The most common deer in the country is the **roe deer**, one of the smaller breeds; it numbers around a million in Sweden. Roe deer are much more likely to be seen in the south and centre of the country than the north. One of the best places to see it, as well as **red deer** and (in particular) **elk** (a close relation of the American moose) is the plateau of Halleberg, just south of Vanersborg in Västergötland. Used as a royal hunting ground for elk since the 1870s, Halleberg has around 140 of these creatures in winter and 200 in summer. The elk, which is the largest species of deer in the world, can be over 2m tall and weigh up to five hundred kilogrammes. The best times to see elk and deer are dawn and dusk, when they emerge to seek food in cleared areas. Also seen in this area are Swedish **woodland hare**, **badgers** and even **lynx** – the only member of the cat family living in the wild in Sweden. It lives off roe deer and hare, and is characterized by its triangular tufted ears. Although it's a rare practice today, some provinces still organise small scale hunting of the creature.

Sweden's **wolves** have been hunted almost to extinction. A rare few – believed to be less

---

ALLEMANSRÄTTEN

The relationship between the Swedish people and their environment is characterized by an intense reverence – as one might expect of the country that produced the world-renowed botanist Carl von Linné, whose system of plant classification is still used today. Many Swedes regard regular communion with the lakes and forests as an absolute necessity, and their respect for the natural world is encapsulated by the **Allemansrätten** or **Right of Common Access**. An unwritten right, it permits anyone to walk anywhere and spend a night anywhere, as long as this does not infringe the privacy of home-owners or impinge upon land where crops

are grown. The only other exceptions are nature reserves and protected wildlife zones at sensitive times of the year, such as bird sanctuaries, which are entirely closed to visitors during breeding season.

The general rules of the Allemansrätten, which appear in English-language leaflets all over the country, forbid such actions as tree felling, the removal of twigs or bark from living trees, the lighting of fires in dry terrain or on bare rock, and off-road driving (unless there is lying snow). Fishing is allowed along the shores of the country's five largest lakes; in all other bodies of water, a permit to fish is required.

than forty – still live in the north, and can on rare occasions be heard howling in groups. Thanks to intensive efforts at conservation, the wolf population is slowly beginning to recover. Also found in the north are **Arctic foxes**, which have adapted to the conditions of extreme cold; they live only in the mountain regions above the tree line. Although the animals were common in Sweden at the beginning of the twentieth century, excessive hunting for their fur has reduced numbers dramatically. Ironically, the recent minor decline in the **fur trade**, due in part to animal rights activism, has posed a danger to Arctic foxes. A five-year project, set to run until 2002, aimed at conserving the Arctic fox in Sweden and Finland has found that where red foxes (also hunted for their fur), are left uncontrolled, they dominate over Arctic foxes, even preying on juvenile Arctic foxes.

Far closer to extinction than the Arctic fox are **wolverines**, placed under protection in 1969; there are now just one hundred individuals left in Sweden, mostly in the north and mountain regions. One of their difficulties is that they depend on offal left by other predators, mainly wolves. The near demise of the wolf has clearly put considerable pressure on wolverines; consequently, wolverines have been known to damage the tame reindeer herds owned by the *Sámi* people.

The Swedish **brown bear** may grow to 2.3 metres in length and weigh around 350 kilogrammes. Though rarely seen, they still live in the northernmost reaches of Sweden; it is estimated that there are around seven hundred of them in the wild.

BIRDS

While Sweden is not particularly noted for its avian wildlife, the variety of its **native birds** is considerable. Sweden is also a staging post for great numbers of **migratory birds**, which make spectacular viewing on their way between the far north and hotter climes.

Unsurprisingly, the country's coastlines are thick with seagulls, ducks and herons, while swans make beautiful additions to inland lakes and coastal inlets. Kingfishers and dippers can be found around the country's rivers and streams. The mountain regions of Sweden are home to capercaillie, mountain grouse, black grouse and a range of owls. Two varieties of **eagle** are seen throughout the country, though

their numbers are small, while hawks and buzzards make an occasional appearance. Many of these birds are threatened with extinction; and so the hunting of all birds of prey is forbidden.

Among the finest bird areas in the country is **Getterön Nature Reserve**, just a few kilometres north of Varberg on the west coast of Halland. The area is seen as hugely valuable for birdlife, due to its large mosaic of wetlands in an otherwise exploited region. The mix of open water and dramatic clumps of reeds and rushes here make an ideal home for **nesting birds**. Among the rare birds which nest at Getterön are the black-tailed godwit and the southern dunlin; also found here are lapwings, redshanks, skylarks and yellow wagtail. The number of birds peaks in April and May (though spring migration begins as early as February) and from August to October. April is the time to see the most ducks; in May, flocks of dunlins and other waders gather in the bay. The last waders head northwards in June, while female curlews and spotted redshanks meet them heading south. This latter southbound migration goes on through July and August. In autumn, Canada geese and greylag geese arrive. During the winter months it's possible to see white-tailed eagles; peregrine falcons are seen all year.

FISH AND REPTILES

Fish play an important role in Swedish life, with almost every restaurant boasting about its local, fresh fish, and fishing a national sport. Pike perch, roach, bream and carp are the most common types of fish in all but northern Swedish lakes, which are home to salmon trout and char. Lake Vättern, being particularly cold for its latitude, is also rich in Arctic char. The country's rivers are filled with trout, salmon and salmon trout. Off the coasts can be found shoals of herring, mackerel, Baltic herring, spiny dogfish and some sharks. **Shellfish** also appear on thousands of tables throughout the land, with crab, lobster, crayfish and oyster all harvested from offshore waters.

The only poisonous **snake** found in Sweden is the **viper**, its bite only comparable to that of a wasp. **Grass snakes** tend to live near the water's edge; in Sweden, neither grass snakes nor vipers reach more than 1m in length. **Frogs** and **toads** are very common, particularly in southern and central Sweden.

BOOKS

English-language books on Sweden are remarkably scant. The books listed below are the pick of a meagre crop; those that are currently out of print (o/p) shouldn't be too difficult to track down. The UK publisher is given first in each listing, followed by the publisher in the US, unless the title is available in one country only, in which case we've specified which country. Where only one publisher is given, with no country indicated, it means the same company publishes the title in both the US and the UK.

TRAVEL AND GENERAL

James William Barnes Steveni, *Unknown Sweden* (Hurst & Blackett, o/p). A fascinating account of journeys through Sweden in the early years of the twentieth century. With its excellent illustrations, this book is a superb social record.

Mary Wollstonecraft, *A Short Residence in Sweden, Norway and Denmark* (Penguin). A searching account of Wollstonecraft's three-month solo journey through southern Scandinavia in 1795.

HISTORY AND MYTHOLOGY

H.R. Ellis Davidson, *The Gods and Myths of Northern Europe* (Penguin). A Who's Who of Norse mythology, including some useful profiles of the more obscure gods. Displaces the classical deities and their world as the most relevant mythological framework for northern and western European culture.

Eric Elstob, *Sweden: A Traveller's History* (Boydell; Rowman & Littlefield; o/p). An introduction to Swedish history from the year dot to

the twentieth century, with useful chapters on art, architecture and cultural life.

Michael Roberts, *The Early Vasas: A History of Sweden 1523–1611* (Cambridge University Press, o/p). A clear account of the period. Complements the same author's *Gustavus Adolphus and the Rise of Sweden* (Addison Wesley Longman) which, more briefly and enthusiastically, covers the period from 1612 to Gustavus's death in 1632.

ART, ARCHITECTURE AND DESIGN

Henrik O. Andersson and Fredric Bedoire, *Swedish Architecture 1640–1970* (Swedish Museum of Architecture). With superb colour plates, this is the definitive survey of the subject, with parallel English/Swedish text.

Katrin Cargill *Creating the Look: Swedish Style* (Frances Lincoln; Pantheon Books). A great book to help you create cheerful Swedish peasant interiors. Includes lots of evocative photographs by Christopher Drake and a long list of stockists of the materials you'll need. A practical guide, the book includes some background information to place the designs in context.

Görel Cavalli-Björkman and Bo Lindwall, *The World of Carl Larsson* (Simon & Schuster, US). A charming and brilliantly illustrated volume, charting the life and work of one of Sweden's most admired painters.

Barbro Klein and Mats Widbom, *Swedish Folk Art* (Abrams). A lavishly illustrated and richly documented history of its subject, relating ancient crafts to modern-day design ideas.

Mereth Lindgren, Louise Lyberg, Birgitta Sandström and Anna Greta Wahlberg, *A History of Swedish Art* (Coronet, US). A fine overview of Swedish painting, sculpture and, to a lesser extent, architecture, from the Stone Age to the present. Clear text and good, mostly monochrome, illustrations.

Lars Sjöberg and Ursula Sjöberg, *The Swedish Room* (Frances Lincoln; Pantheon Books). An exceptionally well-documented journey through developments in the design of Swedish homes, covering the period from 1640 through to the nineteenth century (stopping short of National Romanticism, Art Nouveau and Functionalism). The book sets design patterns in their historical and political context, and includes beautiful photographs by Ingalill

Snitt. There's also a section on achieving classic Swedish decor effects, and a good list of suppliers of decorative materials, though without exception all are in America.

LITERATURE

Stig Dagerman, *A Burnt Child* (Quartet, UK). One of the author's best works, this intense, short narrative concerns the reactions of a Stockholm family to the death of the mother. A prolific young writer, Dagerman had written short stories, travel sketches, four novels and four plays by the time he was 26; he committed suicide in 1954 at the age of 31.

Kerstin Ekman, *Blackwater* (Vintage; St Martin's Press). A tightly written thriller by one of Sweden's most highly rated novelists. Set in the forests of northern Sweden, the plot concerns a woman whose lover is murdered; years later, she sees her daughter wrapped up in the arms of the person she suspects of the killing.

Robert Fulton (trans.), *Preparations for Flight* (Forest Books, UK). Eight Swedish short stories from the last 25 years, including two rare prose outings by the poet Niklas Rådström.

Lars Gustafsson, *The Death of a Beekeeper* (Harvill; New Directions). Keenly observed novel structured around the journal of a dying schoolteacher-turned-beekeeper.

P.C. Jersild, *A Living Soul* (Norvik Press; Dufour). The work of one of Sweden's best novelists, this is a social satire based around the "experiences" of an artificially produced, bodyless human brain floating in liquid. Entertaining, provocative reading.

Selma Lagerlöf, *The Wonderful Adventures of Nils* (Dover). Lagerlöf is Sweden's best-loved children's writer, and it's an indication of her standing in her native land that she's featured on the 20kr banknote. The tales of Nils Holgren, a little boy who flies all over the country on the back of a magic goose, are continued in *The Further Adventures of Nils* (Tomten, US).

Sara Lidman, *Naboth's Stone* (Norvik Press; Dufour). A novel set in 1880s Västerbotten, in Sweden's far north, charting the lives of settlers and farmers as the industrial age – and the railway – approaches.

Torgney Lindgren, *Merab's Beauty* (HarperCollins). Short stories capturing the distinctive flavour of family life in northern Sweden.

Vilhelm Moberg, *The Emigrants* (Minnesota Historical Society, US). A series of highly poignant novels dealing with the emigration of some one million Swedes to the US in the second half of the nineteenth century. Moberg himself stayed behind, and is regarded by Swedes as the finest chronicler of his times.

Leo Perutz, *The Swedish Cavalier* (Harvill; Arcade). Two men meet in a farmer's barn in 1701 – one is a thief, the other an army officer on the run. An adventure story with a moral purpose.

Agneta Pleijel, *The Dog Star* (Peter Owen, UK). By one of Sweden's leading writers, *The Dog Star* is the powerful tale of a young girl's approach to puberty. Pleijel's finest novel yet, full of fantasy and emotion.

Clive Sinclair, *Augustus Rex* (Andre Deutsch, UK). August Strindberg dies in 1912 – and is then brought back to life by the Devil in 1960s Stockholm. Bawdy, imaginative and very funny treatment of Strindberg's well-documented neuroses.

August Strindberg, *Plays: One* (including *The Father*, *Miss Julie* and *The Ghost Sonata*); *Plays: Two* (*The Dance of Death*, *A Dream Play* and *The Stronger*) (both Methuen). The major plays by the country's most provocative and influential playwright, scrutinizing and analysing the roles of the sexes both in and out of marriage. Only a fraction of Strindberg's sixty plays, twelve historical dramas, five novels, numerous short stories, autobiographical volumes and poetry has been translated into English.

Bent Söderberg, *The Mysterious Barricades* (Peter Owen; Dufour). In which a leading Swedish novelist writes of the Mediterranean during the wars – a part of the world he's lived in for many years.

Hjalmar Söderberg, *Short Stories* (Norvik Press; Dufour). Twenty-six short stories from the stylish pen of Söderberg (1869–1941). Brief, ironic and eminently suited to dipping into.

BIOGRAPHY

Peter Cowie, *Ingmar Bergman* (Andre Deutsch; Scribner; both o/p). A fine critical biography of the great director; a well-written, sympathetic account of Bergman's life and career. Bergman's major screenplays are published by Marion Boyars.

Michael Meyer, *Strindberg* (Oxford University Press). The best and most approachable biography of the tormented genius of Swedish literature.

Andrew Oldham, Tony Calder and Colin Irwin, *Abba* (Pan; Music Book Services). The last word on the band, here described as the "greatest composers of the twentieth century".

Alan Palmer, *Bernadotte* (John Murray, o/p). A lively and comprehensive biography of Napoleon's marshal, who later became King Karl XIV Johan of Sweden.

A BRIEF GUIDE
TO SWEDISH

For most foreigners Swedish is nothing more than an obscure, if somewhat exotic, language spoken by a few million people on the fringe of Europe, and whose most famous speaker is the Swedish chef from TV's *The Muppet Show*. Many travellers take their flirtation with the odd hurdy-gurdy sounds of the language no further than that, since there is no need whatsoever to speak Swedish to enjoy a visit to Sweden. Recent surveys have shown that 95 percent of Swedes speak English to some degree. However, Swedish deserves closer inspection, and if you master even a couple of phrases you'll meet with nothing but words of encouragement.

Despite what you might think, Swedish is one of the easiest languages for English speakers to pick up; its grammar has developed along similar lines to that of English and therefore has no case system to speak of (unlike German). Many everyday words are common to both English and Swedish, having been brought over to Britain by the Vikings, and anyone with a knowledge of northern English or lowland Scottish dialects will already be familiar with a good number of Swedish words and phrases. Your biggest problem is likely to be perfecting the "tones", different rising and falling accents which Swedish uses (the hurdy-gurdy sounds you're no doubt already familiar with).

Swedish is a Germanic language and, as such, is related to English in much the same way as French is related to Italian. However its closest cousins are fellow members of the North Germanic group of tongues: Danish, Faroese,

Icelandic, Norwegian. Within that sub-group, Swedish is most closely linked to Danish and Norwegian, and the languages are mutually intelligible to quite an extent. A knowledge of Swedish will therefore open up the rest of Scandinavia to you; in fact Swedish is the second official language of Finland. Unlike Danish though, Swedish spelling closely resembles pronunciation, which means you stand a sporting chance of being able to read words and make yourself understood.

BOOKS

Swedes are always keen to practise their English, so if you're intent on learning Swedish perseverance is the name of the game. The excellent *Colloquial Swedish* by Philip Holmes and Gunilla Serin (published by Routledge) is the best **textbook** around and should be your starting point. It will guide you through everything from pronunciation to the latest slang. Make sure you buy the companion cassette so you get a chance to hear the spoken language.

Of the handful of **grammars** available, by far the most useful is the six-hundred-page *Swedish: A Comprehensive Grammar* by Philip Holmes and Ian Hinchliffe (Routledge) which is head and shoulders above anything else on the market. An abridged version, *Essentials of Swedish Grammar* (Routledge), is handy as a first step on the road to learning the language.

Until just a couple of years ago, it was virtually impossible to buy an English–Swedish **dictionary** outside Sweden; now most bookshops will supply the *Collins Gem Swedish Dictionary*, perfect for checking basic words whilst travelling around. It's also available in Sweden under the title *Norstedts engelska fickordbok* but costs twice as much. With larger dictionaries, the choice in Sweden is greater than outside (unfortunately, so are the prices). *Norstedts lilla engelska ordbok* will give you 80,000 references in one book; but one of the best dictionaries, and much more extensive, is *Norstedts svensk–engelska* (82,000 words and phrases) and its companion *Engelsk–svenska* (60,000). Both volumes together cost around 600–700kr but are often available at a discount. Incidentally, the Swedish word for dictionary, *ordbok* – meaning "wordbook" – is a good example of how Swedish builds new words from existing ones.

Of the **phrasebooks**, the most useful is *Swedish Phrase Book and Dictionary* (Berlitz); alternatively, you can use the forty-page

Swedish section in the *Scandinavian Phrase Book and Dictionary* (also Berlitz).

Swedish **nouns** can have one of two **genders**: common or neuter. The good news is that three out of four nouns have the common gender. The **indefinite article** precedes the noun, and is *en* for common nouns, and *ett* for neuter nouns. The **definite** article, as in all the other Scandinavian languages, is suffixed to the noun, for example, *en katt*, a cat, but *katten*, the cat; *ett hus*, a house, but *huset*, the house. The same principle applies in the plural: *katter*, cats, but *katterna*, the cats; *hus*, houses, but *husen*, the houses. The plural definite article suffix is therefore *-na* for common nouns and *-en* for neuter nouns (and confusingly identical with the definite article suffix for common nouns).

Forming **plurals** is possibly the most complicated feature of Swedish. Regular plurals take one of the following endings: *-or, -ar, -er, -r, -n,* or no ending at all. Issues like the gender of a word, whether its final letter is a vowel or consonant, and stress can all affect which plural ending is used. You should learn each noun with its plural, but to be honest, the chances are

BASIC PHRASES

yes; no	*ja; nej*	open; closed	*öppet; stängt*
hello	*hej/tjänare*	women; men	*kvinnor; män*
good morning	*god morgon*	toilet	*toalett*
good afternoon	*god middag*	bank; change	*bank; växel*
good night	*god natt*	post office	*posten*
today/tomorrow	*idag/imorgon*	stamp(s)	*frimärke(n)*
please	*tack/var så god*	where are you from?	*varifrån kommer du?*
here you are/		I'm English	*jag är engelsman/*
you're welcome	*var så god*		*engelska*
thank you (very much)	*tack (så mycket)*	Scottish	*skotte*
where?; when?	*var; när/ hur dags*	Welsh	*walesare*
what?; why?	*vad; varför*	Irish	*irländare*
how (much)?	*hur (mycket)*	American	*amerikan*
I don't know	*jag vet inte*	Canadian	*kanadensare*
do you know? (a fact)	*vet du...?*	Australian	*australier*
could you...?	*skulle du kunna...?*	a New Zealander	*nyzeeländare*
sorry; excuse me	*förlåt; ursäkta*	what's your name?	*vad heter du?*
here; there	*här; där*	what's this called in	*vad heter det här på*
near; far	*nära; avlägsen*	Swedish?	*svenska?*
this; that	*det här; det där*	do you speak English?	*talar du engelska?*
now; later	*nu; senare*	I don't understand	*jag förstår inte*
more; less	*mera; mindre*	you're speaking too fast	*du talar för snabbt*
big; little	*stor; liten*	how much is it?	*hur mycket kostar det?*

GETTING AROUND

how do I get to...?	*hur kommer jag till...?*	what time does it leave?	*hur dags går det?*
left; right	*till vänster/ till höger*	what time does it arrive	*hur dags är det*
straight ahead	*rakt fram*	in...?	*framme i...?*
where is the bus station?	*var ligger*	which is the road to...?	*vilken är vägen till...?*
	busstationen?	where are you going?	*vart går du?*
the bus stop for...	*busshållplatsen till...*	I'm going to...	*jag går till...*
railway station	*järnvägsstationen*	that's great, thanks a lot	*jättebra, tack så*
where does the bus to	*varifrån går bussen*		*mycket*
.... leave from?	*till...?*	stop here please	*stanna här, tack*
is this the train for	*åker detta tåg till*	ticket to	*biljett till*
Gothenburg?	*Göteborg?*	return ticket	*tur och retur*

you'll forget the plural ending and get it wrong. Swedes have no apparent difficulty in forming plurals and can't understand why you find it so hard. Show them the plurals section in any grammar and savour their reaction.

Adjectives cause few problems. They generally precede the noun they qualify and agree in gender and number with it; *en ung flicka*, a young girl (ie no ending on the adjective); *ett stort hus*, a big house; *fina böcker*, fine books. The *-a* ending is also used after the definite article irrespective of number, *det stora huset*, the big house, *de fina böckerna*, the fine books; and also after a posses-

sive, once again irrespective of number, *min stora trädgård*, my big garden, or *stadens vackra gator*, the town's beautiful streets.

Verbs are something of a mixed blessing. There is only one form for all persons, singular and plural, in all tenses, which means there are no irksome endings to remember: *jag är* – I am, *du är* – you (singular) are, *ni är* – you (plural) are, *han/vi är* – we are, *de är* – they are. All verbs take the auxiliary *att ha* (to have) in the perfect and pluperfect tenses (eg *jag har gått* – I have gone, *jag har talat* – I have spoken; *jag hade gått* – I had gone, *jag hade talat* – I had spoken). The price for

ACCOMMODATION

where's the youth hostel?	*var ligger vandrarhemmet?*	it's too expensive, I don't want it now	*det är för mycket, jag tar det inte*
is there a hotel round here?	*finns det något hotell i närheten?*	can I/we leave the bags here until…?	*kan jag/vi få lämna väskorna här till…?*
I'd like a single/ double room	*jag skulle vilja ha ett enkelrum/dubbelrum*	have you got anything cheaper?	*har du något billigare?*
can I see it?	*får jag se det?*	with a shower	*med dusch*
I'll take it	*jag tar det*	can I/we camp here?	*får jag/vi tälta här?*
how much is it a night?	*hur mycket kostar det per natt?*		

DAYS AND MONTHS

Sunday	*söndag*	April	*april*
Monday	*måndag*	May	*maj*
Tuesday	*tisdag*	June	*juni*
Wednesday	*onsdag*	July	*juli*
Thursday	*torsdag*	August	*augusti*
Friday	*fredag*	September	*september*
Saturday	*lördag*	October	*oktober*
January	*januari*	November	*november*
February	*februari*	December	*december*
March	*mars*		

Days and months are never capitalized.

THE TIME

what time is it?	*vad är klockan?*	one forty	*tjugo i två*
it's….	*den/hon är…*	one forty-five	*kvart i två*
at what time…?	*hur dags…?*	one fifty-five	*fem i två*
at…	*klockan…*	two o'clock	*klockan två*
midnight	*midnatt*	noon	*klockan tolv*
one in the morning	*klockan ett på natten*	in the morning	*på morgonen*
ten past one	*tio över ett*	in the afternoon	*på eftermiddagen*
one fifteen	*kvart över ett*	in the evening	*på kvällen*
one twenty-five	*fem i halv två*	in ten minutes	*om tio minuter*
one thirty	*halv två*	ten minutes ago	*för tio minuter sedan*
one thirty-five	*fem över halv två*		

continued overleaf

NUMBERS

1	*ett*	10	*tio*	19	*nitton*	80	*åttio*
2	*två*	11	*elva*	20	*tjugo*	90	*nittio*
3	*tre*	12	*tolv*	21	*tjugoett*	100	*hundra*
4	*fyra*	13	*tretton*	22	*tjugotvå*	101	*hundraett*
5	*fem*	14	*fjorton*	30	*trettio*	200	*två hundra*
6	*sex*	15	*femton*	40	*fyrtio*	500	*fem hundra*
7	*sjö*	16	*sexton*	50	*femtio*	1000	*tusen*
8	*åtta*	17	*sjutton*	60	*sextio*	10,000	*tio tusen*
9	*nio*	18	*arton*	70	*sjuttio*		

GLOSSARY OF SWEDISH WORDS AND PHRASES

bastu	sauna	*rabatt*	discount
berg	mountain	*rea*	sale
bio	cinema	*ren*	reindeer
björn	bear	*restaurangsvagn*	train buffet
bokhandel	bookshop	*riksdagshus*	parliament building
bro	bridge	*rådhuset*	town hall
brygga	jetty/pier	*simhallen*	swimming pools
båt	boat/ferry	*sjö*	lake
cyckelstig	cycle path	*skog*	forest
dal	valley	*slott*	palace/castle
domkyrka	cathedral	*smörgåsbord*	spread of different dishes
drottning	queen	*sovvagn*	sleeping car
extrapris	special offer	*spår*	track
färja	ferry	*stadshus*	city hall
färjeläge	ferry terminal/berth	*stora*	big
gamla	old	*strand*	beach
gamla stan	old town	*stuga*	cottage
gata (g.)	street	*stängt*	closed
gränd	alley	*torg*	square/market place
hamn	harbour	*tunnelbana*	underground (metro)
järnvägsstation	railway station	*tåg*	train
kapell	chapel	*universitet*	university
klockan (kl.)	o'clock	*väg (v.)*	road
kung	king	*vrakpris*	bargain
kyrka	church	*ångbåt*	steamboat
liggvagn	couchette car	*älg*	elk
lilla	little	*öppet*	open
muséet	museum	*öppettider*	opening hours
pressbyrå	newsagent		

this simplicity is unfortunately four different conjugations which are distinguished by the way they form their past tense. Verbs are always found as the second idea in any Swedish sentence, as in German, which can often lead to the inversion of verb and subject. However there are no "verb scarers" in Swedish which are responsible for the suicidal pile-up of verbs which often occurs at the end of German sentences.

How to say "you" in many Germanic languages poses considerable problems – not so in Swedish. In the 1960s a wave of liberalism and equality swept through the language and the honorific form, *ni* (the equivalent of *Sie* in German), was dropped in favour of the more informal *du*. However the change in the language has left many elderly people behind, and you'll often still hear them using *ni* to people they don't know very well. In modern Swedish *ni* is really only used to express the plural of you (the equivalent of both *ihr* and plural *Sie* in German).

PRONUNCIATION

Rest assured – you're never going to sound Swedish, for not only can **pronunciation** be difficult, but the sing-song **melody** of the language is beyond the reach of most outsiders. Swedish uses two quite different **tones** on words of two or more syllables – one rises throughout the entire word, while the other falls in the middle before peaking at the end of the word. It's this second down-then-up accent which gives Swedish its distinctive melody. Unfortunately identical words can have two different meanings depending on which tone is used. For example, *fem ton* with a rising accent throughout each word means "five tons", whereas *femton* where the accent dips during the *fem-* and rises throughout the *-ton* means "fifteen". A mistake in tones can often have hilarious consequences! Equally, *komma* with a rising tone throughout means "comma", whereas *komma* with a falling tone followed by a rising tone is the verb "to come". In short, try your best, but don't worry if you get it wrong. Swedes are used to foreigners saying one word but meaning another and will generally understand what you're trying to say.

Vowels can be either long (when followed by one consonant or at the end of a word) or short (when followed by two consonants). Unfamiliar or unusually spelt vowels are as follows:

ej as in m**a**te

y as in **ew**e

å when short, as in h**o**t; when long, sort of as in r**aw**

ä as in g**e**t

ö as in f**u**r

Consonants are pronounced approximately as in English except:

g before e, i, y, ä or ö as in **y**et; before a, o, u, å as in **g**ate; sometimes silent

j, dj, gj, lj as in **y**et

k before e, i, y, ä or ö approximately as in **sh**ut and similar to German **ch** in "ich", otherwise hard

qu as in **kv**

rs as in **sh**ut (also when one word ends in *r* and the next begins with *s*, for example *för stor*, pronounced "fur shtoor")

s as in **s**o (never as English z)

sj, skj, stj approximately as in **sh**ut (different from soft k sound and more like an sh-sound made through the teeth but with rounded lips – this sound takes much practice; see below)

tj approximately as in **sh**ut and with same value as a soft **k**

z as in **s**o (never as in **z**oo)

The soft sound produced by **sj, skj** and **stj** is known as the **sj-sound** and is a peculiarity of Swedish. Unfortunately it appears widely and its pronunciation varies with dialect and individual speakers. To confuse matters further there are two variants, a back sj-sound formed by raising the back of the tongue and a front sj-sound formed by raising the middle or front of the tongue. Gain instant respect by mastering this Swedish tongue twister: *sjuttiosju sjuksköterskor skötte sju sjösjuka sjömän på skeppet till Shangai*, meaning seventy-seven nurses nursed seven seasick sailors on the ship to Shanghai.

SWEDISH SAYINGS

Just two generations ago Sweden was a predominantly rural country which had yet to experience the Industrial Revolution. As a result the language is still full of phrases and expressions which refer to the Swedish countryside. When something goes wrong, you'll often hear *det gick åt skogen*, literally "it went to the forest", the implication being that the uncivilized world began at the forest edge; hence also *dra åt skogen!*, "be off to the forest", which is a polite way of telling someone to leave you alone. Animals also feature in Swedish phrases: *gå som katten kring het gröt* is cats walking around hot porridge, as opposed to the hot tin roofs familiar to their English cousins. Equally, every good Swede is told *sälj inte skinnet förrän björnen är skjuten*, "don't sell the skin before the bear is shot". Swedes don't talk of the devil but instead of the trolls (the Swedish word for "devils", *djävlar*, is one of the worst swear-words in the language). When they're in a crowd, Swedes are never packed like sardines but *packade som sillar* – like herrings. If a Swede is singularly unimpressed about something, it's definitely *ingenting att hänga i julgran*, literally "nothing to hang in the Christmas tree".

INDEX

In Swedish, the letters Å, Ä and Ö are considered to come at the end of the alphabet, after Z; the entries in this index are arranged accordingly.

Stay in touch with us!

ROUGHNEWS **is Rough Guides' free newsletter. In four issues a year we give you news, travel issues, music reviews, readers' letters and the latest dispatches from authors on the road.**

I would like to receive ROUGH*NEWS*: please put me on your free mailing list.

NAME . . . .

ADDRESS . . . .

Please clip or photocopy and send to: Rough Guides, 62–70 Shorts Gardens, London WC2H 9AB, England or Rough Guides, 375 Hudson Street, New York, NY 10014, USA.

ROUGH GUIDES:
Reference and Music CDs

REFERENCE
Classical Music
Classical:
  100 Essential CDs
Drum'n'bass
House Music
Jazz
Music USA

Opera
Opera:
  100 Essential CDs
Reggae
Reggae:
  100 Essential CDs
Rock
Rock:
  100 Essential CDs
Techno
World Music
World Music:
  100 Essential CDs
English Football
European Football

Internet
Millennium

ROUGH GUIDE MUSIC CDs
Music of the
  Andes
Australian
  Aboriginal
Brazilian Music
Cajun & Zydeco

Classic Jazz
Music of
  Colombia
Cuban Music
Eastern Europe

Music of Egypt
English Roots
  Music
Flamenco
India & Pakistan
Irish Music
Music of Japan
Kenya & Tanzania
Native American
North African
Music of Portugal

Reggae
Salsa
Scottish Music
South African
  Music
Music of Spain
Tango
Tex-Mex
West African
  Music
World Music
World Music Vol 2
Music of
  Zimbabwe

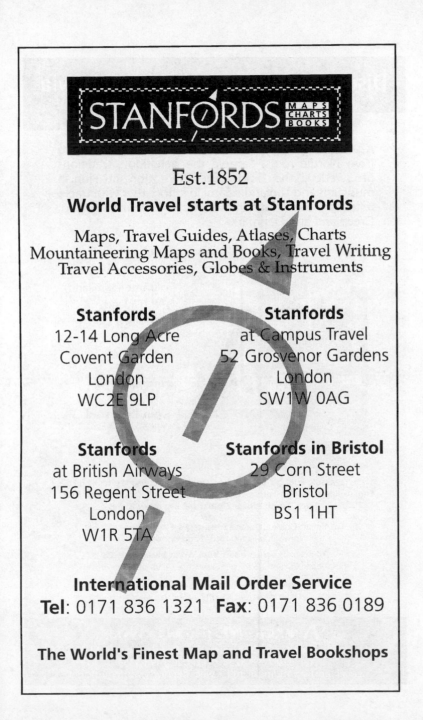